Microsoft® Office

Excel® 2007

Complete Concepts and Techniques

Gary B. Shelly

Thomas J. Cashman

Jeffrey J. Quasney

COURSE TECHNOLOGY
CENGAGE Learning™

Australia • Brazil • Japan • Korea • Mexico • Singapore • Spain • United Kingdom • United States

COURSE TECHNOLOGY
CENGAGE Learning™

Microsoft Office Excel 2007:
Complete Concepts and Techniques
Gary B. Shelly
Thomas J. Cashman
Jeffrey J. Quasney

Executive Editor: Alexandra Arnold

Senior Product Manager: Mali Jones

Associate Product Manager: Klenda Martinez

Editorial Assistant: Jon Farnham

Senior Marketing Manager: Joy Stark-Vancs

Marketing Coordinator: Julie Schuster

Print Buyer: Julio Esperas

Director of Production: Patty Stephan

Senior Production Editor: Catherine G. DiMassa

Developmental Editor: Lyn Markowicz

Proofreader: Green Pen Quality Assurance

Indexer: Rich Carlson

QA Manuscript Reviewers: John Freitas,
    Serge Palladino, Chris Scriver, Danielle Shaw,
    Marianne Snow, Teresa Storch

Art Director: Bruce Bond

Cover and Text Design: Joel Sadagursky

Cover Photo: Jon Chomitz

Compositor: GEX Publishing Services

For product information and technology assistance, contact us at
Cengage Learning Customer & Sales Support, 1-800-354-9706

For permission to use material from this text or product, submit all requests online at **cengage.com/permissions**
Further permissions questions can be emailed to
permissionrequest@cengage.com

ISBN-13: 978-1-4188-4343-4

ISBN-10: 1-4188-4343-1

Course Technology
25 Thomson Place
Boston, Massachusetts 02210
USA

Cengage Learning is a leading provider of customized learning solutions with office locations around the globe, including Singapore, the United Kingdom, Australia, Mexico, Brazil, and Japan. Locate your local office at:
international.cengage.com/region

Cengage Learning products are represented in Canada by Nelson Education, Ltd.

For your lifelong learning solutions, visit **course.cengage.com**

Purchase any of our products at your local college store or at our preferred online store **www.ichapters.com**

Printed in the United States of America
6 7 8 9 10 09

Microsoft® Office

Excel® 2007
Complete Concepts and Techniques

Contents

Appendices

Preface

The Shelly Cashman Series® offers the finest textbooks in computer education. We are proud of the fact that our series of Microsoft Office 4.3, Microsoft Office 95, Microsoft Office 97, Microsoft Office 2000, Microsoft Office XP, and Microsoft Office 2003 textbooks have been the most widely used books in education. With each new edition of our Office books, we have made significant improvements based on the software and comments made by instructors and students.

Microsoft Office 2007 contains more changes in the user interface and feature set than all other previous versions combined. Recognizing that the new features and functionality of Microsoft Office 2007 would impact the way that students are taught skills, the Shelly Cashman Series development team carefully reviewed our pedagogy and analyzed its effectiveness in teaching today's Office student. An extensive customer survey produced results confirming what the series is best known for: its step-by-step, screen-by-screen instructions, its project-oriented approach, and the quality of its content.

We learned, though, that students entering computer courses today are different from students taking these classes just a few years ago. Students today read less, but need to retain more. They need not only to be able to perform skills, but to retain those skills and know how to apply them to different settings. Today's students need to be continually engaged and challenged to retain what they're learning.

As a result, we've renewed our commitment to focusing on the user and how they learn best. This commitment is reflected in every change we've made to our Office 2007 books.

Objectives of This Textbook

Microsoft Office Excel 2007: Complete Concepts and Techniques is intended for a six- to nine-week period in a course that teaches Excel 2007 in conjunction with another application or computer concepts. No experience with a computer is assumed, and no mathematics beyond the high school freshman level is required. The objectives of this book are:

- To offer an in-depth presentation of Microsoft Office Excel 2007
- To expose students to practical examples of the computer as a useful tool
- To acquaint students with the proper procedures to create workbooks and worksheets suitable for coursework, professional purposes, and personal use
- To help students discover the underlying functionality of Excel 2007 so they can become more productive
- To develop an exercise-oriented approach that allows learning by doing

The Shelly Cashman Approach

Features of the Shelly Cashman Series Microsoft Office Excel 2007 books include:

- **Project Orientation** Each chapter in the book presents a project with a practical problem and complete solution in an easy-to-understand approach.

- **Plan Ahead Boxes** The project orientation is enhanced by the inclusion of Plan Ahead boxes. These new features prepare students to create successful projects by encouraging them to think strategically about what they are trying to accomplish before they begin working.

- **Step-by-Step, Screen-by-Screen Instructions** Each of the tasks required to complete a project is clearly identified throughout the chapter. Now, the step-by-step instructions provide a context beyond point-and-click. Each step explains why students are performing a task, or the result of performing a certain action. Found on the screens accompanying each step, call-outs give students the information they need to know when they need to know it. Now, we've used color to distinguish the content in the call-outs. The Explanatory call-outs (in black) summarize what is happening on the screen and the Navigational call-outs (in red) show students where to click.

- **Q&A** Found within many of the step-by-step sequences, Q&As raise the kinds of questions students may ask when working through a step sequence and provide answers about what they are doing, why they are doing it, and how that task might be approached differently.

- **Experimental Steps** These new steps, within our step-by-step instructions, encourage students to explore, experiment, and take advantage of the features of the Office 2007 new user interface. These steps are not necessary to complete the projects, but are designed to increase the confidence with the software and build problem-solving skills.

- **Thoroughly Tested Projects** Unparalleled quality is ensured because every screen in the book is produced by the author only after performing a step, and then each project must pass Course Technology's Quality Assurance program.

- **Other Ways Boxes and Quick Reference Summary** The Other Ways boxes displayed at the end of most of the step-by-step sequences specify the other ways to do the task completed in the steps. Thus, the steps and the Other Ways box make a comprehensive reference unit. A Quick Reference Summary at the end of the book contains all of the tasks presented in the chapters, and all ways identified of accomplishing the tasks.

- **BTW** These marginal annotations provide background information, tips, and answers to common questions that complement the topics covered, adding depth and perspective to the learning process.

- **Integration of the World Wide Web** The World Wide Web is integrated into the Excel 2007 learning experience by (1) BTW annotations that send students to Web sites for up-to-date information and alternative approaches to tasks; (2) a Microsoft Business Certification Program Web page so students can prepare for the certification examinations; (3) a Quick Reference Summary Web page that summarizes the ways to complete tasks (mouse, Ribbon, shortcut menu, and keyboard); and (4) the Learn It Online section at the end of each chapter, which has chapter reinforcement exercises, learning games, and other types of student activities.

- **End-of-Chapter Student Activities** Extensive student activities at the end of each chapter provide the student with plenty of opportunities to reinforce the materials learned in the chapter through hands-on assignments. Several new types of activities have been added that challenge the student in new ways to expand their knowledge, and to apply their new skills to a project with personal relevance.

Organization of This Textbook

Microsoft Office Excel 2007: Complete Concepts and Techniques consists of six chapters on Microsoft Office Excel 2007, two special features, seven appendices, and a Quick Reference Summary.

End-of-Chapter Student Activities

A notable strength of the Shelly Cashman Series Microsoft Office Excel 2007 books is the extensive student activities at the end of each chapter. Well-structured student activities can make the difference between students merely participating in a class and students retaining the information they learn. The activities in the Shelly Cashman Series Office books include the following.

CHAPTER SUMMARY A concluding paragraph, followed by a listing of the tasks completed within a chapter together with the pages on which the step-by-step, screen-by-screen explanations appear.

LEARN IT ONLINE Every chapter features a Learn It Online section that is comprised of six exercises. These exercises include True/False, Multiple Choice, Short Answer, Flash Cards, Practice Test, and Learning Games.

APPLY YOUR KNOWLEDGE This exercise usually requires students to open and manipulate a file from the Data Files that parallels the activities learned in the chapter. To obtain a copy of the Data Files for Students, follow the instructions on the inside back cover of this text.

EXTEND YOUR KNOWLEDGE This exercise allows students to extend and expand on the skills learned within the chapter.

MAKE IT RIGHT This exercise requires students to analyze a document, identify errors and issues, and correct those errors and issues using skills learned in the chapter.

IN THE LAB Three all new in-depth assignments per chapter require students to utilize the chapter concepts and techniques to solve problems on a computer.

CASES AND PLACES Five unique real-world case-study situations, including Make It Personal, an open-ended project that relates to student's personal lives, and one small-group activity.

Instructor Resources CD-ROM

The Shelly Cashman Series is dedicated to providing you with all of the tools you need to make your class a success. Information about all supplementary materials is available through your Course Technology representative or by calling one of the following telephone numbers: Colleges, Universities, and Continuing Ed departments, 1-800-648-7450; High Schools, 1-800-824-5179; and Career Colleges, Business, Government, Library and Resellers, 1-800-477-3692.

The Instructor Resources CD-ROM for this textbook include both teaching and testing aids. The contents of each item on the Instructor Resources CD-ROM (ISBN 1-4239-1226-8) are described on the following pages.

INSTRUCTOR'S MANUAL The Instructor's Manual consists of Microsoft Word files, which include chapter objectives, lecture notes, teaching tips, classroom activities, lab activities, quick quizzes, figures and boxed elements summarized in the chapters, and a glossary page. The new format of the Instructor's Manual will allow you to map through every chapter easily.

LECTURE SUCCESS SYSTEM The Lecture Success System consists of intermediate files that correspond to certain figures in the book, allowing you to step through the creation of a project in a chapter during a lecture without entering large amounts of data.

SYLLABUS Sample syllabi, which can be customized easily to a course, are included. The syllabi cover policies, class and lab assignments and exams, and procedural information.

FIGURE FILES Illustrations for every figure in the textbook are available in electronic form. Use this ancillary to present a slide show in lecture or to print transparencies for use in lecture with an overhead projector. If you have a personal computer and LCD device, this ancillary can be an effective tool for presenting lectures.

POWERPOINT PRESENTATIONS PowerPoint Presentations is a multimedia lecture presentation system that provides slides for each chapter. Presentations are based on chapter objectives. Use this presentation system to present well-organized lectures that are both interesting and knowledge based. PowerPoint Presentations provides consistent coverage at schools that use multiple lecturers.

SOLUTIONS TO EXERCISES Solutions are included for the end-of-chapter exercises, as well as the Chapter Reinforcement exercises. Rubrics and annotated solution files, as described below, are also included.

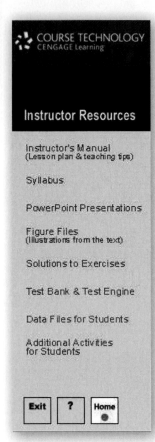

RUBRICS AND ANNOTATED SOLUTION FILES The grading rubrics provide a customizable framework for assigning point values to the laboratory exercises. Annotated solution files that correspond to the grading rubrics make it easy for you to compare students' results with the correct solutions whether you receive their homework as hard copy or via e-mail.

TEST BANK & TEST ENGINE In the ExamView test bank, you will find our standard question types (40 multiple-choice, 25 true/false, 20 completion) and new objective-based question types (5 modified multiple-choice, 5 modified true/false and 10 matching). Critical Thinking questions are also included (3 essays and 2 cases with 2 questions each) totaling the test bank to 112 questions for every chapter with page number references, and when appropriate, figure references. A version of the test bank you can print also is included. The test bank comes with a copy of the test engine, ExamView, the ultimate tool for your objective-based testing needs. ExamView is a state-of-the-art test builder that is easy to use. ExamView enables you to create paper-, LAN-, or Web-based tests from test banks designed specifically for your Course Technology textbook. Utilize the ultra-efficient QuickTest Wizard to create tests in less than five minutes by taking advantage of Course Technology's question banks, or customize your own exams from scratch.

LAB TESTS/TEST OUT The Lab Tests/Test Out exercises parallel the In the Lab assignments and are supplied for the purpose of testing students in the laboratory on the material covered in the chapter or testing students out of the course.

DATA FILES FOR STUDENTS All the files that are required by students to complete the exercises are included. You can distribute the files on the Instructor Resources CD-ROM to your students over a network, or you can have them follow the instructions on the inside back cover of this book to obtain a copy of the Data Files for Students.

ADDITIONAL ACTIVITIES FOR STUDENTS These additional activities consist of Chapter Reinforcement Exercises, which are true/false, multiple-choice, and short answer questions that help students gain confidence in the material learned.

Assessment & Training Solutions
SAM 2007

SAM 2007 helps bridge the gap between the classroom and the real world by allowing students to train and test on important computer skills in an active, hands-on environment.

SAM 2007's easy-to-use system includes powerful interactive exams, training or projects on critical applications such as Word, Excel, Access, PowerPoint, Outlook, Windows, the Internet, and much more. SAM simulates the application environment, allowing students to demonstrate their knowledge and think through the skills by performing real-world tasks.

Designed to be used with the Shelly Cashman series, SAM 2007 includes built-in page references so students can print helpful study guides that match the Shelly Cashman series textbooks used in class. Powerful administrative options allow instructors to schedule exams and assignments, secure tests, and run reports with almost limitless flexibility.

Student Edition Labs

Our Web-based interactive labs help students master hundreds of computer concepts, including input and output devices, file management and desktop applications, computer ethics, virus protection, and much more. Featuring up-to-the-minute content, eye-popping graphics, and rich animation, the highly interactive Student Edition Labs offer students an alternative way to learn through dynamic observation, step-by-step practice, and challenging review questions.

Online Content

Blackboard is the leading distance learning solution provider and class-management platform today. Course Technology has partnered with Blackboard to bring you premium online content. Instructors: Content for use with *Microsoft Office Excel 2007: Complete Concepts and Techniques* is available in a Blackboard Course Cartridge and may include topic reviews, case projects, review questions, test banks, practice tests, custom syllabi, and more.

Course Technology also has solutions for several other learning management systems. Please visit course.com today to see what's available for this title.

Blackboard

CourseCasts Learning on the Go. Always Available...Always Relevant.

Want to keep up with the latest technology trends relevant to you? Visit our site to find a library of podcasts, CourseCasts, featuring a "CourseCast of the Week," and download them to your portable media player at http://coursecasts.course.com.

Our fast-paced world is driven by technology. You know because you are an active participant — always on the go, always keeping up with technological trends, and always learning new ways to embrace technology to power your life.

Ken Baldauf, a faculty member of the Florida State University (FSU) Computer Science Department, is responsible for teaching technology classes to thousands of FSU students each year. He knows what you know; he knows what you want to learn. He is also an expert in the latest technology and will sort through and aggregate the most pertinent news and information so you can spend your time enjoying technology, rather than trying to figure it out.

Visit us at http://coursecasts.course.com to learn on the go!

CourseNotes

Course Technology's CourseNotes are six-panel quick reference cards that reinforce the most important and widely used features of a software application in a visual and user-friendly format. CourseNotes will serve as a great reference tool during and after the student completes the course. CourseNotes for Microsoft Office 2007, Word 2007, Excel 2007, Access 2007, PowerPoint 2007, Windows Vista, and more are available now!

course|notes™
quick reference guide

About Our New Cover Look

Learning styles of students have changed, but the Shelly Cashman Series' dedication to their success has remained steadfast for over 30 years. We are committed to continually updating our approach and content to reflect the way today's students learn and experi-

ence new technology. This focus on the user is reflected in our bold new cover design, which features photographs of real students using the Shelly Cashman Series in their courses. Each book features a different user, reflecting the many ages, experiences, and backgrounds of all of the students learning with our books. When you use the Shelly Cashman Series, you can be assured that you are learning computer skills using the most effective courseware available. We would like to thank the administration and faculty at the participating schools for their help in making our vision a reality. Most of all, we'd like to thank the wonderful students from all over the world who learn from our texts and now appear on our covers.

To the Student . . . Getting the Most Out of Your Book

Welcome to *Microsoft Office Excel 2007: Complete Concepts and Techniques*. You can save yourself a lot of time and gain a better understanding of the Office 2007 programs if you spend a few minutes reviewing the figures and callouts in this section.

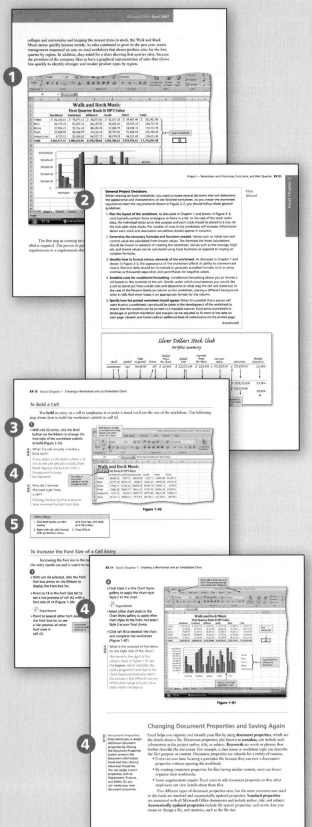

1 PROJECT ORIENTATION
Each chapter's project presents a practical problem and shows the solution in the first figure of the chapter. The project orientation lets you see firsthand how problems are solved from start to finish using application software and computers.

2 PROJECT PLANNING GUIDELINES AND PLAN AHEAD BOXES
Overall planning guidelines at the beginning of a chapter and Plan Ahead boxes throughout encourage you to think critically about how to accomplish the next goal before you actually begin working.

3 CONSISTENT STEP-BY-STEP, SCREEN-BY-SCREEN PRESENTATION
Chapter solutions are built using a step-by-step, screen-by-screen approach. This pedagogy allows you to build the solution on a computer as you read through the chapter. Generally, each step includes an explanation that indicates the result of the step.

4 MORE THAN JUST STEP-BY-STEP
BTW annotations in the margins of the book, Q&As in the steps, and substantive text in the paragraphs provide background information, tips, and answers to common questions that complement the topics covered, adding depth and perspective. When you finish with this book, you will be ready to use the Office programs to solve problems on your own. Experimental steps provide you with opportunities to step out on your own to try features of the programs, and pick up right where you left off in the chapter.

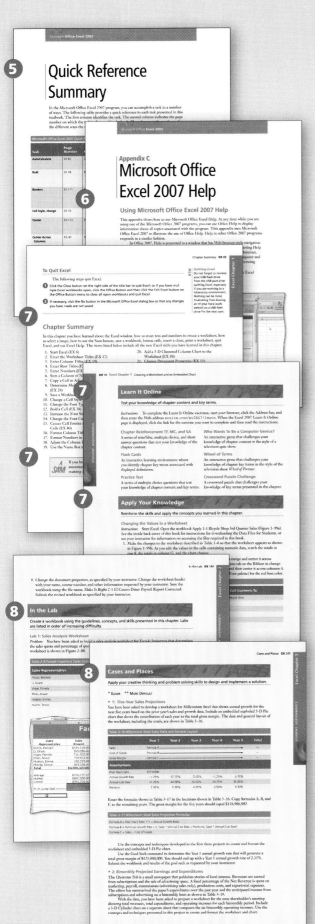

5 OTHER WAYS BOXES AND QUICK REFERENCE SUMMARY
Other Ways boxes that follow many of the step sequences and
a Quick Reference Summary at the back of the book explain the
other ways to complete the task presented, such as using the
mouse, Ribbon, shortcut menu, and keyboard.

6 EMPHASIS ON GETTING HELP WHEN YOU NEED IT
The first project of each application and Appendix C show you
how to use all the elements of Office Help. Being able to answer
your own questions will increase your productivity and reduce
your frustrations by minimizing the time it takes to learn how to
complete a task.

7 REVIEW, REINFORCEMENT, AND EXTENSION
After you successfully step through a project in a chapter, a
section titled Chapter Summary identifies the tasks with which you
should be familiar. Terms you should know for test purposes are
bold in the text. The SAM Training feature provides the opportunity for addional reinforcement on important skills covered in each
chapter. The Learn It Online section at the end of each chapter
offers reinforcement in the form of review questions, learning
games, and practice tests. Also included are exercises that require
you to extend your learning beyond the book.

8 LABORATORY EXERCISES
If you really want to learn how to use the programs, then you
must design and implement solutions to problems on your own.
Every chapter concludes with several carefully developed
laboratory assignments that increase in complexity.

1 Creating a Worksheet and an Embedded Chart

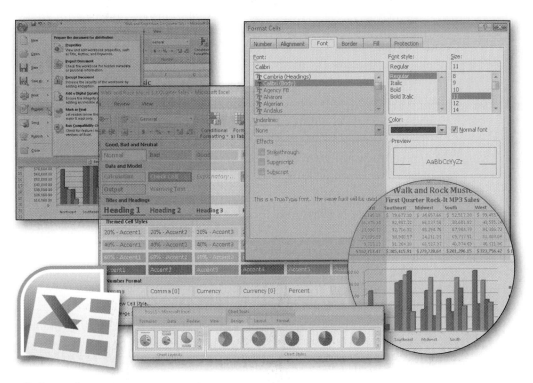

Objectives

You will have mastered the material in this chapter when you can:

- Start and quit Excel
- Describe the Excel worksheet
- Enter text and numbers
- Use the Sum button to sum a range of cells
- Copy the contents of a cell to a range of cells using the fill handle
- Save a workbook
- Format cells in a worksheet
- Create a 3-D Clustered Column chart

- Change document properties
- Save a workbook a second time using the same file name
- Print a worksheet
- Open a workbook
- Use the AutoCalculate area to determine statistics
- Correct errors on a worksheet
- Use Excel Help to answer questions

1 | Creating a Worksheet and an Embedded Chart

What Is Microsoft Office Excel 2007?

Microsoft Office Excel 2007 is a powerful spreadsheet program that allows users to organize data, complete calculations, make decisions, graph data, develop professional looking reports (Figure 1–1), publish organized data to the Web, and access real-time data from Web sites. The four major parts of Excel are:

- **Workbooks and Worksheets** Workbooks are a collection of worksheets. Worksheets allow users to enter, calculate, manipulate, and analyze data such as numbers and text. The terms worksheet and spreadsheet are interchangeable.

- **Charts** Excel can draw a variety of charts.

- **Tables** Tables organize and store data within worksheets. For example, once a user enters data into a worksheet, an Excel table can sort the data, search for specific data, and select data that satisfies defined criteria.

- **Web Support** Web support allows users to save Excel worksheets or parts of a worksheet in HTML format, so a user can view and manipulate the worksheet using a browser. Excel Web support also provides access to real-time data, such as stock quotes, using Web queries.

This latest version of Excel makes it much easier than in previous versions to perform common functions by introducing a new style of user interface. It also offers the capability of creating larger worksheets, improved formatting and printing, improved charting and table functionality, industry-standard XML support that simplifies the sharing of data within and outside an organization, improved business intelligence functionality, and the capability of performing complex tasks on a server.

In this chapter, you will create a worksheet that includes a chart. The data in the worksheet and chart includes sales data for several stores that a company owns and operates.

Project Planning Guidelines

> The process of developing a worksheet that communicates specific information requires careful analysis and planning. As a starting point, establish why the worksheet is needed. Once the purpose is determined, analyze the intended users of the worksheet and their unique needs. Then, gather information about the topic and decide what to include in the worksheet. Finally, determine the worksheet design and style that will be most successful at delivering the message. Details of these guidelines are provided in Appendix A. In addition, each project developed in this book provides practical applications of these planning considerations.

Project — Worksheet with an Embedded Chart

The project in this chapter follows proper design guidelines and uses Excel to create the worksheet shown in Figure 1–1. The worksheet contains sales data for Walk and Rock Music stores. The Walk and Rock Music product line includes a variety of MP3 music players, called Rock-It MP3, including players that show pictures and video, as well as a complete line of headphones and other accessories. The company sells its products at kiosks in several malls throughout the United States. By concentrating its stores near colleges and universities and keeping the newest items in stock, the Walk and Rock Music stores quickly became trendy. As sales continued to grow in the past year, senior management requested an easy-to-read worksheet that shows product sales for the first quarter by region. In addition, they asked for a chart showing first quarter sales, because the president of the company likes to have a graphical representation of sales that allows him quickly to identify stronger and weaker product types by region.

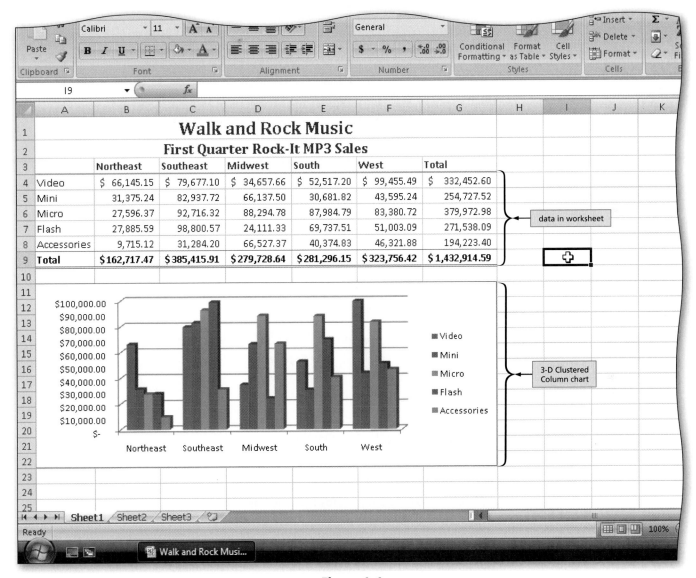

Figure 1–1

The first step in creating an effective worksheet is to make sure you understand what is required. The person or persons requesting the worksheet should supply their requirements in a requirements document. A **requirements document** includes a needs

BTW

Excel 2007 Features
With its what-if analysis tools, research capabilities, collaboration tools, streamlined user interface, smart tags, charting features, Web capabilities, hundreds of functions, and enhanced formatting capabilities, Excel 2007 is one of the easier and more powerful spreadsheet packages available.

statement, source of data, summary of calculations, and any other special requirements for the worksheet, such as charting and Web support. Figure 1–2 shows the requirements document for the new workbook to be created in this chapter.

requirements document →

REQUEST FOR NEW WORKBOOK

Date Submitted:	April 15, 2008
Submitted By:	Trisha Samuels
Worksheet Title:	Walk and Rock Music First Quarter Sales
Needs:	An easy-to-read worksheet that shows Walk and Rock Music's first quarter sales for each of our sales regions in which we operate (Northeast, Southeast, Midwest, South, West). The worksheet also should include total sales for each region, total sales for each product type, and total company sales for the first quarter.
Source of Data:	The data for the worksheet is available for the end of the first quarter from the chief financial officer (CFO) of Walk and Rock Music.
Calculations:	The following calculations must be made for the worksheet: (a) total first quarter sales for each of the five regions; (b) total first quarter sales for each of the five product types; and (c) total first quarter sales for the company.
Chart Requirements:	Below the data in the worksheet, construct a 3-D Clustered Column chart that compares the total sales for each region within each type of product.

Approvals

Approval Status:	X	Approved
		Rejected
Approved By:	Stan Maderbek	
Date:	April 22, 2008	
Assigned To:	J. Quasney, Spreadsheet Specialist	

Figure 1–2

BTW

Worksheet Development Cycle
Spreadsheet specialists do not sit down and start entering text, formulas, and data into a blank Excel worksheet as soon as they have a spreadsheet assignment. Instead, they follow an organized plan, or methodology, that breaks the development cycle into a series of tasks. The recommended methodology for creating worksheets includes: (1) analyze requirements (supplied in a requirements document); (2) design solution; (3) validate design; (4) implement design; (5) test solution; and (6) document solution.

Overview

As you read this chapter, you will learn how to create the worksheet shown in Figure 1–1 by performing these general tasks:

- Enter text in the worksheet
- Add totals to the worksheet
- Save the workbook that contains the worksheet
- Format the text in the worksheet
- Insert a chart in the worksheet
- Save the workbook a second time using the same file name
- Print the worksheet

Plan Ahead

General Project Guidelines
While creating an Excel worksheet, you need to make several decisions that will determine the appearance and characteristics of the finished worksheet. As you create the worksheet shown in Figure 1–1, you should follow these general guidelines:

1. **Select titles and subtitles for the worksheet.** Follow the *less is more* guideline. The less text in the titles and subtitles, the more impact the titles and subtitles will have. Use the fewest words possible to specify the information presented in the worksheet to the intended audience.

(continued)

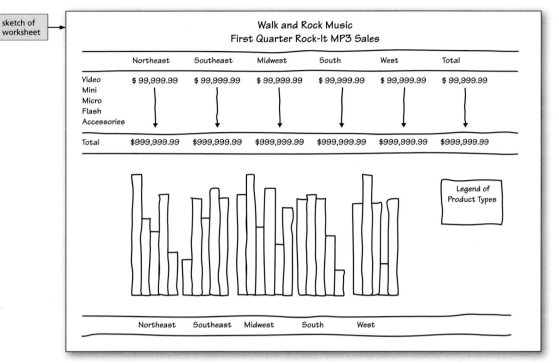

sketch of worksheet

Walk and Rock Music
First Quarter Rock-It MP3 Sales

	Northeast	Southeast	Midwest	South	West	Total
Video Mini Micro Flash Accessories	$ 99,999.99	$ 99,999.99	$ 99,999.99	$ 99,999.99	$ 99,999.99	$ 99,999.99
Total	$999,999.99	$999,999.99	$999,999.99	$999,999.99	$999,999.99	$999,999.99

Legend of Product Types

Northeast   Southeast   Midwest   South   West

Figure 1–3

Plan
Ahead

(continued)

2. **Determine the contents for rows and columns.** Rows typically contain information that is analogous to items in a list, such as the products sold by a company. Columns typically contain descriptive information about items in rows or contain information that helps to group the data in the worksheet, such as company regions.

3. **Determine the calculations that are needed.** You can decide to total data in a variety of ways, such as across rows or in columns. You also can include a grand total.

4. **Determine where to save the workbook.** You can store a workbook permanently, or **save** it, on a variety of storage media including a hard disk, USB flash drive, or CD. You also can indicate a specific location on the storage media for saving the workbook.

5. **Identify how to format various elements of the worksheet.** The overall appearance of a worksheet significantly affects its ability to communicate clearly. Examples of how you can modify the appearance, or **format**, of text include changing its shape, size, color, and position on the worksheet.

6. **Decide on the type of chart needed.** Excel includes the capability of creating many different types of charts, such as bar charts and pie charts. Each chart type relays a different message about the data in the worksheet. Choose a chart type that relays the message that you want to convey.

7. **Establish where to position and how to format the chart.** The position and format of the chart should command the attention of the intended audience. If possible, position the chart so that it prints with the worksheet data on a single page.

When necessary, more specific details concerning the above guidelines are presented at appropriate points in the chapter. The chapter also will identify the actions performed and decisions made regarding these guidelines during the creation of the worksheet shown in Figure 1–1 on page EX 3.

After carefully reviewing the requirements document (Figure 1–2 on page EX 4) and necessary decisions, the next step is to design a solution or draw a sketch of the worksheet based on the requirements, including titles, column and row headings, location of data values, and the 3-D Clustered Column chart, as shown in Figure 1–3 on page EX 5. The dollar signs, 9s, and commas that you see in the sketch of the worksheet indicate formatted numeric values.

With a good understanding of the requirements document, an understanding of the necessary decisions, and a sketch of the worksheet, the next step is to use Excel to create the worksheet and chart.

Starting Excel

If you are using a computer to step through the project in this chapter and you want your screen to match the figures in this book, you should change your computer's resolution to 1024 × 768. For information about how to change a computer's resolution, read Appendix E.

To Start Excel

The following steps, which assume Windows Vista is running, start Excel based on a typical installation of Microsoft Office on your computer. You may need to ask your instructor how to start Excel for your computer.

Note: If you are using Windows XP, see Appendix F for alternate steps.

1

- Click the Start button on the Windows Vista taskbar to display the Start menu.

- Click All Programs at the bottom of left pane on the the Start menu to display the All Programs list.

- Click Microsoft Office in the All Programs list to display the Microsoft Office list (Figure 1–4).

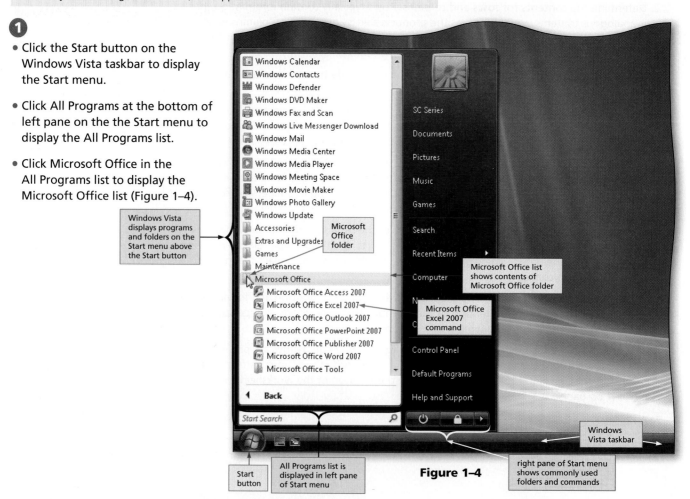

Figure 1–4

2

- Click Microsoft Office Excel 2007 to start Excel and display a new blank workbook titled Book1 in the Excel window (Figure 1–5).

- If the Excel window is not maximized, click the Maximize button next to the Close button on its title bar to maximize the window.

- If the worksheet window in Excel is not maximized, click the Maximize button next to the Close button on its title bar to maximize the worksheet window within Excel.

What is a maximized window?

A maximized window fills the entire screen. When you maximize a window, the Maximize button changes to a Restore Down button. When you restore a maximized window, the window returns to its previous size and the Restore Down button changes to a Maximize button.

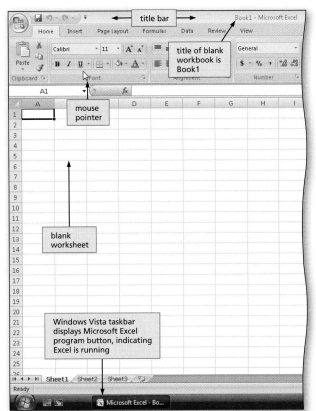

Figure 1–5

The Excel Workbook

The Excel window consists of a variety of components to make your work more efficient and worksheets more professional. These include the document window, Ribbon, Mini toolbar and shortcut menus, Quick Access Toolbar, and Office Button. Some of these components are common to other Microsoft Office 2007 programs; others are unique to Excel.

When Excel starts, it creates a new blank workbook, called Book1. The **workbook** (Figure 1–6) is like a notebook. Inside the workbook are sheets, each of which is called a **worksheet**. Excel opens a new workbook with three worksheets.

If necessary, you can add additional worksheets as long as your computer has enough memory to accommodate them. Each worksheet has a sheet name that appears on a **sheet tab** at the bottom of the workbook. For example, Sheet1 is the name of the active worksheet displayed in the Book1 workbook. If you click the sheet tab labeled Sheet2, Excel displays the Sheet2 worksheet. The project in this chapter uses only the Sheet1 worksheet.

The Worksheet

The worksheet is organized into a rectangular grid containing vertical columns and horizontal rows. A column letter above the grid, also called the **column heading**, identifies each column. A row number on the left side of the grid, also called the **row heading**, identifies

BTW

Excel Help
Help with Excel is no further away than the Help button on the right side of the Ribbon. Click the Help button, type help in the 'Type words to search for' box, and then press the ENTER key. Excel responds with a list of topics you can click to learn about obtaining Help on any Excel-related topic. To find out what is new in Excel 2007, type what is new in Excel in the 'Type words to search for' box.

each row. With the screen resolution set to 1024 × 768 and the Excel window maximized, Excel displays 15 columns (A through O) and 25 rows (1 through 25) of the worksheet on the screen, as shown in Figure 1–6.

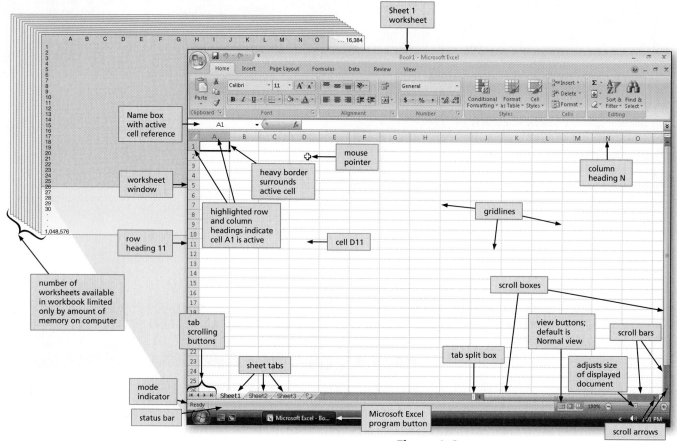

Figure 1–6

BTW

Worksheet Development
The key to developing a useful worksheet is careful planning. Careful planning can reduce your effort significantly and result in a worksheet that is accurate, easy to read, flexible, and useful. When analyzing a problem and designing a worksheet solution, you should follow these steps: (1) define the problem, including need, source of data, calculations, charting, and Web or special requirements; (2) design the worksheet; (3) enter the data and formulas; and (4) test the worksheet.

The intersection of each column and row is a cell. A **cell** is the basic unit of a worksheet into which you enter data. Each worksheet in a workbook has 16,384 columns and 1,048,576 rows for a total of 17,179,869,180 cells. Only a small fraction of the active worksheet appears on the screen at one time.

A cell is referred to by its unique address, or **cell reference**, which is the coordinates of the intersection of a column and a row. To identify a cell, specify the column letter first, followed by the row number. For example, cell reference D11 refers to the cell located at the intersection of column D and row 11 (Figure 1–6).

One cell on the worksheet, designated the **active cell**, is the one into which you can enter data. The active cell in Figure 1–6 is A1. The active cell is identified in three ways. First, a heavy border surrounds the cell; second, the active cell reference shows immediately above column A in the Name box; and third, the column heading A and row heading 1 are highlighted so it is easy to see which cell is active (Figure 1–6).

The horizontal and vertical lines on the worksheet itself are called **gridlines**. Gridlines make it easier to see and identify each cell in the worksheet. If desired, you can turn the gridlines off so they do not show on the worksheet, but it is recommended that you leave them on for now.

The mouse pointer in Figure 1–6 has the shape of a block plus sign. The mouse pointer appears as a block plus sign whenever it is located in a cell on the worksheet. Another common shape of the mouse pointer is the block arrow. The mouse pointer turns into the block arrow whenever you move it outside the worksheet or when you drag cell contents between rows or columns. The other mouse pointer shapes are described when they appear on the screen.

Worksheet Window

You view the portion of the worksheet displayed on the screen through a **worksheet window** (Figure 1–6). The default (preset) view is **normal view**. Below and to the right of the worksheet window are **scroll bars**, **scroll arrows**, and **scroll boxes** that you can use to move the worksheet window around to view different parts of the active worksheet. To the right of the sheet tabs at the bottom of the screen is the tab split box. You can drag the **tab split box** to increase or decrease the view of the sheet tabs (Figure 1–6). When you decrease the view of the sheet tabs, you increase the length of the horizontal scroll bar, and vice versa.

Status Bar

The status bar is located immediately above the Windows Vista taskbar at the bottom of the screen (Figure 1–6). The **status bar** presents information about the worksheet, the function of the button the mouse pointer is pointing to, or the mode of Excel. **Mode indicators**, such as Enter and Ready, appear on the status bar and specify the current mode of Excel. When the mode is **Ready**, Excel is ready to accept the next command or data entry. When the mode indicator reads **Enter**, Excel is in the process of accepting data through the keyboard into the active cell.

Keyboard indicators, such as Scroll Lock, show which toggle keys are engaged. Keyboard indicators appear to the right of the mode indicator. Toward the right edge of the status bar are buttons and controls you can use to change the view of a document and adjust the size of the displayed document.

Ribbon

The **Ribbon**, located near the top of the Excel window, is the control center in Excel (Figure 1–7a). The Ribbon provides easy, central access to the tasks you perform while creating a worksheet. The Ribbon consists of tabs, groups, and commands. Each **tab** surrounds a collection of groups, and each **group** contains related commands.

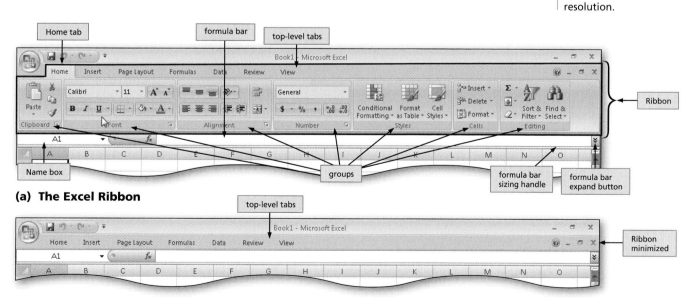

(a) The Excel Ribbon

(b) The Excel Ribbon Minimized

Figure 1–7

BTW

Minimizing the Ribbon
If you want to minimize the Ribbon, right-click the Ribbon and then click Minimize the Ribbon on the shortcut menu, double-click the active tab, or press CTRL+F1. To restore a minimized Ribbon, right-click the Ribbon and then click Minimize the Ribbon on the shortcut menu, double-click any top-level tab, or press CTRL+F1. To use commands on a minimized Ribbon, click the top-level tab.

When you start Excel, the Ribbon displays seven top-level tabs: Home, Insert, Page Layout, Formulas, Data, Review, and View. The **Home tab**, called the primary tab, contains groups with the more frequently used commands. To display a different tab on the Ribbon, click the top-level tab. That is, to display the Insert tab, click Insert on the Ribbon. To return to the Home tab, click Home on the Ribbon. The tab currently displayed is called the **active tab**.

To display more of the document in the document window, some users prefer to minimize the Ribbon, which hides the groups on the Ribbon and displays only the top-level tabs (Figure 1–7b). To use commands on a minimized Ribbon, click the top-level tab.

Each time you start Excel, the Ribbon appears the same way it did the last time you used Excel. The chapters in this book, however, begin with the Ribbon appearing as it did at the initial installation of the software. If you are stepping through this chapter on a computer and you want your Ribbon to match the figures in this book, read Appendix E.

In addition to the top-level tabs, Excel displays other tabs, called **contextual tabs**, when you perform certain tasks or work with objects such as charts or tables. If you insert a chart in the worksheet, for example, the Chart Tools tab and its related subordinate tabs appear (Figure 1–8). When you are finished working with the chart, the Chart Tools and subordinate tabs disappear from the Ribbon. Excel determines when contextual tabs should appear and disappear, based on the tasks you perform.

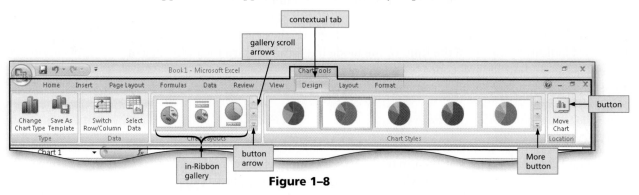

Figure 1–8

Ribbon commands include buttons, boxes (text boxes, check boxes, etc.), and galleries (Figure 1–8). A **gallery** is a set of choices, often graphical, arranged in a grid or in a list. You can scroll through choices on an in-Ribbon gallery by clicking the gallery's scroll arrows. An **in-Ribbon** gallery shows common gallery choices on the Ribbon rather than in a dropdown list. Or, you can click a gallery's More button to view more gallery options on the screen at a time. Some buttons and boxes have arrows that, when clicked, also display a gallery; others always cause a gallery to be displayed when clicked. Most galleries support **live preview**, which is a feature that allows you to point to a gallery choice and see its effect in the worksheet without actually selecting the choice (Figure 1–9).

Some commands on the Ribbon display an image to help you remember their function. When you point to a command on the Ribbon, all or part of the command glows in shades of yellow and orange, and an Enhanced ScreenTip appears on the screen. An **Enhanced ScreenTip** is an on-screen note that provides the name of the command, available keyboard shortcut(s), a description of the command, and sometimes instructions for how to obtain Help about the command (Figure 1–10). Enhanced ScreenTips are more detailed than a typical **ScreenTip**, which usually displays only the name of the command.

The lower-right corner of some groups on the Ribbon has a small arrow, called a **Dialog Box Launcher**, that when clicked displays a dialog box or a task pane (Figure 1–11). A **dialog box** contains additional commands and options for the group. When presented with a dialog box, you make selections and must close the dialog box before returning to the worksheet. A **task pane**, by contrast, is a window that contains additional commands and can stay open and visible while you work on the worksheet.

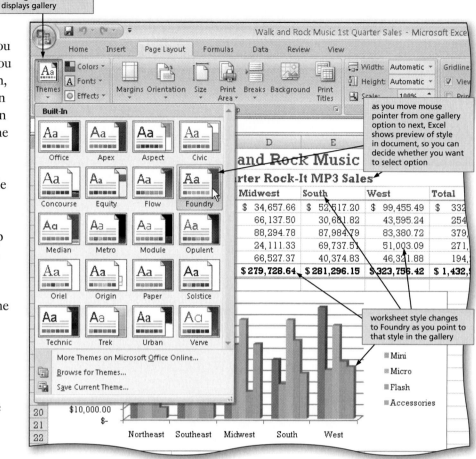

Figure 1–9

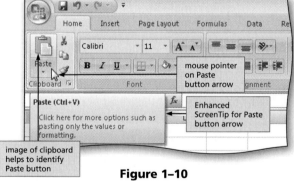

Figure 1–10

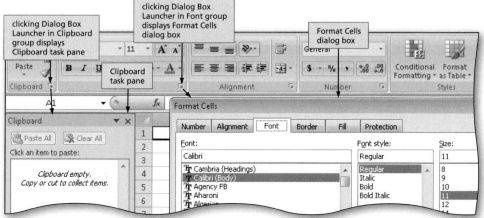

Figure 1–11

Formula Bar

The formula bar appears below the Ribbon (Figure 1–12a). As you type, Excel displays the entry in the **formula bar**. You can make the formula bar larger by dragging the sizing handle (Figure 1–7) on the formula bar or clicking the expand button to the right of the formula bar. Excel also displays the active cell reference in the **Name box** on the left side of the formula bar.

Mini Toolbar and Shortcut Menus

The **Mini toolbar**, which appears automatically based on tasks you perform (such as selecting text), contains commands related to changing the appearance of text in a worksheet. All commands on the Mini toolbar also exist on the Ribbon. The purpose of the Mini toolbar is to minimize mouse movement. For example, if you want to format text using a command that currently is not displayed on the active tab, you can use the command on the Mini toolbar — instead of switching to a different tab to use the command.

When the Mini toolbar appears, it initially is transparent (Figure 1–12a). If you do not use the transparent Mini toolbar, it disappears from the screen. To use the Mini toolbar, move the mouse pointer into the toolbar, which causes the Mini toolbar to change from a transparent to bright appearance (Figure 1–12b).

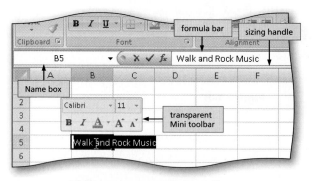

(a) Transparent Mini Toolbar

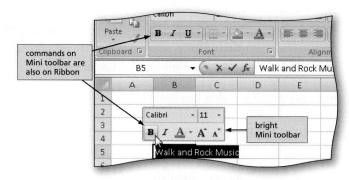

(b) Bright Mini Toolbar

Figure 1–12

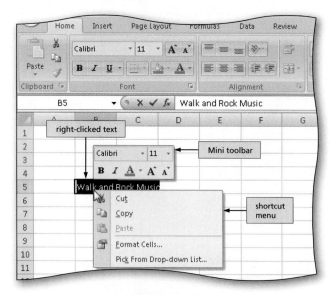

Figure 1–13

A **shortcut menu**, which appears when you right-click an object, is a list of frequently used commands that relate to the right-clicked object. If you right-click an item in the document window such as a cell, Excel displays both the Mini toolbar and a shortcut menu (Figure 1–13).

Quick Access Toolbar

The **Quick Access Toolbar**, located by default above the Ribbon, provides easy access to frequently used commands (Figure 1–14a). The commands on the Quick Access Toolbar always are available, regardless of the task you are performing. Initially, the Quick Access Toolbar contains the Save, Undo, and Redo buttons. If you click the Customize Quick Access Toolbar button, Excel provides a list of commands you quickly can add to and remove from the Quick Access Toolbar (Figure 1–14b).

You also can add other commands to or delete commands from the Quick Access Toolbar so that it contains the commands you use most often. As you add commands to the Quick Access Toolbar, its commands may interfere with the workbook title on the title bar. For this reason, Excel provides an option of displaying the Quick Access Toolbar below the Ribbon (Figure 1–14c).

BTW

Quick Access Toolbar Commands
To add a Ribbon command as a button to the Quick Access Toolbar, right-click the command on the Ribbon and then click Add to Quick Access Toolbar on the shortcut menu. To delete a button from the Quick Access Toolbar, right-click the button on the Quick Access Toolbar and then click Remove from Quick Access Toolbar on the shortcut menu. To display the Quick Access Toolbar below the Ribbon, right-click the Quick Access Toolbar and then click Show Quick Access Toolbar Below the Ribbon on the shortcut menu.

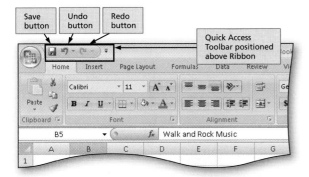

(a) Quick Access Toolbar above Ribbon

(c) Quick Access Toolbar below Ribbon

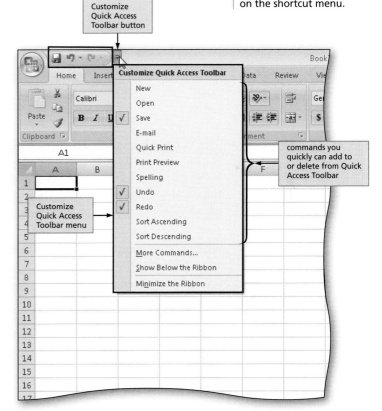

(b) Customize Quick Access Toolbar Menu

Figure 1–14

Each time you start Excel, the Quick Access Toolbar appears the same way it did the last time you used Excel. The chapters in this book, however, begin with the Quick Access Toolbar appearing as it did at the initial installation of the software. If you are stepping through this chapter on a computer and you want your Quick Access Toolbar to match the figures in this book, you should reset your Quick Access Toolbar. For more information about how to reset the Quick Access Toolbar, read Appendix E.

Office Button

While the Ribbon is a control center for creating worksheets, the **Office Button** is a central location for managing and sharing workbooks. When you click the Office Button, located in the upper-left corner of the window, Excel displays the Office Button menu (Figure 1–15). A **menu** contains a list of commands.

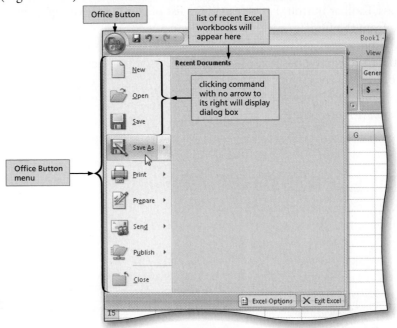

Figure 1–15

When you click the New, Open, Save As, and Print commands on the Office Button menu, Excel displays a dialog box with additional options. The Save As, Print, Prepare, Send, and Publish commands have an arrow to their right. If you point to a button that includes an arrow, Excel displays a **submenu**, which is a list of additional commands associated with the selected command (Figure 1–16). For the Prepare, Send, and Publish commands that do not display a dialog box when clicked, you can point either to the command or the arrow to display the submenu.

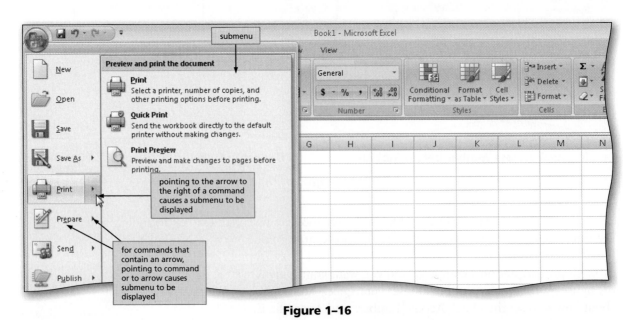

Figure 1–16

Key Tips

If you prefer using the keyboard, instead of the mouse, you can press the ALT key on the keyboard to display a **Key Tip badge**, or keyboard code icon, for certain commands (Figure 1–17). To select a command using the keyboard, press its displayed code letter, or **Key Tip**. When you press a Key Tip, additional Key Tips related to the selected command appear. For example, to select the New command on the Office Button menu, press the ALT key, then press the F key, then press the N key.

Figure 1–17

To remove the Key Tip badges from the screen, press the ALT key or the ESC key on the keyboard until all Key Tip badges disappear or click the mouse anywhere in the Excel window.

Selecting a Cell

To enter data into a cell, you first must select it. The easiest way **to select a cell** (make it active) is to use the mouse to move the block plus sign mouse pointer to the cell and then click.

An alternative method is to use the arrow keys that are located just to the right of the typewriter keys on the keyboard. An arrow key selects the cell adjacent to the active cell in the direction of the arrow on the key.

You know a cell is selected, or active, when a heavy border surrounds the cell and the active cell reference appears in the Name box on the left side of the formula bar. Excel also changes the active cell's column heading and row heading to a gold color.

BTW

Selecting a Cell
You can select any cell by entering its cell reference, such as b4, in the Name box on the left side of the formula bar.

Entering Text

In Excel, any set of characters containing a letter, hyphen (as in a telephone number), or space is considered text. **Text** is used to place titles, such as worksheet titles, column titles, and row titles, on the worksheet.

Plan Ahead	**Select titles and subtitles for the worksheet.**
	As previously stated, worksheet titles and subtitles should be as brief and meaningful as possible. As shown in Figure 1–18, the worksheet title, Walk and Rock Music, identifies the company for whom the worksheet is being created in Chapter 1. The worksheet subtitle, First Quarter Rock-It MP3 Sales, identifies the type of report.

Plan Ahead	**Determine the contents of rows and columns.**
	As previously mentioned, rows typically contain information that is similar to items in a list. For the Walk and Rock Music sales data, the list of product types meets this criterion. It is more likely that in the future, the company will add more product types as opposed to more regions. Each product type, therefore, should be placed in its own row. The row titles in column A (Video, Mini, Micro, Flash, Accessories, and Total) identify the numbers in each row.
	Columns typically contain descriptive information about items in rows or contain information that helps to group the data in the worksheet. In the case of the Walk and Rock Music sales data, the regions classify the sales of each product type. The regions, therefore, are placed in columns. The column titles in row 3 (Northeast, Southeast, Midwest, South, West, and Total) identify the numbers in each column.

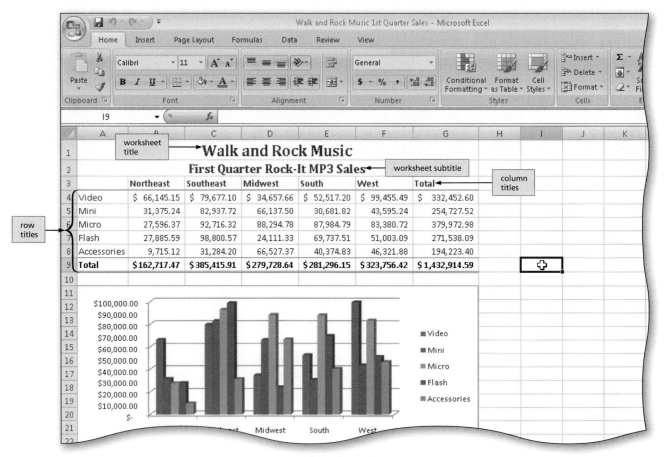

Figure 1–18

To Enter the Worksheet Titles

The following steps show how to enter the worksheet titles in cells A1 and A2. Later in this chapter, the worksheet titles will be formatted so they appear as shown in Figure 1–18.

1

• Click cell A1 to make cell A1 the active cell (Figure 1–19).

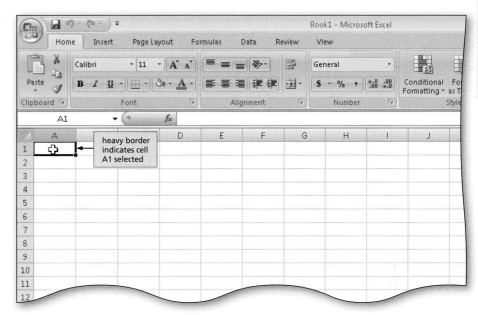

Figure 1–19

2

• Type `Walk and Rock Music` in cell A1, and then point to the Enter box in the formula bar.

Q&A Why did the appearance of the formula bar change?

Excel displays the title in the formula bar and in cell A1. When you begin typing a cell entry, Excel displays two additional boxes in the formula bar: the Cancel box and the Enter box. Clicking the **Enter box** completes an entry. Clicking the **Cancel box** cancels an entry.

Q&A What is the vertical line in cell A1?

In Figure 1–20, the text in cell A1 is followed by the insertion point. The **insertion point** is a blinking vertical line that indicates where the next typed character will appear.

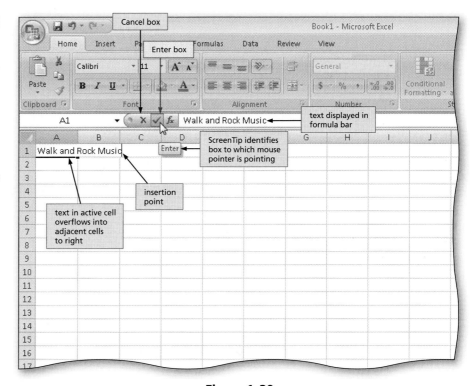

Figure 1–20

- Click the Enter box to complete the entry and enter the worksheet title in cell A1 (Figure 1–21).

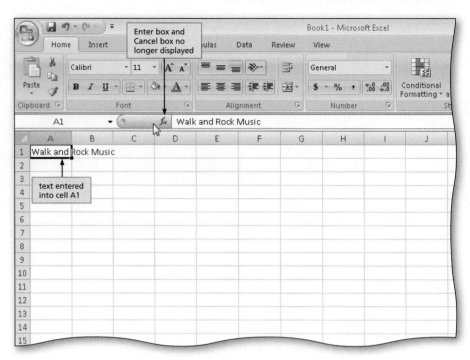

Figure 1–21

- Click cell A2 to select it.

- Type First Quarter Rock-It MP3 Sales as the cell entry.

- Click the Enter box to complete the entry and enter the worksheet subtitle in cell A2 (Figure 1–22).

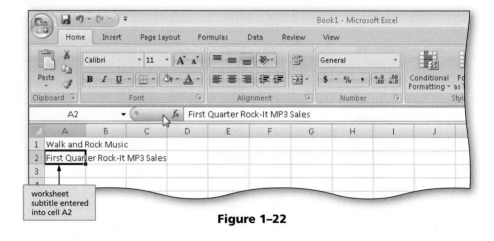

Figure 1–22

Other Ways

1. To complete entry, click any cell other than active cell

2. To complete entry, press ENTER key

3. To complete entry, press HOME, PAGE UP, PAGE DOWN, or END key

4. To complete entry, press UP, DOWN, LEFT, or RIGHT key.

Entering Text in a Cell

When you complete a text entry into a cell, a series of events occurs. First, Excel positions the text left-aligned in the cell. **Left-aligned** means the cell entry is positioned at the far left in the cell. Therefore, the W in the worksheet title, Walk and Rock Music, begins in the leftmost position of cell A1.

Second, when the text is longer than the width of a column, Excel displays the overflow characters in adjacent cells to the right as long as these adjacent cells contain no data. In Figure 1–22, the width of cell A1 is approximately nine characters. The text consists of 19 characters. Therefore, Excel displays the overflow characters from cell A1 in cells B1 and C1, because cells B1 and C1 are empty. If cell B1 contained data, Excel would hide the overflow characters, so that only the first nine characters in cell A1 would appear on the worksheet. Excel stores the overflow characters in cell A1 and displays them in the formula bar whenever cell A1 is the active cell.

Third, when you complete an entry by clicking the Enter box, the cell in which the text is entered remains the active cell.

Correcting a Mistake while Typing

If you type the wrong letter and notice the error before clicking the Enter box or pressing the ENTER key, use the BACKSPACE key to delete all the characters back to and including the incorrect letter. To cancel the entire entry before entering it into the cell, click the Cancel box in the formula bar or press the ESC key. If you see an error in a cell after entering the text, select the cell and retype the entry. Later in this chapter, additional error-correction techniques are discussed.

AutoCorrect

The **AutoCorrect feature** of Excel works behind the scenes, correcting common mistakes when you complete a text entry in a cell. AutoCorrect makes three types of corrections for you:

1. Corrects two initial capital letters by changing the second letter to lowercase.
2. Capitalizes the first letter in the names of days.
3. Replaces commonly misspelled words with their correct spelling. For example, it will change the misspelled word *recieve* to *receive* when you complete the entry. AutoCorrect will correct the spelling of hundreds of commonly misspelled words automatically.

BTW

The ENTER Key
When you first install Excel, the ENTER key not only completes the entry, but it also moves the selection to an adjacent cell. You can instruct Excel not to move the selection after pressing the ENTER key by clicking the Excel Options button on the Office Button menu, clicking the Advanced option, removing the checkmark from the 'After pressing Enter, move selection' check box, and then clicking the OK button.

To Enter Column Titles

To enter the column titles in row 3, select the appropriate cell and then enter the text. The following steps enter the column titles in row 3.

- Click cell B3 to make cell B3 the active cell (Figure 1–23).

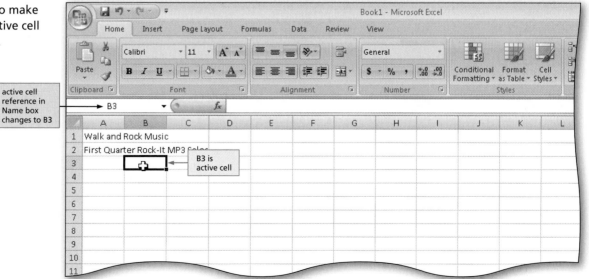

Figure 1–23

2

• Type `Northeast` in cell B3
(Figure 1–24).

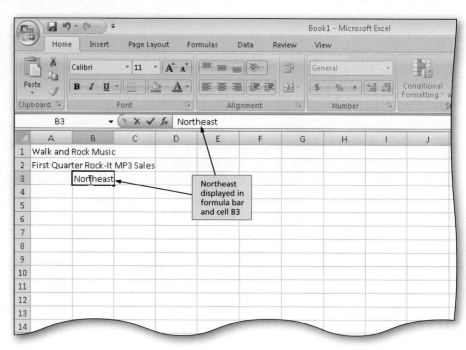

Figure 1–24

3

• Press the RIGHT
ARROW key to
enter the column title,
Northeast, in cell B3
and make cell C3
the active cell
(Figure 1–25).

Q&A

Why is the RIGHT
ARROW key used to
complete the entry in
the cell?

If the next entry is in
an adjacent cell, use
the arrow keys to
complete the entry in a
cell. When you press an
arrow key to complete
an entry, the adjacent
cell in the direction of
the arrow (up, down,
left, or right) becomes
the active cell. If the
next entry is in a
nonadjacent cell, complete an entry by clicking the next cell in which you plan to enter data.
You also can click the Enter box or press the ENTER key and then click the appropriate cell for
the next entry.

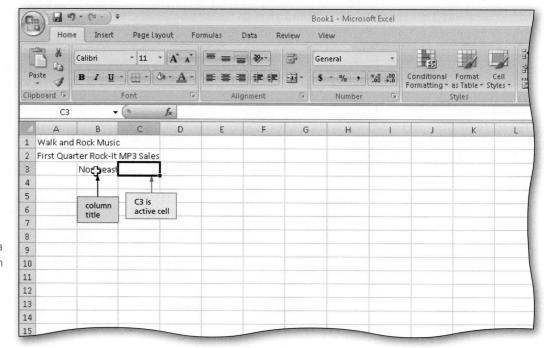

Figure 1–25

- Repeat Steps 2 and 3 to enter the remaining column titles in row 3; that is, enter `Southeast` in cell C3, `Midwest` in cell D3, `South` in cell E3, `West` in cell F3, and `Total` in cell G3 (complete the last entry in cell G3 by clicking the Enter box in the formula bar) (Figure 1–26).

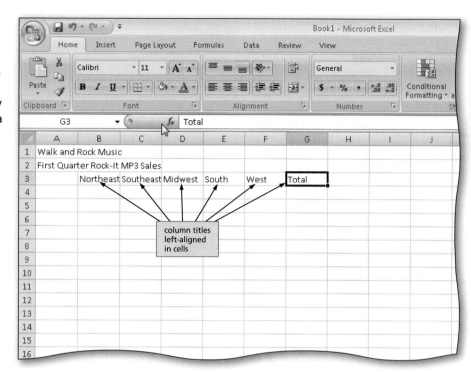

Figure 1–26

To Enter Row Titles

The next step in developing the worksheet for this project is to enter the row titles in column A. This process is similar to entering the column titles. The following steps enter the row titles in the worksheet.

- Click cell A4 to select it.

- Type `Video` and then press the DOWN ARROW key to enter the row title and make cell A5 the active cell (Figure 1–27).

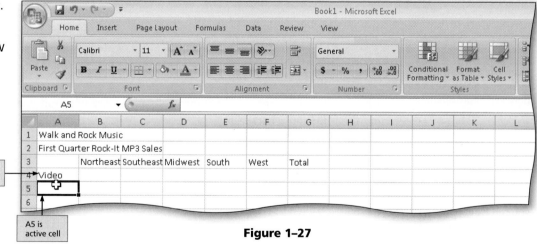

Figure 1–27

2

- Repeat Step 1 to enter the remaining row titles in column A; that is, enter `Mini` in cell A5, `Micro` in cell A6, `Flash` in cell A7, `Accessories` in cell A8, and `Total` in cell A9 (Figure 1–28).

Q&A

Why is the text left-aligned in the cells?

When you enter text, Excel automatically left-aligns the text in the cell. Excel treats any combination of numbers, spaces, and nonnumeric characters as text. For example, the following entries are text:

401AX21, 921-231, 619 321, 883XTY

You can change the text alignment in a cell by realigning it. Several alignment techniques are discussed later in the chapter.

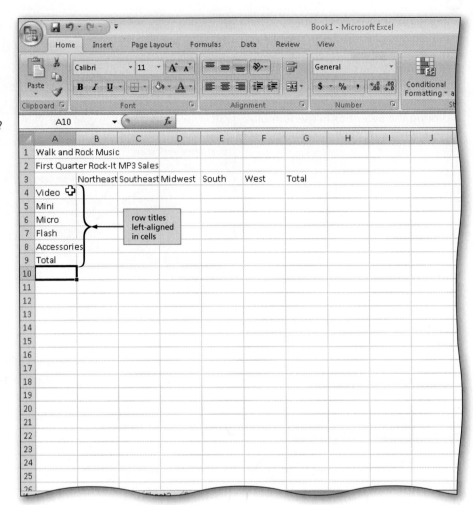

Figure 1–28

BTW

Numeric Limitations
In Excel, a number can be between approximately -1×10^{308} and 1×10^{308}, that is, between a negative 1 followed by 308 zeros and a positive 1 followed by 308 zeros. To enter a number such as 6,000,000,000,000,000, you can type 6,000,000,000,000,000, or you can type 6E15, which stands for 6×10^{15}.

Entering Numbers

In Excel, you can enter numbers into cells to represent amounts. A **number** can contain only the following characters:

0 1 2 3 4 5 6 7 8 9 + - ( ) , / . $ % E e

If a cell entry contains any other keyboard character (including spaces), Excel interprets the entry as text and treats it accordingly. The use of the special characters is explained when they are used in this book.

To Enter Numbers

The Walk and Rock Music First Quarter Rock-It MP3 Sales numbers used in Chapter 1 are summarized in Table 1–1. These numbers, which represent sales revenue for each of the product types and regions, must be entered in rows 4, 5, 6, 7, and 8.

Table 1–1 Walk and Rock Music First Quarter Rock-It MP3 Sales					
	Northeast	**Southeast**	**Midwest**	**South**	**West**
Video	66145.15	79677.10	34657.66	52517.20	99455.49
Mini	31375.24	82937.72	66137.50	30681.82	43595.24
Micro	27596.37	92716.32	88294.78	87984.79	83380.72
Flash	27885.59	98800.57	24111.33	69737.51	51003.09
Accessories	9715.12	31284.20	66527.37	40374.83	46321.88

The following steps enter the numbers in Table 1–1 one row at a time.

1

- Click cell B4.

- Type 66145.15 and then press the RIGHT ARROW key to enter the data in cell B4 and make cell C4 the active cell (Figure 1–29).

Q&A

Do I need to enter dollar signs, commas, or trailing zeros for the quarterly sales numbers?

You are not required to type dollar signs, commas, or trailing zeros. When you enter a dollar value that has cents, however, you must add the decimal point and the numbers representing the cents. Later in this chapter, the numbers will be formatted to use dollar signs, commas, and trailing zeros to improve the appearance and readability of the numbers.

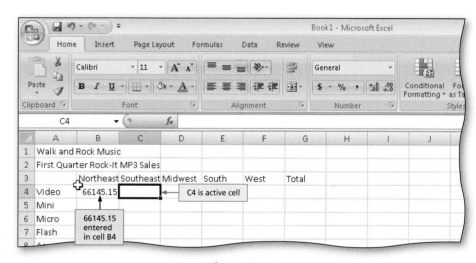

Figure 1–29

2

- Enter 79677.1 in cell C4, 34657.66 in cell D4, 52517.2 in cell E4, and 99455.49 in cell F4 (Figure 1–30).

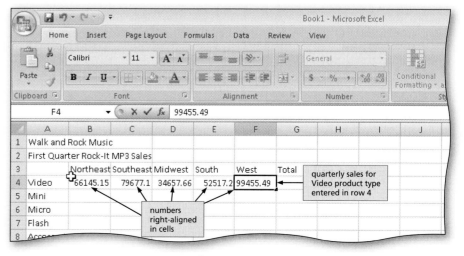

Figure 1–30

3

- Click cell B5.

- Enter the remaining first quarter sales numbers provided in Table 1–1 for each of the four remaining offerings in rows 5, 6, 7, and 8 to display the quarterly sales in the worksheet (Figure 1–31).

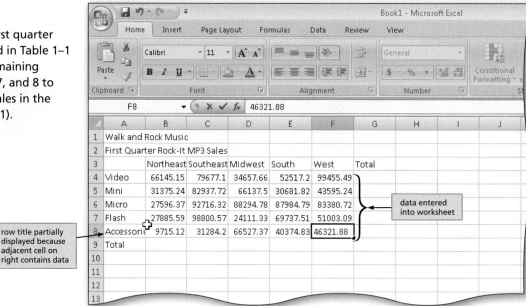

Figure 1–31

Calculating a Sum

The next step in creating the worksheet is to perform any necessary calculations, such as calculating the column and row totals.

Plan Ahead

Determine calculations that are needed.
As stated in the requirements document in Figure 1–2 on page EX 4, totals are required for each region, each product type, and the company. The first calculation is to determine the quarterly sales for the stores in the Northeast region in column B. To calculate this value in cell B9, Excel must add, or sum, the numbers in cells B4, B5, B6, B7, and B8. Excel's **SUM function**, which adds all of the numbers in a range of cells, provides a convenient means to accomplish this task.

A **range** is a series of two or more adjacent cells in a column or row or a rectangular group of cells. For example, the group of adjacent cells B4, B5, B6, B7, and B8 is called a range. Many Excel operations, such as summing numbers, take place on a range of cells.

After the total quarterly sales for the stores in the Northeast region in column B is determined, the totals for the remaining regions and totals for each product type will be determined.

BTW

Entering Numbers as Text
Sometimes, you will want Excel to treat numbers, such as Zip codes and telephone numbers, as text. To enter a number as text, start the entry with an apostrophe (').

BTW

Calculating Sums
Excel calculates sums for a variety of data types. For example, Boolean values, such as TRUE and FALSE, can be summed. Excel treats the value of TRUE as 1 and the value of FALSE as 0. Times also can be summed. For example, Excel treats the sum of 1:15 and 2:45 as 4:00.

To Sum a Column of Numbers

The following steps sum the numbers in column B.

1
- Click cell B9 to make it the active cell and then point to the Sum button on the Ribbon (Figure 1–32).

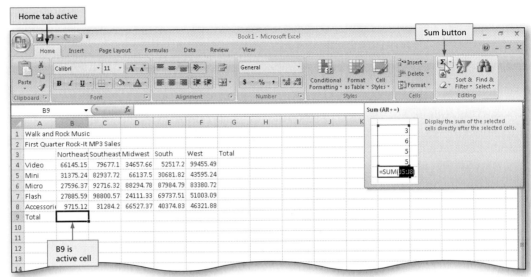

Figure 1–32

2
- Click the Sum button on the Ribbon to display =SUM(B4:B8) in the formula bar and in the active cell B9 (Figure 1–33).

Q&A

How does Excel know which cells to sum?

When you enter the SUM function using the Sum button, Excel automatically selects what it considers to be your choice of the range to sum. When proposing the range to sum, Excel first looks for a range of cells with numbers above the active cell and then to the left. If Excel proposes the wrong range, you can correct it by dragging through the correct range before pressing the ENTER key. You also can enter the correct range by typing the beginning cell reference, a colon (:), and the ending cell reference.

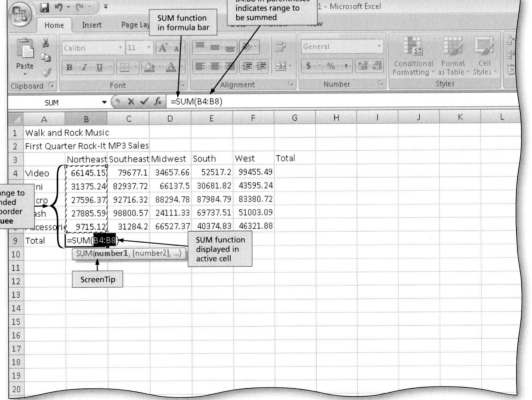

Figure 1–33

3

• Click the Enter box in the formula bar to enter the sum of the first quarter sales for the five product types for the Northeast region in cell B9 (Figure 1-34).

Q&A

What is the purpose of the Sum button arrow?

If you click the Sum button arrow on the right side of the Sum button (Figure 1–34), Excel displays a list of often-used functions from which you can choose. The list includes functions that allow you to determine the average, the number of items in the selected range, the minimum value, or the maximum value of a range of numbers.

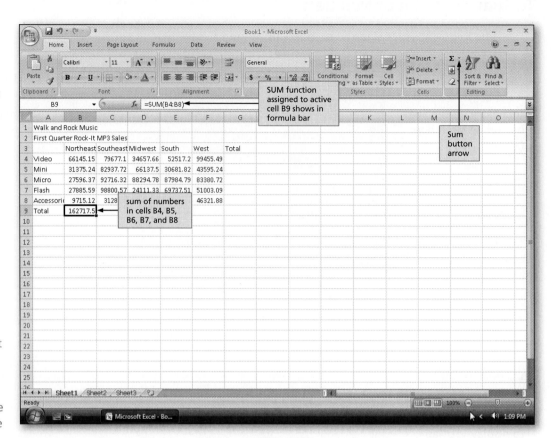

Figure 1–34

Other Ways

1. Click Insert Function button in formula bar, select SUM in Select a function list, click OK button, select range, click OK button

2. Click Sum button arrow on Ribbon, click More Functions, select SUM in Select a function list, click OK button, select range, click OK button

3. Type = s in cell, select SUM from list, select range

4. Press ALT + EQUAL SIGN (=) twice

Using the Fill Handle to Copy a Cell to Adjacent Cells

Excel also must calculate the totals for the Southeast in cell C9, the Midwest in cell D9, the South in cell E9, and for the West in cell F9. Table 1–2 illustrates the similarities between the entry in cell B9 and the entries required to sum the totals in cells C9, D9, E9, and F9.

Table 1–2 Sum Function Entries in Row 9		
Cell	**Sum Function Entries**	**Remark**
B9	=SUM(B4:B8)	Sums cells B4, B5, B6, B7, and B8
C9	=SUM(C4:C8)	Sums cells C4, C5, C6, C7, and C8
D9	=SUM(D4:D8)	Sums cells D4, D5, D6, D7, and D8
E9	=SUM(E4:E8)	Sums cells E4, E5, E6, E7, and E8
F9	=SUM(F4:F8)	Sums cells F4, F5, F6, F7, and F8

To place the SUM functions in cells C9, D9, E9, and F9, you could follow the same steps shown previously in Figures 1–32 through 1–34. A second, more efficient method is to copy the SUM function from cell B9 to the range C9:F9. The cell being copied is called the **source area** or **copy area**. The range of cells receiving the copy is called the **destination area** or **paste area**.

Although the SUM function entries in Table 1–2 are similar, they are not exact copies. The range in each SUM function entry uses cell references that are one column to the right of the previous column. When you copy cell references, Excel automatically adjusts them for each new position, resulting in the SUM function entries illustrated in Table 1–2. Each adjusted cell reference is called a **relative reference**.

To Copy a Cell to Adjacent Cells in a Row

The easiest way to copy the SUM formula from cell B9 to cells C9, D9, E9, and F9 is to use the fill handle. The **fill handle** is the small black square located in the lower-right corner of the heavy border around the active cell. The following steps use the fill handle to copy cell B9 to the adjacent cells C9:F9.

• With cell B9 active, point to the fill handle (Figure 1–35).

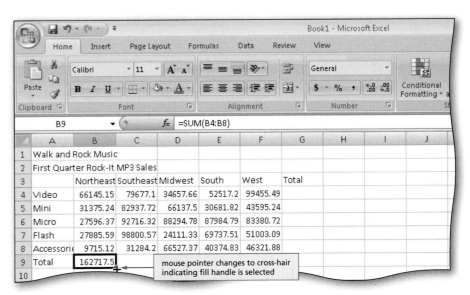

Figure 1–35

• Drag the fill handle to select the destination area, range C9:F9, to display a shaded border around the destination area, range C9:F9, and the source area, cell B9 (Figure 1–36). Do not release the mouse button.

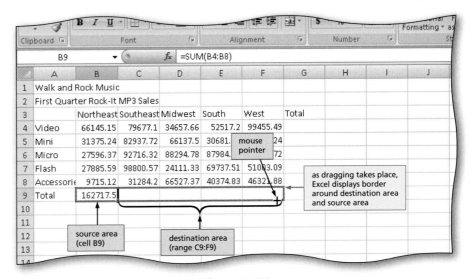

Figure 1–36

- Release the mouse button to copy the SUM function in cell B9 to the range C9:F9 (Figure 1–37) and calculate the sums in cells C9, D9, E9, and F9.

Q&A

What is the purpose of the Auto Fill Options button?

When you copy one range to another, Excel displays an Auto Fill Options button (Figure 1–37). The Auto Fill Options button allows you to choose whether you want to copy the values from the source area to the destination area with formatting, without formatting, or copy only the format. To view the available fill options, click the Auto Fill Options button. The Auto Fill Options button disappears when you begin another activity.

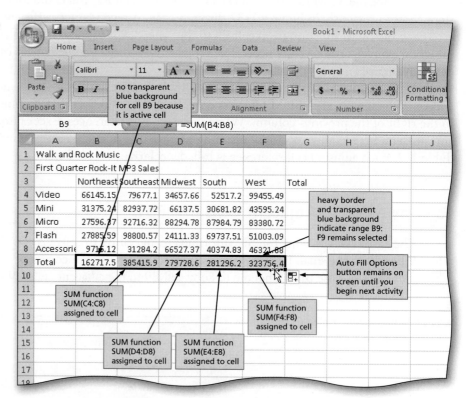

Figure 1–37

Other Ways

1. Select source area, click Copy button on Ribbon, select destination area, click Paste button on Ribbon

2. Right-click source area, click Copy on shortcut menu, right-click destination area, click Paste on shortcut menu

3. Select source area and then point to border of range; while holding down CTRL key, drag source area to destination area

To Determine Multiple Totals at the Same Time

The next step in building the worksheet is to determine the quarterly sales for each product type and total quarterly sales for the company in column G. To calculate these totals, you can use the SUM function much as it was used to total the quarterly sales by region in row 9. In this example, however, Excel will determine totals for all of the rows at the same time. The following steps illustrate this process.

- Click cell G4 to make it the active cell (Figure 1–38).

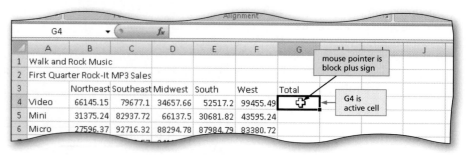

Figure 1–38

2

• With the mouse pointer in cell G4 and in the shape of a block plus sign, drag the mouse pointer down to cell G9 to highlight the range G4:G9 with a transparent view (Figure 1–39).

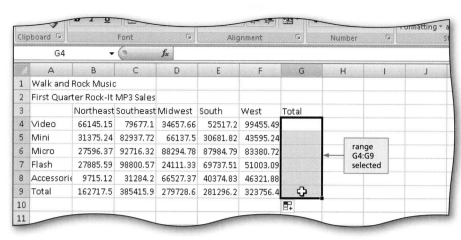

Figure 1–39

3

• Click the Sum button on the Ribbon to calculate and display the sums of the corresponding rows of sales in cells G4, G5, G6, G7, G8, and G9 (Figure 1–40).

4

• Select cell A10 to deselect the range G4:G9.

Q&A

Why does Excel create totals for each row?

If each cell in a selected range is next to a row of numbers, Excel assigns the SUM function to each cell when you click the Sum button.

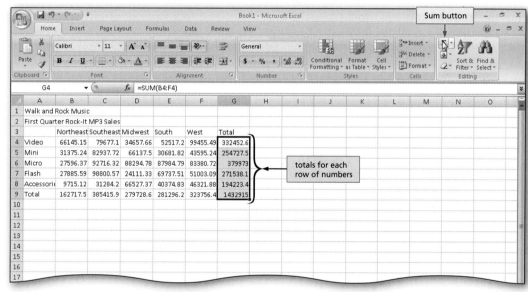

Figure 1–40

Saving the Project

While you are building a worksheet in a workbook, the computer stores it in memory. When you save a workbook, the computer places it on a storage medium such as a USB flash drive, CD, or hard disk. A saved workbook is referred to as a **file**. A **file name** is the name assigned to a file when it is saved. It is important to save the workbook frequently for the following reasons:

• The worksheet in memory will be lost if the computer is turned off or you lose electrical power while Excel is open.

• If you run out of time before completing your workbook, you may finish your worksheet at a future time without starting over.

BTW

Saving
Excel allows you to save a workbook in more than 30 different file formats. Choose the file format by clicking the 'Save as type' box arrow at the bottom of the Save As dialog box (Figure 1–41 on the next page). Excel Workbook is the default file format.

Plan Ahead

Determine where to save the workbook.

When saving a workbook, you must decide which storage medium to use.

- If you always work on the same computer and have no need to transport your projects to a different location, then your computer's hard drive will suffice as a storage location. It is a good idea, however, to save a backup copy of your projects on a separate medium in case the file becomes corrupted or the computer's hard drive fails.

- If you plan to work on your workbooks in various locations or on multiple computers, then you should save your workbooks on a portable medium, such as a USB flash drive or CD. The workbooks used in this book are saved to a USB flash drive, which saves files quickly and reliably and can be reused. CDs are easily portable and serve as good backups for the final versions of workbooks because they generally can save files only one time.

To Save a Workbook

You have performed many tasks while creating this project and do not want to risk losing the work completed thus far. Accordingly, you should save the workbook. The following steps save a workbook on a USB flash drive using the file name, Walk and Rock Music 1st Quarter Sales.

Note: If you are using Windows XP, see Appendix F for alternate steps.

1

- With a USB flash drive connected to one of the computer's USB ports, click the Save button on the Quick Access Toolbar to display the Save As dialog box (Figure 1–41).

- If the Navigation pane is not displayed in the Save As dialog box, click the Browse Folders button to expand the dialog box.

- If a Folders list is displayed below the Folders button, click the Folders button to remove the Folders list.

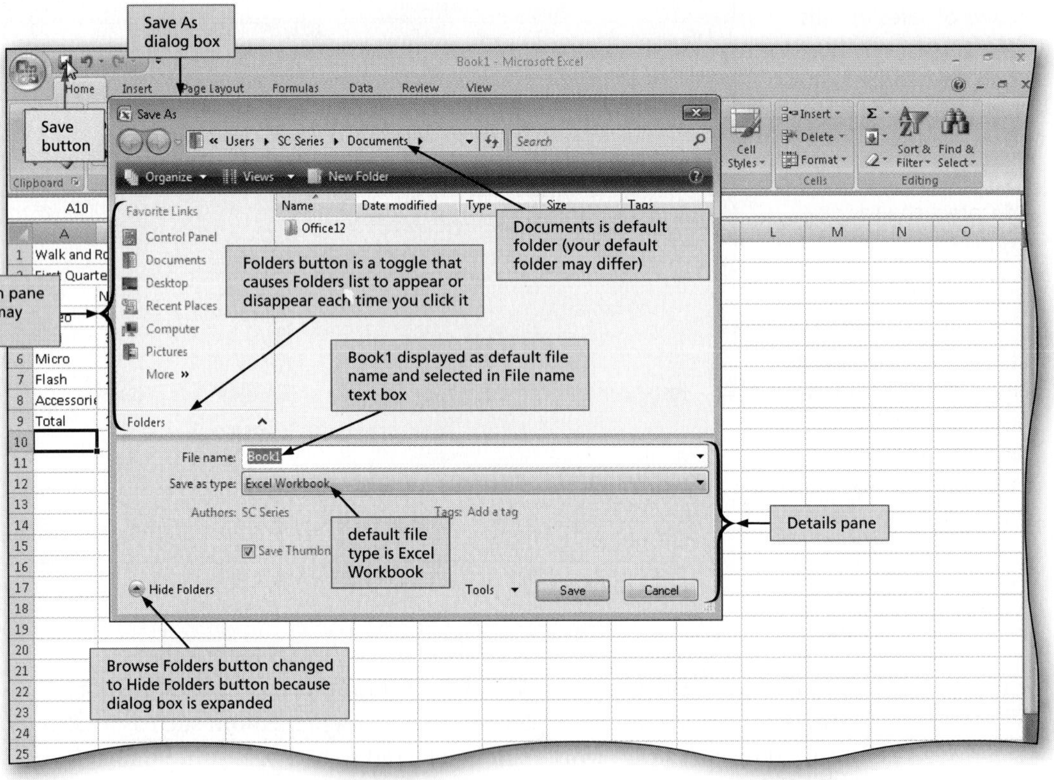

Q&A

Do I have to save to a USB flash drive?

No. You can save to any device or folder. A **folder** is a specific location on a storage medium. You can save to the default folder or a different folder. You also can create your own folders, which is explained later in this book.

Figure 1–41

2

- Type `Walk and Rock Music 1st Quarter Sales` in the File name text box to change the file name. Do not press the ENTER key after typing the file name (Figure 1–42).

Q&A What characters can I use in a file name?

A file name can have a maximum of 255 characters, including spaces. The only invalid characters are the backslash (\), slash (/), colon (:), asterisk (*), question mark (?), quotation mark ("), less than symbol (<), greater than symbol (>), and vertical bar (|).

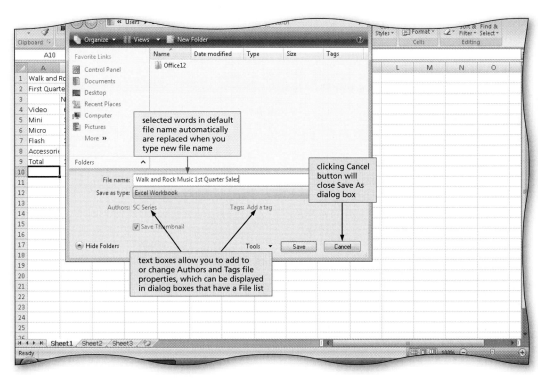

Figure 1–42

3

- If Computer is not displayed in the Favorite Links section, drag the top or bottom edge of the Save As dialog box until Computer is displayed.

- Click Computer in the Favorite Links section to display a list of available drives (Figure 1–43).

- If necessary, scroll until UDISK 2.0 (E :) appears in the list of available drives.

Q&A Why is my list of files, folders, and drives arranged and named differently from those shown in the figure?

Your computer's configuration determines how the list of files and folders is displayed and how drives are named. You can change the save location by clicking links on the **Favorite Links section**.

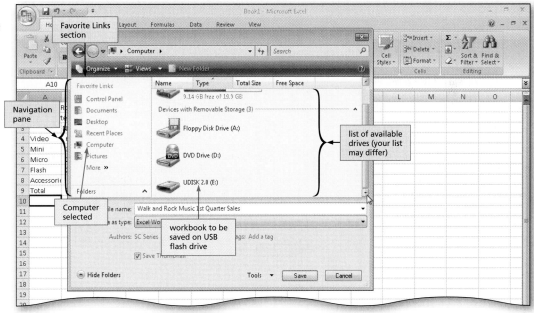

Figure 1–43

Q&A How do I save the file if I am not using a USB flash drive?

Use the same process, but be certain to select your device in the list of available drives.

4

- Double-click UDISK 2.0 (E:) in the Save in list to select the USB flash drive, Drive E in this case, as the new save location (Figure 1–44).

Q&A

What if my USB flash drive has a different name or letter?

It is very likely that your USB flash drive will have a different name and drive letter and be connected to a different port.

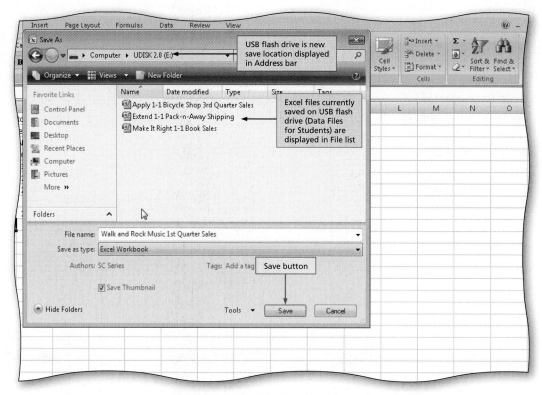

Figure 1–44

5

- Click the Save button in the Save As dialog box to save the workbook on the USB flash drive with the file name, Walk and Rock Music 1st Quarter Sales (Figure 1–45).

Q&A

How do I know that Excel saved the workbook?

While Excel is saving your file, it briefly displays a message on the status bar indicating the amount of the file saved. In addition, your USB drive may have a light that flashes during the save process.

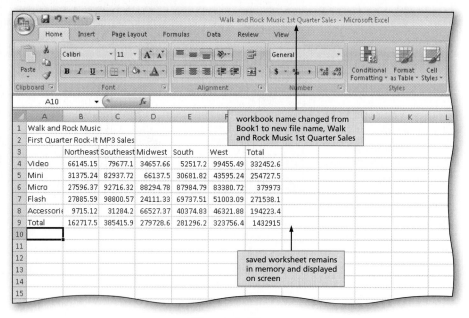

Figure 1–45

Other Ways

1. Click Office Button, click Save, type file name, select drive or folder, click Save button

2. Press CTRL+S or press SHIFT+F12, type file name, select drive or folder, click Save button

Formatting the Worksheet

The text, numeric entries, and functions for the worksheet now are complete. The next step is to format the worksheet. You **format** a worksheet to emphasize certain entries and make the worksheet easier to read and understand.

Figure 1–46a shows the worksheet before formatting. Figure 1–46b shows the worksheet after formatting. As you can see from the two figures, a worksheet that is formatted not only is easier to read but also looks more professional.

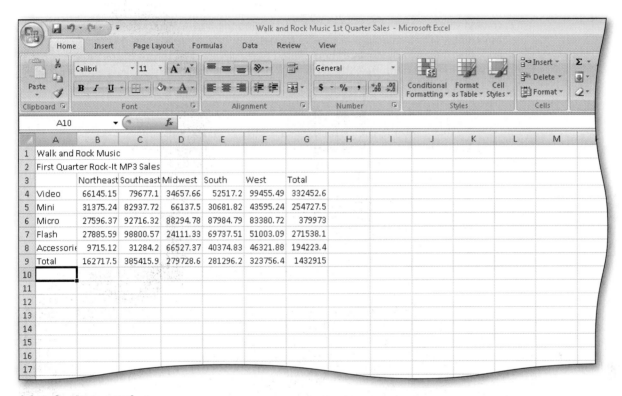

(a) Before Formatting

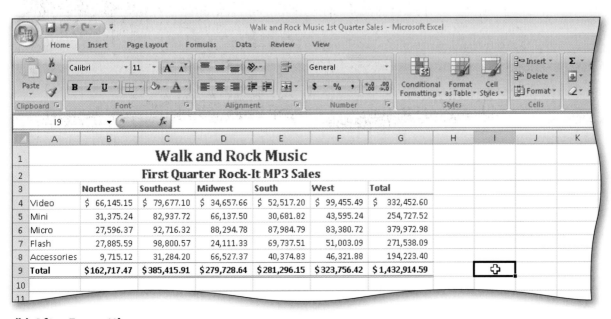

(b) After Formatting

Figure 1–46

<table>
<tr>
<td>Plan
Ahead</td>
<td>

Identify how to format various elements of the worksheet.

To change the unformatted worksheet in Figure 1–46a to the formatted worksheet in Figure 1–46b, the following tasks must be completed:

1. Change the font type, change the font style to bold, increase the font size, and change the font color of the worksheet titles in cells A1 and A2. These changes make the worksheet title prominently display to the user and inform the user of the purpose of the worksheet.

2. Center the worksheet titles in cells A1 and A2 across columns A through G.

3. Format the body of the worksheet. The body of the worksheet, range A3:G9, includes the column titles, row titles, and numbers. Formatting the body of the worksheet changes the numbers to use a dollars-and-cents format, with dollar signs in the first row (row 4) and the total row (row 9); adds underlining that emphasizes portions of the worksheet; and modifies the column widths to make the text and numbers readable.

</td>
</tr>
</table>

The remainder of this section explains the process required to format the worksheet. Although the format procedures are explained in the order described above, you should be aware that you could make these format changes in any order. Modifying the column widths, however, usually is done last.

Font Type, Style, Size, and Color

BTW

Fonts
In general, use no more than two font types in a worksheet.

BTW

Fonts and Themes
Excel uses default recommended fonts based on the workbook's theme. A theme is a collection of fonts and color schemes. The default theme is named Office, and the two recommended fonts for the Office theme are Calibri and Cambria. Excel, however, allows you to apply any font to a cell or range as long as the font is installed on your computer.

The characters that Excel displays on the screen are a specific font type, style, size, and color. The **font type**, or font face, defines the appearance and shape of the letters, numbers, and special characters. Examples of font types include Calibri, Cambria, Times New Roman, Arial, and Courier. **Font style** indicates how the characters are emphasized. Common font styles include regular, bold, underline, or italic. The **font size** specifies the size of the characters on the screen. Font size is gauged by a measurement system called points. A single point is about 1/72 of one inch in height. Thus, a character with a **point size** of 10 is about 10/72 of one inch in height. The **font color** defines the color of the characters. Excel can display characters in a wide variety of colors, including black, red, orange, and blue.

When Excel begins, the preset font type for the entire workbook is Calibri, with a font size, font style, and font color of 11-point regular black. Excel allows you to change the font characteristics in a single cell, a range of cells, the entire worksheet, or the entire workbook.

To Change a Cell Style

Excel includes the capability of changing several characteristics of a cell, such as font type, font size, and font color, all at once by assigning a predefined cell style to a cell. The following steps assign the Title cell style to the worksheet title in cell A1.

1

- Click cell A1 to make cell A1 the active cell.

- Click the Cell Styles button on the Ribbon to display the Cell Styles gallery (Figure 1–47).

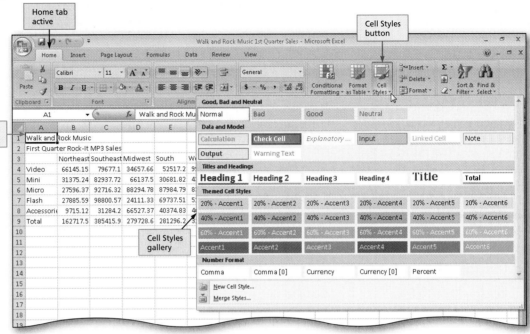

Figure 1–47

2

- Point to the Title cell style in the Titles and Headings area of the Cell Styles gallery to see a live preview of the cell style in cell A1 (Figure 1–48).

  Experiment

- Point to several other cell styles in the Cell Styles gallery to see a live preview of other cell styles in cell A1.

Q&A

Why does the font type, font size, and font color change in cell A1 when I point to it?

The change in cell A1 is a result of live preview. Live preview is a feature of Excel 2007 that allows you to preview cell styles as you point to them in the Cell Styles gallery.

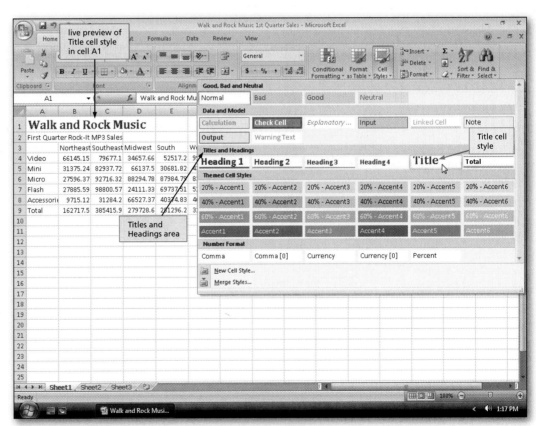

Figure 1–48

- Click the Title cell style to apply the cell style to cell A1 (Figure 1–49).

Q&A

Why do several items in the Font group on the Ribbon change?

The changes to the Font box, Bold button, and Font Size box indicate the font changes applied to the active cell, cell A1, as a result of applying the Title cell style.

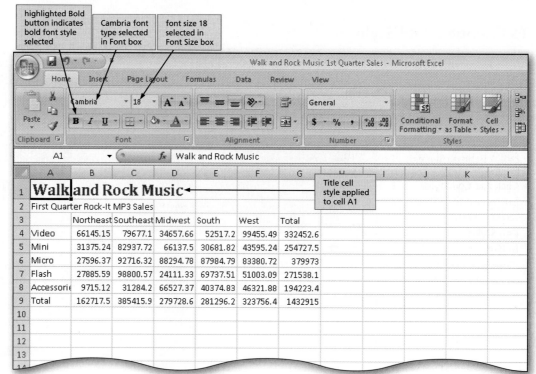

Figure 1–49

To Change the Font Type

Different font types often are used in a worksheet to make it more appealing to the reader. The following steps show how to change the worksheet subtitle's font type from Calibri to Cambria.

- Click cell A2 to make cell A2 the active cell.

- Click the Font box arrow on the Ribbon to display the Font gallery (Figure 1–50).

Q&A

Which fonts are displayed in the Font gallery?

Because many applications supply additional font types beyond what comes with the Windows Vista operating system, the number of font types available on your computer will depend on the applications installed. This book uses only font types that come with the Windows Vista operating system and Microsoft Office.

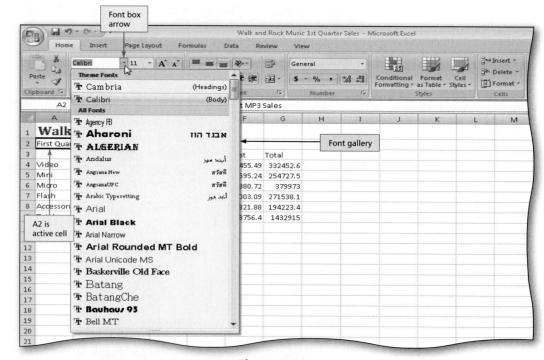

Figure 1–50

2

- Point to Cambria in the Theme Fonts area of the Font gallery to see a live preview of the Cambria font in cell A2 (Figure 1–51).

🔍 **Experiment**

- Point to several other fonts in the Font gallery to see a live preview of other fonts in cell A2.

Q&A

What is the Theme Fonts area?

Excel applies the same default theme to any new workbook that you start. A **theme** is a collection of cell styles and other styles that have common characteristics, such as a color scheme and font type. The default theme for an Excel workbook is the Office theme. The Theme Fonts area of the Font gallery includes the fonts included in the default Office theme. Cambria is recommended for headings and Calibri is recommended for cells in the body of the worksheet (Figure 1–51).

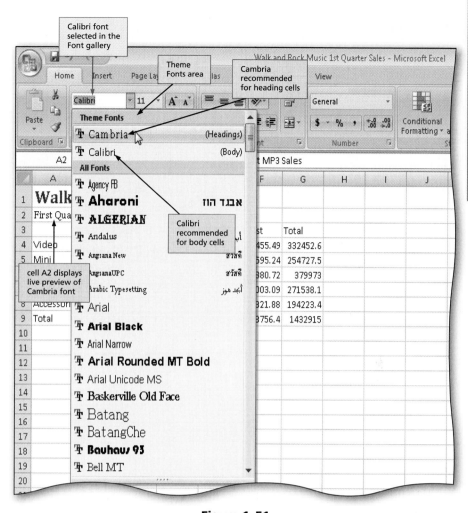

Figure 1–51

3

- Click Cambria in the Theme Fonts area to change the font type of the worksheet subtitle in cell A2 from Calibri to Cambria (Figure 1–52).

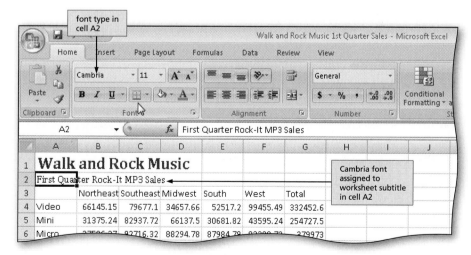

Figure 1–52

Other Ways

1. Select font type from Font list on Mini toolbar

2. Right-click cell, click Format Cells on shortcut menu, click Font tab, click desired font type, click OK button

To Bold a Cell

You **bold** an entry in a cell to emphasize it or make it stand out from the rest of the worksheet. The following step shows how to bold the worksheet subtitle in cell A2.

1

- With cell A2 active, click the Bold button on the Ribbon to change the font style of the worksheet subtitle to bold (Figure 1–53).

Q&A What if a cell already includes a bold style?

If the active cell is already bold, then Excel displays the Bold button with a transparent orange background.

Q&A How do I remove the bold style from a cell?

Clicking the Bold button a second time removes the bold font style.

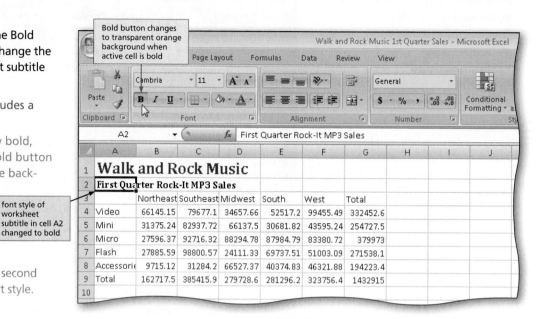

Figure 1–53

Other Ways
1. Click Bold button on Mini toolbar
2. Right-click cell, click Format Cells on shortcut menu, click Font tab, click Bold, click OK button
3. Press CTRL+B

To Increase the Font Size of a Cell Entry

Increasing the font size is the next step in formatting the worksheet subtitle. You increase the font size of a cell so the entry stands out and is easier to read. The following steps increase the font size of the worksheet subtitle in cell A2.

1

- With cell A2 selected, click the Font Size box arrow on the Ribbon to display the Font Size list.

- Point to 14 in the Font Size list to see a live preview of cell A2 with a font size of 14 (Figure 1–54).

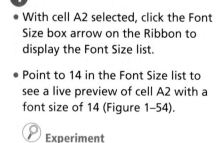 **Experiment**

- Point to several other font sizes in the Font Size list to see a live preview of other font sizes in cell A2.

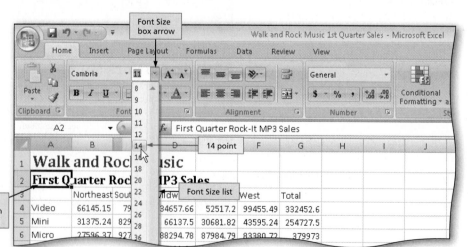

Figure 1–54

2

Q&A

- Click 14 in the Font Size list to change the font in cell A2 from 11 point to 14 point (Figure 1–55).

Can I assign a font size that is not in the Font Size list?

Yes. An alternative to clicking a font size in the Font Size list is to click the Font Size box, type the font size, and then press the ENTER key. This procedure allows you to assign a font size not available in the Font Size list to a selected cell entry.

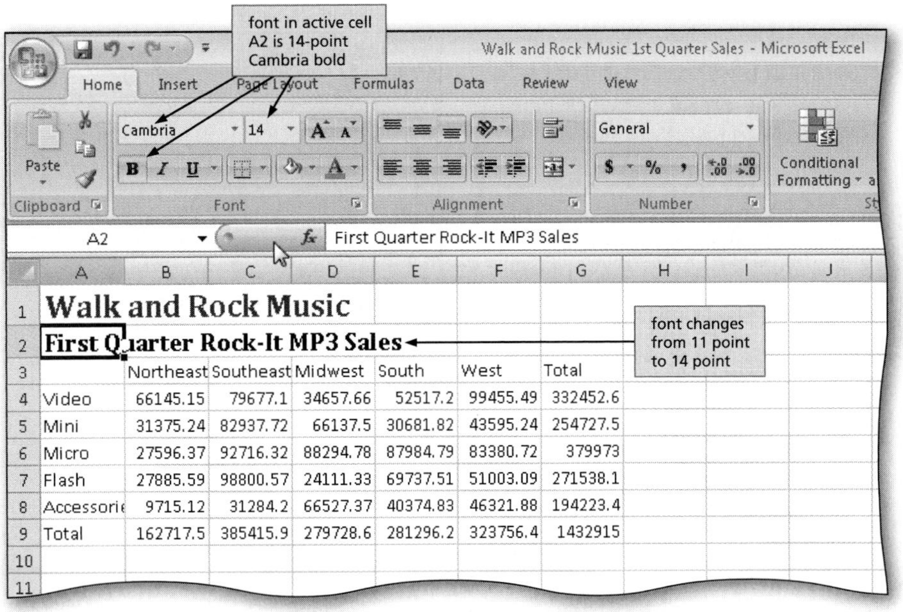

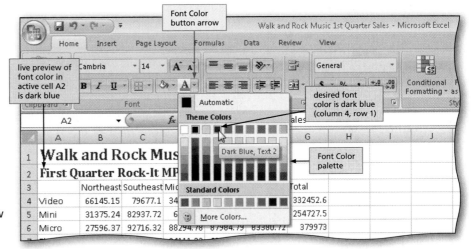

(screenshot annotations: font in active cell A2 is 14-point Cambria bold; Walk and Rock Music 1st Quarter Sales - Microsoft Excel; font changes from 11 point to 14 point)

fx First Quarter Rock-It MP3 Sales

	A	B	C	D	E	F	G
1	Walk and Rock Music						
2	First Quarter Rock-It MP3 Sales						
3		Northeast	Southeast	Midwest	South	West	Total
4	Video	66145.15	79677.1	34657.66	52517.2	99455.49	332452.6
5	Mini	31375.24	82937.72	66137.5	30681.82	43595.24	254727.5
6	Micro	27596.37	92716.32	88294.78	87984.79	83380.72	379973
7	Flash	27885.59	98800.57	24111.33	69737.51	51003.09	271538.1
8	Accessorie	9715.12	31284.2	66527.37	40374.83	46321.88	194223.4
9	Total	162717.5	385415.9	279728.6	281296.2	323756.4	1432915
10							
11							

Figure 1–55

Other Ways

1. Click Increase Font Size button or Decrease Font Size button on Ribbon

2. Select font size from Font Size list on Mini toolbar

3. Right-click cell, click Format Cells on shortcut menu, click Font tab, select font size in Size box, click OK button

To Change the Font Color of a Cell Entry

The next step is to change the color of the font in cell A2 from black to dark blue. The following steps change the font color of a cell entry.

1

- With cell A2 selected, click the Font Color button arrow on the Ribbon to display the Font Color palette.

- Point to Dark Blue, Text 2 (dark blue color in column 4, row 1) in the Theme Colors area of the Font Color palette to see a live preview of the font color in cell A2 (Figure 1–56).

Experiment

- Point to several other colors in the Font Color palette to see a live preview of other font colors in cell A2.

Q&A

Which colors does Excel make available on the Font Color palette?

You can choose from more than 60 different font colors on the Font Color palette (Figure 1–56). Your Font Color palette may have more or fewer colors, depending on color settings of your operating system. The Theme Colors area includes colors that are included in the current workbook's theme.

Figure 1–56

2

- Click Dark Blue, Text 2 (column 4, row 1) on the Font Color palette to change the font of the worksheet subtitle in cell A2 from black to dark blue (Figure 1–57).

Q&A

Why does the Font Color button change after I select the new font color?

When you choose a color on the Font Color palette, Excel changes the Font Color button on the Formatting toolbar to the chosen color. Thus, to change the font color of the cell entry in another cell to the same color, you need only to select the cell and then click the Font Color button.

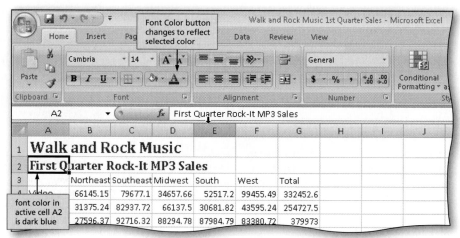

Figure 1–57

Other Ways

1. Select font color from Font Color list on Mini toolbar

2. Right-click cell, click Format Cells on shortcut menu, click Font tab, select color on Font Color palette, click OK button

To Center Cell Entries across Columns by Merging Cells

The final step in formatting the worksheet title and subtitle is to center them across columns A through G. Centering a title across the columns used in the body of the worksheet improves the worksheet's appearance. To do this, the seven cells in the range A1:G1 are combined, or merged, into a single cell that is the width of the columns in the body of the worksheet. The seven cells in the range A2:G2 also are merged in a similar manner. **Merging cells** involves creating a single cell by combining two or more selected cells. The following steps center the worksheet title and subtitle across columns by merging cells.

- Select cell A1 and then drag to cell G1 to highlight the range A1:G1 (Figure 1–58).

Q&A

What if a cell in the range B1:G1 contained data?

For the Merge & Center button to work properly, all the cells except the leftmost cell in the selected range must be empty.

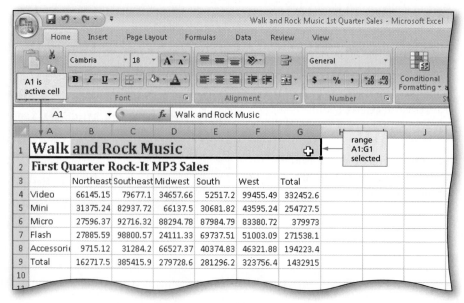

Figure 1–58

2

- Click the Merge & Center button on the Ribbon to merge cells A1 through G1 and center the contents of cell A1 across columns A through G (Figure 1–59).

Q&A What happened to cells B1 through G1?

After the merge, cells B1 through G1 no longer exist. Cell A1 now extends across columns A through G.

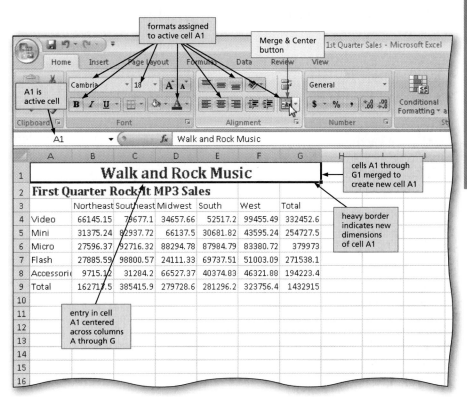

Figure 1–59

3

- Repeat Steps 1 and 2 to merge and center the worksheet subtitle across cells A2 through G2 (Figure 1–60).

Q&A Are cells B1 through G1 and B2 through G2 lost forever?

No. The opposite of merging cells is **splitting a merged cell**. After you have merged multiple cells to create one merged cell, you can unmerge, or split, the merged cell to display the original cells on the worksheet. You split a merged cell by selecting it and clicking the Merge & Center button. For example, if you click the Merge & Center button a second time in Step 2, it will split the merged cell A1 to cells A1, B1, C1, D1, E1, F1, and G1.

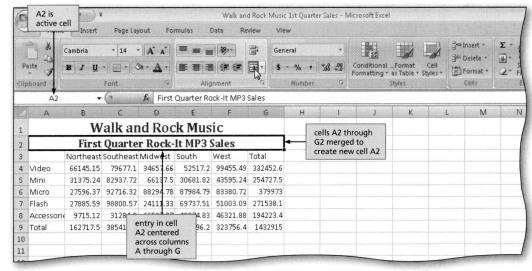

Figure 1–60

Other Ways

1. Right-click selection, click Merge & Center button on Mini toolbar

2. Right-click selection, click Format Cells on shortcut menu, click Alignment tab, select Center Across Selection in Horizontal list, click OK button

To Format Column Titles and the Total Row

The next step to format the worksheet is to format the column titles in row 3 and the total row, row 9. Column titles and the total row should be formatted so anyone who views the worksheet can quickly distinguish the column titles and total row from the data in the body of the worksheet. The following steps format the column titles and total row using cell styles in the default worksheet theme.

1
- Click cell A3 and then drag the mouse pointer to cell G3 to select the range A3:G3.

- Point to the Cell Styles button on the Ribbon (Figure 1–61).

Q&A

Why is cell A3 selected in the range for the column headings?

The style to be applied to the column headings includes an underline that will help to distinguish the column headings from the rest of the worksheet. Including cell A3 in the range ensures that the cell will include the underline, which is visually appealing and further helps to separate the data in the worksheet.

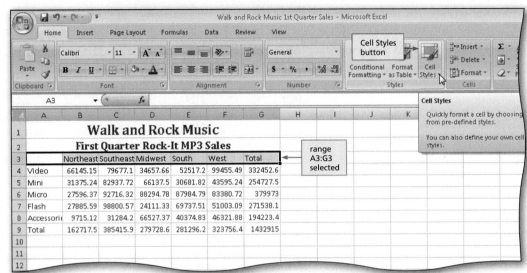

Figure 1–61

2
- Click the Cell Styles button to display the Cell Styles gallery.

- Point to the Heading 3 cell style in the Titles and Headings area of the Cell Styles gallery to see a live preview of the cell style in the range A3:G3 (Figure 1–62).

 Experiment

- Point to other cell styles in the Titles and Headings area of the Cell Styles gallery to see a live preview of other cell styles in the range A3:G3.

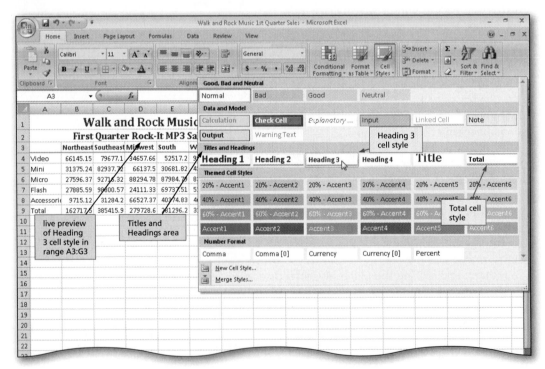

Figure 1–62

3

- Click the Heading 3 cell style to apply the cell style to the range A3:G3.

- Click cell A9 and then drag the mouse pointer to cell G9 to select the range A9:G9.

- Point to the Cell Styles button on the Ribbon (Figure 1–63).

Why should I choose Heading 3 instead of another heading cell style?

Excel includes many types of headings, such as Heading 1 and Heading 2, because worksheets often include many levels of headings above columns. In the case of the worksheet created for this project, the Heading 3 title includes formatting that makes the column titles' font size smaller than the title and subtitle and makes the column titles stand out from the data in the body of the worksheet.

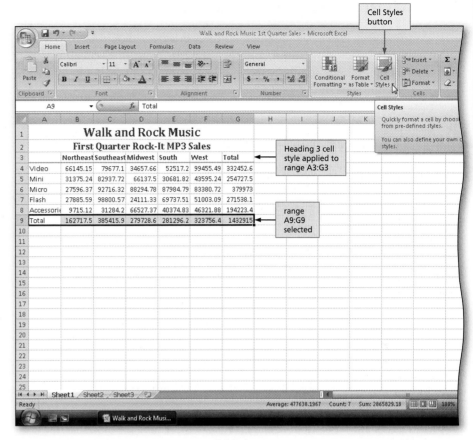

Figure 1–63

4

- Click the Cell Styles button on the Ribbon to display the Cell Styles gallery and then click the Total cell style in the Titles and Headings area to apply the Total cell style to the cells in the range A9:G9.

- Click cell A11 to select the cell (Figure 1–64).

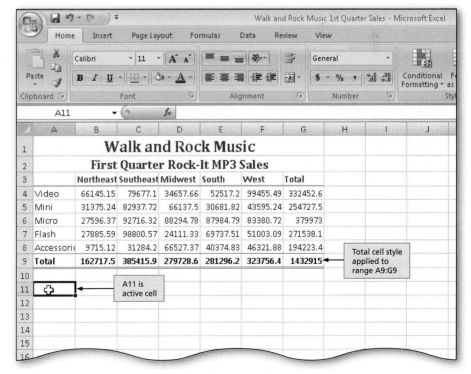

Figure 1–64

To Format Numbers in the Worksheet

As previously noted, the numbers in the worksheet should be formatted to use a dollar-and-cents format, with dollar signs in the first row (row 4) and the total row (row 9). Excel allows you to format numbers in a variety of ways, and these methods are discussed in other chapters in this book. The following steps use buttons on the Ribbon to format the numbers in the worksheet.

- Select cell B4 and drag the mouse pointer to cell G4 to select the range B4:G4.

- Point to the Accounting Number Format button on the Ribbon to display the Enhanced ScreenTip (Figure 1–65).

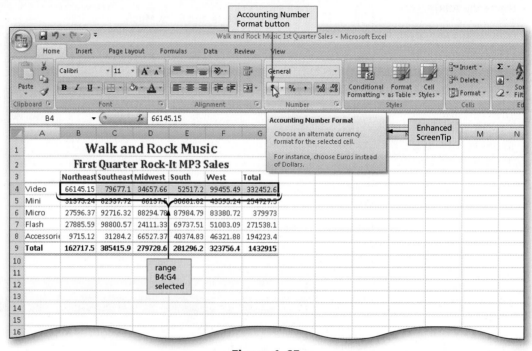

Figure 1–65

- Click the Accounting Number Format button on the Ribbon to apply the Accounting Number format to the cells in the range B4:G4.

- Select the range B5:G8 (Figure 1–66).

Q&A

What effect does the Accounting Number format have on the selected cells?

The Accounting Number format causes the cells to display with two decimal places so that decimal places in cells below the selected cells align vertically. Cell widths are automatically adjusted to accommodate the new formatting.

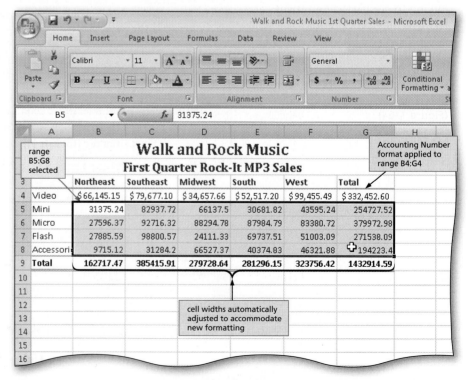

Figure 1–66

3

- Click the Comma Style button on the Ribbon to apply the Comma Style to the range B5:G8.

- Select the range B9:G9 (Figure 1–67).

Q&A What effect does the Comma Style format have on the selected cells?

The Comma Style format causes the cells to display with two decimal places and commas as thousands separators.

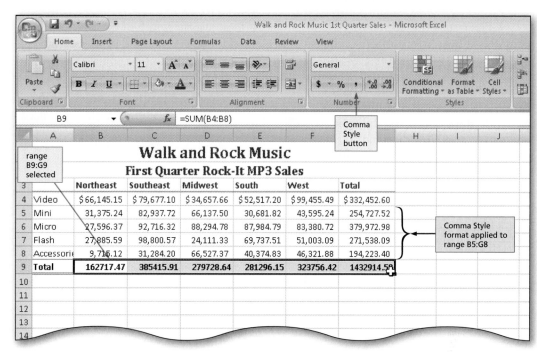

Figure 1–67

4

- Click the Accounting Number Format button on the Ribbon to apply the Accounting Number format to the cells in the range B9:G9.

- Select cell A11 (Figure 1-68).

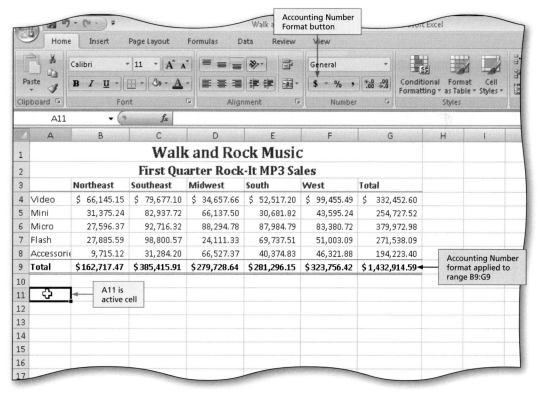

Figure 1–68

Other Ways
1. Click Accounting Number Format or Comma button on Mini toolbar	2. Right-click selection, click Format Cells on the shortcut menu, click Number tab, select Accounting in Category list or select Number and click Use 1000 Separator, click OK button

To Adjust the Column Width

The last step in formatting the worksheet is to adjust the width of column A so that the word Accessories in cell A8 is shown in its entirety in the cell. Excel includes several methods for adjusting cell widths and row heights, and these methods are discussed later in this book. The following steps adjust the width of column A so that the contents of cell A8 are displayed in the cell.

1

- Point to the boundary on the right side of the column A heading above row 1 to change the mouse pointer to a split double arrow (Figure 1–69).

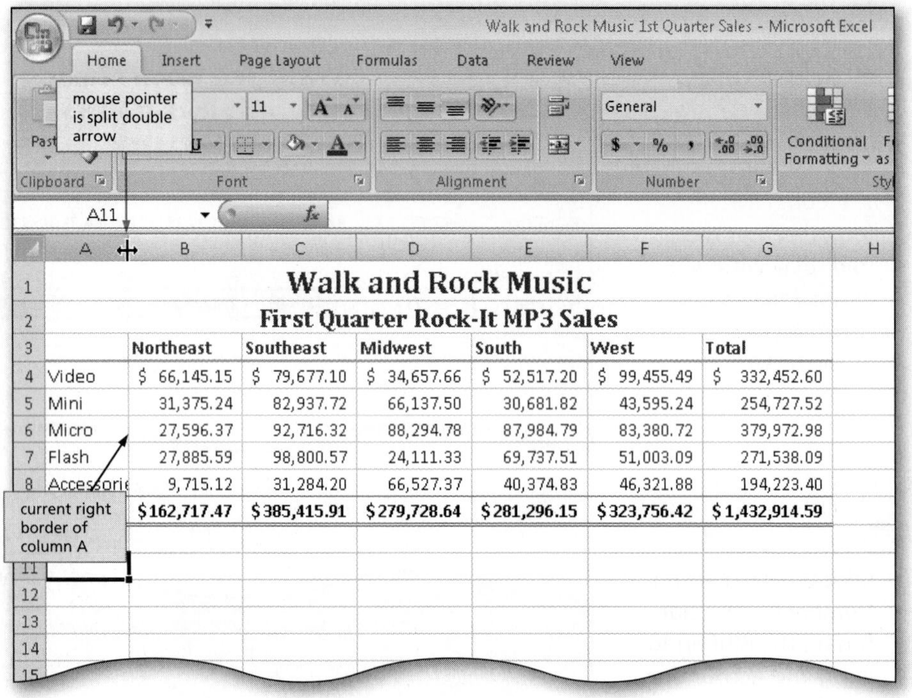

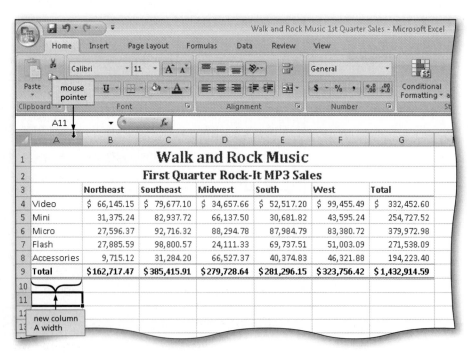

Figure 1–69

2

- Double-click on the boundary to adjust the width of column A to the width of the largest item in the column (Figure 1–70).

Q&A

What if none of the items in column A extended through the entire width of the column?

If all of the items in column A were shorter in length than the width of the column when you double-click the right side of the column A heading, then Excel still would adjust the column width to the largest item in the column. That is, Excel would reduce the width of the column to the largest item.

Figure 1–70

Using the Name Box to Select a Cell

The next step is to chart the quarterly sales for the five product types sold by the company. To create the chart, you must select the cell in the upper-left corner of the range to chart (cell A3). Rather than clicking cell A3 to select it, the next section describes how to use the Name box to select the cell.

To Use the Name Box to Select a Cell

As previously noted, the Name box is located on the left side of the formula bar. To select any cell, click the Name box and enter the cell reference of the cell you want to select. The following steps select cell A3.

1
• Click the Name box in the formula bar and then type a3 as the cell to select (Figure 1–71).

Why is cell A11 still selected?

Even though cell A11 is the active cell, Excel displays the typed cell reference a3 in the Name box until you press the ENTER key.

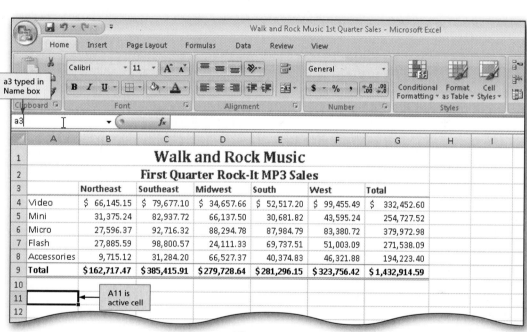

Figure 1–71

2
• Press the ENTER key to change the active cell from A11 to cell A3 (Figure 1–72).

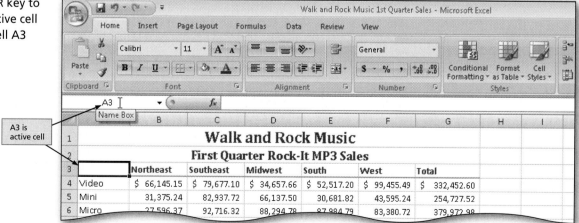

Figure 1–72

Other Ways to Select Cells

As you will see in later chapters, in addition to using the Name box to select any cell in a worksheet, you also can use it to assign names to a cell or range of cells. Excel supports several additional ways to select a cell, as summarized in Table 1–3.

BTW

Find & Select
You can find and select cells based on their content. Click the Find & Select button on the Home tab on the Ribbon. Then, click the Go To Special command. Choose your desired option in the Select area of the Go To Special dialog box and then click the OK button.

Table 1–3 Selecting Cells in Excel

Key, Box, or Command	Function
ALT+PAGE DOWN	Selects the cell one worksheet window to the right and moves the worksheet window accordingly.
ALT+PAGE UP	Selects the cell one worksheet window to the left and moves the worksheet window accordingly.
ARROW	Selects the adjacent cell in the direction of the arrow on the key.
CTRL+ARROW	Selects the border cell of the worksheet in combination with the arrow keys and moves the worksheet window accordingly. For example, to select the rightmost cell in the row that contains the active cell, press CTRL+RIGHT ARROW. You also can press the END key, release it, and then press the appropriate arrow key to accomplish the same task.
CTRL+HOME	Selects cell A1 or the cell one column and one row below and to the right of frozen titles and moves the worksheet window accordingly.
Find command on Find and Select menu or SHIFT+F5	Finds and selects a cell that contains specific contents that you enter in the Find dialog box. If necessary, Excel moves the worksheet window to display the cell. You also can press CTRL+F to display the Find dialog box.
Go To command on Find and Select menu or F5	Selects the cell that corresponds to the cell reference you enter in the Go To dialog box and moves the worksheet window accordingly. You also can press CTRL+G to display the Go To dialog box.
HOME	Selects the cell at the beginning of the row that contains the active cell and moves the worksheet window accordingly.
Name box	Selects the cell in the workbook that corresponds to the cell reference you enter in the Name box.
PAGE DOWN	Selects the cell down one worksheet window from the active cell and moves the worksheet window accordingly.
PAGE UP	Selects the cell up one worksheet window from the active cell and moves the worksheet window accordingly.

Plan Ahead

Decide on the type of chart needed.
Excel includes 11 chart types from which you can choose including column, line, pie, bar, area, X Y (scatter), stock, surface, doughnut, bubble, and radar. The type of chart you choose depends on the type of data that you have, how much data you have, and the message you want to convey.

A column chart is a good way to compare values side-by-side. A Clustered Column chart can go even further in comparing values across categories. In the case of the Walk and Rock Music quarterly sales data, comparisons of product types within each region can be made side-by-side with a Clustered Column chart.

Establish where to position and how to format the chart.
- When possible, try to position charts so that both the data and chart appear on the screen on the worksheet together and so that the data and chart can be printed in the most readable manner possible. By placing the chart below the data on the Walk and Rock Music 1st Quarter Sales worksheet, both of these goals are accomplished.
- When choosing/selecting colors for a chart, consider the color scheme of the rest of the worksheet. The chart should not present colors that are in stark contrast to the rest of the worksheet. If the chart will be printed in color, minimize the amount of dark colors on the chart so that the chart both prints quickly and preserves ink.

Adding a 3-D Clustered Column Chart to the Worksheet

As outlined in the requirements document in Figure 1–2 on page EX 4, the worksheet should include a 3-D Clustered Column chart to graphically represent quarterly sales for each product type that the company sells. The 3-D Clustered Column chart shown in Figure 1–73 is called an **embedded chart** because it is drawn on the same worksheet as the data.

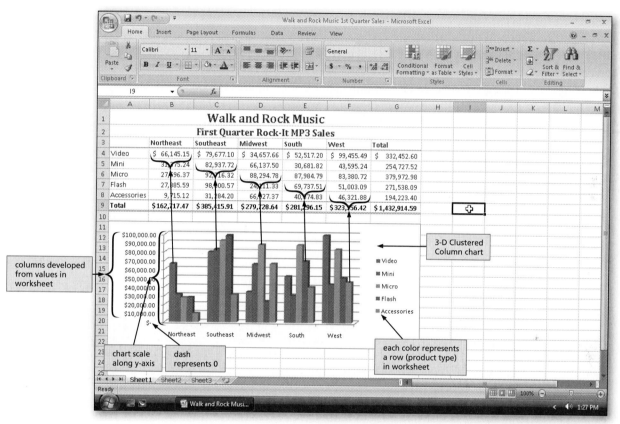

Figure 1–73

The chart uses different colored columns to represent sales for different product types. Each region uses the same color scheme for identifying product types, which allows for easy identification and comparison. For the Northeast sales region, for example, the dark blue column representing Video products shows quarterly sales of $66,145.15; for the Southeast sales region, the maroon column representing Mini products shows quarterly sales of $82,937.72; for the Midwest sales region, the pale green column representing Micro products shows quarterly sales of $88,294.78; for the South sales region, the violet column representing Flash products shows quarterly sales of $69,737.51; and for the West sales region, the light blue column representing Accessories shows quarterly sales of $46,321.88. Because the same color scheme is used in each region to represent the five product types, you easily can compare sales of product types among the sales regions. The totals from the worksheet are not represented, because the totals are not in the range specified for charting.

BTW

Cell Values and Charting
When you change a cell value on which a chart is dependent, Excel redraws the chart instantaneously, unless automatic recalculation is disabled. If automatic recalculation is disabled, then you must press the F9 key to redraw the chart. To enable or disable automatic recalculation, click the Calculations Options button on the Formulas tab on the Ribbon.

Excel derives the chart scale based on the values in the worksheet and then displays the scale along the vertical axis (also called the **y-axis** or **value axis**) of the chart. For example, no value in the range B4:F8 is less than 0 or greater than $100,000.00, so the scale ranges from 0 to $100,000.00. Excel also determines the $10,000.00 increments of the scale automatically. For the numbers along the y-axis, Excel uses a format that includes representing the 0 value with a dash (Figure 1–73 on the previous page).

To Add a 3-D Clustered Column Chart to the Worksheet

The commands to insert a chart are located on the Insert tab. With the range to chart selected, you click the Column button on the Ribbon to initiate drawing the chart. The area on the worksheet where the chart appears is called the chart location. As shown in Figure 1–73, the chart location in this worksheet is the range A11:G22, immediately below the worksheet data.

The following steps draw a 3-D Clustered Column chart that compares the quarterly sales by product type for the five sales regions.

- Click cell A3 and then drag the mouse pointer to the cell F8 to select the range A3:F8 (Figure 1–74).

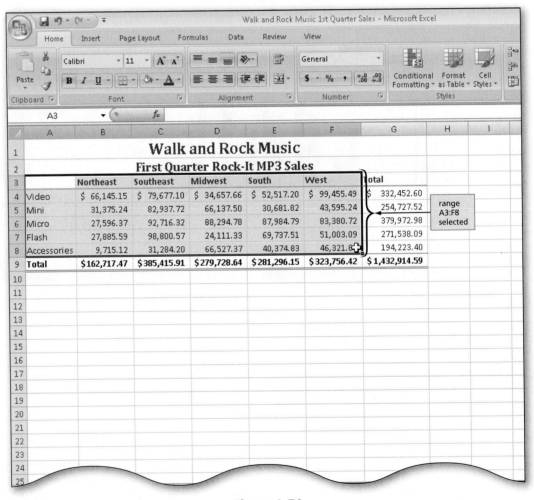

Figure 1–74

2

- Click the Insert tab to make the Insert tab the active tab (Figure 1–75).

What tasks can I perform with the Insert tab?

The Insert tab includes commands that allow you to insert various objects, such as shapes, tables, illustrations, and charts, into a worksheet. These objects will be discussed as they are used throughout this book.

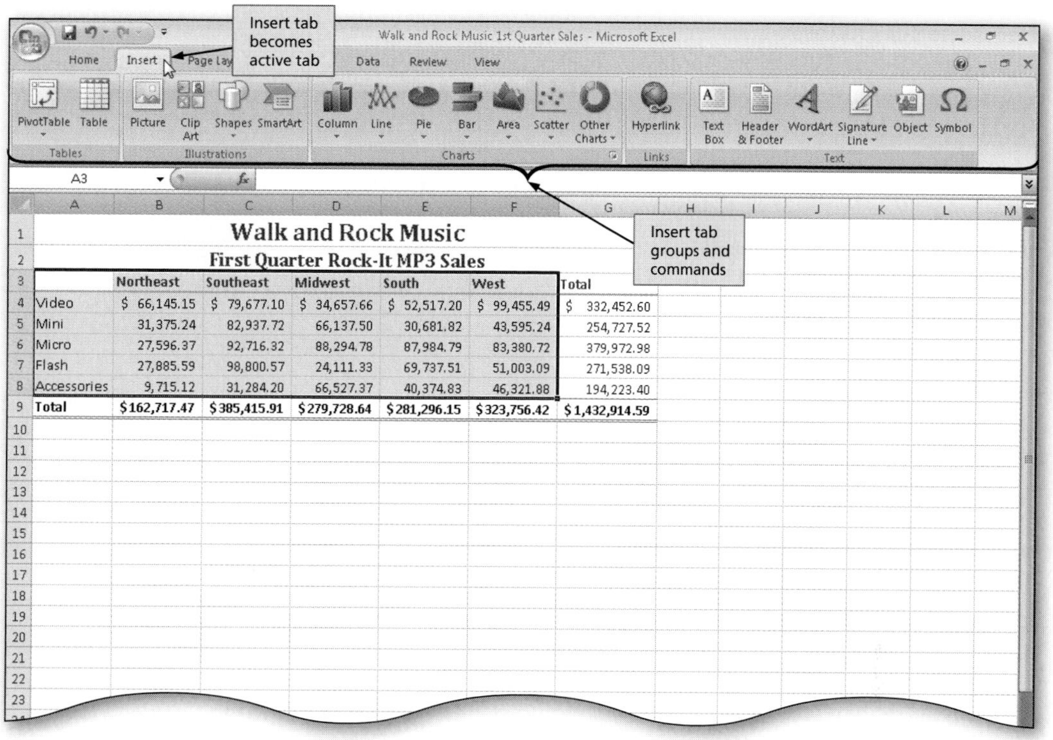

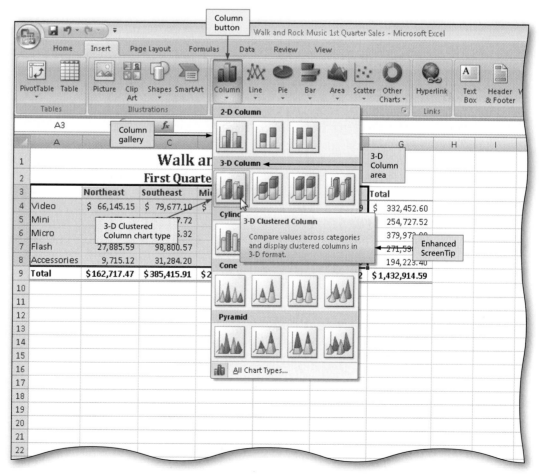

Figure 1–75

3

- Click the Column button on the Ribbon to display the Column gallery.

- Point to the 3-D Clustered Column chart type in the 3-D Column area of the Column gallery (Figure 1–76).

Figure 1–76

4

- Click the 3-D Clustered Column chart type in the 3-D Column area of the Column gallery to add a 3-D Clustered Column chart to the middle of the worksheet in a selection rectangle.

- Click the top-right edge of the selection rectangle but do not release the mouse to grab the chart and change the mouse pointer to a crosshair with four arrowheads (Figure 1–77).

 Why is a new tab displayed on the Ribbon?

When you select objects such as shapes or charts, Excel displays contextual tabs that include special commands that are used to work with the type of object selected. Because a chart is selected, Excel displays the Chart Tools contextual tab. The three tabs below the Chart Tools contextual tab, Design, Layout, and Format, are tabs that include commands to work with charts.

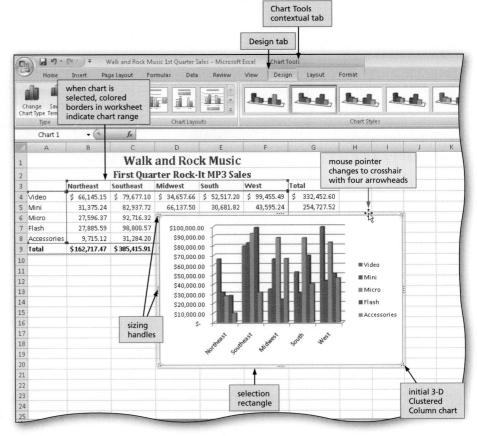

Figure 1–77

5

- Continue holding down the left mouse button while dragging the chart down and to the left to position the upper-left corner of the dotted line rectangle over the upper-left corner of cell A11. Release the mouse button to complete the move of the chart.

- Click the middle sizing handle on the right edge of the chart and do not release the mouse button (Figure 1–78).

How does Excel know how to create the chart?

Excel automatically selects the entries in the topmost row of the chart range (row 3) as the titles for the horizontal axis (also called the **x-axis** or **category axis**) and draws a column for each of the 25 cells in the range containing numbers.

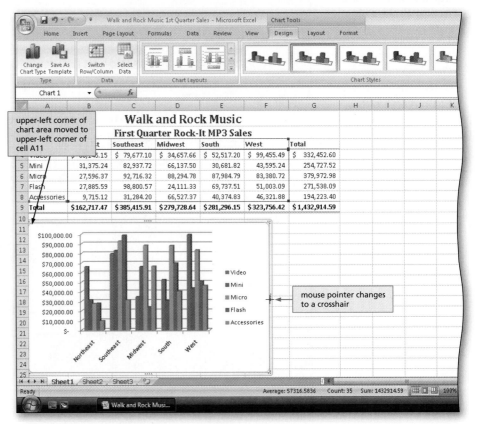

Figure 1–78

6

- While continuing to hold down the mouse button, press the ALT key and drag the right edge of the chart to the right edge of column G and then release the mouse button to resize the chart.

- Point to the middle sizing handle on the bottom edge of the selection rectangle and do not release the mouse button (Figure 1–79).

 Why should I hold the ALT key down while I resize a chart?

Holding down the ALT key while you drag a chart **snaps** (aligns) the edge of the chart area to the worksheet gridlines. If you do not hold down the ALT key, then you can place an edge of a chart in the middle of a column or row.

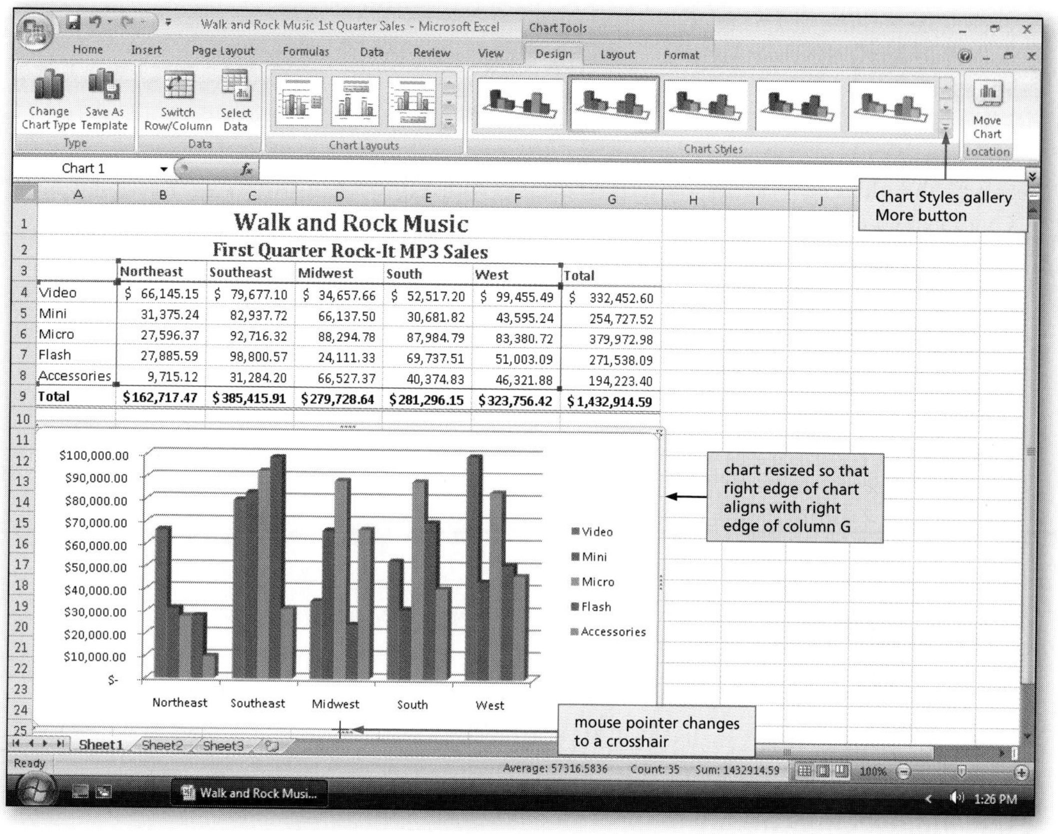

Figure 1–79

7

- While continuing to hold down the mouse button, press the ALT key and drag the bottom edge of the chart up to the bottom edge of row 22 and then release the mouse button to resize the chart.

- Click the More button in the Chart Styles gallery to expand the gallery and point to Style 2 in the gallery (column 2, row 1) (Figure 1–80).

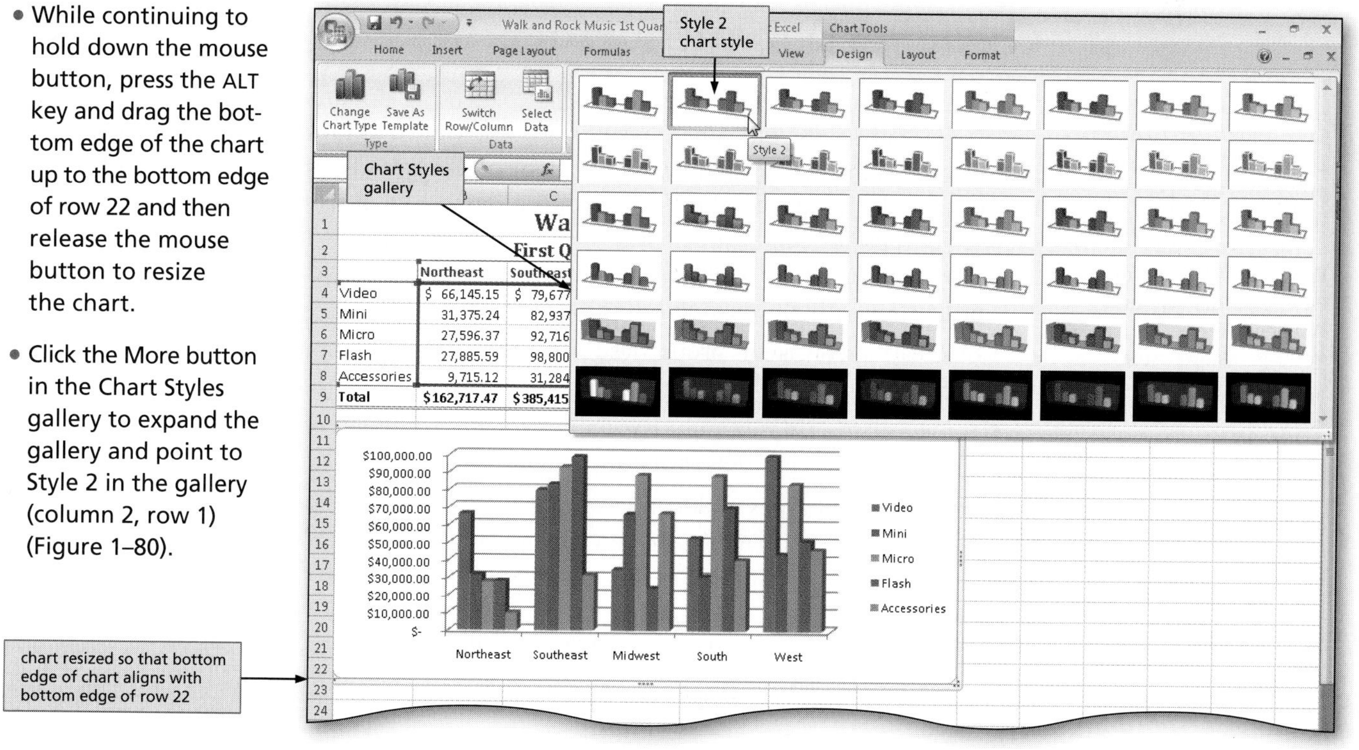

Figure 1–80

8

- Click Style 2 in the Chart Styles gallery to apply the chart style Style 2 to the chart.

Experiment

- Select other chart styles in the Chart Styles gallery to apply other chart styles to the chart, but select Style 2 as your final choice.

- Click cell I9 to deselect the chart and complete the worksheet (Figure 1–81).

Q&A

What is the purpose of the items on the right side of the chart?

The items to the right of the column chart in Figure 1–81 are the **legend**, which identifies the colors assigned to each bar in the chart. Excel automatically selects the entries in the leftmost column of the chart range (column A) as titles within the legend.

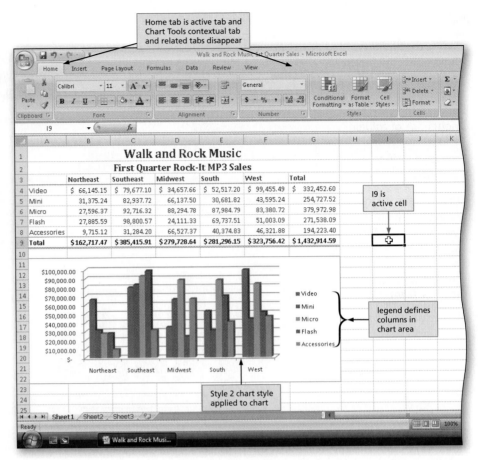

Figure 1–81

Changing Document Properties and Saving Again

BTW

Document Properties
Excel allows you to assign additional document properties by clicking the Document Properties button arrow in the Document Information Panel and then clicking Advanced Properties. You can assign custom properties, such as Department, Purpose, and Editor. Or, you can create your own document properties.

Excel helps you organize and identify your files by using **document properties**, which are the details about a file. Document properties, also known as **metadata**, can include such information as the project author, title, or subject. **Keywords** are words or phrases that further describe the document. For example, a class name or worksheet topic can describe the file's purpose or content. Document properties are valuable for a variety of reasons:

- Users can save time locating a particular file because they can view a document's properties without opening the workbook.

- By creating consistent properties for files having similar content, users can better organize their workbooks.

- Some organizations require Excel users to add document properties so that other employees can view details about these files.

Five different types of document properties exist, but the more common ones used in this book are standard and automatically updated properties. **Standard properties** are associated with all Microsoft Office documents and include author, title, and subject. **Automatically updated properties** include file system properties, such as the date you create or change a file, and statistics, such as the file size.

To Change Document Properties

The **Document Information Panel** contains areas where you can view and enter document properties. You can view and change information in this panel at any time while you are creating your workbook. Before saving the workbook again, you want to add your name and class name as document properties. The following steps use the Document Information Panel to change document properties.

- Click the Office Button to display the Office Button menu.

- Point to Prepare on the Office Button menu to display the Prepare submenu (Figure 1–82).

Q&A

What other types of actions besides changing properties can you take to prepare a document for distribution?

The Prepare submenu provides commands related to sharing a document with others, such as allowing or restricting people to view and modify your document, checking to see if your worksheet will work in earlier versions of Excel, and searching for hidden personal information.

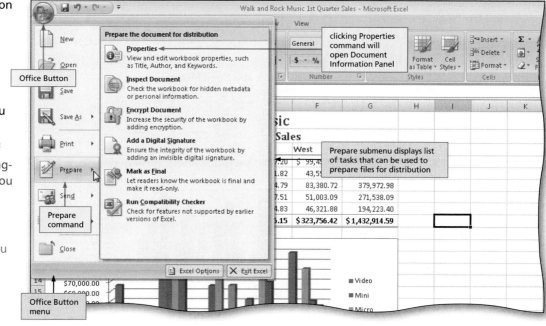

Figure 1–82

- Click Properties on the Prepare submenu to display the Document Information Panel (Figure 1–83).

Q&A

Why are some of the document properties in my Document Information Panel already filled in?

The person who installed Microsoft Office 2007 on your computer or network may have set or customized the properties.

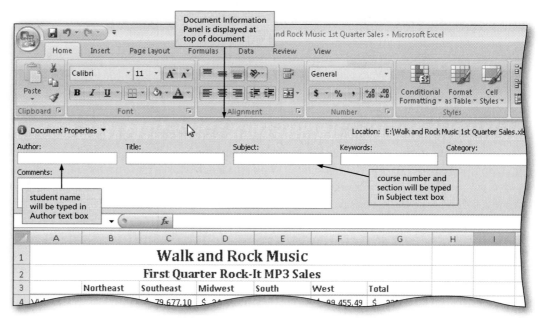

Figure 1–83

3

- Click the Author text box and then type your name as the Author property. If a name already is displayed in the Author text box, delete it before typing your name.

- Click the Subject text box, if necessary delete any existing text, and then type your course and section as the Subject property.

- Click the Keywords text box, if necessary delete any existing text, and then type First Quarter Rock-It MP3 Sales (Figure 1-84).

Q&A

What types of document properties does Excel collect automatically?

Excel records such details as how long you worked at creating your project, how many times you revised the document, and what fonts and themes are used.

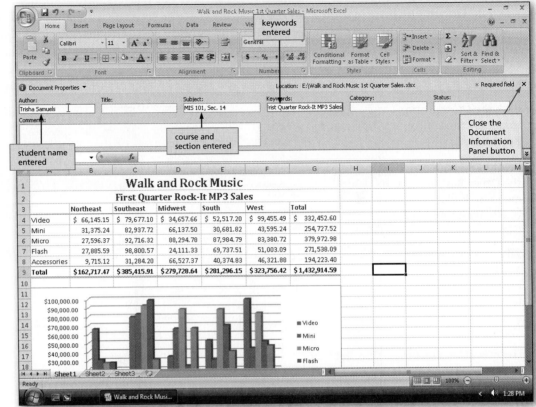

Figure 1-84

4

- Click the Close the Document Information Panel button so that the Document Information Panel no longer is displayed.

To Save an Existing Workbook with the Same File Name

Saving frequently cannot be overemphasized. Several modifications have been made to the workbook since it was saved earlier in the chapter. Earlier in this chapter, the Save button on the Quick Access Toolbar caused the Save As dialog box to appear, and the file name, Walk and Rock Music 1st Quarter Sales, was entered. Clicking the Save button on the Quick Access Toolbar causes Excel to save the changes made to the workbook since the last time it was saved. The following step saves the workbook again.

1

- With your USB flash drive connected to one of the computer's USB ports, click the Save button on the Quick Access Toolbar to overwrite the previous Walk and Rock Music 1st Quarter Sales file on the USB flash drive (Figure 1–85).

Q&A

Why did the Save As dialog box not appear?

Excel overwrites the document using the settings specified the first time the document was saved. To save the file with a different file name or on different media, display the Save As dialog box by clicking the Office Button and then clicking Save As on the Office Button menu. Then, fill in the Save As dialog box as described in Steps 2 through 5 on pages EX 31 and EX 32.

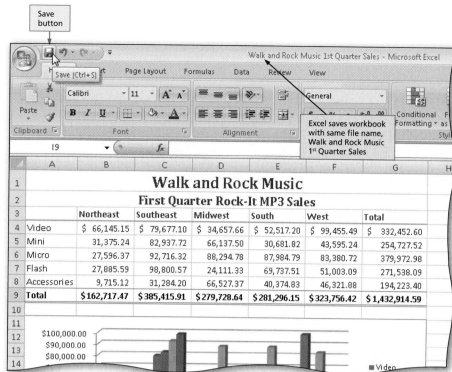

Figure 1–85

Printing a Worksheet

After you create a worksheet, you often want to print it. A printed version of the worksheet is called a **hard copy** or **printout**. Printed copies of your worksheet can be useful for the following reasons:

- Many people prefer proofreading a hard copy of the worksheet rather than viewing the worksheet on the screen to check for errors and readability.
- Someone without computer access can view the worksheet's content.
- Copies can be distributed as handouts to people during a meeting or presentation.
- Hard copies can serve as reference material if your storage medium is lost or becomes corrupted and you need to recreate the worksheet.

It is a good practice to save a workbook before printing it, in the event you experience difficulties with the printer.

To Print a Worksheet

With the completed worksheet saved, you may want to print it. The following steps print the worksheet in the saved Walk and Rock Music 1st Quarter Sales workbook.

- Click the Office Button to display the Office Button menu.

- Point to Print on the Office Button menu to display the Print submenu (Figure 1–86).

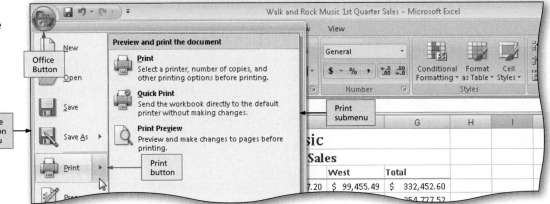

Figure 1–86

- Click Quick Print on the Print submenu to print the worksheet (Figure 1–87).

Q&A

Can I print my worksheet in black and white to conserve ink or toner?

Yes. Click the Office Button and then click the Excel Options button on the Office Button menu. When the Excel Options dialog box is displayed, click Advanced, scroll to the Print area, place a check mark in the Use draft quality check box if it is displayed, and then click the OK button and then click the Close Print Preview button on the Ribbon. Click the Office Button, point to Print, and then click Quick Print.

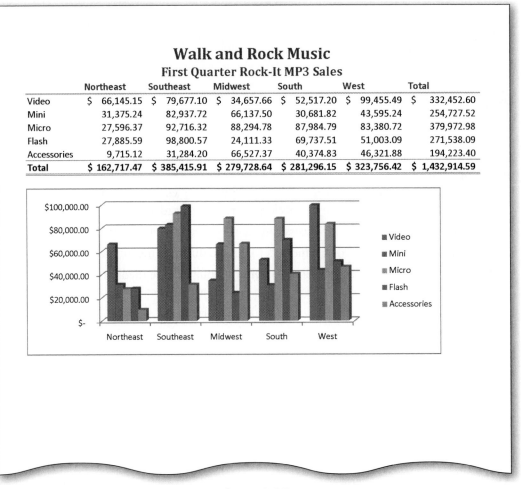

Figure 1–87

Other Ways

1. Press CTRL+P, press ENTER

Quitting Excel

When you quit Excel, if you have made changes to a workbook since the last time the file was saved, Excel displays a dialog box asking if you want to save the changes you made to the file before it closes that window. The dialog box contains three buttons with these resulting actions:

- Yes button — Saves the changes and then quits Excel
- No button — Quits Excel without saving changes
- Cancel button — Closes the dialog box and redisplays the worksheet without saving the changes

If no changes have been made to an open workbook since the last time the file was saved, Excel will close the window without displaying a dialog box.

To Quit Excel with One Workbook Open

The Walk and Rock 1st Quarter Sales worksheet is complete. The following steps quit Excel if only one workbook is open.

1
- Point to the Close button on the right side of the Excel title bar (Figure 1–88).

2
- Click the Close button to quit Excel.

Q&A What if I have more than one Excel workbook open?

You would click the Close button on the Excel title bar for each open workbook. When you click the Close button with the last workbook open, Excel also quits. As an alternative, you could click the Office Button and then click the Exit Excel button on the Office Button menu, which closes all open workbooks and then quits Excel.

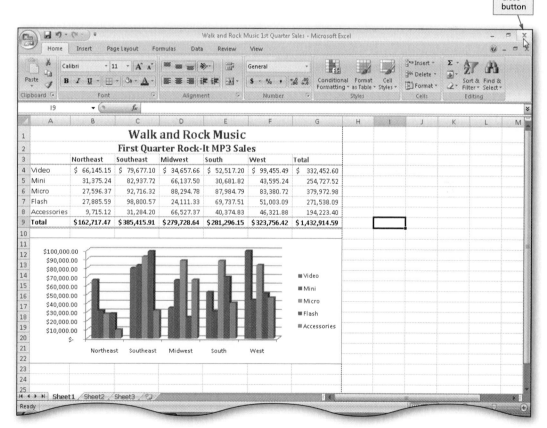
Close button

Figure 1–88

Other Ways
1. Double-click Office Button
2. With multiple workbooks open, click Office Button, click Exit Excel on Office Button menu
3. Right-click Microsoft Excel button on Windows Vista taskbar, click Close on shortcut menu
4. Press ALT+F4

BTW

Print Preview
You can preview the printout on your screen using the Print Preview command on the Print submenu (Figure 1–86 on page EX 58), make adjustments to the worksheet, and then print it only when it appears exactly as you want. Each time you preview rather than print, you save both ink and paper.

Starting Excel and Opening a Workbook

Once you have created and saved a workbook, you may need to retrieve it from your storage medium. For example, you might want to revise a worksheet or reprint it. Opening a workbook requires that Excel is running on your computer.

To Start Excel

The following steps, which assume Windows Vista is running, start Excel.

Note: If you are using Windows XP, please see Appendix F for alternate steps.

1 Click the Start button on the Windows Vista taskbar to display the Start menu.

2 Click All Programs at the bottom of the left pane on the Start menu to display the All Programs list and then click Microsoft Office in the All Programs list to display the Microsoft Office list.

3 Click Microsoft Office Excel 2007 in the Microsoft Office list to start Excel and display a new blank worksheet in the Excel window.

4 If the Excel window is not maximized, click the Maximize button on its title bar to maximize the window.

To Open a Workbook from Excel

Earlier in this chapter, the workbook was saved on a USB flash drive using the file name, Walk and Rock Music 1st Quarter Sales. The following steps open the Walk and Rock Music 1st Quarter Sales file from the USB flash drive.

1

- With your USB flash drive connected to one of the computer's USB ports, click the Office Button to display the Office Button menu (Figure 1–89).

Q&A

What files are shown in the Recent Documents list?

Excel displays the most recently opened document file names in this list. If the name of the file you want to open appears in the Recent Documents list, you could double-click it to open the file.

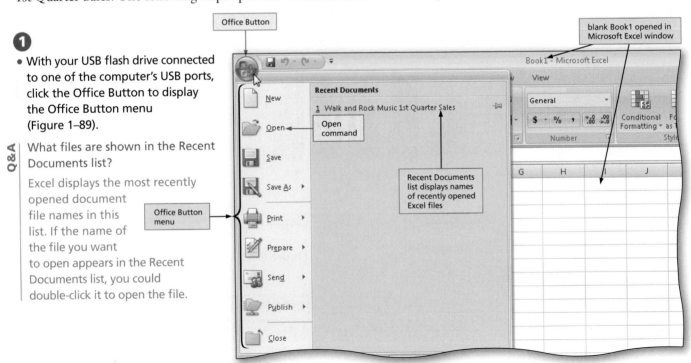

Figure 1–89

2

- Click Open on the Office Button menu to display the Open dialog box.

- If the Folders list is displayed below the Folders button, click the Folders button to remove the Folders list.

- If necessary, click Computer in the Favorite Links section and then scroll until UDISK 2.0 (E:) appears in the list of available drives.

- Double-click UDISK 2.0 (E:) to select the USB flash drive, Drive E in this case, as the new open location.

- Click Walk and Rock Music 1st Quarter Sales to select the file name (Figure 1–90).

 Q&A How do I open the file if I am not using a USB flash drive?

Use the same process, but be certain to select your device in the Computer list.

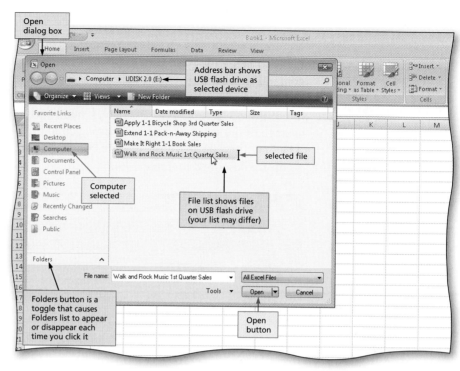

Figure 1–90

3

- Click the Open button to open the selected file and display the worksheet in the Excel window (Figure 1–91).

Q&A Why do I see the Microsoft Excel icon and name on the Windows Vista taskbar?

When you open an Excel file, the application name (Microsoft Excel) is displayed on a selected button on the Windows Vista taskbar. If you point to this button, the file name also appears in a ScreenTip.

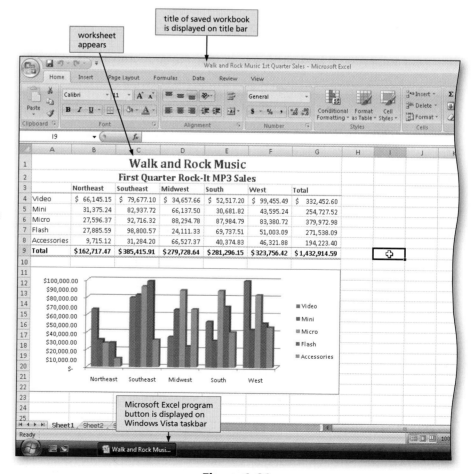

Figure 1–91

Other Ways

1. Click Office Button, double-click file name in Recent Documents list

2. Press CTRL+O, select file name, press ENTER

AutoCalculate
Use the AutoCalculate area on the status bar to check your work as you enter data in a worksheet. If you enter large amounts of data, you select a range of data and then check the AutoCalculate area to provide insight into statistics about the data you entered. Often, you will have an intuitive feel for whether the numbers are accurate or if you may have made a mistake while entering the data.

AutoCalculate

You easily can obtain a total, an average, or other information about the numbers in a range by using the **AutoCalculate area** on the status bar. First, select the range of cells containing the numbers you want to check. Next, right-click the AutoCalculate area to display the Status Bar Configuration shortcut menu (Figure 1–92). The check mark to the left of the active functions (Average, Count, and Sum) indicates that the sum, count, and average of the selected range are displayed in the AutoCalculate area on the status bar. The functions of the AutoCalculate commands on the Status Bar Configuration shortcut menu are described in Table 1–4.

Table 1–4 AutoCalculate Shortcut Menu Commands	
Command	**Function**
Average	AutoCalculate area displays the average of the numbers in the selected range
Count	AutoCalculate area displays the number of nonblank cells in the selected range
Numerical Count	AutoCalculate area displays the number of cells containing numbers in the selected range
Minimum	AutoCalculate area displays the lowest value in the selected range
Maximum	AutoCalculate area displays the highest value in the selected range
Sum	AutoCalculate area displays the sum of the numbers in the selected range

To Use the AutoCalculate Area to Determine a Maximum

The following steps show how to display the largest quarterly sales for any region for the Micro product type.

1

- Select the range B6:F6 and then right-click the AutoCalculate area on the status bar to display the Status Bar Configuration shortcut menu (Figure 1–92).

Q&A

What is displayed on the Status Bar Configuration shortcut menu?

This shortcut menu includes several commands that allow you to control the items displayed on the Customize Status Bar shortcut menu. The AutoCalculate area of the shortcut menu includes six commands as well as the result of the associated calculation on the right side of the menu.

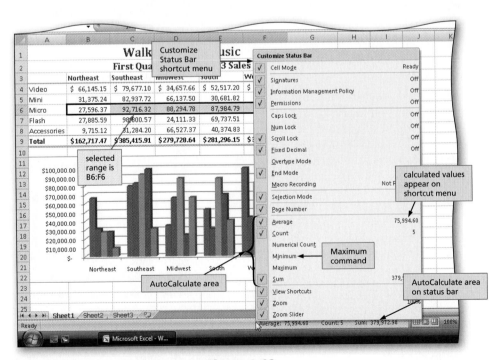

Figure 1–92

2

- Click Maximum on the shortcut menu to display the Maximum value in the range B6:F6 in the AutoCalculate area of the status bar.

- Click anywhere on the worksheet to cause the shortcut menu to disappear (Figure 1–93).

3

- Right-click the AutoCalculate area and then click Maximum on the shortcut menu to cause the Maximum value to no longer appear in the AutoCalculate area.

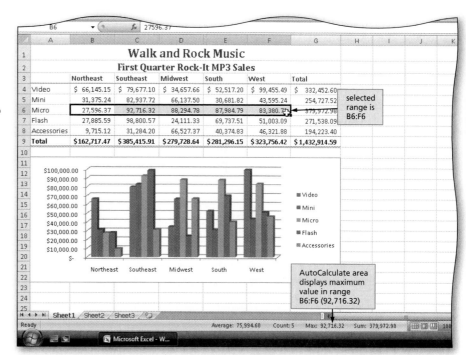

Figure 1–93

Correcting Errors

You can correct errors on a worksheet using one of several methods. The method you choose will depend on the extent of the error and whether you notice it while typing the data or after you have entered the incorrect data into the cell.

Correcting Errors while You Are Typing Data into a Cell

If you notice an error while you are typing data into a cell, press the BACKSPACE key to erase the incorrect characters and then type the correct characters. If the error is a major one, click the Cancel box in the formula bar or press the ESC key to erase the entire entry and then reenter the data from the beginning.

Correcting Errors after Entering Data into a Cell

If you find an error in the worksheet after entering the data, you can correct the error in one of two ways:

1. If the entry is short, select the cell, retype the entry correctly, and then click the Enter box or press the ENTER key. The new entry will replace the old entry.

2. If the entry in the cell is long and the errors are minor, using Edit mode may be a better choice than retyping the cell entry. Use the Edit mode as described below.

   a. Double-click the cell containing the error to switch Excel to Edit mode. In **Edit mode**, Excel displays the active cell entry in the formula bar and a flashing insertion point in the active cell (Figure 1–94). With Excel in Edit mode, you can edit the contents directly in the cell — a procedure called **in-cell editing**.

b. Make changes using in-cell editing, as indicated below.

(1) To insert new characters between two characters, place the insertion point between the two characters and begin typing. Excel inserts the new characters at the location of the insertion point.

(2) To delete a character in the cell, move the insertion point to the left of the character you want to delete and then press the DELETE key or place the insertion point to the right of the character you want to delete and then press the BACKSPACE key. You also can use the mouse to drag through the character or adjacent characters you want to delete and then press the DELETE key or click the Cut button on the Home tab on the Ribbon.

(3) When you are finished editing an entry, click the Enter box or press the ENTER key.

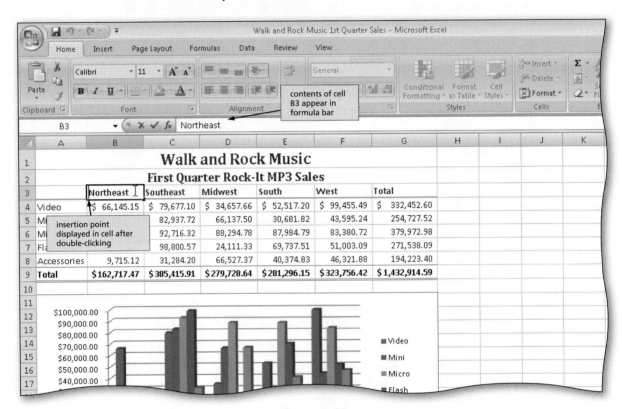

Figure 1–94

When Excel enters the Edit mode, the keyboard usually is in Insert mode. In **Insert mode**, as you type a character, Excel inserts the character and moves all characters to the right of the typed character one position to the right. You can change to Overtype mode by pressing the INSERT key. In **Overtype mode**, Excel overtypes, or replaces, the character to the right of the insertion point. The INSERT key toggles the keyboard between Insert mode and Overtype mode.

While in Edit mode, you may have reason to move the insertion point to various points in the cell, select portions of the data in the cell, or switch from inserting characters to overtyping characters. Table 1–5 summarizes the more common tasks used during in-cell editing.

Table 1–5 Summary of In-Cell Editing Tasks

	Task	Mouse	Keyboard
1	Move the insertion point to the beginning of data in a cell.	Point to the left of the first character and click.	Press HOME
2	Move the insertion point to the end of data in a cell.	Point to the right of the last character and click.	Press END
3	Move the insertion point anywhere in a cell.	Point to the appropriate position and click the character.	Press RIGHT ARROW or LEFT ARROW
4	Highlight one or more adjacent characters.	Drag the mouse pointer through adjacent characters.	Press SHIFT+RIGHT ARROW or SHIFT+LEFT ARROW
5	Select all data in a cell.	Double-click the cell with the insertion point in the cell if there are no spaces in the data in the cell.	
6	Delete selected characters.	Click the Cut button on the Home tab on the Ribbon.	Press DELETE
7	Delete characters to the left of the insertion point.		Press BACKSPACE
8	Delete characters to the right of the insertion point.		Press DELETE
9	Toggle between Insert and Overtype modes.		Press INSERT

Undoing the Last Cell Entry

Excel provides the Undo command on the Quick Access Toolbar (Figure 1–95), which allows you to erase recent cell entries. Thus, if you enter incorrect data in a cell and notice it immediately, click the Undo button and Excel changes the cell entry to what it was prior to the incorrect data entry.

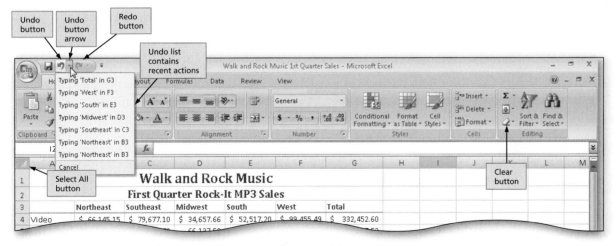

Figure 1–95

Excel remembers the last 100 actions you have completed. Thus, you can undo up to 100 previous actions by clicking the Undo button arrow to display the Undo list and then clicking the action to be undone (Figure 1–95). You can drag through several actions in the Undo list to undo all of them at once. If no actions are available for Excel to undo, then the Undo button is dimmed and inoperative.

The Redo button, next to the Undo button on the Quick Access Toolbar, allows you to repeat previous actions.

BTW

Quick Reference
For a table that lists how to complete the tasks covered in this book using the mouse, Ribbon, shortcut menu, and keyboard, see the Quick Reference Summary at the back of this book, or visit the Excel 2007 Quick Reference Web page (scsite.com/ex2007/qr).

Clearing a Cell or Range of Cells

If you enter data into the wrong cell or range of cells, you can erase, or clear, the data using one of the first four methods listed below. The fifth method clears the formatting from the selected cells.

TO CLEAR CELL ENTRIES USING THE FILL HANDLE

1. Select the cell or range of cells and then point to the fill handle so the mouse pointer changes to a crosshair.
2. Drag the fill handle back into the selected cell or range until a shadow covers the cell or cells you want to erase. Release the mouse button.

TO CLEAR CELL ENTRIES USING THE SHORTCUT MENU

1. Select the cell or range of cells to be cleared.
2. Right-click the selection.
3. Click Clear Contents on the shortcut menu.

TO CLEAR CELL ENTRIES USING THE DELETE KEY

1. Select the cell or range of cells to be cleared.
2. Press the DELETE key.

BTW

Certification
The Microsoft Certified Application Specialist (MCAS) program provides an opportunity for you to obtain a valuable industry credential – proof that you have the Excel 2007 skills required by employers. For more information, see Appendix G or visit the Excel 2007 Certification Web page (scsite.com/ex2007/cert).

TO CLEAR CELL ENTRIES AND FORMATTING USING THE CLEAR BUTTON

1. Select the cell or range of cells to be cleared.
2. Click the Clear button on the Home tab (Figure 1–95 on the previous page).
3. Click Clear Contents on the menu.

TO CLEAR FORMATTING USING THE CELL STYLES BUTTON

1. Select the cell or range of cells from which you want to remove the formatting.
2. Click the Cell Styles button on the Home tab and point to Normal.
3. Click Normal in the Cell Styles Gallery.

The Clear button on the Home tab is the only command that clears both the cell entry and the cell formatting. As you are clearing cell entries, always remember that you should *never press the* SPACEBAR *to clear a cell*. Pressing the SPACEBAR enters a blank character. A blank character is text and is different from an empty cell, even though the cell may appear empty.

Clearing the Entire Worksheet

If required worksheet edits are extremely extensive, you may want to clear the entire worksheet and start over. To clear the worksheet or delete an embedded chart, use the following steps.

BTW

Getting Back to Normal
If you accidentally assign unwanted formats to a range of cells, you can use the Normal cell style selection in the Cell Styles gallery. Click Cell Styles on the Home tab on the Ribbon and then click Normal. Doing so changes the format to Normal style. To view the characteristics of the Normal style, right-click the style in the Cell Styles gallery and then click Modify, or press ALT+APOSTROPHE (').

TO CLEAR THE ENTIRE WORKSHEET

1. Click the Select All button on the worksheet (Figure 1–95).
2. Click the Clear button on the Home tab to delete both the entries and formats.

The Select All button selects the entire worksheet. Instead of clicking the Select All button, you also can press CTRL+A. To clear an unsaved workbook, click the workbook's Close Window button or click the Close command on the Office Button menu. Click the No button if the Microsoft Excel dialog box asks if you want to save changes. To start a new, blank workbook, click the New command on the Office Button menu.

To delete an embedded chart, complete the following steps.

TO DELETE AN EMBEDDED CHART

1. Click the chart to select it.
2. Press the DELETE key.

BTW

Excel Help
The best way to become familiar with Excel Help is to use it. Appendix C includes detailed information about Excel Help and exercises that will help you gain confidence in using it.

Excel Help

At any time while using Excel, you can find answers to questions and display information about various topics through **Excel Help**. This section introduces you to Excel Help.

To Search for Excel Help

Using Excel Help, you can search for information based on phrases such as save a workbook or format a chart, or key terms such as copy, save, or format. Excel Help responds with a list of search results displayed as links to a variety of resources. The following steps, which use Excel Help to search for information about formatting a chart, assume you are connected to the Internet.

1

- Click the Microsoft Office Excel Help button near the upper-right corner of the Excel window to open the Excel Help window.

- Type format a chart in the Type words to search for text box at the top of the Excel Help window (Figure 1–96).

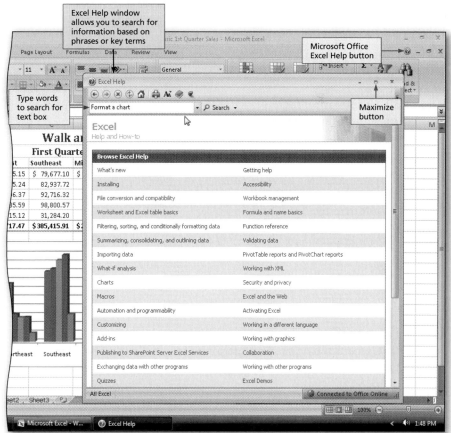

Figure 1–96

2

- Press the ENTER key to display the search results.

- Click the Maximize button on the Excel Help window title bar to maximize the Help window (Figure 1–97).

Q&A Where is the Excel window with the Walk and Rock Music 1st Quarter Sales worksheet?

Excel is open in the background, but the Excel Help window is overlaid on top of the Microsoft Excel window. When the Excel Help window is closed, the worksheet will reappear.

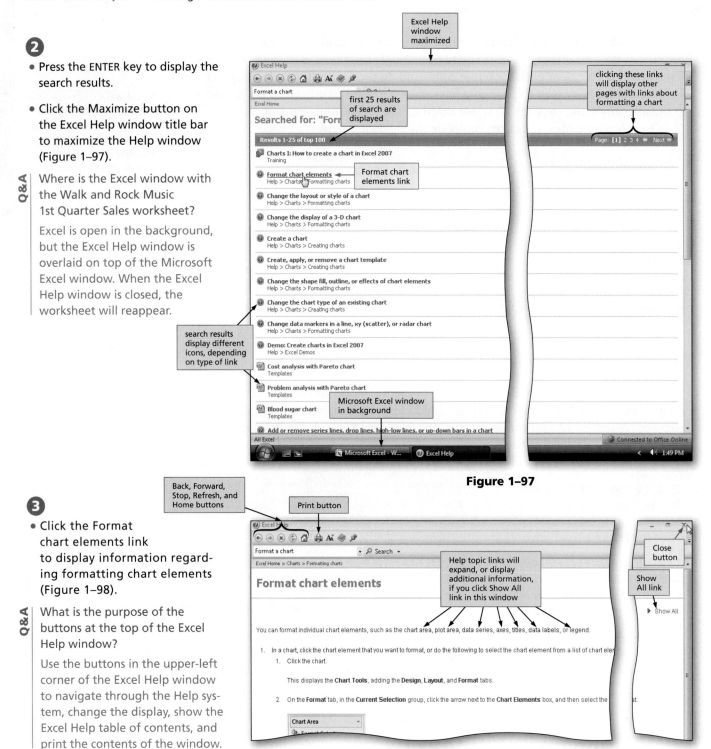

Figure 1–97

3

- Click the Format chart elements link to display information regarding formatting chart elements (Figure 1–98).

Q&A What is the purpose of the buttons at the top of the Excel Help window?

Use the buttons in the upper-left corner of the Excel Help window to navigate through the Help system, change the display, show the Excel Help table of contents, and print the contents of the window.

Figure 1–98

4

- Click the Close button on the Excel Help window title bar to close the Excel Help window and make Excel active.

Other Ways
1. Press F1

To Quit Excel

The following steps quit Excel.

1 Click the Close button on the right side of the title bar to quit Excel; or if you have multiple Excel workbooks open, click the Office Button and then click the Exit Excel button on the Office Button menu to close all open workbooks and quit Excel.

2 If necessary, click the No button in the Microsoft Office Excel dialog box so that any changes you have made are not saved.

BTW | **Quitting Excel**
Do not forget to remove your USB flash drive from the USB port after quitting Excel, especially if you are working in a laboratory environment. Nothing can be more frustrating than leaving all of your hard work behind on a USB flash drive for the next user.

Chapter Summary

In this chapter you have learned about the Excel window, how to enter text and numbers to create a worksheet, how to select a range, how to use the Sum button, save a workbook, format cells, insert a chart, print a worksheet, quit Excel, and use Excel Help. The items listed below include all the new Excel skills you have learned in this chapter.

1. Start Excel (EX 6)
2. Enter the Worksheet Titles (EX 17)
3. Enter Column Titles (EX 19)
4. Enter Row Titles (EX 21)
5. Enter Numbers (EX 23)
6. Sum a Column of Numbers (EX 25)
7. Copy a Cell to Adjacent Cells in a Row (EX 27)
8. Determine Multiple Totals at the Same Time (EX 28)
9. Save a Workbook (EX 30)
10. Change a Cell Style (EX 35)
11. Change the Font Type (EX 36)
12. Bold a Cell (EX 38)
13. Increase the Font Size of a Cell Entry (EX 38)
14. Change the Font Color of a Cell Entry (EX 39)
15. Center Cell Entries across Columns by Merging Cells (EX 40)
16. Format Column Titles and the Total Row (EX 42)
17. Format Numbers in the Worksheet (EX 44)
18. Adjust the Column Width (EX 46)
19. Use the Name Box to Select a Cell (EX 47)
20. Add a 3-D Clustered Column Chart to the Worksheet (EX 50)
21. Change Document Properties (EX 55)
22. Save an Existing Workbook with the Same File Name (EX 58)
23. Print a Worksheet (EX 58)
24. Quit Excel with One Workbook Open (EX 59)
25. Open a Workbook from Excel (EX 60)
26. Use the AutoCalculate Area to Determine a Maximum (EX 62)
27. Clear Cell Entries Using the Fill Handle (EX 66)
28. Clear Cell Entries Using the Shortcut Menu (EX 66)
29. Clear Cell Entries Using the DELETE Key (EX 66)
30. Clear Cell Entries and Formatting Using the Clear Button (EX 66)
31. Clear Formatting Using the Cell Styles Button (EX 66)
32. Clear the Entire Worksheet (EX 66)
33. Delete an Embedded Chart (EX 67)
34. Search for Excel Help (EX 67)

If you have a SAM user profile, you may have access to hands-on instruction, practice, and assessment. Log in to your SAM account (http://sam2007.course.com) to launch any assigned training activities or exams that relate to the skills covered in this chapter.

Learn It Online

Test your knowledge of chapter content and key terms.

Instructions: To complete the Learn It Online exercises, start your browser, click the Address bar, and then enter the Web address scsite.com/ex2007/learn. When the Excel 2007 Learn It Online page is displayed, click the link for the exercise you want to complete and then read the instructions.

Chapter Reinforcement TF, MC, and SA

A series of true/false, multiple choice, and short answer questions that test your knowledge of the chapter content.

Flash Cards

An interactive learning environment where you identify chapter key terms associated with displayed definitions.

Practice Test

A series of multiple choice questions that test your knowledge of chapter content and key terms.

Who Wants To Be a Computer Genius?

An interactive game that challenges your knowledge of chapter content in the style of a television quiz show.

Wheel of Terms

An interactive game that challenges your knowledge of chapter key terms in the style of the television show *Wheel of Fortune*.

Crossword Puzzle Challenge

A crossword puzzle that challenges your knowledge of key terms presented in the chapter.

Apply Your Knowledge

Reinforce the skills and apply the concepts you learned in this chapter.

Changing the Values in a Worksheet

Instructions: Start Excel. Open the workbook Apply 1-1 Bicycle Shop 3rd Quarter Sales (Figure 1–99a). See the inside back cover of this book for instructions for downloading the Data Files for Students, or see your instructor for information on accessing the files required in this book.

1. Make the changes to the worksheet described in Table 1–6 so that the worksheet appears as shown in Figure 1–99b. As you edit the values in the cells containing numeric data, watch the totals in row 8, the totals in column G, and the chart change.

2. Change the worksheet title in cell A1 to the Title cell style and then merge and center it across columns A through G. Use commands in the Font group on the Home tab on the Ribbon to change the worksheet subtitle in cell A2 to 16-point Corbel red, bold font and then center it across columns A through G. Use the Accent 1 theme color (column 5, row 1 on the Font Color palette) for the red font color.

3. Update the document properties with your name, course number, and name for the workbook. Save the workbook using the file name, Apply 1-1 Spoke-Up Bicycle Shop 3rd Quarter Sales. Submit the assignment as requested by your instructor.

Table 1–6 New Worksheet Data	
Cell	**Change Cell Contents To**
A1	Spoke-Up Bicycle Shop
B4	11869.2
E4	9157.83
D6	5217.92
F6	6239.46
B7	3437.64

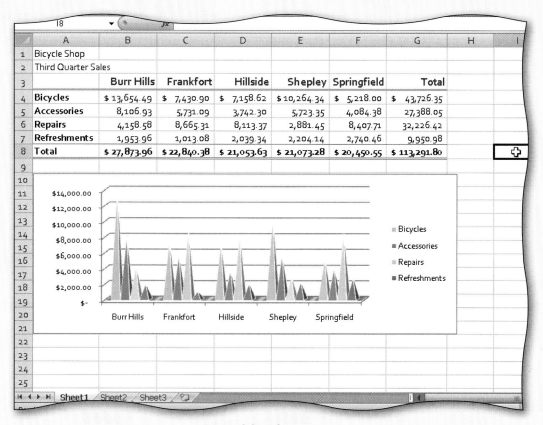

(a) Before

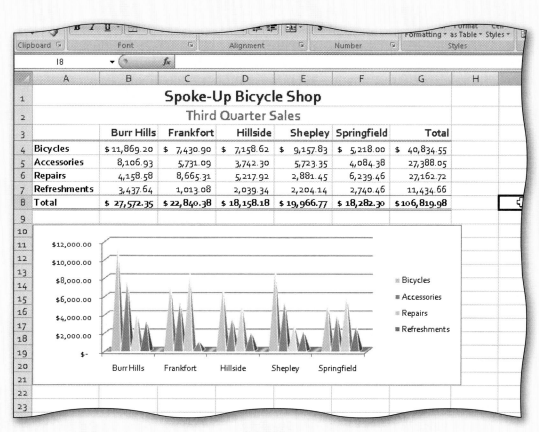

(b) After

Figure 1–99

Extend Your Knowledge

Extend the skills you learned in this chapter and experiment with new skills. You may need to use Help to complete the assignment.

Formatting Cells and Inserting Multiple Charts

Instructions: Start Excel. Open the workbook Extend 1-1 Pack-n-Away Shipping. See the inside back cover of this book for instructions for downloading the Data Files for Students, or see your instructor for information on accessing the files required in this book. Perform the following tasks to format cells in the worksheet and to add two charts to the worksheet.

1. Use the commands in the Font group on the Home tab on the Ribbon to change the font of the title in cell A1 to 24-point Arial, red; bold and subtitle of the worksheet to 16-point Arial Narrow, blue, bold.

2. Select the range A3:E8, click the Insert tab on the Ribbon, and then click the Dialog Box Launcher in the Charts group on the Ribbon to open the Insert Chart dialog box (Figure 1–100).

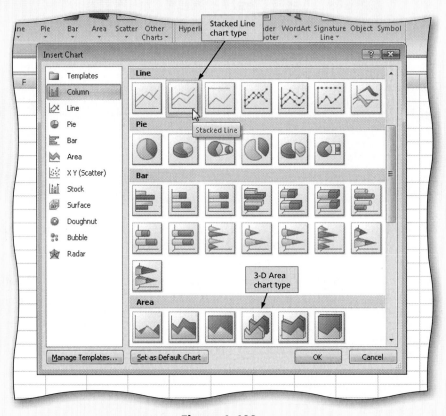

Figure 1–100

3. Insert a Stacked Line chart by clicking the Stacked Line chart in the gallery and then clicking the OK button. Move the chart either below or to the right of the data in the worksheet. Click the Design tab and apply a chart style to the chart.

4. If necessary, reselect the range A3:E8 and follow Step 3 above to insert a 3-D Area chart in the worksheet. You may need to use the scroll box on the right side of the Insert Chart dialog box to view the Area charts in the gallery. Move the chart either below or to the right of the data so that each chart does not overlap the Stacked Line chart. Choose a different chart style for this chart than the one you selected for the Stacked Line chart.

5. Resize each chart so that each snaps to the worksheet gridlines. Make certain that both charts are visible with the worksheet data without the need to scroll the worksheet.

6. Update the document properties with your name, course number, and name for the workbook.

7. Save the workbook using the file name, Extend 1-1 Pack-n-Away Shipping Charts. Submit the assignment as requested by your instructor.

Make It Right

Analyze a workbook and correct all errors and/or improve the design.

Correcting Formatting and Values in a Worksheet

Instructions: Start Excel. Open the workbook Make It Right 1-1 Book Sales. See the inside back cover of this book for instructions for downloading the Data Files for Students, or see your instructor for information on accessing the files required for this book. Correct the following formatting problems and data errors (Figure 1–101) in the worksheet, while keeping in mind the guidelines presented in this chapter.

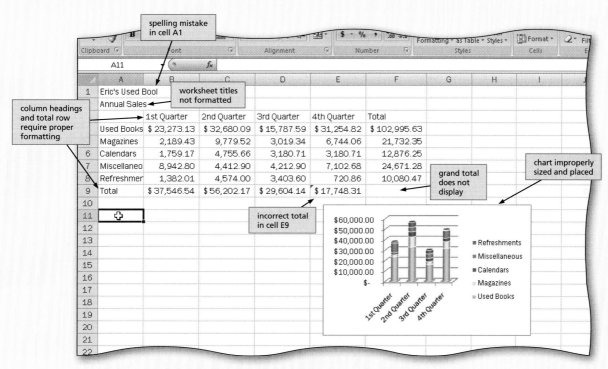

Figure 1–101

1. Merge and center the worksheet title and subtitle appropriately.

2. Format the worksheet title with a cell style appropriate for a worksheet title.

3. Format the subtitle using commands in the Font group on the Ribbon.

4. Correct the spelling mistake in cell A1 by changing Bool to Books.

5. Apply proper formatting to the column headers and total row.

Continued >

Make It Right *continued*

6. Adjust column sizes so that all data in each column is visible.

7. Use the SUM function to create the grand total for annual sales.

8. The SUM function in cell E9 does not sum all of the numbers in the column. Correct this error by editing the range for the SUM function in the cell.

9. Resize and move the chart so that it is below the worksheet data and does not extend past the right edge of the worksheet data. Be certain to snap the chart to the worksheet gridlines by holding down the ALT key as you resize the chart.

10. Update the document properties with your name, course number, and name for the workbook. Save the workbook using the file name, Make It Right 1-1 Eric's Used Books Annual Sales. Submit the assignment as requested by your instructor.

In the Lab

Design and/or create a workbook using the guidelines, concepts, and skills presented in this chapter. Labs 1, 2, and 3 are listed in order of increasing difficulty.

Lab 1: Annual Cost of Goods Worksheet

Problem: You work part-time as a spreadsheet specialist for Kona's Expresso Coffee, one of the up-and-coming coffee franchises in the United States. Your manager has asked you to develop an annual cost of goods analysis worksheet similar to the one shown in Figure 1–102.

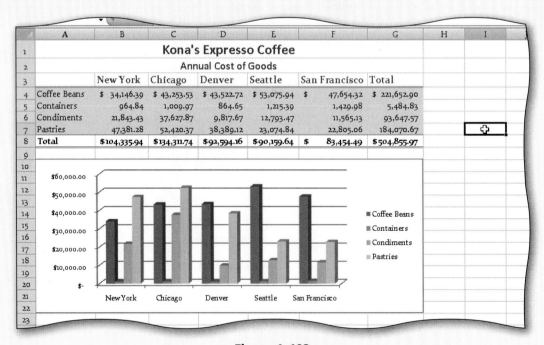

Figure 1–102

Instructions: Perform the following tasks.

1. Start Excel. Enter the worksheet title, Kona's Expresso Coffee, in cell A1 and the worksheet subtitle, Annual Cost of Goods, in cell A2. Beginning in row 3, enter the store locations, costs of goods, and supplies categories shown in Table 1–7.

Table 1–7 Kona's Expresso Coffee Annual Cost of Goods					
	New York	**Chicago**	**Denver**	**Seattle**	**San Franscisco**
Coffee Beans	34146.39	43253.53	43522.72	53075.94	47654.32
Containers	964.84	1009.97	864.65	1215.39	1429.98
Condiments	21843.43	37627.87	9817.67	12793.47	11565.13
Pastries	47381.28	52420.37	38389.12	23074.84	22805.06

2. Use the SUM function to determine the totals for each store location, type of supply, and company grand total.

3. Use Cell Styles in the Styles group on the Home tab on the Ribbon to format the worksheet title with the Title cell style. Center the title across columns A through G. Do not be concerned if the edges of the worksheet title are not displayed.

4. Use buttons in the Font group on the Home tab on the Ribbon to format the worksheet subtitle to 14-point Calibri dark blue, bold font, and center it across columns A through G.

5. Use Cell Styles in the Styles group on the Home tab on the Ribbon to format the range A3:G3 with the Heading 2 cell style, the range A4:G7 with the 20% - Accent1 cell style, and the range A8:G8 with the Total cell style. Use the buttons in the Number group on the Home tab on the Ribbon to apply the Accounting Number format to the range B4:G4 and the range B8:G8. Use the buttons in the Number group on the Home tab on the Ribbon to apply the Comma Style to the range B5:G7. Adjust any column widths to the widest text entry in each column.

6. Select the range A3:F7 and then insert a 3-D Clustered Column chart. Apply the Style 5 chart style to the chart. Move and resize the chart so that it appears in the range A10:G22. If the labels along the horizontal axis (x-axis) do not appear as shown in Figure 1-102, then drag the right side of the chart so that it is displayed in the range A10:G22.

7. Update the document properties with your name, course number, and name for the workbook.

8. Save the workbook using the file name Lab 1-1 Konas Expresso Coffee Annual Cost of Goods.

9. Print the worksheet.

10. Make the following two corrections to the sales amounts: $9,648.12 for Seattle Condiments (cell E6), $12,844.79 for Chicago Pastries (cell C7). After you enter the corrections, the company totals in cell G8 should equal $462,135.04.

11. Print the revised worksheet. Close the workbook without saving the changes. Submit the assignment as requested by your instructor.

In the Lab

Lab 2: Annual Sales Analysis Worksheet

Problem: As the chief accountant for Scissors Office Supply, Inc., you have been asked by the sales manager to create a worksheet to analyze the annual sales for the company by location and customer type category (Figure 1–103). The office locations and corresponding sales by customer type for the year are shown in Table 1–8.

Continued >

In the Lab *continued*

Instructions: Perform the following tasks.

1. Create the worksheet shown in Figure 1–103 using the data in Table 1–8.

2. Use the SUM function to determine totals sales for the four offices, the totals for each customer type, and the company total. Add column and row headings for the totals row and totals column, as appropriate.

Table 1–8 Scissors Office Supply Annual Sales				
	Boston	**Miami**	**St. Louis**	**Santa Fe**
Consumer	206348.81	113861.40	69854.13	242286.82
Small Business	235573.28	133511.24	199158.35	228365.51
Large Business	237317.55	234036.08	126519.10	111773.38
Government	178798.04	144548.80	135470.86	132599.75
Nonprofit	15180.63	28837.75	63924.48	21361.42

3. Format the worksheet title with the Title cell style and center it across columns A through F. Use the Font group on the Ribbon to format the worksheet subtitle to 16-point Cambria green, and bold font. Center the title across columns A through F.

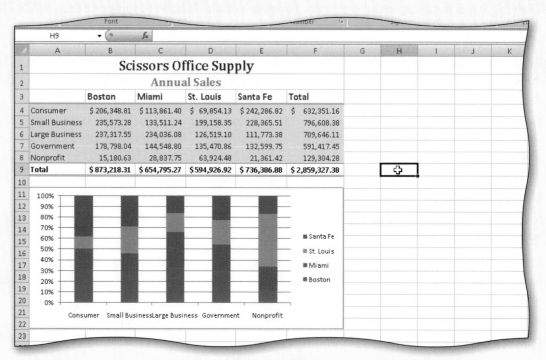

Figure 1–103

4. Format the range A3:F3 with the Heading 2 cell style, the range A4:F8 with the 20% - Accent3 cell style, and the range A9:F9 with the Total cell style. Use the Number group on the Ribbon to format cells B4:F4 and B9:F9 with the Accounting Number Format and cells B5:F8 with the Comma Style numeric format. Adjust the width of column A in order to fit contents of the column.

5. Chart the range A3:E8. Insert a 100% Stacked Column chart for the range A3:E8, as shown in Figure 1–103, by using the Column button on the Insert tab on the Ribbon. Use the chart location A11:F22.

Hey! You just saved serious money by purchasing your used textbooks from Bookbyte.

Smart Move! Now, what to do next?

Our suggestions:

First
Bask in the glow of all the money you saved

Next
Consider all you can do with the money you saved

Third
Do all the things you just considered

Finally
Follow Bookbyte on Facebook and Twitter to keep up to date with special promotions and deals
www.facebook.com/bookbyte and
www.twitter.com/bookbyte
for getting you the cash

And after you're done with your used textbooks, why not make some money from them?
Check the other side for more details.

Bookbyte
The Textbook Way to Save

Once you're done with your textbooks, why hold on to them?

It's easy to sell your books back to Bookbyte once you've finished your courses.

First
Go online to Bookbyte.com

Next
Enter your book's ISBN to see how much your book is worth

Third
Print off the shipping label for free, pre-paid shipping

Finally
Cash the check we send you once we process your book

It's that simple!

Bookbyte
The Textbook Way to Save

6. Update the document properties with your name, course number, and name for the workbook.

7. Save the workbook using the file name, Lab 1-2 Scissors Office Supply Annual Sales. Print the worksheet.

8. Two corrections to the figures were sent in from the accounting department. The correct sales are $98,342.16 for Miami's annual Small Business sales (cell C5) and $48,933.75 for St. Louis's annual Nonprofit sales (cell D8). After you enter the two corrections, the company total in cell F9 should equal $2,809,167.57. Print the revised worksheet.

9. Use the Undo button to change the worksheet back to the original numbers in Table 1–8. Use the Redo button to change the worksheet back to the revised state.

10. Close Excel without saving the latest changes. Start Excel and open the workbook saved in Step 7. Double-click cell E6 and use in-cell editing to change the Santa Fe annual Large Business sales (cell E6) to $154,108.49. Write the company total in cell F9 at the top of the first printout. Click the Undo button.

11. Click cell A1 and then click the Merge & Center button to split cell A1 into cells A1, B1, C1, D1, E1, and F1. To merge the cells into one again, select the range A1:F1 and then click the Merge & Center button on the Home tab on the Ribbon.

12. Close the workbook without saving the changes. Submit the assignment as requested by your instructor.

In the Lab

Lab 3: College Cost and Financial Support Worksheet

Problem: Attending college is an expensive proposition and your resources are limited. To plan for your four-year college career, you have decided to organize your anticipated resources and costs in a worksheet. The data required to prepare your worksheet is shown in Table 1–9.

Table 1–9 College Cost and Resources				
Cost	**Freshman**	**Sophomore**	**Junior**	**Senior**
Books	450.00	477.00	505.62	535.95
Room & Board	7500.00	7950.00	8427.00	8932.62
Tuition	8200.00	8692.00	9213.52	9766.33
Entertainment	1325.00	1404.50	1488.77	1578.10
Miscellaneous	950.00	1007.00	1067.42	1131.47
Clothes	725.00	768.50	814.61	863.49
Financial Support	**Freshman**	**Sophomore**	**Junior**	**Senior**
Job	3400.00	3604.00	3820.24	4049.45
Savings	4350.00	4611.00	4887.66	5180.92
Parents	4700.00	4982.00	5280.92	5597.78
Financial Aid	5500.00	5830.00	6179.80	6550.59
Other	1200.00	1272.00	1348.32	1429.22

Continued >

In the Lab *continued*

Instructions Part 1: Using the numbers in Table 1–9, create the worksheet shown in columns A through F in Figure 1–104. Format the worksheet title as Calibri 24-point bold red. Merge and center the worksheet title in cell A1 across columns A through F. Format the worksheet subtitles in cells A2 and A11 as Calibri 16-point bold green. Format the ranges A3:F3 and A12:F12 with the Heading 2 cell style, the ranges A4:F9 and A13:F17 with the 20% - Accent1 cell style, and the ranges A10:F10 and A18:F18 with the Total cell style.

Update the document properties, including the addition of at least one keyword to the properties, and save the workbook using the file name, Lab 1-3 Part 1 College Cost and Financial Support. Print the worksheet. Submit the assignment as requested by your instructor.

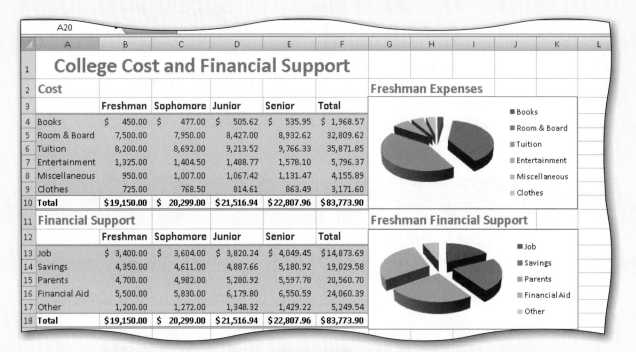

Figure 1–104

After reviewing the numbers, you realize you need to increase manually each of the Junior-year expenses in column D by $600. Change the Junior-year expenses to reflect this change. Manually change the financial aid for the Junior year in cell D16 by the amount required to cover the increase in costs. The totals in cells F10 and F18 should equal $87,373.90. Print the worksheet. Close the workbook without saving changes.

Instructions Part 2: Open the workbook Lab 1-3 Part 1 College Cost and Financial Support and then save the workbook using the file name, Lab 1-3 Part 2 College Cost and Financial Support. Insert an Exploded pie in 3-D chart in the range G3:K10 to show the contribution of each category of cost for the Freshman year. Chart the range A4:B9 and apply the Style 8 chart style to the chart. Add the Pie chart title as shown in cell G2 in Figure 1–104. Insert an Exploded pie in 3-D chart in the range G12:K18 to show the contribution of each category of financial support for the Freshman year. Chart the range A13:B17 and apply the Style 8 chart style to the chart. Add the Pie chart title shown in cell G11 in Figure 1–104. Update the identification area with the exercise part number and save the workbook. Print the worksheet. Submit the assignment as requested by your instructor.

Instructions Part 3: Open the workbook Lab 1-3 Part 2 College Cost and Financial Support. Do not save the workbook in this part. A close inspection of Table 1–9 shows that both cost and financial support figures increase 6% each year. Use Excel Help to learn how to enter the data for the last three years using a formula and the Copy and Paste buttons on the Home tab on the Ribbon. For example, the formula to enter in cell C4 is =B4*1.06. Enter formulas to replace all the numbers in the range C4:E9 and C13:E17. If necessary, reformat the tables, as described in Part 1. The worksheet should appear as shown in Figure 1–104, except that some of the totals will be off by 0.01 due to rounding errors. Save the worksheet using the file name, Lab 1-3 Part 3 College Cost and Financial Support. Print the worksheet. Press CTRL+ACCENT MARK (`) to display the formulas. Print the formulas version. Submit the assignment as requested by your instructor. Close the workbook without saving changes.

Cases and Places

Apply your creative thinking and problem solving skills to design and implement a solution.

● EASIER   ●● MORE DIFFICULT

● **1: Design and Create a Workbook to Analyze Yearly Sales**
You are working as a summer intern for Hit-the-Road Mobile Services. Your manager has asked you to prepare a worksheet to help her analyze historical yearly sales by type of product (Table 1–10). Use the concepts and techniques presented in this chapter to create the worksheet and an embedded 3-D Clustered Column chart.

Table 1–10 Hit-the-Road Mobile Services Sales				
	2005	**2006**	**2007**	**2008**
Standard Mobile Phones	87598	99087	129791	188785
Camera Phones	71035	75909	96886	100512
Music Phones	65942	24923	34590	15696
Wireless PDAs	67604	58793	44483	35095
Satellite Radios	15161	27293	34763	43367
Headsets	9549	6264	2600	4048
Other Accessories	47963	108059	100025	62367

● **2: Design and Create a Worksheet and Chart to Analyze a Budget**
To estimate the funds needed by your school's Environmental Club to make it through the upcoming year, you decide to create a budget for the club itemizing the expected quarterly expenses. The anticipated expenses are listed in Table 1–11. Use the concepts and techniques presented in this chapter to create the worksheet and an embedded 3-D Column chart using an appropriate chart style that compares the quarterly cost of each expense. Use the AutoCalculate area to determine the average amount spent per quarter on each expense. Manually insert the averages with appropriate titles in an empty area on the worksheet.

Table 1–11 Quarterly Environmental Club Budget				
	Jan – Mar	**April – June**	**July – Sept**	**Oct – Dec**
Meeting Room Rent	300	300	150	450
Copies and Supplies	390	725	325	640
Travel	450	755	275	850
Refreshments	105	85	215	155
Speaker Fees	200	200	0	500
Miscellaneous	125	110	75	215

Continued >

Cases and Places *continued*

•• 3: Create a 3-D Pie Chart to Analyze Quarterly Revenue

In-the-Villa DVD Rental is a DVD movie rental store. The owner of the store is trying to decide if it is feasible to hire more employees during certain times of the year. You have been asked to develop a worksheet totaling all the revenue received last year by quarter. The revenue per quarter is: Quarter 1, $52,699.23; Quarter 2, $111,244.32; Quarter 3, $70,905.03; and Quarter 4, $87,560.10. Create a 3-D Pie chart to illustrate quarterly revenue contribution by quarter. Use the AutoCalculate area to find the average, maximum, and minimum quarterly revenue and manually enter them and their corresponding identifiers in an empty area of the worksheet.

•• 4: Design and Create a Workbook to Analyze Your Field of Interest

Make It Personal

Based on your college major, area of interest, or career, use an Internet search engine or other research material to determine the total number of people employed in your chosen field of interest in the country over the past five years. For each year, break the yearly number down into two or more categories. For example, the number for each year can be broken into management and nonmanagement employees. Create an Excel worksheet that includes this data. Place the data in appropriate rows and columns for each year and category. Create totals for each row, totals for each column, and a grand total. Format the worksheet title, column headings, and data using the concepts presented in this chapter. Create a properly formatted Clustered Cone chart for the data and place it below the data in the worksheet. Make certain that years are on the X axis and number of employees is on the Y axis.

•• 5: Design and Create a Workbook to Analyze Your School

Working Together

Visit the registrar's office at your school and obtain data, such as age, gender, and full-time versus part-time status, for the students majoring in at least six different academic departments this semester. Have each member of your team divide the data into different categories. For example, separate the data by:

1. Age, divided into four different age groups

2. Gender, divided into male and female

3. Status, divided into full-time and part-time

After coordinating the data as a group, have each member independently use the concepts and techniques presented in this chapter to create a worksheet and appropriate chart to show the total students by characteristics by academic department. As a group, critique each worksheet and have each member modify his or her worksheet based on the group recommendations.

2 Formulas, Functions, Formatting, and Web Queries

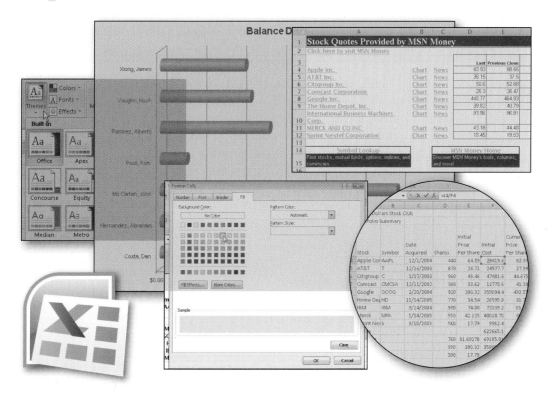

Objectives

You will have mastered the material in this chapter when you can:

- Enter formulas using the keyboard and Point mode
- Apply the AVERAGE, MAX, and MIN functions
- Verify a formula using Range Finder
- Apply a theme to a workbook
- Add conditional formatting to cells
- Change column width and row height
- Check the spelling of a worksheet

- Set margins, headers and footers in Page Layout View
- Preview and print versions of a worksheet
- Use a Web query to get real-time data from a Web site
- Rename sheets in a workbook
- E-mail the active workbook from within Excel

2 | Formulas, Functions, Formatting, and Web Queries

Introduction

In Chapter 1, you learned how to enter data, sum values, format the worksheet to make it easier to read, and draw a chart. You also learned about using Help and saving, printing, and opening a workbook. This chapter continues to highlight these topics and presents some new ones.

The new topics covered in this chapter include using formulas and functions to create a worksheet. A **function** is a prewritten formula that is built into Excel. Other new topics include smart tags and option buttons, verifying formulas, applying a theme to a worksheet, adding borders, formatting numbers and text, using conditional formatting, changing the widths of columns and heights of rows, spell checking, e-mailing from within an application, renaming worksheets, using alternative types of worksheet displays and printouts, and adding page headers and footers to a worksheet. One alternative worksheet display and printout shows the formulas in the worksheet, instead of the values. When you display the formulas in the worksheet, you see exactly what text, data, formulas, and functions you have entered into it. Finally, this chapter covers Web queries to obtain real-time data from a Web site.

Project — Worksheet with Formulas, Functions, and Web Queries

The project in the chapter follows proper design guidelines and uses Excel to create the two worksheets shown in Figure 2–1. The Silver Dollars Stock Club was started and is owned by a national academic fraternity, which pools contributions from a number of local chapters. Each local chapter contributes $150 per month; the money is then invested in the stock market for the benefit of the organization and as a tool to help members learn about investing. At the end of each month, the club's treasurer summarizes the club's financial status in a portfolio summary. This summary includes information such as the stocks owned by the club, the cost of the stocks to the club, and the gain or loss that the club has seen over time on the stock. As the complexity of the task of creating the summary increases, the treasurer wants to use Excel to create the monthly portfolio summary. The treasurer also sees an opportunity to use Excel's built-in capability to access real-time stock quotes over the Internet.

Recall that the first step in creating an effective worksheet is to make sure you understand what is required. The people who will use the worksheet usually provide requirements. The requirements document for the Silver Dollars Stock Club Portfolio Summary worksheet includes the following: needs, source of data, summary of calculations, Web requirements, and other facts about its development (Figure 2–2 on page EX 84). The real-time stock quotes (shown in Figure 2–1b) will be accessed via a Web query. The stock quotes will be returned to the active workbook on a separate worksheet. Microsoft determines the content and format of the Real-Time Stock Quotes worksheet.

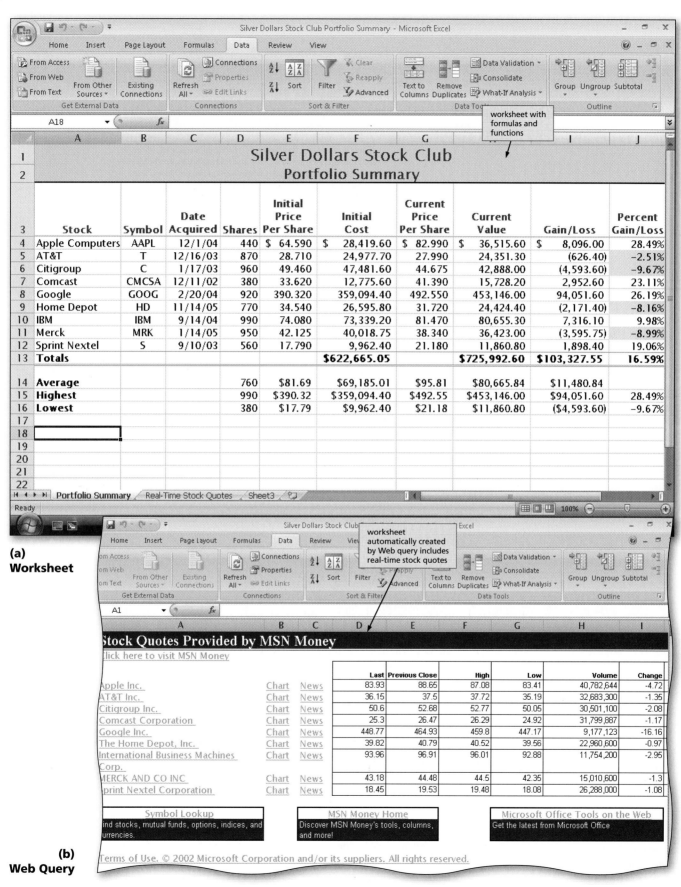

(a) Worksheet

(b) Web Query

Figure 2–1

REQUEST FOR NEW WORKSHEET

Date Submitted:	April 8, 2008
Submitted By:	Juan Castillo
Worksheet Title:	Silver Dollars Stock Club Portfolio Summary
Needs:	An easy-to-read worksheet that summarizes the club's investments (Figure 2-3). For each stock, the worksheet is to include the stock name, stock symbol, date acquired, shares, initial price per share, initial cost, current price per share, current value, gain/loss, and percent gain/loss. Also include totals and the average, highest value, and lowest value for each column of numbers. Use the import data capabilities of Excel to access real-time stock quotes using Web queries.
Source of Data:	The data supplied by Juan includes the stock names, symbols, dates acquired, number of shares, initial price per share, and current price per share. This data is shown in Table 2-1 on page EX 89.
Calculations:	The following calculations must be made for each of the stocks: 1. Initial Cost = Shares × Initial Price Per Share 2. Current Value = Shares × Current Price Per Share 3. Gain/Loss = Current Value – Initial Cost 4. Percent Gain/Loss = Gain/Loss / Initial Cost 5. Compute the totals for initial cost, current value, and gain/loss. 6. Use the AVERAGE function to determine the average for the number of shares, initial price per share, initial cost per share, current price per share, current value, and gain/loss. 7. Use the MAX and MIN functions to determine the highest and lowest values for the number of shares, initial price per share, initial cost per share, current price per share, current value, gain/loss, and percent gain/loss.
Web Requirements:	Use the Web query feature of Excel to get real-time stock quotes for the stocks owned by the Silver Dollars Stock Club.

Approvals

Approval Status:	X	Approved
		Rejected
Approved By:	Members of the Silver Dollars Stock Club	
Date:	April 15, 2008	
Assigned To:	J. Quasney, Spreadsheet Specialist	

Figure 2–2

BTW

Aesthetics versus Function

In designing a worksheet, functional considerations should come first, before visual aesthetics. The function, or purpose, of a worksheet is to provide a user with direct ways to accomplish tasks. Avoid the temptation to use flashy or confusing visual elements within the worksheet, unless they will help the user more easily complete a task.

Overview

As you read this chapter, you will learn how to create the worksheet shown in Figure 2–1 by performing these general tasks:

- Enter formulas and apply functions in the worksheet
- Add conditional formatting to the worksheet
- Apply a theme to the worksheet
- Work with the worksheet in Page Layout View
- Print a part of the worksheet
- Perform a Web query to get real-time data from a Web site and create a new worksheet
- E-mail the worksheet

Plan Ahead

General Project Decisions

While creating an Excel worksheet, you need to make several decisions that will determine the appearance and characteristics of the finished worksheet. As you create the worksheet required to meet the requirements shown in Figure 2–2, you should follow these general guidelines:

1. **Plan the layout of the worksheet.** As discussed in Chapter 1 and shown in Figure 2–3, rows typically contain items analogous to items in a list. In the case of the stock club's data, the individual stocks serve this purpose and each stock should be placed in a row. As the club adds more stocks, the number of rows in the worksheet will increase. Information about each stock and associated calculations should appear in columns.

2. **Determine the necessary formulas and functions needed.** Values such as initial cost and current value are calculated from known values. The formulas for these calculations should be known in advance of creating the worksheet. Values such as the average, highest, and lowest values can be calculated using Excel functions as opposed to relying on complex formulas.

3. **Identify how to format various elements of the worksheet.** As discussed in Chapter 1 and shown in Figure 2–3, the appearance of the worksheet affects its ability to communicate clearly. Numeric data should be formatted in generally accepted formats, such as using commas as thousands separators and parentheses for negative values.

4. **Establish rules for conditional formatting.** Conditional formatting allows you to format a cell based on the contents of the cell. Decide under which circumstances you would like a cell to stand out from similar cells and determine in what way the cell will stand out. In the case of the Percent Gain/Loss column on the worksheet, placing a different background color in cells that show losses is an appropriate format for the column.

5. **Specify how the printed worksheet should appear.** When it is possible that a person will want to print a worksheet, care should be taken in the development of the worksheet to ensure that the contents can be printed in a readable manner. Excel prints worksheets in landscape or portrait orientation and margins can be adjusted to fit more or less data on each page. Headers and footers add an additional level of customization to the printed page.

(continued)

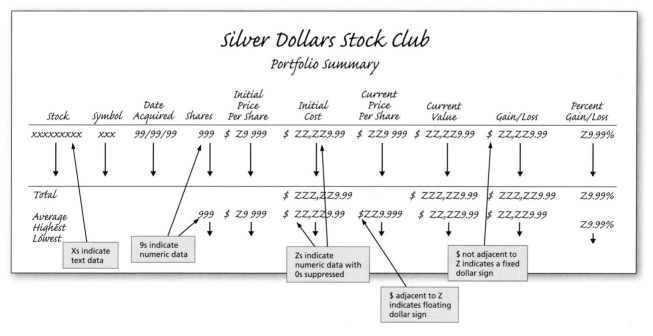

Figure 2–3

**Plan
Ahead**

(continued)

6. **Gather information regarding the needed Web query.** You must also know what information the Web query requires in order for it to generate results that you can use in Excel.

7. **Choose names for the worksheets.** When a workbook includes multiple worksheets, each worksheet should be named. A good worksheet name is succinct, unique to the workbook, and meaningful to any user of the workbook.

In addition, using a sketch of the worksheet can help you visualize its design. The sketch for Silver Dollars Stock Club Portfolio Summary worksheet (Figure 2–3 on the previous page) includes a title, a subtitle, column and row headings, and the location of data values. It also uses specific characters to define the desired formatting for the worksheet as follows:

1. The row of Xs below the leftmost column defines the cell entries as text, such as stock names and stock symbols.

2. The rows of Zs and 9s with slashes, dollar signs, decimal points, commas, and percent signs in the remaining columns define the cell entries as numbers. The Zs indicate that the selected format should instruct Excel to suppress leading 0s. The 9s indicate that the selected format should instruct Excel to display any digits, including 0s.

3. The decimal point means that a decimal point should appear in the cell entry and indicates the number of decimal places to use.

4. The commas indicate that the selected format should instruct Excel to display a comma separator only if the number has enough digits to the left of the decimal point.

5. The slashes in the third column identify the cell entry as a date.

6. The dollar signs that are not adjacent to the Zs in the first row below the column headings and in the total row signify a fixed dollar sign. The dollar signs that are adjacent to the Zs below the total row signify a floating dollar sign, or one that appears next to the first significant digit.

7. The percent sign (%) in the far right column indicates a percent sign should appear after the number.

When necessary, more specific details concerning the above guidelines are presented at appropriate points in the chapter. The chapter also will identify the actions you perform and decisions made regarding these guidelines during the creation of the worksheet shown in Figure 2–3 on page EX 85.

With a good understanding of the requirements document, an understanding of the necessary decisions, and a sketch of the worksheet, the next step is to use Excel to create the worksheet.

To Start Excel

If you are using a computer to step through the project in this chapter and you want your screen to match the figures in this book, you should change your computer's resolution to 1024 × 768. For information about how to change a computer's resolution, read Appendix E.

The following steps, which assume Windows Vista is running, start Excel based on a typical installation of Microsoft Office on your computer. You may need to ask your instructor how to start Excel for your computer.

Note: If you are using Windows XP, see Appendix F for alternate steps.

1 Click the Start button on the Windows Vista taskbar to display the Start menu.

2 Point to All Programs at the bottom of the left pane on the Start menu to display the All Programs list.

3 Click Microsoft Office in the All Programs list to display the Microsoft Office list.

4 Click Microsoft Office Excel to start Excel and display a blank worksheet in the Excel window.

5 If the Excel window is not maximized, click the Maximize button next to the Close button on its title bar to maximize the window.

6 If the worksheet window in Excel is not maximized, click the Maximize button next to the Close button on its title bar to maximize the worksheet window within Excel.

BTW

Starting Excel
You can use a command-line switch to start Excel and control how it starts. First, click the Start button on the Windows Vista taskbar, and then click the Start Search box. Next, enter the complete path to Excel's application file including the switch (for example, C:\Program Files\Microsoft Office\ Office12\Excel.exe/e). The switch /e starts Excel without opening a new workbook; /i starts Excel with a maximized window; /p "folder" sets the active path to folder and ignores the default folder; /r "filename" opens filename in read-only mode; and /s starts Excel in safe mode.

Entering the Titles and Numbers into the Worksheet

The first step in creating the worksheet is to enter the titles and numbers into the worksheet.

To Enter the Worksheet Title and Subtitle

The following steps enter the worksheet title and subtitle into cells A1 and A2.

1 If necessary, select cell A1. Type `Silver Dollars Stock Club` in the cell and then press the DOWN ARROW key to enter the worksheet title in cell A1.

2 Type `Portfolio Summary` in cell A2 and then press the DOWN ARROW key to enter the worksheet subtitle in cell A2 (Figure 2–4 on page EX 89).

To Enter the Column Titles

The column titles in row 3 begin in cell A3 and extend through cell J3. The column titles in Figure 2–3 include multiple lines of text. To start a new line in a cell, press ALT+ENTER after each line, except for the last line, which is completed by clicking the Enter box, pressing the ENTER key, or pressing one of the arrow keys. When you see ALT+ENTER in a step, press the ENTER key while holding down the ALT key and then release both keys.

The stock names and the row titles Totals, Average, Highest, and Lowest in the leftmost column begin in cell A4 and continue down to cell A16. This data is entered into rows 4 through 12 of the worksheet. The remainder of this section explains the steps required to enter the column titles, stock data, and row titles as shown in Figure 2–4 on page EX 89 and then save the workbook.

1 With cell A3 selected, type `Stock` and then press the RIGHT ARROW key.

2 Type `Symbol` in cell B3 and then press the RIGHT ARROW key.

Wrapping Text
If you have a long text entry, such as a paragraph, you can instruct Excel to wrap the text in a cell, rather than pressing ALT+ENTER to end a line. To wrap text, right-click in the cell, click Format Cells on the shortcut menu, click the Alignment tab, click Wrap text, and then click OK. Excel will increase the height of the cell automatically so the additional lines will fit. If you want to control where each line ends in the cell, rather than letting Excel wrap based on the cell width, however, then you must end each line with ALT+ENTER.

③ In cell C3, type `Date` and then press ALT+ENTER. Type `Acquired` and then press the RIGHT ARROW key.

④ In cell D3, type `Shares` and then press the RIGHT ARROW key.

⑤ In cell E3, type `Initial` and then press ALT+ENTER. Type `Price` and then press ALT+ENTER. Type `Per Share` and then press the RIGHT ARROW key.

⑥ Type `Initial` in cell F3 and then press ALT+ENTER. Type `Cost` and then press the RIGHT ARROW key.

⑦ In cell G3, type `Current` and then press ALT+ENTER. Type `Price` and then press ALT+ENTER. Type `Per Share` and then press the RIGHT ARROW key.

⑧ Type `Current` in cell H3 and then press ALT+ENTER. Type `Value` and then press the RIGHT ARROW key.

⑨ In cell I3, type `Gain/Loss` and then press the RIGHT ARROW key.

⑩ In cell J3, type `Percent` and then press ALT+ENTER. Type `Gain/Loss`.

To Enter the Portfolio Summary Data

The portfolio summary data in Table 2–1 includes a purchase date for each stock. Excel considers a date to be a number and, therefore, it displays the date right-aligned in the cell. The following steps enter the portfolio summary data shown in Table 2–1.

① Select cell A4, type `Apple Computers`, and then press the RIGHT ARROW key.

② Type `AAPL` in cell B4 and then press the RIGHT ARROW key.

③ Type `12/1/04` in cell C4 and then press the RIGHT ARROW key.

④ Type `440` in cell D4 and then press the RIGHT ARROW key.

⑤ Type `64.59` in cell E4 and then click cell G4.

⑥ Type `82.99` in cell G4 and then click cell A5.

⑦ Enter the portfolio summary data in Table 2–1 for the eight remaining stocks in rows 5 through 12 (Figure 2–4).

Two-Digit Years
When you enter a two-digit year value, Excel changes a two-digit year less than 30 to 20xx and a two-digit year of 30 and greater to 19xx. Use four-digit years to ensure that Excel interprets year values the way you intend, if necessary.

Formatting a Worksheet
With early worksheet programs, users often skipped rows to improve the appearance of the worksheet. With Excel it is not necessary to skip rows because you can increase row heights to add white space between information.

To Enter the Row Titles

① Select cell A13. Type `Totals` and then press the DOWN ARROW key. Type `Average` in cell A14 and then press the DOWN ARROW key.

② Type `Highest` in cell A15 and then press the DOWN ARROW key. Type `Lowest` in cell A16 and then press the ENTER key. Select cell F4 (Figure 2–4).

Table 2–1 Silver Dollars Stock Club Portfolio Summary Data					
Stock	Symbol	Date Acquired	Shares	Initial Price Per Share	Current Price Per Share
Apple Computers	AAPL	12/1/04	440	64.59	82.99
AT&T	T	12/16/03	870	28.71	27.99
Citigroup	C	1/17/03	960	49.46	44.675
Comcast	CMCSA	12/11/02	380	33.62	41.39
Google	GOOG	2/20/04	920	390.32	492.55
Home Depot	HD	11/14/05	770	34.54	31.72
IBM	IBM	9/14/04	990	74.08	81.47
Merck	MRK	1/14/05	950	42.125	38.34
Sprint Nextel	S	9/10/03	560	17.79	21.18

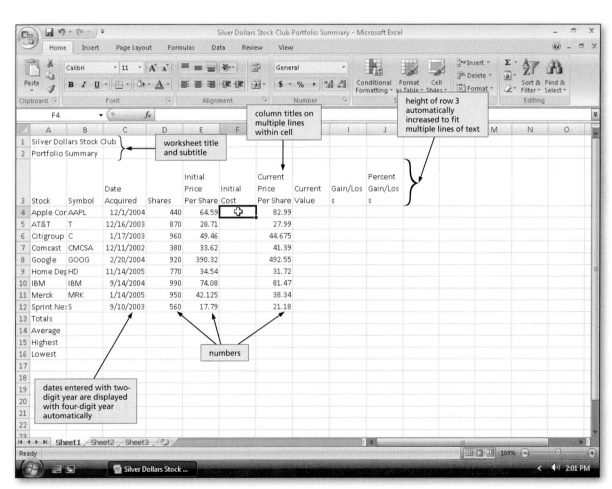

Figure 2–4

To Change Workbook Properties and Save the Workbook

With the data entered into the worksheet, the following steps save the workbook using the file name, Silver Dollars Stock Club Portfolio Summary. As you are building a workbook, it is a good idea to save it often so that you do not lose your work if the computer is turned off or if you lose electrical power. The first time you save a workbook, you should change the workbook properties.

1 Click the Office Button, click Prepare on the Office Button menu, and then click Properties.

2 Update the document properties with your name and any other information required.

3 Click the Close button on the Document Properties pane.

Note: If you are using Windows XP, see Appendix F for alternate steps.

4 With a USB flash drive connected to one of the computer's USB ports, click the Save button on the Quick Access Toolbar.

5 When Excel displays the Save As dialog box, type `Silver Dollars Stock Club Portfolio Summary` in the File name text box.

6 If the Folders list is displayed below the Folders button, click the Folders button to remove the Folders list.

7 If Computer is not displayed in the Favorite Links section, drag the top or bottom edge of the Save As dialog box until Computer is displayed.

8 Click Computer in the Favorite Links section. If necessary, scroll until UDISK 2.0 (E:) appears in the list of available drives. Double-click UDISK 2.0 (E:) (your USB flash drive may have a different name and letter). Click the Save button in the Save As dialog box to save the workbook on the USB flash drive using the file name, Silver Dollars Stock Club Portfolio Summary.

Entering Formulas

One of the reasons Excel is such a valuable tool is that you can assign a **formula** to a cell and Excel will calculate the result. Consider, for example, what would happen if you had to multiply 440×64.59 and then manually enter the product, 28,419.60, in cell F4. Every time the values in cells D4 or E4 changed, you would have to recalculate the product and enter the new value in cell F4. By contrast, if you enter a formula in cell F4 to multiply the values in cells D4 and E4, Excel recalculates the product whenever new values are entered into those cells and displays the result in cell F4.

Plan Ahead

> **Determine the necessary formulas and functions needed.**
> The formulas needed in the worksheet are noted in the requirements document as follows:
>
> 1. Initial Cost (column F) = Shares $\times$ Initial Price Per Share
>
> 2. Current Value (column H) = Shares $\times$ Current Price Per Share
>
> 3. Gain/Loss (column I) = Current Value – Initial Cost
>
> 4. Percent Gain/Loss (column J) = Gain/Loss / Initial Cost
>
> The necessary functions to determine the average, highest, and lowest numbers are discussed shortly.

To Enter a Formula Using the Keyboard

The initial cost for each stock, which appears in column F, is equal to the number of shares in column D times the initial price per share in column E. Thus, the initial cost for Apple Computers in cell F4 is obtained by multiplying 440 (cell D4) by 64.59 (cell E4) or =D4*E4. The following steps enter the initial cost formula in cell F4 using the keyboard.

1

• With cell F4 selected, type =d4*e4 in the cell to display the formula in the formula bar and in cell F4 and to display colored borders around the cells referenced in the formula (Figure 2–5).

Q&A

What is happening on the worksheet as I enter the formula?

The **equal sign** (=) preceding d4*e4 is an important part of the formula. It alerts Excel that you are entering a formula or function and not text. Because the most common error when entering a formula is to reference the wrong cell in a formula mistakenly, Excel colors the borders of the cells referenced in the formula. The coloring helps in the reviewing process to ensure the cell references are correct. The **asterisk** (*) following d4 is the arithmetic operator that directs Excel to perform the multiplication operation.

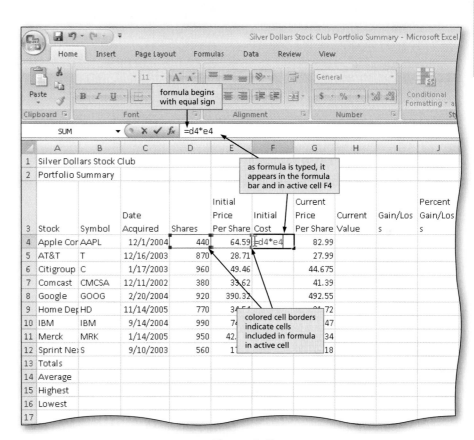

Figure 2–5

2

• Press the RIGHT ARROW key twice to complete the arithmetic operation indicated by the formula, display the result, 28419.6, and to select cell H4 (Figure 2–6).

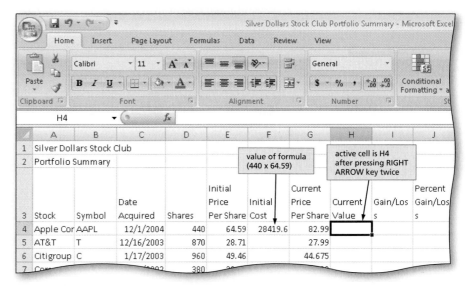

Figure 2–6

Arithmetic Operations

Table 2–2 describes multiplication and other valid Excel arithmetic operators.

Table 2–2 Summary of Arithmetic Operators

Arithmetic Operator	Meaning	Example of Usage	Meaning
–	Negation	–34	Negative 34
%	Percentage	=72%	Multiplies 72 by 0.01
^	Exponentiation	=4 ^ 6	Raises 4 to the sixth power
*	Multiplication	=22.6 * F4	Multiplies the contents of cell F4 by 22.6
/	Division	=C3 / C6	Divides the contents of cell C3 by the contents of cell C6
+	Addition	=7 + 3	Adds 7 and 3
–	Subtraction	=F12 – 22	Subtracts 22 from the contents of cell F12

BTW

Troubling Formulas
If Excel does not accept a formula, remove the equal sign from the left side and complete the entry as text. Later, after you have entered additional data or determined the error, reinsert the equal sign to change the text back to a formula and edit the formula as needed.

You can enter the cell references in formulas in uppercase or lowercase, and you can add spaces before and after arithmetic operators to make the formulas easier to read. The formula, =d4*e4, is the same as the formulas, =d4 * e4, =D4 * e4, or =D4 * E4.

Order of Operations

When more than one arithmetic operator is involved in a formula, Excel follows the same basic order of operations that you use in algebra. Moving from left to right in a formula, the **order of operations** is as follows: first negation (–), then all percentages (%), then all exponentiations (^), then all multiplications (*) and divisions (/), and finally, all additions (+) and subtractions (–).

You can use parentheses to override the order of operations. For example, if Excel follows the order of operations, 5 * 9 + 8 equals 53. If you use parentheses, however, to change the formula to 5 * (9 + 8), the result is 85, because the parentheses instruct Excel to add 9 and 8 before multiplying by 5. Table 2–3 illustrates several examples of valid Excel formulas and explains the order of operations.

Table 2–3 Examples of Excel Formulas

Formula	Meaning
=K12	Assigns the value in cell K12 to the active cell.
=10 + 4^2	Assigns the sum of 10 + 16 (or 26) to the active cell.
=3 * C20 or =C20 * 3 or =(3 * C20)	Assigns three times the contents of cell C20 to the active cell.
=50% * 12	Assigns the product of 0.50 times 12 (or 6) to the active cell.
– (H3 * Q30)	Assigns the negative value of the product of the values contained in cells H3 and Q30 to the active cell.
=12 * (N8 – O8)	Assigns the product of 12 times the difference between the values contained in cells N8 and O8 to the active cell.
=M9 / Z8 – C3 * Q19 + A3 ^ B3	Completes the following operations, from left to right: exponentiation (A3 ^ B3), then division (M9 / Z8), then multiplication (C3 * Q19), then subtraction (M9 / Z8) – (C3 * Q19), and finally addition (M9 / Z8 – C3 * Q19) + (A3 ^ B3). If cells A3 = 2, B3 = 4, C3 = 6, M9 = 3, Q19 = 4, and Z8 = 3, then Excel assigns the active cell the value 18; that is, 3 / 3 – 6 * 4 + 2 ^ 4 = -7.

To Enter Formulas Using Point Mode

The sketch of the worksheet in Figure 2–3 on page EX 85 calls for the current value, gain/loss, and percent gain/loss of each stock to appear in columns H, I, and J respectively. All three of these values are calculated using formulas in row 4:

Current Value (cell H4) = Shares $\times$ Current Price Per Share or =D4*G4

Gain/Loss (cell I4) = Current Value – Initial Cost or H4-F4

Percent Gain/Loss (cell J4) = Gain/Loss / Initial Cost or I4/F4

An alternative to entering the formulas in cells H4, I4, and J4 using the keyboard is to enter the formulas using the mouse and Point mode. **Point mode** allows you to select cells for use in a formula by using the mouse. The following steps enter formulas using Point mode.

1

- With cell H4 selected, type = (equal sign) to begin the formula and then click cell D4 to add a reference to cell D4 to the formula (Figure 2–7).

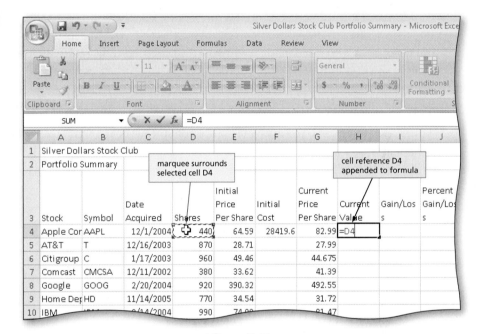

Figure 2–7

2

- Type * (asterisk) and then click cell G4 to add a multiplication operator and reference to cell G4 to the formula (Figure 2–8).

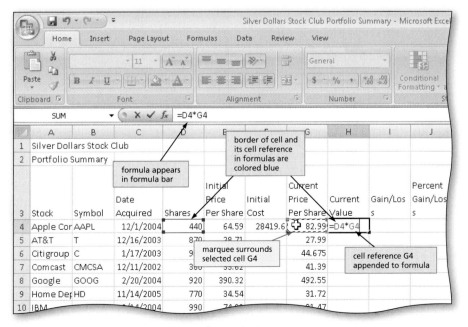

Figure 2–8

3

- Click the Enter box and then click cell I4 to select cell I4.

- Type = (equal sign) and then click cell H4 to add a reference to cell H4 to the formula.

- Type – (minus sign) and then click cell F4 to add a subtraction operator and reference to cell F4 to the formula (Figure 2–9).

Q&A

When should I use Point mode to enter formulas?

Using Point mode to enter formulas often is faster and more accurate than using the keyboard to type the entire formula when the cell you want to select does not require you to scroll. In many instances, as in these steps, you may want to use both the keyboard and mouse when entering a formula in a cell. You can use the keyboard to begin the formula, for example, and then use the mouse to select a range of cells.

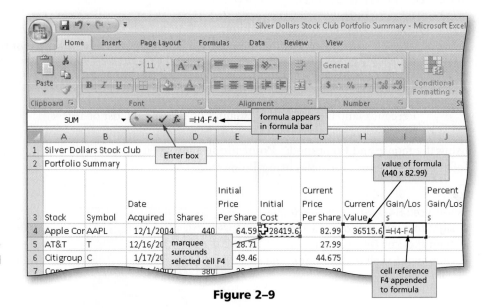

Figure 2–9

4

- Click the Enter box to enter the formula in cell I4.

- Select cell J4. Type = (equal sign) and then click cell I4 to add a reference to cell I4 to the formula.

- Type / (forward slash) and then click cell F4 to add a reference to cell F4 to the formula.

- Click the Enter box to enter the formula in cell J4 (Figure 2–10).

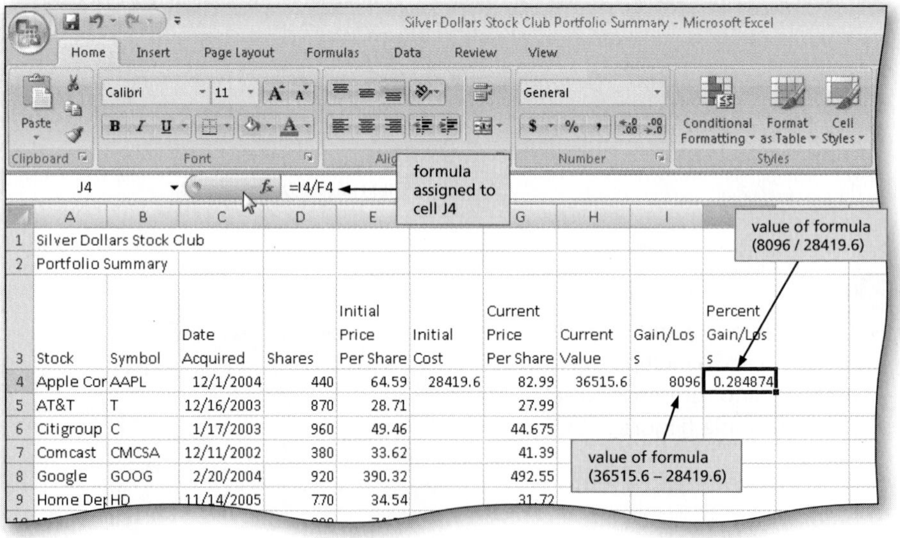

Q&A

Why do only six decimal places show in cell J4?

The actual value assigned by Excel to cell J4 from the division operation in Step 4 is 0.284873819. While not all the decimal places appear in Figure 2–10, Excel maintains all of them for computational purposes. Thus, if referencing cell J4 in a formula, the value used for computational purposes is 0.284873819, not 0.284874. Excel displays the value in cell J4 as 0.284874 because the cell formatting is set to display only six digits after the decimal point. If you change the cell formatting of column J to display nine digits after the decimal point, then Excel displays the true value 0.284873819.

Figure 2–10

To Copy Formulas Using the Fill Handle

The four formulas for Apple Computers in cells F4, H4, I4, and J4 now are complete. You could enter the same four formulas one at a time for the eight remaining stocks. A much easier method of entering the formulas, however, is to select the formulas in row 4 and then use the fill handle to copy them through row 12. Recall from Chapter 1 that the fill handle is a small rectangle in the lower-right corner of the active cell or active range. The following steps copy the formulas using the fill handle.

1

- Select cell F4 and then point to the fill handle.

- Drag the fill handle down through cell F12 and continue to hold the mouse button to select the destination range (Figure 2–11).

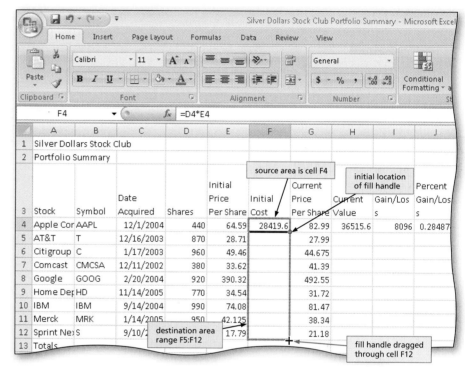

Figure 2–11

2

- Release the mouse button to copy the formula in cell F4 to the cells in the range F5:F12.

- Select the range H4:J4 and then point to the fill handle (Figure 2–12).

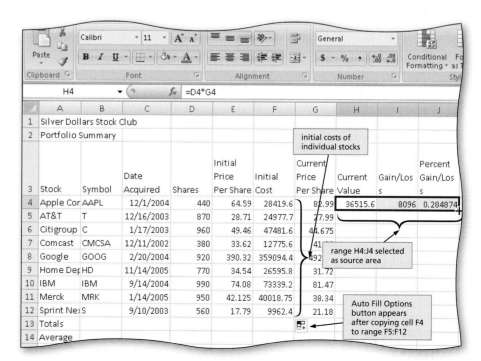

Figure 2–12

3

- Drag the fill handle down through the range H5:J12 to copy the three formulas =D4*G4 in cell H4, =H4-F4 in cell I4, and =I4/F4 in cell J4 to the range H5:J12 (Figure 2–13).

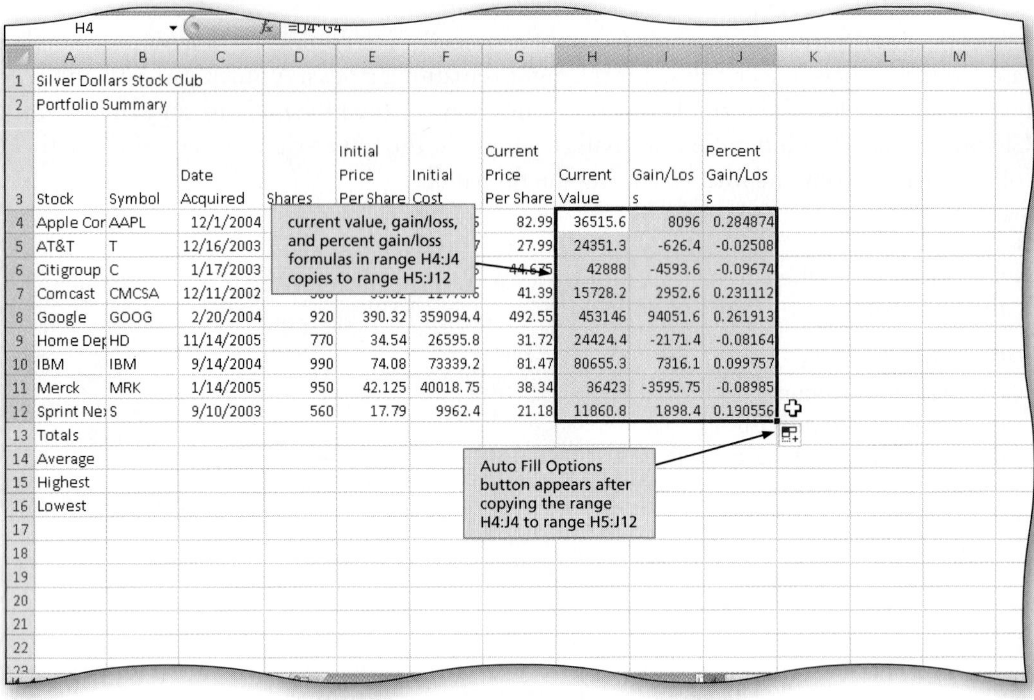

How does Excel adjust the cell references in the formulas in the destination area?

Recall that when you copy a formula, Excel adjusts the cell references so the new formulas contain references corresponding to the new location and performs calculations using the appropriate

	H4		▼		*fx*	=D4*G4							
	A	B	C	D	E	F	G	H	I	J	K	L	M
1	Silver Dollars Stock Club												
2	Portfolio Summary												
3	Stock	Symbol	Date Acquired	Shares	Initial Price Per Share	Initial Cost	Current Price Per Share	Current Value	Gain/Loss	Percent Gain/Loss			
4	Apple Cor	AAPL	12/1/2004				82.99	36515.6	8096	0.284874			
5	AT&T	T	12/16/2003				27.99	24351.3	-626.4	-0.02508			
6	Citigroup	C	1/17/2003			44.6		42888	-4593.6	-0.09674			
7	Comcast	CMCSA	12/11/2002				41.39	15728.2	2952.6	0.231112			
8	Google	GOOG	2/20/2004	920	390.32	359094.4	492.55	453146	94051.6	0.261913			
9	Home Dep	HD	11/14/2005	770	34.54	26595.8	31.72	24424.4	-2171.4	-0.08164			
10	IBM	IBM	9/14/2004	990	74.08	73339.2	81.47	80655.3	7316.1	0.099757			
11	Merck	MRK	1/14/2005	950	42.125	40018.75	38.34	36423	-3595.75	-0.08985			
12	Sprint Ne	S	9/10/2003	560	17.79	9962.4	21.18	11860.8	1898.4	0.190556			
13	Totals												
14	Average												
15	Highest												
16	Lowest												
17													
18													
19													
20													
21													
22													

current value, gain/loss, and percent gain/loss formulas in range H4:J4 copies to range H5:J12

Auto Fill Options button appears after copying the range H4:J4 to range H5:J12

Figure 2–13

values. Thus, if you copy downward, Excel adjusts the row portion of cell references. If you copy across, then Excel adjusts the column portion of cell references. These cell references are called **relative cell references**.

Other Ways

1. Select source area, click Copy button on Ribbon, select destination area, click Paste button on Ribbon

2. Select source area, right-click copy area, click Copy on shortcut menu, select destination area, right-click paste area, click Paste on shortcut menu

Automatic Recalculation Every time you enter a value into a cell in the worksheet, Excel automatically recalculates all formulas. You can change to manual recalculation by clicking the Calculation Options button on the Formulas tab on the Ribbon and then clicking Manual. In manual calculation mode, press the F9 key to instruct Excel to recalculate all formulas.

Smart Tags and Option Buttons

Excel can identify certain actions to take on specific data in workbooks using **smart tags**. Data labeled with smart tags includes dates, financial symbols, people's names, and more. To use smart tags, you must turn on smart tags using the AutoCorrect Options in the Excel Options dialog box. To change AutoCorrect options, click the Office Button, click the Excel Options button on the Office Button menu, click Proofing, and then click AutoCorrect Options. Once smart tags are turned on, Excel places a small purple triangle, called a **smart tag indicator**, in a cell to indicate that a smart tag is available. When you move the insertion point over the smart tag indicator, the Smart Tag Actions button appears. Clicking the Smart Tag Actions button arrow produces a list of actions you can perform on the data in that specific cell.

In addition to smart tags, Excel also displays Options buttons in a workbook while you are working on it to indicate that you can complete an operation using automatic features such as AutoCorrect, Auto Fill, error checking, and others. For example, the Auto Fill Options button shown in Figure 2–13 appears after a fill operation, such as dragging the fill handle. When an error occurs in a formula in a cell, Excel displays the Trace Error button next to the cell and identifies the cell with the error by placing a green triangle in the upper left of the cell.

Table 2–4 summarizes the smart tag and Options buttons available in Excel. When one of these buttons appears on your worksheet, click the button arrow to produce the list of options for modifying the operation or to obtain additional information.

Table 2–4 Smart Tag and Options Buttons in Excel

Button	Name	Menu Function
	Auto Fill Options	Gives options for how to fill cells following a fill operation, such as dragging the fill handle.
	AutoCorrect Options	Undoes an automatic correction, stops future automatic corrections of this type, or causes Excel to display the AutoCorrect Options dialog box.
	Insert Options	Lists formatting options following an insertion of cells, rows, or columns.
	Paste Options	Specifies how moved or pasted items should appear (for example, with original formatting, without formatting, or with different formatting).
	Smart Tag Actions	Lists information options for a cell containing data recognized by Excel, such as a stock symbol.
	Trace Error	Lists error checking options following the assignment of an invalid formula to a cell.

To Determine Totals Using the Sum Button

The next step is to determine the totals in row 13 for the initial cost in column F, current value in column H, and gain/loss in column I. To determine the total initial cost in column F, the values in the range F4 through F12 must be summed. To do so, enter the function =sum(f4:f12) in cell F13 or select cell F13 and then click the Sum button on the Ribbon and then press the ENTER key. Recall that a function is a prewritten formula that is built into Excel. Similar SUM functions or the Sum button can be used in cells H13 and I13 to determine total current value and total gain/loss, respectively.

1 Select cell F13. Click the Sum button on the Ribbon and then click the Enter button.

2 Select the range H13:I13. Click the Sum button on the Ribbon to display the totals in row 13 as shown in Figure 2–14.

BTW

Selecting a Range
You can select a range using the keyboard. Press the F8 key and then use the arrow keys to select the desired range. After you are finished, make sure to press the F8 key to turn off the selection or you will continue to select ranges.

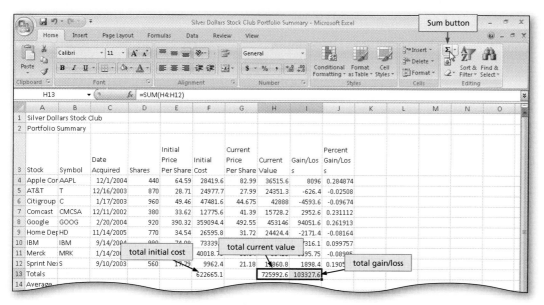

Figure 2–14

To Determine the Total Percent Gain/Loss

With the totals in row 13 determined, the next step is to copy the percent gain/loss formula in cell J12 to cell J13 as performed in the following steps.

1 Select cell J12 and then point to the fill handle.

2 Drag the fill handle down through cell J13 to copy the formula in cell J12 to cell J13 (Figure 2–15).

Q&A

Why was the formula I13/F13 not copied to cell J13 earlier?

The formula, I13/F13, was not copied to cell J13 when cell J4 was copied to the range J5:J12 because both cells involved in the computation (I13 and F13) were blank, or zero, at the time. A **blank cell** in Excel has a numerical value of zero, which would have resulted in an error message in cell J13. Once the totals were determined, both cells I13 and F13 (especially F13, because it is the divisor) had nonzero numerical values.

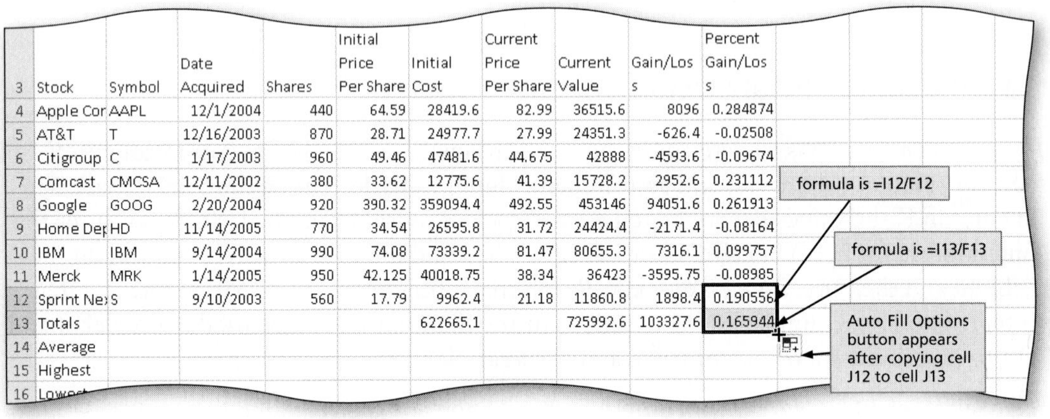

	Stock	Symbol	Date Acquired	Shares	Initial Price Per Share	Initial Cost	Current Price Per Share	Current Value	Gain/Loss	Percent Gain/Loss
3	Stock	Symbol	Date Acquired	Shares	Initial Price Per Share	Initial Cost	Current Price Per Share	Current Value	Gain/Loss	Percent Gain/Loss
4	Apple Cor	AAPL	12/1/2004	440	64.59	28419.6	82.99	36515.6	8096	0.284874
5	AT&T	T	12/16/2003	870	28.71	24977.7	27.99	24351.3	-626.4	-0.02508
6	Citigroup	C	1/17/2003	960	49.46	47481.6	44.675	42888	-4593.6	-0.09674
7	Comcast	CMCSA	12/11/2002	380	33.62	12775.6	41.39	15728.2	2952.6	0.231112
8	Google	GOOG	2/20/2004	920	390.32	359094.4	492.55	453146	94051.6	0.261913
9	Home Dep	HD	11/14/2005	770	34.54	26595.8	31.72	24424.4	-2171.4	-0.08164
10	IBM	IBM	9/14/2004	990	74.08	73339.2	81.47	80655.3	7316.1	0.099757
11	Merck	MRK	1/14/2005	950	42.125	40018.75	38.34	36423	-3595.75	-0.08985
12	Sprint Nex	S	9/10/2003	560	17.79	9962.4	21.18	11860.8	1898.4	0.190556
13	Totals					622665.1		725992.6	103327.6	0.165944
14	Average									
15	Highest									
16	Lowest									

formula is =I12/F12

formula is =I13/F13

Auto Fill Options button appears after copying cell J12 to cell J13

Figure 2–15

BTW

Entering Functions
You can drag the Function Arguments dialog box (Figure 2–20 on page EX 101) out of the way in order to select a range. You also can click the Collapse Dialog button to the right of the Number 1 box to hide the Function Arguments dialog box. After selecting the range, click the Collapse Dialog button a second time.

BTW

Statistical Functions
Excel usually considers a blank cell to be equal to 0. The statistical functions, however, ignore blank cells. Excel thus calculates the average of 3 cells with values of 7, blank, and 5 to be 6 or (7 + 5) / 2 and not 4 or (7 + 0 + 5) / 3.

Using the AVERAGE, MAX, and MIN Functions

The next step in creating the Silver Dollars Stock Club Portfolio Summary worksheet is to compute the average, highest value, and lowest value for the number of shares listed in the range D4:D12 using the AVERAGE, MAX, and MIN functions in the range D14:D16. Once the values are determined for column D, the entries can be copied across to the other columns.

Excel includes prewritten formulas called functions to help you compute these statistics. A **function** takes a value or values, performs an operation, and returns a result to the cell. The values that you use with a function are called **arguments**. All functions begin with an equal sign and include the arguments in parentheses after the function name. For example, in the function =AVERAGE(D4:D12), the function name is AVERAGE, and the argument is the range D4:D12.

With Excel, you can enter functions using one of five methods: (1) the keyboard or mouse; (2) the Insert Function box in the formula bar; (3) the Sum menu; (4) the AutoSum command on the Formulas tab on the Ribbon; and (5) the Name box area in the formula bar (Figure 2–16). The method you choose will depend on your typing skills and whether you can recall the function name and required arguments.

In the following pages, each of the first three methods will be used. The keyboard and mouse method will be used to determine the average number of shares (cell D14). The Insert Function button in the formula bar method will be used to determine the highest number of shares (cell D15). The Sum menu method will be used to determine the lowest number of shares (cell D16).

To Determine the Average of a Range of Numbers Using the Keyboard and Mouse

The **AVERAGE function** sums the numbers in the specified range and then divides the sum by the number of nonzero cells in the range. The following steps use the AVERAGE function to determine the average of the numbers in the range D4:D12.

- Select cell D14.

- Type =av in the cell to display the Formula AutoComplete list.

- Point to the AVERAGE function name (Figure 2–16).

Q&A

What is happening as I type?

As you type the equal sign followed by the characters in the name of a function, Excel displays the Formula AutoComplete list. This list contains those functions that alphabetically match the letters you have typed. Because you typed =av, Excel displays all the functions that begin with the letters av.

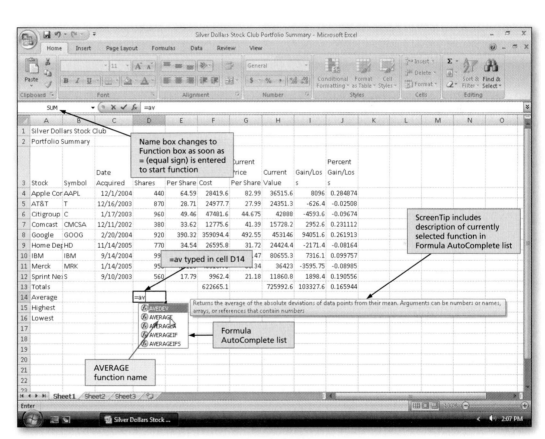

Figure 2–16

2

- Double-click AVERAGE in the Formula AutoComplete list to select the AVERAGE function.

- Select the range D4:D12 to insert the range as the argument to the AVERAGE function (Figure 2–17).

Q&A As I drag, why does the function in cell D14 change?

When you click cell D4, Excel appends cell D4 to the left parenthesis in the formula bar and surrounds cell D4 with a marquee. When you begin dragging, Excel appends to the argument a colon (:) and the cell reference of the cell where the mouse pointer is located.

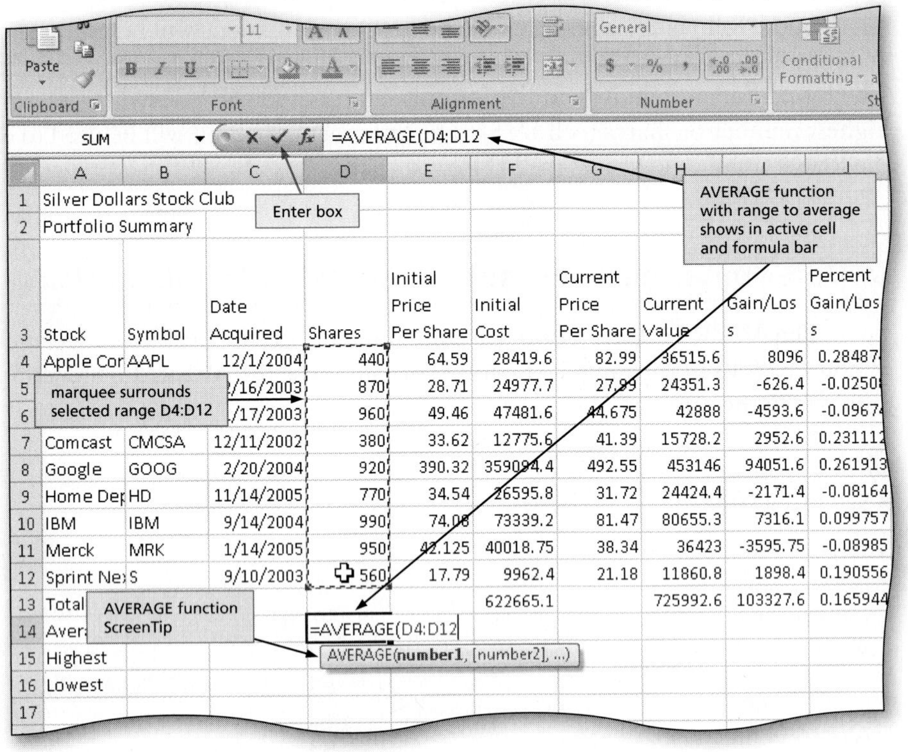

3

- Click the Enter box to compute the average of the nine numbers in the range D4:D12 and display the result in cell D14 (Figure 2–18).

Q&A Can I use the arrow keys to complete the entry instead?

No. When you use Point mode you cannot use the arrow keys to complete the entry. While in Point mode, the arrow keys change the selected cell reference in the range you are selecting.

Q&A What is the purpose of the parentheses in the function?

The AVERAGE function requires that the argument (in this case, the range D4:D12) be included within parentheses following the function name. Excel automatically appends the right parenthesis to complete the AVERAGE function when you click the Enter box or press the ENTER key.

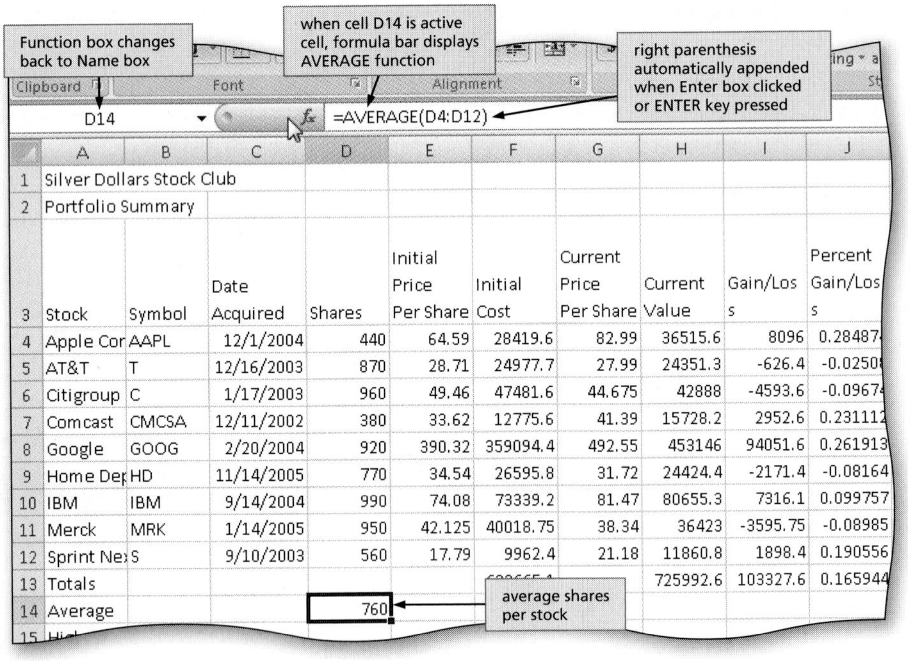

Figure 2–17

Figure 2–18

Other Ways

1. Click Insert Function box in formula bar, click AVERAGE function

2. Click Sum button arrow on Ribbon, click Average function

3. Click Formulas tab on Ribbon, click AutoSum button arrow, click Average function

To Determine the Highest Number in a Range of Numbers Using the Insert Function Box

The next step is to select cell D15 and determine the highest (maximum) number in the range D4:D12. Excel has a function called the **MAX function** that displays the highest value in a range. Although you could enter the MAX function using the keyboard and Point mode as described in the previous steps, an alternative method to entering the function is to use the Insert Function box in the formula bar, as performed in the following steps.

1

- Select cell D15.

- Click the Insert Function box in the formula bar to display the Insert Function dialog box.

- When Excel displays the Insert Function dialog box, click MAX in the 'Select a function' list (Figure 2–19).

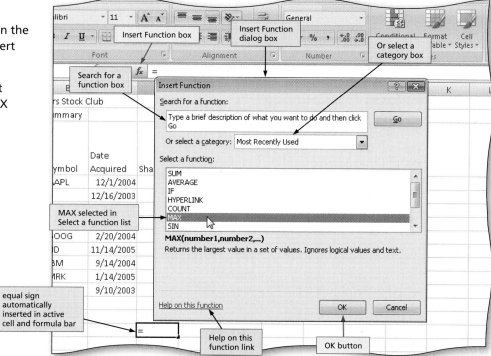

Figure 2–19

2

- Click the OK button.

- When Excel displays the Function Arguments dialog box, type d4:d12 in the Number1 box (Figure 2–20).

Q&A

Why did numbers appear in the Function Arguments dialog box?

As shown in Figure 2–20, Excel displays the value the MAX function will return to cell D15 in the Function Arguments dialog box. It also lists the first few numbers in the selected range, next to the Number1 box.

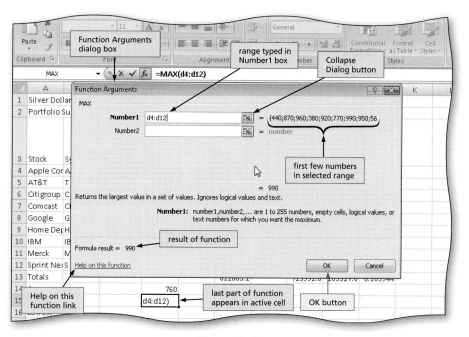

Figure 2–20

- Click the OK button to display the highest value in the range D4:D12 in cell D15 (Figure 2–21).

Q&A

Why should I not just enter the highest value that I see in the range D4:D12 in cell D15?

In this example, rather than entering the MAX function, you easily could scan the range D4:D12, determine that the highest number of shares is 990, and manually enter the number 990 as a constant in cell D15. Excel would display the number the same as in Figure 2–21. Because it contains a constant, however, Excel will continue to display 990 in cell D15, even if the values in the range D4:D12 change. If you use the MAX function, Excel will recalculate the highest value in the range D4:D9 each time a new value is entered into the worksheet.

	A	B	C	D	E	F	G	H	I	J
1	Silver Dollars Stock Club									
2	Portfolio Summary									
3	Stock	Symbol	Date Acquired	Shares	Initial Price Per Share	Initial Cost	Current Price Per Share	Current Value	Gain/Loss	Percent Gain/Loss
4	Apple Cor	AAPL	12/1/2004	440	64.59	28419.6	82.99	36515.6	8096	0.28487
5	AT&T	T	12/16/2003	870	28.71	24977.7	27.99	24351.3	-626.4	-0.0250
6	Citigroup	C	1/17/2003	960	49.46	47481.6	44.675	42888	-4593.6	-0.0967
7	Comcast	CMCSA	12/11/2002	380	33.62	12775.6	41.39	15728.2	2952.6	0.231112
8	Google	GOOG	2/20/2004	920	390.32	359094.4	492.55	453146	94051.6	0.261913
9	Home Dep	HD	11/14/2005	770	34.54	26595.8	31.72	24424.4	-2171.4	-0.08164
10	IBM	IBM	9/14/2004	990	74.08	73339.2	81.47	80655.3	7316.1	0.099757
11	Merck	MRK	1/14/2005	950	42.125	40018.75	38.34	36423	-3595.75	-0.08985
12	Sprint Ne	S	9/10/2003	560	17.79	9962.4	21.18	11860.8	1898.4	0.190556
13	Totals					622665.1		725992.6	103327.6	0.165944
14	Average			760						
15	Highest			990						
16	Lowest									

D15   =MAX(D4:D12)

MAX function determines highest value in range D4:D12

highest value in range D4:D12

Figure 2–21

Other Ways

1. Click Sum button arrow on Ribbon, click Max function
2. Click Formulas tab on Ribbon, click AutoSum button arrow, click Max function
3. Type =MAX in cell

To Determine the Lowest Number in a Range of Numbers Using the Sum Menu

The next step is to enter the **MIN function** in cell D16 to determine the lowest (minimum) number in the range D4:D12. Although you can enter the MIN function using either of the methods used to enter the AVERAGE and MAX functions, the following steps perform an alternative using the Sum button on the Ribbon.

- Select cell D16.

- Click the Sum button arrow on the Ribbon to display the Sum button menu (Figure 2–22).

Q&A

Why should I use the Sum button menu?

Using the Sum button menu allows you to enter one of five often-used functions easily into a cell, without having to memorize its name or the required arguments.

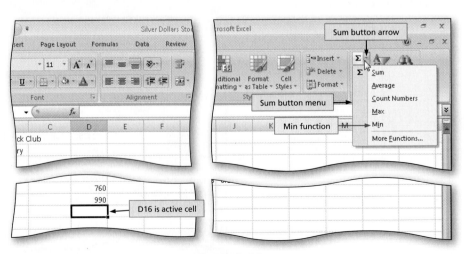

Figure 2–22

2

- Click Min to display the function =MIN(D14:D15) in the formula bar and in cell D16 (Figure 2–23).

Q&A

Why does Excel select the range D14:D15?

The range D14:D15 automatically selected by Excel is not correct. Excel attempts to guess which cells you want to include in the function by looking for adjacent ranges to the selected cell that contain numeric data.

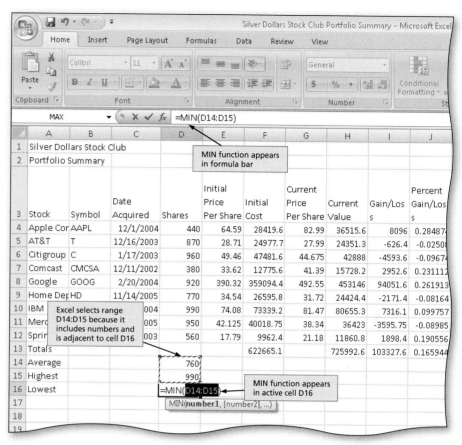

Figure 2–23

3

- Click cell D4 and then drag through cell D12 to display the function in the formula bar and in cell D14 with the new range (Figure 2–24).

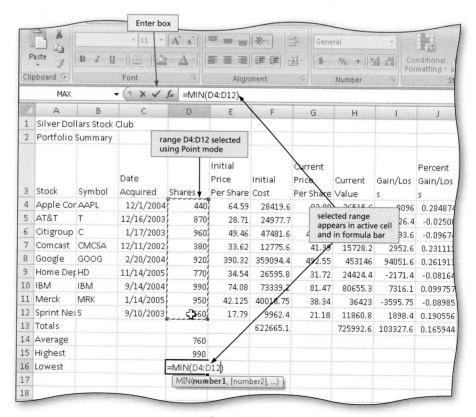

Figure 2–24

4

- Click the Enter box to determine the lowest value in D4:D12 and display the result in the formula bar and in cell D14 (Figure 2–25).

Q&A

How can I use other functions?

Excel has more than 400 additional functions that perform just about every type of calculation you can imagine. These functions are categorized in the Insert Function dialog box shown in Figure 2–19 on page EX 101. To view the categories, click the 'Or select a category' box arrow. To obtain a description of a selected function, select its name in the Insert Function dialog box. Excel displays the description of the function below the Select a function list in the dialog box.

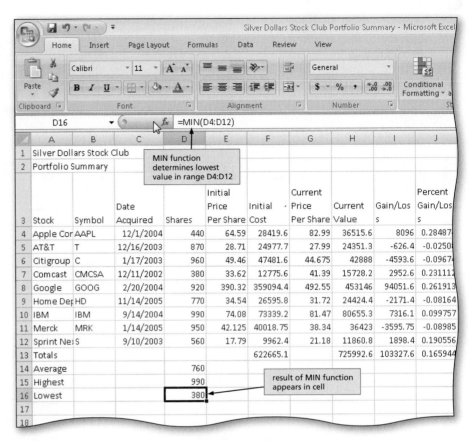

Figure 2–25

Other Ways
1. Click Insert Function box in formula bar, click MIN function	2. Click Formulas tab on Ribbon, click AutoSum button arrow, click Min function	3. Type =MIN in cell

To Copy a Range of Cells across Columns to an Adjacent Range Using the Fill Handle

The next step is to copy the AVERAGE, MAX, and MIN functions in the range D14:D16 to the adjacent range E14:J16. The following steps use the fill handle to copy the functions.

1

- Select the range D14:D16.

- Drag the fill handle in the lower-right corner of the selected range through cell J16 and continue to hold down the mouse button (Figure 2–26).

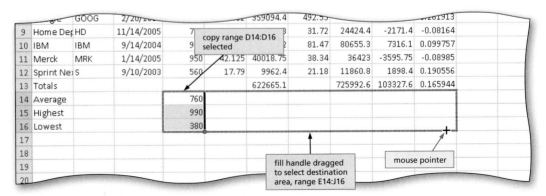

Figure 2–26

2

- Release the mouse button to copy the three functions to the range E14:J16 (Figure 2–27).

How can I be sure that the function arguments are proper for the cells in range E14:J16?

Remember that Excel adjusts the cell references in the copied functions so each function refers to the range of numbers above it in the same column. Review the numbers in rows 14 through 16 in Figure 2–27. You should see that the functions in each column return the appropriate values, based on the numbers in rows 4 through 12 of that column.

		Date			Initial	Price	Current	Gain/Los	Percent Gain/Los
3 Stock	Symbol	Acquired	Shares	Per Share	Cost	Per Share	Value	s	s
4 Apple Cor	AAPL	12/1/2004	440	64.59	28419.6	82.99	36515.6	8096	0.284874
5 AT&T	T	12/16/2003	870	28.71	24977.7	27.99	24351.3	-626.4	-0.02508
6 Citigroup	C	1/17/2003	960	49.46	47481.6	44.675	42888	-4593.6	-0.09674
7 Comcast	CMCSA	12/11/2002	380	33.62	12775.6	41.39	15728.2	2952.6	0.231112
8 Google	GOOG	2/20/2004	920	390.32	359094.4	492.55	453146	94051.6	0.261913
9 Home Dep	HD	11/14/2005	770	34.54	26595.8	31.72	24424.4	-2171.4	-0.08164
10 IBM	IBM	9/14/2004	990	74.08	73339.2	81.47	80655.6	7316.1	0.099757
11 Merck	MRK	1/14/2005	950	42.125	40018.75	38.34	36423	-3595.75	-0.08985
12 Sprint Nex	S	9/10/2003	560	17.79	9962.4	21.18	11860.8	1898.4	0.190556
13 Totals					622665.1		725992.6	103327.6	0.165944
14 Average			760	81.69278	69185.01	95.81167	80665.84	11480.84	0.086099
15 Highest			990	390.32	359094.4	492.55	453146	94051.6	0.284874
16 Lowest			380	17.79	9962.4	21.18	11860.8	-4593.6	-0.09674
17									
18									
19									
20									
21									
22									

AVERAGE, MAX, and MIN functions in range D14:D16 copied to range E14:J16

Auto Fill Options button

I◄ ◄ ► ►I   Sheet1 ╱ Sheet2 ╱ Sheet3 ╱ ♪

Ready   Count: 21   Max: 453146   Sum: 1088082.908

Silver Dollars Stock ...

Figure 2–27

3

- Select cell J14 and press the DELETE key to delete the average of the percent gain/loss (Figure 2–28).

Why is the formula in cell J14 deleted?

The average of the percent gain/loss in cell J14 is deleted because an average of percentages of this type is mathematically invalid.

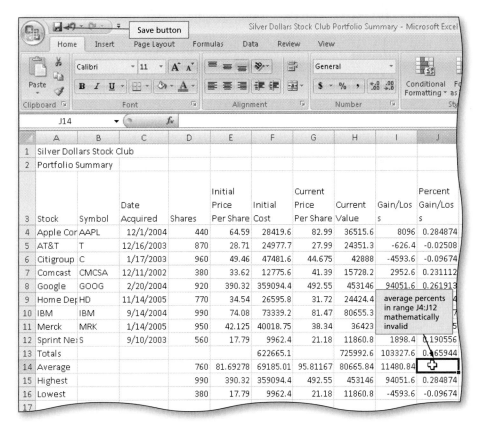

Other Ways

1. Select source area and point to border of range, while holding down CTRL key, drag source area to destination area
2. Select source area, on Ribbon click Copy button, select destination area, on Ribbon click Paste button
3. Right-click source area, click Copy on shortcut menu, right-click destination area, click Paste on shortcut menu
4. Select source area, press CTRL+C, select destination area, press CTRL+V

Figure 2–28

To Save a Workbook Using the Same File Name

Earlier in this project, an intermediate version of the workbook was saved using the file name, Silver Dollars Stock Club Portfolio Summary. The following step saves the workbook a second time using the same file name.

1 Click the Save button on the Quick Access Toolbar to save the workbook on the USB flash drive using the file name, Silver Dollars Stock Club Portfolio Summary.

Q&A

Why did Excel not display the Save As dialog box?

When you save a workbook a second time using the same file name, Excel will not display the Save As dialog box as it does the first time you save the workbook. Excel automatically stores the latest version of the workbook using the same file name, Silver Dollars Stock Club Portfolio Summary. You also can click Save on the Office Button menu or press SHIFT+F12 or CTRL+S to save a workbook again.

Verifying Formulas Using Range Finder

One of the more common mistakes made with Excel is to include a wrong cell reference in a formula. An easy way to verify that a formula references the cells you want it to reference is to use Excel's Range Finder. Use the **Range Finder** to check which cells are referenced in the formula assigned to the active cell. Range Finder allows you to make immediate changes to the cells referenced in a formula.

To use Range Finder to verify that a formula contains the intended cell references, double-click the cell with the formula you want to check. Excel responds by highlighting the cells referenced in the formula so you can check that the cell references are correct.

To Verify a Formula Using Range Finder

The following steps use Range Finder to check the formula in cell J4.

1
- Double-click cell J4 to activate Range Finder (Figure 2–29).

2
- Press the ESC key to quit Range Finder and then select cell A18.

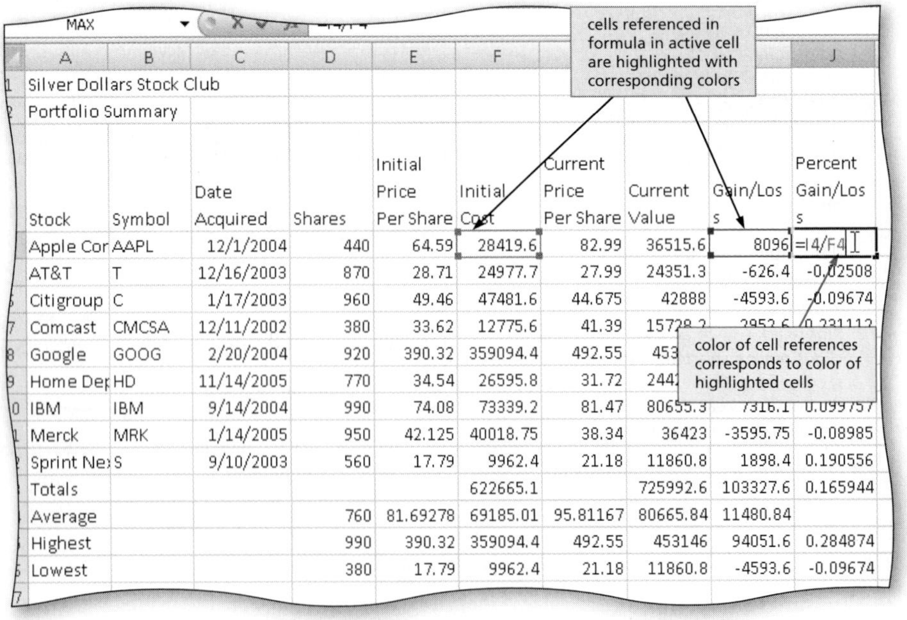

Figure 2–29

Formatting the Worksheet

Although the worksheet contains the appropriate data, formulas, and functions, the text and numbers need to be formatted to improve their appearance and readability.

In Chapter 1, cell styles were used to format much of the worksheet. This section describes how to change the unformatted worksheet in Figure 2–30a to the formatted worksheet in Figure 2–30b using a theme and other commands on the Ribbon. A **theme** is a predefined set of colors, fonts, chart styles, cell styles, and fill effects that can be applied to an entire workbook. Every new workbook that you create is assigned a default theme named Office. The colors and fonts that are used in the worksheet shown in Figure 2–30b are those that are associated with the Concourse theme.

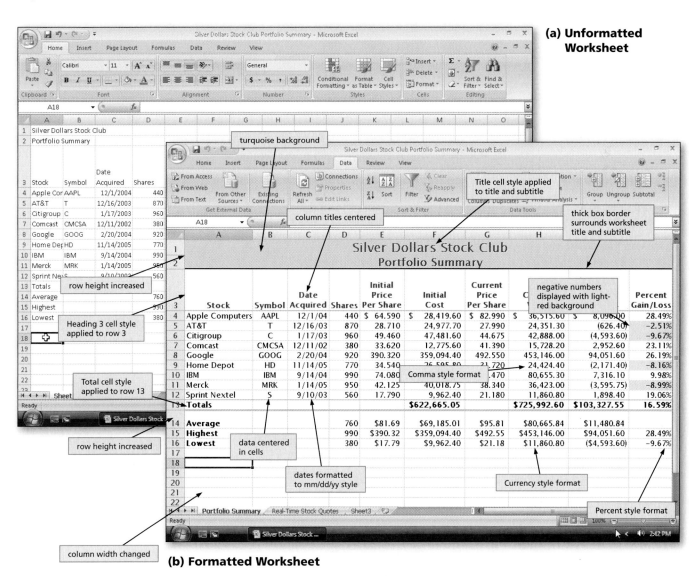

(a) Unformatted Worksheet

(b) Formatted Worksheet

Figure 2–30

Plan
Ahead

Identify how to format various elements of the worksheet.
The following outlines the formatting suggested in the sketch of the worksheet in Figure 2–3 on page EX 85:

1. Workbook theme - Concourse

2. Worksheet title and subtitle

   a. Alignment — center across columns A through J

   b. Cell style —Title

   c. Font size — title 18; subtitle 16

   d. Background color (range A1:J2) — Turquoise Accent 1, Lighter 60%

   e. Border — thick box border around range A1:J2

3. Column titles

   a. Cell style — Heading 3

   b. Alignment — center

4. Data

   a. Alignment — center data in column B

   b. Dates in column C — mm/dd/yy format

   c. Numbers in top row (range E4:I4) — Accounting style

   d. Numbers below top row (range E5:I12) — Comma style and decimal places

5. Total line

   a. Cell style — Total

   b. Numbers — Accounting style

6. Average, Highest, and Lowest rows

   a. Font style of row titles in range A14:A16 — bold

   b. Numbers — Currency style with floating dollar sign in the range E14:I16

7. Percentages in column J

   a. Numbers — Percentage style with two decimal places; if a cell in range J4:J12 is less than zero, then cell appears with background color of light red

8. Column widths

   a. Column A — 14.11 characters

   b. Columns B and C — best fit

   c. Column D — 6.00 characters

   d. Column E, G, and J — 9.00 characters

   e. Columns F, H, and I — 12.67 characters

9. Row heights

   a. Row 3 — 60.00 points

   b. Row 14 — 26.25 points

   c. Remaining rows — default

BTW

Colors
Knowing how people perceive colors helps you emphasize parts of your worksheet. Warmer colors (red and orange) tend to reach toward the reader. Cooler colors (blue, green, and violet) tend to pull away from the reader. Bright colors jump out of a dark background and are easiest to see. White or yellow text on a dark blue, green, purple, or black background is ideal.

To Change the Workbook Theme

The Concourse theme includes fonts and colors that provide the worksheet a professional and subtly colored appearance. The following steps change the workbook theme to the Concourse theme.

1

- Click the Page Layout tab on the Ribbon.

- Click the Themes button on the Ribbon to display the Theme gallery (Figure 2–31).

🔎 **Experiment**

- Point to several themes in the Theme gallery to see a live preview of the themes.

Q&A Why should I change the theme of a workbook?

A company or department may standardize on a specific theme so that all of their documents have a similar appearance. Similarly, an individual may want to have a theme that sets their work apart from others. Other Office applications, such as Word and PowerPoint, include the same themes included with Excel, meaning that all of your Microsoft Office documents can share a common theme.

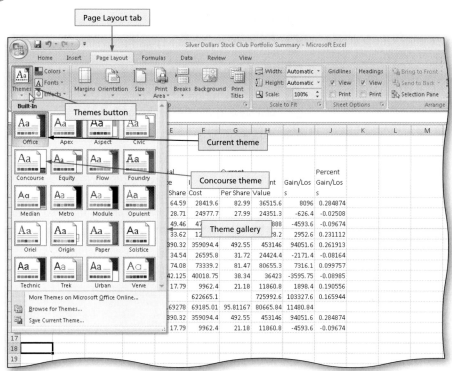

Figure 2–31

2

- Click Concourse in the Theme gallery to change the workbook theme to Concourse (Figure 2–32).

Q&A Why did the cells in the worksheet change?

The cells in the worksheet originally were formatted with the default font for the default Office theme. The default font for the Concourse theme is different than that of the default font for the Office theme and therefore changed on the worksheet when you changed the theme. If you had modified the font for any of the cells, those cells would not receive the default font for the Concourse theme.

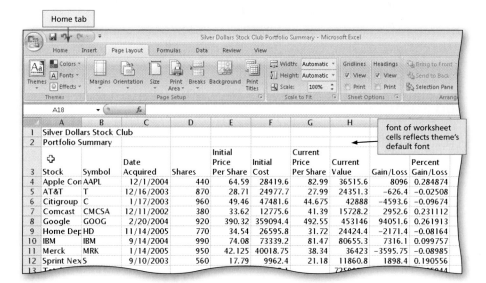

Figure 2–32

To Format the Worksheet Titles

The following steps merge and center the worksheet titles, apply the Title cells style to the worksheet titles, and decrease the font of the worksheet subtitle.

1 Click the Home tab on the Ribbon.

2 Select the range A1:J1 and then click the Merge & Center button on the Ribbon.

3 Select the range A2:J2 and then click the Merge & Center button on the Ribbon.

4 Select the range A1:A2, click the Cell Styles button on the Ribbon, and then click the Title cell style in the Cell Styles gallery.

5 Select cell A2 and then click the Decrease Font Size button on the Ribbon (Figure 2–33).

Q&A What is the effect of clicking the Decrease Font Size button?

When you click the Decrease Font Size button Excel assigns the next lowest font size in the Font Size gallery to the selected range. The Increase Font Size button works in a similar manner, but causes Excel to assign the next highest font size in the Font Size gallery to the selected range.

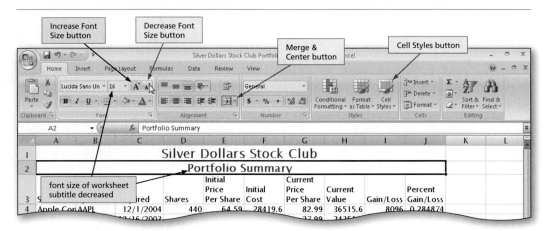

Figure 2–33

To Change the Background Color and Apply a Box Border to the Worksheet Title and Subtitle

The final formats assigned to the worksheet title and subtitle are the turquoise background color and thick box border (Figure 2–30b on page EX 107). The following steps complete the formatting of the worksheet titles.

• Select the range A1:A2 and then click the Fill Color button arrow on the Ribbon to display the Fill Color palette (Figure 2–34).

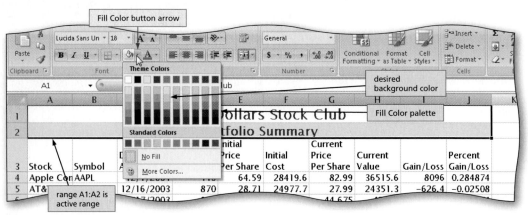

Figure 2–34

2

• Click Turquoise Accent 1, lighter 60% (column 5, row 3) on the Fill Color palette to change the background color of cells A1 and A2 from white to turquoise (Figure 2–35).

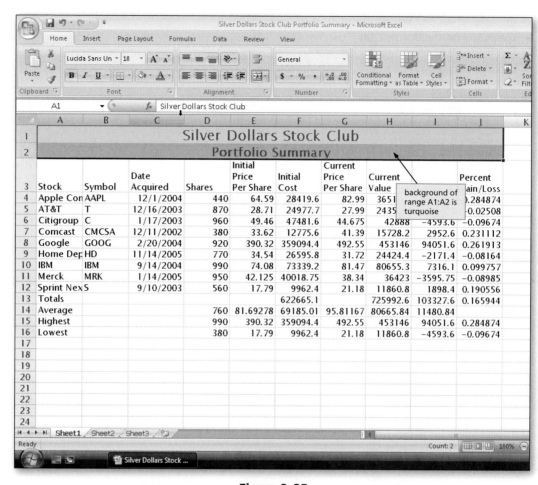

Figure 2–35

3

• Click the Borders button arrow on the Ribbon to display the Borders gallery (Figure 2–36).

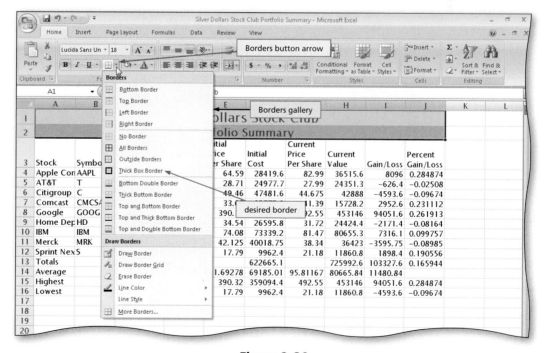

Figure 2–36

- Click the Thick Box Border command on the Borders gallery to display a thick box border around the range A1:A2.

- Click cell A18 to deselect the range A1:A2 (Figure 2–37).

Other Ways

1. On Ribbon click Format Cells Dialog Box Launcher, click appropriate tab, click desired format, click OK button

2. Right-click range, click Format Cells on shortcut menu, click appropriate tab, click desired format, click OK button

3. Press CTRL+1, click appropriate tab, click desired format, click OK button

Figure 2–37

To Apply a Cell Style to the Column Headings and Format the Total Rows

As shown in Figure 2–30b on page EX 107, the column titles (row 3) have the Heading 3 cell style and the total row (row 13) has the Total cell style. The summary information headings in the range A14:A16 should be bold. The following steps assign these styles to row 3 and row 13 and the range A14:A16.

1 Select the range A3:J3.

2 Apply the Heading 3 cell style to the range A3:J3.

3 Apply the Total cell style to the range A13:J13.

4 Select the range A14:A16 and then click the Bold button on the Ribbon (Figure 2–38).

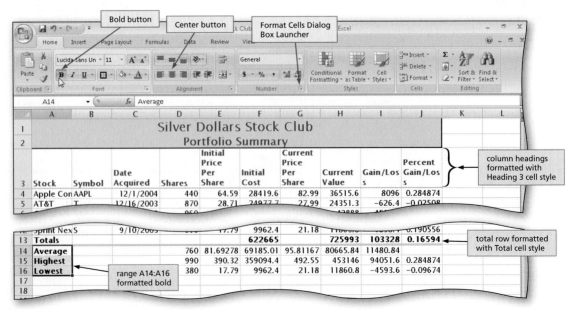

Figure 2–38

To Center Data in Cells and Format Dates

With the column titles and total rows formatted, the next step is to center the stock symbols in column B and format the dates in column C. If a cell entry is short, such as the stock symbols in column B, centering the entries within their respective columns improves the appearance of the worksheet. The following steps center the data in the range B4:B12 and format the dates in the range C4:C12.

1

- Select the range B4:B12 and then click the Center button on the Ribbon to center the data in the range B4:B12.

2

- Select the range C4:C12.

- Click the Format Cells: Number Dialog Box Launcher on the Ribbon to display the Format Cells dialog box.

- When Excel displays the Format Cells dialog box, if necessary click the Number tab, click Date in the Category list, and then click 3/14/01 in the Type list to choose the format for the range C4:C12 (Figure 2–39).

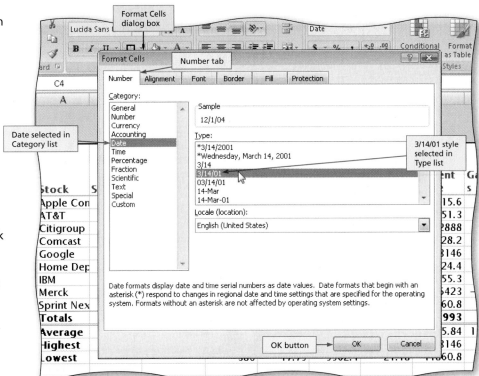

Figure 2–39

3

- Click the OK button to format the dates in column C using the date format style, mm/dd/yy.

- Select cell E4 to deselect the range C4:C12 (Figure 2–40).

Q&A

Can I format an entire column at once?

Yes. Rather than selecting the range B4:B12 in Step 1, you could have clicked the column B heading immediately above cell B1, and then clicked the Center button on the Ribbon. In this case, all cells in column B down to the last cell in the worksheet would have been formatted to use center alignment. This same procedure could have been used to format the dates in column C.

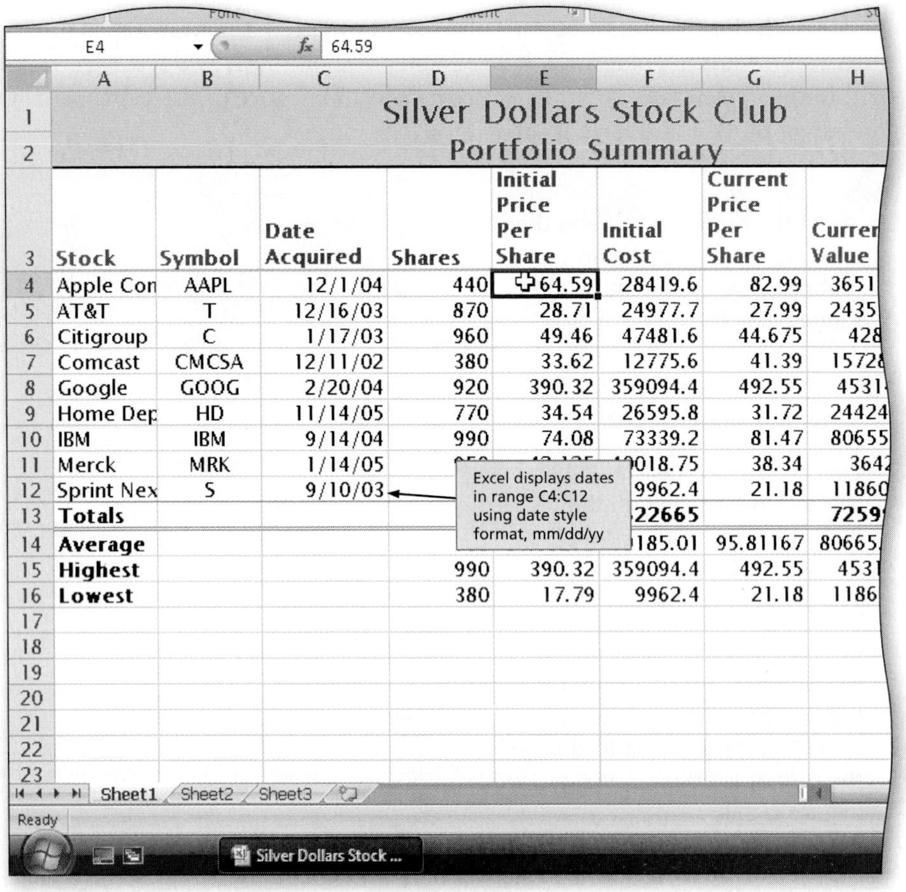

	E4		f_x	64.59			
	A	B	C	D	E	F	G	H

	A	B	C	D	E	F	G	H
1				Silver Dollars Stock Club				
2				Portfolio Summary				
3	Stock	Symbol	Date Acquired	Shares	Initial Price Per Share	Initial Cost	Current Price Per Share	Currer Value
4	Apple Con	AAPL	12/1/04	440	64.59	28419.6	82.99	3651
5	AT&T	T	12/16/03	870	28.71	24977.7	27.99	2435
6	Citigroup	C	1/17/03	960	49.46	47481.6	44.675	428
7	Comcast	CMCSA	12/11/02	380	33.62	12775.6	41.39	15728
8	Google	GOOG	2/20/04	920	390.32	359094.4	492.55	4531
9	Home Dep	HD	11/14/05	770	34.54	26595.8	31.72	24424
10	IBM	IBM	9/14/04	990	74.08	73339.2	81.47	80655
11	Merck	MRK	1/14/05			018.75	38.34	3642
12	Sprint Nex	S	9/10/03			9962.4	21.18	11860
13	Totals					22665		7259
14	Average					185.01	95.81167	80665.
15	Highest				990	390.32	359094.4	492.55	4531
16	Lowest				380	17.79	9962.4	21.18	1186
17								

Excel displays dates in range C4:C12 using date style format, mm/dd/yy

Sheet1 / Sheet2 / Sheet3

Ready

Silver Dollars Stock ...

Figure 2–40

BTW

Rotating and Shrinking Entries in Cells

In addition to aligning entries horizontally and vertically, you also can rotate and shrink entries to fit in a cell. To rotate or shrink entries to fit in a cell, click Format Cells on the shortcut menu, click the Alignment tab in the Format Cells dialog box, and then select the type of control you want.

Formatting Numbers Using the Ribbon

As shown in Figure 2–30b on page EX 107, the worksheet is formatted to resemble an accounting report. For example, in columns E through I, the numbers in the first row (row 4), the totals row (row 13), and the rows below the totals (rows 14 through 16) have dollar signs, while the remaining numbers (rows 5 through 12) in columns E through I do not.

To append a dollar sign to a number, you should use the Accounting number format. Excel displays numbers using the **Accounting number format** with a dollar sign to the left of the number, inserts a comma every three positions to the left of the decimal point, and displays numbers to the nearest cent (hundredths place). Clicking the Accounting Number Format button on the Ribbon assigns the desired Accounting number format. When you use the Accounting Number Format button to assign the Accounting number format, Excel displays a **fixed dollar sign** to the far left in the cell, often with spaces between it and the first digit. To assign a **floating dollar sign** that appears immediately to the left of the first digit with no spaces, use the Currency style in the Format Cells dialog box.

The Comma style format is used to instruct Excel to display numbers with commas and no dollar signs. The **Comma style format**, which can be assigned to a range of cells by clicking the Comma Style button on the Ribbon, inserts a comma every three positions to the left of the decimal point and causes numbers to be displayed to the nearest hundredths.

To Apply an Accounting Style Format and Comma Style Format Using the Ribbon

The following steps show how to assign formats using the Accounting Number Format button and the Comma Style button on the Ribbon.

1
- Select the range E4:I4.

- While holding down the CTRL key, select the ranges F13:I13.

- Click the Accounting Number Format button on the Ribbon (Figure 2–41) to apply the Accounting style format with fixed dollar signs to the nonadjacent ranges E4:I4 and F13:I13 (Figure 2–41).

Q&A

What is the effect of applying the Accounting style format?

The Accounting Number Format button assigns a fixed dollar sign to the numbers in the ranges E4:I4 and F13:I13. In each cell in these ranges, Excel displays the dollar sign to the far left with spaces between it and the first digit in the cell.

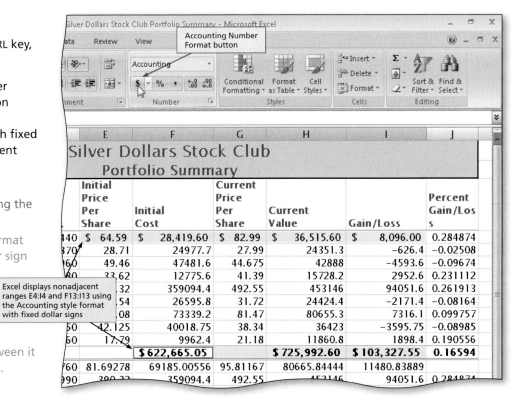

Figure 2–41

2
- Select the range E5:I12.

- Click the Comma Style button on the Ribbon to assign the Comma style format to the range E5:I12 (Figure 2–42).

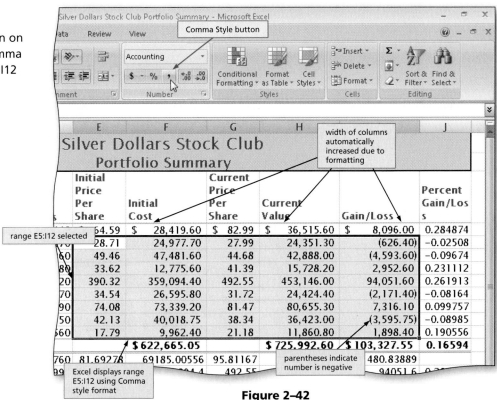

Figure 2–42

③

- Click cell E4.

- While holding down the CTRL key, select cell G4.

- Click the Increase Decimal button on the Ribbon to increase the number of decimal places displayed in cell E4 and G4.

- Select the range E5:E12. While holding down the CTRL key, select the range G5:G12.

- Click the Increase Decimal button on the Ribbon to increase the number of decimal places displayed in selected ranges (Figure 2–43).

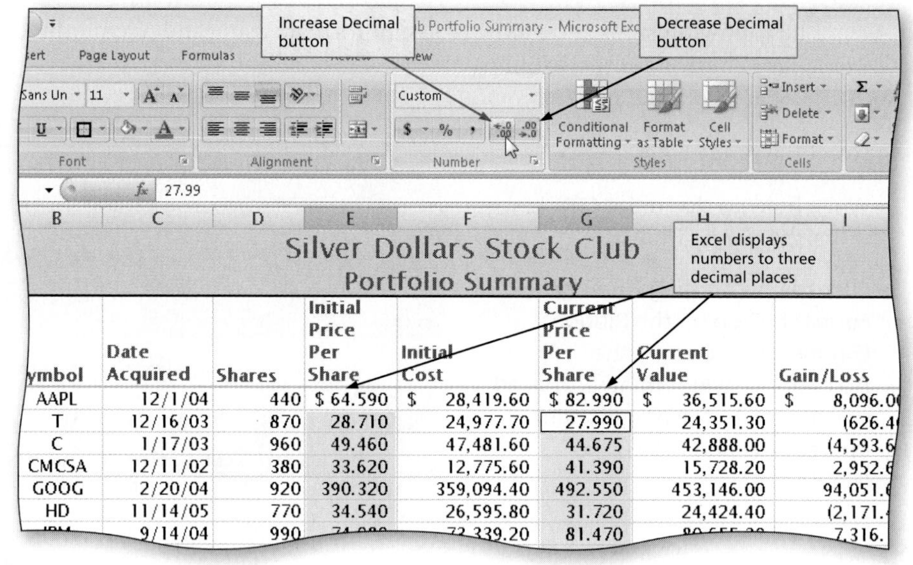

Q&A

What is the effect of clicking the Increase Decimal button?

The Increase Decimal button instructs Excel to display additional decimal places in a cell. Each time you click the Increase Decimal button, Excel adds a decimal place to the selected cell.

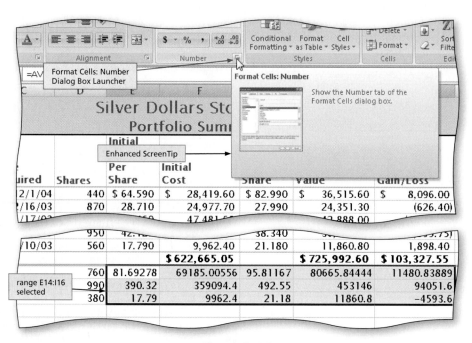

Figure 2–43

To Apply a Currency Style Format with a Floating Dollar Sign Using the Format Cells Dialog Box

The following steps use the Format Cells dialog box to apply the Currency style format with a floating dollar sign to the numbers in the ranges E14:I16.

①

- Select the range E14:I16 and then point to the Format Cells: Number Dialog Box Launcher on the Ribbon (Figure 2–44).

Figure 2–44

2

- Click the Format Cells: Number Dialog Box Launcher.

- If necessary, click the Number tab in the Format Cells dialog box.

- Click Currency in the Category list and then click the third style ($1,234.10) in the Negative numbers list (Figure 2–45).

Q&A How do I select the proper format?

You can choose from 12 categories of formats. Once you select a category, you can select the number of decimal places, whether or not a dollar sign should be displayed, and how negative numbers should appear. Selecting the appropriate negative numbers format is important, because doing so adds a space to the right of the number in order to align the numbers in the worksheet on the decimal points. Some of the available negative number formats do not align the numbers in the worksheet on the decimal points.

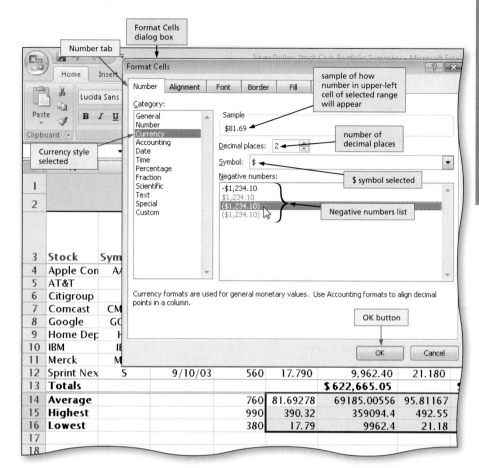

Figure 2–45

3

- Click the OK button to assign the Currency style format with a floating dollar sign to the range E14:I16 (Figure 2–46).

Q&A Should I click the Accounting Number Style button on the Ribbon or use the Format Cells dialog box?

Recall that a floating dollar sign always appears immediately to the left of the first digit, and the fixed dollar sign always appears on the left side of the cell. Cell E4, for example, has a fixed dollar sign, while cell E14 has a floating dollar sign. The Currency style was assigned to cell E14 using the Format Cells dialog box and the result is a floating dollar sign.

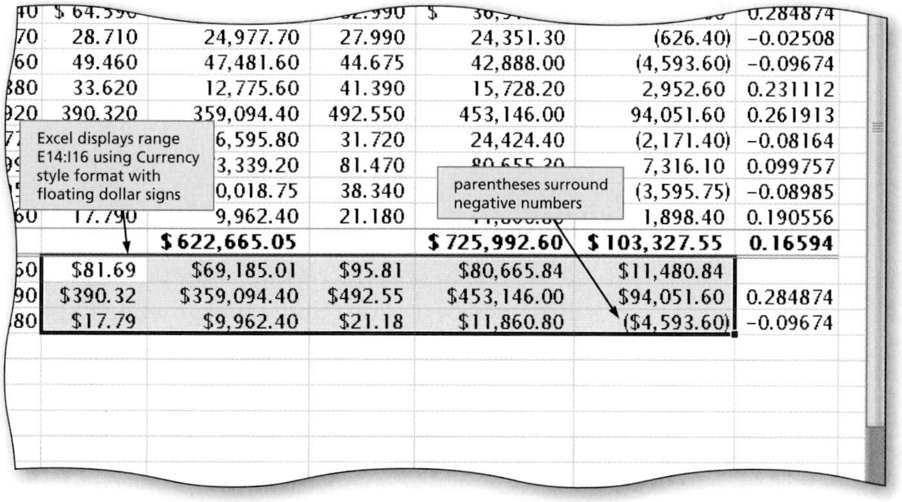

Figure 2–46

Other Ways

1. Press CTRL+1, click Number tab, click Currency in Category list, select format, click OK button

2. Press CTRL+SHIFT+ DOLLAR SIGN ($)

To Apply a Percent Style Format and Use the Increase Decimal Button

The next step is to format the percent gain/loss in column J. Currently, Excel displays the numbers in column J as a decimal fraction (for example, 0.284874 in cell J4). The following steps format the range J4:J16 to the Percent style format with two decimal places.

- Select the range J4:J16.
- Click the Percent Style button on the Ribbon to display the numbers in column J as a rounded whole percent.

Q&A

What is the result of clicking the Percent Style button?

The Percent Style button instructs Excel to display a value as a percentage, determined by multiplying the cell entry by 100, rounding the result to the nearest percent, and adding a percent sign. For example, when cell J4 is formatted using the Percent Style and Increase Decimal buttons, Excel displays the actual value 0.284874 as 28.49%.

- Click the Increase Decimal button on the Ribbon two times to display the numbers in column J with the Percent style format and two decimal places (Figure 2–47).

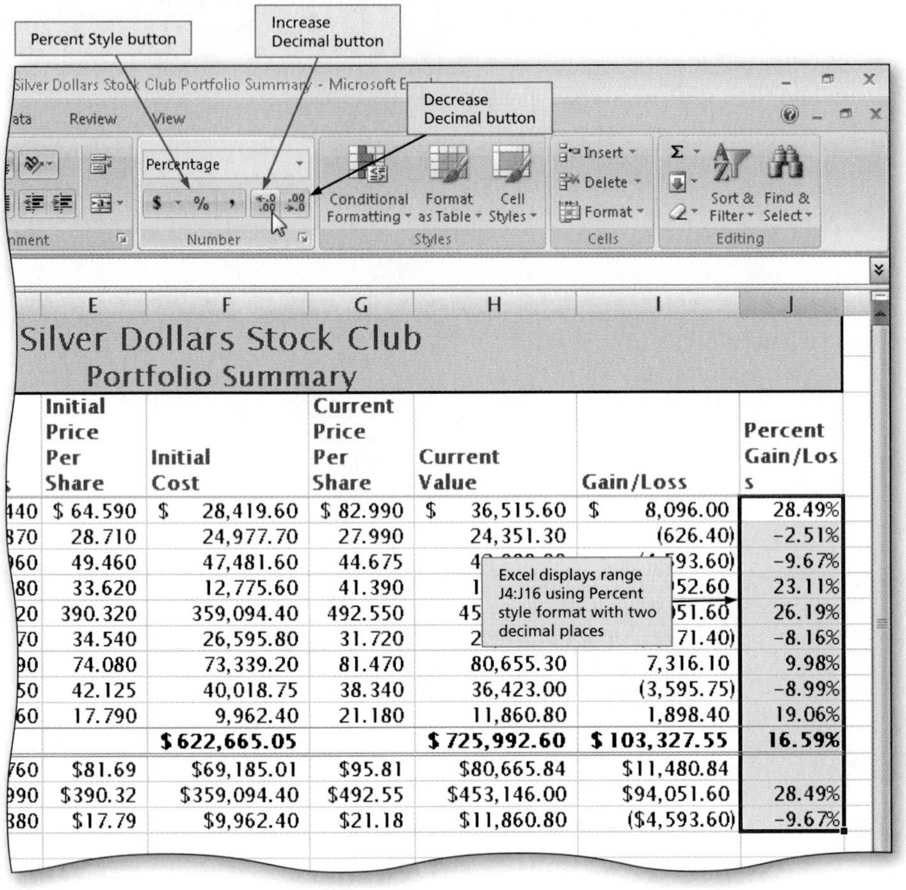

Figure 2–47

Other Ways

1. Right-click range, click Format Cells on shortcut menu, click Number tab, click Percentage in Category list, select format, click OK button
2. Press CTRL+1, click Number tab, click Percentage in Category list, select format, click OK button
3. Press CTRL+SHIFT+ PERCENT SIGN (%)

Conditional Formatting

The next step is to emphasize the negative percentages in column J by formatting them to appear with a tinted background. The Conditional Formatting button on the Ribbon will be used to complete this task.

Excel lets you apply formatting that appears only when the value in a cell meets conditions that you specify. This type of formatting is called **conditional formatting**. You can apply conditional formatting to a cell, a range of cells, the entire worksheet, or the entire workbook. Usually, you apply conditional formatting to a range of cells that contains values you want to highlight, if conditions warrant. For example, you can instruct Excel to change the color of the background of a cell if the value in the cell meets a condition, such as being less than 0 as shown in Figure 2–48.

A **condition**, which is made up of two values and a relational operator, is true or false for each cell in the range. If the condition is true, then Excel applies the formatting. If the condition is false, then Excel suppresses the formatting. What makes conditional formatting so powerful is that the cell's appearance can change as you enter new values in the worksheet.

To Apply Conditional Formatting

The following steps assign conditional formatting to the range J4:J12, so that any cell value less than zero will cause Excel to display the number in the cell with a light red background.

- Select the range J4:J12.

- Click the Conditional Formatting button on the Ribbon to display the Conditional Formatting gallery (Figure 2–48).

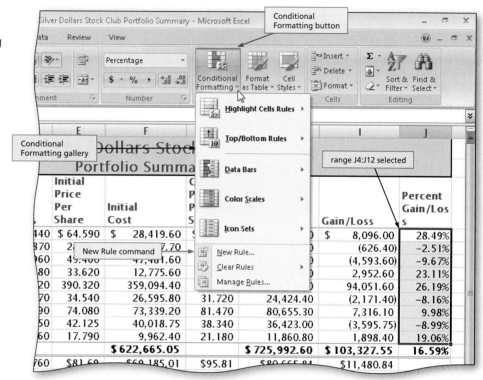

Figure 2–48

- Click New Rule in the Conditional Formatting gallery to display the New Formatting Rule dialog box.

- Click 'Format only cells that contain' in the Select a Rule Type area.

- In the Edit the Rule Description area, click the box arrow in the relational operator box (second text box) and then select less than.

- Type 0 (zero) in the rightmost box in the Edit the Rule Description area (Figure 2–49).

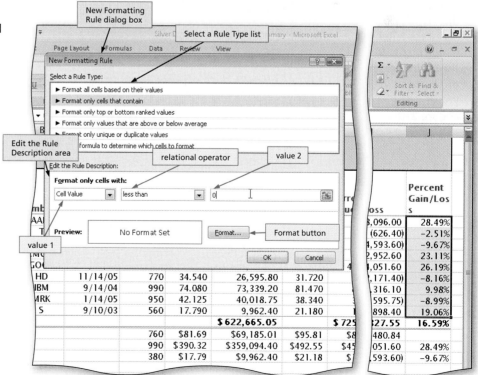

Figure 2–49

- Click the Format button.

- When Excel displays the Format Cells dialog box, click the Fill tab and then click the light red color in column 7, row 2 (Figure 2–50).

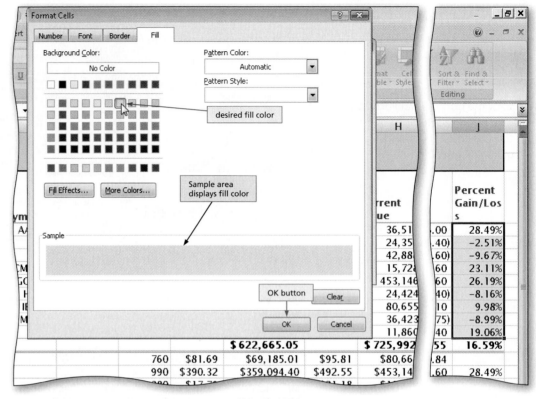

Figure 2–50

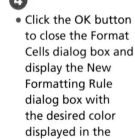

- Click the OK button to close the Format Cells dialog box and display the New Formatting Rule dialog box with the desired color displayed in the Preview box (Figure 2–51).

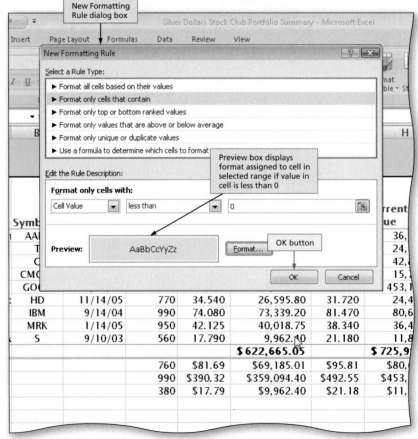

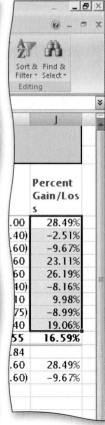

Figure 2–51

5

- Click the OK button to assign the conditional format to the range J4:J12.

- Click cell A18 to deselect the range J4:J12 (Figure 2–52).

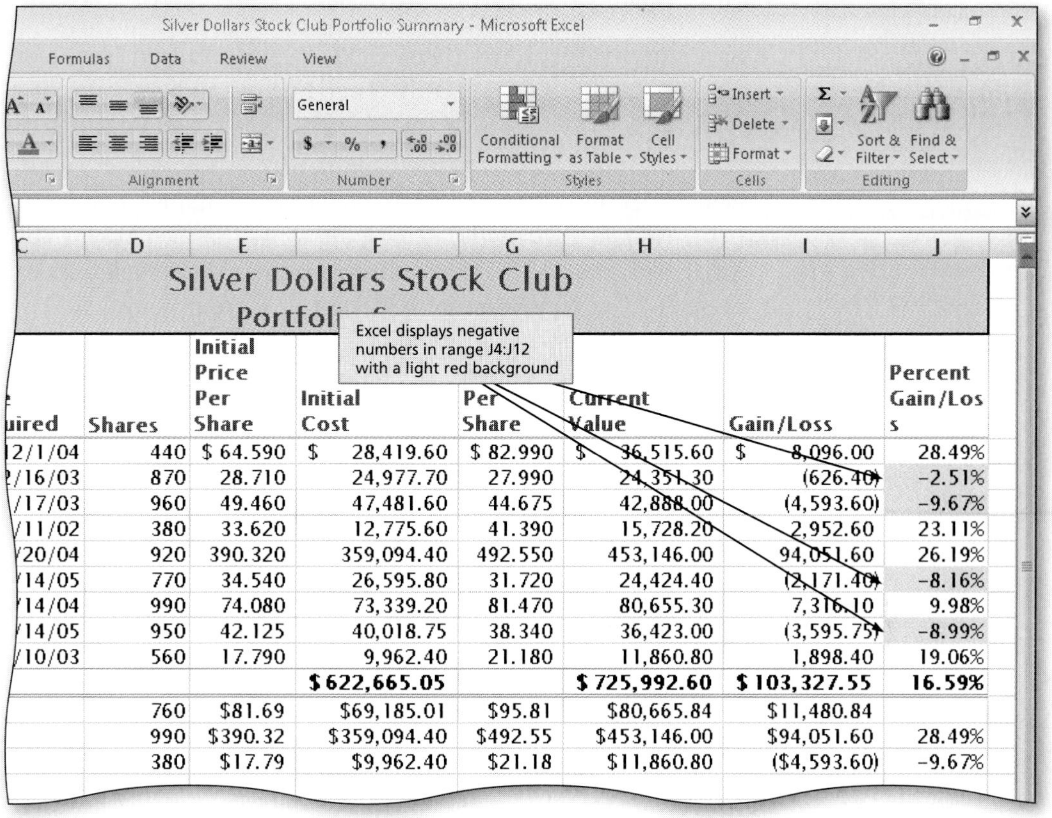

Figure 2–52

Conditional Formatting Operators

As shown in Figure 2–49 on page EX 119, the second text box in the New Formatting Rule dialog box allows you to select a relational operator, such as less than, to use in the condition. The eight different relational operators from which you can choose for conditional formatting in the New Formatting Rule dialog box are summarized in Table 2–5.

Table 2–5 Summary of Conditional Formatting Relational Operators	
Relational Operator	**Description**
Between	Cell value is between two numbers
Not between	Cell value is not between two numbers
Equal to	Cell value is equal to a number
Not equal to	Cell value is not equal to a number
Greater than	Cell value is greater than a number
Less than	Cell value is less than a number
Greater than or equal to	Cell value is greater than or equal to a number
Less than or equal to	Cell value is less than or equal to a number

BTW

Conditional Formatting
You can assign any format to a cell, a range of cells, a worksheet, or an entire workbook conditionally. If the value of the cell changes and no longer meets the specified condition, Excel suppresses the conditional formatting.

Hidden Columns
Trying to unhide a range of columns using the mouse can be frustrating. An alternative is to use the keyboard: select the columns to the right and left of the hidden columns and then press CTRL+SHIFT+) (RIGHT PARENTHESIS). To use the keyboard to hide a range of columns, press CTRL+0 (ZERO).

Changing the Widths of Columns and Heights of Rows

When Excel starts and displays a blank worksheet on the screen, all of the columns have a default width of 8.43 characters, or 64 pixels. A character is defined as a letter, number, symbol, or punctuation mark in 11-point Calibri font, the default font used by Excel. An average of 8.43 characters in 11-point Calibri font will fit in a cell.

Another measure of the height and width of cells is pixels, which is short for picture element. A **pixel** is a dot on the screen that contains a color. The size of the dot is based on your screen's resolution. At a common resolution of 1024 × 768, 1024 pixels appear across the screen and 768 pixels appear down the screen for a total of 786,432 pixels. It is these 786,432 pixels that form the font and other items you see on the screen.

The default row height in a blank worksheet is 15 points (or 20 pixels). Recall from Chapter 1 that a point is equal to 1/72 of an inch. Thus, 15 points is equal to about 1/5 of an inch. You can change the width of the columns or height of the rows at any time to make the worksheet easier to read or to ensure that Excel displays an entry properly in a cell.

To Change the Widths of Columns

When changing the column width, you can set the width manually or you can instruct Excel to size the column to best fit. **Best fit** means that the width of the column will be increased or decreased so the widest entry will fit in the column. Sometimes, you may prefer more or less white space in a column than best fit provides. Excel thus allows you to change column widths manually.

When the format you assign to a cell causes the entry to exceed the width of a column, Excel automatically changes the column width to best fit. If you do not assign a format to a cell or cells in a column, the column width will remain 8.43 characters. To set a column width to best fit, double-click the right boundary of the column heading above row 1.

The following steps change the column widths: column A to 14.11 characters; columns B and C to best fit; column D to 6.00 characters; columns E, G, and J to 9.00 characters; and columns F, H, and I to 12.67 characters.

1

• Point to the boundary on the right side of the column A heading above row 1.

• When the mouse pointer changes to a split double arrow, drag until the ScreenTip indicates Width: 14.11 (134 pixels). Do not release the mouse button (Figure 2–53).

Q&A

What happens if I change the column width to zero (0)?

If you decrease the column width to 0, the column is hidden. **Hiding cells** is a technique you can use to hide data that might not be relevant to a particular report or sensitive data that you do not want others to see. To instruct Excel to display a hidden column, position the mouse pointer to the right of the column heading boundary where the hidden column is located and then drag to the right.

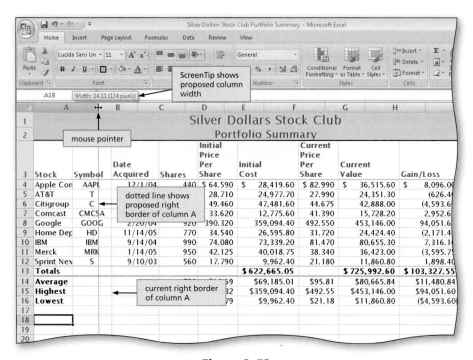

Figure 2–53

2

- Release the mouse button.

- Drag through column headings B and C above row 1.

- Point to the boundary on the right side of column heading C to cause the mouse pointer to become a split double arrow (Figure 2–54).

Q&A

What if I want to make a large change to the column width?

If you want to increase or decrease column width significantly, you can right-click a column heading and then use the Column Width command on the shortcut menu to change the column's width. To use this command, however, you must select one or more entire columns.

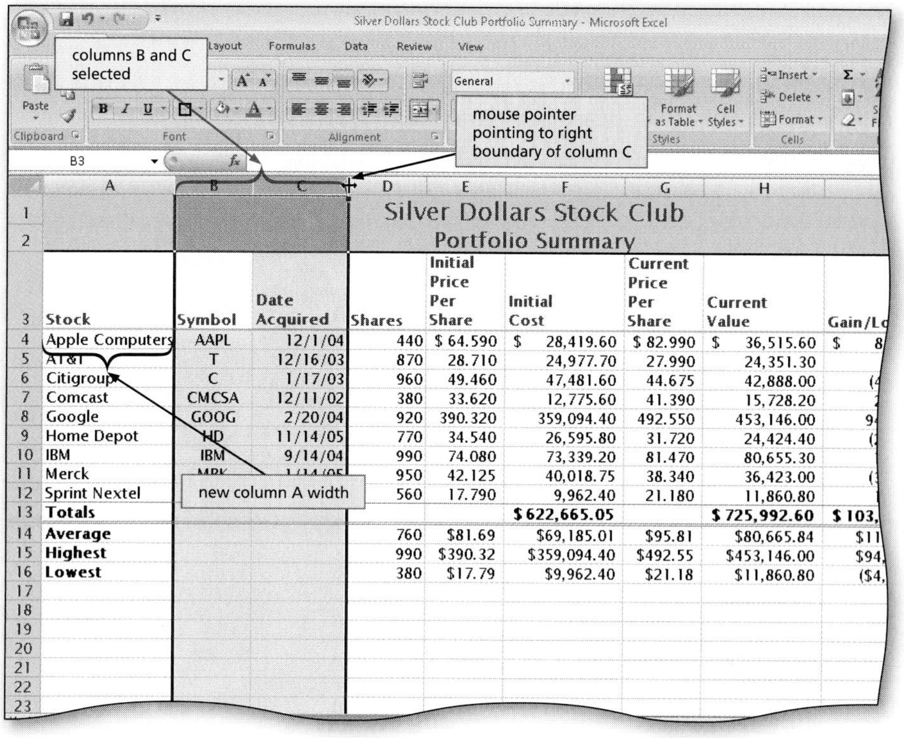

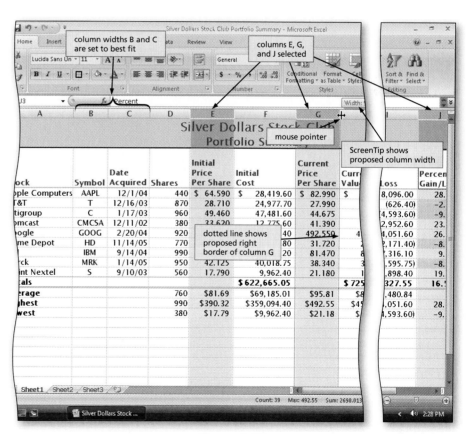

Figure 2–54

3

- Double-click the right boundary of column heading C to change the width of columns B and C to best fit.

- Click the column E heading above row 1.

- While holding down the CTRL key, click the column G heading and then the column J heading above row 1 so that columns E, G, and J are selected.

- If necessary, scroll the worksheet to the right so that the right border of column J is visible. Point to the boundary on the right side of the column J heading above row 1.

- Drag until the ScreenTip indicates Width: 9.00 (88 pixels). Do not release the mouse button (Figure 2–55).

Figure 2–55

4

- Release the mouse button.

- Click the column F heading above row 1 to select column F.

- While holding down the CTRL key, click the column H heading and then the column I heading above row 1, to select columns F, H, and I.

- Point to the boundary on the right side of the column I heading above row 1.

- Drag to the left until the ScreenTip indicates Width: 12.67 (121 pixels). Do not release the mouse button (Figure 2–56).

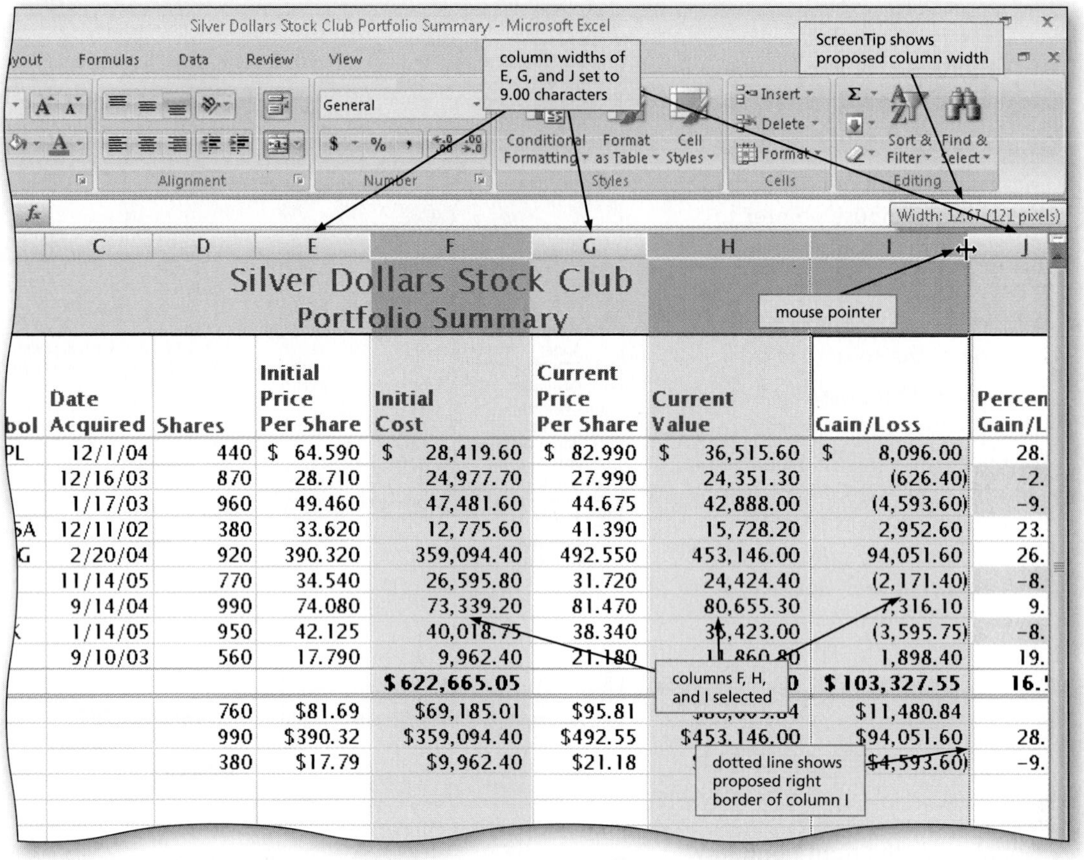

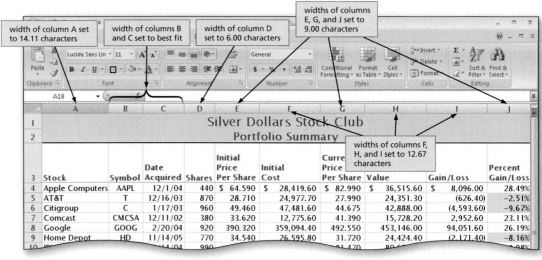

Figure 2–56

5

- Release the mouse button.

- Point to the boundary on the right side of the column D heading above row 1.

- Drag to the left until the ScreenTip indicates Width: 6.00 (61 pixels) and then release the mouse button to display the worksheet with the new column widths.

- Click cell A18 to deselect columns F, H, and I (Figure 2–57).

Figure 2–57

Other Ways

1. Right-click column heading or drag through multiple column headings and right-click, click Column Width on shortcut menu, enter desired column width, click OK button

2. Right-click column heading or drag through multiple column headings and right-click, click Format button on Ribbon, click Column Width in Format gallery, enter desired column width, click OK button

To Change the Heights of Rows

When you increase the font size of a cell entry, such as the title in cell A1, Excel automatically increases the row height to best fit so it can display the characters properly. Recall that Excel did this earlier when multiple lines were entered in a cell in row 3, and when the cell style of the worksheet title and subtitle was changed.

You also can increase or decrease the height of a row manually to improve the appearance of the worksheet. The following steps show how to improve the appearance of the worksheet by increasing the height of row 3 to 60.00 points, and increasing the height of row 14 to 26.25 points.

1

- Point to the boundary below row heading 3.

- Drag down until the ScreenTip indicates Height: 60.00 (80 pixels). Do not release the mouse button (Figure 2–58).

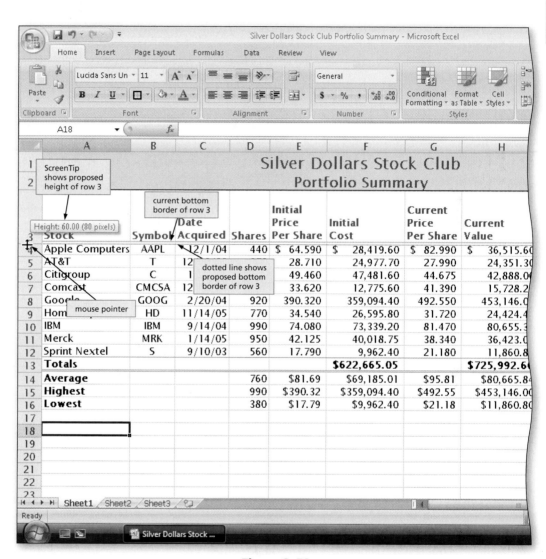

Figure 2–58

2

- Release the mouse button.

- Point to the boundary below row heading 14.

- Drag down until the ScreenTip indicates Height: 26.25 (35 pixels). Do not release the mouse button (Figure 2–59).

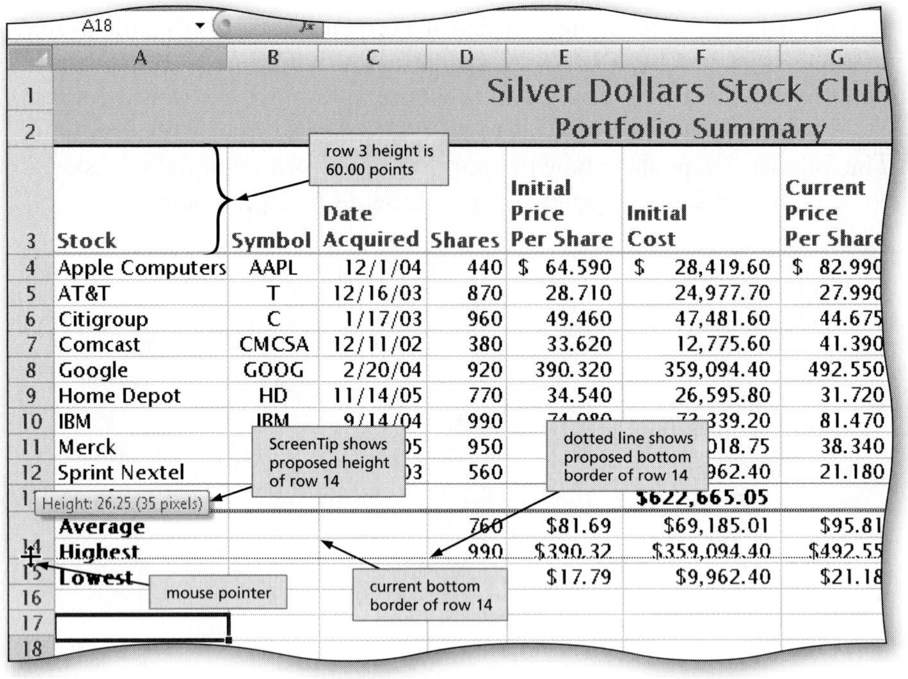

Figure 2–59

3

- Release the mouse button to change the row height of row 14 to 26.25.

- Select cells A3:J3 and then click the Center button on the Ribbon to center the column headings.

- Select cell A18 (Figure 2–60).

Q&A

Can I hide a row?

Yes. As with column widths, when you decrease the row height to 0, the row is hidden. To instruct Excel to display a hidden row, position the mouse pointer just below the row heading boundary where the row is hidden and then drag down. To set a row height to best fit, double-click the bottom boundary of the row heading.

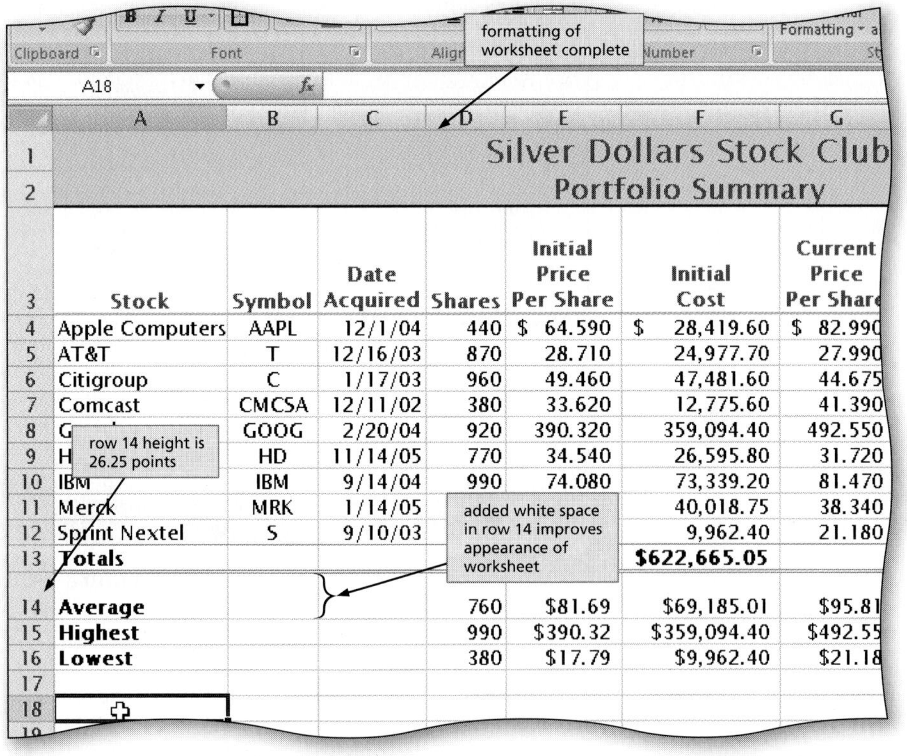

Figure 2–60

Other Ways

1. Right-click row heading or drag through multiple row headings and right-click, click Row Height

   on shortcut menu, enter desired row height, click OK button

Checking Spelling

Excel has a **spell checker** you can use to check the worksheet for spelling errors. The spell checker looks for spelling errors by comparing words on the worksheet against words contained in its standard dictionary. If you often use specialized terms that are not in the standard dictionary, you may want to add them to a custom dictionary using the Spelling dialog box.

When the spell checker finds a word that is not in either dictionary, it displays the word in the Spelling dialog box. You then can correct it if it is misspelled.

BTW

Hidden Rows
You can use the keyboard to unhide a range of rows by selecting the rows immediately above and below the hidden rows and then pressing CTRL+SHIFT+((LEFT PARENTHESIS). To use the keyboard to hide a range of rows, press CTRL+9.

To Check Spelling on the Worksheet

To illustrate how Excel responds to a misspelled word, the word, Stock, in cell A3 is misspelled purposely as the word, Stcok, as shown in Figure 2–61.

1

- Click cell A3 and then type Stcok to misspell the word Stock.

- Click cell A1.

- Click the Review tab on the Ribbon.

- Click the Spelling button on the Ribbon to run the spell checker and display the misspelled word, Stcok, in the Spelling dialog box (Figure 2–61).

Q&A

What happens when the spell checker finds a misspelled word?

When the spell checker identifies that a cell contains a word not in its standard or custom dictionary, it selects that cell as the active cell and displays the Spelling dialog box. The Spelling dialog box (Figure 2–61) lists the word not found in the dictionary and a list of suggested corrections.

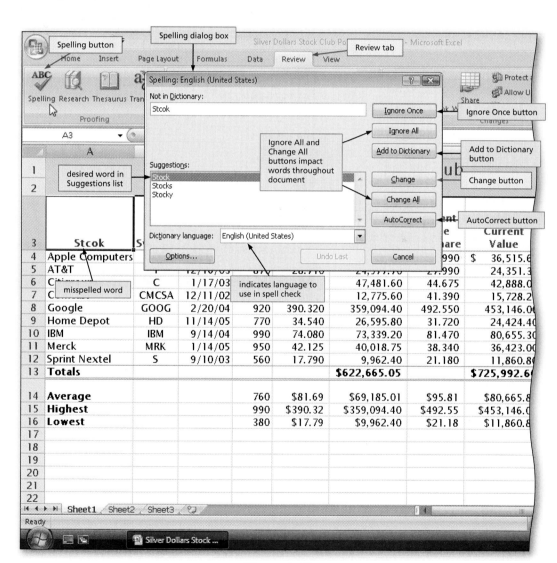

Figure 2–61

Additional Spell Checker Considerations

Consider these additional guidelines when using the spell checker:

- To check the spelling of the text in a single cell, double-click the cell to make the formula bar active and then click the Spelling button on the Review tab on the Ribbon.

- If you select a single cell so that the formula bar is not active and then start the spell checker, Excel checks the remainder of the worksheet, including notes and embedded charts.

- If you select a cell other than cell A1 before you start the spell checker, Excel will display a dialog box when the spell checker reaches the end of the worksheet, asking if you want to continue checking at the beginning.

- If you select a range of cells before starting the spell checker, Excel checks the spelling of the words only in the selected range.

- To check the spelling of all the sheets in a workbook, click Select All Sheets on the sheet tab shortcut menu and then start the spell checker. To instruct Excel to display the sheet tab shortcut menu, right-click any sheet tab.

- To add words to the dictionary such as your last name, click the Add to Dictionary button in the Spelling dialog box (Figure 2–61 on page EX 127) when Excel identifies the word as not in the dictionary.

- Click the AutoCorrect button (Figure 2–61) to add the misspelled word and the correct version of the word to the AutoCorrect list. For example, suppose you misspell the word, do, as the word, dox. When the spell checker displays the Spelling dialog box with the correct word, do, in the Change to box, click the AutoCorrect button. Then, anytime in the future that you type the word, dox, Excel automatically will change it to the word, do.

Preparing to Print the Worksheet

Excel allows for a great deal of customization in how a worksheet appears when printed. For example, the margins on the page can be adjusted. A header or footer can be added to each printed page as well. Excel also has the capability to work on the worksheet in Page Layout View. **Page Layout View** allows you to create or modify a worksheet while viewing how it will look in printed format. The default view that you have worked in up until this point in the book is called **Normal View**.

Specify how the printed worksheet should appear.
Before printing a worksheet, you should consider how the worksheet will appear when printed. In order to fit as much information on the printed page as possible, the margins of the worksheet should be set to a reasonably small width and height. The current Portfolio Summary worksheet will print on one page. If, however, the club added more data to the worksheet, then it may extend to multiple pages. It is, therefore, a good idea to add a page header to the worksheet that prints in the top margin of each page.

In Chapter 1, the worksheet was printed in **portrait orientation**, which means the printout is printed across the width of the page. **Landscape orientation** means the printout is printed across the length of the page. Landscape orientation is a good choice for the Silver Dollars Stock Club Portfolio Summary because the printed worksheet's width is greater than its length.

BTW Spell Checking
While Excel's spell checker is a valuable tool, it is not infallible. You should proofread your workbook carefully by pointing to each word and saying it aloud as you point to it. Be mindful of misused words such as its and it's, through and though, and to and too. Nothing undermines a good impression more than a professional looking report with misspelled words.

BTW Error Checking
Always take the time to check the formulas of a worksheet before submitting it to your supervisor. You can check formulas by clicking the Error Checking button on the Formulas tab on the Ribbon. You also should test the formulas by employing data that tests the limits of formulas. Experienced spreadsheet specialists spend as much time testing a workbook as they do creating it, before placing it into production.

Plan Ahead

BTW Certification
The Microsoft Certified Application Specialist (MCAS) program provides an opportunity for you to obtain a valuable industry credential – proof that you have the Excel 2007 skills required by employers. For more information, see Appendix G or visit the Excel 2007 Certification Web page (scsite.com/ex2007/cert).

To Change the Worksheet's Margins, Header, and Orientation in Page Layout View

The following steps change to Page Layout View, narrow the margins of the worksheet, change the header of the worksheet, and set the orientation of the worksheet to landscape.

- Click the Page Layout View button on the status bar to view the worksheet in Page Layout (Figure 2–63).

Q&A

What are some key features of Page Layout View?

Page Layout View shows the worksheet divided into pages. A blue background separates each page. The white areas surrounding each page indicate the print margins. The top of each page includes a Header area, and the bottom of each page includes a Footer area. Page Layout View also includes a ruler at the top of the page that assists you in placing objects on the page, such as charts and pictures.

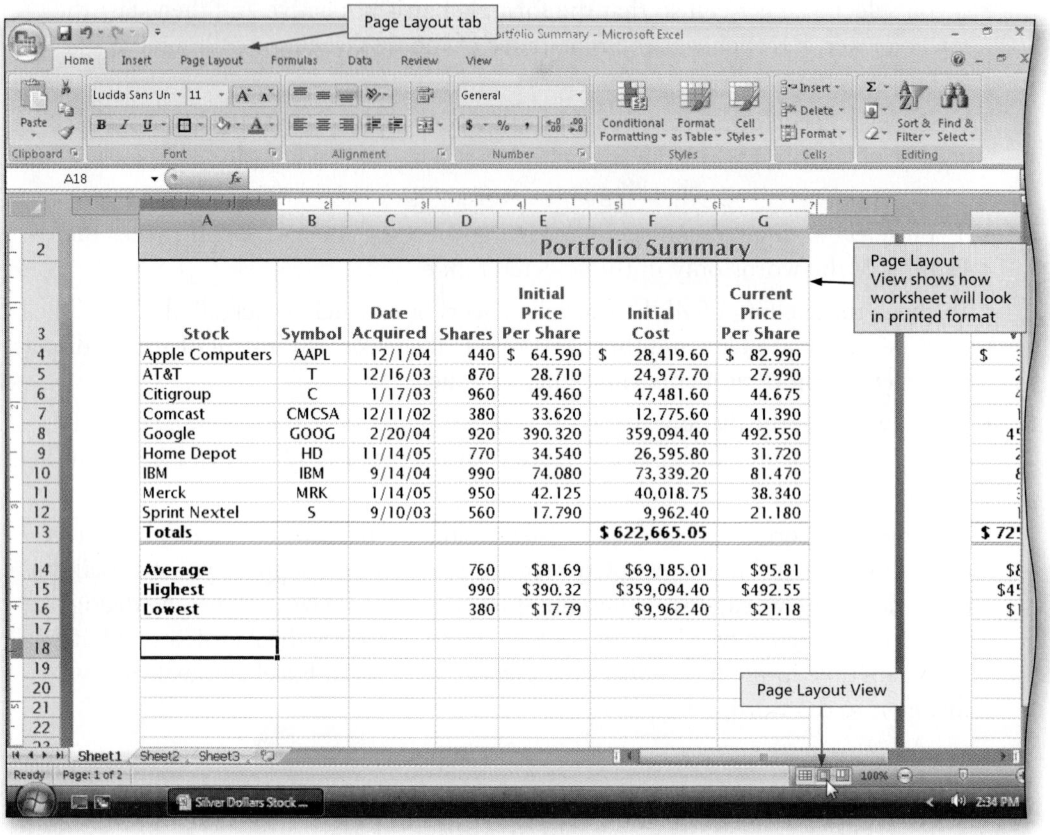

Figure 2–63

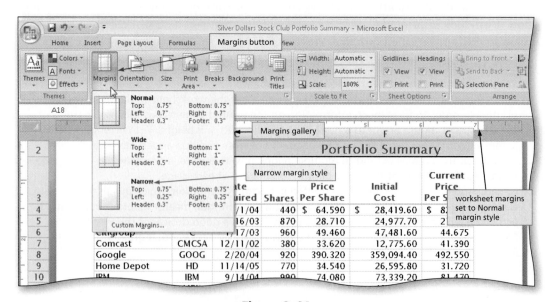

- Click the Page Layout tab on the Ribbon.

- Click the Margins button on the Ribbon to display the Margins gallery (Figure 2–64).

Figure 2–64

3

- Click Narrow in the Margins gallery to change the worksheet margins to the Narrow margin style.

- Drag the scroll bar on the right side of the worksheet to the top so that row 1 of the worksheet is displayed.

- Click above the worksheet title in cell A1 in the Header area.

- Type Treasurer: Juan Castillo and then press the ENTER key. Type castillo_juan37@hotmail.com to complete the worksheet header (Figure 2–65).

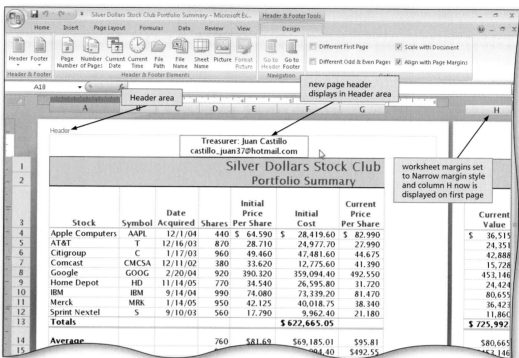

Figure 2–65

4

- Select cell B16 to deselect the header. Click the Orientation button on the Ribbon to display the Orientation gallery.

- Point to Landscape but do not click the mouse button (Figure 2–66).

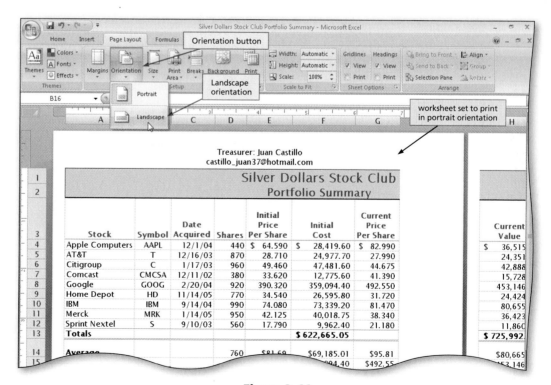

Figure 2–66

5

- Click Landscape in the Orientation gallery to change the worksheet's orientation to landscape (Figure 2–67).

Q&A

Do I need to change the orientation every time I want to print the worksheet?

No. Once you change the orientation and save the workbook, Excel will save the orientation setting for that workbook until you change it. When you open a new workbook, Excel sets the orientation to portrait.

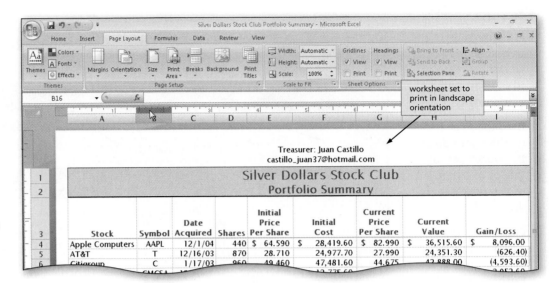

Figure 2–67

Other Ways

1. Click Page Layout tab on Ribbon, click Page Setup Dialog Box Launcher, click Page tab, click Portrait or Landscape, click OK button

Previewing and Printing the Worksheet

In Chapter 1, the worksheet was printed without first previewing it on the screen. By **previewing the worksheet**, however, you see exactly how it will look without generating a printout. Previewing a worksheet using the Print Preview command can save time, paper, and the frustration of waiting for a printout only to discover it is not what you want.

To Preview and Print a Worksheet

The following steps preview and then print the worksheet.

1

- Click the Office Button and then point to Print on the Office Button menu to display the Print submenu (Figure 2–68).

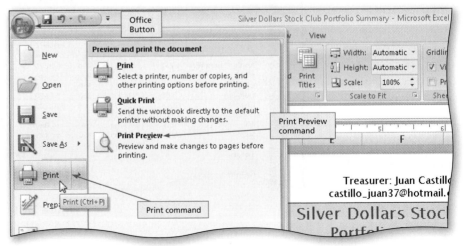

Figure 2–68

2

- Click Print Preview on the Print sub-menu to display a preview of the worksheet in land-scape orientation (Figure 2–69).

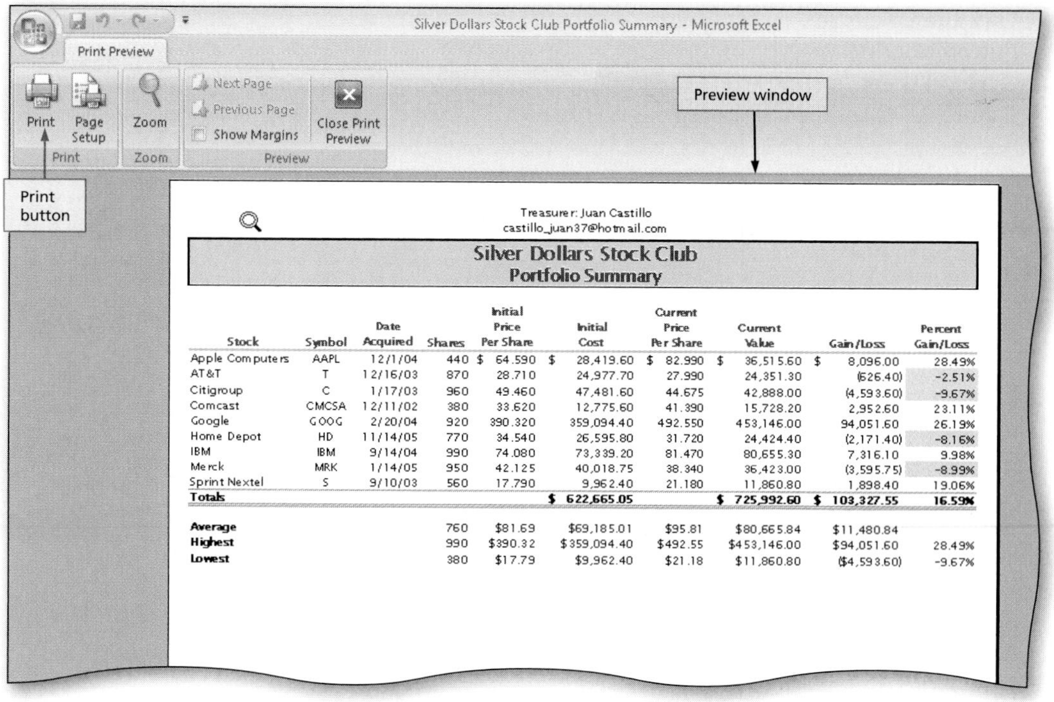

Q&A

What is the purpose of the buttons in the Print Preview area?

The Print button displays the Print dialog box and allows you to print the worksheet. The Page Setup button displays the Page Setup dialog box. The Zoom button allows you to zoom in and out of the page displayed in the Preview win-dow. You also can click the previewed page in the Preview window when the mouse pointer shape is a magnifying glass to carry out the function of the Zoom button.

3

- Click the Print button to display the Print dialog box (Figure 2–70).

Q&A

How can I use the Print dialog box?

When you click the Print command on the Print submenu of the Office Button menu or a Print but-ton in a dialog box or Preview window, Excel displays the Print dialog box shown in Figure 2–70. Excel does not display the Print dialog box when you use the Print button on the Quick Access Toolbar, as was the case in Chapter 1. The Print dialog box allows you to select a printer, instruct Excel what to print, and indicate how many copies of the printout you want.

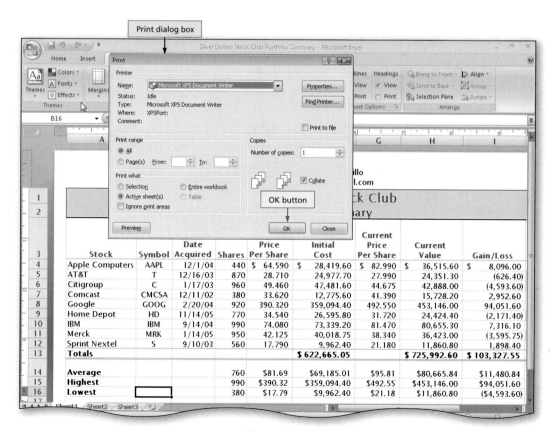

Figure 2–69

Figure 2–70

- Click the OK button to print the worksheet (Figure 2–71).

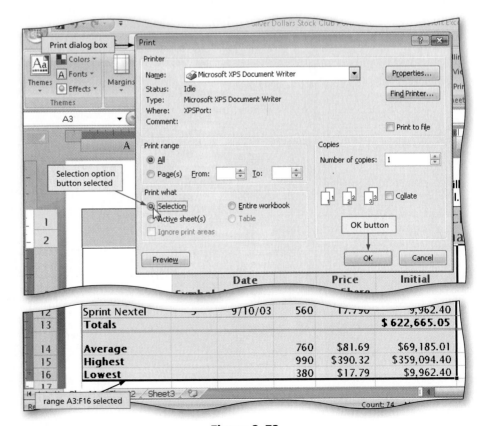

worksheet printed in landscape orientation

Treasurer: Juan Castillo
castillo_juan37@hotmail.com

Silver Dollars Stock Club
Portfolio Summary

Stock	Symbol	Date Aquired	Shares	Initial Price Per Share	Initial Cost	Current Price Per Share	Current Value	Gain/Loss
Apple Computers	AAPL	12/1/04	440	$ 64.590	$ 28,419.60	$ 82.990	$ 36,515.60	$ 8,096.00
AT&T	T	12/16/03	870	28.710	24,977.70	27.990	24,351.30	(626.40)
Citigroup	C	1/17/04	960	49.460	47,481.60	44.675	42,888.00	(4,593.60)
Comcast	CMCSA	2/11/02	380	33.620	12,775.60	41.390	15,728.20	2,952.60
Google	GOOG	2/20/04	920	390.320	359,094.40	492.550	453,146.00	94,051.60
Home Depot	HD	11/14/05	770	34.540	26,595.80	31.720	24,424.40	(2,171.40)
IBM	IBM	9/14/04	990	74.080	73,339.20	81.470	80,655.30	7,316.10
Merck	MRK	1/14/05	950	42.125	40,018.75	38.340	36,423.00	(3,595.75)
Sprint Nextel	S	9/10/03	560	17.790	9,962.40	21.180	11,860.80	1,898.40
Totals					$ 622,665.05		$ 725,992.60	$ 103,327.55
Average			760	$81.69	$69,185.01	$95.81	$80,665.84	$11,480.84
Highest			990	$390.32	$359,094.40	$492.55	$453,146.00	$94,051.60
Lowest			380	$17.79	$9,962.40	$21.18	$11,860.80	($4,593.60)

Figure 2–71

Other Ways

1. Click Page Layout tab on Ribbon, click Page Setup Dialog Box Launcher, click appropriate tab, change desired options, click Print, click OK button

To Print a Section of the Worksheet

You might not always want to print the entire worksheet. You can print portions of the worksheet by selecting the range of cells to print and then clicking the Selection option button in the Print what area in the Print dialog box. The following steps print the range A3:F16.

- Select the range A3:F16.

- Click the Office Button and then click Print on the Office Button menu to display the Print dialog box.

- Click Selection in the Print what area to instruct Excel to print only the selected range (Figure 2–72).

Figure 2–72

2

- Click the OK button to print the selected range of the worksheet on the printer (Figure 2–73).

- Click the Normal View button on the status bar.

- Click cell A18 to deselect the range A3:F13.

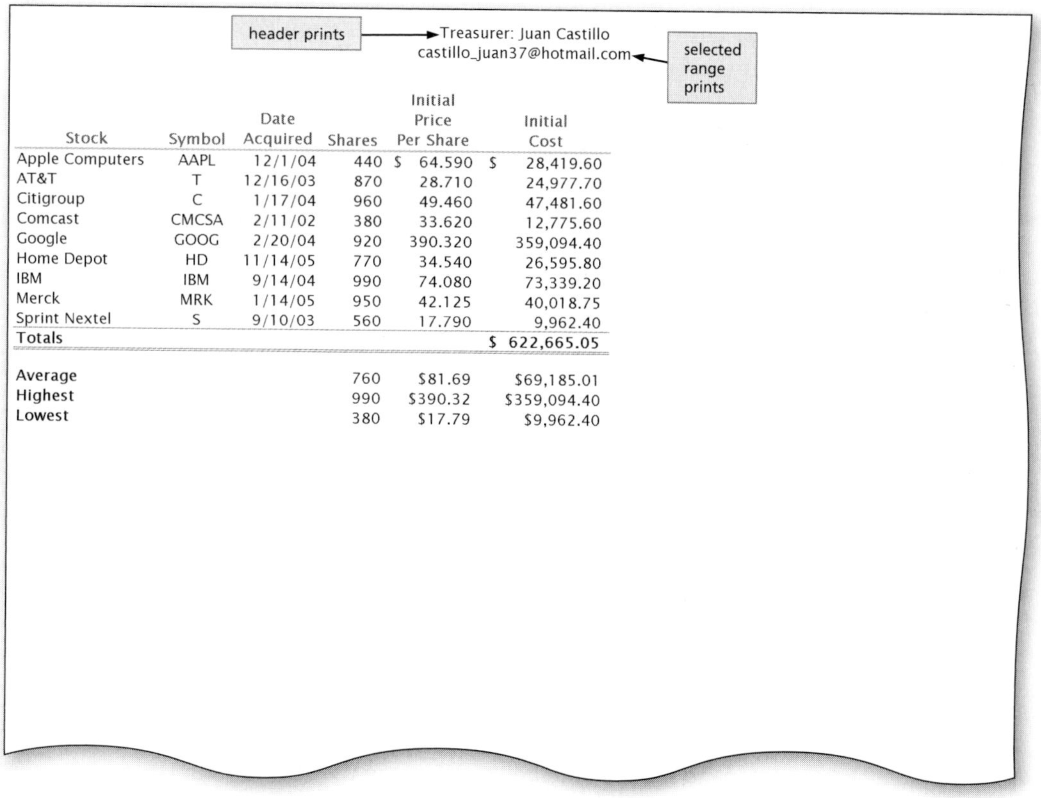

What are the options in the Print what area?

The Print what area of the Print dialog box includes four option buttons (Figure 2–72). As shown in the previous steps, the Selection option button instructs Excel to print the selected range. The Active sheet(s) option button instructs Excel to print the active worksheet (the worksheet currently on the screen) or the selected worksheets. Finally, the Entire workbook option button instructs Excel to print all of the worksheets in the workbook.

| header prints | Treasurer: Juan Castillo | selected range prints |

Treasurer: Juan Castillo
castillo_juan37@hotmail.com

Stock	Symbol	Date Acquired	Shares	Initial Price Per Share	Initial Cost
Apple Computers	AAPL	12/1/04	440	$ 64.590	$ 28,419.60
AT&T	T	12/16/03	870	28.710	24,977.70
Citigroup	C	1/17/04	960	49.460	47,481.60
Comcast	CMCSA	2/11/02	380	33.620	12,775.60
Google	GOOG	2/20/04	920	390.320	359,094.40
Home Depot	HD	11/14/05	770	34.540	26,595.80
IBM	IBM	9/14/04	990	74.080	73,339.20
Merck	MRK	1/14/05	950	42.125	40,018.75
Sprint Nextel	S	9/10/03	560	17.790	9,962.40
Totals					$ 622,665.05
Average			760	$81.69	$69,185.01
Highest			990	$390.32	$359,094.40
Lowest			380	$17.79	$9,962.40

Figure 2–73

Displaying and Printing the Formulas Version of the Worksheet

Thus far, you have been working with the **values version** of the worksheet, which shows the results of the formulas you have entered, rather than the actual formulas. Excel also can display and print the **formulas version** of the worksheet, which shows the actual formulas you have entered, rather than the resulting values. You can toggle between the values version and formulas version by holding down the CTRL key while pressing the ACCENT MARK (`) key, which is located to the left of the number 1 key on the keyboard.

The formulas version is useful for debugging a worksheet. **Debugging** is the process of finding and correcting errors in the worksheet. Viewing and printing the formulas version instead of the values version makes it easier to see any mistakes in the formulas.

When you change from the values version to the formulas version, Excel increases the width of the columns so the formulas and text do not overflow into adjacent cells on the right. The formulas version of the worksheet thus usually is significantly wider than the values version. To fit the wide printout on one page, you can use landscape orientation, which has already been selected for the workbook, and the Fit to option in the Page sheet in the Page Setup dialog box.

To Display the Formulas in the Worksheet and Fit the Printout on One Page

The following steps change the view of the worksheet from the values version to the formulas version of the worksheet and then print the formulas version on one page.

- Press CTRL+ACCENT MARK (`).

- When Excel displays the formulas version of the worksheet, click the right horizontal scroll arrow until column J appears to display the worksheet with formulas (Figure 2–74).

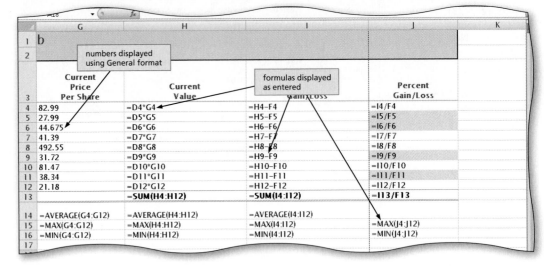

Figure 2–74

- If necessary, click the Page Layout tab on the Ribbon and then click the Page Setup Dialog Box Launcher to display the Page Setup dialog box.

- If necessary, click Landscape to select it and then click Fit to in the Scaling area.

- Click the Print button in the Page Setup dialog box to print the formulas in the worksheet on one page in landscape orientation (Figure 2–75).

- When Excel displays the Print dialog box, click the OK button.

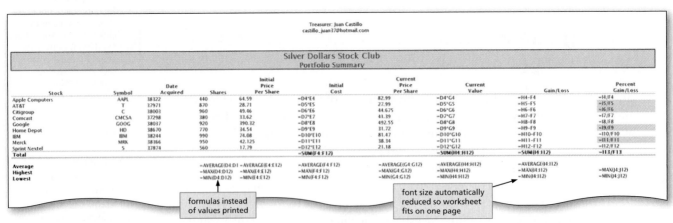

Figure 2–75

- After viewing and printing the formulas version, press CTRL+ACCENT MARK (`) to instruct Excel to display the values version.

- Click the left horizontal scroll arrow until column A appears.

Other Ways

1. Click Show Formulas button on Formulas tab on Ribbon

To Change the Print Scaling Option Back to 100%

Depending on your printer, you may have to change the Print Scaling option back to 100% after using the Fit to option. The following steps reset the Print Scaling option so future worksheets print at 100%, instead of being resized to print on one page.

1 If necessary, click the Page Layout tab on the Ribbon and then click the Page Setup Dialog Box Launcher to display the Page Setup dialog box.

2 Click Adjust to in the Scaling area.

3 If necessary, type 100 in the Adjust to box.

4 Click the OK button to set the print scaling to normal.

5 Click the Home tab on the Ribbon.

Q&A What is the purpose of the Adjust to box in the Page Setup dialog box?

The Adjust to box allows you to specify the percentage of reduction or enlargement in the printout of a worksheet. The default percentage is 100%. When you click the Fit to option, this percentage automatically changes to the percentage required to fit the printout on one page.

Importing External Data from a Web Source Using a Web Query

One of the major features of Excel is its capability of importing external data from Web sites. To import external data from a Web site, you must have access to the Internet. You then can import data stored on a Web site using a **Web query**. When you run a Web query, Excel imports the external data in the form of a worksheet. As described in Table 2–6, three Web queries are available when you first install Excel. All three Web queries relate to investment and stock market activities.

BTW
Web Queries
Most Excel specialists that build Web queries use the worksheet returned from the Web query as an engine to supply data to another worksheet in the workbook. With 3-D cell references, you can create a worksheet similar to the Silver Dollars Stock Club worksheet to feed the Web query stock symbols and get refreshed stock prices in return.

Table 2–6 Excel Web Queries

Query	External Data Returned
MSN MoneyCentral Investor Currency Rates	Currency rates
MSN MoneyCentral Investor Major Indices	Major indices
MSN MoneyCentral Investor Stock Quotes	Up to 20 stocks of your choice

Gather information regarding the needed Web query.
As shown in Table 2–6, the MSN Money Central Investor Stock Quotes feature that is included with Excel allows you to retrieve information on up to 20 stocks of your choice. The Web query requires that you supply the stock symbols. The stock symbols are located in column B of the Portfolio Summary worksheet.

Plan Ahead

To Import Data from a Web Source Using a Web Query

Although you can have a Web query return data to a blank workbook, the following steps have the data for the nine stock symbols in column B of the Portfolio Summary worksheet returned to a blank worksheet in the Silver Dollars Stock Club Portfolio Summary workbook. The data returned by the stock-related Web queries is real time in the sense that it is no more than 20 minutes old during the business day.

- With the Silver Dollars Stock Club Portfolio Summary workbook open, click the Sheet2 tab at the bottom of the window.

- With cell A1 active, click the Data tab on the Ribbon, and then click the Existing Connections button to display the Existing Connections dialog box (Figure 2–76).

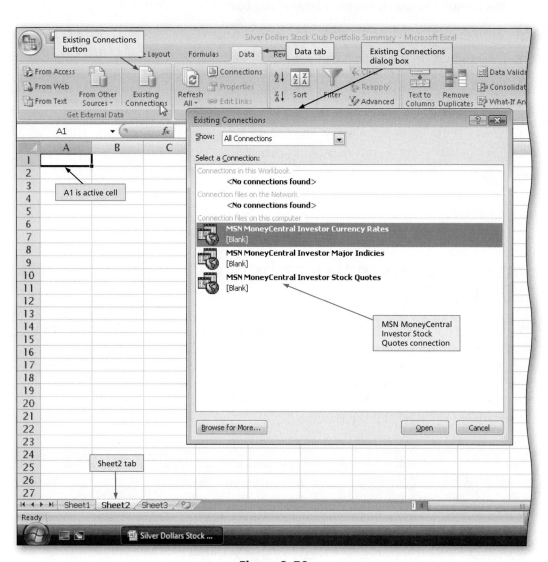

Figure 2–76

2

- Double-click MSN MoneyCentral Investor Stock Quotes to display the Import Data dialog box (Figure 2–77).

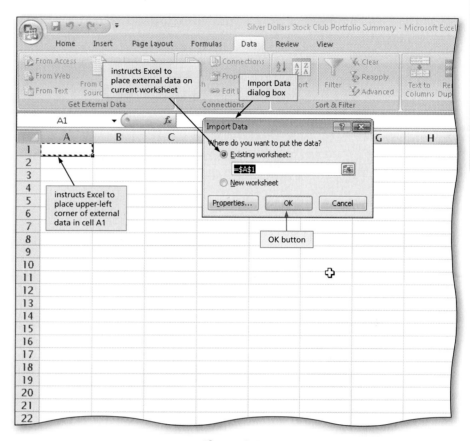

Figure 2–77

3

- Click the OK button.

- When Excel displays the Enter Parameter Value dialog box, type the nine stock symbols `aapl t c cmcsa goog hd ibm mrk s` in the text box.

- Click the 'Use this value/reference for future refreshes' check box to select it (Figure 2–78).

Q&A

What is the purpose of clicking the check box?

Once Excel displays the worksheet, you can refresh the data as often as you want. To refresh the data for all the stocks, click the Refresh All button on the Data tab on the Ribbon. Because the 'Use this value/reference for future refreshes' check box was selected, Excel will continue to use the same stock symbols each time it refreshes.

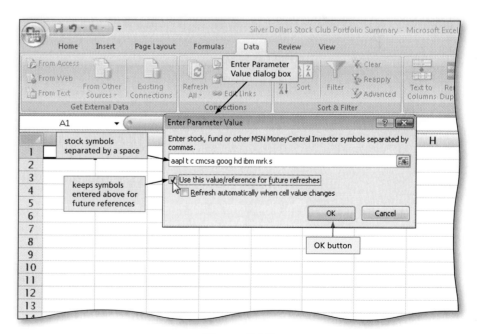

Figure 2–78

4

• Click the OK button to retrieve the stock quotes and display a new worksheet with the desired data (Figure 2–79).

Q&A

What composes the new worksheet?

As shown in Figure 2–79, Excel displays the data returned from the Web query in an organized, formatted worksheet, which has a worksheet title, column titles, and a row of data for each stock symbol entered. Other than the first column, which contains the stock name and stock symbol, you have no control over the remaining columns of data returned. The latest price of each stock appears in column D.

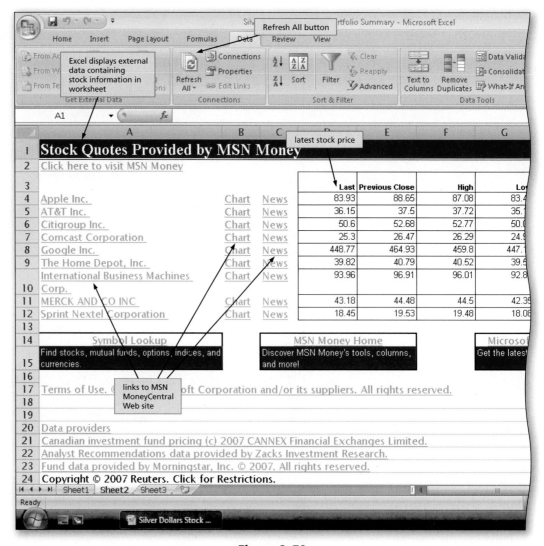

Figure 2–79

Other Ways

1. Press ALT+A, X, select data source

Changing the Worksheet Names

The sheet tabs at the bottom of the window allow you to view any worksheet in the workbook. You click the sheet tab of the worksheet you want to view in the Excel window. By default, Excel presets the names of the worksheets to Sheet1, Sheet2, and so on. The worksheet names become increasingly important as you move towards more sophisticated workbooks, especially workbooks in which you reference cells between worksheets.

Plan Ahead

Choose names for the worksheets.
Use simple, meaningful names for each worksheet. Name the first worksheet that includes the portfolio summary Portfolio Summary. The second worksheet that includes the stock quotes should be named Real-Time Stock Quotes to reflect its contents.

To Change the Worksheet Names

The following steps show how to rename worksheets by double-clicking the sheet tabs.

1

- Double-click the sheet tab labeled Sheet2 in the lower-left corner of the window.

- Type `Real-Time Stock Quotes` as the worksheet name and then press the ENTER key to display the new worksheet name on the sheet tab (Figure 2–80).

What is the maximum length for a worksheet tab?

Worksheet names can be up to 31 characters (including spaces) in length. Longer worksheet names, however, mean that fewer sheet tabs will show. To view more sheet tabs, you can drag the tab split box (Figure 2–81) to the right. This will reduce the size of the scroll bar at the bottom of the screen. Double-click the tab split box to reset it to its normal position.

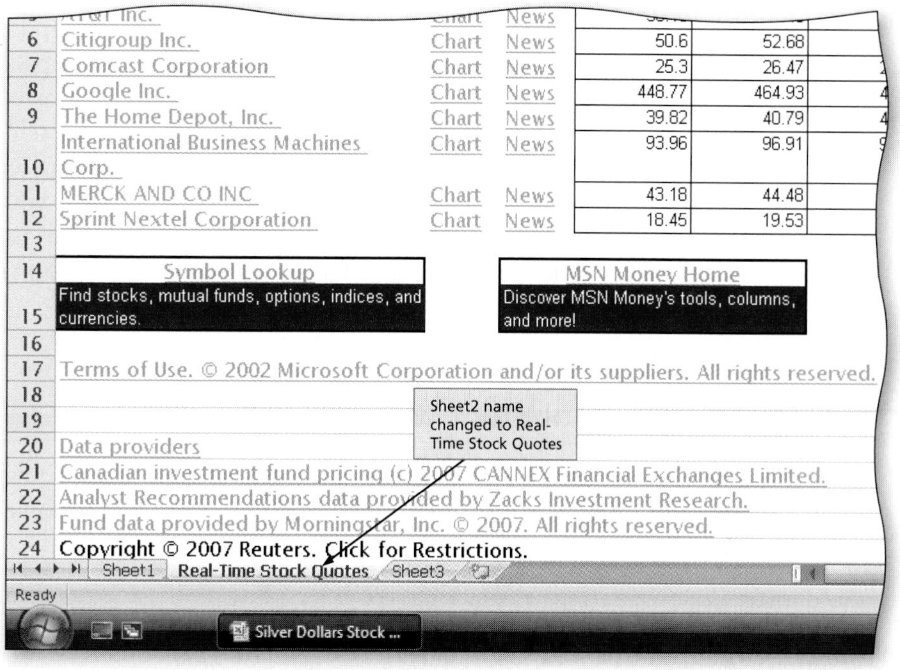

6	Citigroup Inc.	Chart	News	50.6	52.68	
7	Comcast Corporation	Chart	News	25.3	26.47	
8	Google Inc.	Chart	News	448.77	464.93	
9	The Home Depot, Inc.	Chart	News	39.82	40.79	
10	International Business Machines Corp.	Chart	News	93.96	96.91	
11	MERCK AND CO INC	Chart	News	43.18	44.48	
12	Sprint Nextel Corporation	Chart	News	18.45	19.53	
13						
14	Symbol Lookup			MSN Money Home		
15	Find stocks, mutual funds, options, indices, and currencies.			Discover MSN Money's tools, columns, and more!		
16						
17	Terms of Use. © 2002 Microsoft Corporation and/or its suppliers. All rights reserved.					
18						
19						
20	Data providers					
21	Canadian investment fund pricing (c) 2007 CANNEX Financial Exchanges Limited.					
22	Analyst Recommendations data provided by Zacks Investment Research.					
23	Fund data provided by Morningstar, Inc. © 2007. All rights reserved.					
24	Copyright © 2007 Reuters. Click for Restrictions.					

Sheet2 name changed to Real-Time Stock Quotes

Sheet1 **Real-Time Stock Quotes** Sheet3

Ready

Silver Dollars Stock ...

Figure 2–80

2

- Double-click the sheet tab labeled Sheet1 in the lower-left corner of the window.

- Type `Portfolio Summary` as the worksheet name and then press the ENTER key to change the name of the worksheet from Sheet 1 to Portfolio Summary (Figure 2–81).

How can I quickly move between worksheet tabs?

You can use the tab scrolling buttons to the left of the sheet tabs (Figure 2–81) to move between worksheets. The leftmost and rightmost scroll buttons move to the first or last worksheet in the workbook. The two middle scroll buttons move one worksheet to the left or right.

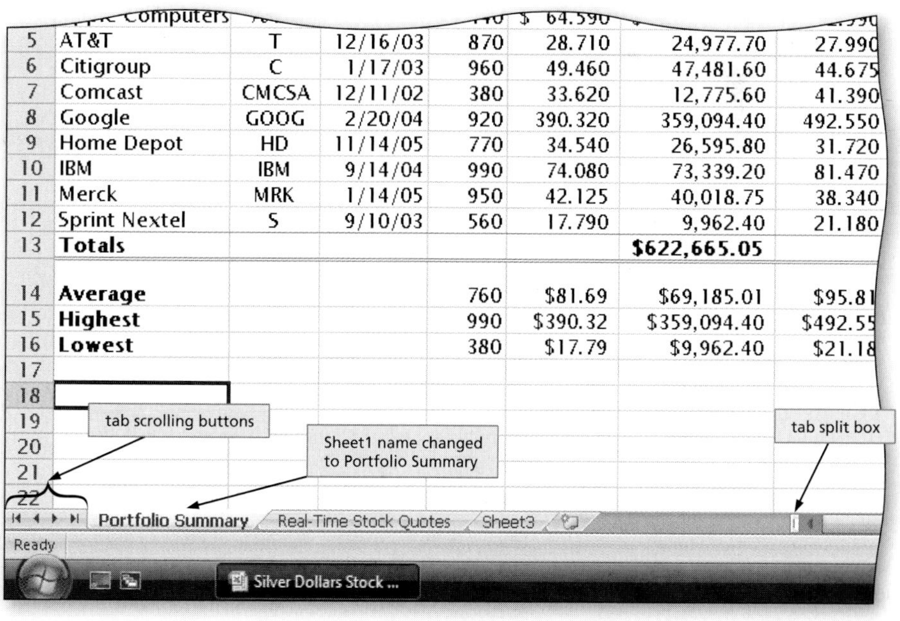

5	AT&T	T	12/16/03	870	28.710	24,977.70	27.990
6	Citigroup	C	1/17/03	960	49.460	47,481.60	44.675
7	Comcast	CMCSA	12/11/02	380	33.620	12,775.60	41.390
8	Google	GOOG	2/20/04	920	390.320	359,094.40	492.550
9	Home Depot	HD	11/14/05	770	34.540	26,595.80	31.720
10	IBM	IBM	9/14/04	990	74.080	73,339.20	81.470
11	Merck	MRK	1/14/05	950	42.125	40,018.75	38.340
12	Sprint Nextel	S	9/10/03	560	17.790	9,962.40	21.180
13	**Totals**					**$622,665.05**	
14	**Average**			760	$81.69	$69,185.01	$95.81
15	**Highest**			990	$390.32	$359,094.40	$492.55
16	**Lowest**			380	$17.79	$9,962.40	$21.18

tab scrolling buttons

Sheet1 name changed to Portfolio Summary

tab split box

Portfolio Summary Real-Time Stock Quotes Sheet3

Ready

Silver Dollars Stock ...

Figure 2–81

3

- Click the Home tab on the Ribbon.

BTW

Obtaining an E-Mail Account
Several Web sites that allow you to sign up for free e-mail are available. Some choices are MSN Hotmail, Yahoo! Mail, and Google Gmail.

E-Mailing a Workbook from within Excel

The most popular service on the Internet is electronic mail, or **e-mail**, which is the electronic transmission of messages and files to and from other computers using the Internet. Using e-mail, you can converse with friends across the room or on another continent. One of the features of e-mail is the capability to attach Office files, such as Word documents or Excel workbooks, to an e-mail message and send it to a coworker. In the past, if you wanted to e-mail a workbook, you saved the workbook, closed the file, started your e-mail program, and then attached the workbook to the e-mail message before sending it. With Excel, you have the capability of e-mailing a worksheet or workbook directly from within Excel. For these steps to work properly, you must have an e-mail address and one of the following as your e-mail program: Microsoft Outlook, Microsoft Outlook Express, Microsoft Exchange Client, or another 32-bit e-mail program compatible with Messaging Application Programming Interface.

To E-Mail a Workbook from within Excel

The following steps show how to e-mail the Silver Dollars Stock Club Portfolio Summary workbook from within Excel to Juan Castillo at the e-mail address castillo_juan37@hotmail.com.

1

- With the Silver Dollars Stock Club Portfolio Summary workbook open, click the Office Button and then click Send to display the Send submenu (Figure 2–82).

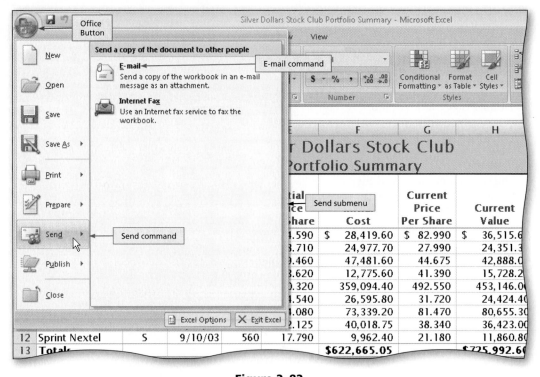

Figure 2–82

2

- Click E-mail on the Send submenu.

- When the e-mail Message window appears, type castillo_ juan37@hotmail. com in the To text box.

- Type the message shown in the message area in Figure 2–83.

3

- Click the Send button to send the e-mail with the attached workbook to castillo_juan37@ hotmail.com.

Q&A How can the recipient use the attached workbook?

Because the workbook was sent as an attachment, Juan Castillo can double-click the attachment in the e-mail to open it in Excel, or he can save it on disk and then open it later.

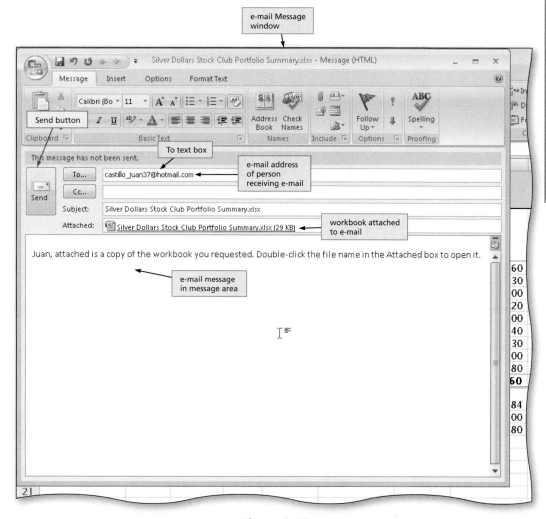

Figure 2–83

To Save the Workbook and Quit Excel

With the workbook complete and e-mailed, the following steps save the workbook and quit Excel.

1 Click the Save button on the Quick Access Toolbar.

2 Click the Close button on the upper-right corner of the title bar.

BTW

Quick Reference
For a table that lists how to complete the tasks covered in this book using the mouse, Ribbon, shortcut menu, and keyboard, see the Quick Reference Summary at the back of this book, or visit the Excel 2007 Quick Reference Web page (scsite.com/ex2007/qr).

Chapter Summary

In creating the Silver Dollars Stock Club Portfolio Summary workbook, you learned how to enter formulas, calculate an average, find the highest and lowest numbers in a range, verify formulas using Range Finder, draw borders, align text, format numbers, change column widths and row heights, and add conditional formatting to a range of numbers. In addition, you learned to spell check a worksheet, preview a worksheet, print a section of a worksheet, display and print the formulas version of the worksheet using the Fit to option, complete a Web query, rename sheet tabs, and send an e-mail directly from within Excel with the opened workbook as an attachment. The items listed below include all the new Excel skills you have learned in this chapter.

1. Enter a Formula Using the Keyboard (EX 91)
2. Enter Formulas Using Point Mode (EX 93)
3. Copy Formulas Using the Fill Handle (EX 95)
4. Determine the Average of a Range of Numbers Using the Keyboard and Mouse (EX 99)
5. Determine the Highest Number in a Range of Numbers Using the Insert Function Box (EX 101)
6. Determine the Lowest Number in a Range of Numbers Using the Sum Menu (EX 102)
7. Copy a Range of Cells across Columns to an Adjacent Range Using the Fill Handle (EX 104)
8. Verify a Formula Using Range Finder (EX 106)
9. Change the Workbook Theme (EX 109)
10. Change the Background Color and Apply a Box Border to the Worksheet Title and Subtitle (EX 110)
11. Center Data in Cells and Format Dates (EX 113)
12. Apply an Accounting Number Format and Comma Style Format Using the Ribbon (EX 115)
13. Apply a Currency Style Format with a Floating Dollar Sign Using the Format Cells Dialog Box (EX 116)
14. Apply a Percent Style Format and Use the Increase Decimal Button (EX 118)
15. Apply Conditional Formatting (EX 119)
16. Change the Widths of Columns (EX 122)
17. Change the Heights of Rows (EX 125)
18. Check Spelling on the Worksheet (EX 127)
19. Change the Worksheet's Margins, Header, and Orientation in Page Layout View (EX 130)
20. Preview and Print a Worksheet (EX 132)
21. Print a Section of the Worksheet (EX 134)
22. Display the Formulas in the Worksheet and Fit the Printout on One Page (EX 136)
23. Import Data from a Web Source Using a Web Query (EX 138)
24. Change the Worksheet Names (EX 141)
25. E-Mail a Workbook from within Excel (EX 142)

If you have a SAM user profile, you may have access to hands-on instruction, practice, and assessment. Log in to your SAM account (http://sam2007.course.com) to launch any assigned training activities or exams that relate to the skills covered in this chapter.

Learn It Online

Learn It Online is a series of online student exercises that test your knowledge of chapter content and key terms.

Instructions: To complete the Learn It Online exercises, start your browser, click the Address bar, and then enter the Web address `scsite.com/ex2007/learn`. When the Excel 2007 Learn It Online page is displayed, click the link for the exercise you want to complete and then read the instructions.

Chapter Reinforcement TF, MC, and SA
A series of true/false, multiple choice, and short answer questions that test your knowledge of the chapter content.

Flash Cards
An interactive learning environment where you identify chapter key terms associated with displayed definitions.

Practice Test
A series of multiple choice questions that test your knowledge of chapter content and key terms.

Who Wants To Be a Computer Genius?
An interactive game that challenges your knowledge of chapter content in the style of a television quiz show.

Wheel of Terms
An interactive game that challenges your knowledge of chapter key terms in the style of the television show *Wheel of Fortune*.

Crossword Puzzle Challenge
A crossword puzzle that challenges your knowledge of key terms presented in the chapter.

Apply Your Knowledge

Reinforce the skills and apply the concepts you learned in this chapter.

Profit Analysis Worksheet

Instructions Part 1: Start Excel. Open the workbook Apply 2-1 Car-B-Clean Profit Analysis. See the inside back cover of this book for instructions for downloading the Data Files for Students or see your instructor for information on accessing the files required in this book. The purpose of this exercise is to open a partially completed workbook, enter formulas and functions, copy the formulas and functions, and then format the worksheet titles and numbers. As shown in Figure 2–84, the completed worksheet analyzes profits by product.

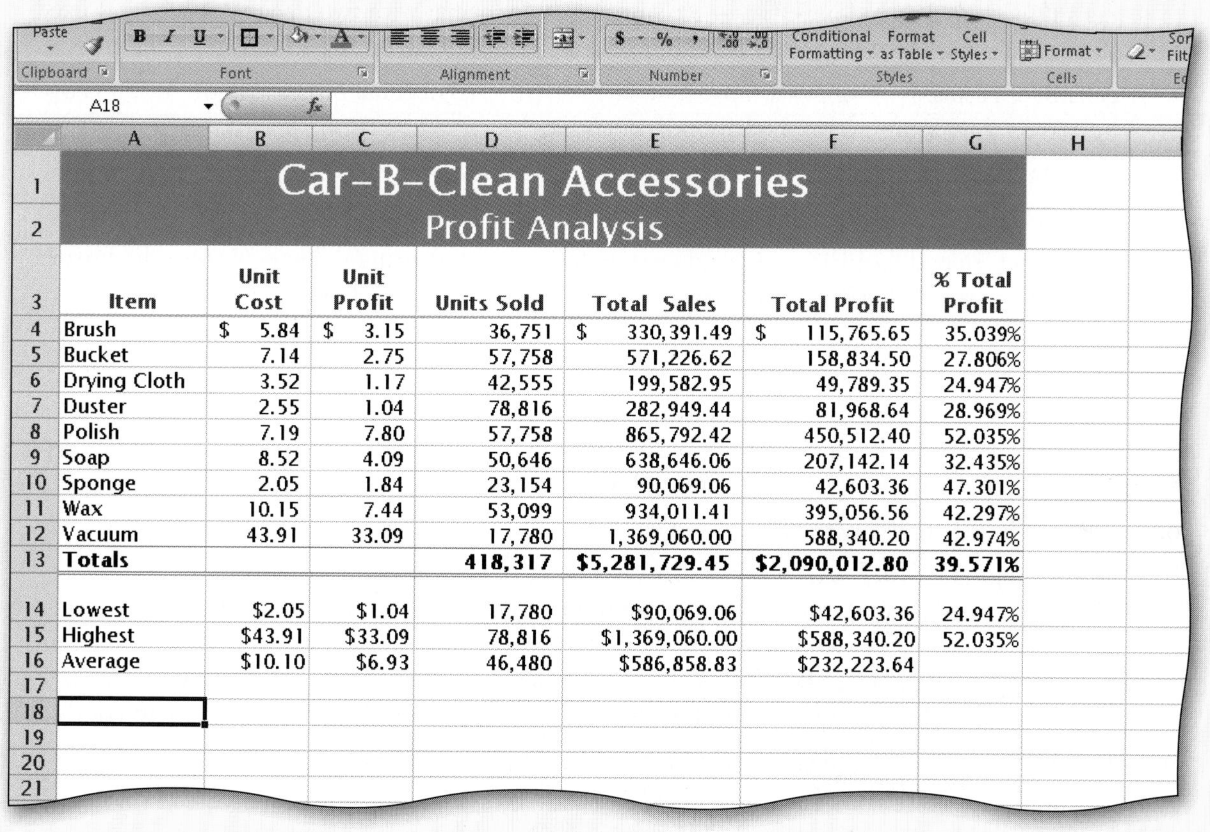

	A	B	C	D	E	F	G	H
1			Car-B-Clean Accessories					
2			Profit Analysis					
3	Item	Unit Cost	Unit Profit	Units Sold	Total Sales	Total Profit	% Total Profit	
4	Brush	$ 5.84	$ 3.15	36,751	$ 330,391.49	$ 115,765.65	35.039%	
5	Bucket	7.14	2.75	57,758	571,226.62	158,834.50	27.806%	
6	Drying Cloth	3.52	1.17	42,555	199,582.95	49,789.35	24.947%	
7	Duster	2.55	1.04	78,816	282,949.44	81,968.64	28.969%	
8	Polish	7.19	7.80	57,758	865,792.42	450,512.40	52.035%	
9	Soap	8.52	4.09	50,646	638,646.06	207,142.14	32.435%	
10	Sponge	2.05	1.84	23,154	90,069.06	42,603.36	47.301%	
11	Wax	10.15	7.44	53,099	934,011.41	395,056.56	42.297%	
12	Vacuum	43.91	33.09	17,780	1,369,060.00	588,340.20	42.974%	
13	Totals			418,317	$5,281,729.45	$2,090,012.80	39.571%	
14	Lowest	$2.05	$1.04	17,780	$90,069.06	$42,603.36	24.947%	
15	Highest	$43.91	$33.09	78,816	$1,369,060.00	$588,340.20	52.035%	
16	Average	$10.10	$6.93	46,480	$586,858.83	$232,223.64		
17								
18								
19								
20								
21								

Figure 2–84

Perform the following tasks.

1. Use the following formulas in cells E4, F4, and G4:

   Total Sales (cell E4) = Units Sold * (Unit Cost + Unit Profit) or =D4 * (B4 + C4)

   Total Profit (cell F4) = Units Sold * Unit Profit or = D4 * C4

   % Total Profit (cell G4) = Total Profit / Total Sales or = F4 / E4

   Use the fill handle to copy the three formulas in the range E4:G4 to the range E5:G12.

2. Determine totals for the units sold, total sales, and total profit in row 13. Copy cell G12 to G13 to assign the formula in cell G12 to G13 in the total line.

Continued >

Apply Your Knowledge *continued*

3. In the range B14:B16, determine the lowest value, highest value, and average value, respectively, for the values in the range B4:B12. Use the fill handle to copy the three functions to the range C14:G16. Delete the average from cell G16, because an average of percentages of this type is mathematically invalid.

4. Format the worksheet as follows:

   a. change the workbook theme to Concourse by using the Themes button on the Page Layout tab on the Ribbon

   b. cell A1 — change to font size 24 with a green (column 6 of standard colors) background and white font color by using the buttons in the Font group on the Home tab on the Ribbon

   c. cell A2 — change to a green (column 6 of standard colors) background and white font color

   d. cells B4:C4, E4:F4, and E13:F13 — Accounting style format with two decimal places and fixed dollar signs (use the Accounting Style button on the Home tab on the Ribbon)

   e. cells B5:C12 and E5:F12 — Comma style format with two decimal places (use the Comma Style button on the Home tab on the Ribbon)

   f. cells D4:D16 — Comma style format with no decimal places

   g. cells G4:G15 — Percent style format with three decimal places

   h. cells B14:C16 and E14:F16 — Currency style format with floating dollar signs (use the Format Cells: Number Dialog Box Launcher on the Home tab on the Ribbon)

5. Switch to Page Layout View and enter your name, course, laboratory assignment number (Apply 2-1), date, and any other information requested by your instructor in the Header area. Preview and print the worksheet in landscape orientation. Change the document properties, as requested by your instructor. Save the workbook using the file name, Apply 2-1 Car-B-Clean Profit Analysis Complete in the format as requested by your instructor.

6. Use Range Finder to verify the formula in cell F4.

7. Print the range A3:E16. Press CTRL+ACCENT MARK (`) to change the display from the values version of the worksheet to the formulas version. Print the formulas version in landscape orientation on one page (Figure 2–85) by using the Fit to option in the Page sheet in the Page Setup dialog box. Press CTRL+ACCENT MARK (`) to change the display of the worksheet back to the values version. Do not save the workbook. If requested, submit the three printouts to your instructor.

Instructions Part 2:

1. Do not save the workbook in this part. In column C, use the keyboard to add manually $1.00 to the profit of each product with a unit profit less than $7.00 and $3.00 to the profits of all other products. You should end up with $2,765,603.80 in cell F13.

2. Print the worksheet. Do not save the workbook. If requested, submit the revised workbook in the format as requested by your instructor.

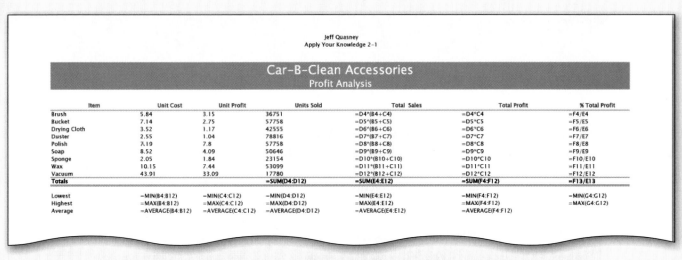

Jeff Quasney
Apply Your Knowledge 2–1

Car-B-Clean Accessories
Profit Analysis

Item	Unit Cost	Unit Profit	Units Sold	Total Sales	Total Profit	% Total Profit
Brush	5.84	3.15	36751	=D4*(B4+C4)	=D4*C4	=F4/E4
Bucket	7.14	2.75	57758	=D5*(B5+C5)	=D5*C5	=F5/E5
Drying Cloth	3.52	1.17	42555	=D6*(B6+C6)	=D6*C6	=F6/E6
Duster	2.55	1.04	78816	=D7*(B7+C7)	=D7*C7	=F7/E7
Polish	7.19	7.8	57758	=D8*(B8+C8)	=D8*C8	=F8/E8
Soap	8.52	4.09	50646	=D9*(B9+C9)	=D9*C9	=F9/E9
Sponge	2.05	1.84	23154	=D10*(B10+C10)	=D10*C10	=F10/E10
Wax	10.15	7.44	53099	=D11*(B11+C11)	=D11*C11	=F11/E11
Vacuum	43.91	33.09	17780	=D12*(B12+C12)	=D12*C12	=F12/E12
Totals			=SUM(D4:D12)	=SUM(E4:E12)	=SUM(F4:F12)	=F13/E13
Lowest	=MIN(B4:B12)	=MIN(C4:C12)	=MIN(D4:D12)	=MIN(E4:E12)	=MIN(F4:F12)	=MIN(G4:G12)
Highest	=MAX(B4:B12)	=MAX(C4:C12)	=MAX(D4:D12)	=MAX(E4:E12)	=MAX(F4:F12)	=MAX(G4:G12)
Average	=AVERAGE(B4:B12)	=AVERAGE(C4:C12)	=AVERAGE(D4:D12)	=AVERAGE(E4:E12)	=AVERAGE(F4:F12)	

Figure 2–85

Extend Your Knowledge

Extend the skills you learned in this chapter and experiment with new skills. You may need to use Help to complete the assignment.

Applying Conditional Formatting to Cells

Instructions: Start Excel. Open the workbook Extend 2-1 Biology 201 Midterm Scores. See the inside back cover of this book for instructions for downloading the Data Files for Students, or see your instructor for information on accessing the files required in this book. Perform the following tasks to apply new conditional formatting to the worksheet.

1. Select the range C4:C18. Click the Conditional Formatting button on the Home tab on the Ribbon and then select New Rule in the Conditional Formatting gallery. Select 'Format only top or bottom ranked values' in the Select a Rule Type area (Figure 2–86). Enter a value between 20 and 35 of your choosing in the text box in the Edit the Rule Description area and click the '% of the selected range' check box to select it. Click the Format button and choose a format to assign to this conditional format. Click the OK button in each dialog box to close the dialog boxes and view the worksheet.

2. With range C4:C18 selected, apply a conditional format to the range that highlights scores that are below average.

3. With range D4:D18 selected, apply a conditional format to the range that highlights any grade that is a D or an F.

4. With range B4:B18 selected, apply a conditional format to the range that uses a red color to highlight any duplicate student names.

5. Change the document properties, as requested by your instructor. Change the worksheet header with your name, course number, and other information requested by your instructor. Save the workbook using the file name, Extend 2-1 Biology 201 Midterm Scores Complete, and submit the revised workbook as requested by your instructor.

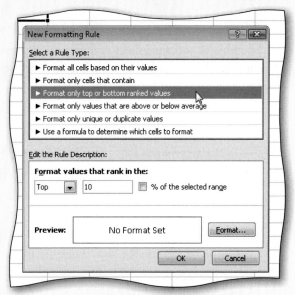

Figure 2–86

Make It Right

Analyze a workbook and correct all errors and/or improve the design.

Correcting Functions and Formulas in a Worksheet

Instructions: Start Excel. Open the workbook Make It Right 2-1 El Centro Diner Payroll Report. See the inside back cover of this book for instructions for downloading the Data Files for Students, or see your instructor for information on accessing the files required for this book. Correct the following formatting, function, and formula problems (Figure 2–87) in the worksheet.

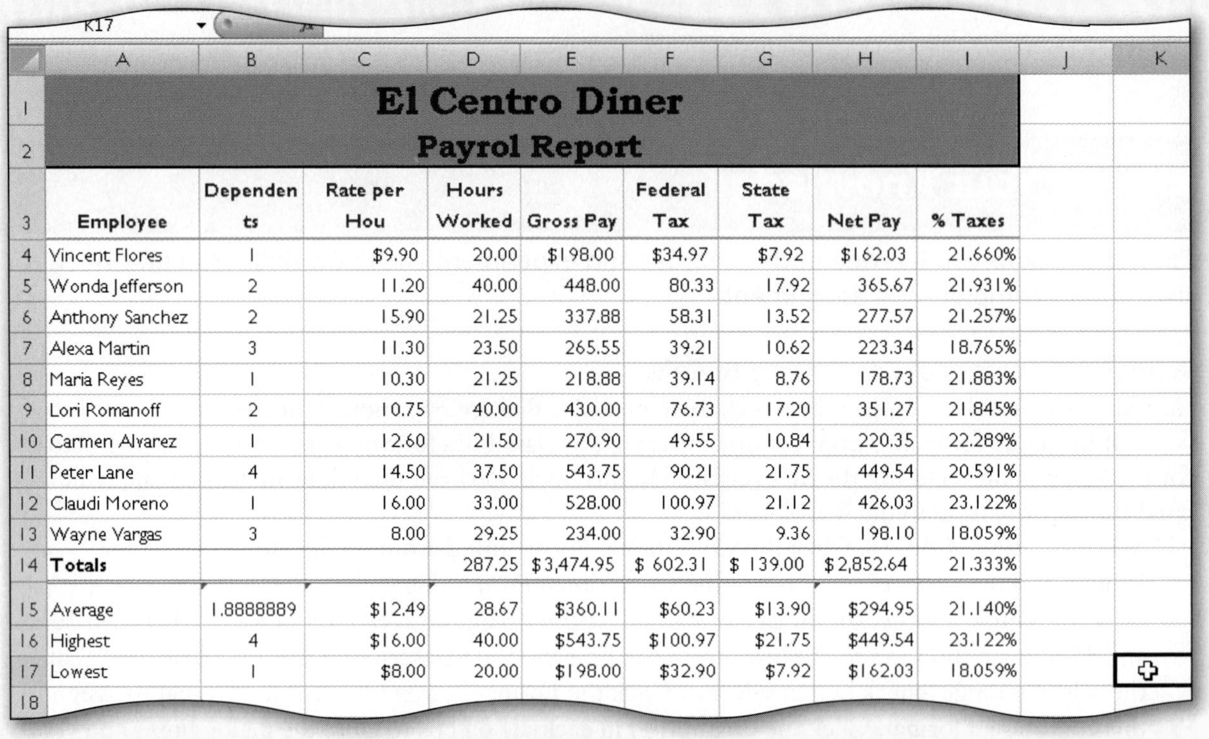

El Centro Diner
Payrol Report

Employee	Dependents	Rate per Hou	Hours Worked	Gross Pay	Federal Tax	State Tax	Net Pay	% Taxes
Vincent Flores	1	$9.90	20.00	$198.00	$34.97	$7.92	$162.03	21.660%
Wonda Jefferson	2	11.20	40.00	448.00	80.33	17.92	365.67	21.931%
Anthony Sanchez	2	15.90	21.25	337.88	58.31	13.52	277.57	21.257%
Alexa Martin	3	11.30	23.50	265.55	39.21	10.62	223.34	18.765%
Maria Reyes	1	10.30	21.25	218.88	39.14	8.76	178.73	21.883%
Lori Romanoff	2	10.75	40.00	430.00	76.73	17.20	351.27	21.845%
Carmen Alvarez	1	12.60	21.50	270.90	49.55	10.84	220.35	22.289%
Peter Lane	4	14.50	37.50	543.75	90.21	21.75	449.54	20.591%
Claudi Moreno	1	16.00	33.00	528.00	100.97	21.12	426.03	23.122%
Wayne Vargas	3	8.00	29.25	234.00	32.90	9.36	198.10	18.059%
Totals			287.25	$3,474.95	$ 602.31	$ 139.00	$2,852.64	21.333%
Average	1.8888889	$12.49	28.67	$360.11	$60.23	$13.90	$294.95	21.140%
Highest	4	$16.00	40.00	$543.75	$100.97	$21.75	$449.54	23.122%
Lowest	1	$8.00	20.00	$198.00	$32.90	$7.92	$162.03	18.059%

Figure 2–87

1. Adjust the width of column B to 11.25 pixels so that the word in the column header does not wrap.
2. Spell check the worksheet and correct any spelling mistakes that are found, but ignore any spelling mistakes found with the worksheet title and the employee names.
3. The averages in several columns do not include the employee in row 13. Adjust the functions in these cells so that all employees are included in the calculation.
4. The net pay calculation should be:

    Net Pay = Gross Pay – (Federal Taxes + State Taxes)

    Adjust the formulas in the range H4:H13 so that the correct formula is used.
5. The value for the highest value in column C was entered as a number rather than as a function. Replace the value with the appropriate function.
6. The currency values in row 4 should be formatted with the Accounting Number Format button on the Home tab on the Ribbon. They are currently formatted with the Currency format.
7. Delete the function in the cell containing the average of % Taxes because it is mathematically invalid.

8. Change the document properties, as specified by your instructor. Change the worksheet header with your name, course number, and other information requested by your instructor. Save the workbook using the file name, Make It Right 2-1 El Centro Diner Payroll Report Corrected. Submit the revised workbook as specified by your instructor.

In the Lab

Create a workbook using the guidelines, concepts, and skills presented in this chapter. Labs are listed in order of increasing difficulty.

Lab 1: Sales Analysis Worksheet

Problem: You have been asked to build a sales analysis worksheet for Facade Importers that determines the sales quota and percentage of quota met for the sales representatives in Table 2–8. The desired worksheet is shown in Figure 2–88.

Table 2–8 Facade Importers Sales Data

Sales Representative	Sales Amount	Sales Return	Sales Quota
Polizzi, Bernard	591518	12638	765130
Li, Grace	895050	12015	776381
Volpe, Pamela	716502	18141	733309
Khan, Anwer	709672	22326	566940
Hudson, Emma	802525	11138	712222
Huerta, Teresa	885156	18721	778060

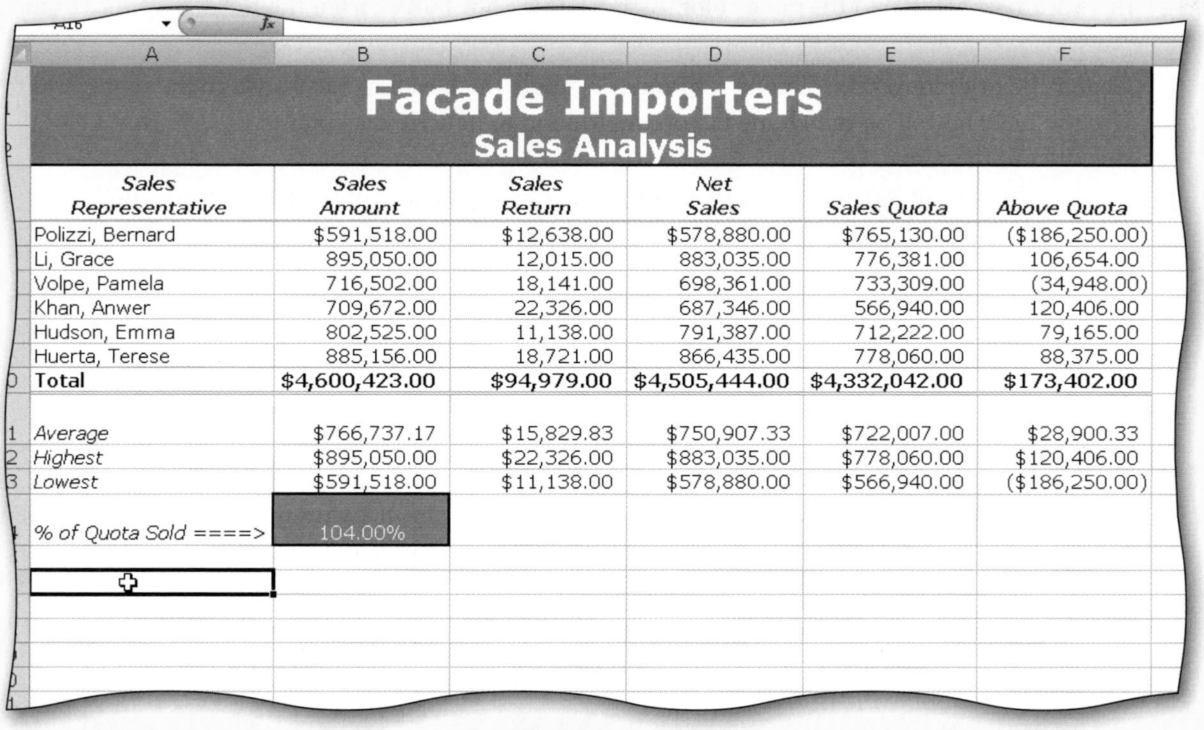

	A	B	C	D	E	F
	— **Facade Importers**					
		Sales Analysis				
	Sales Representative	*Sales Amount*	*Sales Return*	*Net Sales*	*Sales Quota*	*Above Quota*
	Polizzi, Bernard	$591,518.00	$12,638.00	$578,880.00	$765,130.00	($186,250.00)
	Li, Grace	895,050.00	12,015.00	883,035.00	776,381.00	106,654.00
	Volpe, Pamela	716,502.00	18,141.00	698,361.00	733,309.00	(34,948.00)
	Khan, Anwer	709,672.00	22,326.00	687,346.00	566,940.00	120,406.00
	Hudson, Emma	802,525.00	11,138.00	791,387.00	712,222.00	79,165.00
	Huerta, Terese	885,156.00	18,721.00	866,435.00	778,060.00	88,375.00
	Total	$4,600,423.00	$94,979.00	$4,505,444.00	$4,332,042.00	$173,402.00
	Average	$766,737.17	$15,829.83	$750,907.33	$722,007.00	$28,900.33
	Highest	$895,050.00	$22,326.00	$883,035.00	$778,060.00	$120,406.00
	Lowest	$591,518.00	$11,138.00	$578,880.00	$566,940.00	($186,250.00)
	% of Quota Sold ====>	104.00%				

Figure 2–88

Continued >

In the Lab *continued*

Instructions Part 1: Perform the following tasks to build the worksheet shown in Figure 2–88.

1. Apply the Aspect theme to the worksheet by using the Themes button on the Page Layout tab on the Ribbon.

2. Increase the width of column A to 19.00 points and the width of columns B through F to 13.50 points.

3. Enter the worksheet title Facade Importers in cell A1 and the worksheet subtitle Sales Analysis in cell A2. Enter the column titles in row 3 as shown in Figure 2–88. In row 3, use ALT+ENTER to start a new line in a cell.

4. Enter the sales data described in Table 2–8 in columns A, B, C, and E in rows 4 through 9. Enter the row titles in the range A10:A14 as shown in Figure 2–88 on the previous page.

5. Obtain the net sales in column D by subtracting the sales returns in column C from the sales amount in column B. Enter the formula in cell D4 and copy it to the range D5:D9.

6. Obtain the above quota amounts in column F by subtracting the sales quota in column E from the net sales in column D. Enter the formula in cell F4 and copy it to the range F5:F9.

7. Obtain the totals in row 10 by adding the column values for each salesperson. In the range B11:B13, use the AVERAGE, MAX, and MIN functions to determine the average, highest value, and lowest value in the range B4:B9. Copy the range B11:B13 to the range C11:F13.

8. Determine the percent of quota sold in cell B14 by dividing the total net sales amount in cell D10 by the total sales quota amount in cell E10. Center this value in the cell.

9. If necessary, click the Home tab on the Ribbon. One at a time, merge and center the worksheet title and subtitle across columns A through F. Select cells A1 and A2 and change the background color to red (column 2 in the Standard Colors area on the Fill Color palette). Apply the Title cell style to cells A1 and B1 by clicking the Cell Styles button on the Home tab on the Ribbon and clicking the Title cell style in the Titles and Headings area in the Cell Styles gallery. Change the worksheet title in cell A1 to 28-point white (column 1, row 1 on the Font Color gallery). Change the worksheet subtitle to the same color. Assign a thick box border from the Borders gallery to the range A1:A2.

10. Center the titles in row 3, columns A through F. Apply the Heading 3 cell style to the range A3:F3. Use the Italic button on the Home tab on the Ribbon to italicize the column titles in row 3 and the row titles in the range A10:A14.

11. Apply the Total cell style to the range A10:F10. Assign a thick box to cell B14. Change the background and font colors for cell B14 to the same colors applied to the worksheet title in Step 9.

12. Change the row heights of row 3 to 33.00 points and rows 11 and 14 to 30.00 points.

13. Select cell B14 and then click the Percent Style button on the Home tab on the Ribbon. Click the Increase Decimal button on the Ribbon twice to display the percent in cell B14 to hundredths.

14. Use the CTRL key to select the ranges B4:F4 and B10:F13. That is, select the range B4:F4 and then while holding down the CTRL key, select the range B10:F13. Use the Format Cells: Number Dialog Box Launcher button on the Home tab on the Ribbon to display the Format Cells dialog box to assign the selected ranges a Floating Dollar Sign style format with two decimal places and parentheses to represent negative numbers. Select the range B5:F9 and click the Comma Style button on the Home tab on the Ribbon.

15. Rename the sheet tab as Sales Analysis. Change the document properties, as specified by your instructor. Change the worksheet header with your name, course number, and other information requested by your instructor.

16. Save the workbook using the file name Lab 2-1 Part 1 Facade Importers Sales Analysis. Print the entire worksheet in landscape orientation. Print only the range A3:B10.

17. Display the formulas version by pressing CTRL+ACCENT MARK (`). Print the formulas version using the Fit to option button in the Scaling area on the Page tab in the Page Setup dialog box. After printing the worksheet, reset the Scaling option by selecting the Adjust to option button on the Page tab in the Page Setup dialog box and changing the percent value to 100%. Change the display from the formulas version to the values version by pressing CTRL+ACCENT MARK (`). Do not save the workbook.

18. Submit the assignment as requested by your instructor.

Instructions Part 2: Open the workbook created in Part 1 and save the workbook as Lab 2-1 Part 2 Facade Importers Sales Analysis. Manually decrement each of the six values in the sales amount column by $10,000.00 until the percent of quota sold in cell B14 is below, yet as close as possible to, 100%. All six values in column B must be incremented the same number of times. The percent of quota sold in B14 should equal 99.85%. Update the worksheet header and save the workbook. Print the worksheet. Submit the assignment as requested by your instructor.

Instructions Part 3: Open the workbook created in Part 2 and then save the workbook as Lab 2-1 Part 3 Facade Importers Sales Analysis. With the percent of quota sold in cell B14 equal to 99.85% from Part 2, manually decrement each of the six values in the sales return column by $1,000.00 until the percent of quota sold in cell B14 is above, yet as close as possible to, 100%. Decrement all six values in column C the same number of times. Your worksheet is correct when the percent of quota sold in cell B14 is equal to 100.12%. Update the worksheet header and save the workbook. Print the worksheet. Submit the assignment as requested by your instructor.

In the Lab

Lab 2: Balance Due Worksheet

Problem: You are a spreadsheet intern for Jackson's Bright Ideas, a popular Denver-based light fixture store with outlets in major cities across the western United States. You have been asked to use Excel to generate a report (Figure 2–89) that summarizes the monthly balance due. A graphic breakdown of the data also is desired. The customer data in Table 2–9 is available for test purposes.

Table 2–9 Jackson's Bright Ideas Monthly Balance Due Data				
Customer	**Beginning Balance**	**Credits**	**Payments**	**Purchases**
Costa, Dan	160.68	18.70	99.33	68.28
Hernandez, Abraham	138.11	48.47	75.81	46.72
Mc Cartan, John	820.15	32.11	31.23	29.19
Paoli, Pam	167.35	59.32	52.91	33.90
Ramirez, Alberto	568.34	55.17	18.53	36.34
Vaughn, Noah	449.92	25.90	82.05	99.77
Xiong, James	390.73	48.12	19.35	92.13

Continued >

In the Lab *continued*

Instructions Part 1: Create a worksheet similar to the one shown in Figure 2–89. Include the five columns of customer data in Table 2–9 in the report, plus two additional columns to compute a service charge and a new balance for each customer. Assume no negative unpaid monthly balances.

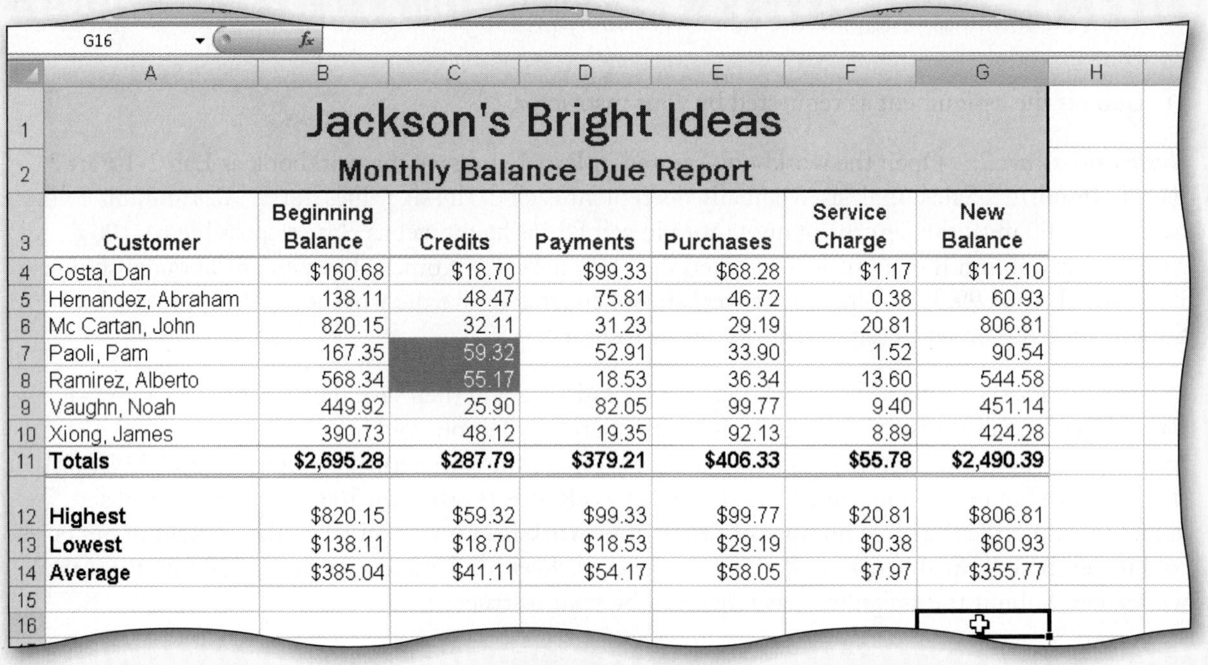

	A	B	C	D	E	F	G
1	Jackson's Bright Ideas						
2	Monthly Balance Due Report						
3	Customer	Beginning Balance	Credits	Payments	Purchases	Service Charge	New Balance
4	Costa, Dan	$160.68	$18.70	$99.33	$68.28	$1.17	$112.10
5	Hernandez, Abraham	138.11	48.47	75.81	46.72	0.38	60.93
6	Mc Cartan, John	820.15	32.11	31.23	29.19	20.81	806.81
7	Paoli, Pam	167.35	59.32	52.91	33.90	1.52	90.54
8	Ramirez, Alberto	568.34	55.17	18.53	36.34	13.60	544.58
9	Vaughn, Noah	449.92	25.90	82.05	99.77	9.40	451.14
10	Xiong, James	390.73	48.12	19.35	92.13	8.89	424.28
11	**Totals**	**$2,695.28**	**$287.79**	**$379.21**	**$406.33**	**$55.78**	**$2,490.39**
12	**Highest**	$820.15	$59.32	$99.33	$99.77	$20.81	$806.81
13	**Lowest**	$138.11	$18.70	$18.53	$29.19	$0.38	$60.93
14	**Average**	$385.04	$41.11	$54.17	$58.05	$7.97	$355.77

Figure 2–89

Perform the following tasks:

1. Enter and format the worksheet title `Jackson's Bright Ideas` and worksheet subtitle `Monthly Balance Due Report` in cells A1 and A2. Change the theme of the worksheet to the Technic theme. Apply the Title cell style to cells A1 and A2. Change the font size in cell A1 to 28 points. One at a time, merge and center the worksheet title and subtitle across columns A through G. Change the background color of cells A1 and A2 to yellow (column 4 in the Standard Colors area in the Font Color palette). Draw a thick box border around the range A1:A2.
2. Change the width of column A to 20.00 characters. Change the widths of columns B through G to 12.00. Change the heights of row 3 to 36.00 and row 12 to 30.00 points.
3. Enter the column titles in row 3 and row titles in the range A11:A14 as shown in Figure 2–89. Center the column titles in the range A3:G3. Apply the Heading 3 cell style to the range A3:G3. Bold the titles in the range A11:A14. Apply the Total cell style to the range A11:G11. Change the font size of the cells in the range A3:G14 to 12 points.
4. Enter the data in Table 2–9 in the range A4:E10.
5. Use the following formulas to determine the service charge in column F and the new balance in column G for the first customer. Copy the two formulas down through the remaining customers.
   a. Service Charge (cell F4) = 2.75% * (Beginning Balance – Payments – Credits) or = 0.0275 * (B4 – D4 – C4)
   b. New Balance (G4) = Beginning Balance + Purchases – Credits – Payments + Service Charge or =B4 + E4 – C4 – D4 + F4
6. Determine the totals in row 11.

7. Determine the maximum, minimum, and average values in cells B12:B14 for the range B4:B10 and then copy the range B12:B14 to C12:G14.

8. Use the Format Cells command on the shortcut menu to format the numbers as follows: (a) assign the Currency style with a floating dollar sign to the cells containing numeric data in the ranges B4:G4 and B11:G14; and (b) assign the Comma style (currency with no dollar sign) to the range B5:G10.

9. Use conditional formatting to change the formatting to white font on a red background in any cell in the range C4:C10 that contains a value greater than 50.

10. Change the worksheet name from Sheet1 to Balance Due. Change the document properties, as specified by your instructor. Change the worksheet header with your name, course number, and other information requested by your instructor.

11. Spell check the worksheet. Preview and then print the worksheet in landscape orientation. Save the workbook using the file name, Lab 2-2 Part 1 Jackson's Bright Ideas Monthly Balance Due Report.

12. Print the range A3:D14. Print the formulas version on one page. Close the workbook without saving the changes. Submit the assignment as requested by your instructor.

Instructions Part 2: This part requires that a 3-D Bar chart with a cylindrical shape be inserted on a new worksheet in the workbook. If necessary, use Excel Help to obtain information on inserting a chart on a separate sheet in the workbook.

1. With the Lab 2-2 Part 1 Jackson's Bright Ideas Monthly Balance Due Report workbook open, save the workbook using the file name, Lab 2-2 Part 2 Jackson's Bright Ideas Monthly Balance Due Report. Draw the 3-D Bar chart with cylindrical shape showing each customer's total new balance as shown in Figure 2–90.

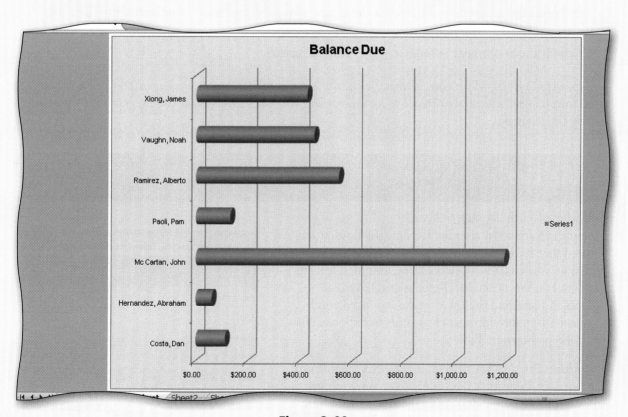

Figure 2–90

2. Use the CTRL key and mouse to select the nonadjacent chart ranges A4:A10 and G4:G10. That is, select the range A4:A10 and then while holding down the CTRL key, select the range G4:G10. The customer names in the range A4:A10 will identify the cylindrical bars, while the data series in the range G4:G10 will determine the length of the bars.

Continued >

3. Click the Insert tab on the Ribbon. Click the Bar button in the Charts group on the Ribbon and then select Clustered Horizontal Cylinder in the Cylinder area. When the chart is displayed on the worksheet, click the Move Chart button on the Ribbon. When the Move Chart dialog box appears, click New sheet and then type Bar Chart for the sheet name. Click the OK button.

4. When the chart is displayed on the new worksheet, click the chart area, which is a blank area near the edge of the chart, and then click the Format contextual tab. Click the Shape Fill button on the Ribbon and then select Gold, Accent 2, Lighter 80% in the gallery (column 6, row 2). Click the Layout contextual tab. Click the Chart Title button on the Ribbon and then select Above Chart in the Chart Title gallery. If necessary, use the scroll bar on the right side of the worksheet to scroll to the top of the chart. Click the edge of the chart title to select it and then type Balance Due as the chart title.

5. Drag the Balance Due tab at the bottom of the worksheet to the left of the Bar Chart tab to reorder the sheets in the workbook. Preview and print the chart.

6. Click the Balance Due sheet tab. Change the following purchases: customer John Mc Cartan to $406.58, and customer Pam Paoli to $74.99. The company also decided to change the service charge from 2.75% to 3.25% for all customers. After copying the adjusted formula in cell F4 to the range F5:F10, click the Auto Fill Options button and then click Fill without Formatting to maintain the original formatting in the range F5:F10. The total new balance in cell G11 should equal $2,919.01.

7. Select both sheets by holding down the SHIFT key and then clicking the Bar Chart tab. Preview and print the selected sheets. Submit the assignment as requested by your instructor. Save the workbook.

8. Submit the assignment as requested by your instructor.

Instructions Part 3: With your instructor's permission, e-mail the workbook created in this exercise with the changes indicated in Part 2 as an attachment to your instructor. Close the workbook without saving the changes.

In the Lab

Lab 3: Equity Web Queries

Problem: A friend of your family, Benson Yackley, has learned that Excel can connect to the Web, download real-time stock data into a worksheet, and then refresh the data as often as needed. Because you have had courses in Excel and the Internet, he has hired you as a consultant to develop a stock analysis workbook. His portfolio is shown in Table 2–10.

Table 2–10 Benson Yackley's Stock Portfolio	
Company	**Stock Symbol**
Exxon Mobil	XOM
Dell	DELL
Hewlett-Packard	HPQ
Intel	INTC
MetLife	MET
PepsiCo	PEP

Instructions Part 1: Start Excel. If necessary, connect to the Internet. Perform a Web query to obtain multiple stock quotes (Figure 2–91), using the stock symbols in the second column of Table 2–10. Place the results of the Web query in a new worksheet. Rename the worksheet Real-Time Stock Quotes. Change the document properties, as specified by your instructor. Add a header with your name, course number, and other information requested by your instructor. Save the workbook using the file name, Lab 2-3 Part 1 Benson Yackley Equities Online. Preview and then print the worksheet in landscape orientation using the Fit to option.

Click the following links and print the Web page that appears in the browser window: Click here to visit MSN Money; Dell Inc.; Chart (to the right of MetLife, Inc.); and News (to the right of PepsiCo, Inc.). Submit the assignment as requested by your instructor.

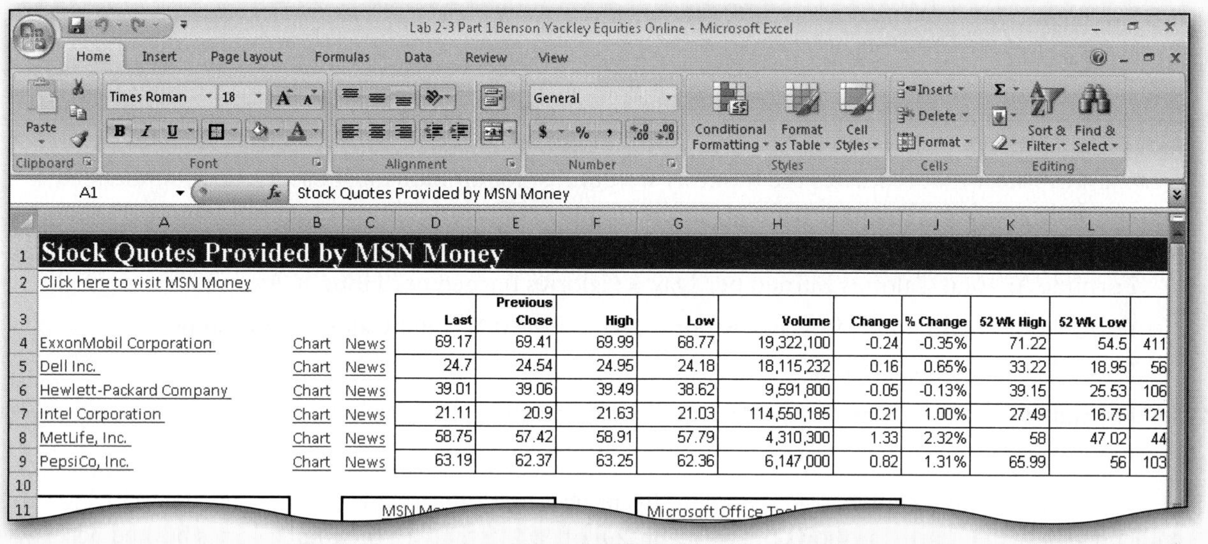

	A	B	C	D	E	F	G	H	I	J	K	L	
1	Stock Quotes Provided by MSN Money												
2	Click here to visit MSN Money												
3				Last	Previous Close	High	Low	Volume	Change	% Change	52 Wk High	52 Wk Low	
4	ExxonMobil Corporation	Chart	News	69.17	69.41	69.99	68.77	19,322,100	-0.24	-0.35%	71.22	54.5	411
5	Dell Inc.	Chart	News	24.7	24.54	24.95	24.18	18,115,232	0.16	0.65%	33.22	18.95	56
6	Hewlett-Packard Company	Chart	News	39.01	39.06	39.49	38.62	9,591,800	-0.05	-0.13%	39.15	25.53	106
7	Intel Corporation	Chart	News	21.11	20.9	21.63	21.03	114,550,185	0.21	1.00%	27.49	16.75	121
8	MetLife, Inc.	Chart	News	58.75	57.42	58.91	57.79	4,310,300	1.33	2.32%	58	47.02	44
9	PepsiCo, Inc.	Chart	News	63.19	62.37	63.25	62.36	6,147,000	0.82	1.31%	65.99	56	103

Figure 2–91

Instructions Part 2: While connected to the Internet and with the Lab 2-3 Benson Yackley Equities Online workbook open, create a worksheet listing the major indices and their current values on Sheet2 of the workbook (Figure 2–92). After clicking the Sheet2 tab, create the worksheet by double-clicking MSN MoneyCentral Investor Major Indices in the Existing Connections dialog box. The dialog box is displayed when you click the Existing Connections button on the Data tab on the Ribbon. Rename the worksheet Major Indices. Preview and then print the Major Indices worksheet in landscape orientation using the Fit to option. Save the workbook using the same file name as in Part 1. Submit the assignment as requested by your instructor.

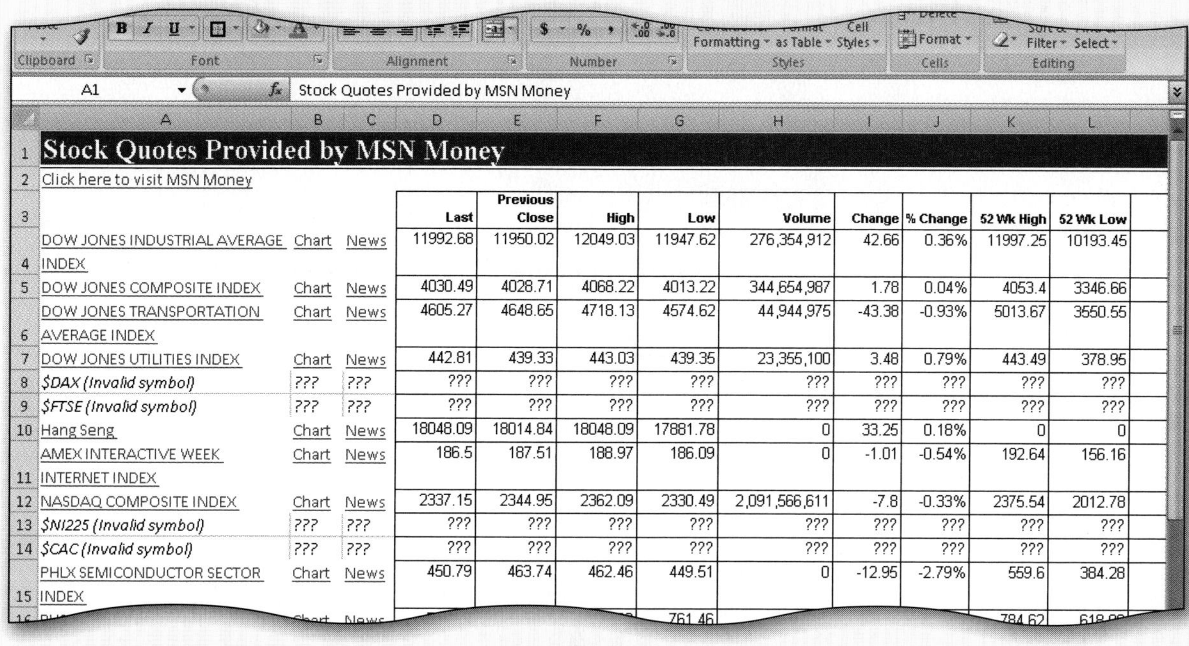

	A	B	C	D	E	F	G	H	I	J	K	L
1	Stock Quotes Provided by MSN Money											
2	Click here to visit MSN Money											
3				Last	Previous Close	High	Low	Volume	Change	% Change	52 Wk High	52 Wk Low
4	DOW JONES INDUSTRIAL AVERAGE INDEX	Chart	News	11992.68	11950.02	12049.03	11947.62	276,354,912	42.66	0.36%	11997.25	10193.45
5	DOW JONES COMPOSITE INDEX	Chart	News	4030.49	4028.71	4068.22	4013.22	344,654,987	1.78	0.04%	4053.4	3346.66
6	DOW JONES TRANSPORTATION AVERAGE INDEX	Chart	News	4605.27	4648.65	4718.13	4574.62	44,944,975	-43.38	-0.93%	5013.67	3550.55
7	DOW JONES UTILITIES INDEX	Chart	News	442.81	439.33	443.03	439.35	23,355,100	3.48	0.79%	443.49	378.95
8	*$DAX (Invalid symbol)*	???	???	???	???	???	???	???	???	???	???	???
9	*$FTSE (Invalid symbol)*	???	???	???	???	???	???	???	???	???	???	???
10	Hang Seng	Chart	News	18048.09	18014.84	18048.09	17881.78	0	33.25	0.18%	0	0
11	AMEX INTERACTIVE WEEK INTERNET INDEX	Chart	News	186.5	187.51	188.97	186.09	0	-1.01	-0.54%	192.64	156.16
12	NASDAQ COMPOSITE INDEX	Chart	News	2337.15	2344.95	2362.09	2330.49	2,091,566,611	-7.8	-0.33%	2375.54	2012.78
13	*$NI225 (Invalid symbol)*	???	???	???	???	???	???	???	???	???	???	???
14	*$CAC (Invalid symbol)*	???	???	???	???	???	???	???	???	???	???	???
15	PHLX SEMICONDUCTOR SECTOR INDEX	Chart	News	450.79	463.74	462.46	449.51	0	-12.95	-2.79%	559.6	384.28

Figure 2–92

Cases and Places

Apply your creative thinking and problem solving skills to design and implement a solution.

• EASIER •• MORE DIFFICULT

• 1: Design and Create a Weight-Loss Plan Worksheet

As a summer intern working for Choose to Lose, a local weight-loss clinic, you have been asked to create a worksheet that estimates the monthly weight lost for an individual based on recommended average daily activities. You have been given the numbers of calories burned per hour and the average number of hours for each activity (Table 2–11). Use the following formulas:

Formula A: Total Calories Burned per Day = Calories burned per Hour × Average Hours Daily

Formula B: Total Pounds Lost per Month (30 days) = 30 × Total Calories Burned per Day / 3500

Formula C: Average function

Formula D: Max function

Formula E: Min function

Use the concepts and techniques presented in this project to create and format the worksheet. Include an embedded 3-D Pie chart that shows the contribution of each activity to the total calories burned per day. Use Microsoft Excel Help to create a professional looking 3-D Pie chart with title and data labels.

Table 2–11 Activities with Corresponding Calories Burned per Hour and Worksheet Layout

Activity	Calories Burned per Hour	Average Hours Daily	Total Calories Burned per Day	Total Pounds Lost per Month (30 Days)
Aerobics class	450	0.50	Formula A	Formula B
Brisk walking	350	0.50		
House work	150	1.00		
Office work/sitting	120	6.00		
Sleeping	70	9.00		
Standing	105	2.00		
Swimming	290	0.50		
Tennis	315	0.25		
Walking	240	4.25		
Totals	—		—	—
Average	Formula C			
Highest	Formula D			
Lowest	Formula E			

• **2: Create a Profit Potential Worksheet**

You work part-time for Doze-Now, a retailer of sleep-related products. Your manager wants to know the profit potential of their inventory based on the categories of inventory in Table 2–12. Table 2–12 contains the format of the desired report. The required formulas are shown in Table 2–13. Use the concepts and techniques developed in this project to create and format the worksheet. Submit a printout of the values version and formulas version of the worksheet. The company just received a shipment of 175 additional comforters and 273 items of sleepwear. Update the appropriate cells in the Units on Hand column.

Table 2–12 Doze-Now Profit Potential Data and Worksheet Layout

Item	Units on Hand	Average Unit Cost	Total Cost	Average Unit Price	Total Value	Potential Profit
Comforters	216	46.52	Formula A	Formula B	Formula C	Formula D
Night lights	4,283	6.89				
Pillows	691	47.64				
Sleep sound machines	103	45.06				
Sleepwear	489	16.77				
Total	—		—	—	—	—
Average	Formula E					
Lowest	Formula F					
Highest	Formula G					

Table 2–13 Doze-Now Profit Potential Formulas

Formula A = Units on Hand * Average Unit Cost

Formula B = Average Unit Cost * (1 / (1 − .58))

Formula C = Units on Hand * Average Unit Price

Formula D = Total Value − Total Cost

Formula E = AVERAGE function

Formula F = MIN function

Formula G = MAX function

Continued >

Cases and Places *continued*

•• 3: Create a Fund-Raising Analysis Worksheet

You are the chairperson of the fund-raising committee for a local charity. You want to compare various fund-raising ideas to determine which will give you the best profit. The data obtained from six businesses about their products and the format of the desired report are shown in Table 2–14. The required formulas are shown in Table 2–15. Use the concepts and techniques presented in this project to create and format the worksheet.

Table 2–14 Fund-Raising Data and Worksheet Layout

Product	Company	Cost per Unit	Margin	Selling Price	Profit per 2000 Sales	Profit per 5000 Sales
Candles	Woodland Farms	$4.75	40%	Formula A	Formula B	Formula C
Candy	Polkandy	3.00	70%			
Coffee	Garcia Coffee	6.50	45%			
Cookie dough	Oh, Dough!	2.90	65%			
Flower bulbs	Early Bloom	2.40	50%			
T-shirts	Zed's Sports	5.75	42%			
Minimum		Formula D				
Maximum		Formula E				

Table 2–15 Band Fund-Raising Formulas

Formula A = Cost per Unit / (1 – Margin)

Formula B = 2000 * (Selling Price – Cost per Unit)

Formula C = 5000 *110% * (Selling Price – Cost per Unit)

Formula D = MIN function

Formula E = MAX function

•• 4: Design and Create a Projected Budget

Make It Personal

For the next six-month period, forecast your income for each month, your base expenditures for each month, and your special expenditures for each month. Base expenditures include expenses that occur each month, such as food and loan payments. Special expenditures include expenses that are out of the ordinary, such as the purchase of gifts, automobile insurance, and medical expenses. With this data, develop a worksheet calculating the amount of remaining money at the end of each month. You can determine this amount by subtracting both expenses from the anticipated income.

Include a total, average value, highest value, and lowest value for income, base expenditures, special expenditures, and remaining money. Use the concepts and techniques presented in this project to create and format the worksheet.

Create a 3-D Pie chart on a separate sheet illustrating the portion each month's special expenditures deducts from the total remaining money after all six months have passed. Use Microsoft Excel Help to create a professional looking 3-D Pie chart with title and data labels.

•• 5: Design and Create a Stock Analysis Worksheet

Working Together

Have each member of your team select six stocks — two bank stocks, two communications stocks, and two Internet stocks. Each member should submit the stock names, stock symbols, and an approximate six-month-old price. Create a worksheet that lists the stock names, symbols, price, and number of shares for each stock (use 350 shares as the number of shares for all stocks). Format the worksheet so that it has a professional appearance and is as informative as possible.

Have the group do research on the use of 3-D references, which is a reference to a range that spans two or more worksheets in a workbook (use Microsoft Excel Help). Use what the group learns to create a Web query on the Sheet2 worksheet by referencing the stock symbols on the Sheet1 worksheet. On the Sheet1 worksheet, change the cells that list current price per share numbers on the Sheet1 worksheet so that they use 3-D cell references that refer to the worksheet created by the Web query on the Sheet2 worksheet. Present your workbook and findings to the class.

3 | What-If Analysis, Charting, and Working with Large Worksheets

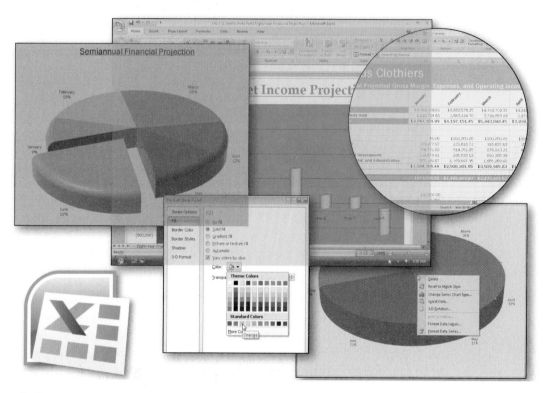

Objectives

You will have mastered the material in this chapter when you can:

- Rotate text in a cell
- Create a series of month names
- Copy, paste, insert, and delete cells
- Format numbers using format symbols
- Freeze and unfreeze titles
- Show and format the system date
- Use absolute cell references in a formula
- Use the IF function to perform a logical test

- Use the Format Painter button to format cells
- Create a 3-D Pie chart on a separate chart sheet
- Color and rearrange worksheet tabs
- Change the worksheet view
- Answer what-if questions
- Goal seek to answer what-if questions

3 | What-If Analysis, Charting, and Working with Large Worksheets

Introduction

Worksheets normally are much larger than those created in the previous chapters, often extending beyond the size of the window. Because you cannot see the entire worksheet on the screen at one time, working with a large worksheet sometimes can be frustrating. This chapter introduces several Excel commands that allow you to control what displays on the screen so you can view critical parts of a large worksheet at one time. One command lets you freeze the row and column titles so Excel always displays them on the screen. Another command splits the worksheet into separate window panes so you can view different parts of a worksheet on the screen at one time. Hiding the Ribbon will allow a larger portion of the worksheet to be visible.

When you set up a worksheet, you should use cell references in formulas whenever possible, rather than constant values. The use of a cell reference allows you to change a value in multiple formulas by changing the value in a single cell. The cell references in a formula are called assumptions. Assumptions are values in cells that you can change to determine new values for formulas. This chapter emphasizes the use of assumptions and shows how to use Excel to answer what-if questions such as, what happens to the semi-annual operating income if you decrease the marketing expenses assumption by 2%? Being able to analyze quickly the effect of changing values in a worksheet is an important skill in making business decisions.

This chapter also introduces you to techniques that will enhance your ability to create worksheets and draw charts. From your work in Chapter 1, you are aware of how easily you can create charts. This chapter covers additional charting techniques that allow you to convey your message in a dramatic pictorial fashion such as an exploded 3-D Pie chart. This chapter also covers other methods for entering values in cells, such as allowing Excel to enter values for you based on a pattern of values that you create, and formatting these values. In addition, you will learn how to use absolute cell references and how to use the IF function to assign a value to a cell based on a logical test.

Project — Financial Projection Worksheet with What-If Analysis and Chart

The project in the chapter follows proper design guidelines and uses Excel to create the worksheet and pie chart shown in Figure 3–1. Campus Clothiers manufactures and sells customized clothing to college students on campuses around the country. Each June and December, the director of finance and accounting submits a plan to the management team to show projected monthly revenues, costs of goods, gross margin, expenses, and operating income for the next six months. The director requires an easy-to-read worksheet that shows financial projections for the next six months. The worksheet should allow for quick analysis if projections for certain numbers change, such as the percentage of expenses allocated to marketing. In addition, a 3-D Pie chart is required that shows the projected operating income contribution for each of the six months.

Campus Clothiers

Semiannual Projected Gross Margin, Expenses, and Operating Income   11/5/2008

	January	February	March	April	May	June	Total
Sales	$3,383,909.82	$6,880,576.15	$9,742,702.37	$4,818,493.53	$4,566,722.63	$8,527,504.39	$37,919,908.89
Cost of Goods Sold	1,319,724.83	2,683,424.70	3,799,653.92	1,879,212.48	1,781,021.83	3,325,726.71	14,788,764.47
Gross Margin	$2,064,184.99	$4,197,151.45	$5,943,048.45	$2,939,281.05	$2,785,700.80	$5,201,777.68	$23,131,144.42
Expenses							
Bonus	$0.00	$100,000.00	$100,000.00	$100,000.00	$0.00	$100,000.00	$400,000.00
Commission	109,977.07	223,618.72	316,637.83	156,601.04	148,418.49	277,143.89	1,232,397.04
Marketing	304,551.88	619,251.85	876,843.21	433,664.42	411,005.04	767,475.40	3,412,791.80
Research and Development	194,574.81	395,633.13	560,205.39	277,063.38	262,586.55	490,331.50	2,180,394.76
Support, General, and Administrative	575,264.67	1,169,697.95	1,656,259.40	819,143.90	776,342.85	1,449,675.75	6,446,384.51
Total Expenses	$1,184,368.44	$2,508,201.65	$3,509,945.83	$1,786,472.74	$1,598,352.92	$3,084,626.54	$13,671,968.11
Operating Income	$879,816.55	$1,688,949.80	$2,433,102.62	$1,152,808.32	$1,187,347.88	$2,117,151.14	$9,459,176.31
What-if Assumptions							
Bonus		100,000.00					
Commission		3.25%					
Margin		61.00%					
Marketing		9.00%					
Research and Development		5.75%					
Revenue for Bonus		4,750,000.00					
Support, General, and Administrative		17.00%					

(a) Worksheet

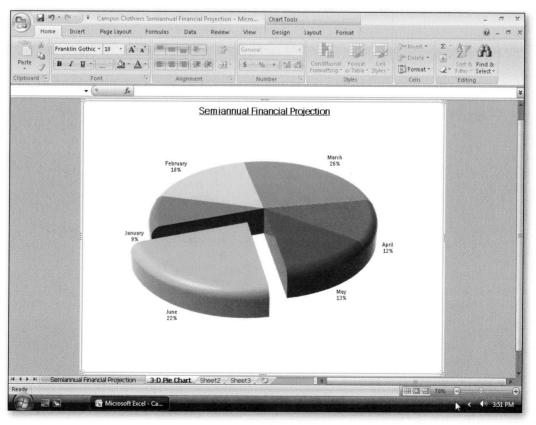

(b) 3-D Pie Chart

Figure 3–1

BTW

Correctness
Studies have shown that more than 25 percent of all business worksheets have errors. If you are not careful entering data and formulas, then your worksheet is prone to errors. You can ensure correctness in your formulas by carefully checking them using Range Finder. The Formula Auditing group on the Formulas tab on the Ribbon also can be helpful when verifying formulas.

The requirements document for the Campus Clothiers Semiannual Financial Projection worksheet is shown in Figure 3–2. It includes the needs, source of data, summary of calculations, chart requirements, and other facts about its development.

REQUEST FOR NEW WORKBOOK

Date Submitted:	October 27, 2008
Submitted By:	Norm Armand
Worksheet Title:	Campus Clothiers Semiannual Projected Gross Margin, Expenses, and Operating Income
Needs:	The needs are: (1) a worksheet (Figure 3-3a) that shows Campus Clothiers's projected monthly sales, cost of goods, gross margin, expenses, and operating income for a six-month period; and (2) a 3-D Pie chart (Figure 3-3b) that shows the projected contribution of each month's operating income to the six-month period operating income.
Source of Data:	The data supplied by the Finance department includes projections of the monthly sales and expenses (Table 3-1) that are based on prior years. All the remaining numbers in the worksheet are determined from these 13 numbers using formulas.
Calculations:	The following calculations must be made for each month: 1. Cost of Goods = Sales – Sales * Margin 2. Gross Margin = Sales – Cost of Goods 3. Bonus Expense = $100,000.00 if the Sales exceeds the Revenue for Bonus; otherwise Bonus Expense = 0 4. Commission Expense = Commission Assumption * Sales 5. Marketing Expense = Marketing Assumption * Sales 6. Research and Development = Research and Development Assumption * Sales 7. Support, General, and Administrative Expense = Support, General, and Administrative Assumption * Sales 8. Total Expenses = Sum of Expenses 9. Operating Income = Gross Margin – Total Expenses
Chart Requirements:	A 3-D Pie chart is required on a separate sheet (Figure 3-3b) to show the contribution of each month's operating income to the six-month period operating income. The chart should also emphasize the month with the greatest operating income.

Approvals

Approval Status:	X	Approved
		Rejected
Approved By:	Shauna Hendricks, CFO	
Date:	November 1, 2008	
Assigned To:	J. Quasney, Spreadsheet Specialist	

Figure 3–2

BTW

Excel's Usefulness
Just a few short years ago, a what-if question of any complexity only could be answered using a large, expensive computer programmed by highly paid computer professionals. Generating a result could take days. Excel gives the noncomputer professional the ability to get complex business-related questions answered instantaneously and economically.

Overview

As you read this chapter, you will learn how to create the worksheet shown in Figure 3–1 by performing these general tasks:

- Create a series of month names
- Use absolute cell references in a formula
- Use the IF function to perform a logical test
- Use the Format Painter button to format cells
- Create a 3-D Pie chart on a separate chart sheet
- Answer what-if questions
- Manipulate large worksheets

General Project Decisions

Plan Ahead

While creating an Excel worksheet, you need to make several decisions that will determine the appearance and characteristics of the finished worksheet. As you create the worksheet required to meet the requirements shown in Figure 3–2, you should follow these general guidelines:

1. Plan the layout of the worksheet. The requirements state that six months are necessary in the worksheet. It is therefore sensible to place the months across columns so that the financial headings can be placed in rows. The what-if assumptions should not clutter the worksheet, but they should be placed in an easily located portion of the worksheet.

2. Determine the necessary formulas and functions needed. Except for the monthly sales numbers, the remaining numbers in the main portion of the worksheet are calculated based on the numbers in the what-if portion of the worksheet. The formulas are stated in the requirements document (Figure 3–2). The Bonus expense is included only if a certain condition is met. A function can check for the condition and include the bonus when necessary.

3. Identify how to format various elements of the worksheet. Sales and Expenses are two distinct categories of financial data and should be separated visually. Gross Margin and Total Expenses should stand out because they are subtotals. The Operating Income is the key piece of information being calculated in the worksheet and, therefore, should be formatted in such a manner as to draw the reader's attention. The what-if assumptions should be formatted in a manner which indicates that they are separate from the main area of the worksheet.

4. Specify how the chart should convey necessary information. The requirements document indicates that the chart should be a 3-D Pie chart and emphasize the month with the greatest operating income. A 3-D Pie chart is a good way to compare visually a small set of numbers. The month, which is emphasized, also should appear closer to the reader in order to draw the reader's attention.

5. Perform what-if analysis and goal seeking using the best techniques. What-if analysis allows you quickly to answer questions regarding various predictions. In Campus Clothiers Semiannual Financial Projection worksheet, the only cells that you should change when performing what-if analysis are those in the what-if portion of the worksheet. All other values in the worksheet, except for the projected sales, are calculated. Goal seeking allows you automatically to modify values in the what-if area of the worksheet based on a goal that you have for another cell in the worksheet.

(continued)

Plan Ahead

(continued)

In addition, using a sketch of the worksheet can help you visualize its design. The sketch of the worksheet (Figure 3-3a) consists of titles, column and row headings, location of data values, calculations, and a rough idea of the desired formatting. The sketch of the 3-D Pie chart (Figure 3–3b) shows the expected contribution of each month's operating income to the semiannual operating income. The projected monthly sales will be entered in row 4 of the worksheet. The assumptions will be entered below the operating income (Figure 3–3a). The projected monthly sales and the assumptions will be used to calculate the remaining numbers in the worksheet.

When necessary, more specific details concerning the above guidelines are presented at appropriate points in the chapter. The chapter also will identify the actions you perform and decisions made regarding these guidelines during the creation of the worksheet shown in Figure 3–1 on page EX 163.

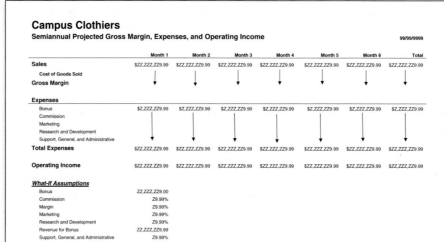

(a) Worksheet

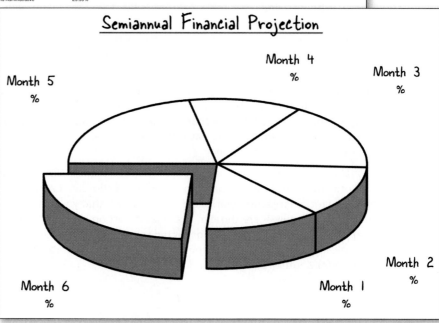

(b) 3-D Pie Chart

Figure 3–3

With a good understanding of the requirements document, an understanding of the necessary decisions, and a sketch of the worksheet, the next step is to use Excel to create the worksheet.

Table 3–1 Campus Clothiers Semiannual Financial Projections Data and What-If Assumptions	
Projected Monthly Total Net Revenues	
January	$3,383,909.82
February	6,880,576.15
March	9,742,702.37
April	4,818,493.53
May	4,566,722.63
June	8,527,504.39
What-If Assumptions	
Bonus	$100,000.00
Commission	3.25%
Margin	61.00%
Marketing	9.00%
Research and Development	5.75%
Revenue for Bonus	$4,750,000.00
Support, General, and Administrative	17.00%

To Start Excel

If you are using a computer to step through the project in this chapter and you want your screen to match the figures in this book, you should change your computer's resolution to 1024 × 768. For information about how to change a computer's resolution, see page APP 36 in Appendix E.

The following steps, which assume Windows Vista is running, start Excel based on a typical installation of Microsoft Office on your computer. You may need to ask your instructor how to start Excel for your computer.

Note: If you are using Windows XP, see Appendix F for alternate steps.

1. Click the Start button on the Windows Vista taskbar to display the Start menu.

2. Click All Programs at the bottom of the left pane on the Start menu to display the All Programs list.

3. Click Microsoft Office in the All Programs list to display the Microsoft Office list.

4. Click Microsoft Office Excel 2007 to start Excel and display a blank worksheet in the Excel window.

5. If the Excel window is not maximized, click the Maximize button next to the Close button on its title bar to maximize the window.

6. If the worksheet window in Excel is not maximized, click the Maximize button next to the Close button on its title bar to maximize the worksheet window within Excel.

To Enter the Worksheet Titles, Change Workbook Properties, Apply a Theme, and Save the Workbook

The worksheet contains two titles, one in cell A1 and another in cell A2. In the previous chapters, titles were centered across the worksheet. With large worksheets that extend beyond the size of a window, it is best to enter titles in the upper-left corner as shown in the sketch of the worksheet in Figure 3–3a. The following steps enter the worksheet titles and save the workbook.

1 Click cell A1 and then enter `Campus Clothiers` as the worksheet title.

2 Click cell A2 and then enter `Semiannual Projected Gross Margin, Expenses, and Operating Income` as the worksheet subtitle and then press the ENTER key.

3 Click the Office Button, click Prepare on the Office Button menu, and then click Properties.

4 Update the document properties with your name and any other relevant information.

5 Click the Close button in the Document Properties pane.

6 Apply the Trek theme to the worksheet by clicking the Themes button on the Page Layout tab on the Ribbon and then return to the Home tab on the Ribbon.

7 With a USB flash drive connected to one of the computer's USB ports, click the Save button on the Quick Access Toolbar.

8 When Excel displays the Save As dialog box, type `Campus Clothiers Semiannual Financial Projection` in the File name text box.

9 If the Folders list is displayed below the Folders button, click the Folders button to remove the Folders list.

10 If Computer is not displayed in the Favorite Links section, drag the top or bottom edge of the Save As dialog box until Computer is displayed.

11 Click Computer in the Favorite Links section. If necessary, scroll until UDISK 2.0 (E:) appears in the list of available drives. Double-click UDISK 2.0 (E:) (your USB flash drive may have a different name and letter). Click the Save button in the Save As dialog box to save the workbook.

Note: If you are using Windows XP, see Appendix F for alternate steps.

BTW

Rotating Text in a Cell
In Excel, you use the Alignment sheet of the Format Cells dialog box, as shown in Figure 3–5, to position data in a cell by centering, left-aligning, or right-aligning; indenting; aligning at the top, bottom, or center; and rotating. If you enter 90 in the Degrees box in the Orientation area, the text will appear vertically and read from bottom to top in the cell.

Rotating Text and Using the Fill Handle to Create a Series

The data on the worksheet, including month names and the What-If Assumptions section, now can be added to the worksheet.

Plan Ahead

Plan the layout of the worksheet.
The design of the worksheet calls specifically for only six months of data. Because there always will be only six months of data in the worksheet, the months should be placed across the top of the worksheet as column headings rather than as row headings. There are more data items regarding each month than there are months, and it is possible that more expense categories could be added in the future. A proper layout, therefore, includes placing the data items for each month as row headings. The What-If Assumptions section should be placed in an area of the worksheet that is easily accessible, yet does not impair the view of the main section of the worksheet. As shown in Figure 3–3a, the What-If Assumptions should be placed below the calculations in the worksheet.

When you first enter text, its angle is zero degrees (0°), and it reads from left to right in a cell. Text in a cell can be rotated counterclockwise by entering a number between 1° and 90° in the Alignment sheet in the Format Cells dialog box.

To Rotate Text and Use the Fill Handle to Create a Series of Month Names

Chapters 1 and 2 used the fill handle to copy a cell or a range of cells to adjacent cells. The fill handle also can be used to create a series of numbers, dates, or month names automatically. The following steps enter the month name, January, in cell B3; format cell B3 (including rotating the text); and then use the fill handle to enter the remaining month names in the range C3:G3.

1

- Select cell B3.

- Type January as the cell entry and then click the Enter box.

- Click the Format Cells: Alignment Dialog Box Launcher on the Ribbon to display the Format Cells dialog box (Figure 3– 4).

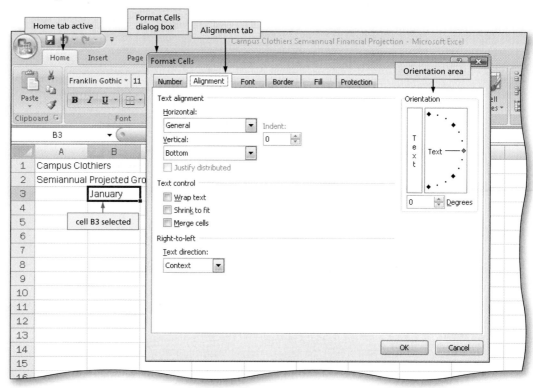

Figure 3–4

2

- Click the 45° point in the Orientation area to move the Text hand in the Orientation area to the 45° point and to display 45 in the Degrees box (Figure 3–5).

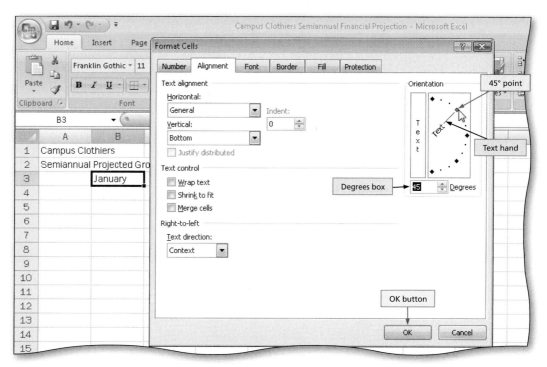

Figure 3–5

- Click the OK button to rotate the text in cell B3 at a 45° angle and automatically increase the height of row 3 to best fit the rotated text (Figure 3–6).

- Point to the fill handle on the lower-right corner of cell B3.

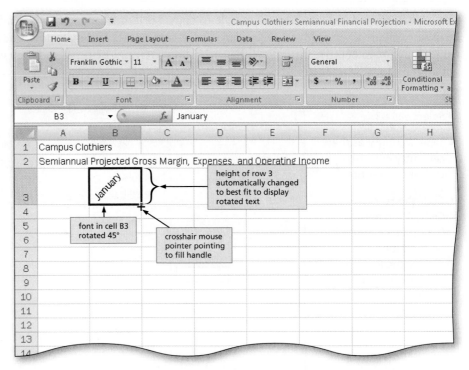

Figure 3–6

- Drag the fill handle to the right to select the range C3:G3. Do not release the mouse button (Figure 3–7).

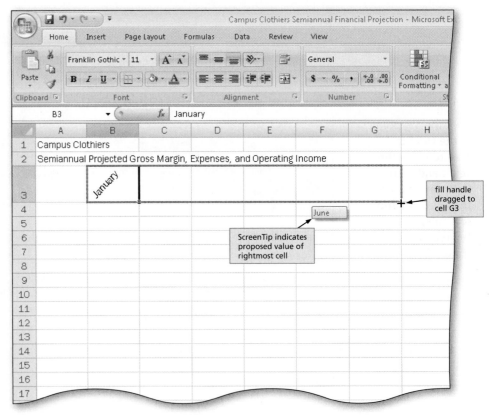

Figure 3–7

5

- Release the mouse button to create a month name series January through June in the range B3:G3 and copy the format in cell B3 to the range C3:G3.

- Click the Auto Fill Options button below the lower-right corner of the fill area to display the Auto Fill Options menu (Figure 3–8).

 Q&A What if I do not want to copy the format of cell B3 during the auto fill operation?

In addition to creating a series of values, dragging the fill handle instructs Excel to copy the format of cell B3 to the range C3:G3. With some fill operations, you may not want to copy the formats of the source cell or range to the destination cell or range. If this is the case, click the Auto Fill Options button after the range fills (Figure 3–8) and then select the option you desire on the Auto Fill Options menu.

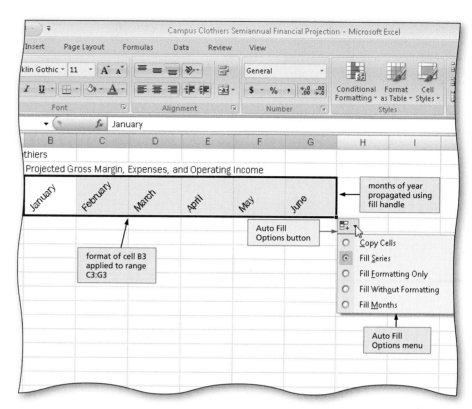

Figure 3–8

6

- Click the Auto Fill Options button to hide the Auto Fill Options menu.

- Click cell H3, type Total, and then press the RIGHT ARROW key.

Q&A Why is the word Total automatically formatted with the Heading 3 cell style and 45° rotation?

Excel tries to save you time by automatically recognizing the adjacent cell format in cell G3 and applying it to cell H3. The Heading 3 cell style in cell G3 causes this action to occur.

Using the Auto Fill Options Menu

As shown in Figure 3–8, Fill Series is the default option that Excel uses to fill the area, which means it fills the destination area with a series, using the same formatting as the source area. If you choose another option on the Auto Fill Options menu, then Excel immediately changes the contents of the destination range. Following the use of the fill handle, the Auto Fill Options button remains active until you begin the next Excel operation. Table 3–2 summarizes the options on the Auto Fill Options menu.

Other Ways

1. Enter start month in cell, apply formatting, right-drag fill handle in direction to fill, click Fill Months on shortcut menu

2. Enter start month in cell, apply formatting, select range, click Fill button on Home tab on Ribbon, click Series, click AutoFill

The Mighty Fill Handle
If you drag the fill handle to the left or up, Excel will decrement the series rather than increment the series. To copy a word, such as January or Monday, which Excel might interpret as the start of a series, hold down the CTRL key while you drag the fill handle to a destination area. If you drag the fill handle back into the middle of a cell, Excel erases the contents.

Table 3–2 Options Available on the Auto Fill Options Menu

Auto Fill Option	Description
Copy Cells	Fill destination area with contents using format of source area. Do not create a series.
Fill Series	Fill destination area with series using format of source area. This option is the default.
Fill Formatting Only	Fill destination area using format of source area. No content is copied unless fill is series.
Fill Without Formatting	Fill destination area with contents, without the formatting of source area.
Fill Months	Fill destination area with series of months using format of source area. Same as Fill Series and shows as an option only if source area contains a month.

You can use the fill handle to create a series longer than the one shown in Figure 3–8. If you drag the fill handle past cell G3 in Step 4, Excel continues to increment the months and logically will repeat January, February, and so on, if you extend the range far enough to the right.

You can create several different types of series using the fill handle. Table 3–3 illustrates several examples. Notice in examples 4 through 7, 9, and 11 that, if you use the fill handle to create a series of numbers or nonsequential months, you must enter the first item in the series in one cell and the second item in the series in an adjacent cell. Next, select both cells and drag the fill handle through the destination area.

Table 3–3 Examples of Series Using the Fill Handle

Example	Contents of Cell(s) Copied Using the Fill Handle	Next Three Values of Extended Series
1	2:00	3:00, 4:00, 5:00
2	Qtr3	Qtr4, Qtr1, Qtr2
3	Quarter 1	Quarter 2, Quarter 3, Quarter 4
4	5-Jan, 5-Mar	5-May, 5-Jul, 5-Sep
5	2007, 2008	2009, 2010, 2011
6	1, 2	3, 4, 5
7	430, 410	390, 370, 350
8	Sun	Mon, Tue, Wed
9	Sunday, Tuesday	Thursday, Saturday, Monday
10	4th Section	5th Section, 6th Section, 7th Section
11	−205, −208	−211, −214, −217

To Increase Column Widths and Enter Row Titles

In Chapter 2, the column widths were increased after the values were entered into the worksheet. Sometimes, you may want to increase the column widths before you enter the values and, if necessary, adjust them later. The following steps increase the column widths and then enter the row titles in column A down to What-If Assumptions in cell A18.

- Move the mouse pointer to the boundary between column heading A and column heading B so that the mouse pointer changes to a split double arrow.

- Drag the mouse pointer to the right until the ScreenTip displays, Width: 35.00 (322 pixels). Do not release the mouse button (Figure 3–9).

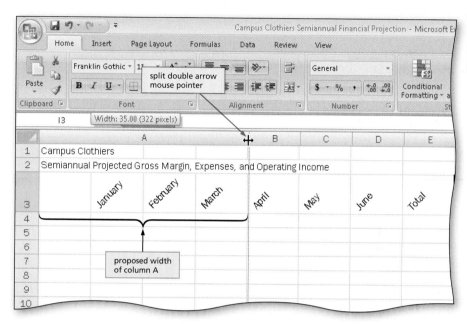

Figure 3–9

- Release the mouse button to change the width of column A.

- Click column heading B and then drag through column heading G to select columns B through G.

- Move the mouse pointer to the boundary between column headings B and C and then drag the mouse to the right until the ScreenTip displays, Width: 14.00 (133 pixels). Do not release the mouse button (Figure 3–10).

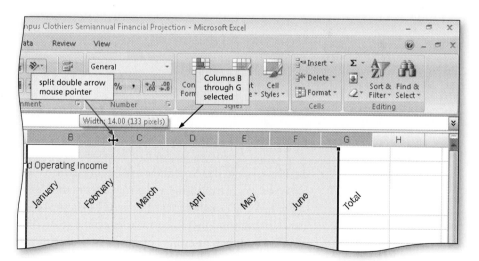

Figure 3–10

3

- Release the mouse button to change the width of columns B through G.

- Use the technique described in Step 1 to increase the width of column H to 15.00.

- Enter the row titles in the range A4:A18 as shown in Figure 3–11, but without the indents.

- Click cell A5 and then click the Increase Indent button on the Ribbon.

- Select the range A9:A13 and then click the Increase Indent button on the Ribbon.

- Click cell A19 to finish entering the row titles (Figure 3–11).

Q&A

What happens when I click the Increase Indent button?

The Increase Indent button indents the contents of a cell to the right by three spaces each time you click it. The Decrease Indent button decreases the indent by three spaces each time you click it.

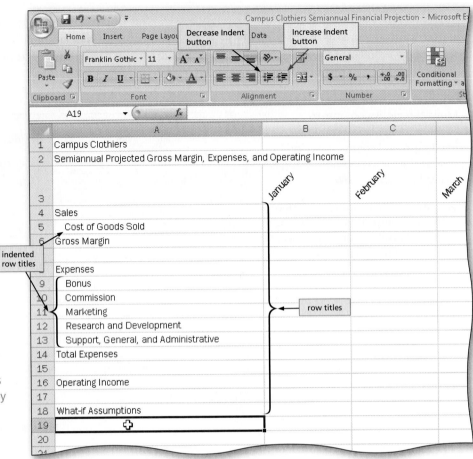

Figure 3–11

Other Ways

1. To indent, right-click range, click Format Cells on shortcut menu, click Alignment tab, click Left (Indent) in Horizontal list, type number of spaces to indent in Indent text box, click OK button

BTW

Fitting Entries in a Cell
An alternative to increasing the column widths or row heights is to shrink the characters in the cell to fit the current width of the column. To shrink to fit, click Format Cells: Alignment Dialog Box Launcher on the Ribbon, and click Shrink to fit in the Text control area. After shrinking entries to fit in a cell, consider using the Zoom slider on the status bar to make the entries more readable.

Copying a Range of Cells to a Nonadjacent Destination Area

As shown in the sketch of the worksheet (Figure 3–3a on page EX 166), the row titles in the Expenses area are the same as the row titles in the What-If Assumptions table, with the exception of the two additional entries in cells A21 (Margin) and A24 (Revenue for Bonus). Hence, the What-If Assumptions table row titles can be created by copying the range A9:A13 to the range A19:A23 and then inserting two rows for the additional entries in cells A21 and A24. The source area (range A9:A13) is not adjacent to the destination area (range A19:A23). The first two chapters used the fill handle to copy a source area to an adjacent destination area. To copy a source area to a nonadjacent destination area, however, you cannot use the fill handle.

A more versatile method of copying a source area is to use the Copy button and Paste button on the Home tab on the Ribbon. You can use these two buttons to copy a source area to an adjacent or nonadjacent destination area.

The Copy button copies the contents and format of the source area to the **Office Clipboard**, a reserved place in the computer's memory that allows you to collect text and graphic items from an Office document and then paste them into any Office document. The Copy command on the Edit menu or shortcut menu works the same as the Copy button. The Paste button copies the item from the Office Clipboard to the destination area.

To Copy a Range of Cells to a Nonadjacent Destination Area

The following steps use the Copy and Paste buttons to copy the range A9:A13 to the nonadjacent range A19:A23.

1

- Select the range A9:A13 and then click the Copy button on the Home tab on the Ribbon to copy the values and formats of the range A9:A13 to the Office Clipboard.

- Click cell A19, the top cell in the destination area (Figure 3–12).

Q&A

Why do I not need to select the entire destination area?

You are not required to select the entire destination area (range A19:A23) before clicking the Paste button. Excel needs to know only the upper-left cell of the destination area. In the case of a single column range, such as A19:A23, the top cell of the destination area (cell A19) also is the upper-left cell of the destination area.

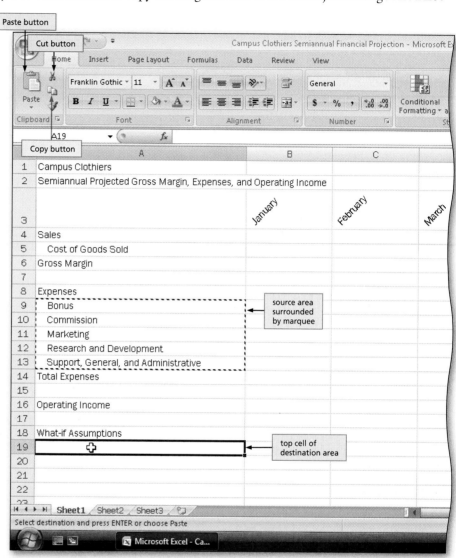

Figure 3–12

2

- Click the Paste button on the Ribbon to copy the values and formats of the last item placed on the Office Clipboard (range A9:A13) to the destination area A19:A23.

- Scroll down so row 5 appears at the top of the window (Figure 3–13).

Q&A

What if data already existed in the destination area?

When you complete a copy, the values and formats in the destination area are replaced with the values and formats of the source area. Any data contained in the destination area prior to the copy and paste is lost. If you accidentally delete valuable data, immediately click the Undo button on the Quick Access Toolbar.

3

- Press the ESC key to remove the marquee from the source area and disable the Paste button on the Ribbon.

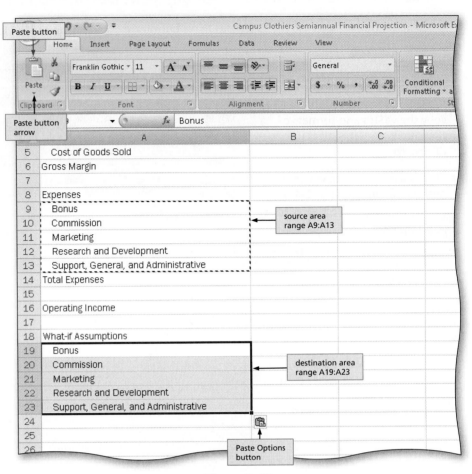

Figure 3–13

Other Ways

1. Right-click source area, click Copy on shortcut menu, right-click destination area, click Paste on shortcut menu

2. Select source area and point on border of range; while holding down CTRL key, drag source area to destination area

3. Select source area, press CTRL+C, select destination area, press CTRL+V

Using the Paste Options Menu

After the Paste button is clicked, Excel immediately displays the Paste Options button, as shown in Figure 3–13. If you click the Paste Options button arrow and select an option on the Paste Options menu, Excel modifies the most recent paste operation based on your selection. Table 3–4 summarizes the options available on the Paste Options menu.

Table 3–4 Options Available on the Paste Options Menu

Paste Option	Description
Keep Source Formatting	Copy contents and format of source area. This option is the default.
Match Destination Formatting	Copy contents of source area, but not the format.
Values and Number Formatting	Copy contents and format of source area for numbers or formulas, but use format of destination area for text.
Keep Source Column Widths	Copy contents and format of source area. Change destination column widths to source column widths.
Formatting Only	Copy format of source area, but not the contents.
Link Cells	Copy contents and format and link cells so that a change to the cells in source area updates the corresponding cells in destination area.

The Paste button on the Ribbon (Figure 3–13) includes an arrow, which displays a list of advanced paste options (Paste, Paste Special, and Paste as Hyperlink). These options will be discussed when they are used.

An alternative to clicking the Paste button is to press the ENTER key. The ENTER key completes the paste operation, removes the marquee from the source area, and disables the Paste button so that you cannot paste the copied source area to other destination areas. The ENTER key was not used in the previous set of steps so that the capabilities of the Paste Options button could be discussed. The Paste Options button does not appear on the screen when you use the ENTER key to complete the paste operation.

Using Drag and Drop to Move or Copy Cells

You also can use the mouse to move or copy cells. First, you select the source area and point to the border of the cell or range. You know you are pointing to the border of the cell or range when the mouse pointer changes to a block arrow. To move the selected cell or cells, drag the selection to the destination area. To copy a selection, hold down the CTRL key while dragging the selection to the destination area. You know Excel is in copy mode when a small plus sign appears next to the block arrow mouse pointer. Be sure to release the mouse button before you release the CTRL key. Using the mouse to move or copy cells is called **drag and drop**.

Using Cut and Paste to Move Cells

Another way to move cells is to select them, click the Cut button on the Ribbon (Figure 3–12 on page EX 175) to remove them from the worksheet and copy them to the Office Clipboard, select the destination area, and then click the Paste button on the Ribbon or press the ENTER key. You also can use the Cut command on the shortcut menu, instead of the Cut button.

Inserting and Deleting Cells in a Worksheet

At any time while the worksheet is on the screen, you can insert cells to enter new data or delete cells to remove unwanted data. You can insert or delete individual cells; a range of cells, rows, columns; or entire worksheets.

To Insert a Row

The Insert command on the shortcut menu allows you to insert rows between rows that already contain data. According to the sketch of the worksheet in Figure 3–3a on page EX 166, two rows must be inserted in the What-If Assumptions table, one between Commission and Marketing for the Margin assumption and another between Research and Development and Support, General, and Administrative for the Revenue for Bonus assumption. The following steps accomplish the task of inserting the new rows into the worksheet.

BTW

Move It or Copy It
You may hear someone say, "Move it or copy it, it's all the same." No, it is not the same! When you move a cell, the data in the original location is cleared and the format is reset to the default. When you copy a cell, the data and format of the copy area remain intact. In short, you should copy cells to duplicate entries and move cells to rearrange entries.

BTW

Cutting
When you cut a cell or range of cells using the Cut command or Cut button, Excel copies the cells to the Office Clipboard, but does not remove the cells from the source area until you paste the cells in the destination area by clicking the Paste button or pressing the ENTER key. When you complete the paste, Excel clears the cell entry and its formats from the source area.

BTW

Inserting Multiple Rows
If you want to insert multiple rows, you have two choices. First, you can insert a single row by using the Insert command on the shortcut menu and then repeatedly press F4 to keep inserting rows. Alternatively, you can select any number of existing rows before inserting new rows. For instance, if you want to insert five rows, select five existing rows in the worksheet, right-click the rows, and then click Insert on the shortcut menu.

• Right-click row heading 21, the row below where you want to insert a row, to display the shortcut menu and the Mini toolbar (Figure 3–14).

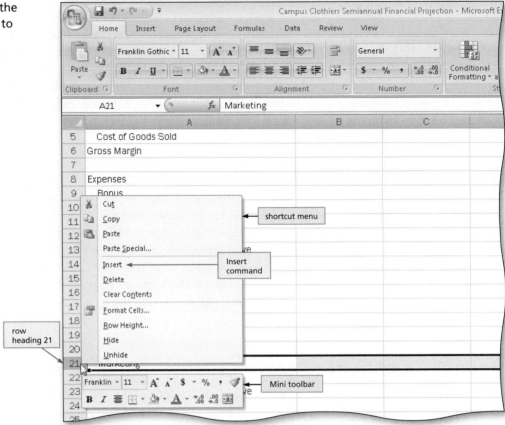

Figure 3–14

• Click Insert on the shortcut menu to insert a new row in the worksheet by shifting the selected row 21 and all rows below it down one row.

• Click cell A21 in the new row and then enter Margin as the row title (Figure 3–15).

Q&A

What is the resulting format of the new row?

The cells in the new row inherit the formats of the cells in the row above them. You can change this by clicking the Insert Options button that appears immediately above the inserted row. Following the insertion of a row, the Insert Options button lets you select from the following options: (1) Format Same As Above; (2) Format Same As Below; and (3) Clear Formatting. The Format Same as Above option is the default. The Insert Options button remains active until you begin the next Excel operation.

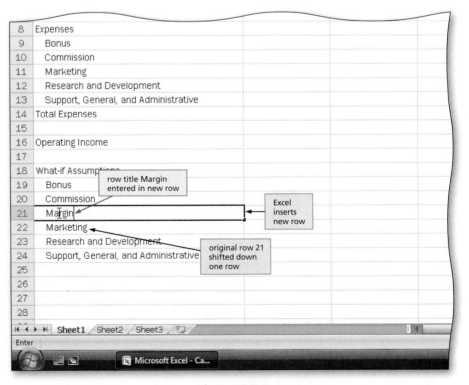

Figure 3–15

3

- Right-click row heading 24 and then click Insert on the shortcut menu to insert a new row in the worksheet.

- Click cell A24 in the new row and then enter Revenue for Bonus as the row title (Figure 3–16).

Q&A

What would happen if cells in the shifted rows are included in formulas?

If the rows that are shifted down include cell references in formulas located in the worksheet, Excel automatically adjusts the cell references in the formulas to their new locations. Thus, in Step 2, if a formula in the worksheet references a cell in row 21 before the insert, then the cell reference in the formula is adjusted to row 22 after the insert.

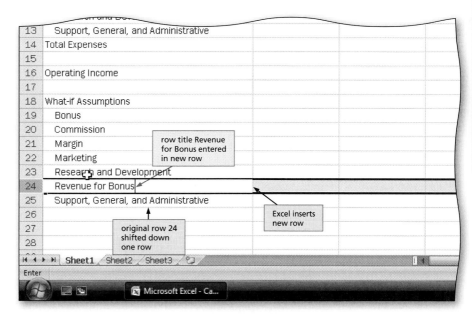

Figure 3–16

Other Ways

1. On Home tab on Ribbon, click Insert button arrow, click Insert Sheet Rows

2. Press CTRL+SHIFT+PLUS SIGN, click Entire Row, click OK button

Inserting Columns

You insert columns into a worksheet in the same way you insert rows. To insert columns, select one or more columns immediately to the right of where you want Excel to insert the new column or columns. Select the number of columns you want to insert. Next, click the Home tab on the Ribbon and then click Insert Sheet Rows in the Insert gallery or click Insert on the shortcut menu. The Insert command on the shortcut menu requires that you select an entire column (or columns) to insert a column (or columns). Following the insertion of a column, Excel displays the Insert Options button, which allows you to modify the insertion in a fashion similar to that discussed earlier when inserting rows.

Inserting Single Cells or a Range of Cells

The Insert command on the shortcut menu or the Insert Cells command on the Insert gallery of the Insert button on the Ribbon allows you to insert a single cell or a range of cells. You should be aware that if you shift a single cell or a range of cells, however, it no longer may be lined up with its associated cells. To ensure that the values in the worksheet do not get out of order, it is recommended that you insert only entire rows or entire columns. When you insert a single cell or a range of cells, Excel displays the Insert Options button so that you can change the format of the inserted cell, using options similar to those for inserting rows and columns.

BTW

Dragging Ranges
You can move and insert a selected cell or range between existing cells by holding down the SHIFT key while you drag the selection to the gridline where you want to insert. You also can copy and insert by holding down the CTRL+SHIFT keys while you drag the selection to the desired gridline.

BTW

The Insert Options Button
When you insert columns or rows, Excel only displays the Insert Options button if formats are assigned to the leftmost column or top row of the selection.

Deleting Columns and Rows

The Delete button on the Ribbon or the Delete command on the shortcut menu removes cells (including the data and format) from the worksheet. Deleting cells is not the same as clearing cells. The Clear command, which was described earlier in Chapter 1 on page EX 66, clears the data from the cells, but the cells remain in the worksheet. The Delete command removes the cells from the worksheet and shifts the remaining rows up (when you delete rows) or shifts the remaining columns to the left (when you delete columns). If formulas located in other cells reference cells in the deleted row or column, Excel does not adjust these cell references. Excel displays the error message **#REF!** in those cells to indicate a cell reference error. For example, if cell A7 contains the formula =A4+A5 and you delete row 5, Excel assigns the formula =A4+#REF! to cell A6 (originally cell A7) and displays the error message #REF! in cell A6. It also displays an Error Options button when you select the cell containing the error message #REF!, which allows you to select options to determine the nature of the problem.

Deleting Individual Cells or a Range of Cells

Although Excel allows you to delete an individual cell or range of cells, you should be aware that if you shift a cell or range of cells on the worksheet, it no longer may be lined up with its associated cells. For this reason, it is recommended that you delete only entire rows or entire columns.

Entering Numbers with Format Symbols

The next step in creating the Semiannual Financial Projection worksheet is to enter the what-if assumptions values in the range B19:B25. The numbers in the table can be entered and then formatted as in Chapters 1 and 2, or each one can be entered with format symbols. When a number is entered with a **format symbol**, Excel immediately displays it with the assigned format. Valid format symbols include the dollar sign ($), comma (,), and percent sign (%).

If you enter a whole number, it appears without any decimal places. If you enter a number with one or more decimal places and a format symbol, Excel displays the number with two decimal places. Table 3–5 illustrates several examples of numbers entered with format symbols. The number in parentheses in column 4 indicates the number of decimal places.

Table 3–5 Numbers Entered with Format Symbols			
Format Symbol	**Typed in Formula Bar**	**Displays in Cell**	**Comparable Format**
,	83,341	83,341	Comma (0)
	1,675.8	1,675.80	Comma (2)
$	$278	$278	Currency (0)
	$3818.54	$3,818.54	Currency (2)
	$45,612.3	$45,612.30	Currency (2)
%	23%	23%	Percent (0)
	97.50%	97.50%	Percent (2)
	39.833%	39.83%	Percent (2)

To Enter Numbers with Format Symbols

The following step enters the numbers in the What-If Assumptions table with format symbols.

1

• Enter 100,000.00 in cell B19, 3.25% in cell B20, 61.00% in cell B21, 9.00% in cell B22, 5.75% in cell B23, 4,750,000.00 in cell B24, and 17.00% in cell B25 to display the entries using a format based on the format symbols entered with the numbers (Figure 3–17).

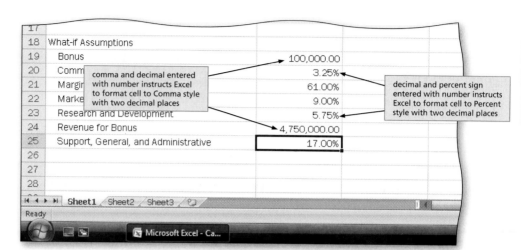

Figure 3–17

Other Ways

1. Right-click range, click Format Cells on shortcut menu, click Number tab, click category in Category list, [select desired format], click OK button

2. Press CTRL+1, click Number tab, click category in Category list, [select desired format], click OK button

---

Freezing Worksheet Titles

Freezing worksheet titles is a useful technique for viewing large worksheets that extend beyond the window. Normally, when you scroll down or to the right, the column titles in row 3 and the row titles in column A that define the numbers no longer appear on the screen. This makes it difficult to remember what the numbers in these rows and columns represent. To alleviate this problem, Excel allows you to **freeze the titles**, so that Excel displays the titles on the screen, no matter how far down or to the right you scroll.

BTW

Freezing Titles
If you want to freeze only column headings, select the appropriate cell in column A before you click the Freeze Panes button on the View tab on the Ribbon. If you only want to freeze row titles, then select the appropriate cell in row 1. To freeze both column headings and row titles, select the cell that is the intersection of the column and row titles before you click the Freeze Panes button on the View tab on the Ribbon.

To Freeze Column and Row Titles

The following steps use the Freeze Panes button on the View tab on the Ribbon to freeze the worksheet title and column titles in rows 1, 2, and 3, and the row titles in column A.

- Press CTRL+HOME to select cell A1 and ensure that Excel displays row 1 and column A on the screen.

- Select cell B4.

- Click the View tab on the Ribbon and then click the Freeze Panes button on the Ribbon to display the Freeze Panes gallery (Figure 3–18).

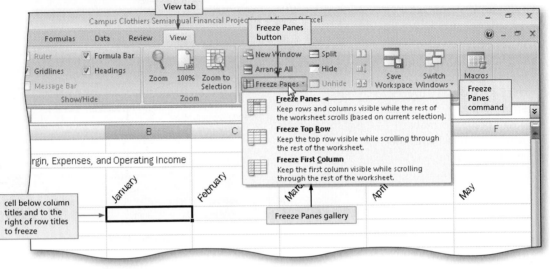

Figure 3–18

Q&A Why is cell A1 selected first?

Before freezing the titles, it is important that Excel displays cell A1 in the upper-left corner of the screen. For example, if cell B4 was selected without first selecting cell A1 to ensure Excel displays the upper-left corner of the screen, then Excel would freeze the titles and also hide rows 1 and 2. Excel thus would not be able to display rows 1 and 2 until they are unfrozen.

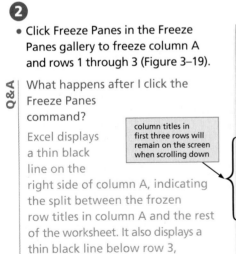

- Click Freeze Panes in the Freeze Panes gallery to freeze column A and rows 1 through 3 (Figure 3–19).

Q&A What happens after I click the Freeze Panes command?

Excel displays a thin black line on the right side of column A, indicating the split between the frozen row titles in column A and the rest of the worksheet. It also displays a thin black line below row 3, indicating the split between the frozen column titles in rows 1 through 3 and the rest of the worksheet (Figure 3–19).

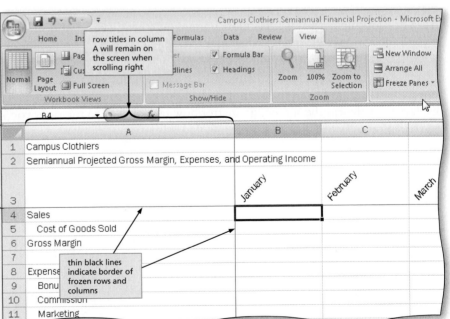

Figure 3–19

Other Ways
1. Press ALT+W, F

To Enter the Projected Monthly Sales

The following steps enter the projected monthly sales, listed earlier in Table 3–1 on page EX 167, in row 4 and compute the projected semiannual sales in cell H4.

1 If necessary, click the Home tab on the Ribbon.

2 Enter 3383909.82 in cell B4, 6880576.15 in cell C4, 9742702.37 in cell D4, 4818493.53 in cell E4, 4566722.63 in cell F4, and 8527504.39 in cell G4.

3 Click cell H4 and then click the Sum button on the Ribbon twice to total the semiannual sales in cell H4 (Figure 3–20).

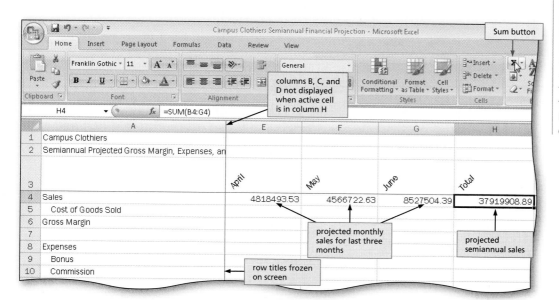

Figure 3–20

BTW

Your Age in Days
How many days have you been alive? Enter today's date (e.g., 12/5/2008) in cell A1. Next, enter your birth date (e.g., 6/22/1986) in cell A2. Select cell A3 and enter the formula =A1 - A2. Format cell A3 to the General style using the Number Dialog Box Launcher. Cell A3 will display your age in days.

Displaying a System Date

The sketch of the worksheet in Figure 3–3a on page EX 166 includes a date stamp on the right side of the heading section. A **date stamp** shows the date a workbook, report, or other document was created or the period it represents. In business, a report often is meaningless without a date stamp. For example, if a printout of the worksheet in this chapter were distributed to the company's analysts, the date stamp would show when the six-month projections were made, as well as what period the report represents.

A simple way to create a date stamp is to use the NOW function to enter the system date tracked by your computer in a cell in the worksheet. The **NOW function** is one of 14 date and time functions available in Excel. When assigned to a cell, the NOW function returns a number that corresponds to the system date and time beginning with December 31, 1899. For example, January 1, 1900 equals 1, January 2, 1900 equals 2, and so on. Noon equals .5. Thus, noon on January 1, 1900 equals 1.5 and 6 P.M. on January 1, 1900 equals 1.75. If the computer's system date is set to the current date, which normally it is, then the date stamp is equivalent to the current date.

Excel automatically formats this number as a date, using the date and time format, mm/dd/yyyy hh:mm, where the first mm is the month, dd is the day of the month, yyyy is the year, hh is the hour of the day, and mm is the minutes past the hour.

BTW

Updating the System Date and Time
If the system date and time appear in an active worksheet, Excel will not update the date and time in the cell until you enter data in another cell or complete some other activity, such as undoing a previous activity or pressing function key F9.

To Enter and Format the System Date

The following steps enter the NOW function and change the format from mm/dd/yyyy hh:mm to mm/dd/yyyy.

1

- Click cell H2 and then click the Insert Function box in the formula bar.

- When Excel displays the Insert Function dialog box, click the 'Or select a category' box arrow, and then select Date & Time in the list.

- Scroll down in the Select a function list and then click NOW (Figure 3–21).

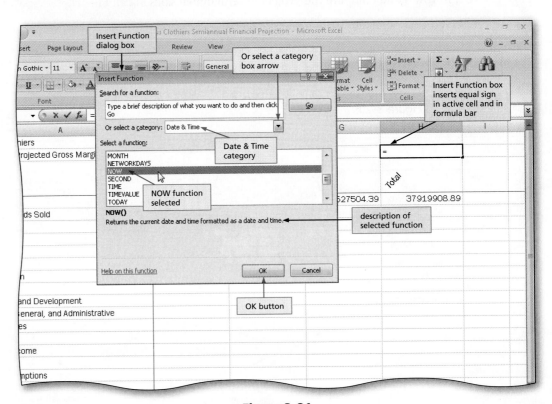

Figure 3–21

2

- Click the OK button.

- When Excel displays the Function Arguments dialog box, click the OK button to display the system date and time in cell H2, using the default date and time format mm/dd/yyyy hh:mm.

- Right-click cell H2 to display the shortcut menu (Figure 3–22).

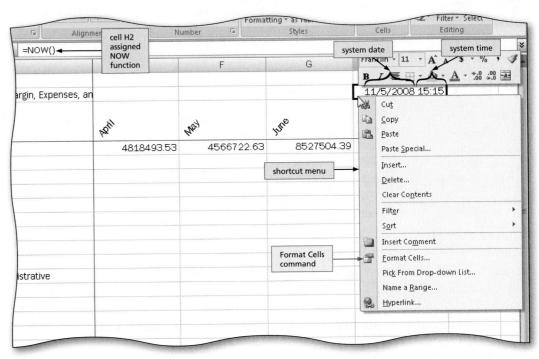

Figure 3–22

• Click Format Cells on the shortcut menu.

• When Excel displays the Format Cells dialog box, if necessary, click the Number tab.

• Click Date in the Category list. Scroll down in the Type list and then click 3/14/2001 to display a sample of the data in the active cell (H2) using the selected format in the Sample area (Figure 3–23).

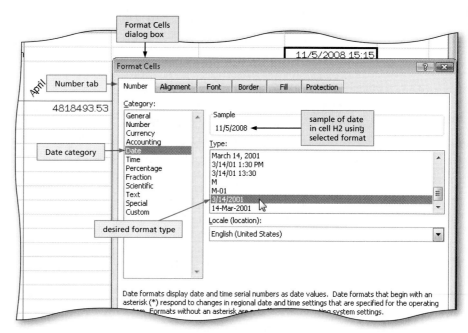

Figure 3–23

④

• Click the OK button in the Format Cells dialog box to display the system date in the form mm/dd/yyyy (Figure 3–24).

Q&A

How does Excel format a date?

In Figure 3–24, the date is displayed right-aligned in the cell because Excel treats a date as a number formatted to display as a date. If you assign the General format (Excel's default format for numbers) to a date in a cell, the date is displayed as a number with two decimal places. For example, if the system time and date is 6:00 PM on December 28, 2007 and the cell containing the NOW function is assigned the General format, then Excel displays the following number in the cell:

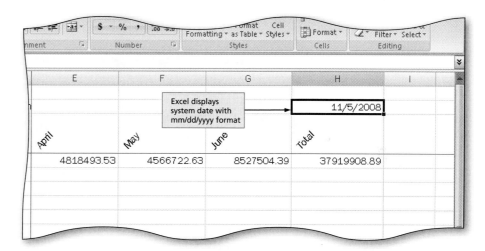

Figure 3–24

39444.75

Number of days since   time of day is 6:00 PM
December 31, 1899   (portion of day complete)

The whole number portion of the number (39444) represents the number of days since December 31, 1899. The decimal portion of the number (.75) represents 6:00 PM as the time of day, at which point 3/4 of the day is complete. To assign the General format to a cell, click General in the Category list in the Format Cells dialog box (Figure 3–23).

Other Ways

1. On Formulas tab on Ribbon, click Date & Time, click NOW
2. Press CTRL+SEMICOLON (not a volatile date)
3. Press CTRL+SHIFT+# to format date to day-month-year

Absolute versus Relative Addressing

The next sections describe the formulas and functions needed to complete the calculations in the worksheet.

Plan Ahead

> **Determine necessary formulas and functions needed.**
> The next step is to enter the formulas that calculate the following values for January: cost of goods sold (cell B5), gross margin (cell B6), expenses (range B9:B13), total expenses (cell B14), and the operating income (cell B16). The formulas are based on the projected monthly sales in cell B4 and the assumptions in the range B19:B25.
>
> The formulas for each column (month) are the same, except for the reference to the projected monthly sales in row 4, which varies according to the month (B4 for January, C4 for February, and so on). Thus, the formulas for January can be entered in column B and then copied to columns C through G. Table 3–6 shows the formulas for determining the January costs of goods, gross margin, expenses, total expenses, and operating income in column B.
>
> If the formulas are entered as shown in Table 3–6 in column B for January and then copied to columns C through G (February through June) in the worksheet, Excel will adjust the cell references for each column automatically. Thus, after the copy, the February Commission expense in cell C10 would be =C4 * C20. While the cell reference C4 (February Sales) is correct, the cell reference C20 references an empty cell. The formula for cell C10 should read =C4 * B20, rather than =C4 * C20, because B20 references the Commission % value in the What-If Assumptions table. In this instance, a way is needed to keep a cell reference in a formula the same, or constant, when it is copied.

Table 3–6 Formulas for Determining Cost of Goods, Margin, Expenses, Total Expenses, and Operating Income for January			
Cell	**Row Title**	**Formula**	**Comment**
B5	Cost of Goods Sold	=B4 * (1 − B21)	Sales times (1 minus Margin %)
B6	Gross Margin	= B4 − B5	Sales minus Cost of Goods
B9	Bonus	=IF(B4 >= B24, B19, 0)	Bonus equals value in B19 or 0
B10	Commission	=B4 * B20	Sales times Commission %
B11	Marketing	=B4 * B22	Sales times Marketing %
B12	Research and Development	=B4 * B23	Sales times Research and Development %
B13	Support, General, and Administrative	=B4 * B25	Sales times Support, General, and Administrative %
B14	Total Expenses	=SUM(B9:B13)	Sum of January Expenses
B16	Operating Income	=B6 − B14	Gross Margin minus Total Expense

BTW

Absolute Referencing
Absolute referencing is one of the more difficult worksheet concepts to understand. One point to keep in mind is that the paste operation is the only operation affected by an absolute cell reference. An absolute cell reference instructs the paste operation to keep the same cell reference as it copies a formula from one cell to another.

To keep a cell reference constant when copying a formula or function, Excel uses a technique called absolute cell referencing. To specify an absolute cell reference in a formula, enter a dollar sign ($) before any column letters or row numbers you want to keep constant in formulas you plan to copy. For example, $B$20 is an absolute cell reference, while B20 is a relative cell reference. Both reference the same cell. The difference becomes apparent when they are copied to a destination area. A formula using the **absolute cell reference** $B$20 instructs Excel to keep the cell reference B20 constant (absolute) in the formula as it copies it to the destination area. A formula using the **relative cell reference** B20 instructs Excel to adjust the cell reference as it copies it to the destination area. A cell reference with only one dollar sign before either the column or the row is called a **mixed cell reference**. Table 3–7 gives some additional examples of absolute, relative, and mixed cell references.

Table 3–7 Examples of Absolute, Relative, and Mixed Cell References

Cell Reference	Type of Reference	Meaning
$B$20	Absolute cell reference	Both column and row references remain the same when you copy this cell, because the cell references are absolute.
B$20	Mixed reference	This cell reference is mixed. The column reference changes when you copy this cell to another column because it is relative. The row reference does not change because it is absolute.
$B20	Mixed reference	This cell reference is mixed. The column reference does not change because it is absolute. The row reference changes when you copy this cell reference to another row because it is relative.
B20	Relative cell reference	Both column and row references are relative. When copied to another cell, both the column and row in the cell reference are adjusted to reflect the new location.

To Enter a Formula Containing Absolute Cell References

The following steps enter the cost of goods formula = B4*(1 − $B$21) in cell B5 using Point mode. To enter an absolute cell reference, you can type the dollar sign ($) as part of the cell reference or enter it by pressing F4 with the insertion point in or to the right of the cell reference to change to absolute.

1

- Press CTRL+HOME and then click cell B5.

- Type = (equal sign), click cell B4, type *(1−b21 and then press F4 to change b21 from a relative cell reference to an absolute cell reference.

- Type) to complete the formula (Figure 3–25).

Q&A

Is an absolute reference required in this formula?

No, because a mixed cell reference could have been used. The formula in cell B4 will be copied across columns, rather than down rows. So, the formula entered in cell B4 in Step 1 could have been entered as =B4*(1-$B21), rather than =B4*(1-$B$21). That is, the formula could have included the mixed cell reference $B21, rather than the absolute cell reference $B$21. When you copy a formula across columns, the row does not change anyway. The key is to ensure that column B remains constant as you copy the formula across rows. To change the absolute cell reference to a mixed cell reference, continue to press the F4 key until you get the desired cell reference.

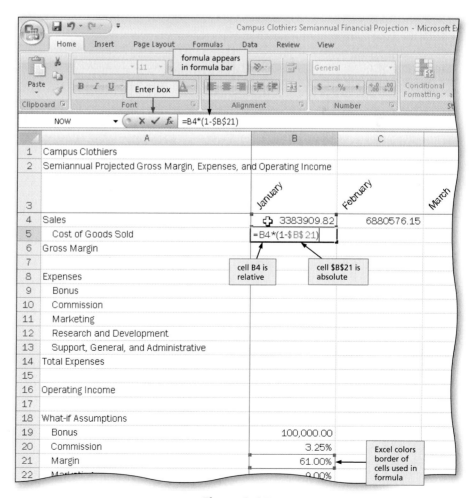

Figure 3–25

2

- Click the Enter box in the formula bar to display the result, 1319724.83, in cell B5, instead of the formula (Figure 3–26).

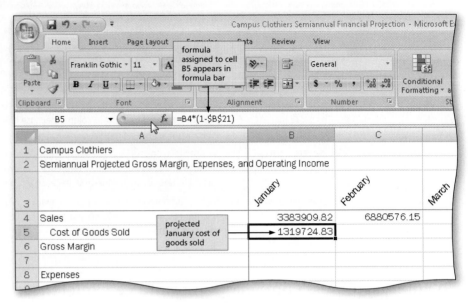

Figure 3–26

3

- Click cell B6, type = (equal sign), click cell B4, type − (minus sign), and then click cell B5.

- Click the Enter box in the formula bar to display the gross margin for January, 2064184.99, in cell B6 (Figure 3-27).

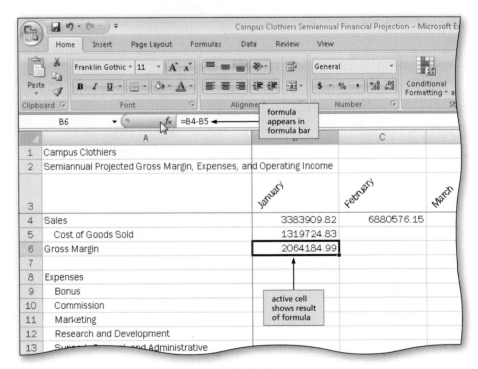

Figure 3–27

Making Decisions — The IF Function

According to the Request for New Workbook in Figure 3–2 on page EX 164, if the projected January sales in cell B4 is greater than or equal to the revenue for bonus in cell B24 (4,750,000.00), then the January bonus value in cell B9 is equal to the bonus value in cell B19 (100,000.00); otherwise, cell B9 is equal to 0. One way to assign the January bonus value in cell B9 is to check to see if the sales in cell B4 equal or exceed the revenue for bonus amount in cell B24 and, if so, then to enter 100,000.00 in cell B9. You can use this manual process for all six months by checking the values for the corresponding month.

Because the data in the worksheet changes each time a report is prepared or the figures are adjusted, however, it is preferable to have Excel assign the monthly bonus to the entries in the appropriate cells automatically. To do so, cell B9 must include a formula or function that displays 100,000.00 or 0.00 (zero), depending on whether the projected January sales in cell B4 is greater than, equal to, or less than the revenue for bonus value in cell B24.

The **IF function** is useful when you want to assign a value to a cell based on a logical test. For example, using the IF function, cell B9 can be assigned the following IF function:

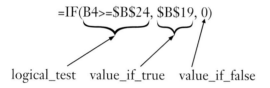

logical_test   value_if_true   value_if_false

The IF function instructs Excel that, if the projected January sales in cell B4 is greater than or equal to the revenue for bonus value in cell B24, then Excel should display the value 100000 in cell B19, in cell B9. If the projected January sales in cell B4 is less than the revenue for bonus value in cell B24, then Excel displays a 0 (zero) in cell B9.

The general form of the IF function is:

$$=IF(logical\_test, value\_if\_true, value\_if\_false)$$

The argument, logical_test, is made up of two expressions and a comparison operator. Each expression can be a cell reference, a number, text, a function, or a formula. Valid comparison operators, their meaning, and examples of their use in IF functions are shown in Table 3–8. The argument, value_if_true, is the value you want Excel to display in the cell when the logical test is true. The argument, value_if_false, is the value you want Excel to display in the cell when the logical test is false.

Table 3–8 Comparison Operators		
Comparison Operator	**Meaning**	**Example**
=	Equal to	=IF(H7 = 0, J6 ^ H4, L9 + D3)
<	Less than	=IF(C34 * W3 < K7, $K$6, L33 - 5)
>	Greater than	=IF(MIN(K8:K12) > 75, 1, 0)
>=	Greater than or equal to	=IF(P8 >= $H$6, J7 / V4, 7.5)
<=	Less than or equal to	=IF(G7 - G2 <= 23, L$9, 35 / Q2)
<>	Not equal to	=IF(B1 <> 0, "No","Yes")

BTW

Logical Operators in IF Functions
IF functions can use logical operators, such as AND, OR, and NOT. For example, the three IF functions =IF(AND(B3>C3, D3<C5), "OK", "Not OK") and =IF(OR(C3>G5, D2<X3), "OK", "Not OK") and =IF(NOT(A6<H7), "OK", "Not OK") use logical operators. In the first example, both logical tests must be true for the value_if_true OK to be assigned to the cell. In the second example, one or the other logical tests must be true for the value_if_true OK to be assigned to the cell. In the third example, the logical test A6<H7 must be false for the value_if_true OK to be assigned to the cell.

To Enter an IF Function

The following steps assign the IF function =IF(B4>=$B$24,$B$19,0) to cell B9. This IF function determines whether or not the worksheet assigns a bonus for January.

1
- Click cell B9. Type `=if(b4>=$b$24, $b$19,0)` in the cell (Figure 3–28).

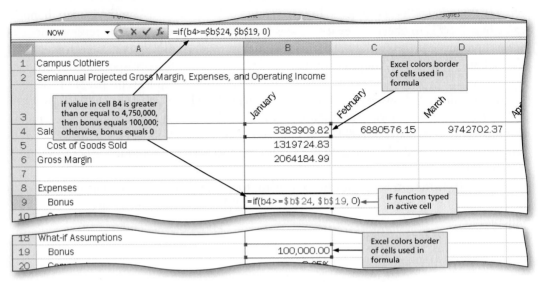

Figure 3–28

2
- Click the Enter box in the formula bar to display 0 in cell B9 (Figure 3–29), because the value in cell B4 (3383909.82) is less than the value in cell B24 (4,750,000) (Figure 3–29).

Q&A

Why does the value 0 display in cell B9?

The value that Excel displays in cell B9 depends on the values assigned to cells B4, B19, and B24. For example, if the value for January sales in cell B4 is reduced below 4,750,000.00, then the IF function in cell B9 will cause Excel to display a 0. If you change the bonus in cell B19 from 100,000.00 to another number and the value in cell B4 is greater than or equal to the value in cell B24, it will change the results in cell B9 as well. Finally, increasing the revenue for bonus in cell B24 so that it is greater than the value in cell B4 will change the result in cell B9.

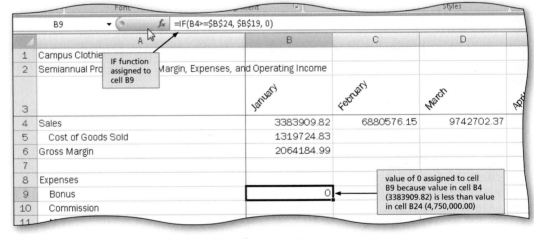

Figure 3–29

Other Ways

1. On Formulas tab on Ribbon, click Logical button, click IF
2. Click Insert Function box in formula bar, click Logical in 'Or select a category list', click IF in drop-down list, click OK button

To Enter the Remaining January Formulas

The January commission expense in cell B10 is equal to the sales in cell B4 times the commission assumption in cell B20 (3.25%). The January marketing expense in cell B11 is equal to the projected January sales in cell B4 times the marketing assumption in cell B22 (9.00%). Similar formulas determine the remaining January expenses in cells B12 and B13.

The total expenses value in cell B14 is equal to the sum of the expenses in the range B9:B13. The operating income in cell B16 is equal to the gross margin in cell B6 minus the total expenses in cell B14. The formulas are short, and therefore, they are typed in the following steps, rather than entered using Point mode.

1 Click cell B10. Type =b4*b20 and then press the DOWN ARROW key. Type =b4*b22 and then press the DOWN ARROW key. Type =b4*b23 and then press the DOWN ARROW key. Type =b4*b25 and then press the DOWN ARROW key.

2 With cell B14 selected, click the Sum button on the Home tab on the Ribbon twice. Click cell B16. Type =b6-b14 and then press the ENTER key (Figure 3–30a).

3 Press CTRL+ACCENT MARK (`) to instruct Excel to display the formulas version of the worksheet (Figure 3–30b).

4 When you are finished viewing the formulas version, press CTRL+ACCENT MARK (`) to instruct Excel to display the values version of the worksheet.

Q&A Why should I view the formulas version of the worksheet?

Viewing the formulas version (Figure 3–30b) of the worksheet allows you to check the formulas assigned to the range B5:B16. Recall that formulas were entered in lowercase. You can see that Excel converts all the formulas from lowercase to uppercase.

BTW

Replacing a Formula with a Constant
You can replace a formula with its result so it remains constant. Do the following: (1) Click the cell with the formula; (2) press F2 or click in the formula bar; (3) press F9 to display the value in the formula bar; and (4) press the ENTER key.

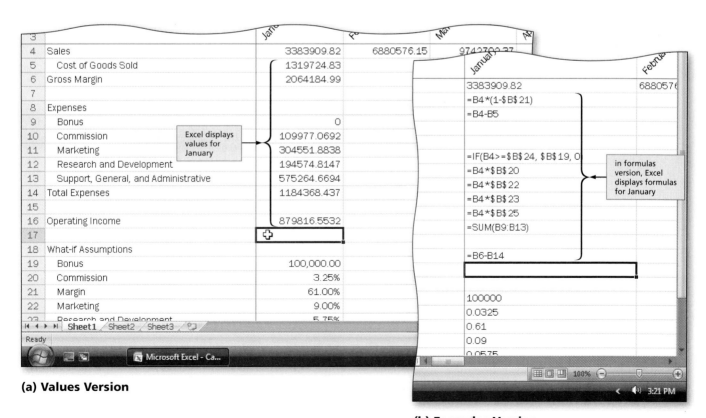

(a) Values Version

(b) Formulas Version

Figure 3–30

To Copy Formulas with Absolute Cell References Using the Fill Handle

The following steps show how to use the fill handle to copy the January formulas in column B to the other five months in columns C through G.

- Select the range B5:B16 and then point to the fill handle in the lower-right corner of cell B16 (Figure 3–31).

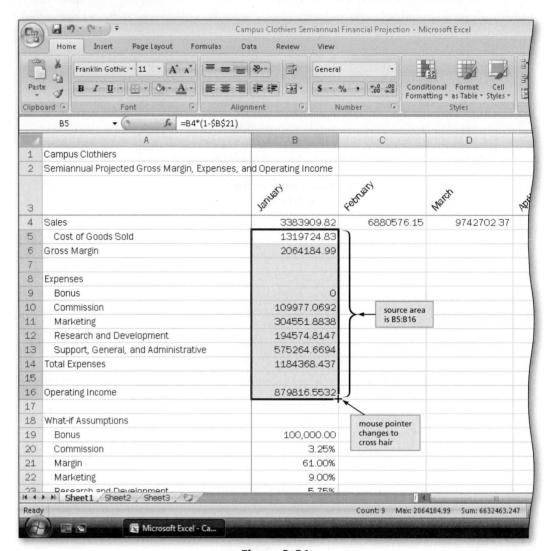

Figure 3–31

or Messages

en Excel cannot
:ulate a formula, it
plays an error message
a cell. These error
ssages always begin
h a number sign (#).
more commonly
urring error messages
: #DIV/0! (tries to
ide by zero); #NAME?
es a name Excel does
t recognize); #N/A
fers to a value not
ilable); #NULL!
ecifies an invalid
ersection of two
as); #NUM! (uses a
mber incorrectly); #REF
fers to a cell that is
t valid); #VALUE! (uses
incorrect argument
operand); and #####
ll not wide enough to
play entire entry).

To Determine Row Totals in Nonadjacent Cells

The following steps determine the row totals in column H. To determine the row totals using the Sum button, select only the cells in column H containing numbers in adjacent cells to the left. If, for example, you select the range H5:H16, Excel will display 0s as the sum of empty rows in cells H7, H8, and H15.

1 Select the range H5:H6. Hold down the CTRL key and select the range H9:H14 and cell H16 as shown in Figure 3–33.

2 Click the Sum button on the Ribbon to display the row totals in column H (Figure 3–33).

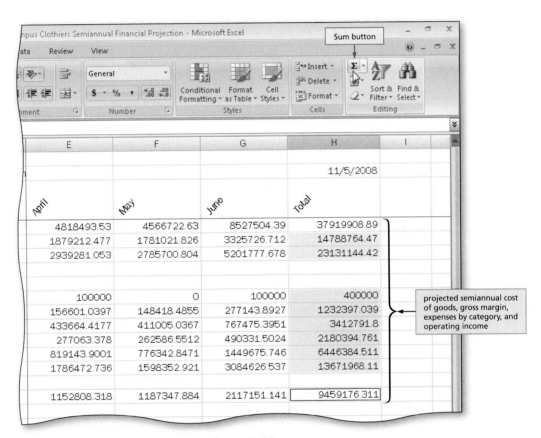

Figure 3–33

ggle Commands

any of the commands
the Ribbon, in
e galleries, and the
ortcut keys function as
toggle. For example,
you click the Freeze
anes command on the
eeze Panes gallery, the
mmand changes to
nfreeze Panes the next
me you view the gallery.
hese types of commands
ork like an on-off
vitch, or toggle.

To Unfreeze the Worksheet Titles and Save the Workbook

All the text, data, and formulas have been entered into the worksheet. The following steps unfreeze the titles and save the workbook using its current file name, Campus Clothiers Semiannual Financial Projection.

1 Press CTRL+HOME to select cell B4 and view the upper-left corner of the screen.

2 Click the View tab on the Ribbon and then click the Freeze Panes button on the Ribbon to display the Freeze Panes gallery (Figure 3–34).

3 Click Unfreeze Panes in the Freeze Panes gallery to unfreeze the titles.

2

- Drag the fill handle to the right to select the destination area C5:G16 to copy the formulas from the source area (B5:B16) to the destination area (C5:G16) and display the calculated amounts and Auto Fill Options button (Figure 3–32).

Q&A

What happens to the formulas after the copy is made?

Because the formulas in the range B5:B16 use absolute cell references, the formulas still refer to the current values in the Assumptions table when the formulas are copied to the range C5:G16.

Q&A

What happened to columns B, C, and D?

As shown in Figure 3–32, as the fill handle is dragged to the right, columns B, C, and D no longer appear on the screen. Column A, however, remains on the screen, because the row titles were frozen earlier in this chapter.

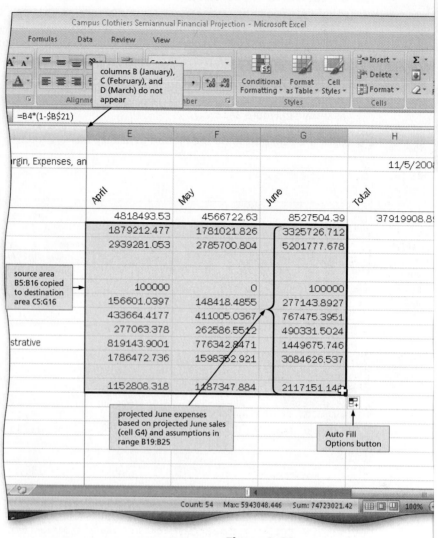

Figure 3–32

④ Click the Home tab on the Ribbon and then click the Save button on the Quick Access Toolbar.

Q&A

Why does pressing CTRL+HOME select cell B4?

When the titles are frozen and you press CTRL+HOME, Excel selects the upper-left cell of the unfrozen section of the worksheet. For example, in Step 1 of the previous steps, Excel selected cell B4. When the titles are unfrozen, then pressing CTRL+HOME selects cell A1.

BTW

Work Days
Assume that you have two dates: one in cell F3 and the other in cell F4. The date in cell F3 is your starting date and the date in cell F4 is the ending date. To calculate the work days between the two dates (excludes weekends), use the following formula: =NETWORKDAYS(F3, F4). For this function to work, make sure the Analysis ToolPak add-in is installed. You can install it on the Add-Ins page of the Excel Options dialog box.

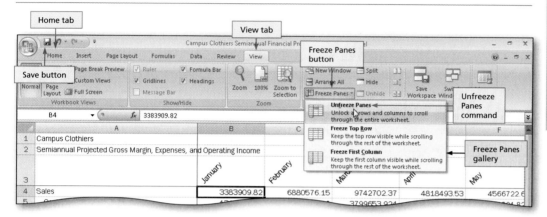

Figure 3–34

Nested Forms of the IF Function

A **nested IF function** is one in which the action to be taken for the true or false case includes yet another IF function. The second IF function is considered to be nested, or layered, within the first. Study the nested IF function below, which determines the eligibility of a person to vote. Assume the following in this example: (1) the nested IF function is assigned to cell K12, which instructs Excel to display one of three messages in the cell; (2) cell H12 contains a person's age; and (3) cell I12 contains a Y or N, based on whether the person is registered to vote.

=IF(H12>=18, IF(I12="Y","Registered","Eligible and Not Registered"),"Not Eligible to Register")

The nested IF function instructs Excel to display one, and only one, of the following three messages in cell K12: (1) Registered; or (2) Eligible and Not Registered; or (3) Not Eligible to Register.

You can nest IF functions as deep as you want, but after you get beyond a nest of three IF functions, the logic becomes difficult to follow and alternative solutions, such as the use of multiple cells and simple IF functions, should be considered.

BTW

Using IFERROR
Similar to the IF function, the IFERROR function checks a formula for correctness. For example, =IFERROR(Formula, "Message") examines the Formula argument. If an error appears (such as #DIV/0!), Excel displays the Message text instead of the Excel error.

Formatting the Worksheet

The worksheet created thus far shows the financial projections for the six-month period, from January to June. Its appearance is uninteresting, however, even though some minimal formatting (formatting assumptions numbers, changing the column widths, and formatting the date) was performed earlier. This section will complete the formatting of the worksheet to make the numbers easier to read and to emphasize the titles, assumptions, categories, and totals.

Plan
Ahead

Identify how to format various elements of the worksheet.
The worksheet will be formatted in the following manner so it appears as shown in Figure 3–35: (1) format the numbers; (2) format the worksheet title, column titles, row titles, and operating income row; and (3) format the assumptions table. Numbers in heading rows and total rows should be formatted with a currency symbol. Other dollar amounts should be formatted with a Comma style. The assumptions table should be diminished in its formatting so it does not distract from the main calculations and data in the worksheet. Assigning the data in the assumptions table a font size of 8 point would set it apart from other data formatted with a font size of 11 point.

Selecting Nonadjacent Ranges
One of the more difficult tasks to learn is selecting nonadjacent ranges. To complete this task, do not hold down the CTRL key when you select the first range because Excel will consider the current active cell to be the first selection. Once the first range is selected, hold down the CTRL key and drag through the nonadjacent ranges. If a desired range is not visible in the window, use the scroll arrows to view the range. It is not necessary to hold down the CTRL key while you scroll.

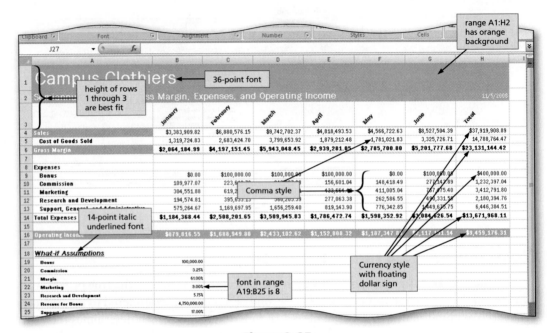

Figure 3–35

To Assign Formats to Nonadjacent Ranges

The numbers in the range B4:H16 are to be formatted as follows:
1. Assign the Currency style with a floating dollar sign to rows 4, 6, 9, 14, and 16.
2. Assign a Comma style to rows 5 and 10 through 13.

To assign a Currency style with a floating dollar sign, use the Format Cells dialog box rather than the Accounting Style button on the Ribbon, which assigns a fixed dollar sign. Also use the Format Cells dialog box to assign the Comma style, because the Comma Style button on the Ribbon assigns a format that displays a dash (-) when a cell has a value of 0. The specifications for this worksheet call for displaying a value of 0 as 0.00 (see cell B9 in Figure 3–35), rather than as a dash. To create a Comma style using the Format Cells dialog box, you can assign a Currency style with no dollar sign. The following steps assign formats to the numbers in rows 4 through 16.

1

- Select the range B4:H4.

- While holding down the CTRL key, select the nonadjacent ranges B6:H6, B9:H9, B14:H14, and B16:H16, and then release the CTRL key.

- Click the Format Cells: Number Dialog Box Launcher on the Ribbon to display the Format Cells dialog box (Figure 3–36).

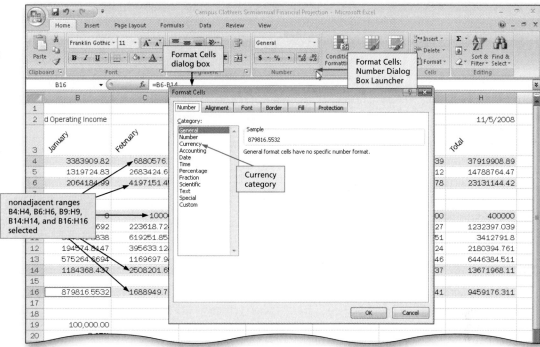

Figure 3–36

2

- Click Currency in the Category list, select 2 in the Decimal places box, click $ in the Symbol list to ensure a dollar sign shows, and click the black font color ($1,234.10) in the Negative numbers list (Figure 3–37).

Q&A

Why was the particular style chosen for the negative numbers?

In accounting, negative numbers often are shown with parentheses surrounding the value rather than with a negative sign preceding the value. Thus, the format (1,234.10) in the Negative numbers list was clicked. The data being used in this chapter contains no negative numbers. However, you must select a format for negative numbers, and you must be consistent if you are choosing different formats in a column, otherwise the decimal points may not line up.

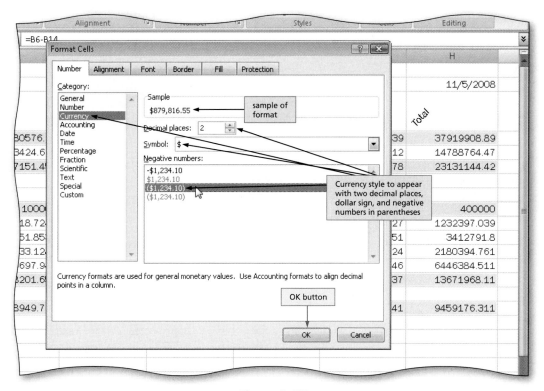

Figure 3–37

3

- Click the OK button.

- Select the range B5:H5.

- While holding down the CTRL key, select the range B10:H13, and then release the CTRL key.

- Click the Format Cells: Number Dialog Box Launcher on the Ribbon to display the Format Cells dialog box.

- When Excel displays the Format Cells dialog box, click Currency in the Category list, select 2 in the Decimal places box, click None in the Symbol list so a dollar sign does not show, and click the black font color (1,234.10) in the Negative numbers list (Figure 3–38).

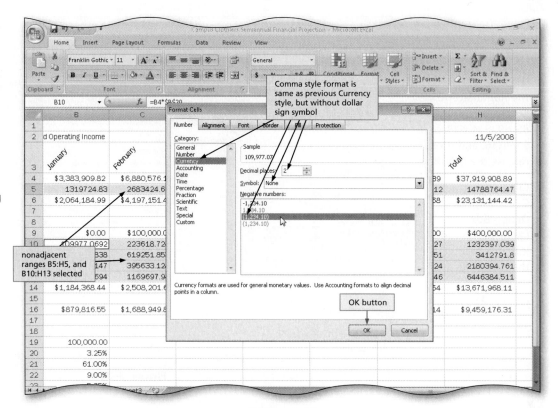

Figure 3–38

4

- Click the OK button.

- Press CTRL+HOME to select cell A1 to display the formatted numbers as shown in Figure 3–39.

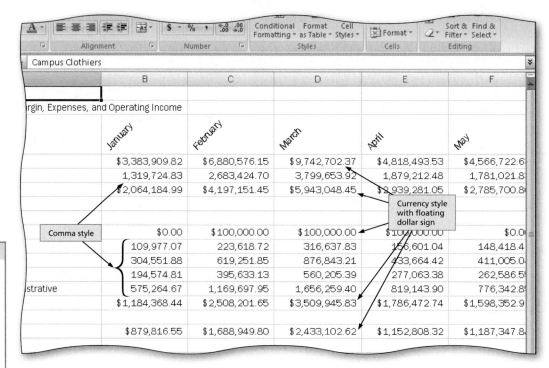

Figure 3–39

Other Ways

1. Right-click range, click Format Cells on shortcut menu, click Number tab, click category in Category list, select format, click OK button

2. Press CTRL+1, click Number tab, click category in Category list, select format, click OK button

To Format the Worksheet Titles

The following steps emphasize the worksheet titles in cells A1 and A2 by changing the font type, size, and color. The steps also format all of the row headers in column A with a Bold font style.

- Click the column A heading to select column A.

- Click the Bold button on the Ribbon to bold all of the data in column A (Figure 3–40).

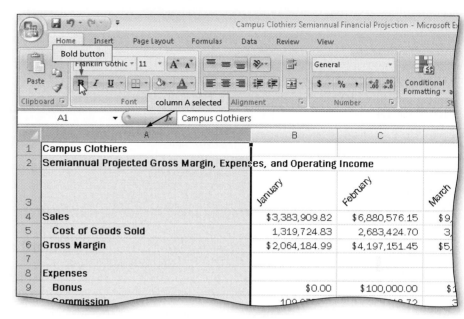

Figure 3–40

2

- Click cell A1 to select it. Click the Font Size box arrow on the Ribbon, and then click 36 in the Font Size list.

- Click cell A2, click the Font Size box arrow, and then click 18 in the Font Size list (Figure 3–41).

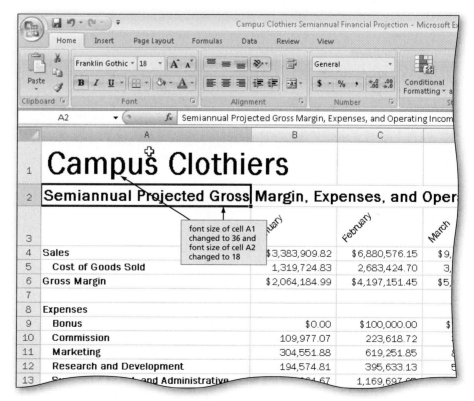

Figure 3–41

3

- Select the range A1:H2 and then click the Fill Color button arrow on the Ribbon.

- Click Orange, Accent 1 (column 5, row 1) on the Fill Color palette.

- Click the Font Color button arrow on the Ribbon and then select White, Background 1 (column 1, row 1) on the Font Color palette (Figure 3–42).

Figure 3–42

Other Ways

1. Right-click range, click Format Cells on shortcut menu, click Fill tab to color background (or click Font tab to color font), click OK button

2. Press CTRL+1, click Fill tab to color background (or click Font tab to color font), click OK button

To Assign Cell Styles to Nonadjacent Rows and Colors to a Cell

The next step to improving the appearance of the worksheet is to format the heading in row 3 and the totals in rows 4, 14, and 16. The following steps format the heading in row 3 with the Heading 3 cell style and the totals in rows 4, 14, and 16 with the Total cell style. Cell A4 also is formatted.

1 Select the range A3:H3 and apply the Heading 3 cell style.

2 Select the range A6:H6 and while holding down the CTRL key, select the ranges A14:H14 and A16:H16.

3 Apply the Total cell style.

4 Click cell A4, click the Fill Color button arrow on the Ribbon, and then click the Orange, Accent 1 color (column 5, row 1) on the Fill Color palette.

5 Click the Font Color button arrow on the Ribbon, and then click the White, Background 1 color (column 1, row 1) on the Font Color palette (Figure 3–43).

BTW

The Fill and Font Color Button
You may have noticed that the color bar at the bottom of the Fill Color and Font Color buttons on the Home tab on the Ribbon (Figure 3-42) changes to the most recently selected color. To apply this same color to a cell background or text, select a cell and then click the Fill Color button to use the color as a background or click the Font Color button to use the color as a font color.

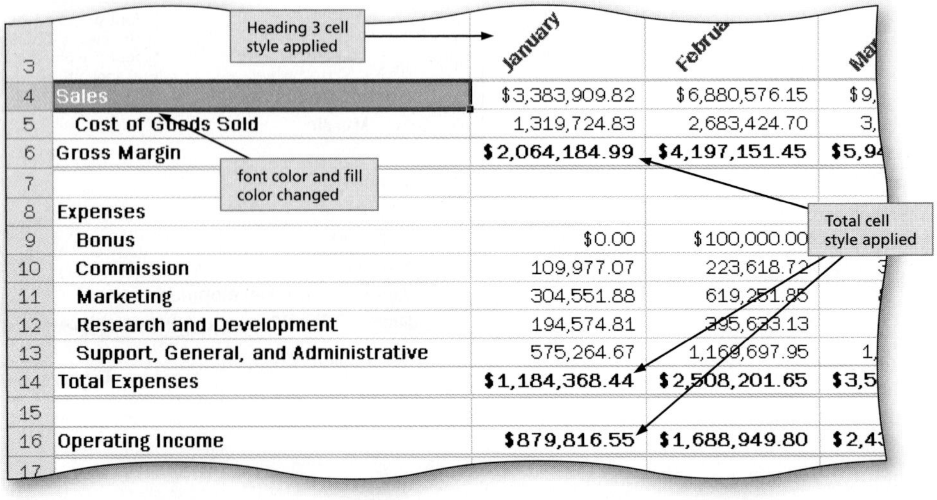

		January	Februa	Ma
3				
4	Sales	$3,383,909.82	$6,880,576.15	$9,
5	Cost of Goods Sold	1,319,724.83	2,683,424.70	3,
6	Gross Margin	$2,064,184.99	$4,197,151.45	$5,94
7				
8	Expenses			
9	Bonus	$0.00	$100,000.00	
10	Commission	109,977.07	223,618.72	3
11	Marketing	304,551.88	619,251.85	
12	Research and Development	194,574.81	395,633.13	
13	Support, General, and Administrative	575,264.67	1,168,697.95	1,
14	Total Expenses	$1,184,368.44	$2,508,201.65	$3,5
15				
16	Operating Income	$879,816.55	$1,688,949.80	$2,4
17				

Heading 3 cell style applied

font color and fill color changed

Total cell style applied

Figure 3–43

Copying a Cell's Format Using the Format Painter Button

Using the Format Painter button on the Ribbon, you can format a cell quickly by copying a cell's format to another cell or a range of cells.

To Copy a Cell's Format Using the Format Painter Button

The following steps format cells A6, A14, and the range A16:H16 using the Format Painter button.

1

- Select cell A4.

- Click the Format Painter button on the Ribbon and then move the mouse pointer onto the worksheet to cause the mouse pointer to change to a block plus sign with a paintbrush (Figure 3–44).

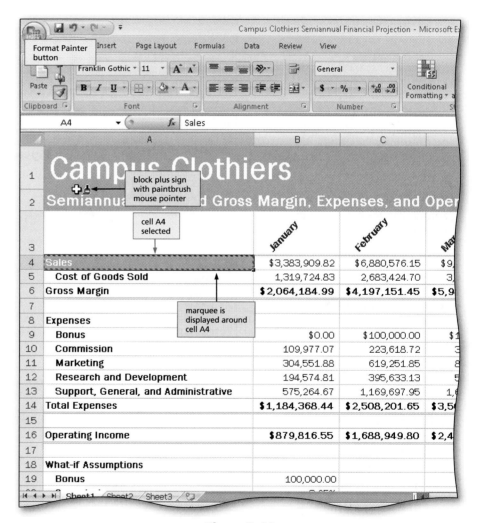

Figure 3–44

2

- Click cell A6 to assign the format of cell A4 to cell A6 (Figure 3–45).

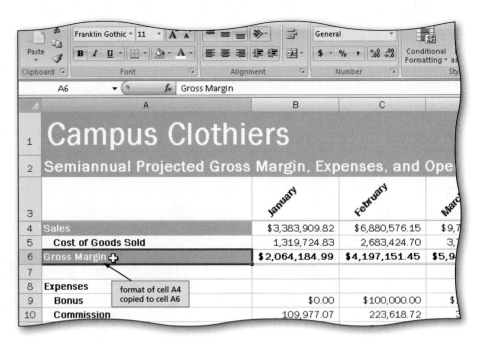

Figure 3–45

3

- With cell A6 selected, click the Format Painter button on the Ribbon and then click cell A16.

- Select the range B16:H16, click the Fill Color button on the Ribbon, and then click the Orange, Accent 1 color (column 5, row 1) on the Fill Color palette.

- Click the Font Color button on the Ribbon, and then click the White, Background 1 color (column 1, row 1) on the Font Color palette (Figure 3–46).

- If necessary, apply the Currency style to the range B16:G16.

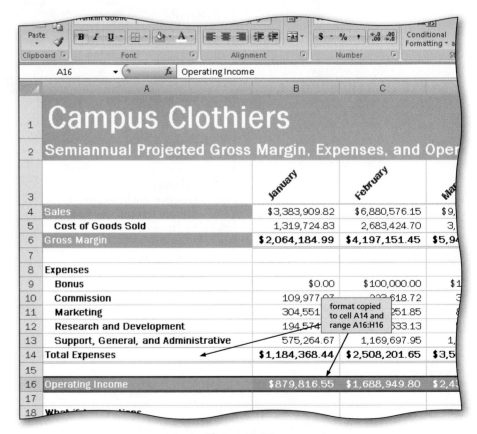

Figure 3–46

Other Ways

1. Click Copy button, select cell, click Paste button, click Paste Special command on Paste menu, click Formats, click OK button

2. Double-click Format Painter button

To Format the What-If Assumptions Table and Save the Workbook

The last step to improving the appearance of the worksheet is to format the What-If Assumptions table in the range A18:B25. The specifications in Figure 3–35 on page EX 196 require a 14-point italic underlined font for the title in cell A18 and 8-point font in the range A19:B25. The following steps format the What-If Assumptions table.

1 Scroll down to view rows 18 through 25 and then click cell A18.

2 Click the Font Size box arrow on the Ribbon and then click 14 in the Font Size list. Click the Italic button and then click the Underline button on the Ribbon.

3 Select the range A19:B25, click the Font Size button on the Ribbon, and then click 8 in the Font Size list.

4 Click cell D25 to deselect the range A19:B25 and display the What-If Assumptions table as shown in Figure 3–47.

5 Click the Save button on the Quick Access Toolbar.

Q&A What happens when I click the Italic and Underline buttons?

Recall that when you assign the italic font style to a cell, Excel slants the characters slightly to the right as shown in cell A18 in Figure 3–47. The **underline** format underlines only the characters in the cell, rather than the entire cell, as is the case when you assign a cell a bottom border.

BTW

Painting a Format to Nonadjacent Ranges
Double-click the Format Painter button on the Home tab on the Ribbon and then drag through the nonadjacent ranges to paint the formats to the ranges. Click the Format Painter button to deactivate it.

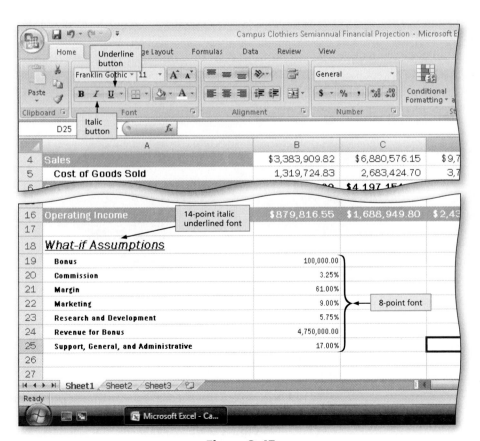

Figure 3–47

Adding a 3-D Pie Chart to the Workbook

The next step in the chapter is to draw the 3-D Pie chart on a separate sheet in the workbook, as shown in Figure 3–48. Use a **Pie chart** to show the relationship or proportion of parts to a whole. Each slice (or wedge) of the pie shows what percent that slice contributes to the total (100%).

Plan Ahead

> **Specify how the chart should convey necessary information.**
> The 3-D Pie chart in Figure 3–48 shows the contribution of each month's projected operating income to the six-month projected operating income. The 3-D Pie chart makes it easy to evaluate the contribution of one month in comparison to the other months.
>
> Unlike the 3-D Column chart created in Chapter 1, the 3-D Pie chart shown in Figure 3–48 is not embedded in the worksheet. Instead, the Pie chart resides on a separate sheet, called a **chart sheet**, which contains only the chart.
>
> In this worksheet, the ranges to chart are the nonadjacent ranges B3:G3 (month names) and B16:G16 (monthly operating incomes). The month names in the range B3:G3 will identify the slices of the Pie chart; these entries are called **category names**. The range B16:G16 contains the data that determines the size of the slices in the pie; these entries are called the **data series**. Because six months are being charted, the 3-D Pie chart contains six slices.
>
> The sketch of the 3-D Pie chart in Figure 3–3b on page EX 166 also calls for emphasizing the month of June by offsetting its slice from the main portion. A Pie chart with one or more slices offset is called an **exploded Pie chart**.

BTW

Charts
You are aware that, when you change a value on which a chart is dependent, Excel immediately redraws the chart based on the new value. Did you know that, with bar charts, you can drag the bar in the chart in one direction or another to change the corresponding value in the worksheet, as well?

BTW

Certification
The Microsoft Certified Application Specialist (MCAS) program provides an opportunity for you to obtain a valuable industry credential – proof that you have the Excel 2007 skills required by employers. For more information, see Appendix G or visit the Excel 2007 Certification Web page (scsite.com/ex2007/cert).

BTW

Chart Items
When you rest the mouse pointer over a chart item, such as a legend, bar, or axis, Excel displays a chart tip containing the name of the item.

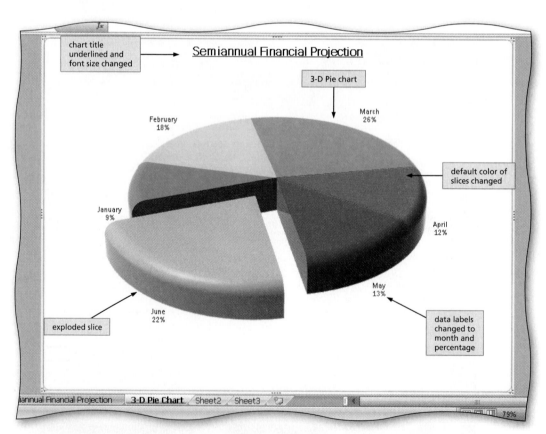

Figure 3–48

As shown in Figure 3–48, the default 3-D Pie chart also has been enhanced by rotating it, changing the colors of the slices, adding a bevel, and modifying the chart title and labels that identify the slices.

6
- Click the Close button to close the Format Data Labels dialog box and display the chart as shown in Figure 3–57.

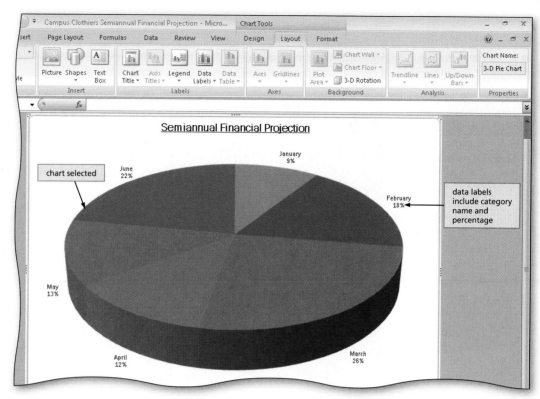

Figure 3–57

To Rotate the 3-D Pie Chart

With a three-dimensional chart, you can change the view to better show the section of the chart you are trying to emphasize. Excel allows you to control the rotation angle, elevation, perspective, height, and angle of the axes by using the Format Chart Area dialog box.

When Excel initially draws a Pie chart, it always positions the chart so that one of the dividing lines between two slices is a straight line pointing to 12 o'clock (or 0°). As shown in Figure 3–57, the line that divides the January and June slices currently is set to 0°. This line defines the rotation angle of the 3-D Pie chart.

To obtain a better view of the offset June slice, the 3-D Pie chart can be rotated 250° to the right. The following steps show how to rotate the 3-D Pie chart.

1

- Click the 3-D Rotation button on the Ribbon to display the Format Chart Area dialog box.

- Click the Increase X Rotation button in the Rotation area of the Format Chart Area dialog box until the X rotation is at 250° (Figure 3–58).

Q&A

What happens as I click the Increase X Rotation button?

Excel rotates the chart 10° in a clockwise direction each time you click the Increase X Rotation button. The Y box in the Rotation area allows you to control the tilt, or elevation, of the chart. You can tilt the chart towards or away from your view in order to enhance the view of the chart.

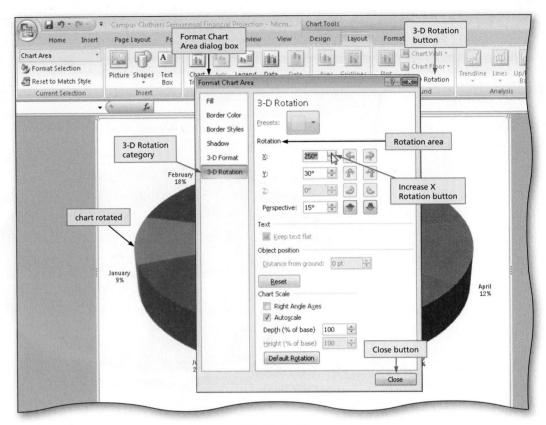

Figure 3–58

2

- Click the Close button in the Format Chart Area dialog box to display the rotated chart (Figure 3–59).

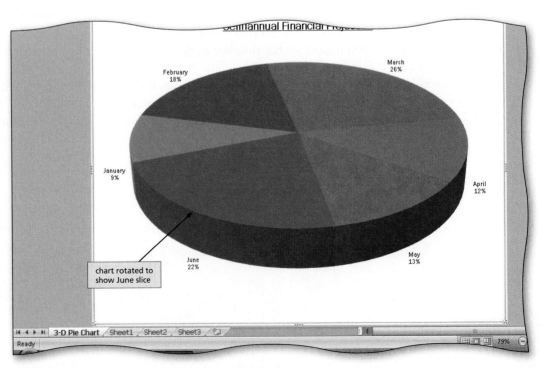

Figure 3–59

To Apply a 3-D Format to the Pie Chart

Excel allows you to apply dramatic 3-D visual effects to charts. The chart shown in Figure 3–59 could be enhanced with a bevel along the top edge. A bevel is a curve that is applied to soften the appearance of a straight edge. Excel also allows you to change the appearance of the material from which the surface of the chart appears to be constructed. The following steps apply a bevel to the chart and change the surface of the chart to a softer-looking material.

- Right-click the chart to display the shortcut menu (Figure 3–60).

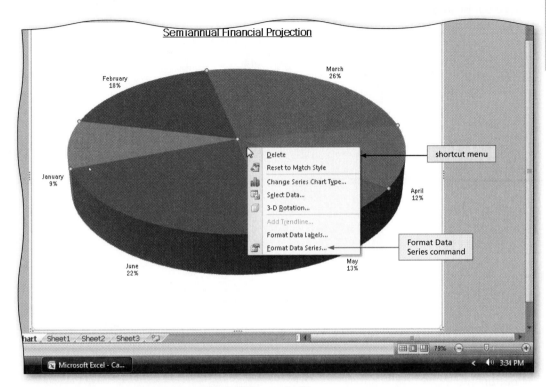

Figure 3–60

- Click the Format Data Series command on the shortcut menu to display the Format Data Series dialog box and then click the 3-D Format category on the left side of the dialog box.

- Click the Top button in the Bevel area to display the Bevel gallery (Figure 3–61).

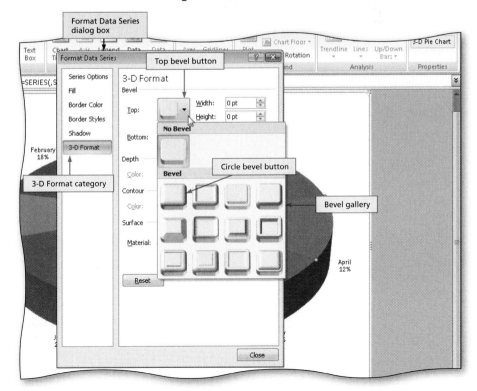

Figure 3–61

- Click the Circle bevel button (column 1, row 1) in the Bevel gallery to add a bevel to the chart.

- Type 50 pt in the top Width box in the Bevel area of the dialog box and then type 50 pt in the uppermost Height box in the Bevel area of the dialog box to increase the width and height of the bevel on the chart (Figure 3–62).

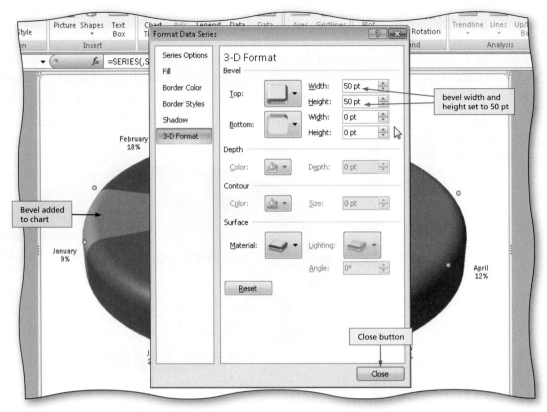

Figure 3–62

4

- Click the Material button in the Surface area of the Format Data Series dialog box and then point to the Soft Edge button (column 2, row 2) in the Material gallery (Figure 3–63).

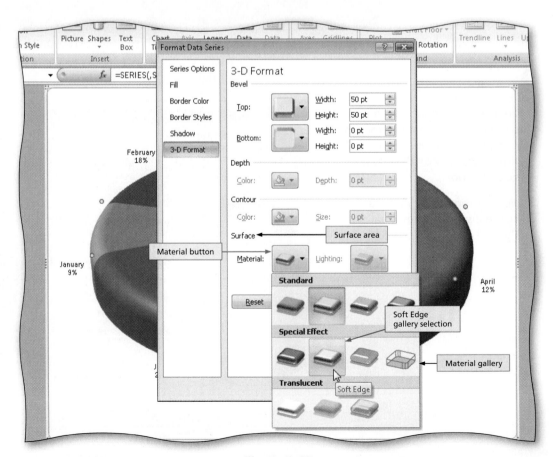

Figure 3–63

5

• Click the Soft Edge button and then click the Close button in the Format Data Series dialog box (Figure 3-64).

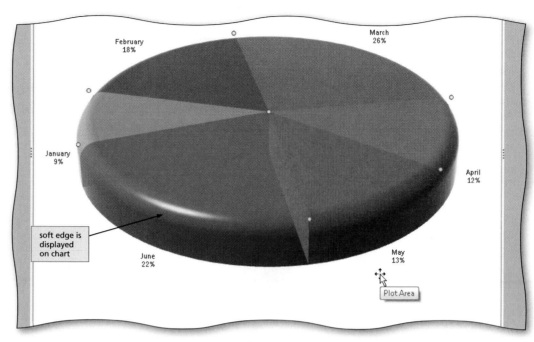

Figure 3–64

To Explode the 3-D Pie Chart and Change the Color of a Slice

The next step is to emphasize the slice representing June by **offsetting**, or exploding, it from the rest of the slices so that it stands out. The following steps explode a slice of the 3-D Pie chart and then change its color.

1

• Click the slice labeled June twice (do not double-click) to select only the June slice.

• Right-click the slice labeled June to display the shortcut menu and then point to Format Data Point (Figure 3-65).

• Click Format Data Point.

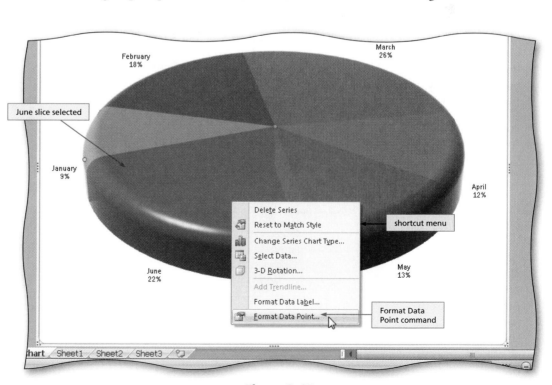

Figure 3–65

2

- When Excel displays the Format Data Point dialog box, drag the Point Explosion slider to the right until the Point Explosion box reads 28% (Figure 3–66).

Q&A

Should I offset more slices?

You can offset as many slices as you want, but remember that the reason for offsetting a slice is to emphasize it. Offsetting multiple slices tends to reduce the impact on the reader and reduces the overall size of the Pie chart.

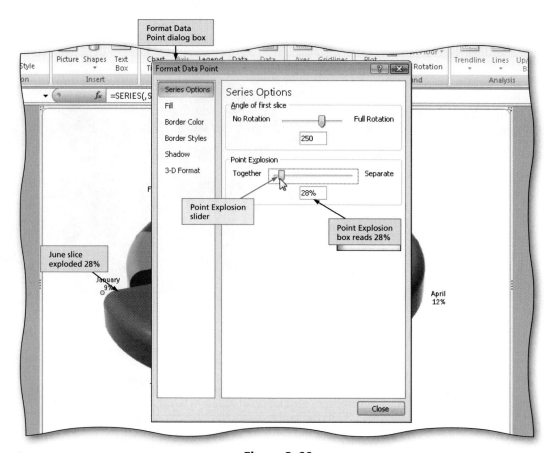

Figure 3–66

3

- Click the Fill category on the left side of the dialog box.

- Click the Solid fill option button and then click the Color button to display the color palette.

- Point to the Orange color in the Standard Colors area (Figure 3–67).

4

- Click the Orange color on the color palette and then click the Close button on the Format Data Point dialog box to change the color of the slice labeled June to orange.

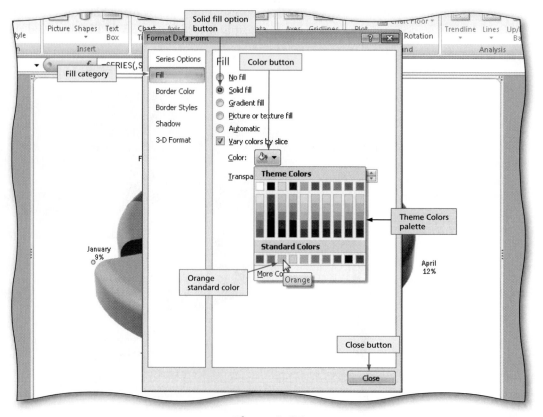

Figure 3–67

To Change the Colors of the Remaining Slices

BTW

Exploding a 3-D Pie Chart
If you click the 3-D Pie chart so that all of the slices are selected, you can drag one of the slices to explode all of the slices.

The colors of the remaining slices also can be changed to enhance the appeal of the chart. The following steps change the color of the remaining five chart slices.

1 Click the slice labeled January twice (do not double-click) to select only the January slice.

2 Right-click the slice labeled January to display the shortcut menu and then click Format Data Point.

3 Click the Fill category on the left side of the dialog box.

4 Click the Solid fill option button and then click the Color button to display the color palette.

5 Click the Green color on the color palette and then click the Close button in the Format Data Point dialog box to change the color of the slice labeled January to green.

6 Repeat steps 1 through 5 for the remaining four slices. Assign the following colors in the Standard Colors area of the color palette to each slice: February – Yellow; March – Light Blue; April – Red; May – Blue. The completed chart appears as shown in Figure 3–68.

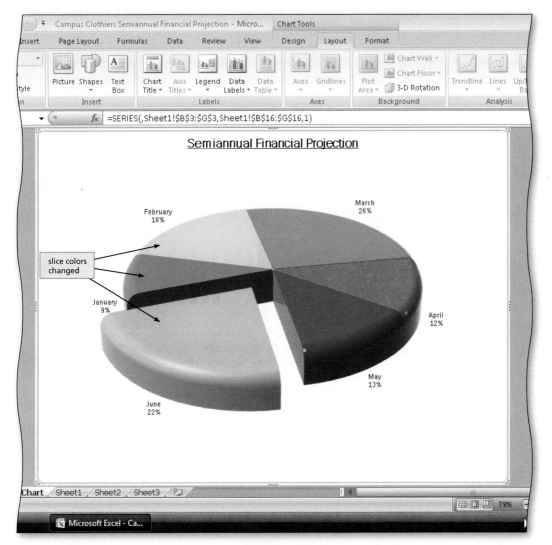

Figure 3–68

Renaming and Reordering the Sheets and Coloring Their Tabs

The final step in creating the workbook is to reorder the sheets and modify the tabs at the bottom of the screen.

To Rename and Reorder the Sheets and Color Their Tabs

The following steps rename the sheets, color the tabs, and reorder the sheets so the worksheet precedes the chart sheet in the workbook.

- Right-click the tab labeled 3-D Pie Chart at the bottom of the screen to display the shortcut menu.

- Point to the Tab Color command to display the color palette (Figure 3–69).

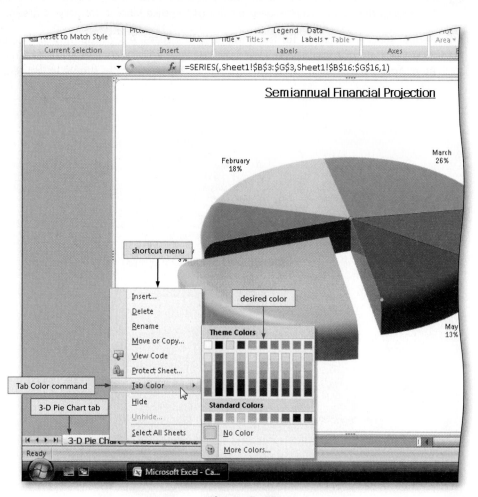

Figure 3–69

2

- Click Brown, Accent 2 (column 6, row 1) in the Theme Colors area to change the color of the tab to brown.

- Double-click the tab labeled Sheet1 at the bottom of the screen.

- Type Semiannual Financial Projection as the new sheet name and then press the ENTER key.

- Right-click the tab and then click Tab Color on the shortcut menu.

- Point to the Orange, Accent 1 (column 5, row 1) color in the Theme Colors area of the palette (Figure 3–70).

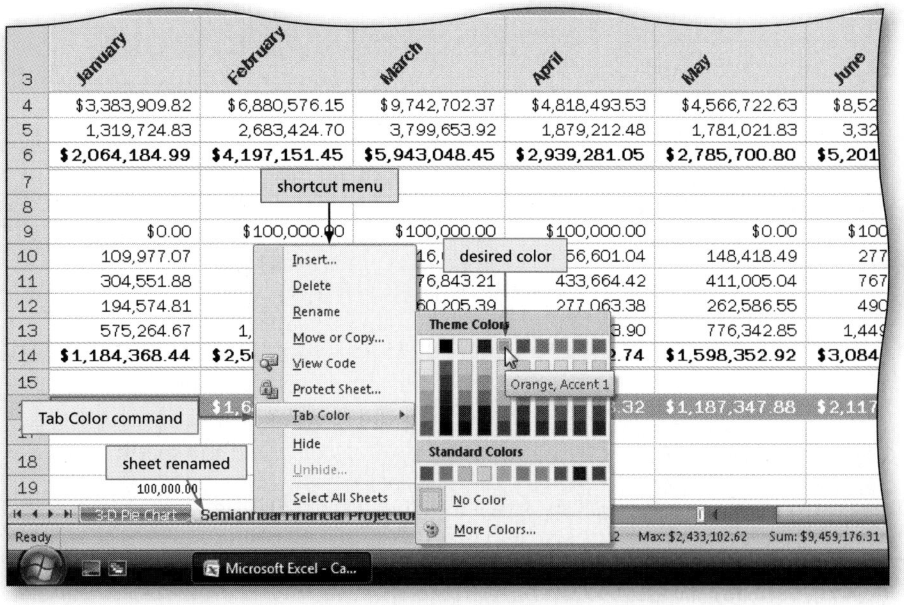

3

- Click Orange, Accent 1 (column 5, row 1) in the Theme Colors area to change the color of the tab to orange.

- Drag the Semiannual Financial Projection tab to the left in front of the 3-D Pie Chart tab to rearrange the sequence of the sheets and then click cell E18 (Figure 3–71).

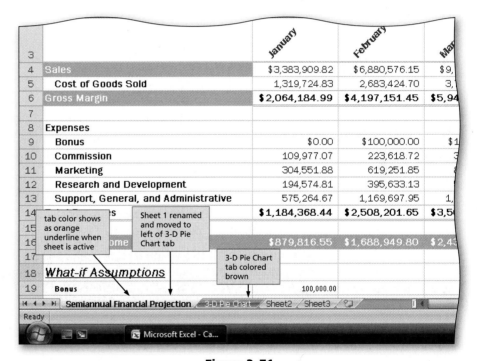

Figure 3–70

Figure 3–71

Other Ways
1. To rename sheet, right-click sheet tab, click Rename on shortcut menu
2. To move sheet, right-click sheet tab, click Move or Copy on shortcut menu

BTW

Checking Spelling
Unless you first select a range of cells or an object before starting the spell checker, Excel checks the selected worksheet, including all cell values, cell comments, embedded charts, text boxes, buttons, and headers and footers.

Checking Spelling, Saving, Previewing, and Printing the Workbook

With the workbook complete, this section checks spelling, saves, previews, and then prints the workbook. Each set of steps concludes with saving the workbook to ensure that the latest changes are saved.

To Check Spelling in Multiple Sheets

By default, the spell checker checks the spelling only in the selected sheets. It will check all the cells in the selected sheets, unless you select a range of two or more cells. Before checking the spelling, the following steps select the 3-D Pie Chart sheet so that the entire workbook is checked for spelling errors.

1 With the Semiannual Financial Projection sheet active, press CTRL+HOME to select cell A1. Hold down the CTRL key and then click the 3-D Pie Chart tab.

2 Click the Review tab on the Ribbon and then click the Spelling button on the Ribbon.

3 Correct any errors and then click the OK button when the spell check is complete.

4 Click the Save button on the Quick Access Toolbar.

BTW

Printing in Black and White
You can speed up the printing process and save ink if you print worksheets with color in black and white. To print a worksheet in black and white on a color printer, do the following: (1) Click the Page Setup Dialog Box Launcher on the Page Layout tab on the Ribbon, click the Sheet tab, and then click 'Black and white' in the Print area. (2) Click the Preview button to see that Excel has removed the colored backgrounds, click the Close button, and then click the OK button. You are now ready to print economically, in black and white.

To Preview and Print the Workbook

After checking the spelling, the next step is to preview and print the sheets. As with spelling, Excel previews and prints only the selected sheets. In addition, because the worksheet is too wide to print in portrait orientation, the orientation must be changed to landscape. The following steps adjust the orientation and scale, preview the workbook, and then print the workbook.

1 Ready the printer. If both sheets are not selected, hold down the CTRL key and then click the tab of the inactive sheet.

2 Click the Page Layout tab on the Ribbon and then click the Page Setup Dialog Box Launcher. Click the Page tab and then click Landscape. Click Fit to in the Scaling area.

3 Click the Print Preview button in the Page Setup dialog box. When the preview of the first of the selected sheets appears, click the Next Page button at the top of the Print Preview window to view the next sheet. Click the Previous Page button to redisplay the first sheet.

4 Click the Print button at the top of the Print Preview window. When Excel displays the Print dialog box, click the OK button to print the worksheet and chart (Figure 3–72).

5 Right-click the Semiannual Financial Projection tab. Click Ungroup Sheets on the shortcut menu to deselect the 3-D Pie Chart tab.

6 Click the Save button on the Quick Access Toolbar.

BTW

Quick Reference
For a table that lists how to complete the tasks covered in this book using the mouse, Ribbon, shortcut menu, and keyboard, see the Quick Reference Summary at the back of this book, or visit the Excel 2007 Quick Reference Web page (scsite.com/ex2007/qr).

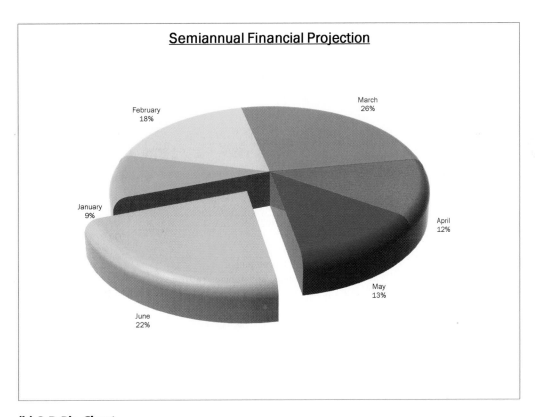

Campus Clothiers
Semiannual Projected Gross Margin, Expenses, and Operating Income

	January	February	March	April	May	June	Total
Sales	$3,383,909.82	$6,880,576.15	$9,742,702.37	$4,818,493.53	$4,566,722.63	$8,527,504.39	$37,919,908.89
Cost of Goods Sold	1,319,724.83	2,683,424.70	3,799,653.92	1,879,212.48	1,781,021.83	3,325,726.71	14,788,764.47
Gross Margin	$2,064,184.99	$4,197,151.45	$5,943,048.45	$2,939,281.05	$2,785,700.80	$5,201,777.68	$23,131,144.42
Expenses							
Bonus	$0.00	$100,000.00	$100,000.00	$100,000.00	$0.00	$100,000.00	$400,000.00
Commission	109,977.07	223,618.72	316,637.83	156,601.04	148,418.49	277,143.89	1,232,397.04
Marketing	304,551.88	619,251.85	876,843.21	433,664.42	411,005.04	767,475.40	3,412,791.80
Research and Development	194,574.81	395,633.13	560,205.39	277,063.38	262,586.55	490,331.50	2,180,394.76
Support, General, and Administrative	575,264.67	1,169,697.95	1,656,259.40	819,143.90	776,342.85	1,449,675.75	6,446,384.51
Total Expenses	$1,184,368.44	$2,508,201.65	$3,509,945.83	$1,786,472.74	$1,598,352.92	$3,084,626.54	$13,671,968.11
Operating Income	$879,816.55	$1,688,949.80	$2,433,102.62	$1,152,808.32	$1,187,347.88	$2,117,151.14	$9,459,176.31

What-If Assumptions

Bonus	100,000.00
Commission	3.25%
Margin	61.00%
Marketing	9.00%
Research and Development	5.75%
Revenue for Bonus	4,750,000.00
Support, General, and Administrative	17.00%

(a) Worksheet

Semiannual Financial Projection

February 18%
March 26%
January 9%
April 12%
June 22%
May 13%

(b) 3-D Pie Chart

Figure 3–72

BTW

Zooming
You can use the Zoom In and Zoom Out buttons on the status bar to zoom from 10% to 400% to reduce or enlarge the display of the worksheet.

Changing the View of the Worksheet

With Excel, you easily can change the view of the worksheet. For example, you can magnify or shrink the worksheet on the screen. You also can view different parts of the worksheet through window panes.

To Shrink and Magnify the View of a Worksheet or Chart

You can magnify (zoom in) or shrink (zoom out) the appearance of a worksheet or chart by using the Zoom button on the View tab on the Ribbon. When you magnify a worksheet, Excel enlarges the view of the characters on the screen, but displays fewer columns and rows. Alternatively, when you shrink a worksheet, Excel is able to display more columns and rows. Magnifying or shrinking a worksheet affects only the view; it does not change the window size or printout of the worksheet or chart. The following steps shrink and magnify the view of the worksheet.

1

- If cell A1 is not active, press CTRL+HOME.

- Click the View tab on the Ribbon and then click the Zoom button on the Ribbon to display a list of Magnifications in the Zoom dialog box (Figure 3–73).

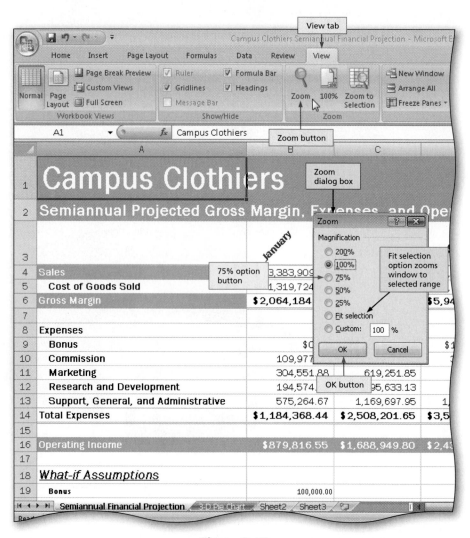

Figure 3–73

2

- Click 75% and then click the OK button to shrink the display of the worksheet to 75% of its normal display (Figure 3–74).

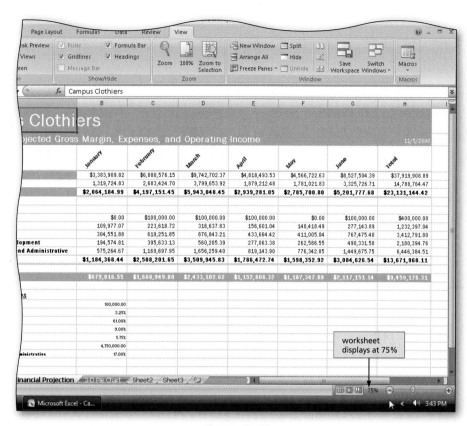

worksheet displays at 75%

Figure 3–74

3

- Click the Zoom In button on the status bar until the worksheet displays at 100% (Figure 3–75).

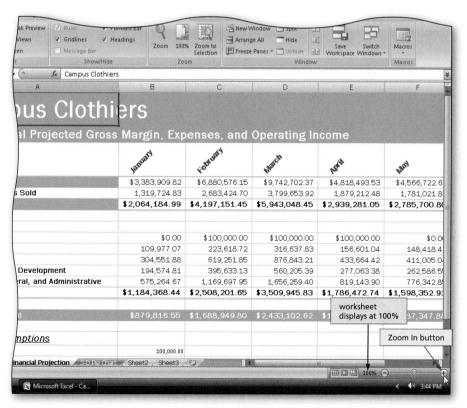

worksheet displays at 100%

Zoom In button

Figure 3–75

To Split a Window into Panes

When working with a large worksheet, you can split the window into two or four panes to view different parts of the worksheet at the same time. Splitting the Excel window into four panes at cell D7 allows you to view all four corners of the worksheet easily. The following steps split the Excel window into four panes.

- Select cell D7, the intersection of the four proposed panes.

- If necessary, click the View tab on the Ribbon and then point to the Split button on the Ribbon (Figure 3–76).

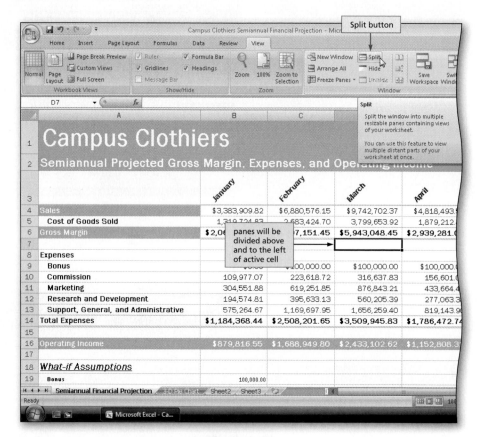

Figure 3–76

2

• Click the Split button to divide the window into four panes.

• Use the scroll arrows to show the four corners of the worksheet at the same time (Figure 3–77).

Q&A

What is shown in the four panes?

The four panes in Figure 3–77 are used to show the following: (1) range A1:C6 in the upper-left pane; (2) range G1:I6 in the upper-right pane; (3) range A14:C26 in the lower-left pane; and (4) range G14:I26 in the lower-right pane. The vertical split bar is the vertical bar going up and down the middle of the window. The horizontal split bar is the horizontal bar going across the middle of the window. If you use the scroll bars below the window and to the right of the window to scroll the window, you will see that the panes split by the horizontal split bar scroll together vertically. The panes split by the vertical split bar scroll together horizontally. To resize the panes, drag either split bar to the desired location in the window.

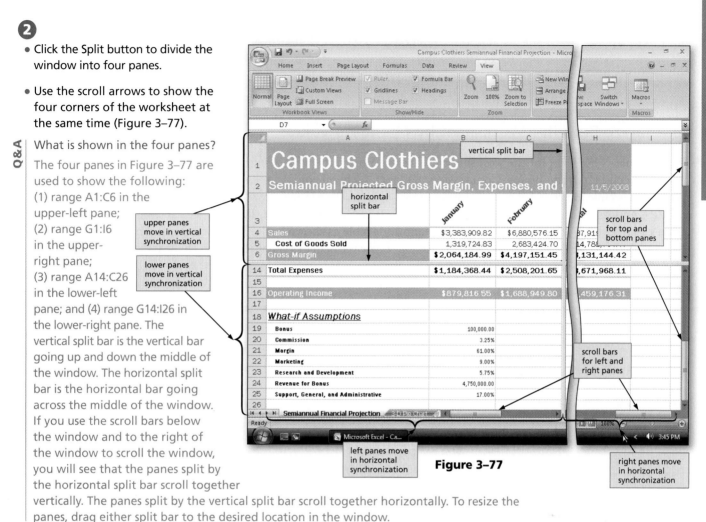

Figure 3–77

To Remove the Panes from the Window

1 Position the mouse pointer at the intersection of the horizontal and vertical split bars.

2 When the mouse pointer changes to a four-headed arrow, double-click to remove the four panes from the window.

What-If Analysis

The automatic recalculation feature of Excel is a powerful tool that can be used to analyze worksheet data. Using Excel to scrutinize the impact of changing values in cells that are referenced by a formula in another cell is called **what-if analysis** or **sensitivity analysis**. When new data is entered, Excel not only recalculates all formulas in a worksheet, but also redraws any associated charts.

BTW

Window Panes
If you want to split the window into two panes, rather than four, drag the vertical split box to the far left of the window or horizontal split box to the top of the window (Figure 3–78 on the next page). You also can drag the center of the four panes in any direction to change the size of the panes.

In the workbook created in this chapter, many of the formulas are dependent on the assumptions in the range B19:B25. Thus, if you change any of the assumption values, Excel immediately recalculates all formulas. Excel redraws the 3-D Pie chart as well, because it is based on these numbers.

To Analyze Data in a Worksheet by Changing Values

A what-if question for the worksheet in Chapter 3 might be *what* would happen to the semiannual operating income in cell H16 *if* the Bonus, Commission, Support, General, and Administrative assumptions in the What-If Assumptions table are changed as follows: Bonus $100,000.00 to $75,000.00; Commission 3.25% to 2.25%; Support, General, and Administrative 17.00% to 14.50%? To answer a question like this, you need to change only the first, second, and seventh values in the What-If Assumptions table as shown in the following steps. The steps also divide the window into two vertical panes. Excel instantaneously recalculates the formulas in the worksheet and redraws the 3-D Pie chart to answer the question.

- Use the vertical scroll bar to move the window so cell A6 is in the upper-left corner of the screen.

- Drag the vertical split box from the lower-right corner of the screen to the left so that the vertical split bar is positioned as shown in Figure 3–78.

- Use the right scroll arrow to view the totals in column H in the right pane.

- Enter 75000 in cell B19, 2.25 in cell B20, and 14.50 in cell B25 (Figure 3–78), which causes the semiannual operating income in cell H16 to increase from $9,459,176.31 to $10,886,373.12.

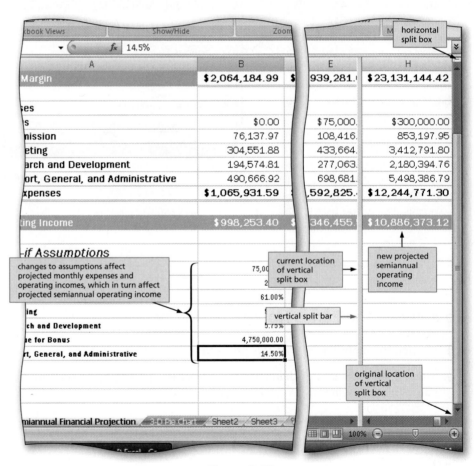

Figure 3–78

To Goal Seek

If you know the result you want a formula to produce, you can use **goal seeking** to determine the value of a cell on which the formula depends. The following steps close and reopen the Campus Clothiers Semiannual Financial Projection workbook. They then show how to use the Goal Seek command on the Data tab on the Ribbon to determine the Support, General, and Administrative percentage in cell B25 that will yield a semiannual operating income of $10,500,000 in cell H16, rather than the original $9,459,176.31.

1

- Close the workbook without saving changes and then reopen it.

- Drag the vertical split box so that the vertical split bar is positioned as shown in Figure 3–79.

- Show column H in the right pane.

- Click cell H16, the cell that contains the semiannual operating income.

- Click the Data tab on the Ribbon and then click the What-If Analysis button on the Ribbon to display the What-If Analysis menu (Figure 3–79).

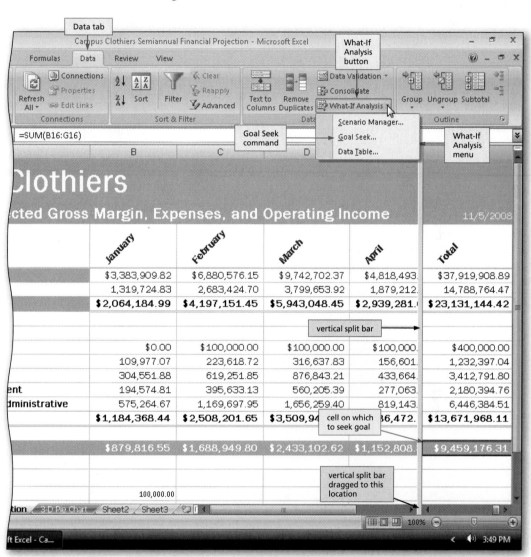

Figure 3–79

2

- Click Goal Seek to display the Goal Seek dialog box with the Set cell box set to the selected cell, H16.

- When Excel displays the Goal Seek dialog box, click the To value text box, type 10,500,000 and then click the By changing cell box.

- Scroll down so row 4 is at the top of the screen.

- Click cell B25 on the worksheet to assign cell B25 to the By changing cell box (Figure 3–80).

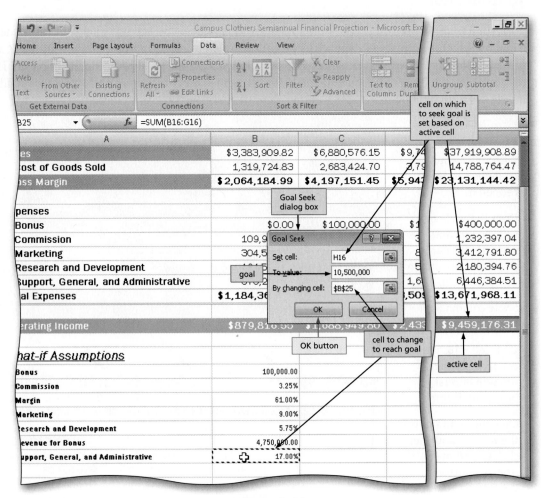

Figure 3–80

3

- Click the OK button to goal seek for the value $10,500,000.00 in cell H16 (Figure 3–81).

Q&A

What happens when I click the OK button?

Excel immediately changes cell H16 from $9,459,176.31 to the desired value of $10,500,000.00. More importantly, Excel changes the Support, General, and Administrative assumption in cell B25 from 17.00% to 14.26% (Figure 3–81). Excel also displays the Goal Seek Status dialog box. If you click the OK button, Excel keeps the new values in the worksheet. If you click the Cancel button, Excel redisplays the original values.

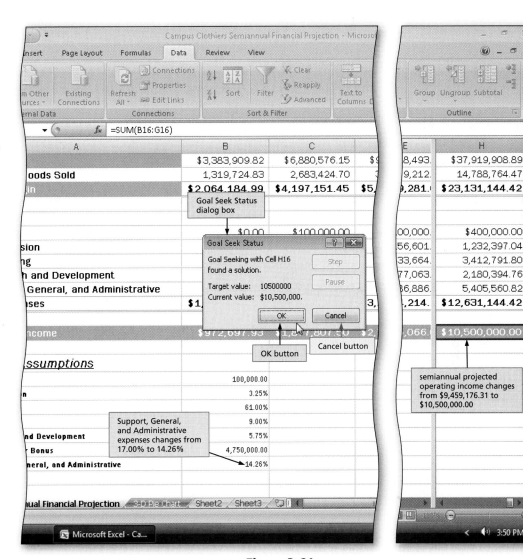

Figure 3–81

4

- Click the Cancel button in the Goal Seek Status dialog box.

Other Ways
1. Press ALT+T, G

Goal Seeking

Goal seeking assumes you can change the value of only one cell referenced directly or indirectly to reach a specific goal for a value in another cell. In this example, to change the semiannual operating income in cell H16 to $10,500,000.00, the Support, General, and Administrative percentage in cell B25 must decrease by 2.74% from 17.00% to 14.26%.

You can see from this goal seeking example that the cell to change (cell B25) does not have to be referenced directly in the formula or function. For example, the semiannual operating income in cell H16 is calculated by the function =SUM(B16:G16). Cell B25 is not referenced in this function. Instead, cell B25 is referenced in the formulas in rows 9 through 13, on which the monthly operating incomes in row 16 are based. Excel thus is capable of goal seeking on the semiannual operating income by varying the value for the Support, General, and Administrative assumption.

BTW

Undoing What You Did
The Undo button is ideal for returning the worksheet to its original state after you have changed the values in a worksheet to answer a what-if question. To view the original worksheet after answering a what-if question, click the Undo button on the Quick Access Toolbar for each value you changed.

To Quit Excel

To quit Excel, complete the following steps.

1 Click the Close button on the title bar.

2 If the Microsoft Excel dialog box is displayed, click the No button.

Chapter Summary

In this chapter you learned how to work with large worksheets that extend beyond the window, how to use the fill handle to create a series, new formatting techniques, about the difference between absolute cell references and relative cell references, how to use the IF function, how to rotate text in a cell, freeze titles, change the magnification of the worksheet, show different parts of the worksheet at the same time through multiple panes, create a 3-D Pie chart, and improve the appearance of a 3-D Pie chart. This chapter also introduced you to using Excel to do what-if analysis by changing values in cells and goal seeking. The items listed below include all the new Excel skills you have learned in this chapter.

1. Rotate Text and Use the Fill Handle to Create a Series of Month Names (EX 169)
2. Increase Column Widths and Enter Row Titles (EX 173)
3. Copy a Range of Cells to a Nonadjacent Destination Area (EX 175)
4. Insert a Row (EX 177)
5. Enter Numbers with Format Symbols (EX 181)
6. Freeze Column and Row Titles (EX 182)
7. Enter and Format the System Date (EX 184)
8. Enter a Formula Containing Absolute Cell References (EX 187)
9. Enter an IF Function (EX 190)
10. Copy Formulas with Absolute Cell References Using the Fill Handle (EX 192)
11. Unfreeze the Worksheet Titles and Save the Workbook (EX 194)
12. Assign Formats to Nonadjacent Ranges (EX 196)
13. Format the Worksheet Titles (EX 199)
14. Copy a Cell's Format Using the Format Painter Button (EX 201)
15. Draw a 3-D Pie Chart on a Separate Chart Sheet (EX 205)
16. Insert a Chart Title and Data Labels (EX 206)
17. Rotate the 3-D Pie Chart (EX 209)
18. Apply a 3-D Format to the Pie Chart (EX 211)
19. Explode the 3-D Pie Chart and Change the Color of a Slice (EX 213)
20. Rename and Reorder the Sheets and Color Their Tabs (EX 216)
21. Check Spelling in Multiple Sheets (EX 218)
22. Shrink and Magnify the View of a Worksheet or Chart (EX 220)
23. Split a Window into Panes (EX 222)
24. Analyze Data in a Worksheet by Changing Values (EX 224)
25. Goal Seek (EX 225)

If you have a SAM user profile, you may have access to hands-on instruction, practice, and assessment. Log in to your SAM account (http://sam2007.course.com) to launch any assigned training activities or exams that relate to the skills covered in this chapter.

Learn It Online

Learn It Online is a series of online student exercises that test your knowledge of chapter content and key terms.

Instructions: To complete the Learn It Online exercises, start your browser, click the Address bar, and then enter the Web address scsite.com/off2007/learn. When the Office 2007 Learn It Online page is displayed, click the link for the exercise you want to complete and then read the instructions.

Chapter Reinforcement TF, MC, and SA
A series of true/false, multiple choice, and short answer questions that test your knowledge of the chapter content.

Flash Cards
An interactive learning environment where you identify chapter key terms associated with displayed definitions.

Practice Test
A series of multiple choice questions that test your knowledge of chapter content and key terms.

Who Wants To Be a Computer Genius?
An interactive game that challenges your knowledge of chapter content in the style of a television quiz show.

Wheel of Terms
An interactive game that challenges your knowledge of chapter key terms in the style of the television show *Wheel of Fortune*.

Crossword Puzzle Challenge
A crossword puzzle that challenges your knowledge of key terms presented in the chapter.

Apply Your Knowledge

Reinforce the skills and apply the concepts you learned in this chapter.

Understanding Logical Tests and Absolute Cell Referencing

Instructions Part 1: Determine the truth value (true or false) of the following logical tests, given the following cell values: X4 = 25; Y3 = 28; K7 = 110; Z2 = 15; and Q9 = 35. Enter true or false.

a. $Y3 < X4$ Truth value: _____

b. $Q9 = K7$ Truth value: _____

c. $X4 + 15 * Z2 / 5 <> K7$ Truth value: _____

d. $K7 / Z2 > X4 - Y3$ Truth value: _____

e. $Q9 * 2 - 42 < (X4 + Y3 - 8) / 9$ Truth value: _____

f. $K7 + 300 <= X4 * Z2 + 10$ Truth value: _____

g. $Q9 + K7 > 2 * (Q9 + 25)$ Truth value: _____

h. $Y3 = 4 * (Q9 / 5)$ Truth value: _____

Instructions Part 2: Write cell K23 as a relative reference, absolute reference, mixed reference with the row varying, and mixed reference with the column varying.

_____   _____   _____   _____

Instructions Part 3: Start Excel. Open the workbook Apply 3-1 Absolute Cell References. See the inside back cover of this book for instructions for downloading the Data Files for Students, or see your instructor for information on accessing the files required in this book. You will recreate the numerical grid pictured in Figure 3–82 on the next page.

Continued >

Apply Your Knowledge *continued*

Perform the following tasks:

1. Enter a formula in cell C7 that multiplies cell C2 times the sum of cells C3 through C6. Write the formula so that when you copy it to cells D7 and E7, cell C2 remains absolute. Verify your formula by checking it with the values found in cells C7, D7, and E7 in Figure 3–82.

2. Enter a formula in cell F3 that multiplies cell B3 times the sum of cells C3 through E3. Write the formula so that when you copy the formula to cells F4, F5, and F6, cell B3 remains absolute. Verify your formula by checking it with the values found in cells F3, F4, F5, and F6 in Figure 3–82.

3. Enter a formula in cell C8 that multiplies cell C2 times the sum of cells C3 through C6. Write the formula so that when you copy the formula to cells D8 and E8, Excel adjusts all the cell references according to the destination cells. Verify your formula by checking it with the values found in cells C8, D8, and E8 in Figure 3–82.

4. Enter a formula in cell G3 that multiplies cell B3 times the sum of cells C3, D3, and E3. Write the formula so that when you copy the formula to cells G4, G5, and G6, Excel adjusts all the cell references according to the destination cells. Verify your formula by checking it with the values found in cells G3, G4, G5, and G6 in Figure 3–82.

5. Change the document properties, as specified by your instructor. Change the worksheet header with your name, course number, and other information as specified by your instructor. Save the workbook using the file name, Apply 3-1 Absolute Cell References Complete, and submit the revised workbook as requested by your instructor.

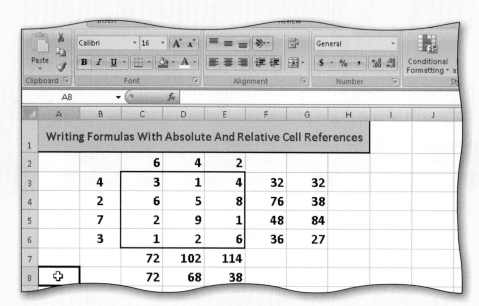

Figure 3–82

Extend Your Knowledge

Extend the skills you learned in this chapter and experiment with new skills. You may need to use Help to complete the assignment.

Nested IF Functions and More About the Fill Handle

Instructions Part 1: Start Excel. You will use nested IF functions to determine values for sets of data.

Perform the following tasks:

1. Enter the following IF function in cell C1:
    =IF(B1="CA","West", IF(B1="NJ","East", IF(B1="IL","Midwest","State Error")))

2. Use the fill handle to copy the nested IF function down through cell C7. Enter the following data in the cells in the range B1:B7 and then write down the results that display in cells C1 through C7 for each set. Set 1: B1 = CA; B2 = NY; B3 = NJ; B4 = MI; B5 = IL; B6 = CA; B7 = IL. Set 2: B1= WI; B2 = NJ; B3 = IL; B4 = CA; B5 = NJ; B6 = NY; B7 = CA.

Set 1 Results: ____

Set 2 Results: ____

Instructions Part 2: Start Excel. Open the workbook Extend 3-1 Create Series. See the inside back cover of this book for instructions for downloading the Data Files for Students, or see your instructor for information on accessing the files required in this book.

Perform the following tasks:

1. Use the fill handle on one column at a time to propagate the fourteen series through row 16 as shown in Figure 3–83. For example, in column A, select cell A2 and drag the fill handle down to cell A16. In column C, hold down the CTRL key to repeat Monday through cell C16. In column D, select the range D2:D3 and drag the fill handle down to cell D16. Likewise, in columns F and I through K, select the two adjacent cells in rows 2 and 3 before dragging the fill handle down to the corresponding cell in row 16.
2. Select cell D21. While holding down the CTRL key, one at a time drag the fill handle three cells to the right, to the left, up, and down to generate four series of numbers beginning with zero and incremented by one.
3. Select cell I21. Point to the cell border so that the mouse pointer changes to a plus sign with four arrows. Drag the mouse pointer down to cell I22 to move the contents of cell I21 to cell I22.
4. Select cell I22. Point to the cell border so that the mouse pointer changes to a plus sign with four arrows. While holding down the CTRL key, drag the mouse pointer to cell M22 to copy the contents of cell I22 to cell M22.
5. Select cell M21. Drag the fill handle in to the center of cell M21 so that the cell is shaded in order to delete the cell contents.
6. Change the document properties, as specified by your instructor. Change the worksheet header with your name, course number, and other information requested by your instructor. Save the workbook using the file name, Extend 3-1 Create Series Complete, and submit the revised workbook as requested by your instructor.

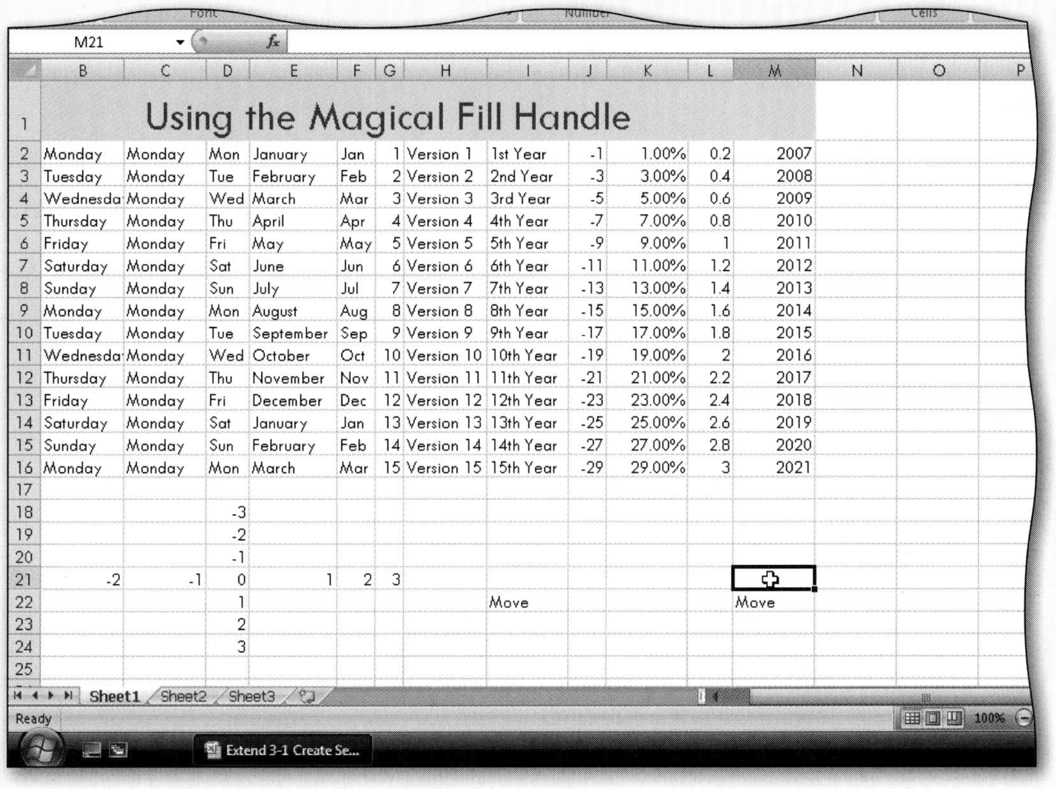

	B	C	D	E	F	G	H	I	J	K	L	M
1	Using the Magical Fill Handle											
2	Monday	Monday	Mon	January	Jan	1	Version 1	1st Year	-1	1.00%	0.2	2007
3	Tuesday	Monday	Tue	February	Feb	2	Version 2	2nd Year	-3	3.00%	0.4	2008
4	Wednesda	Monday	Wed	March	Mar	3	Version 3	3rd Year	-5	5.00%	0.6	2009
5	Thursday	Monday	Thu	April	Apr	4	Version 4	4th Year	-7	7.00%	0.8	2010
6	Friday	Monday	Fri	May	May	5	Version 5	5th Year	-9	9.00%	1	2011
7	Saturday	Monday	Sat	June	Jun	6	Version 6	6th Year	-11	11.00%	1.2	2012
8	Sunday	Monday	Sun	July	Jul	7	Version 7	7th Year	-13	13.00%	1.4	2013
9	Monday	Monday	Mon	August	Aug	8	Version 8	8th Year	-15	15.00%	1.6	2014
10	Tuesday	Monday	Tue	September	Sep	9	Version 9	9th Year	-17	17.00%	1.8	2015
11	Wednesda	Monday	Wed	October	Oct	10	Version 10	10th Year	-19	19.00%	2	2016
12	Thursday	Monday	Thu	November	Nov	11	Version 11	11th Year	-21	21.00%	2.2	2017
13	Friday	Monday	Fri	December	Dec	12	Version 12	12th Year	-23	23.00%	2.4	2018
14	Saturday	Monday	Sat	January	Jan	13	Version 13	13th Year	-25	25.00%	2.6	2019
15	Sunday	Monday	Sun	February	Feb	14	Version 14	14th Year	-27	27.00%	2.8	2020
16	Monday	Monday	Mon	March	Mar	15	Version 15	15th Year	-29	29.00%	3	2021
17												
18			-3									
19			-2									
20			-1									
21	-2	-1	0	1	2	3						
22			1					Move				Move
23			2									
24			3									
25												

Figure 3–83

Make It Right

Analyze a workbook and correct all errors and/or improve the design.

Inserting Rows, Moving a Range, and Correcting Formulas in a Worksheet
Instructions: Start Excel. Open the workbook Make It Right 3-1 e-MusicPro.com Annual Projected Net Income. See the inside back cover of this book for instructions for downloading the Data Files for Students, or see your instructor for information on accessing the files required for this book. Correct the following design and formula problems (Figure 3–84a) in the worksheet.

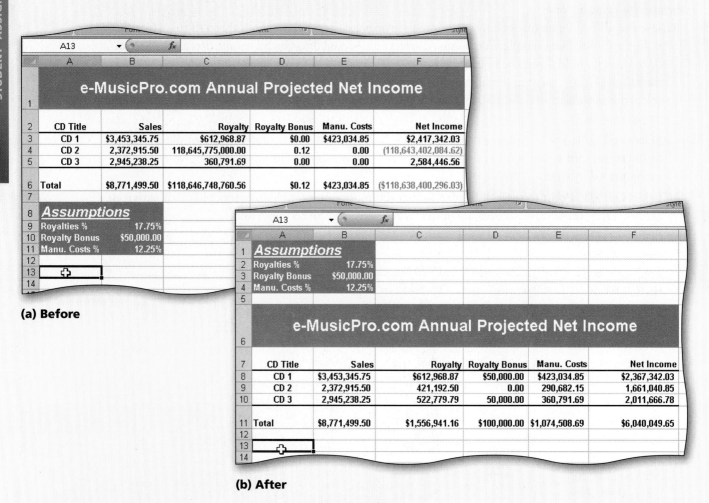

(a) Before

(b) After

Figure 3–84

1. The Royalty in cell C3 is computed using the formula =B9*B3 (Royalties % × Sales). Similar formulas are used in cells C4 and C5. The formula in cell C3 was entered and copied to cells C4 and C5. Although the result in cell C3 is correct, the results in cells C4 and C5 are incorrect. Edit the formula in cell C3 by changing cell B9 to an absolute cell reference. Copy the corrected formula in cell C3 to cells C4 and C5. After completing the copy, click the Auto Fill Options button arrow that displays below and to the right of cell C5 and choose Fill Without Formatting.

2. The Royalty Bonus amounts in cells D3, D4, and D5 are computed using the IF function. The Royalty Bonus should equal the amount in cell B10 ($50,000) if the corresponding Sales in column B is greater than or equal to $2,750,000. If the corresponding Sales in column B is less than $2,750,000, then the Royalty Bonus is zero ($0). The IF function in cell D3 was entered and

copied to cells D4 and D5. The current IF functions in cells D3, D4, and D5 are incorrect. Edit and correct the IF function in cell D3. Copy the corrected formula in cell D3 to cells D4 and D5. After completing the copy, click the Auto Fill Options button arrow that displays below and to the right of cell D5 and choose Fill Without Formatting.

3. The Manufacturing Costs in cell E3 is computed using the formula =B11*B3 (Manu. Costs % x Sales). The formula in cell E3 was entered and copied to cells E4 and E5. Although the result in cell E3 is correct, the results in cells E4 and E5 are incorrect. Edit and correct the formula in cell E3 by changing cell B11 to an absolute cell reference. Copy the corrected formula in cell E3 to cells E4 and E5. After completing the copy, click the Auto Fill Options button arrow that displays below and to the right of cell E5 and choose Fill Without Formatting.

4. Change the design of the worksheet by moving the Assumptions table in the range A8:B11 to the range A1:B4 as shown in Figure 3–84b. To complete the move, insert five rows above row 1 and then drag the Assumptions table to the range A1:B4. Use Figure 3–84b to verify that Excel automatically adjusted the cell references based on the move. Use the Undo button and Redo button on the Quick Access Toolbar to move the Assumptions table back and forth while the results of the formulas remain the same.

5. Change the document properties, as specified by your instructor. Change the worksheet header with your name, course number, and other information as specified by your instructor. Save the workbook using the file name, Make It Right 3-1 e-MusicPro.com Annual Projected Net Income Complete, and submit the revised workbook as specified by your instructor.

In the Lab

Create a workbook using the guidelines, concepts, and skills presented in this chapter. Labs are listed in order of increasing difficulty.

Lab 1: Eight-Year Financial Projection

Problem: Your supervisor in the Finance department at Salioto Auto Parts has asked you to create a worksheet that will project the annual gross margin, expenses, total expenses, operating income, income taxes, and net income for the next ten years based on the assumptions in Table 3–9. The desired worksheet is shown in Figure 3–85 on the next page. In Part 1 you will create the worksheet. In Part 2 you will create a chart to present the data, shown in Figure 3–86 on page 236. In Part 3 you will use Goal Seek to analyze three different sales scenarios.

Table 3–9 Salioto Auto Parts Financial Projection Assumptions	
Units Sold in Prior Year	11,459,713
Unit Cost	$13.40
Annual Sales Growth	4.50%
Annual Price Decrease	4.25%
Margin	39.25%

Continued >

In the Lab *continued*

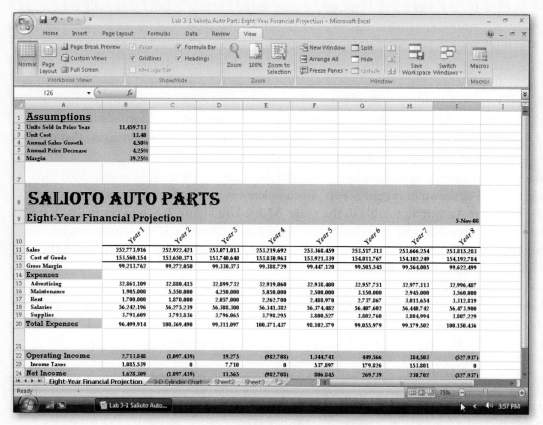

Figure 3–85

Instructions Part 1:

1. Start Excel. Apply the Apex theme to the worksheet by using the Themes button on the Page Layout tab on the Ribbon. Bold the entire worksheet by selecting the entire worksheet and using the Bold button on the Home tab on the Ribbon.

2. Enter the worksheet title Salioto Auto Parts in cell A8 and the subtitle Eight-Year Financial Projection in cell A9. Format the worksheet title in cell A8 to 36-point Algerian (or a similar font). Format the worksheet subtitle in cell A9 to 20-point Rockwell (or a similar font). Enter the system date in cell I9 using the NOW function. Format the date to the 14-Mar-01 style.

3. Change the following column widths: A = 25.00 characters; B through I = 15.00 characters. Change the heights of rows 7, 10, and 21 to 42.00 points.

4. Enter the eight column titles Year 1 through Year 8 in the range B10:I10 by entering Year 1 in cell B10 and then dragging cell B10's fill handle through the range C10:I10. Format cell B10 as follows: (a) increase the font size to 14; (b) center and italicize; and (c) rotate its contents 45°. Use the Format Painter button to copy the format assigned to cell B10 to the range C10:I10.

5. Enter the row titles in the range A11:A24. Change the font in cells A14, A20, A22, and A24 to 14-point Rockwell (or a similar font). Add thick bottom borders to the ranges B10:I10 and B12:I12. Use the Increase Indent button on the Home tab on the Ribbon to increase the indent of the row titles in cell A12, the range A15:A19, and cell A23.

6. Enter the table title Assumptions in cell A1. Enter the assumptions in Table 3-9 in the range A2:B6. Use format symbols when entering the numbers. Change the font size of the table title to 14-point Rockwell and underline it.

7. Select the range B11:I24 and then click the Format Cells: Number Dialog Box Launcher on the Home tab on the Ribbon to display the Format Cells dialog box. Use the Number category in the Format Cells dialog box to assign the Comma style with no decimal places and negative numbers enclosed in parentheses to the range B11:I24.

8. Complete the following entries:

   a. Year 1 Sales (cell B11) = Units Sold in Prior Year * (Unit Cost / (1 − Margin)) or =B2 * (B3 / (1 − B6))

   b. Year 2 Sales (cell C11) = Year 1 Sales * (1 + Annual Sales Growth) * (1 − Annual Price Decrease) or =B11 * (1 + $B$4) * (1 − $B$5)

   c. Copy cell C11 to the range D11:I11.

   d. Year 1 Cost of Goods (cell B12) = Year 1 Sales * (1 − Margin) or =B11 * (1 − $B$6)

   e. Copy cell B12 to the range C12:I12.

   f. Gross Margin (cell B13) = Year 1 Sales − Year 1 Cost of Goods or =B11 − B12

   g. Copy cell B13 to the range C13:I13.

   h. Year 1 Advertising (cell B15) = 500 + 13% * Year 1 Sales or =500 + 13% * B11

   i. Copy cell B15 to the range C15:I15.

   j. Maintenance (row 16): Year 1 = 1,905,000; Year 2 = 5,550,000; Year 3 = 4,250,000; Year 4 = 5,050,000; Year 5 = 2,500,000; Year 6 = 3,150,000; Year 7 = 2,945,000; and Year 8 = 3,560,000.

   k. Year 1 Rent (cell B17) = 1,700,000

   l. Year 2 Rent (cell C17) = Year 1 Rent + (10% * Year 1 Rent) or =B17 * (1 + 10%)

   m. Copy cell C17 to the range D17:I17.

   n. Year 1 Salaries (cell B18) = 22.25% * Year 1 Sales or =22.25% * B11

   o. Copy cell B18 to the range C18:I18.

   p. Year 1 Supplies (cell B19) = 1.5% * Year 1 Sales or =1.5% * B11

   q. Copy cell B19 to the range C19:I19.

   r. Year 1 Total Expenses (cell B20) or =SUM(B15:B19)

   s. Copy cell B20 to the range C20:I20.

   t. Year 1 Operating Income (cell B22) = Year 1 Gross Margin − Year 1 Total Expenses or =B13 − B20

   u. Copy cell B22 to the range C22:I22.

   v. Year 1 Income Taxes (cell B23): If Year 1 Operating Income is less than 0, then Year 1 Income Taxes equal 0; otherwise Year 1 Income Taxes equal 40% * Year 1 Operating Income or =IF(B22 < 0, 0, 40% * B22)

   w. Copy cell B23 to the range C23:I23.

   x. Year 1 Net Income (cell B24) = Year 1 Operating Income − Year 1 Income Taxes or =B22 − B23

   y. Copy cell B24 to the range C24:I24.

9. Change the background colors as shown in Figure 3-85. Use Orange (column 3 under Standard Colors) for the background colors.

10. Zoom to: (a) 200%; (b) 75%; (c) 25%; and (d) 100%.

11. Change the document properties, as specified by your instructor. Change the worksheet header with your name, course number, and other information requested by your instructor. Save the workbook using the file name, Lab 3-1 Salioto Auto Parts Eight-Year Financial Projection.

12. Preview the worksheet. Use the Page Setup button to fit the printout on one page in landscape orientation. Preview the formulas version (CTRL+`) of the worksheet in landscape orientation using the Fit to option. Press CTRL+` to instruct Excel to display the values version of the worksheet. Save the workbook again and close the workbook.

13. Submit the workbook as requested by your instructor.

Instructions Part 2:

1. Start Excel. Open the workbook Lab 3-1 Salioto Auto Parts Eight-Year Financial Projection.

2. Use the nonadjacent ranges B10:I10 and B24:I24 to create a 3-D Cylinder chart. Draw the chart by clicking the Column button on the Insert tab on the Ribbon. When the Column gallery is displayed, click the Clustered Cylinder chart type (column 1, row 3). When the chart is displayed, click the Move Chart button on the Ribbon to move the chart to a new sheet.

Continued >

In the Lab *continued*

3. Select the legend on the right side of the chart and delete it. Add the chart title by clicking the Layout tab on the Ribbon, then clicking the Chart Title button. Click Above Chart in the Chart Title gallery. Format the chart title as shown in Figure 3–86.

4. To change the color of the cylinders, click one of the cylinders and use the Shape Fill button on the Format tab on the Ribbon. To change the color of the wall, click the wall behind the cylinders and use the Shape Fill button on the Format tab on the Ribbon. Use the same procedure to change the color of the base of the wall.

5. Rename the sheet tabs Eight-Year Financial Projection and 3-D Cylinder Chart. Rearrange the sheets so that the worksheet is leftmost, and color their tabs as shown in Figure 3–86.

6. Click the Eight-Year Financial Projection tab to display the worksheet. Save the workbook using the same file name (Lab 3-1 Salioto Auto Parts Eight-Year Financial Projection) as defined in Part 1. Submit the workbook as requested by your instructor.

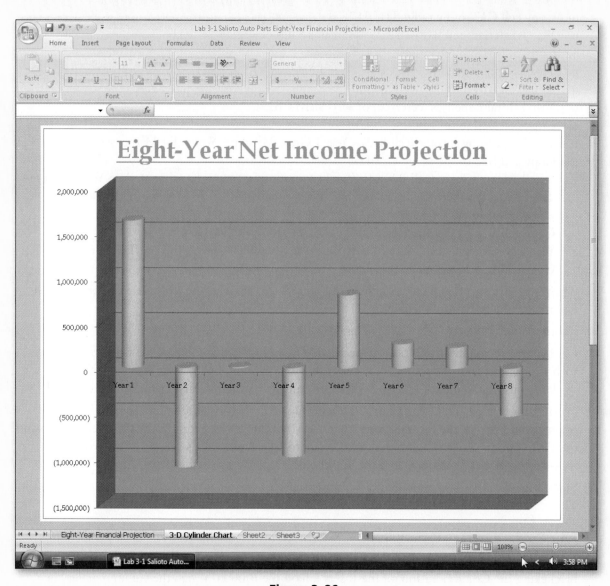

Figure 3–86

Instructions Part 3:

1. Start Excel. Open the workbook Lab 3-1 Salioto Auto Parts Eight-Year Financial Projection. Do not save the workbook in this part. Divide the window into two panes by dragging the horizontal split box between rows 6 and 7. Use the scroll bars to show both the top and bottom of the worksheet. Using the numbers in columns 2 and 3 of Table 3-10, analyze the effect of changing the annual sales growth (cell B4) and annual price decrease (cell B5) on the net incomes in row 24. The resulting answers are in column 4 of Table 3–10. Submit the workbook or results of the what-if analysis for each case as requested by your instructor.

Table 3–10 Salioto Auto Parts Data to Analyze and Results

Case	Annual Sales Growth	Annual Price Decrease	Year 8 Resulting Net Income in Cell I24
1	7.45%	5.25%	174,568
2	12.75%	−3.00%	6,677,903
3	−7.25%	1.65%	(3,552,156)

2. Close the workbook without saving it, and then reopen it. Use the What-If Analysis button on the Data tab on the Ribbon to goal seek. Determine a margin (cell B6) that would result in a Year 8 net income of $2,000,000 (cell I24). You should end up with a margin of 40.68% in cell B6. Submit the workbook with the new values or the results of the goal seek as requested by your instructor. Do not save the workbook with the latest changes.

In the Lab

Lab 2: Modifying a Weekly Payroll Worksheet

Problem: As a summer intern at Britney's Music Emporium, you have been asked to modify the weekly payroll report shown in Figure 3–87a on the next page. The workbook, Lab 3-2 Britney's Music Emporium Weekly Payroll Report, is included with the Data Files for Students. See the inside back cover of this book for instructions for downloading the Data Files for Students, or see your instructor for information on accessing the files required for this book.

The major modifications to the payroll report to be made in this exercise include: (1) reformatting the worksheet; (2) adding computations of time-and-a-half for hours worked greater than 40; (3) adding calculations to charge no federal tax in certain situations; (4) adding Social Security and Medicare deductions; (5) adding and deleting employees; and (6) changing employee information. The final payroll report is shown in Figure 3–87b on the next page.

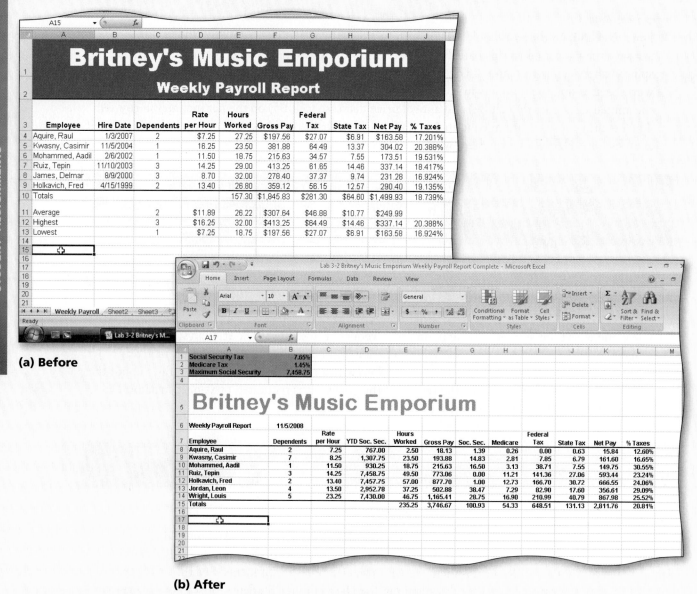

(a) Before

(b) After

Figure 3–87

Instructions Part 1:

1. Start Excel. Open the workbook, Lab 3-2 Britney's Music Emporium Weekly Payroll Report and then save the workbook using the file name Lab 3-2 Britney's Music Emporium Weekly Payroll Report Complete.

2. Select the worksheet by clicking the Select All button. Click the Clear button on the Home tab on the Ribbon and then click Clear Formats on the Clear menu to clear the formatting. Bold the entire worksheet.

3. Delete rows 11 through 13 to remove the statistics below the Totals row. Change all the row heights back to the default height (12.75).

4. Insert four rows above row 1 by selecting rows 1 through 4, right-clicking the selection, and clicking Insert on the shortcut menu.

5. Change the row heights as follows: row 5 = 48.00; rows 6 and 7 = 25.50. One at a time, select cells D7, E7, and G7. For each cell, press the F2 key and then the ENTER key to display the column headings on multiple rows. Center the range B7:J7.

6. Delete column B by right-clicking the column heading and clicking Delete on the shortcut menu.

7. Insert a new column between columns C and D. Change the column widths as follows: A = 25.00; D = 13.00; and E through K = 9.71. Enter the new column D title **YTD Soc. Sec.** in cell D7.

8. Insert two new columns between columns F and G. Enter the new column G title **Soc. Sec.** in cell G7. Enter the new column H title **Medicare** in cell H7.

9. Enhance the worksheet title in cell A5 by using a 36-point light blue Arial Rounded MT Bold (or a similar font) font style as shown in Figure 3–87b.

10. Assign the NOW function to cell B6 and format it to the 3/14/2001 style.

11. Delete employee James, Delmar (row 12). Change Raul Aquire's (row 8) hours worked to 2.5. Change Casimir Kwasny's (row 9) number of dependents to 7 and rate per hour to $8.25. Change Tepin Ruiz's (row 11) hours worked to 49.5 and Fred Holkavich's (row 12) hours worked to 57.

12. Freeze column A and rows 1 through 7 by selecting cell B8, clicking the Freeze Panes button on the View tab on the Ribbon, and then clicking Freeze Panes on the Freeze Panes menu.

13. In column D, enter the YTD Soc. Sec. values listed in Table 3–11.

14. Insert two new rows immediately above the Totals row. Add the new employee data as listed in Table 3–12.

Table 3–11 The Britney Music Emporium's YTD Social Security Values

Employee	YTD Soc. Sec.
Aquire, Raul	767.00
Kwasny, Casimir	1307.75
Mohammed, Aadil	930.25
Ruiz, Tepin	7458.75
Holkavich, Fred	7457.75

Table 3–12 The Britney Music Emporium's New Employee Data

Employee	Dependents	Rate per Hour	YTD Soc. Sec.	Hours Worked
Jordan, Leon	4	13.50	2952.78	37.25
Wright, Louis	5	23.25	7430.00	46.75

15. Center the range B6:B14. Use the Currency category in the Format Cells dialog box to assign a Comma style (no dollar signs) with two decimal places and negative numbers within parentheses to the range C8:K15. Assign a Percent style and two decimal places to the range L8:L15. Draw a thick bottom border in the ranges A7:L7 and A14:L14.

16. As shown in Figure 3–87b, enter and format the Social Security (7.65% with a maximum of $7,458.75) and Medicare tax (1.45%) information in the range A1:B3. Use format symbols where applicable.

17. Change the formulas to determine the gross pay in column F and the federal tax in column I as follows:

    a. In cell F8, enter an IF function that applies the following logic and then copy it to the range F9:F14. If Hours Worked <= 40, then Rate per Hour * Hours Worked, otherwise Rate per Hour * Hours Worked + 0.5 * Rate per Hour * (Hours Worked − 40) or =IF(E8 <= 40, C8 * E8, C8 * E8 + 0.5 * C8 *(E8 − 40))

    b. In cell I8, enter the IF function that applies the following logic and then copy it to the range I9:I14. If (Gross Pay − Dependents * 22.09 > 0, then 20% * (Gross Pay − Dependents * 22.09), otherwise 0 or =IF(F8 − B8 * 22.09 > 0, 20% * (F8 − B8 * 22.09), 0)

Continued >

In the Lab continued

18. An employee pays Social Security tax only if his or her YTD Soc. Sec. in column D is less than the Maximum Social Security value in cell B3. Use the following logic to determine the Social Security tax for Raul Aquire in cell G8 and then copy it to the range G9:G14.

    Soc. Sec. (cell G8): If Social Security Tax * Gross Pay + YTD Soc. Sec. > Maximum Social Security, then Maximum Social Security − YTD Soc. Sec., otherwise Social Security Tax * Gross Pay or =IF($B$1 * F8 + D8 >= $B$3, $B$3 − D8, $B$1 * F8)

19. In cell H8, enter the following formula and then copy it to the range H9:H14:

    Medicare (cell H8) = Medicare Tax * Gross Pay or =$B$2 * F8

20. In cell K8, enter the following formula and copy it to the range K9:K14:

    Net Pay (K8) = Gross Pay − (Soc. Sec. + Medicare + Federal Tax + State Tax) or =F8 − (G8 + H8 + I8 + J8)

21. In cell L8, enter the following formula and copy it to the range L9:L14:

    % Taxes (cell L8) = (Soc. Sec. + Medicare + Federal Tax + State Tax) / Gross Pay or =(G8 + H8 + I8 + J8) / F8

22. Use the Range Finder (double-click cell) to verify the new totals as shown in row 15 in Figure 3–87b. Unfreeze the worksheet by clicking the Freeze Panes button on the View tab on the Ribbon, and then clicking Unfreeze Panes on the Freeze Panes menu.

23. Preview the worksheet. Use the Page Setup button to change the orientation to landscape and fit the report on one page.

24. Change the document properties, as specified by your instructor. Change the worksheet header with your name, course number, and other information requested by your instructor. Save the workbook.

25. Use the Zoom button on the View tab on the Ribbon to change the view of the worksheet. One by one, select all the percents on the Zoom dialog box. When you are done, return the worksheet to 100% magnification.

26. Preview the formulas version (CTRL+`) in landscape orientation. Close the worksheet without saving the latest changes.

27. Submit the workbook as requested by your instructor.

Instructions Part 2: Start Excel. Open Lab 3-2 Britney's Music Emporium Weekly Payroll Report Complete. Do not save the workbook in this part. Using the numbers in Table 3–13, analyze the effect of changing the Medicare tax in cell B2. The first case should result in a total Medicare tax in cell H15 of $106.78. The second case should result in a total Medicare tax of $166.73. Close the workbook without saving changes. Submit the results of the what-if analysis as requested by your instructor.

Table 3–13 The Britney Music Emporium's Medicare Tax Cases	
Case	**Medicare Tax**
1	2.85%
2	4.45%

Instructions Part 3: Submit results for this part as requested by your instructor.

1. Start Excel. Open Lab 3-2 Britney's Music Emporium Weekly Payroll Report Complete. Select cell F8. Write down the formula that Excel displays in the formula bar. Select the range C8:C14. Point to the border surrounding the range and drag the selection to the range D17:D23. Click cell F8, and write down the formula that Excel displays in the formula bar below the one you wrote down earlier. Compare the two formulas. What can you conclude about how Excel responds when you move cells involved in a formula? Click the Undo button on the Quick Access Toolbar.

2. Right-click the range C8:C14 and then click Delete on the shortcut menu. When Excel displays the Delete dialog box, click Shift cells left and then click the OK button. What does Excel display in cell F8? Click cell F8 and then point to the Trace Error button that is displayed to the left of the cell. Write down the ScreenTip that is displayed. Click the Undo button on the Quick Access Toolbar.

3. Right-click the range C8:C14 and then click Insert on the shortcut menu. When Excel displays the Insert dialog box, click Shift cells right and then click the OK button. What does Excel display in the formula bar when you click cell F8? What does Excel display in the formula bar when you click cell G8? What can you conclude about how Excel responds when you insert cells next to cells involved in a formula? Close the workbook without saving the changes.

In the Lab

Lab 3: Analysis of Indirect Expense Allocations

Problem: Your classmate works part time as a consultant for RockieView Resort and Spa. She has asked you to assist her in creating an indirect expense allocation worksheet (Figure 3–88) that will help the resort and spa administration better evaluate the profit centers described in Table 3–14 on the next page.

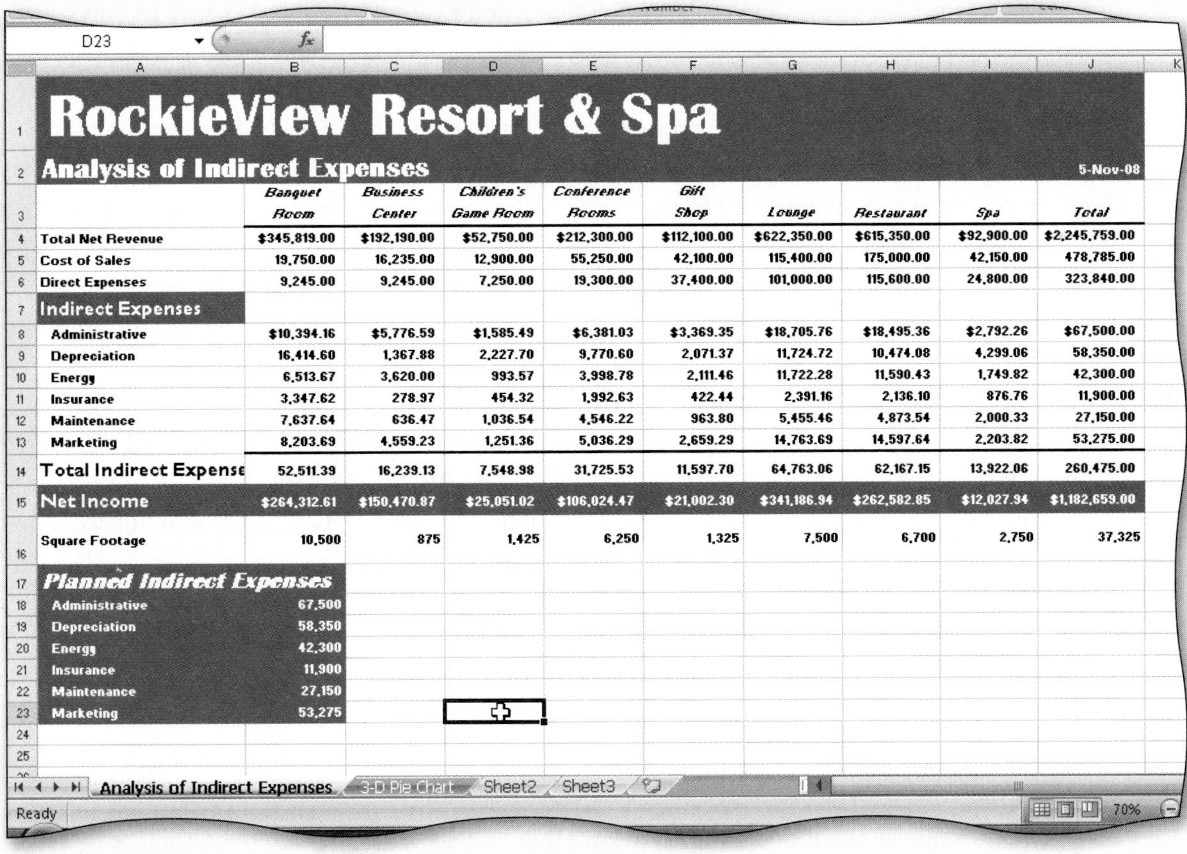

	Banquet Room	Business Center	Children's Game Room	Conference Rooms	Gift Shop	Lounge	Restaurant	Spa	Total
RockieView Resort & Spa									
Analysis of Indirect Expenses									5-Nov-08
Total Net Revenue	$345,819.00	$192,190.00	$52,750.00	$212,300.00	$112,100.00	$622,350.00	$615,350.00	$92,900.00	$2,245,759.00
Cost of Sales	19,750.00	16,235.00	12,900.00	55,250.00	42,100.00	115,400.00	175,000.00	42,150.00	478,785.00
Direct Expenses	9,245.00	9,245.00	7,250.00	19,300.00	37,400.00	101,000.00	115,600.00	24,800.00	323,840.00
Indirect Expenses									
Administrative	$10,394.16	$5,776.59	$1,585.49	$6,381.03	$3,369.35	$18,705.76	$18,495.36	$2,792.26	$67,500.00
Depreciation	16,414.60	1,367.88	2,227.70	9,770.60	2,071.37	11,724.72	10,474.08	4,299.06	58,350.00
Energy	6,513.67	3,620.00	993.57	3,998.78	2,111.46	11,722.28	11,590.43	1,749.82	42,300.00
Insurance	3,347.62	278.97	454.32	1,992.63	422.44	2,391.16	2,136.10	876.76	11,900.00
Maintenance	7,637.64	636.47	1,036.54	4,546.22	963.80	5,455.46	4,873.54	2,000.33	27,150.00
Marketing	8,203.69	4,559.23	1,251.36	5,036.29	2,659.29	14,763.69	14,597.64	2,203.82	53,275.00
Total Indirect Expense	52,511.39	16,239.13	7,548.98	31,725.53	11,597.70	64,763.06	62,167.15	13,922.06	260,475.00
Net Income	$264,312.61	$150,470.87	$25,051.02	$106,024.47	$21,002.30	$341,186.94	$262,582.85	$12,027.94	$1,182,659.00
Square Footage	10,500	875	1,425	6,250	1,325	7,500	6,700	2,750	37,325
Planned Indirect Expenses									
Administrative	67,500								
Depreciation	58,350								
Energy	42,300								
Insurance	11,900								
Maintenance	27,150								
Marketing	53,275								

Figure 3–88

Continued >

In the Lab *continued*

Table 3–14 RockieView Resort and Spa Worksheet Data

	Banquet Room	Business Center	Children's Game Room	Conference Rooms	Gift Shop	Lounge	Restaurant	Spa
Total Net Revenue	345819	192190	52750	212300	112100	622350	615350	92900
Cost of Sales	19750	16235	12900	55250	42100	115400	175000	42150
Direct Expenses	9245	9245	7250	19300	37400	101000	115600	24800
Square Footage	10500	875	1425	6250	1325	7500	6700	2750

Instructions Part 1: Do the following to create the worksheet shown in Figure 3–88.

1. Apply the Solstice theme to the worksheet. Bold the entire worksheet by selecting the entire worksheet and using the Bold button on the Ribbon.

2. Change the following column widths: A = 28.00; B through I = 13.00; J = 14.00.

3. Enter the worksheet titles in cells A1 and A2 and the system date in cell J2. Format the date to the 14-Mar-01 style.

4. Enter the column titles, row titles, and the first three rows of numbers in Table 3–14 in rows 3 through 6. Center and italicize the column headings in the range B3:J3. Add a thick bottom border to the range B3:J3. Sum the individual rows 4, 5, and 6 in the range J4:J6.

5. Enter the Square Footage row in Table 3–14 with the comma format symbol in row 16. Sum row 16 in cell J16. Use the Format Painter button to format cell J16. Change the height of row 16 to 39.00. Vertically center the range A16:J16 through the use of the Format Cells dialog box.

6. Enter the remaining row titles in the range A7:A17 as shown in Figure 3–88. Increase the font size in cells A7, A14, and A15 to 16 point.

7. Copy the row titles in range A8:A13 to the range A18:A23. Enter the numbers shown in the range B18:B23 of Figure 3–88 with format symbols.

8. The planned indirect expenses in the range B18:B23 are to be prorated across the profit center as follows: Administrative (row 8), Energy (row 10), and Marketing (row 13) on the basis of Total Net Revenue (row 4); Depreciation (row 9), Insurance (row 11), and Maintenance (row 12) on the basis of Square Footage (row 16). Use the following formulas to accomplish the prorating:

   a. Banquet Room Administrative (cell B8) = Administrative Expenses * Banquet Room Total Net Revenue / Resort Total Net Revenue or =$B$18 * B4 / $J$4

   b. Banquet Room Depreciation (cell B9) = Depreciation Expenses * Banquet Room Square Footage / Total Square Footage or =$B$19 * B16 / $J$16

   c. Banquet Room Energy (cell B10) = Energy Expenses * Banquet Room Total Net Revenue / Resort Total Net Revenue or =$B$20 * B4 / $J$4

   d. Banquet Room Insurance (cell B11) = Insurance Expenses * Banquet Room Square Feet / Total Square Footage or =$B$21 * B16 / $J$16

   e. Banquet Room Maintenance (cell B12) = Maintenance Expenses * Banquet Room Square Footage / Total Square Footage or =$B$22 * B16 / $J$16

   f. Banquet Room Marketing (cell B13) = Marketing Expenses * Banquet Room Total Net Revenue / Resort Total Net Revenue or =$B$23 * B4 / $J$4

   g. Banquet Room Total Indirect Expenses (cell B14) = SUM(B8:B13)

   h. Banquet Room Net Income (cell B15) = Total Net Revenue − (Cost of Sales + Direct Expenses + Total Indirect Expenses) or =B4 − (B5 + B6 + B14)

   i. Copy the range B8:B15 to the range C8:I15.

   j. Sum the individual rows 8 through 15 in the range J8:J15.

9. Add a thick bottom border to the range B13:J13. Assign the Currency style with two decimal places and show negative numbers in parentheses to the following ranges: B4:J4; B8:J8; and B14:J15. Assign the Comma style with two decimal places and show negative numbers in parentheses to the following ranges: B5:J6 and B9:J13.

10. Change the font in cell A1 to 48-point Britannic Bold (or a similar font). Change the font in cell A2 to 22-point Britannic Bold (or a similar font). Change the font in cell A17 to 18-point italic Britannic Bold.

11. Use the background color blue and the font color white for the ranges A1:J2; A7; A15:J15; and A17:B23 as shown in Figure 3–88.

12. Rename the Sheet1 sheet, Analysis of Indirect Expenses, and color its tab blue.

13. Update the document properties with your name, course number, and name for the workbook. Change the worksheet header with your name, course number, and other information as specified by your instructor. Save the workbook using the file name, Lab 3-3 RockieView Resort and Spa Indirect Expenses Allocations.

14. Preview the worksheet. Use the Page Setup button to change the orientation to landscape and fit the report on one page. Preview the formulas version (CTRL+`) of the worksheet in landscape orientation using the Fit to option button in the Page Setup dialog box. Press CTRL+` to show the values version of the worksheet. Save the workbook again.

15. Divide the window into four panes and show the four corners of the worksheet. Remove the four panes. Close the workbook but do not save the workbook.

Instructions Part 2: Start Excel. Open Lab 3-3 RockieView Resort and Spa Indirect Expenses Allocations. Draw a 3-D Pie chart (Figure 3–89) on a separate sheet that shows the contribution of each category of indirect expense to the total indirect expenses. That is, chart the nonadjacent ranges A8:A13 (category names) and J8:J13 (data series). Show labels that include category names and percentages. Do not show the legend. Format the 3-D Pie chart as shown in Figure 3–89. Rename the chart sheet 3-D Pie Chart and color the tab red. Move the chart tab to the right of the worksheet tab. Save the workbook using the file name, Lab 3-3 RockieView Resort and Spa Indirect Expenses Allocations. Submit the workbook as requested by your instructor.

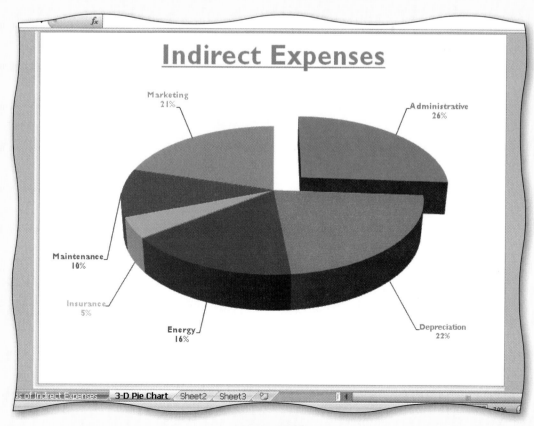

Figure 3–89

Continued >

STUDENT ASSIGNMENTS

In the Lab *continued*

Instructions Part 3:   Start Excel. Open Lab 3-3 RockieView Resort and Spa Indirect Expenses Allocations.
1. Using the numbers in Table 3–15, analyze the effect of changing the planned indirect expenses in the range B18:B23 on the net incomes for each profit center. You should end with the following totals in cell J15: Case 1 = $892,684.00 and Case 2 = $869,634.00. Submit the workbook or results for each case as requested by your instructor.

2. Use the What-If Analysis button on the Data tab on the Ribbon to goal seek. Determine a planned indirect Administrative expense (cell B18) that would result in a total net income of $1,200,000 (cell J15). You should end up with a planned indirect Administrative expense of $50,159 in cell B18. Submit the workbook with the new values or the results of the goal seek as requested by your instructor.

Table 3–15 RockieView Resort and Spa Indirect Expense Allocations What-If Data		
	Case 1	**Case 2**
Administrative	234000	210000
Depreciation	123500	152000
Energy	67750	48000
Insurance	26200	53000
Maintenance	42000	38000
Marketing	57000	72500

Cases and Places

Apply your creative thinking and problem solving skills to design and implement a solution.

• Easier •• More Difficult

• 1: Five-Year Sales Projections

You have been asked to develop a worksheet for Millennium Steel that shows annual growth for the next five years based on the prior year's sales and growth data. Include an embedded exploded 3-D Pie chart that shows the contribution of each year to the total gross margin. The data and general layout of the worksheet, including the totals, are shown in Table 3–16.

Table 3–16 Millennium Steel Sales Data and General Layout						
	Year 1	**Year 2**	**Year 3**	**Year 4**	**Year 5**	**Total**
Sales	Formula A ──────────────────────────────→					—
Cost of Goods	Formula B ──────────────────────────────→					—
Gross Margin	Formula C ──────────────────────────────→					—
Assumptions						
Prior Year's Sales	35234500					
Annual Growth Rate	−1.75%	12.35%	5.00%	−1.25%	8.75%	
Annual Cost Rate	41.25%	44.00%	33.00%	43.75%	34.25%	
Premium	2.90%	3.10%	4.95%	2.50%	4.50%	

Enter the formulas shown in Table 3–17 in the locations shown in Table 3–16. Copy formulas A, B, and C to the remaining years. The gross margin for the five years should equal $118,986,982.

Table 3–17 Millennium Steel Sales Projection Formulas
Formula A = Prior Year's Sales * (1 + Annual Growth Rate)
Formula B = IF(Annual Growth Rate < 0, Sales * (Annual Cost Rate + Premium), Sales * Annual Cost Rate)
Formula C = Sales − Cost of Goods

Use the concepts and techniques developed in the first three projects to create and format the worksheet and embedded 3-D Pie chart.

Use the Goal Seek command to determine the Year 1 annual growth rate that will generate a total gross margin of $125,000,000. You should end up with a Year 1 annual growth rate of 2.35%. Submit the workbook and results of the goal seek as requested by your instructor.

• 2: Bimonthly Projected Earnings and Expenditures

The *Chesterton Trib* is a small newspaper that publishes stories of local interest. Revenues are earned from subscriptions and the sale of advertising space. A fixed percentage of the Net Revenue is spent on marketing, payroll, commissions (advertising sales only), production costs, and reportorial expenses. The editor has summarized the paper's expenditures over the past year and the anticipated income from subscriptions and advertising on a bimonthly basis as shown in Table 3–18.

With the data, you have been asked to prepare a worksheet for the next shareholder's meeting showing total revenues, total expenditures, and operating incomes for each bimonthly period. Include a 3-D Cylinder chart on a separate sheet that compares the six bimonthly operating incomes. Use the concepts and techniques presented in this chapter to create and format the worksheet and chart.

Table 3–18 Chesterton Trib Bimonthly Projected Earnings and Expenditures

Revenue	February	April	June	August	October	December
Subscriptions	12178.30	8391.50	15714.50	16340.10	12567.25	12800.15
Advertising	4130.20	6425.00	4123.15	5023.30	7015.75	9273.20
Assumptions						
Marketing	15.60%					
Payroll	21.50%					
Commissions on Advertising	3.25%					
Production Costs	12.50%					
Reportorial Expenses	5.00%					

One shareholder lobbied to reduce marketing expenditures by 3% and payroll costs by 5%. Perform a what-if-analysis reflecting the proposed changes in expenditure assumptions. The reduction in expenditures should result in a total operating income of $59,696.91 or an increase of $9,118.59. Submit the workbook and results of the what-if analysis as requested by your instructor.

•• 3: Projected Used-Truck Savings

Cousin Abe and Aunt Esther own a paint company. Their good friend Billie Bob is retiring after 35 years of delivering the morning newspaper. Billie Bob has offered them the opportunity to take his place next year. The job requires, however, that they own a truck. They need to save enough money over the next six months to buy a $10,000 used truck.

They have job orders at their paint company for the next six months: $22,150 in July, $22,480 in August, $42,900 in September, $31,200 in October, $45,301 in November, and $32,190 in December. Each month, they spend 34.55% of the job order income on material, 3.00% on rollers and brushes, 4.75% on their retirement account, and 39.5% on food and clothing. They plan to save 25% of each month's profit for the purchase of the truck. Aunt Esther's retired parents have agreed to provide a bonus of $250 whenever the monthly savings for the truck exceeds $2,000. Use the concepts and techniques presented in this project to create and format the worksheet. Your initial worksheet should show savings of $9,178.06 over the 6 months.

Cousin Abe has asked you to create a worksheet that shows orders, expenses, profits, bonuses, and savings for the next six months, and totals for each category. Aunt Esther would like to save for another used truck for $17,000. She has asked you to (a) perform a what-if analysis to determine the effect on the savings by reducing the percentage spent on material to 25% (answer total savings = $14,612.83), and (b) with the original assumptions, goal seek to determine what percentage of profits to spend on food and clothing if $15,000 is needed for the used truck (answer = 29.16%). Submit the workbook and results of the what-if analysis as requested by your instructor.

•• 4: College Expense and Resource Projections

Make It Personal

Attending college with limited resources can be a trying experience. One way to alleviate some of the financial stress is to plan ahead. Develop a worksheet following the general layout in Table 3–19 that shows the projected expenses and resources for four years of college. Use the formulas listed in Table 3–20 and the concepts and techniques presented in this chapter to create the worksheet.

Table 3–19 College Expense and Resource Projections

Expenses	Freshman	Sophomore	Junior	Senior	Total
Room & Board	$6,125.00	Formula A	⟶		—
Tuition & Books	8,750.00	Formula A	⟶		—
Clothes	750.00	Formula A	⟶		—
Entertainment	1,025.00	Formula A	⟶		—
Miscellaneous	675.00	Formula A	⟶		—
Total Expenses	—	—	—	—	—
Resources	**Freshman**	**Sophomore**	**Junior**	**Senior**	**Total**
Savings	Formula B	⟶			—
Parents	Formula B	⟶			—
Job	Formula B	⟶			—
Loans	Formula B	⟶			—
Scholarships	Formula B	⟶			—
Total Resources	—	—	—	—	—

Assumptions	
Savings	10.00%
Parents	20.00%
Job	10.00%
Loans	30.00%
Scholarships	30.00%
Annual Rate Increase	7.50%

After creating the worksheet: (a) perform what-if analysis by changing the percents of the resource assumptions; (b) perform a what-if analysis to determine the effect on the resources by increasing the Annual Rate Increase to 9%; and (c) with the original assumptions, goal seek to determine what the Annual Rate Increase would be for the total expenses to be $100,000. Submit the workbook and results of the what-if analysis as requested by your instructor.

Table 3–20 College Expense and Resource Projections Formulas

Formula A = Prior Year's Expense * (1 + Annual Rate Increase)

Formula B = Total Expenses for Year * Corresponding Assumption

•• 5: Cost of Storing Radio Isotopes

Working Together

A government agency plans to conduct experiments that will result in some radioactive waste. Although the isotopes will break apart into atoms of other elements over time, agency watchdogs are concerned about containment costs while the material still is radioactive. The agency director has asked your group to prepare a worksheet showing the amount of radioactive material remaining, containment costs, estimated agency appropriations, and the percentage of appropriations that will be spent on containment every year for the next decade. The director has outlined the desired worksheet as shown in Table 3–21 on the next page.

Continued >

Cases and Places *continued*

These formulas have been supplied:

Formula A: Amount Remaining = Original Amount $\times$ 0.5 ^(Number of Years Stored / Half-Life)

Formula B: Containment Costs = Containment Cost Per Kilogram $\times$ Total Amount Remaining

Formula C: Estimated Appropriations = Appropriations $\times$ (1 + Estimated Yearly Increase)^ Number of Years Stored

Formula D: Percentage Spent on Containment = Containment Costs / Estimated Appropriations

The director has asked your group to include a function that prints "Acceptable" below the percentage spent on containment whenever the percentage is less than 1%, otherwise print "Not Acceptable."

Have each member of your team submit a sketch of the proposed worksheet and then implement the best one. Use the concepts and techniques presented in this project to create and format the worksheet. Submit the sketches and workbook as requested by your instructor.

Table 3–21 Cost of Storing Radioactive Isotopes

	Number of Years Stored				
Number of Years Stored	1	2	3	....	10
Amount of Isotope X Remaining (in kg)	Formula A				→
Amount of Isotope Y Remaining (in kg)	Formula A				→
Total Remaining (in kg)	—	—	—	....	—
Containment Costs	Formula B				→
Estimated Appropriations	Formula C				→
Percentage Spent on Containment	Formula D				→
	Message				→

Assumptions	
Original Amount of Isotope X Remaining (in kg)	650
Half-Life of Isotope X (in years)	1
Containment Cost per Kilogram	1000
Estimated Yearly Increase	10.00%
Original Amount of Isotope Y Remaining (in kg)	3000
Half-Life of Isotope Y (in years)	0.45
Appropriations	6000000

Web Feature

Creating Web Pages Using Excel

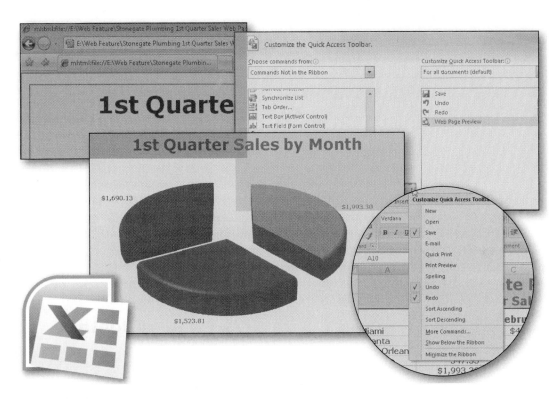

Objectives

You will have mastered the material in this Web feature when you can:

- Customize the Quick Access Toolbar
- Publish a worksheet and chart as a Web page
- Display Web pages published in Excel in a browser
- Complete file management tasks within Excel

Web Feature Introduction

Excel provides fast, easy methods for saving workbooks as Web pages that can be stored on the World Wide Web, a company's intranet, or a local hard disk. A user then can display the workbook using a browser, rather than Excel.

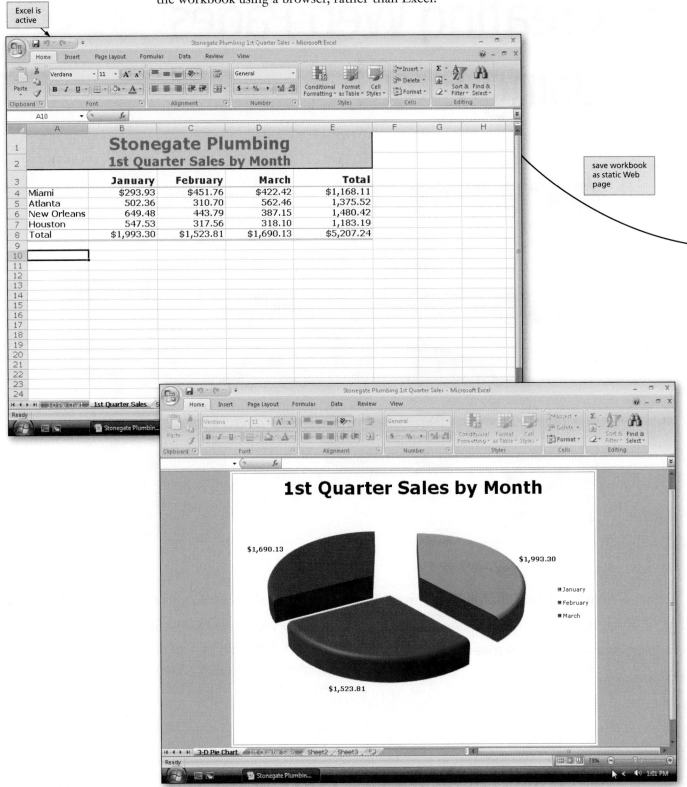

(a) Workbook Viewed in Excel

Figure 1

Project — Workbook with Chart Saved as a Web Page

Figure 1a shows the workbook for Stonegate Plumbing's 1st quarter sales by month. The chief financial officer for the company requests that the information in the worksheet, including the chart, be made available on the company's intranet for others in the company to view. In order to accomplish this task, you must save the workbook as a Web page.

You can save a workbook, or a portion of a workbook, as a Web page. The saved **Web page** is a snapshot of the workbook. It is similar to a printed report in that you can view it, but you cannot modify it. In the browser window, the workbook appears as it would in Microsoft Excel, including sheet tabs that you can click to switch between worksheets. As illustrated in Figure 1, this Web feature shows you how to save a workbook (Figure 1a) as a Web page (Figure 1b) and view it using your browser.

When you use the Save As command on the Office Button menu and choose to save a workbook as a Web page, Excel allows you to **publish workbooks**, which is the process of making a workbook available to others; for example, on the World Wide Web or on a

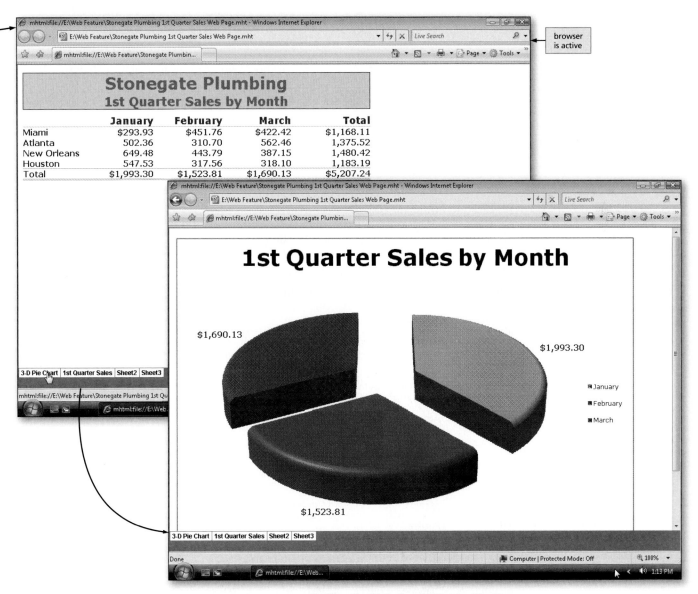

(b) Static Web Page Viewed in Browser

Web Folders and FTP Locations
You can save any type of file to a Web folder or on an FTP location, just as you would save to a folder on your hard disk. Web folders and FTP locations are particularly useful because they appear as standard folders in Windows Explorer or in the Address bar list. For additional information, see Appendix D.

company's intranet. If you have access to a Web server, you can publish Web pages by saving them on a Web server or on an FTP location. To learn more about publishing Web pages on a Web server or on an FTP location using Microsoft Office applications, refer to Appendix D.

This Web feature illustrates how to create and save the Web pages on a USB flash drive, rather than on a Web server. This feature also demonstrates how to preview a workbook as a Web page and create a new folder using the Save As dialog box.

Overview

As you read through this Web feature, you will learn how to create the worksheet shown in Figure 1 on pages EX 250 and 251 by performing these general tasks:

- Save a Workbook as a Web page
- Preview the Workbook in a Web browser
- Complete file management tasks within Excel

Using Web Page Preview and Saving an Excel Workbook as a Web Page

At any time during the construction of a workbook, you can preview it as a Web page by using the Web Page Preview command. The Web Page Preview command is not available on the Ribbon, but you can add the command to the Quick Access Toolbar. When you invoke the Web Page Preview command, it starts your browser and displays the active sheet in the workbook as a Web page. If the preview is acceptable, then you can save the workbook as a Web page.

To Add a Button to the Quick Access Toolbar

Many commands available in Excel are not included on any of the tabs on the Ribbon. You can, however, add such commands to the Quick Access Toolbar. One such command allows you to preview a document in a Web browser. This command, Web Page Preview, needs to be added to the Quick Access Toolbar so that the Web page can be previewed. The following steps add the Web Page Preview command to the Quick Access Toolbar.

- Connect a USB flash drive with the Data Files for Students on it to one of the computer's USB ports.

- Start Excel and then open the workbook, Stonegate Plumbing 1st Quarter Sales, from the Data Files for Students.

- Click the Customize Quick Access Toolbar button to display the Customize Quick Access Toolbar menu (Figure 2).

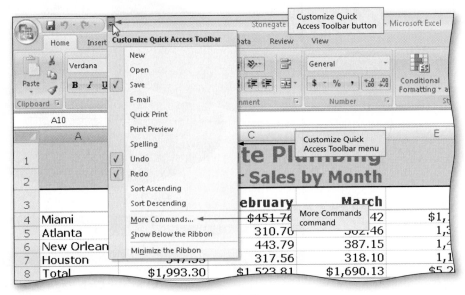

Figure 2

3

- Click the More Commands command on the Customize Quick Access Toolbar menu.
- When the Excel Options dialog box is displayed, click the 'Choose commands from' box arrow to display the 'Choose commands from' list (Figure 3).

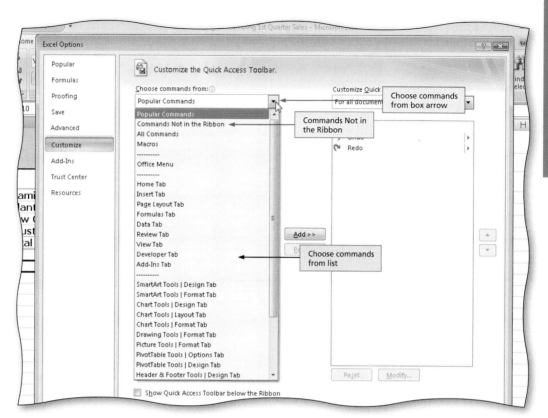

Figure 3

4

- Click Commands Not in the Ribbon in the 'Choose commands from' list to display a list of commands not in the Ribbon (Figure 4).

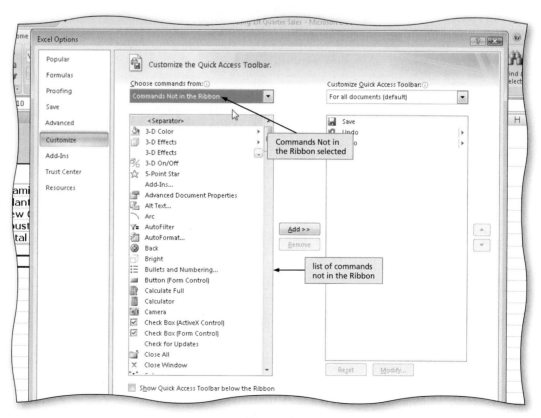

Figure 4

• Scroll to the bottom of the list, click Web Page Preview, and then click the Add button to add the button to the Quick Access Toolbar (Figure 5).

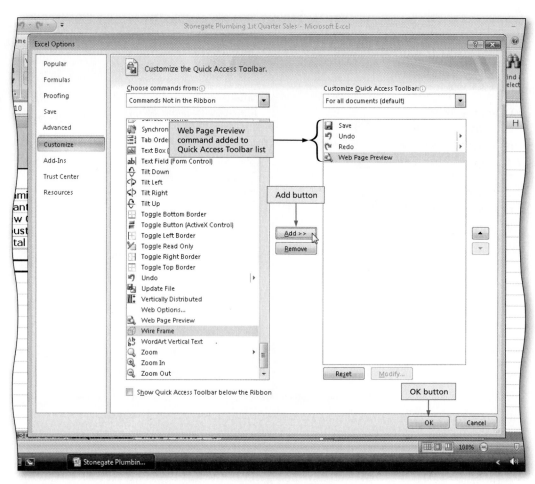

Figure 5

• Click the OK button to close the Excel Options dialog box and display the Quick Access Toolbar with the Web Page Preview button added to it (Figure 6).

Will the Web Page Preview command be on the Quick Access Toolbar the next time that I start Excel?

Yes. When you change the Quick Access Toolbar, the changes remain even after you restart Excel. If you share a computer with somebody else or if the Quick Access Toolbar becomes cluttered, Excel allows you to remove commands from the Quick Access Toolbar. The Web Page Preview button is removed from the Quick Access Toolbar later in this Web feature.

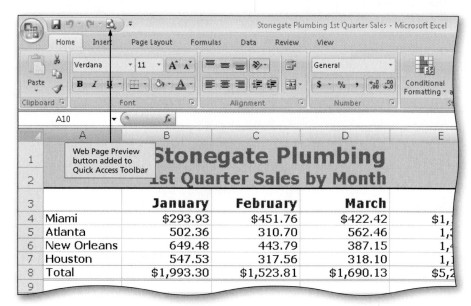

Figure 6

To Preview the Web Page

The following steps preview the Web page version of the workbook in a browser.

1

- Click the Web Page Preview button on the Quick Access Toolbar to display the Web page in your browser. If the security warning appears in the Information bar at the top of the Web page, click its Close button.

- If necessary, click the Maximize button on your browser's title bar (Figure 7).

Q&A

What happens when I click the Web Page Preview button?

Excel starts your browser. The browser displays a preview of how the 1st Quarter Sales sheet will appear as a Web page (Figure 7). The Web page preview in the browser is nearly identical to the display of the worksheet in Excel. A highlighted browser button appears on the Windows Vista taskbar indicating it is active. The Excel button on the Windows Vista taskbar no longer is highlighted.

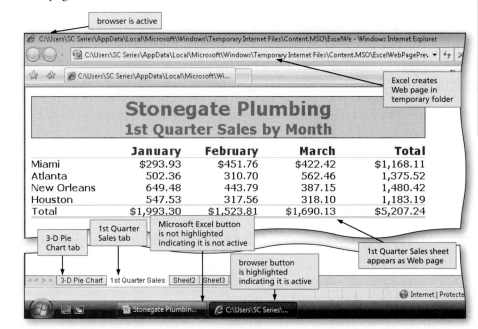

Figure 7

2

- Click the 3-D Pie Chart tab at the bottom of the Web page to display the 3-D Pie chart in the browser (Figure 8).

3

- After viewing the Web page preview of the Stonegate Plumbing 1st Quarter Sales workbook, click the Close button on the right side of the browser title bar to close the browser and make Excel active again.

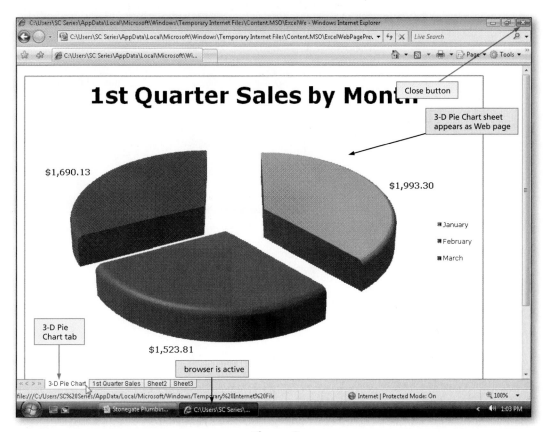

Figure 8

To Save an Excel Workbook as a Web Page in a Newly Created Folder

Once the preview of the workbook as a Web page is acceptable, you can save the workbook as a Web page so that others can view it using a Web browser, such as Internet Explorer or Mozilla Firefox.

Two Web page formats exist in which you can save workbooks. Both formats convert the contents of the workbook into HTML (HyperText Markup Language), which is a language browsers can interpret. One format is called **Single File Web Page format**, which saves all of the components of the Web page in a single file with an .mht extension. This format is useful particularly for e-mailing workbooks in HTML format. The second format, called **Web Page format**, saves the Web page in a file and some of its components in a folder. This format is useful if you need access to the components, such as images, that make up the Web page.

Experienced users organize the files saved on a storage medium, such as a USB flash drive or hard disk, by creating folders. They then save related files in a common folder. Excel allows you to create folders before saving a file using the Save As dialog box. The following steps create a new folder on the USB flash drive and save the workbook as a Web page in the new folder.

- With the Stonegate Plumbing 1st Quarter Sales workbook open, click the Office Button.

- Click Save As on the Office Button menu to display the Save As dialog box (Figure 9).

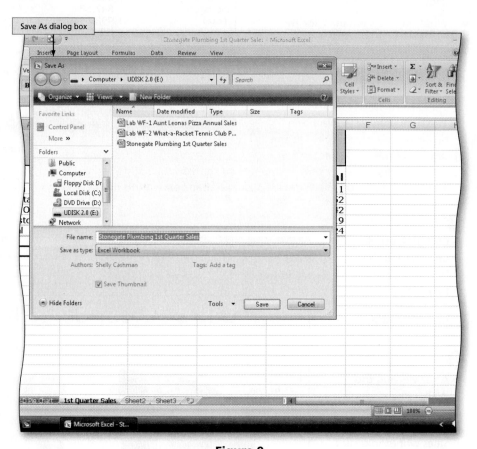

Figure 9

- Type Stonegate Plumbing 1st Quarter Sales Web Page in the File name box.

- Click the 'Save as type' box arrow and then click Single File Web Page.

- Click the Address bar arrow, select UDISK 2.0 (E:) (your USB flash drive name and letter may be different), and then click the New Folder button to create a new folder.

- When Excel displays the new folder with the name New Folder, type Web Feature in the text box (Figure 10).

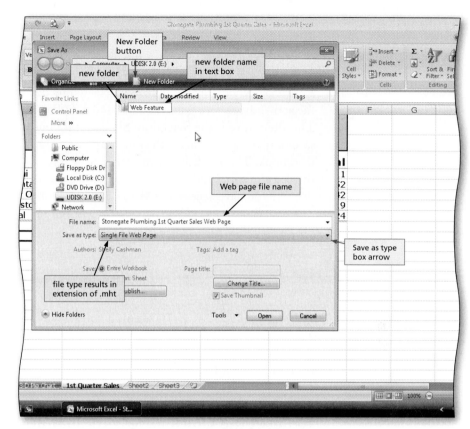

Figure 10

- Press the ENTER key. If the Microsoft Office Excel dialog box appears, click the Yes button.

Q&A

What does Excel do when I press the ENTER key?

Excel automatically selects the new folder named Web Feature in the Address bar (Figure 11). The Entire Workbook option button in the Save area instructs Excel to save all sheets in the workbook as Web pages.

- Click the Save button in the Save As dialog box to save the workbook in a single file in HTML format in the Web Feature folder on the USB flash drive.

- If the Microsoft Office Excel dialog box is displayed, click the Yes button.

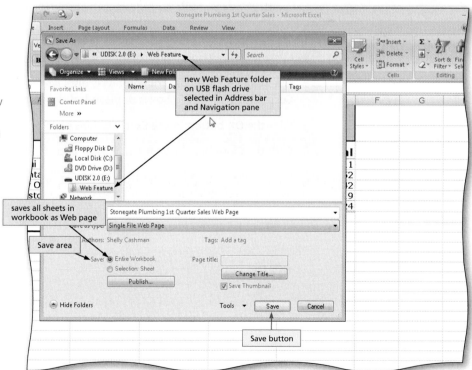

Figure 11

BTW

Creating Links
You can add hyperlinks to an Excel workbook before you save it as a Web page. The hyperlinks in the Excel workbook can link to a Web page, a location in a Web page, or an e-mail address that automatically starts the viewer's e-mail program.

Saving Workbooks as Web Pages

The Save As dialog box changes when you select Single File Web Page, which is in MHTML format, in the 'Save as type' box. When you use the Single File Web Page format, a Save area appears in the dialog box. Within the Save area are two option buttons and a Publish button (Figure 11). You can select only one of the option buttons. The Entire Workbook option button is selected by default. This indicates Excel will save all the active sheets (1st Quarter Sales and 3-D Pie Chart) in the workbook as a Web page. The alternative is the Selection: Sheet option button. If you select this option, Excel will save only the active sheet (the one that currently is displaying in the Excel window) in the workbook. The Publish button in the Save As dialog box in Figure 11 is an alternative to the Save button. It allows you to customize the Web page further.

If you have access to a Web server and it allows you to save files in a Web folder, then you can save the Web page directly on the Web server by clicking the Network icon in the Folders list in the Save As dialog box (Figure 11). If you have access to a Web server that allows you to save on an FTP site, then you can select the FTP site below FTP locations in the Address bar just as you select any folder in which to save a file. To learn more about publishing Web pages in a Web folder or on an FTP location using Office applications, refer to Appendix D.

After Excel saves the workbook in Step 4, it displays the MHTML file in the Excel window. Excel can continue to display the workbook in HTML format, because, within the MHTML file that it created, it also saved the Excel formats that allow it to display the MHTML file in Excel.

BTW

Viewing Source Code
To view the HTML source code for a Web page created in Excel, use your browser to display the Web page, click the Page button and then click View Source.

To Reset the Quick Access Toolbar and Quit Excel

The necessary work with the Excel workbook is complete. The following steps remove the Web Page Preview button from the Quick Access Toolbar and quit Excel.

1 Click the Customize the Quick Access Toolbar button on the Ribbon.

2 Click the More Commands command.

3 When the Excel Options dialog box is displayed, click the Reset button. If the Reset Customizations dialog box is displayed, click the Yes button.

4 Click the OK button in the Excel Options dialog box to close it.

5 Click the Close button on the Microsoft Excel title bar.

Q&A Do I need to remove the button from the Quick Access Toolbar?

No. For consistency, in this book the Quick Access Toolbar is reset after the added buttons no longer are needed. If you share a computer with others, you should reset the Quick Access Toolbar when you are finished using the computer.

File Management Tools in Excel

In the previous set of steps, Excel automatically navigates to the new folder name in the Save in box when you press the ENTER key after typing the new folder name (Figure 11 on page EX 257). It actually was not necessary to create a new folder earlier in this Web feature; the Web page could have been saved on the USB flash drive in the same manner files were saved on the USB flash drive in the previous projects. Creating a new folder, however, allows you to organize your work.

Finally, once you create a folder, you can right-click it while the Save As dialog box is active and perform many file management tasks directly in Excel (Figure 12). For example, once the shortcut menu appears, you can rename the selected folder, delete it, copy it, display its properties, and perform other file management functions.

BTW

Quick Reference
For a table that lists how to complete the tasks covered in this book using the mouse, Ribbon, shortcut menu, and keyboard, see the Quick Reference Summary at the back of this book, or visit the Excel 2007 Quick Reference Web page (scsite.com/ex2007/qr).

BTW

Certification
The Microsoft Certified Application Specialist (MCAS) program provides an opportunity for you to obtain a valuable industry credential – proof that you have the Excel 2007 skills required by employers. For more information, see Appendix G or visit the Excel 2007 Certification Web page (scsite.com/ex2007/cert).

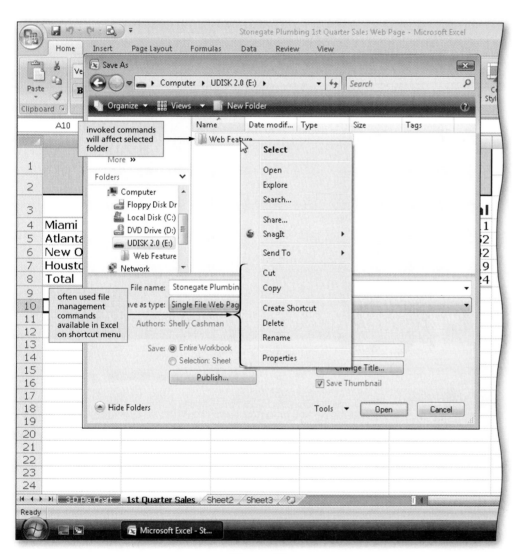

Figure 12

To View and Manipulate the Web Page Using a Browser

With the Web page saved in the Web Feature folder on the USB flash drive, you can now view it using a browser, as shown in the following steps.

- If necessary, connect the USB flash drive with the Data Files for Students to one of the computer's USB ports.

- Click the Start button on the Windows Vista taskbar, click All Programs on the Start menu, and then click Internet Explorer in the All Programs list.

- When the Internet Explorer window opens, type e:\web feature\ stonegate plumbing 1st quarter sales web page.mht in the Address box and then press the ENTER key to display the Web page in your browser (Figure 13). (Your USB flash drive may have a different name and letter.)

- If the Internet Explorer dialog box appears, click the OK button, right-click the first Internet Explorer button on the Windows Vista taskbar, and then click Close on the shortcut menu. If a security warning appears in the Information bar at the top of the Web page, click its Close button.

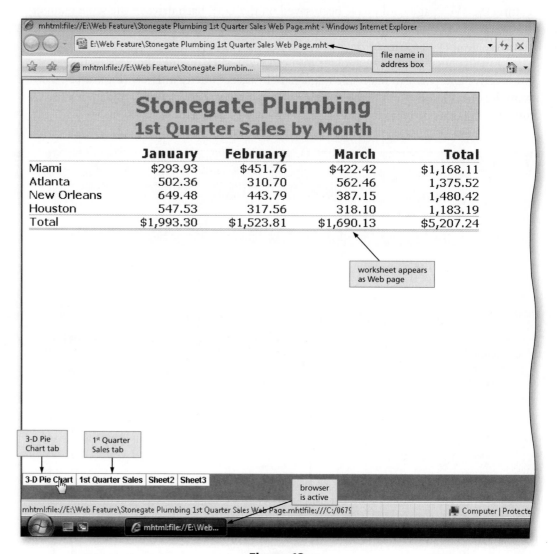

Figure 13

- Click the 3-D Pie Chart sheet tab at the bottom of the window to display the 3-D Pie chart in your browser (Figure 14). If the security warning appears in the Information bar at the top of the Web page, click its Close button.

- Use the scroll arrows to display the lower portion of the chart.

Q&A

What are the benefits of using a browser to view a workbook?

You can see from Figures 13 and 14 that a Web page is an ideal way to distribute information to a large group of people. For example, the Web page could be published on a Web server connected to the Internet and made available to anyone with a computer, browser, and the address of the Web page. It also can be e-mailed easily, because the Web page resides in a single file, rather than in a file and folder. Publishing a workbook as a Web page, therefore, is an excellent alternative to distributing printed copies of the workbook.

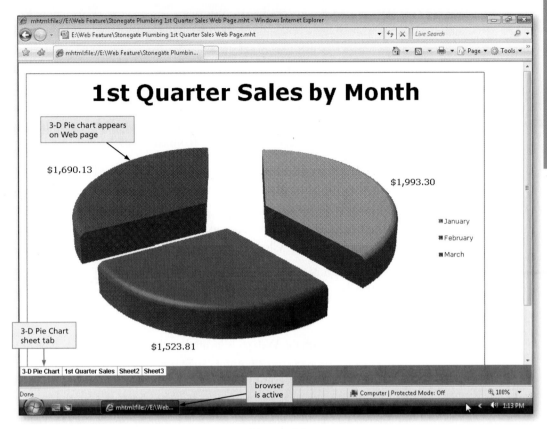

Figure 14

- Click the Close button on the right side of the browser title bar to close the browser.

Feature Summary

This Web feature introduced you to customizing the Quick Access Toolbar, previewing a workbook as a Web page, creating a new folder on a USB flash drive, and publishing and viewing a Web page. The items listed below include all the new Office 2007 skills you have learned in this Web feature.

1. Add a Button to the Quick Access Toolbar (EX 252)
2. Preview the Web Page (EX 255)
3. Save an Excel Workbook as a Web Page in a Newly Created Folder (EX 256)
4. View and Manipulate the Web Page Using a Browser (EX 260)

In the Lab

Create a Web page using the guidelines, concepts, and skills presented in this Web feature. Labs are listed in order of increasing difficulty.

1 Creating a Web Page I

Problem: You are a spreadsheet specialist for Aunt Leona's Pizza, a national chain of pizzerias. Your manager has asked you to create a Web page from the company's annual sales workbook.

Instructions Part 1:   Start Excel and open the Lab WF-1 Aunt Leonas Pizza Annual Sales workbook from the Data Files for Students. Perform the following tasks:

1. Add the Web Page Preview command to the Quick Access Toolbar.

2. Review the worksheet and chart so you have an idea of what the workbook contains. Preview the workbook as a Web page. Close the browser.

3. Save the workbook as a single file Web page in a new folder titled Web Feature Exercises using the file name, Lab WF-1 Aunt Leonas Pizza Annual Sales Web Page. Make sure you select Entire Workbook in the Save area before you click the Save button. Reset the Quick Access Toolbar and then quit Excel.

4. Start your browser. With the Web page located on the USB flash drive, type `e:\web feature exercises\ lab wf-1 aunt leonas pizza annual sales web page.mht` in the Address box (your USB flash drive may have a different name and letter). When the browser displays the Web page, click the tabs at the bottom of the window to view the sheets. Close the browser. Submit the assignment as requested by your instructor.

In the Lab

2 Creating a Web Page II

Problem: You work part-time as a spreadsheet analyst for What-a-Racket Tennis Club. You have been asked to create a Web page from the workbook that the company uses to project membership dues and payroll expenses.

Instructions Part 1:   Start Excel and open the Lab WF-2 What-a-Racket Tennis Club Projections workbook from the Data Files for Students. Perform the following tasks:

1. Add the Web Page Preview command to the Quick Access Toolbar.

2. Review the 3-D Bar Chart sheet and the Projected Expenses sheet in Excel. Preview the workbook as a Web page. Close the browser.

3. Save the workbook as a Web page (select Web Page in the Save as type box) in the Web Feature Exercises folder using the file name, Lab WF-2 What-a-Racket Tennis Club Projections Web Page. Make sure you select Entire Workbook in the Save area before you click the Save button. Reset the Quick Access Toolbar and then quit Excel. Saving the workbook as a Web page, rather than a single file Web page, will result in an additional folder being added to the Web Feature Exercises folder.

4. Start your browser. Type `e:\web feature exercises\lab wf-2 what-a-racket tennis club projections web page.htm` in the Address box (your USB flash drive may have a different name and letter). When the browser displays the Web page, click the tabs at the bottom of the window to view the sheets. Close the browser. Submit the assignment as requested by your instructor.

In the Lab

3 File Management within Excel

Problem: Your manager at What-a-Racket Tennis Club has asked you to teach her to complete basic file management tasks from within Excel.

Instructions: Start Excel and click the Open command on the Office Button menu. When Excel displays the Open dialog box, create a new folder called In the Lab 3. Click the Back to button to reselect the drive in the Address bar. Use the shortcut menu to complete the following tasks: (1) rename the In the Lab 3 folder to In the Lab 3A; (2) show the properties of the In the Lab 3A folder; and (3) delete the In the Lab 3A folder.

4

Financial Functions, Data Tables, and Amortization Schedules

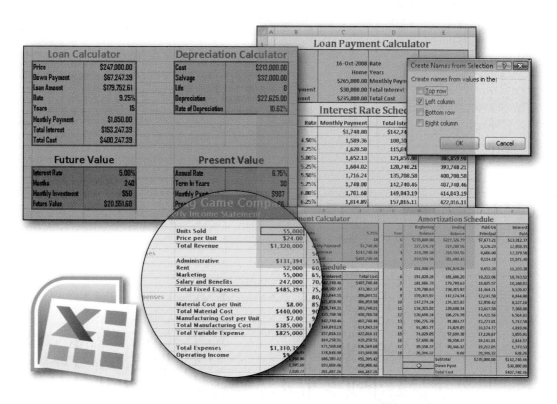

Objectives

You will have mastered the material in this chapter when you can:

- Control the color and thickness of outlines and borders

- Assign a name to a cell and refer to the cell in a formula using the assigned name

- Determine the monthly payment of a loan using the financial function PMT

- Use the financial functions PV (present value) and FV (future value)

- Create a data table to analyze data in a worksheet

- Add a pointer to a data table

- Create an amortization schedule

- Analyze worksheet data by changing values

- Use names and the Set Print Area command to print sections of a worksheet

- Set print options

- Protect and unprotect cells in a worksheet

- Use the formula checking features of Excel

- Hide and unhide cell gridlines, rows, columns, sheets, and workbooks

4 | Financial Functions, Data Tables, and Amortization Schedules

Introduction

Two of the more powerful aspects of Excel are its wide array of functions and its capability of organizing answers to what-if questions. In this chapter, you will learn about financial functions such as the PMT function, which allows you to determine a monthly payment for a loan, and the PV function, which allows you to determine the present value of an investment.

In earlier chapters, you learned how to analyze data by using Excel's recalculation feature and goal seeking. This chapter introduces an additional what-if analysis tool, called data tables. You use a data table to automate data analyses and organize the answers returned by Excel. Another important loan analysis tool is the Amortization Schedule section. An amortization schedule shows the beginning and ending balances and the amount of payment that applies to the principal and interest over a period.

In previous chapters, you learned how to print in a variety of ways. This chapter continues with a discussion about additional methods of printing using names and the Set Print Area command.

Finally, this chapter introduces you to cell protection; hiding and unhiding rows, columns, sheets, and workbooks; and formula checking. **Cell protection** ensures that users do not change values inadvertently that are critical to the worksheet. **Hiding** portions of a workbook lets you show only the parts of the workbook that the user needs to see. The **formula checker** checks the formulas in a workbook in a manner similar to the way the spell checker checks for misspelled words.

Project — Loan Payment Calculator with Data Table and Amortization Schedule

The project in the chapter follows proper design guidelines and uses Excel to create the worksheet shown in Figure 4–1. Braden Mortgage operates as a small home loan institution. The company's Chief Financial Officer has asked for a workbook that calculates loan payment information, displays an amortization schedule, and displays a table that shows loan payments for varying interest rates. To ensure that the loan officers do not delete the formulas in the worksheet, she has asked that cells in the worksheet be protected so they cannot be changed accidently.

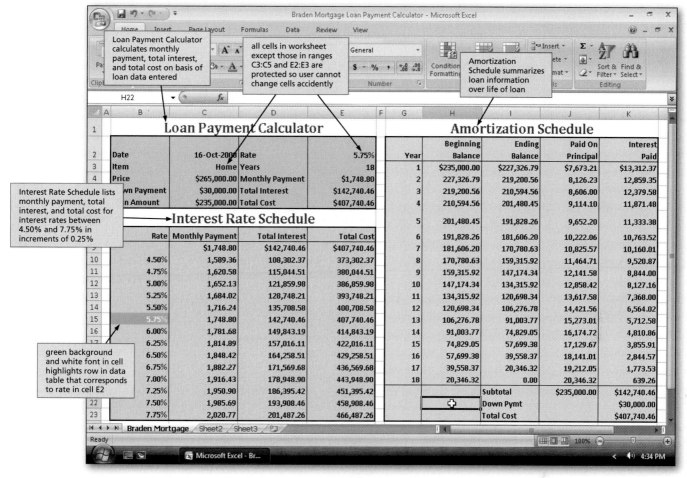

Figure 4–1

The requirements document for the Braden Mortgage Loan Payment Calculator worksheet is shown in Figure 4–2 on the next page. It includes the needs, source of data, summary of calculations, special requirements, and other facts about its development.

Overview

As you read this chapter, you will learn how to create the worksheet shown in Figure 4–1 by performing these general tasks:

- Create and format the Loan Payment Calculator section and use the payment function
- Create and format a data table that includes the interest rate schedule
- Create and format the amortization schedule and use the present value and future value functions
- Create and test print areas in the worksheet
- Protect cells in the worksheet
- Check the formulas in the worksheet

REQUEST FOR NEW WORKBOOK

Date Submitted:	May 5, 2008
Submitted By:	Elana Hughes
Worksheet Title:	Loan Payment Calculator
Needs:	An easy-to-read worksheet (Figure 4-3) that: 1. determines the monthly payment, total interest, and total cost for a loan; 2. shows a data table that answers what-if questions based on changing interest rates; 3. highlights the rate in the data table that matches the actual interest rate; and 4. shows an amortization schedule that lists annual summaries.
Source of Data:	The data (item, price of the item, down payment, interest rate, and term of the loan in years) is determined by the loan officer and customer when they initially meet to review the loan. The Excel Data Table command creates the data table.

Calculations:	1. The following calculations must be made for each loan:
	    a. Loan Amount = Price – Down Payment
	    b. Monthly Payment = PMT function
	    c. Total Interest = 12 × Years × Monthly Payment – Loan Amount
	    d. Total Cost = 12 × Years x Monthly Payment + Down Payment
	2. The amortization schedule involves the following calculations:
	    a. Beginning Balance = Loan Amount
	    b. Ending Balance = PV function or 0
	    c. Paid on Principal = Beginning Balance – Ending Balance
	    d. Interest Paid = 12 × Monthly Payment – Paid on Principal or 0
	    e. Paid on Principal Subtotal = SUM function
	    f. Interest Paid Subtotal = SUM function

Special Requirements	1. Assign names to the ranges of the three major sections of the worksheet and the worksheet itself, so that the names can be used to print each section separately. 2. Protect the worksheet in such a way that the loan officers cannot enter data into wrong cells mistakenly.

Approvals

Approval Status:	X	Approved
		Rejected
Approved By:		Jorge Martin, Chief Information Officer
Date:		May 12, 2008
Assigned To:		J. Quasney, Spreadsheet Specialist

Figure 4–2

Plan
Ahead

General Project Decisions

While creating an Excel worksheet, you need to make several decisions that will determine the appearance and characteristics of the finished worksheet. As you create the worksheet required to meet the requirements shown in Figure 4–2, you should follow these general guidelines:

1. Create and format the Loan Payment Calculator section of the worksheet. The Loan Payment Calculator section requires a compact and understandable interface where both loan officers and customers can view the results of possible loan situations quickly. This section requires complex financial calculations such as present value and future value of a loan. Excel's financial functions can be used to solve these problems. As with the other two sections of the worksheet, this section of the worksheet should be formatted to make it distinct from the other two sections of the worksheet.

2. Create and format the Interest Rate Schedule section of the worksheet. The Interest Rate Schedule depends on values in the Loan Payment Calculator section of the worksheet. If those values are placed in the top row of the Interest Rate Schedule, then payment, interest, and cost values for various interest rates can be computed in the columns in this section.

3. Create and format the Amortization Schedule section of the worksheet. The amortization schedule relies on formulas specified in the requirements document (Figure 4–2). This section of the worksheet also should include subtotals and a total to provide additional insight to the users of the worksheet.

4. Specify and name print areas of the worksheet. As specified in the requirements document, users of the worksheet require the option to print the individual sections of the worksheet. Excel allows you to name these sections and then print the sections by name.

5. Determine which cells to protect and unprotect in the worksheet. When creating a workbook that will be used by others, the spreadsheet designer should consider which cells another user should be able to manipulate. For the Loan Payment Calculator, the user needs to modify only the item, price, down payment, rate, and number of years of the loan. All other cells in the worksheet should be protected from input by the user of the worksheet.

In addition, using a sketch of the worksheet can help you visualize its design. The sketch of the worksheet (Figure 4–3) consists of titles, column and cell headings, location of data values, and a general idea of the desired formatting.

As shown in the worksheet sketch shown in Figure 4–3, the three basic sections of the worksheet are (1) the Loan Payment Calculator on the upper–left side, (2) the Interest Rate Schedule data table on the lower–left side, and (3) the Amortization Schedule on the right side. The worksheet will be created in this order.

(continued)

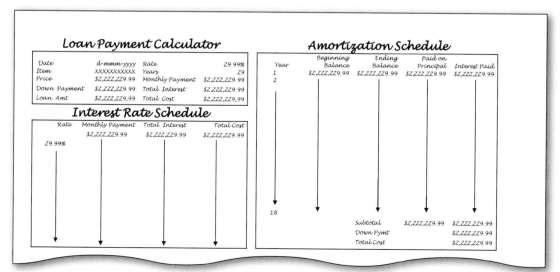

Figure 4–3

Plan Ahead

(continued)

When necessary, more specific details concerning the above guidelines are presented at appropriate points in the chapter. The chapter also will identify the actions you perform and decisions made regarding these guidelines during the creation of the worksheet shown in Figure 4–1 on page EX 267.

Good Worksheet Design
Do not create worksheets as if you are going to use them only once. Carefully design worksheets as if they will be on display and evaluated by your fellow workers. Smart worksheet design starts with visualizing the results you need. A well-designed worksheet often is used for many years.

With a good understanding of the requirements document, an understanding of the necessary decisions, and a sketch of the worksheet, the next step is to use Excel to create the worksheet.

To Start Excel

If you are using a computer to step through the project in this chapter and you want your screen to match the figures in this book, you should change your computer's resolution to 1024×768. For information about how to change a computer's resolution, see page APP 21 in Appendix E.

The following steps, which assume Windows is running, start Excel based on a typical installation of Microsoft Office on your computer. You may need to ask your instructor how to start Excel for your computer.

1 Click the Start button on the Windows Vista taskbar to display the Start menu.

2 Click All Programs at the bottom of the left pane on the Start menu to display the All Programs list.

3 Click Microsoft Office in the All Programs list to display the Microsoft Office list.

4 Click Microsoft Office Excel 2007 to start Excel and display a blank worksheet in the Excel window.

5 If the Excel window is not maximized, click the Maximize button next to the Close button on its title bar to maximize the window.

6 If the worksheet window in Excel is not maximized, click the Maximize button next to the Close button on its title bar to maximize the worksheet window within Excel.

Multiple Worksheets
You can have more than one instance of Excel running. Besides opening multiple workbooks in Excel, you can run multiple instances of Excel. Each instance of Excel will show as a button on the Windows Vista taskbar. When you first install Excel, Excel shows all open workbooks in the taskbar. To change this behavior, click the Excel Options button on the Office Button menu, click Advanced, remove the checkmark from the 'Show all windows in the Taskbar' check box, and then click the OK button.

To Bold the Entire Worksheet

The following steps assign a bold format to the entire worksheet so that all entries will be emphasized.

1 Click the Select All button immediately above row heading 1 and to the left of column heading A.

2 Click the Bold button on the Home tab on the Ribbon.

To Enter the Section Title, Row Titles, System Date, Document Properties, and Save the Workbook

The next step is to enter the Loan Payment Calculator section title, row titles, system date, document properties, and then save the workbook. To make the worksheet easier to read, the width of column A will be decreased to 1.57 characters and used as a separator between the Loan Payment Calculator section and the row headings on the left. Using a column as a separator between sections on a worksheet is a common technique employed by spreadsheet specialists. The width of columns B through E will be increased so the intended values fit. The height of row 1, which contains the title, will be increased so it stands out. The worksheet title also will be changed to the Title cell style.

The following steps enter the section title, row titles, system date, document properties, and then save the workbook.

① Select cell B1. Enter `Loan Payment Calculator` as the section title. Select the range B1:E1. Click the Merge & Center button on the Ribbon.

② With cell B1 active, click the Cell Styles button on the Ribbon and then select the Title cell style in the Cell Styles gallery.

③ Position the mouse pointer on the bottom boundary of row heading 1. Drag down until the ScreenTip indicates Height: 23.25 (31 pixels). Position the mouse pointer on the bottom boundary of row heading 2. Drag down until the ScreenTip indicates Height: 30.00 (40 pixels).

④ Select cell B2 and then enter `Date` as the row title and then press the TAB key.

⑤ With cell C2 selected, enter `=now()` to display the system date.

⑥ Right–click cell C2 and then click Format Cells on the shortcut menu. When Excel displays the Format Cells dialog box, click the Number tab, click Date in the Category list, scroll down in the Type list, and then click 14–Mar–2001. Click the OK button.

⑦ Enter the following row titles:

Cell	Entry	Cell	Entry
B3	Item	D2	Rate
B4	Price	D3	Years
B5	Down Payment	D4	Monthly Payment
B6	Loan Amount	D5	Total Interest
		D6	Total Cost

⑧ Position the mouse pointer on the right boundary of column heading A and then drag to the left until the ScreenTip indicates Width: 1.57 (16 pixels).

⑨ Position the mouse pointer on the right boundary of column heading B and then drag to the right until the ScreenTip indicates Width: 13.86 (102 pixels).

⑩ Click column heading C to select it and then drag through column headings D and E. Position the mouse pointer on the right boundary of column heading C and then drag until the ScreenTip indicates Width: 16.29 (119 pixels).

⑪ Double–click the Sheet1 tab and then enter `Braden Mortgage` as the sheet name. Right–click the tab and then click Tab Color. Click Light Green (column 5, row 1) in the Standard Colors area and then select cell D6 (Figure 4–4 on the next page).

BTW

Global Formatting
To assign formats to all the cells in all the worksheets in a workbook, click the Select All button, right-click a tab, and click Select All Sheets on the shortcut menu. Next, assign the formats. To deselect the sheets, hold down the SHIFT key and click the Sheet1 tab. You also can select a cell or a range of cells and then select all sheets to assign formats to that cell or a range of cells on all sheets in a workbook.

BTW

Concatenation
You can concatenate text, numbers, or text and numbers from two or more cells into a single cell. The ampersand (&) is the concatenation operator. For example, if cell A1 = AB, cell A2 = CD, cell A3 = 25, and you assign cell A4 the formula =A1&A2&A3, then ABCD25 displays in cell A4.

⑫ Update the document properties with your name and any other relevant information.

⑬ With a USB flash drive connected to one of the computer's USB ports, click the Save button on the Quick Access Toolbar. Save the workbook using the file name `Braden Mortgage Loan Payment Calculator` on the USB flash drive.

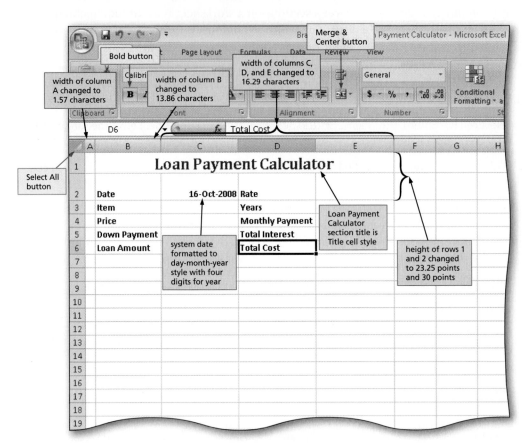

Figure 4–4

Adding Custom Borders and a Background Color to a Range

In previous projects, you were introduced to outlining a range using the Borders button on the Home tab on the Ribbon. The Borders button, however, offers only a limited selection of border thicknesses. To control the color and thickness, Excel requires that you use the Border sheet in the Format Cells dialog box.

To Add Custom Borders and a Background Color to a Range

The following steps add a thick black border and a light blue background color to the Loan Payment Calculator section. Rather than using the Fill Color button to color the background of a range as was done in previous projects, the steps use the Fill sheet in the Format Cells dialog box. To subdivide the row titles and numbers further, light borders also are added within the section as shown in Figure 4–1 on page EX 267.

To Format Cells before Entering Values

While usually you format cells after you enter values in cells, Excel also allows you to format cells before you enter the values. For example, at the beginning of this project, bold was applied to all the cells in the blank worksheet. The steps on the next page assign the Currency style format with a floating dollar sign to the ranges C4:C6 and E4:E6 before the values are entered.

1 Select the range C4:C6. While holding down the CTRL key, select the nonadjacent range E4:E6.

2 Right–click one of the selected ranges and then click Format Cells on the shortcut menu.

3 When Excel displays the Format Cells dialog box, click the Number tab. Click Currency in the Category list and then click the second format, $1,234.10, in the Negative numbers list. Click the OK button to assign the Currency style format with a floating dollar sign to the ranges C4:C6 and E4:E6.

Q&A

What will happen when I enter values in those cells?

As you enter numbers into these cells, Excel will display the numbers using the Currency style format. You also could have selected the range B4:E6 rather than the nonadjacent ranges and assigned the Currency style format to this range, which includes text. The Currency style format has no impact on text in a cell.

BTW

When to Format
Excel lets you format (1) before you enter data; (2) when you enter data, through the use of format symbols; (3) incrementally after entering sections of data; and (4) after you enter all the data. Spreadsheet specialists usually format a worksheet in increments as they build the worksheet, but occasions do exist where it makes sense to format cells before you enter any data.

To Enter the Loan Data

As shown in the Source of Data section of the Request for New Workbook document in Figure 4–2 on page EX 268, five items make up the loan data in the worksheet: the item to be purchased, the price of the item, the down payment, the interest rate, and the number of years until the loan is paid back (also called the term of the loan). These items are entered into cells C3 through C5 and cells E2 and E3. The steps below describe how to enter the following loan data: Item — Home; Price — $265,000.00; Down Payment — $30,000.00; Interest Rate — 5.75%; and Years — 18.

1 Select cell C3. Type Home and then click the Enter box in the formula bar. With cell C3 still active, click the Align Text Right button on the Ribbon. Select cell C4 and then enter 265000 for the price of the house. Select cell C5 and then enter 30000 for the down payment.

2 Select cell E2. Enter 5.75% for the interest rate. Select cell E3 and then enter 18 for the number of years to complete the entry of loan data in the worksheet (Figure 4–9 on the next page).

Q&A

Why are the entered values already formatted?

The values in cells C4 and C5 in Figure 4–9 are formatted using the Currency style with two decimal places, because this format was assigned to the cells prior to entering the values. Excel also automatically formats the interest rate in cell E2 to the Percent style with two decimal places, because the percent sign (%) was appended to 5.75 when it was entered.

BTW

Entering Percents
When you format a cell to display percentages, Excel assumes that whatever you enter into that cell in the future will be a percentage. Thus, if you enter the number .5, Excel translates the value as 50%. A potential problem arises, however, when you start to enter numbers greater than or equal to one. For instance, if you enter the number 25, do you mean 25% or 2500%? If you want Excel to treat the number 25 as 25% instead of 2500% and Excel interprets the number 25 as 2500%, click the Excel Options button on the Office Button menu. When the Excel Options dialog box is displayed, click the Advanced button and make sure the 'Enable automatic percent entry' check box is selected.

BTW

Managing Range Names

When you insert a column into a worksheet range that includes a named range, Excel automatically updates the named range to include the inserted column. To delete a named range, click the Name Manager button on the Formulas tab, select the name in the Name Manager dialog box, and then click the Delete button (Figure 4-12 on page EX 278).

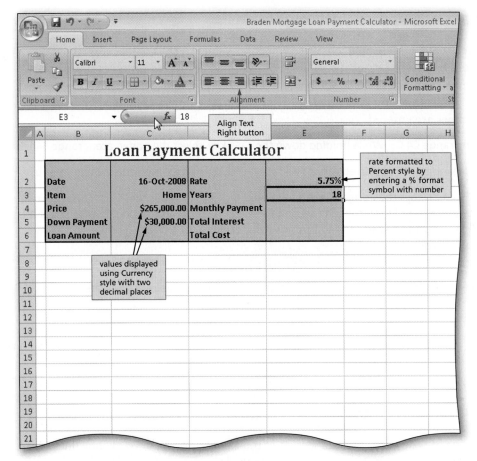

Figure 4–9

BTW

Cell References in Formulas

Are you tired of writing formulas that make no sense when you read them because of cell references? The Name Manager can help add clarity to your formulas by allowing you to assign names to cells. You then can use the names, such as Amount, rather than the cell reference, such as H10, in the formulas you create. To access the Name Manager, click the Formulas tab on the Ribbon and then click the Name Manager button.

Creating Cell Names Based on Row Titles

Worksheets often have column titles at the top of each column and row titles to the left of each row that describe the data within the worksheet. You can use these titles within formulas when you want to refer to the related data by name. A cell **name** is created from column and row titles through the use of the Name command on the Insert menu. You also can use the same command to define descriptive names that are not column titles or row titles to represent cells, ranges of cells, formulas, or constants.

Naming a cell that you plan to reference in a formula helps make the formula easier to read and remember. For example, the loan amount in cell C6 is equal to the price in cell C4 minus the down payment in cell C5. Therefore, according to what you learned in earlier projects, you can enter the loan amount formula in cell C6 as =C4 – C5. By naming cells C4 and C5 using the corresponding row titles in cells B4 and B5, however, you can enter the loan amount formula as =Price – Down Payment, which is clearer and easier to understand than =C4 – C5.

To Create Names Based on Row Titles

The following steps assign the row titles in the range B4:B6 to their adjacent cell in column C and assigns the row titles in the range D2:D6 to their adjacent cell in column E.

1

- Select the range B4:C6.

- Click the Formulas tab on the Ribbon (Figure 4–10).

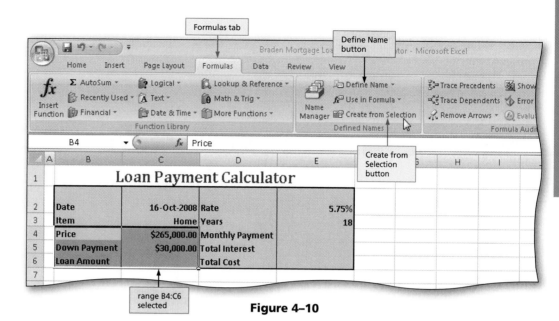

range B4:C6 selected

Figure 4–10

2

- Click the Create from Selection button on the Ribbon to display the Create Names from Selection dialog box (Figure 4–11).

Q&A

How does Excel determine which option to automatically select in the the Create Names from Selection dialog box?

Excel automatically selects the Left column check box in the 'Create names from values in the' area because the left column of the cells selected in Step 1 contains text.

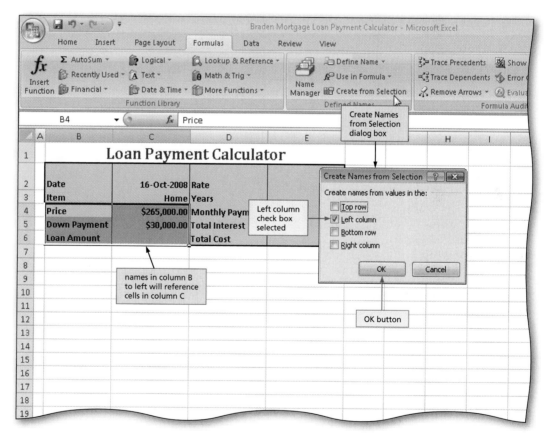

Figure 4–11

3

- Click the OK button.

- Select the range D2:E6 and then click the Create from Selection button on the Ribbon.

- Click the OK button on the Create Names from Selection dialog box to assign names to the range E2:E6.

4

- Select cell B8 to deselect the range D2:E6 and then click the Name box arrow in the formula bar to view the names created (Figure 4–12a).

Q&A

How can the cell names be used?

You now can use the assigned names in formulas to reference cells in the ranges C4:C6 or E2:E6. Excel is not case–sensitive with respect to names of cells. Hence, you can enter the names of cells in formulas in uppercase or lowercase letters. To use a name that is made up of two or more words in a formula, you should replace any space with the underscore character (_). For example, the name, Down Payment, is written as down_payment or Down_Payment when you want to reference the adjacent cell C5. Figure 4–12b shows the Name Manager dialog box that displays when you click the Name Manager button.

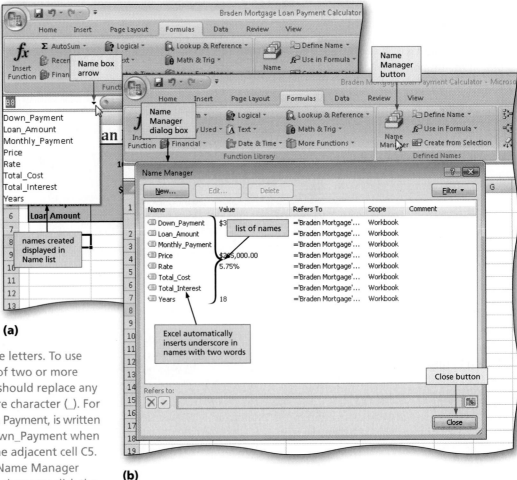

(a)

(b)

Figure 4–12

Other Ways

1. Select cell or range, type name in Name box, press ENTER key
2. Select cell or range, on Formulas tab on Ribbon click Define Name button, [type name], click OK button
3. Select cell or range, on Formulas tab on Ribbon click Name Manager button, click New, [type name], click OK button, click Close button

More About Cell Names

If you enter a formula using Point mode and click a cell that has an assigned name, then Excel will insert the name of the cell rather than the cell reference. Consider these additional points regarding the assignment of names to cells:

1. A name can be a minimum of 1 character to a maximum of 255 characters.
2. If you want to assign a name that is not a text item in an adjacent cell, use the Define Name button on the Formulas tab on the Ribbon (Figure 4–10 on the previous page) or select the cell or range and then type the name in the Name box in the formula bar.
3. Names are absolute cell references. This is important to remember if you plan to copy formulas that contain names, rather than cell references.
4. Excel displays the names in alphabetical order in the Name list when you click the Name box arrow and in the Name Manager dialog box when you click the Name Manager button on the Formulas tab on the Ribbon (Figures 4–12a and 4–12b).

5. Names are **global** to the workbook. That is, a name assigned to a cell or cell range on one worksheet in a workbook can be used on other sheets in the same workbook to reference the named cell or range.

Spreadsheet specialists often assign names to a cell or range of cells so they can select them quickly. If you want to select a cell or range of cells using the assigned name, you can click the Name box arrow (Figure 4–12a) and then click the name of the cell you want to select. This method is similar to using the F5 key to select a cell, but it is much quicker. When you select a name that references a range in the Name list, Excel highlights the range on the worksheet.

BTW

Entering Interest Rates
An alternative to requiring the user to enter an interest rate in percent form, such as 7.75%, is to allow the user to enter the interest rate as a number without an appended percent sign (7.75) and then divide the interest rate by 1200, rather than 12.

To Enter the Loan Amount Formula Using Names

To determine the loan amount in cell C6, subtract the down payment in cell C5 from the price in cell C4. As indicated earlier, this can be done by entering the formula =C4 – C5 or by entering the formula =price – down_payment in cell C6. You also can use Point mode to enter the formula, as shown in the following steps.

1

- Select cell C6.

- Type = (equal sign), click cell C4, type – (minus sign), and then click cell C5 to display the formula in cell C6 and in the formula bar using the names of the cells rather then the cell references (Figure 4–13).

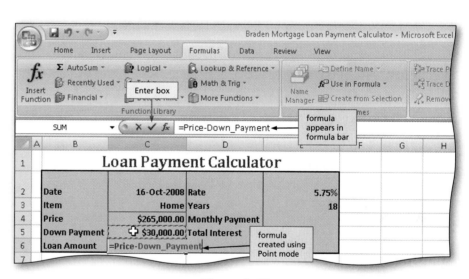

Figure 4–13

2

- Click the Enter box to assign the formula =Price – Down_Payment to cell C6 (Figure 4–14).

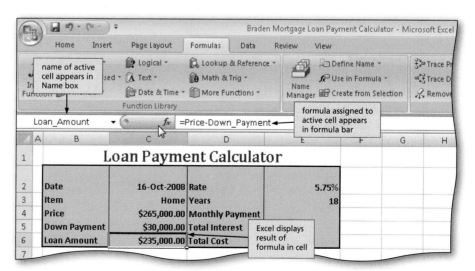

Figure 4–14

To Enter the PMT Function

The next step is to determine the monthly payment for the loan in cell E4. You can use Excel's PMT function to determine the monthly payment. The **PMT function** has three arguments — rate, payment, and loan amount. Its general form is:

=PMT(rate, periods, loan amount)

where rate is the interest rate per payment period, periods is the number of payments, and loan amount is the amount of the loan.

In the worksheet shown in Figure 4–14 on the previous page, Excel displays the annual interest rate in cell E2. Financial institutions, however, calculate interest on a monthly basis. Therefore, the rate value in the PMT function is rate / 12 (cell E2 divided by 12), rather than just rate (cell E2). The periods (or number of payments) in the PMT function is 12 * years (12 times cell E3) because there are 12 months, or 12 payments, per year.

Excel considers the value returned by the PMT function to be a debit and, therefore, returns a negative number as the monthly payment. To display the monthly payment as a positive number, begin the function with a negative sign instead of an equal sign. The PMT function for cell E4 is:

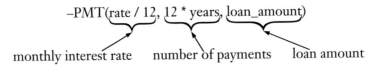

–PMT(rate / 12, 12 * years, loan_amount)

monthly interest rate   number of payments   loan amount

The following steps use the keyboard, rather than Point mode, to enter the PMT function to determine the monthly payment in cell E4.

1

• Select cell E4. Type –pmt(rate / 12, 12*years, loan_amount as the function to display the PMT function in cell E4 and in the formula bar (Figure 4–15).

Q&A

What happens as I enter the function?

The ScreenTip shows the general form of the PMT function. The arguments in brackets in the ScreenTip are optional and not required for the computation described here. The Formula AutoComplete list shows functions and cell names that match the letters that you type on the keyboard. You can type the complete cell name, such as Loan_Amount, or select the cell name from the list. Excel will add the closing parenthesis to the function automatically. Excel also may scroll the worksheet to the right in order to accommodate the display of the ScreenTip.

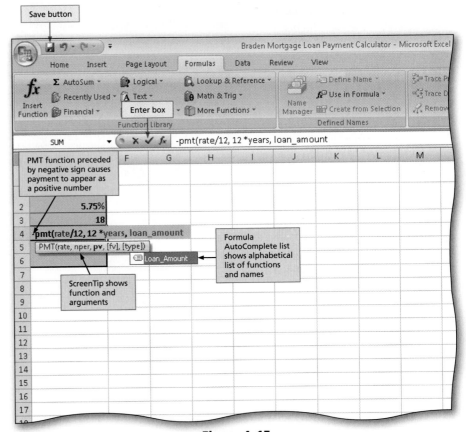

Figure 4–15

2

- If necessary, scroll the worksheet to the left using the horizontal scrollbar.

- Click the Enter box in the formula bar to complete the function (Figure 4–16).

Q&A

What does Excel display after I click the Enter box?

Excel displays the monthly payment $1,748.80 in cell E4, based on a loan amount of $235,000.00 (cell C6) with an annual interest rate of 5.75% (cell E2) for a term of 18 years (cell E3), as shown in Figure 4–16.

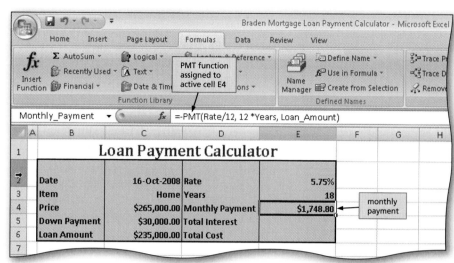

Figure 4–16

Other Ways

1. Click Formulas tab on Ribbon, click Financial button on Ribbon, select PMT function, enter arguments, click OK button

2. Click Insert Function button in formula bar, select Financial category, select PMT function, click OK button, enter arguments, click OK button

Other Financial Functions

In addition to the PMT function, Excel provides more than 50 additional financial functions to help you solve the most complex finance problems. These functions save you from entering long, complicated formulas to obtain needed results. Table 4–1 summarizes three of the more frequently used financial functions.

Table 4–1 Financial Functions

Function	Description
FV (rate, periods, payment)	Returns the future value of an investment based on periodic, constant payments, and a constant interest rate.
PMT (rate, periods, loan amount)	Calculates the payment for a loan based on the loan amount, constant payments, and a constant interest rate.
PV (rate, periods, payment)	Returns the present value of an investment. The present value is the total amount that a series of future payments is worth now.

To Determine the Total Interest and Total Cost

The next step is to determine the total interest the borrower will pay on the loan (the lending institution's gross profit on the loan) and the total cost the borrower will pay for the item being purchased. The total interest (cell E5) is equal to the number of payments times the monthly payment, less the loan amount:

=12 * years * monthly_payment – loan_amount

The total cost of the item to be purchased (cell E6) is equal to the price plus the total interest:

=price + total_interest

The steps on the next page enter formulas to determine the total interest and total cost using names.

BTW

Range Finder
Remember to check all formulas carefully. You can double-click a cell with a formula and Excel will use Range Finder to highlight the cells that provide data to the formula. While Range Finder is active, you can drag the outlines from one cell to another to change the cells referenced in the formula, provided the cells have not been named.

1 Select cell E5. Use Point mode and the keyboard to enter the formula =12 * years * monthly_payment - loan_amount to determine the total interest.

2 Select cell E6. Use Point mode and the keyboard to enter the formula =price + total_interest to determine the total cost.

3 Select cell B8 to deselect cell E6 (Figure 4–17).

4 Click the Save button on the Quick Access Toolbar to save the workbook using the file name Braden Mortgage Loan Payment Calculator.

Q&A

What are the new values displayed by Excel?

Excel displays a total interest (the lending institution's gross profit) of $142,740.46 in cell E5 and a total cost of $407,740.46 in cell E6, which is the total cost of the home to the borrower (Figure 4–17).

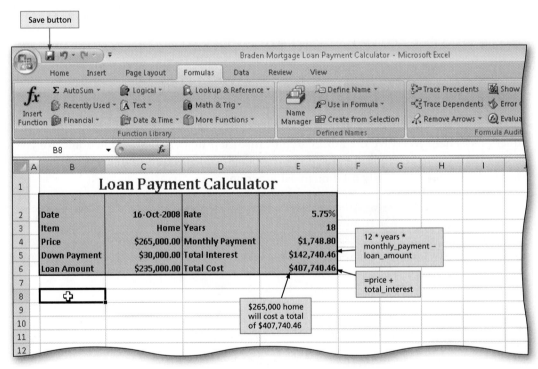

Figure 4–17

To Enter New Loan Data

Assume you want to purchase a Prius for $25,500.00. You have $5,280.00 for a down payment and you want the loan for a term of five years. Braden Mortgage currently is charging 10.25% interest for a five–year auto loan. The following steps show how to enter the new loan data.

1 Select cell C3. Type Prius and then press the DOWN ARROW key.

2 In cell C4, type 25500 and then press the DOWN ARROW key.

3 In cell C5, type 5280 and then select cell E2.

4 In cell E2, type 10.25% and then press the DOWN ARROW key.

5 In cell E3, type 5 and then select cell B8 to recalculate the loan information in cells C6, E4, E5, and E6 (Figure 4–18).

Q&A What do the results of the new calculation mean?

As you can see from Figure 4–18, the monthly payment for the Prius is $432.11. By paying for the car over a five–year period at an interest rate of 10.25%, you will pay total interest of $5,706.40 on the loan and pay a total cost of $31,206.40 for a $25,500.00 Prius.

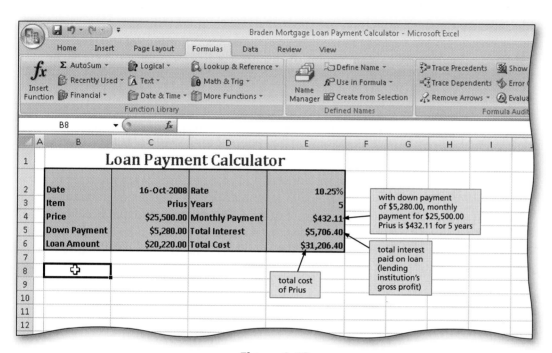

Figure 4–18

To Enter the Original Loan Data

The following steps re–enter the original loan data.

1 Select cell C3. Type Home and then press the DOWN ARROW key.

2 In cell C4, type 265000 and then press the DOWN ARROW key.

3 In cell C5, type 30000 and then select cell E2.

4 In cell E2, type 5.75 and then press the DOWN ARROW key.

5 In cell E3, type 18 and then select cell B8.

Q&A What is happening on the worksheet as I enter the original data?

Excel instantaneously recalculates all formulas in the worksheet each time you enter a value. Excel displays the original loan information as shown in Figure 4–17.

Q&A Can the Undo button on the Quick Access Toolbar be used to change back to the original data?

Yes, but the Undo button must be clicked five times, once for each data item.

BTW

Testing a Worksheet
It is good practice to test the formulas in a worksheet over and over again until you are confident they are correct. Use data that tests the limits of the formulas. For example, you should enter negative numbers, zero, and large positive numbers to test the formulas.

Using a Data Table to Analyze Worksheet Data

You already have seen that if you change a value in a cell, Excel immediately recalculates and displays the new results of any formulas that reference the cell directly or indirectly. But what if you want to compare the results of the formula for several different values? Writing down or trying to remember all the answers to the what–if questions would be unwieldy. If you use a data table, however, Excel will organize the answers in the worksheet for you automatically.

A **data table** is a range of cells that shows the answers generated by formulas in which different values have been substituted. Data tables are built in an unused area of the worksheet (in this case, the range B7:E23). Figure 4–19 illustrates the makeup of a one–input data table. With a **one–input data table**, you vary the value in one cell (in this worksheet, cell E2, the interest rate). Excel then calculates the results of one or more formulas and fills the data table with the results.

An alternative to a one–input table is a two–input data table. A **two–input data table** allows you to vary the values in two cells, but you can apply it to only one formula. A two–input data table example is illustrated in the Extend Your Knowledge exercise on page EX 325.

The interest rates that will be used to analyze the loan formulas in this project range from 4.50% to 7.75%, increasing in increments of 0.25%. The one–input data table shown in Figure 4–20 illustrates the impact of varying the interest rate on three formulas: the monthly payment (cell E4), total interest paid (cell E5), and the total cost of the item to be purchased (cell E6). The series of interest rates in column B are called **input values**.

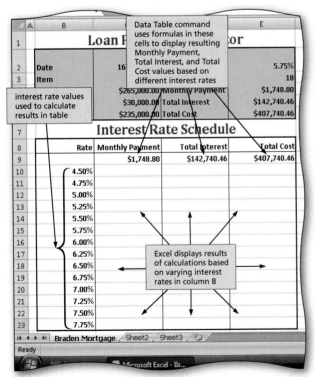

Figure 4–19

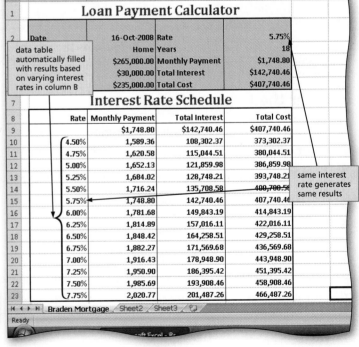

Figure 4–20

To Enter the Data Table Title and Column Titles

The first step in constructing the data table shown in Figure 4–20 is to enter the data table section title and column titles in the range B7:E8 and adjust the heights of rows 7 and 8.

1 Click the Home tab on the Ribbon. Select cell B7. Enter `Interest Rate Schedule` as the data table section title.

2 Select cell B1. Click the Format Painter button on the Ribbon. Select cell B7 to copy the format of cell B1.

3 Enter the column titles in the range B8:E8 as shown in Figure 4–21. Select the range B8:E8 and then click the Align Text Right button on the Ribbon to right–align the column titles.

4 Position the mouse pointer on the bottom boundary of row heading 7. Drag down until the ScreenTip indicates Height: 23.25 (31 pixels). Position the mouse pointer on the bottom boundary of row heading 8. Drag down until the ScreenTip indicates Height: 18.00 (24 pixels). Click cell B10 to deselect the range B8:E8 (Figure 4–21).

BTW

Selecting Cells
If you double-click the top of the heavy black border surrounding an active cell, Excel will make the first nonblank cell in the column active. If you double-click the left side of the heavy black border surrounding the active cell, Excel will make the first nonblank cell in the row the active cell. This procedure works in the same fashion for the right border and the bottom border of the active cell.

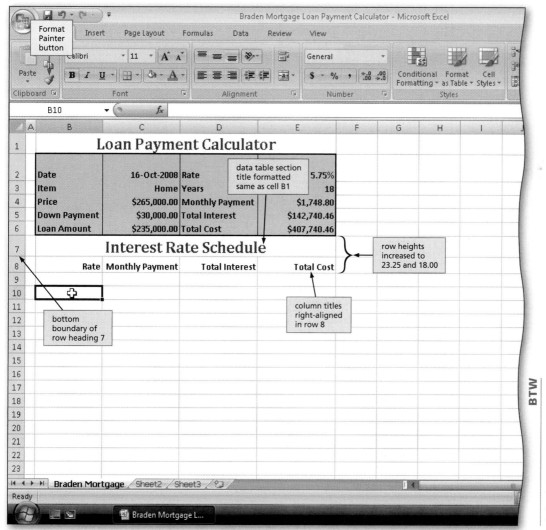

Figure 4–21

BTW

Expanding Tables
The data table you see in Figure 4–22 on the next page is relatively small. You can continue the series of percents to the bottom of the worksheet and insert additional formulas in columns to create as large a data table as you want.

To Create a Percent Series Using the Fill Handle

The next step is to create the percent series in column B using the fill handle. These percent figures will serve as the input data for the data table.

- With cell B10 selected, enter 4.50% as the first number in the series.
- Select cell B11 and then enter 4.75% as the second number in the series.
- Select the range B10:B11.
- Drag the fill handle through cell B23 to create the border of the fill area as indicated by the shaded border (Figure 4–22). Do not release the mouse button.

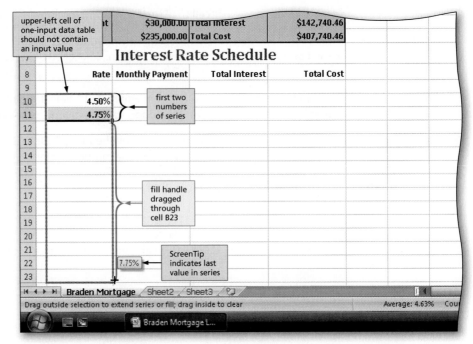

Figure 4–22

- Release the mouse button to generate the percent series from 4.50 to 7.75% and display the Auto Fill Options button. Click cell C9 to deselect the range B10:B23 (Figure 4–23).

Q&A

What is the purpose of the percent figures in column B?

Excel will use the percent figures in column B to calculate the formulas to be evaluated and entered at the top of the data table in row 9. This series begins in cell B10, not cell B9, because the cell immediately to the left of the formulas in a one–input data table should not include an input value.

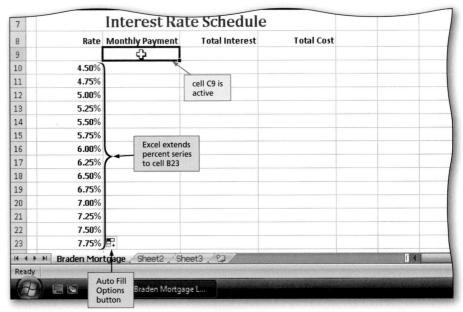

Figure 4–23

Other Ways

1. Right–drag fill handle in direction to fill, click Fill Series on shortcut menu
2. Select range, click Fill button on Home tab on Ribbon, click Down

To Enter the Formulas in the Data Table

BTW

Formulas in Data Tables
Any experienced Excel user will tell you that to enter the formulas at the top of the data table, you should enter the cell reference or name of the cell preceded by an equal sign (Figure 4–24). This ensures that if you change the original formula in the worksheet, Excel automatically will change the corresponding formula in the data table. If you use a cell reference, Excel also copies the format to the cell. If you use a name, Excel does not copy the format to the cell.

The next step in creating the data table is to enter the three formulas at the top of the table in cells C9, D9, and E9. The three formulas are the same as the monthly payment formula in cell E4, the total interest formula in cell E5, and the total cost formula in cell E6. The number of formulas you place at the top of a one–input data table depends on the application. Some one–input data tables will have only one formula, while others might have several. In this case, three formulas are affected when the interest rate changes.

Excel provides four ways to enter these formulas in the data table: (1) retype the formulas in cells C9, D9, and E9; (2) copy cells E4, E5, and E6 to cells C9, D9, and E9, respectively; (3) enter the formulas =monthly_payment in cell C9, =total_interest in cell D9, and =total_cost in cell E9; or (4) enter the formulas =e4 in cell C9, =e5 in cell D9, and =e6 in cell E9.

The best alternative to define the formulas in the data table is the fourth one, which involves using the cell references preceded by an equal sign. This is the best method because: (1) it is easier to enter the cell references; (2) if you change any of the formulas in the range E4:E6, the formulas at the top of the data table are updated automatically; and (3) Excel automatically assigns the format of the cell reference (Currency style format) to the cell. Using the names of the cells in formulas is nearly as good an alternative, but if you use cell names, Excel will not assign the format to the cells. The following steps enter the formulas of the data table in row 9.

1 With cell C9 active, type =e4 and then press the RIGHT ARROW key.

2 Type =e5 in cell D9 and then press the RIGHT ARROW key.

3 Type =e6 in cell E9 and then click the Enter box to complete the assignment of the formulas and Currency style format in the range C9:E9 (Figure 4–24).

Q&A Why are these cells assigned the values of cells in the Loan Payment Calculator area of the worksheet?

It is important to understand that the entries in the top row of the data table (row 9) refer to the formulas that the loan department wants to evaluate using the series of percentages in column B. Furthermore, recall that when you assign a formula to a cell, Excel applies the format of the first cell reference in the formula to the cell. Thus, Excel applies the Currency style format to cells C9, D9, and E9 because that is the format of cells E4, E5, and E6.

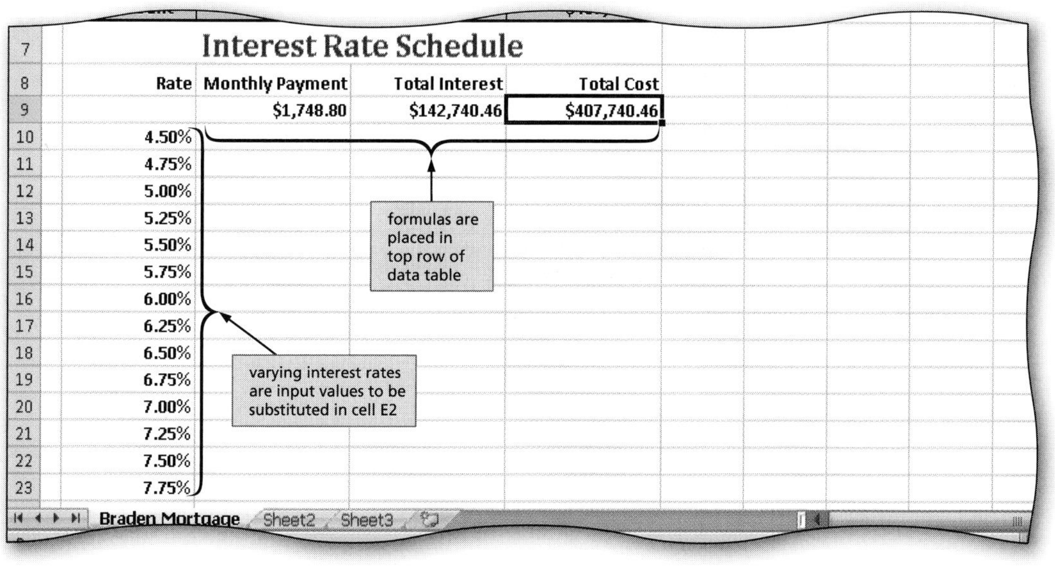

	Rate	Monthly Payment	Total Interest	Total Cost
7		**Interest Rate Schedule**		
8	Rate	Monthly Payment	Total Interest	Total Cost
9		$1,748.80	$142,740.46	$407,740.46
10	4.50%			
11	4.75%			
12	5.00%			
13	5.25%		formulas are placed in top row of data table	
14	5.50%			
15	5.75%			
16	6.00%			
17	6.25%			
18	6.50%			
19	6.75%		varying interest rates are input values to be substituted in cell E2	
20	7.00%			
21	7.25%			
22	7.50%			
23	7.75%			

Braden Mortgage   Sheet2   Sheet3

Figure 4–24

To Define a Range as a Data Table

After creating the interest rate series in column B and entering the formulas in row 9, the next step is to define the range B9:E23 as a data table. The Data Table command on the What–If Analysis button on the Data tab on the Ribbon is used to define the range B9:E23 as a data table. Cell E2 is the input cell, which means it is the cell in which values from column B in the data table are substituted in the formulas in row 9.

1

- Select the range B9:E23.

- Click the Data tab on the Ribbon and then click the What–If Analysis button on the Ribbon to display the What–If Analysis menu (Figure 4–25).

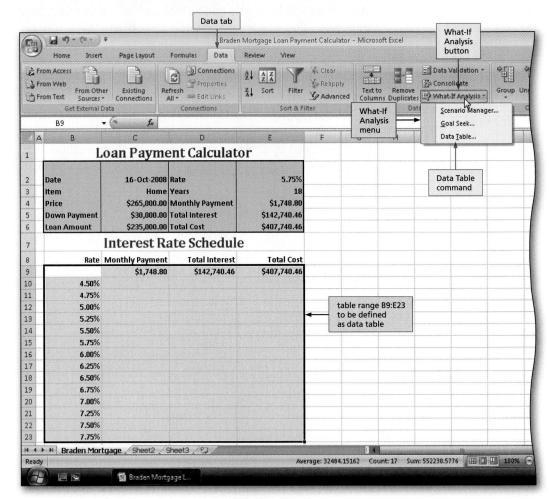

Figure 4–25

2

- Click Data Table on the What–If Analysis menu.

- When Excel displays the Data Table dialog box, click the 'Column input cell' box, and then click cell E2 in the Loan Payment Calculator section (Figure 4–26).

Q&A

What is the purpose of clicking cell E2?

The purpose of clicking cell E2 is to select it for the Column input cell. A marquee surrounds the selected cell E2, indicating it will be the input cell in which values from column B in the data table are substituted in the formulas in row 9. $E$2 now appears in the Column input cell box in the Data Table dialog box.

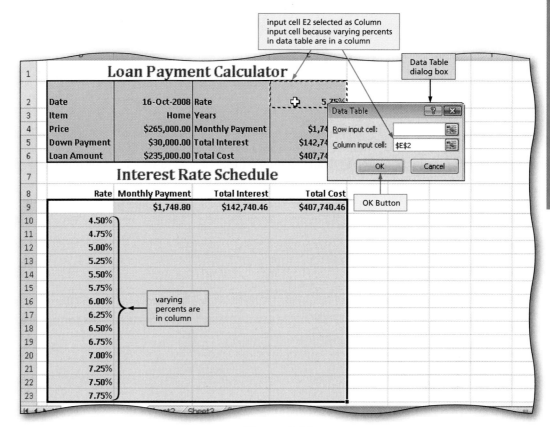

Figure 4–26

3

- Click the OK button to create the data table (Figure 4–27).

Q&A

How does Excel create the data table?

Excel calculates the results of the three formulas in row 9 for each interest rate in column B and immediately fills columns C, D, and E of the data table. The resulting values for each interest rate are displayed in the corresponding rows.

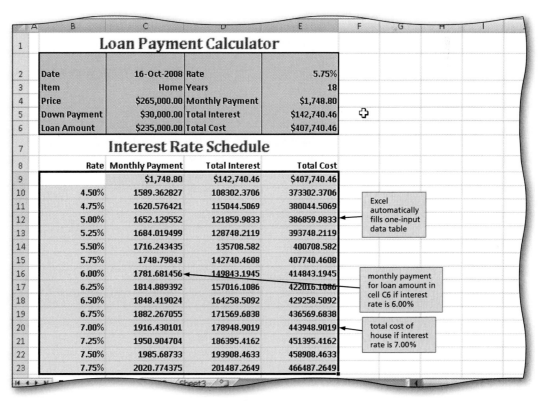

Figure 4–27

More About Data Tables

In Figure 4–27, the data table shows the monthly payment, total interest, and total cost for the interest rates in the range B10:B23. For example, if the interest rate is 5.75% (cell E2), the monthly payment is $1,748.80 (cell E4). If the interest rate is 7.75% (cell B23), however, the monthly payment is $2,020.77 rounded to the nearest cent (cell C23). If the interest rate is 7.00% (cell B20), then the total cost of the house is $443,948.90 rounded to the nearest cent (cell E20), rather than $407,740.46 (cell E6). Thus, a 1.25% increase from the interest rate of 5.75% to 7.00% results in a $36,208.44 increase in the total cost of the house.

The following list details important points you should know about data tables:

1. The formula(s) you are analyzing must include a cell reference to the input cell.

2. You can have as many active data tables in a worksheet as you want.

3. While only one value can vary in a one–input data table, the data table can analyze as many formulas as you want.

4. To include additional formulas in a one–input data table, enter them in adjacent cells in the same row as the current formulas (row 9 in Figure 4–27 on the previous page) and then define the entire new range as a data table by using the Table command on the Data menu.

5. You delete a data table as you would delete any other item on a worksheet. That is, select the data table and then press the DELETE key.

To Format the Data Table

The following steps format the data table to improve its readability.

1 Select the range B8:E23. Right–click the selected range and then click Format Cells on the shortcut menu. When Excel displays the Format Cells dialog box, click the Border tab, and then click the medium line style in the Style area (column 2, row 5). Click the Outline button in the Presets area. Click the light border in the Style area (column 1, row 7) and then click the Vertical Line button in the Border area to preview the black vertical border in the Border area.

2 Click the Fill tab and then click the light red color box (column 6, row 2). Click the OK button.

3 Select the range B8:E8. Click the Home tab on the Ribbon and then click the Borders button to assign a light bottom border.

4 Select the range C10:E23 and right–click. Click Format Cells on the shortcut menu. When Excel displays the Format Cells dialog box, click the Number tab. Click Currency in the Category list, click the Symbol box arrow, click None, and then click the second format, 1,234.10, in the Negative numbers list. Click the OK button to display the worksheet as shown in Figure 4–28.

5 Click the Save button on the Quick Access Toolbar to save the workbook using the file name Braden Mortgage Loan Payment Calculator.

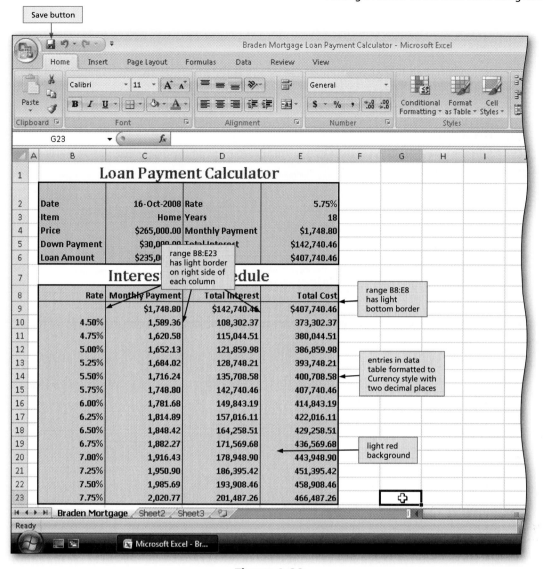

Figure 4–28

Adding a Pointer to the Data Table Using Conditional Formatting

If the interest rate in cell E2 is between 4.50% and 7.75% and its decimal portion is a multiple of 0.25 (such as 6.25%), then one of the rows in the data table agrees exactly with the monthly payment, interest paid, and total cost in the range E4:E6. For example, in Figure 4–28, row 15 (5.75%) in the data table agrees with the results in the range E4:E6, because the interest rate in cell B15 is the same as the interest rate in cell E2. Analysts often look for the row in the data table that agrees with the input cell results.

BTW

Conditional Formatting
You can add as many conditional formats to a range as you like. After adding the first condition, click the Conditional Formatting button on the Home tab on the Ribbon and then click New Rule to add more conditions. If more than one condition is true for a cell, then Excel applies the formats of each condition, beginning with the first.

To Add a Pointer to the Data Table

To make the row stand out, you can add formatting that serves as a pointer to a row. To add a pointer, you can use conditional formatting to make the cell in column B that agrees with the input cell (cell E2) stand out, as shown in the following steps.

1

- Select the range B10:B23.

- Click the Conditional Formatting button on the Home tab on the Ribbon to display the Conditional Formatting menu (Figure 4–29).

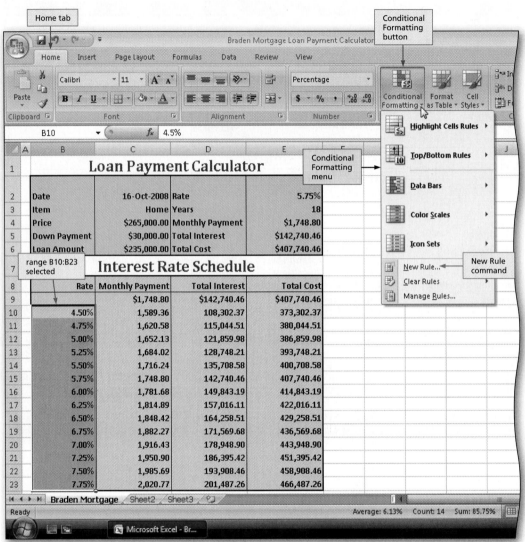

Figure 4–29

②

- Click New Rule on the Conditional Formatting menu.

- When Excel displays the New Formatting Rule dialog box, click 'Format only cells that contain' in the Select a Rule Type box. Select Cell Value in the left list in the 'Format only cells with' area and then select equal to in the middle list.

- Type =$E$2 in the right box.

- Click the Format button, click the Fill tab, and then click Green (column 5, row 7) on the Background color palette.

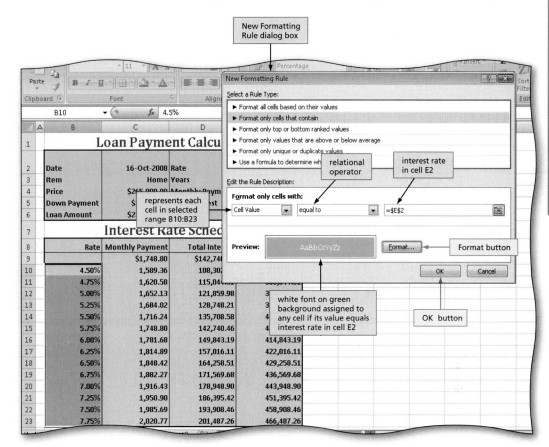

Figure 4–30

- Click the Font tab, click the Color box arrow, and then click White (column 1, row 1) on the Color palette in the Theme area.

- Click the OK button in the Format Cells dialog box to display the New Formatting Rule dialog box as shown in Figure 4–30.

③

- Click the OK button in the New Formatting Rule dialog box. Click cell G23 to deselect the range B10:B23 (Figure 4–31).

Q&A

How does Excel apply the conditional formatting?

Cell B15 in the data table, which contains the value, 5.75%, appears with white font on a green background, because the value 5.75% is the same as the interest rate value in cell E2.

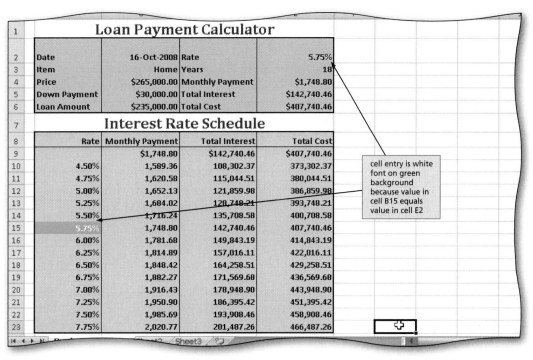

Figure 4–31

4

- Select cell E2 and then enter `7.25` as the interest rate (Figure 4–32).

5

- Enter `5.75` in cell E2 to return the Loan Payment Calculator section and Interest Rate Schedule section to their original states as shown in Figure 4–31.

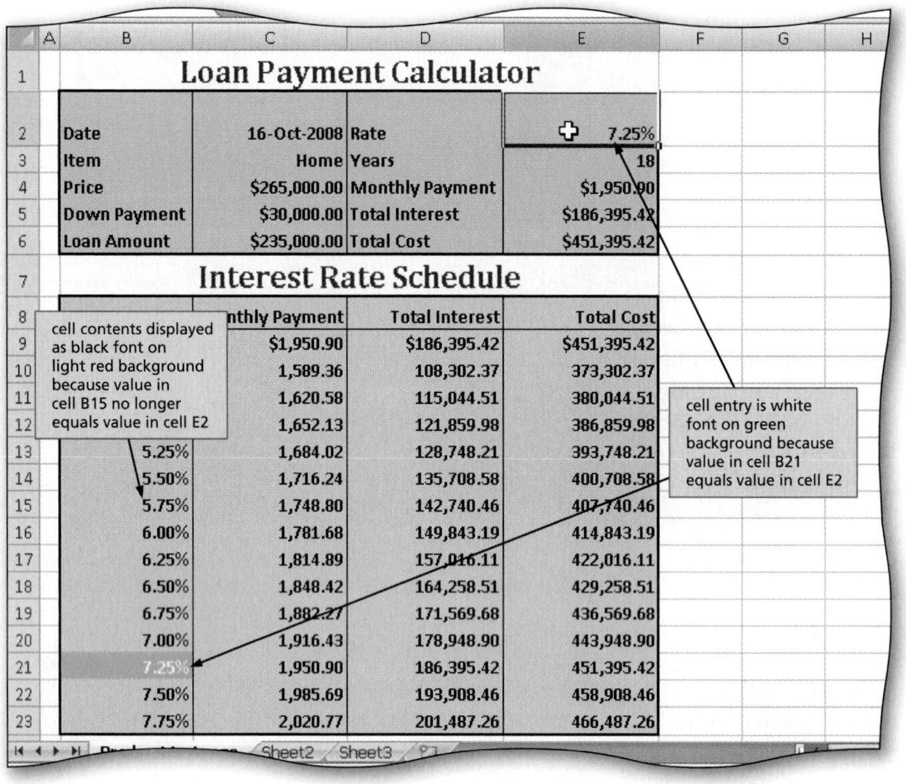

Figure 4–32

Q&A What happens when the interest rate is changed from 5.75?

Excel immediately displays the cell containing the new rate with a white font on a green background and displays cell B15 with black bold font on a light red background (Figure 4–32). Thus, the white font on a green background serves as a pointer in the data table to indicate the row that agrees with the input cell (cell E2). When the loan officer using this worksheet enters a different percent in cell E2, the pointer will move or disappear. It will disappear whenever the interest rate in cell E2 is outside the range of the data table or its decimal portion is not a multiple of 0.25, such as when the interest rate is 8.25% or 5.80%.

Other Ways

1. Press ALT+O, D

Creating an Amortization Schedule

BTW **Amortization Schedules**
Hundreds of Web sites offer amortization schedules. To find these Web sites, use a search engine, such as Google at google.com, and search using the keywords, amortization schedule.

The next step in this project is to create the Amortization Schedule section on the right side of Figure 4–33. An **amortization schedule** shows the beginning and ending balances of a loan, and the amount of payment that applies to the principal and interest for each year over the life of the loan. For example, if a customer wanted to pay off the loan after six years, the Amortization Schedule section tells the loan officer what the payoff would be (cell I8 in Figure 4–33). The Amortization Schedule section shown in Figure 4–33 will work only for loans of up to 18 years. You could, however, extend the table to any number of years. The Amortization Schedule section also contains summaries in rows 21, 22, and 23. These summaries should agree exactly with the corresponding amounts in the Loan Payment Calculator section in the range B1:E6.

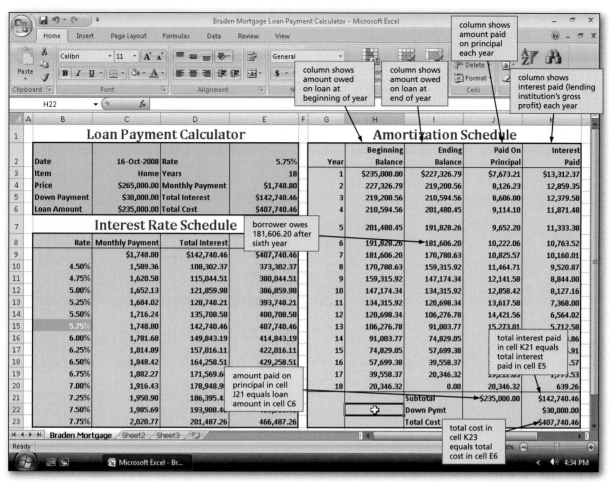

Figure 4–33

To Change Column Widths and Enter Titles

The first step in creating the Amortization Schedule section is to adjust the column widths and enter the Amortization Schedule section title and column titles, as shown in the following steps.

1 Position the mouse pointer on the right boundary of column heading F and then drag to the left until the ScreenTip shows Width: 1.57 (16 pixels).

2 Position the mouse pointer on the right boundary of column heading G and then drag to the left until the ScreenTip shows Width: 8.43 (64 pixels).

3 Drag through column headings H through K to select them. Position the mouse pointer on the right boundary of column heading K and then drag to the right until the ScreenTip shows Width: 14.00 (103 pixels).

4 Select cell G1. Type Amortization Schedule as the section title. Press the ENTER key.

BTW

Column Borders
In this chapter, columns A and F are used as column borders to divide sections of the worksheet from one another, as well as from the row headings. A column border is an unused column with a significantly reduced width. You also can use row borders to separate sections of a worksheet.

5 Select cell B1. Click the Format Painter button on the Ribbon. Click cell G1 to copy the format of cell B1. Click the Merge & Center button on the Ribbon to split cell G1. Select the range G1:K1 and then click the Merge & Center button on the Ribbon.

6 Enter the column titles in the range G2:K2 as shown in Figure 4–34. Where appropriate, press ALT+ENTER to enter the titles on two lines. Select the range G2:K2 and then click the Align Text Right button on the Ribbon. Select cell G3 to display the section title and column headings as shown in Figure 4–34.

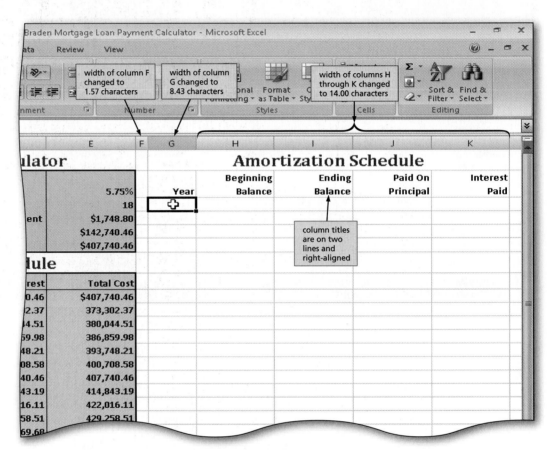

Figure 4–34

To Create a Series of Integers Using the Fill Handle

The next step is to create a series of numbers, using the fill handle, that represent the years during the life of the loan. The series begins with 1 (year 1) and ends with 18 (year 18).

1 With cell G3 active, enter 1 as the initial year. Select cell G4 and then enter 2 to represent the next year.

2 Select the range G3:G4 and then point to the fill handle. Drag the fill handle through cell G20 to create the series of integers 1 through 18 in the range G3:G20 (Figure 4–35).

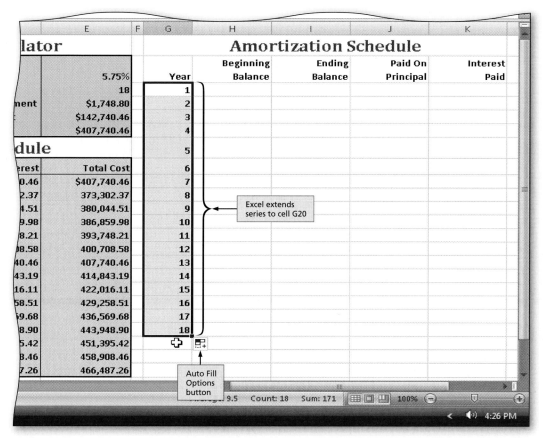

Figure 4–35

To Enter the Formulas in the Amortization Schedule

The next step is to enter the four formulas that form the basis of the amortization schedule in row 3. Later, these formulas will be copied through row 20. The formulas are summarized in Table 4–2.

Table 4–2 Formulas for the Amortization Schedule			
Tab Stop	**Tab Marker**	**Result of Pressing Tab Key**	**Example**
H3	Beginning Balance	=C6	The beginning balance (the balance at the end of a year) is the initial loan amount in cell C6.
I3	Ending Balance	=IF(G3 <= $E$3, PV($E$2 /12, 12 * ($E$3 – G3), –$E$4), 0)	The ending balance (the balance at the end of a year) is equal to the present value of the payments paid over the remaining life of the loan.
J3	Paid On Principal	=H3 – I3	The amount paid on the principal at the end of the year is equal to the beginning balance (cell H3) less the ending balance (cell I3).
K3	Interest Paid	=IF(H3 > 0, 12 * $E$4 – J3, 0)	The interest paid during the year is equal to 12 times the monthly payment (cell E4) less the amount paid on the principal (cell J3).

Of the four formulas in Table 4–2, the most difficult to understand is the PV function that will be assigned to cell I3. The **PV function** returns the present value of an annuity. An **annuity** is a series of fixed payments (such as the monthly payment in cell E4) made at the end of each of a fixed number of periods (months) at a fixed interest rate. You can use the PV function to determine how much the borrower of the loan still owes at the end of each year.

The PV function can determine the ending balance after the first year (cell I3) by using a term equal to the number of months for which the borrower still must make payments. For example, if the loan is for 18 years (216 months), then the borrower still owes 204 payments after the first year (216 months – 12 months). The number of payments outstanding can be determined from the formula 12 * (E3 – G3) or 12 * (18 – 1), which equals 204. Recall that column G contains integers that represent the years of the loan. After the second year, the number of payments remaining is 192, and so on.

If you assign the PV function as shown in Table 4–2 to cell I3 and then copy it to the range I4:I20, the ending balances for each year will display properly. If the loan is for less than 18 years, however, then the ending balances displayed for the years beyond the time the loan is due are invalid. For example, if a loan is taken out for 5 years, then the rows representing years 6 through 18 in the amortization schedule should be 0. The PV function, however, will display negative numbers even though the loan already has been paid off.

To avoid this, the worksheet should include a formula that assigns the PV function to the range I3:I20 as long as the corresponding year in column G is less than or equal to the number of years in cell E3. If the corresponding year in column G is greater than the number of years in cell E3, then the ending balance for that year and the remaining years should be 0. The following IF function causes the value of the PV function or 0 to display in cell I3 depending on whether the corresponding value in column G is less than or equal to the number of years in cell E3. Recall that the dollar signs within the cell references indicate the cell reference is absolute and, therefore, will not change as you copy the function downward.

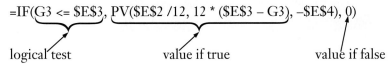

=IF(G3 <= $E$3, PV($E$2 /12, 12 * ($E$3 – G3), –$E$4), 0)

logical test   value if true   value if false

In the above formula, the logical test determines if the year in column G is less than or equal to the term of the loan in cell E3. If the logical test is true, then the IF function assigns the PV function to the cell. If the logical test is false, then the IF function assigns zero (0) to the cell.

The PV function in the IF function includes absolute cell references (cell references with dollar signs) to ensure that the references to cells in column E do not change when the IF function later is copied down the column.

The following steps enter the four formulas shown in Table 4–2 into row 3. Row 3 represents year 1 of the loan.

1

- Select cell H3 and then enter =c6 as the beginning balance of the loan.

- Select cell I3 and then type =if(g3 <= e3, pv(e2 / 12, 12 * (e3 – g3), –e4), 0) as the entry (Figure 4-36).

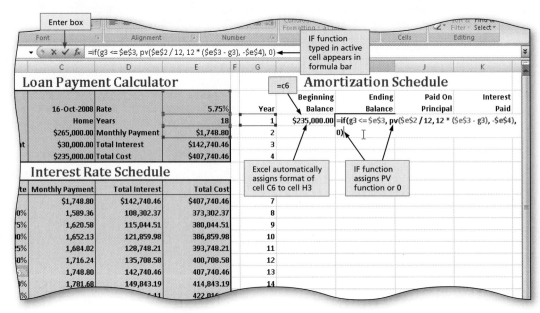

Figure 4–36

2

- Click the Enter box in the formula bar to insert the formula (Figure 4–37).

What happens when the Enter box is clicked?

Excel evaluates the IF function in cell I3 and displays the result of the PV function (227326.7922) because the value in cell G3 (1) is less than or equal to the term of the loan in cell E3 (18). With cell I3 active, Excel also displays the formula in the formula bar. If the borrower wanted to pay off the loan after one year, the cost would be $227,326.79.

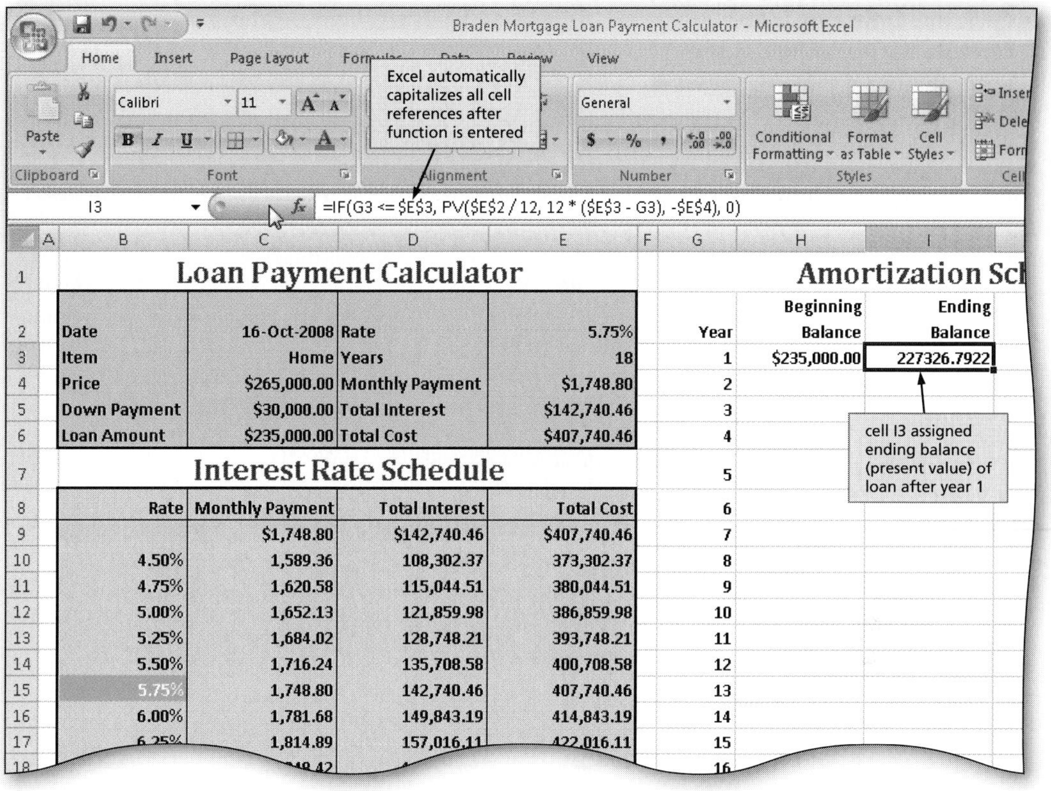

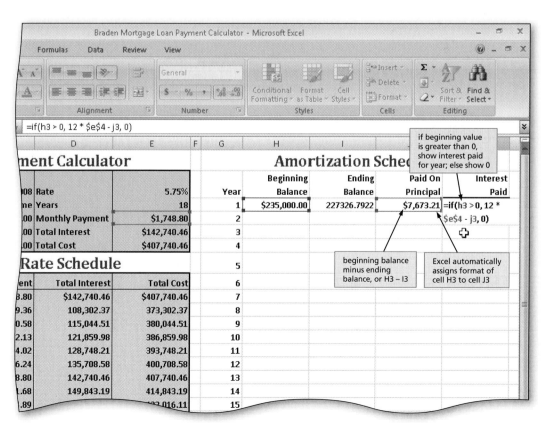

Figure 4–37

3

- Select cell J3. Type =h3 - i3 and then press the RIGHT ARROW key.

- Type =if(h3 > 0, 12 * e4 - j3, 0) in cell K3 to display the amount paid on the principal after 1 year ($7,673.21) in cell J3, using the same format as in cell H3 (Figure 4–38).

Figure 4–38

4

- Click the Enter box in the formula bar to complete the entry (Figure 4–39).

Q&A

What happens when the Enter box is clicked?

Excel displays the interest paid after 1 year (13312.37332) in cell K3. Thus, the lending institution's gross profit for the first year of the loan is $13,312.37.

Q&A

Why are some of the cells in the range H3:K3 formatted?

When you enter a formula in a cell, Excel assigns the cell the same format as the first cell reference in the formula. For example, when you enter =c6 in cell H3, Excel assigns the format in cell C6 to cell H3. The same applies to cell J3. Although this method of formatting also works for most functions, it does not work for the IF function. Thus, the results of the IF functions in cells I3 and K3 are displayed using the General style format, which is the format of all cells when you open a new workbook.

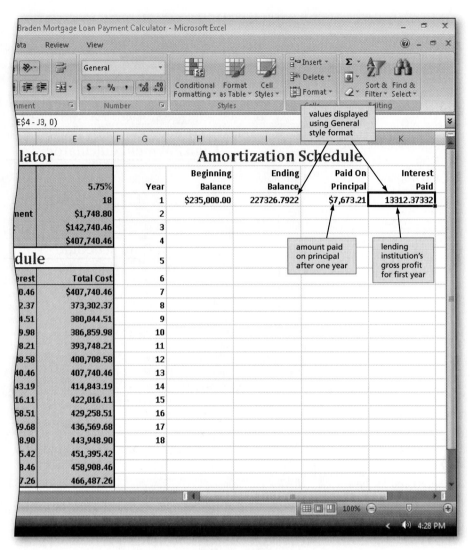

Figure 4–39

To Copy the Formulas to Fill the Amortization Schedule

With the formulas entered into the first row, the next step is to copy them to the remaining rows in the amortization schedule. The required copying is straightforward, except for the beginning balance column. To obtain the next year's beginning balance (cell H4), last year's ending balance (cell I3) must be used. After cell I3 is copied to cell H4, then H4 can be copied to the range H5:H20.

1

- Select the range I3:K3 and then drag the fill handle down through row 20 to copy the formulas in cells I3, J3, and K3 to the range I4: K20 (Figure 4–40).

Q&A Why do some of the numbers seem incorrect?

Many of the numbers displayed are incorrect because most of the cells in column H do not contain beginning balances.

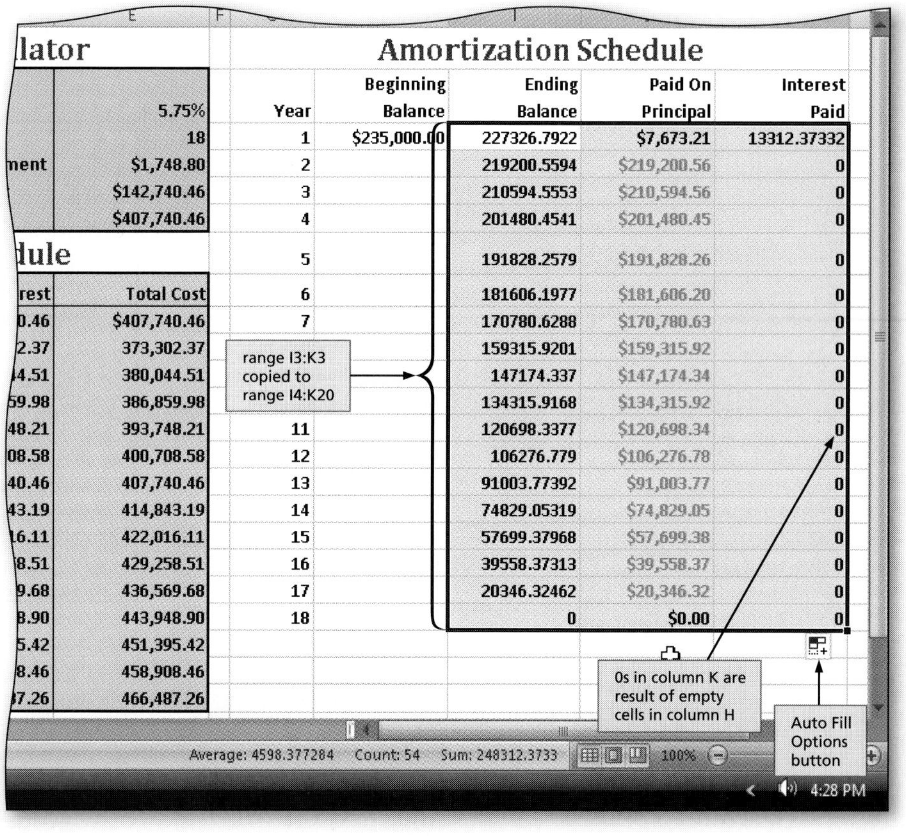

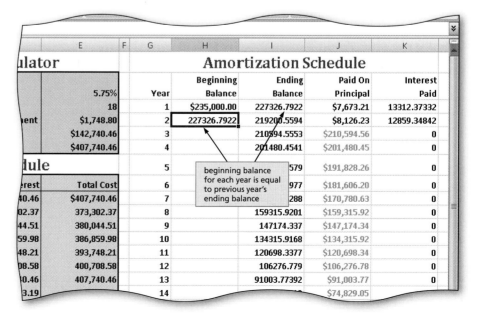

Figure 4–40

2

- Select cell H4, type `=i3` as the cell entry, and then click the Enter box in the formula bar to display the ending balance (227326.7922) for year 1 as the beginning balance for year 2 (Figure 4–41).

Figure 4–41

3

- With cell H4 active, drag the fill handle down through row 20 to copy the formula in cell H4 (=I3) to the range H5:H20 (Figure 4–42).

Q&A

What happens after the fill operation is complete?

Because the cell reference I3 is relative, Excel adjusts the row portion of the cell reference as it is copied downward. Thus, each new beginning balance in column H is equal to the ending balance of the previous year.

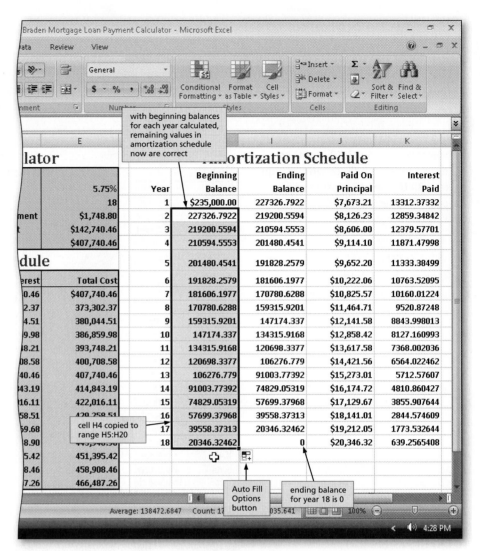

Figure 4–42

To Enter the Total Formulas in the Amortization Schedule

The next step is to determine the amortization schedule totals in rows 21 through 23. These totals should agree with the corresponding totals in the Loan Payment Calculator section (range B1:E6). The following steps show how to enter the total formulas in the amortization schedule.

1 Select cell I21. Enter `Subtotal` as the row title. Select the range J21:K21. Click the Sum button on the Ribbon.

2 Select cell I22. Type `Down Pymt` as the row title. Select cell K22 and then enter `=c5` as the down payment.

3 Select cell I23. Type `Total Cost` as the row title. Select cell K23, type `=j21 + k21 + k22` as the total cost, and then click the Enter box in the formula bar to complete the amortization schedule totals (Figure 4–43).

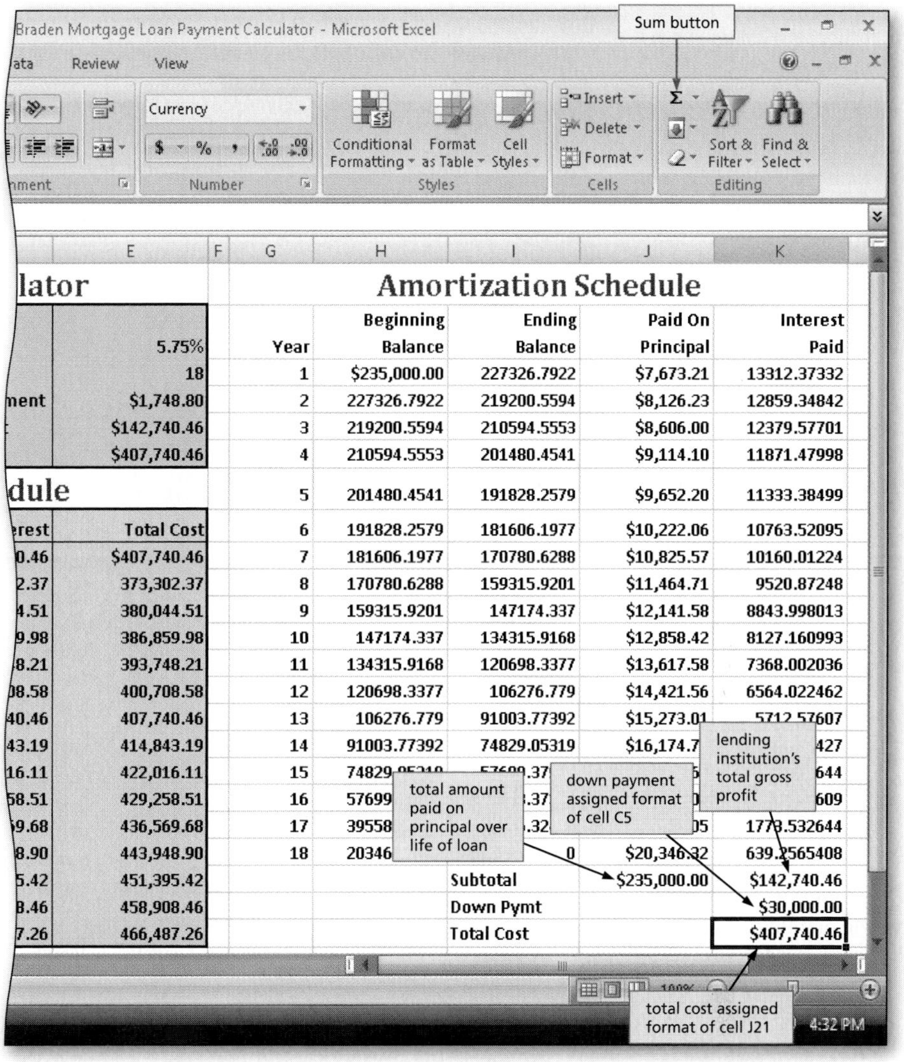

Q&A

What was accomplished in the previous steps?

The formula assigned to cell K23 (=j21 + k21 + k22) sums the total amount paid on the principal (cell J21), the total interest paid (cell K21), and the down payment (cell K22). Excel assigns cell J21 the same format as cell J3, because cell J3 is the first cell reference in =SUM(J3:J20). Furthermore, because cell J21 was selected first when the range J21:K21 was selected to determine the sum, Excel assigned cell K21 the same format it assigned to cell J21. Finally, cell K22 was assigned the Currency style format, because cell K22 was assigned the formula =c5, and cell C5 has a Currency style format. For the same reason, the value in cell K23 appears in Currency style format.

Figure 4–43

To Format the Numbers in the Amortization Schedule

The final step in creating the amortization schedule is to format it so it is easier to read. The formatting is divided into two parts: (1) formatting the numbers and (2) adding borders and background.

When the beginning balance formula (=c6) was entered earlier into cell H3, Excel automatically copied the Currency style format along with the value from cell C6 to cell H3. The steps on the next page use the Format Painter button to copy the Currency style format from cell H3 to the range I3:K3. Then the Comma style will be assigned to the range H4:K20.

The Magical Fill Handle
If there is a column with entries adjacent to the range you plan to drag the fill handle down through, then you can double-click the fill handle instead of dragging. For example, in Step 3 on page EX 302, you could have double-clicked the fill handle instead of dragging the fill handle down through column 20 to copy the formula in cell H4 to the range H5:H20, because of the numbers in column G. This feature also applies to copying a range using the fill handle.

Round-Off Errors
If you manually add the numbers in column K (range K3:K20) and compare it to the sum in cell K21, you will notice that the total interest paid is $0.01 off. This round-off error is due to the fact that some of the numbers involved in the computations have additional decimal places that do not appear in the cells. You can use the ROUND function on the formula entered into cell K3 to ensure that the total is exactly correct. For information on the ROUND function, click the Insert Function button in the formula bar, click Math & Trig in the 'Or select a category' list, scroll down in the 'Select a function' list, and then click ROUND.

1 Select cell H3. Click the Format Painter button on the Home tab on the Ribbon. Drag through the range I3:K3 to assign the Currency style format to the cells.

2 Select the range H4:K20 and then right–click. Click Format Cells on the shortcut menu. When Excel displays the Format Cells dialog box, click the Number tab. Click Currency in the Category list, click the Symbol box arrow, click None, and then click the second format, 1,234.10, in the Negative numbers list. Click the OK button.

3 Select cell H21 to deselect the range H4:K20 to display the numbers in the amortization schedule as shown in Figure 4–44.

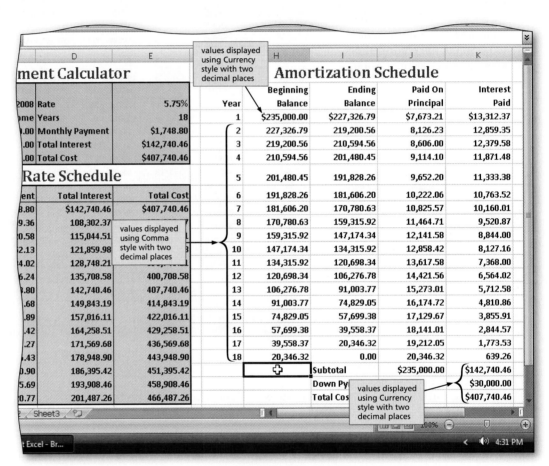

Figure 4–44

To Add Borders and a Background to the Amortization Schedule

The following steps add the borders and a background to the amortization schedule.

1 Select the range G2:K23. Right–click the selected range and then click Format Cells on the shortcut menu. When Excel displays the Format Cells dialog box, click the Border tab.

2 Click the medium line style in the Style area (column 2, row 5). Click the Outline button in the Presets area.

3 Click the light line style in the Style area (column 1, row 7). Click the vertical line button in the Border area.

4 Click the Fill tab and then click light blue (column 5, row 2). Click the OK button.

5 Select the range G2:K2. Click the Borders button on the Home tab on the Ribbon to assign the range a light bottom border.

6 Select the range G20:K20 and then click the Borders button on the Home tab on the Ribbon to assign the range a light bottom border. Select cell H22 to display the worksheet as shown in Figure 4–45.

7 Click the Save button on the Quick Access Toolbar to save the workbook using the file name, Braden Mortgage Loan Payment Calculator.

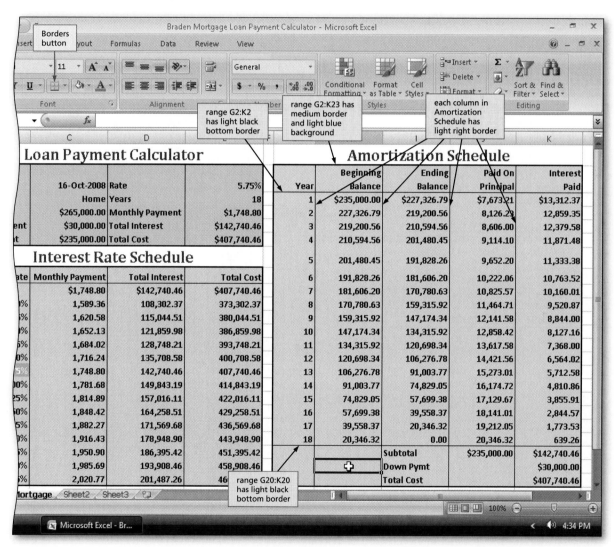

Figure 4–45

To Enter New Loan Data

With the Loan Payment Calculator, Interest Rate Schedule, and Amortization Schedule sections of the worksheet complete, you can use them to generate new loan information. For example, assume you want to purchase a pontoon boat for $41,550.00. You have $6,000.00 for a down payment and want the loan for 5 years. Braden Mortgage currently is charging 7.25% interest for a 5–year loan. The steps on the next page enter the new loan data.

1 Select cell C3. Type `Pontoon Boat` and then press the DOWN ARROW key.

2 In cell C4, type `41550` and then press the DOWN ARROW key.

3 In cell C5, type `6000` as the down payment.

4 Select cell E2, type `7.25` and then press the DOWN ARROW key.

5 In cell E3, type `5` and then press the DOWN ARROW key. Select cell H22 to display the worksheet as shown in Figure 4–46.

Q&A What happens on the worksheet when the new data is entered?

As shown in Figure 4–46, the monthly payment for the pontoon boat is $708.13 (cell E4). The total interest is $6,938.00 (cell E5) and the total cost for the boat is $48,488.00 (cell E6). Because the term of the loan is for 5 years, the rows for years 6 through 18 in the Amortization Schedule section display 0.00.

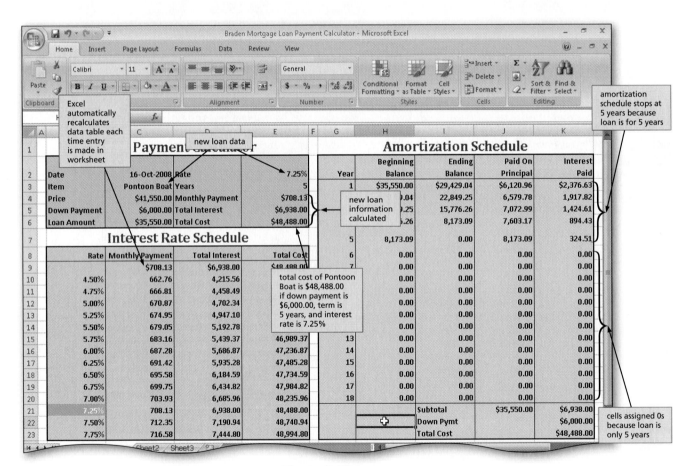

Figure 4–46

To Enter the Original Loan Data

The following steps enter the original loan data.

1 Select cell C3. Type `Home` and then press the DOWN ARROW key.

2 In cell C4, type `265000` and then press the DOWN ARROW key.

3 In cell C5, type `30000` as the down payment.

4 Select cell E2, type 5.75 and then press the DOWN ARROW key.

5 In cell E3, type 18 and then click the Enter box in the formula bar or press the ENTER key to complete the entry of the original load data. Select cell H22.

Printing Sections of the Worksheet

In Chapter 2, you learned to print a section of a worksheet by selecting it and using the Selection option in the Print dialog box (see page EX 134). If you find yourself continually selecting the same range in a worksheet to print, you can set a specific range to print each time you print the worksheet by using the Set Print Area command. When you set a range to print using the Set Print Area command, Excel will continue to print only that range until you clear it using the Clear Print Area command.

To Set Up a Worksheet to Print

This section describes print options available in the Sheet sheet in the Page Setup dialog box (Figure 4–47). These print options pertain to the way the worksheet will appear in the printed copy or when previewed. One of the more important print options is the capability of printing in black and white. Printing in black and white not only speeds up the printing process, but also saves ink. This is especially true if you have a color printer and need only a black and white printed copy of the worksheet. The following steps ensure any printed copy fits on one page and prints in black and white.

- Click the Page Layout tab on the Ribbon and then click the Page Setup Dialog Box Launcher on the Ribbon.

- When Excel displays the Page Setup dialog box, click the Page tab and then click Fit to in the Scaling area to set the worksheet to print on one page (Figure 4–47).

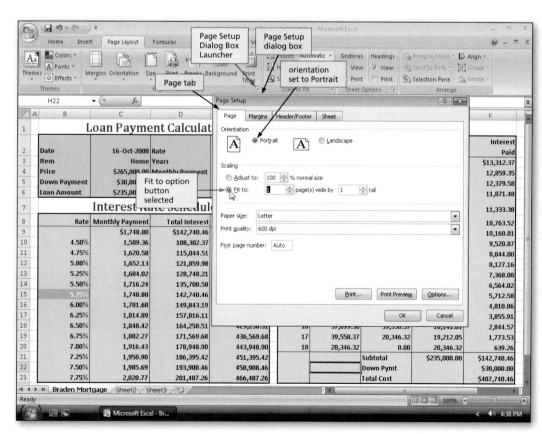

Figure 4–47

2

• Click the Sheet tab and then click 'Black and white' in the Print area to select the check box (Figure 4–48).

3

• Click the OK button.

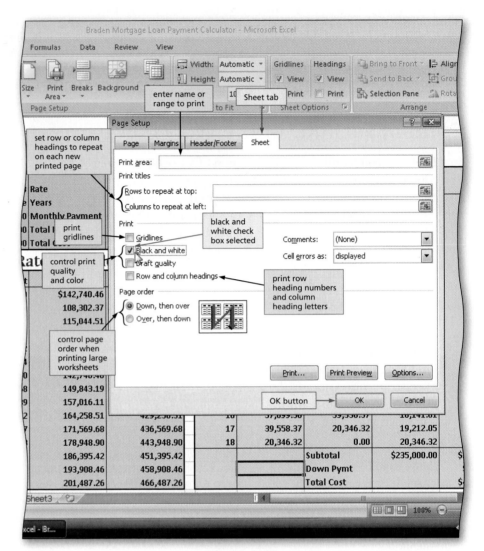

Figure 4–48

More About Print Options

Table 4–3 summarizes the print options available on the Sheet sheet in the Page Setup dialog box.

Table 4–3 Print Options Available Using the Sheet Sheet in the Page Setup Dialog Box	
Print Option	**Description**
Print area box	Excel prints from cell A1 to the last occupied cell in a worksheet unless you instruct it to print a selected area. You can select a range to print with the mouse, or you can enter a range or name of a range in the Print area box. Nonadjacent ranges will print on a separate page.

Table 4–3 Print Options Available Using the Sheet Tab in the Page Setup Dialog Box (continued)	
Print Option	**Description**
Print titles area	This area is used to instruct Excel to print row titles and column titles on each printed page of a worksheet. You must specify a range, even if you are designating one column (e.g., 1:4 means the first four rows).
Gridlines check box	A check mark in this check box instructs Excel to print gridlines.
Black and white check box	A check mark in this check box speeds up printing and saves colored ink if you have colors in a worksheet and a color printer.
Draft quality check box	A check mark in this check box speeds up printing by ignoring formatting and not printing most graphics.
Row and column headings check box	A check mark in this check box instructs Excel to include the column heading letters (A, B, C, etc.) and row heading numbers (1, 2, 3, etc.) in the printout.
Comments box	Indicates where comments are to be displayed on the printout.
Cell errors as box	Indicates how errors in cells should be displayed on the printout.
Page order area	Determines the order in which multipage worksheets will print.

To Set the Print Area

The following steps print only the Loan Payment Calculator section by setting the print area to the range B1:E6.

- Select the range B1:E6 and then click the Print Area button on the Ribbon to display the Print Area menu (Figure 4–49).

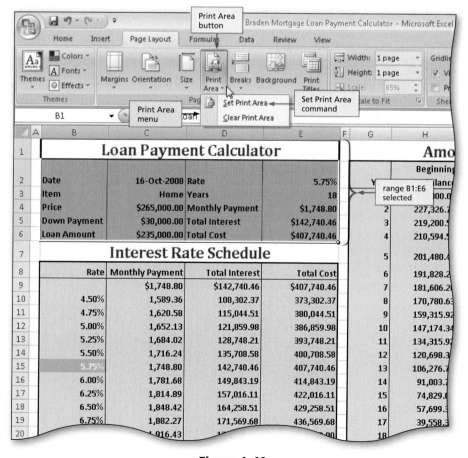

Figure 4–49

2

- Click Set Print Area on the Print Area menu.

- Click the Office Button and then click Print on the Office Button menu. When Excel displays the Print dialog box, click the OK button to print the selected area (Figure 4–50).

3

- Click the Print Area button on the Ribbon and then click the Clear Print Area command on the Print Area menu to reset the print area to the entire worksheet.

Q&A

What happens when I set a print area?

Once you set a print area, Excel will continue to print the specified range, rather than the entire worksheet. If you save the workbook with the print area set, then Excel will remember the settings the next time you open the workbook and print only the specified range. To remove the print area so that the entire worksheet prints, click Clear Print Area on the Print Area menu as described in Step 3.

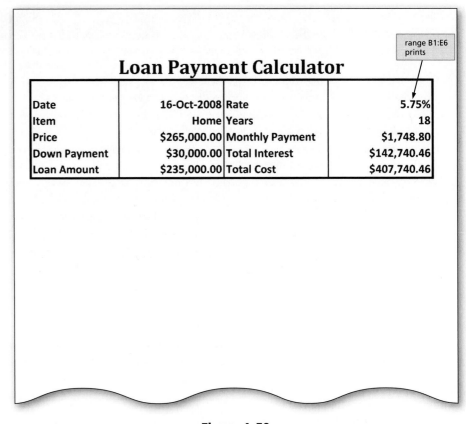

Figure 4–50

Other Ways

1. Press ALT+F, T, S

To Name and Print Sections of a Worksheet

With some spreadsheet applications, you will want to print several different areas of a worksheet, depending on the request. Rather than using the Set Print Area command or manually selecting the range each time you want to print, you can name the ranges using the Name box in the formula bar. You then can use one of the names to select an area before using the Set Print Area command or Selection option button. The following steps name the Loan Payment Calculator section, the Interest Rate Schedule section, the Amortization Schedule section, and the entire worksheet, and then print each section using the Selection option button in the Print dialog box.

1

- Click the Page Setup Dialog Box Launcher, click the sheet tab, and, if necessary, click 'Black and white' to deselect the check box.

- Click the OK button to close the Page Setup dialog box.

- If necessary, select the range B1:E6, click the Name box, and then type `Loan_Payment` as the name of the range (Figure 4–51).

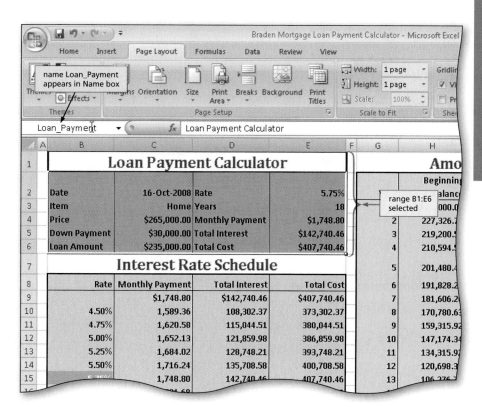

Figure 4–51

2

- Press the ENTER key.

- Select the range B7:E23, click the Name box, type `Interest_Schedule` as the name of the range, and then press the ENTER key.

- Select the range G1:K23, click the Name box, type `Amortization_Schedule` as the name of the range, and then press the ENTER key.

- Select the range B1:K23, click the Name box, type `All_Sections` as the name of the range, and then press the ENTER key.

- Select cell H22 and then click the Name box arrow in the formula bar to display the Name list with the new range names (Figure 4–52).

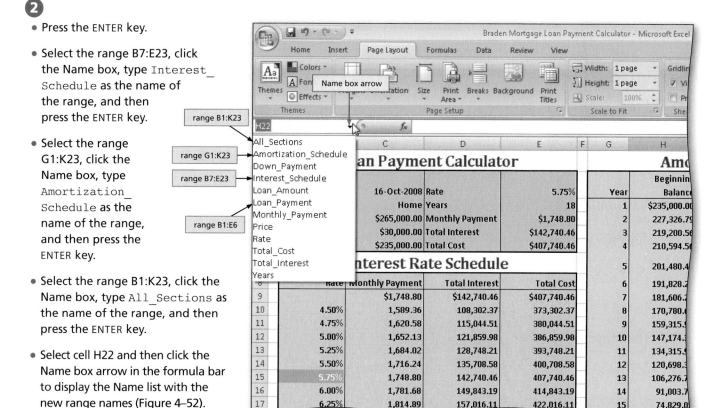

Figure 4–52

3

- Click Loan_Payment in the Name list to select the range B1:E6.

- Click the Office Button and then click Print on the Office Button menu to display the Print dialog box.

- When Excel displays the Print dialog box, click Selection in the Print what area (Figure 4–53).

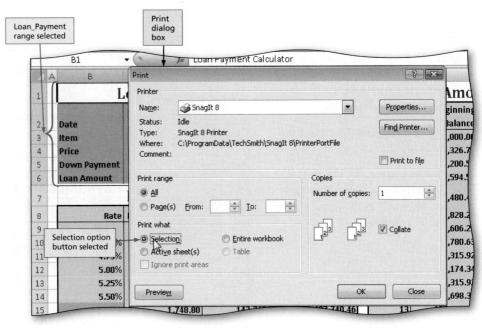

Figure 4–53

4

- Click the OK button to print the Loan_Payment range.

- One at a time, use the Name box to select the names Interest_Schedule, Amortization_Schedule, and All_Sections, and then print them following the instructions in Step 3 (Figure 4–54).

5

- Click the Save button on the Quick Access Toolbar to save the workbook using the file name, Braden Mortgage Loan Payment Calculator.

Q&A

Why does the All_Sections range print on one page?

Recall that the Fit to option was selected earlier (Figure 4–47 on page EX 307). This selection ensures that each of the printouts fits across the page in portrait orientation.

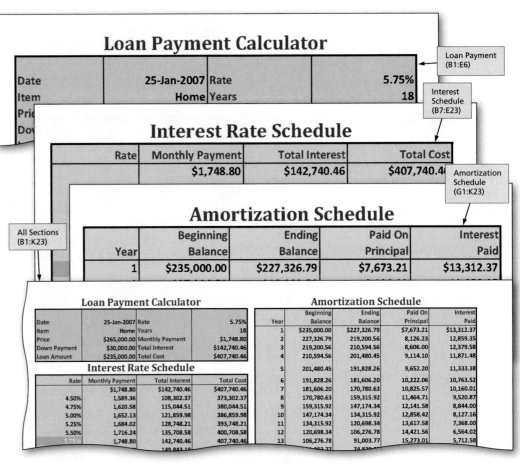

Figure 4–54

Other Ways

1. Select cell or range, on Formulas tab on Ribbon, click Define Name button, [type name], click OK button

2. Select cell or range, on Formulas tab on Ribbon, click Name Manager button, click New, [type name], click OK button, click Close button

Protecting the Worksheet

When building a worksheet for novice users, you should protect the cells in the worksheet that you do not want changed, such as cells that contain text or formulas.

When you create a new worksheet, all the cells are assigned a locked status, but the lock is not engaged, which leaves cells unprotected. **Unprotected cells** are cells whose values you can change at any time. **Protected cells** are cells that you cannot change.

You should protect cells only after the worksheet has been tested fully and the correct results appear. Protecting a worksheet is a two–step process:

1. Select the cells you want to leave unprotected and then change their cell protection settings to an unlocked status.

2. Protect the entire worksheet.

At first glance, these steps may appear to be backwards. Once you protect the entire worksheet, however, you cannot change anything, including the locked status of individual cells.

BTW

Naming Ranges
A name can be assigned to two or more nonadjacent ranges. After selecting the first range, hold down the CTRL key and drag through the additional ranges of cells to select them before entering the name in the Name box.

To Protect a Worksheet

In the Loan Payment Calculator worksheet (Figure 4–55), the user should be able to make changes to only five cells: the item in cell C3; the price in cell C4; the down payment in cell C5; the interest rate in cell E2; and the years in cell E3. These cells must remain unprotected so that users can enter the correct data. The remaining cells in the worksheet should be protected so that the user cannot change them.

The following steps show how to protect the Loan Payment Calculator worksheet.

1

- Select the range C3:C5.

- Hold down the CTRL key and then select the nonadjacent range E2:E3.

- Right–click one of the selected ranges to display the shortcut menu (Figure 4–55).

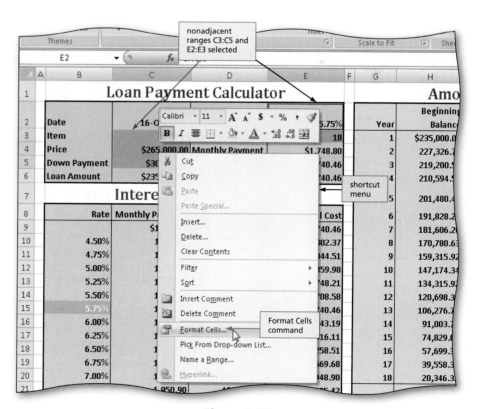

Figure 4–55

2

- Click Format Cells on the shortcut menu.

- When Excel displays the Custom Lists dialog box, click the Protection tab, and then click Locked to remove the check mark (Figure 4–56).

What is the meaning of the Locked check box ?

Excel displays the Protection sheet in the Custom Lists dialog box with the check mark removed from the Locked check box (Figure 4–56). This means the selected cells (C3:C5 and E2:E3) will not be protected when the Protect command is invoked later.

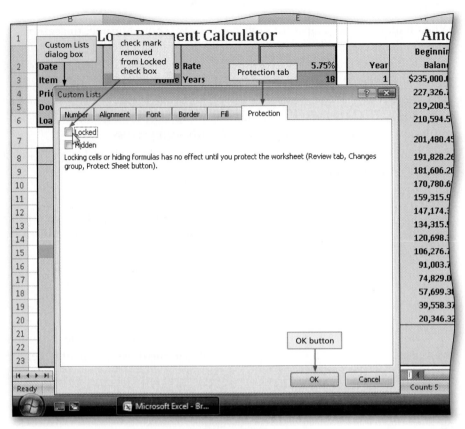

Figure 4–56

3

- Click the OK button and then select cell H22 to deselect the ranges C3:C5 and E2:E3.

- Click the Review tab on the Ribbon (Figure 4–57).

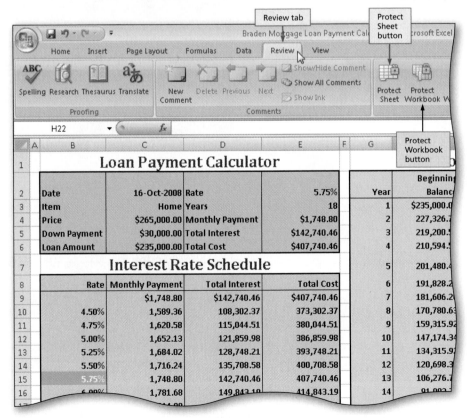

Figure 4–57

4

- Click the Protect Sheet button on the Ribbon to display the Protect Sheet dialog box.

- When Excel displays the Protect Sheet dialog box, make sure the Protect worksheet and contents of locked cells check box at the top of the dialog box and the first two check boxes in the list contain check marks (Figure 4–58).

What do the three checked check boxes mean?

With all three check boxes selected, the worksheet is protected from changes to contents (except the cells left unlocked). The two check boxes in the list allow the user to select any cell on the worksheet, but the user can change only unlocked cells.

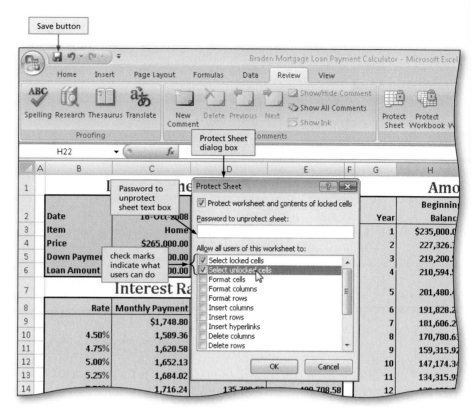

Figure 4–58

5

- Click the OK button in the Protect Sheet dialog box.

- Click the Save button on the Quick Access Toolbar.

Other Ways

1. Click Format Cells Dialog Box Launcher, click Protection tab, remove check mark from Locked check box, click OK button

More About Worksheet Protection

All the cells in the worksheet are protected, except for the ranges C3:C5 and E2:E3. The Protect Sheet dialog box in Figure 4–58 lets you enter a password that can be used to unprotect the sheet. You should create a **password** when you want to keep others from changing the worksheet from protected to unprotected. The check boxes in the list in the Protect Sheet dialog box also give you the option to modify the protection so that the user can make certain changes, such as formatting cells or inserting hyperlinks.

If you want to protect more than one sheet in a workbook, select each sheet before you begin the protection process or click the Protect Workbook button on the Review tab on the Ribbon, instead of clicking the Protect Sheet button (Figure 4–57). If you want to unlock cells for specific users, you can use the Allow Users to Edit Ranges button on the Review tab on the Ribbon.

When this workbook is put into production, users will be able to enter data in only the unprotected cells. If they try to change any protected cell, such as the monthly payment in cell E4, Excel displays a dialog box with an error message as shown in Figure 4–59 on the next page. An alternative to displaying this dialog box is to remove the check mark from the 'Select unlocked cells' check box in the Protect Sheet dialog box (Figure 4–58). With the check mark removed, the user cannot select a locked cell.

To unprotect the worksheet so that you can change all cells in the worksheet, unprotect the document by clicking the Unprotect Sheet button on the Review tab on the Ribbon.

BTW | **Using Protected Worksheets**
You can move from one unprotected cell to another unprotected cell in a worksheet by using the tab and SHIFT+TAB keys. This is especially useful when the cells are not adjacent to one another.

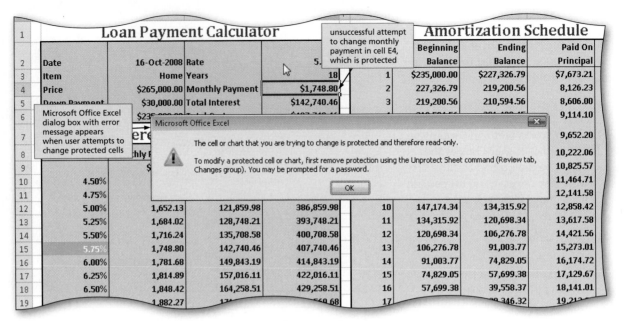

Figure 4–59

To Hide and Unhide a Sheet

You can hide rows, columns, and sheets that contain sensitive data. Sheets are hidden by first selecting one or more of them and then using the Hide command on the sheet tab's shortcut menu (Figure 4–60). Later, you can use the Unhide command on the same shortcut menu to unhide sheets. You also learned earlier in Chapter 2 (page EX 126) that you can use the mouse and keyboard to hide and unhide rows and columns. The following steps show how to hide and then unhide a sheet.

- If the Braden Mortgage sheet is not active, click its sheet tab.

- Right–click the sheet tab to display the shortcut menu (Figure 4–60).

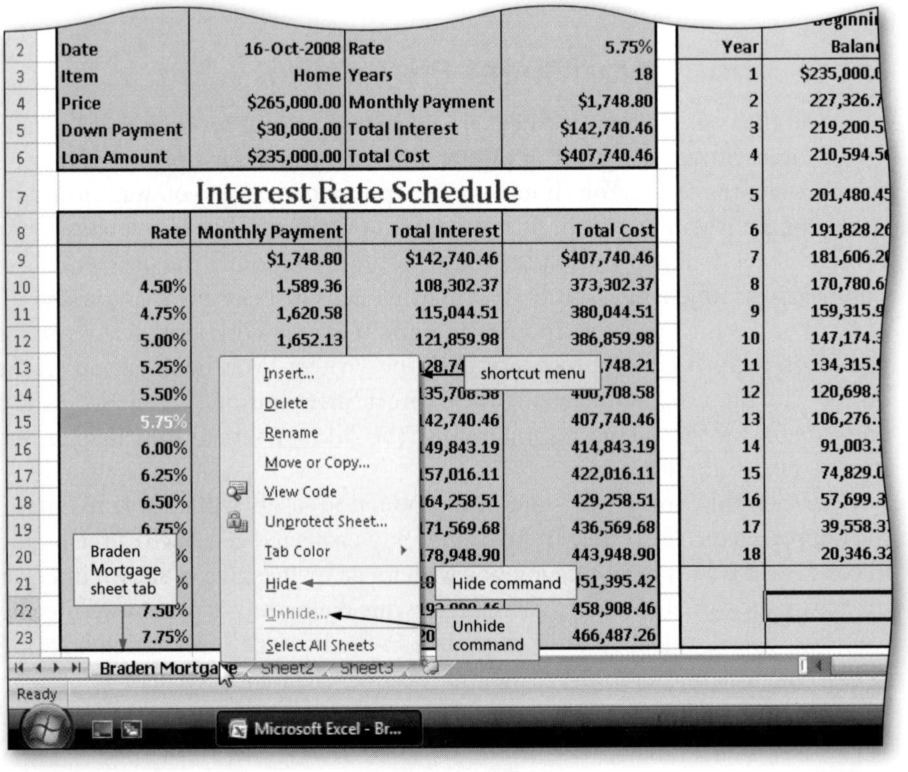

Figure 4–60

2

- Click Hide on the shortcut menu to hide the Braden Mortgage sheet.

3

- Right–click any sheet tab to display the shortcut menu.

4

- Click Unhide on the shortcut menu to open the Unhide dialog box.

5

- When Excel displays the Unhide dialog box, if necessary, click Braden Mortgage in the Unhide sheet list (Figure 4–61).

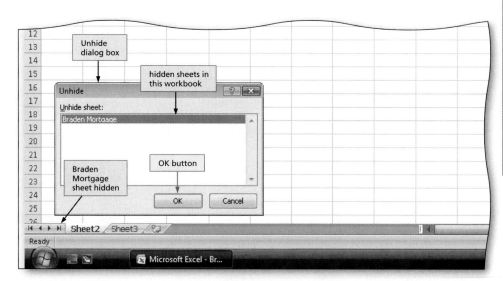

Figure 4–61

Q&A When should I hide a sheet?

Hiding sheets in a workbook is not uncommon when working with complex workbooks that have one sheet with the results the user needs to see and one or more sheets with essential data that is unimportant to the user, and thus hidden from view. The fact that a sheet is hidden does not mean the data and formulas on the hidden sheets are unavailable for use on other sheets in the workbook. This same logic applies to hidden rows and columns.

6

- Click the OK button to unhide the Braden Mortgage sheet as it was shown in Figure 4–60.

To Hide and Unhide a Workbook

You hide an entire workbook by using the Hide button on the View tab on the Ribbon. Some users employ this command when they leave a workbook up on an unattended computer and do not want others to be able to see the workbook. The Hide command is also useful when you have several workbooks opened simultaneously and want the user to be able to view only one of them. The following steps show how to hide and unhide a workbook.

1

- Click the View tab on the Ribbon (Figure 4–62).

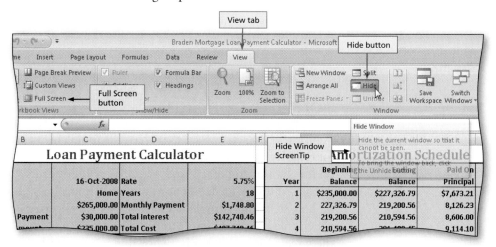

Figure 4–62

2

- Click the Hide button on the Ribbon to hide the Braden Mortgage workbook.

3

- Click the Unhide button on the Ribbon.

- When Excel displays the Unhide dialog box, if necessary, click Braden Mortgage Loan Payment Calculator in the Unhide workbook list (Figure 4–63).

Q&A

What else can I hide?

You can hide most window elements in order to display more rows of worksheet data. These window elements include the Ribbon, formula bar, and status bar. The Excel window elements can be hidden by using the Full Screen button on the View tab on the Ribbon (Figure 4–62 on the previous page). These elements remain hidden only as long as the workbook is open. They redisplay when you close the workbook and open it again.

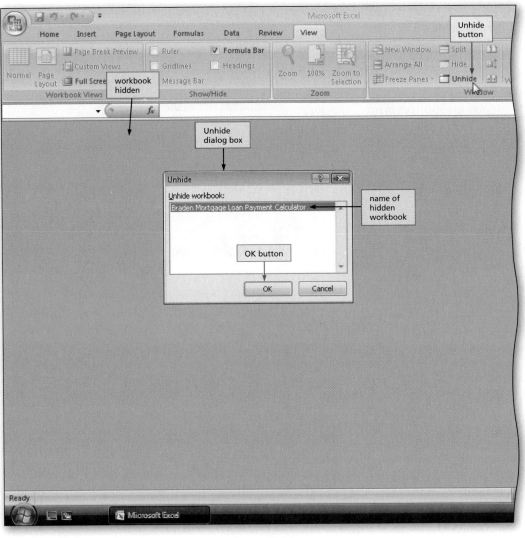

Figure 4–63

4

- Click the OK button to unhide the Braden Mortgage Loan Payment Calculator workbook as it was shown in Figure 4–62 on the previous page.

Formula Checking

Similar to the spell checker, Excel has a **formula checker** that checks formulas in a worksheet for rule violations. You invoke the formula checker by clicking the Error Checking command on the Tools menu. Each time Excel encounters a cell with a formula that violates one of its rules, it displays a dialog box containing information about the formula and a suggestion on how to fix the formula. Table 4–4 lists Excel's error checking rules. You can choose which rules you want Excel to use by enabling and disabling them in the Formulas area in the Excel Options dialog box shown in Figure 4–64 on page EX 320.

Table 4–4 Error Checking Rules		
Rule	**Name of Rule**	**Description**
1	Cells containing formulas that result in an error	The cell contains a formula that does not use the expected syntax, arguments, or data types.
2	Inconsistent calculated column formula in tables	The cell contains formulas or values that are inconsistent with the column formula or tables.
3	Cells containing years represented as 2 digits	The cell contains a text date with a two–digit year that can be misinterpreted as the wrong century.
4	Numbers formatted as text or preceded by an apostrophe	The cell contains numbers stored as text.
5	Formulas inconsistent with other formulas in the region	The cell contains a formula that does not match the pattern of the formulas around it.
6	Formula that omits cells in a region	The cell contains a formula that does not include a correct cell or range reference.
7	Unlocked cells containing formulas	The cell with a formula is unlocked in a protected worksheet.
8	Formulas referring to empty cell	The cells referred to in a formula are empty.
9	Data entered in a table is invalid	The cell has a data validation error.

To Enable Background Formula Checking

Through the Excel Options dialog box, you can enable background formula checking. **Background formula checking** means that Excel continually will review the workbook for errors in formulas as you create or manipulate it. The following steps enable background formula checking.

1 Click the Office Button on the Ribbon, click the Excel Options button, and then click the Formulas button.

2 If necessary, click 'Enable background error checking' in the Error Checking area to select it.

3 Click any check box in the 'Error checking rules' area that does not contain a check mark (Figure 4–64 on the next page).

4 Click the OK button.

Q&A How can I decide which rules to have the background formula checker check?

You can decide which rules you want the background formula checker to highlight by adding and removing check marks from the check boxes in the 'Error checking rules' area (Figure 4–64). If you add or remove check marks, then you should click the Reset Ignored Errors button to reset error checking.

BTW

Excel Help
The best way to become familiar with Excel Help is to use it. Appendix C includes detailed information about Excel Help and exercises that will help you gain confidence in using it.

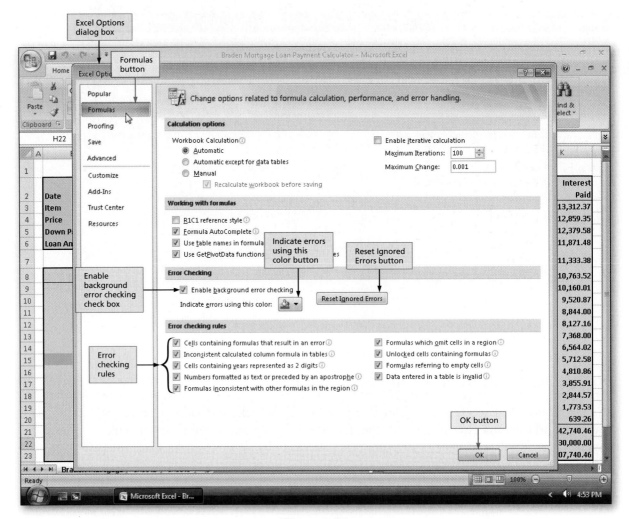

Figure 4–64

More About Background Formula Checking

BTW

Quick Reference
For a table that lists how to complete the tasks covered in this book using the mouse, Ribbon, shortcut menu, and keyboard, see the Quick Reference Summary at the back of this book, or visit the Excel 2007 Quick Reference Web page (scsite.com/ex2007/qr).

When a formula fails to pass one of the rules and background formula checking is enabled, then Excel displays a small green triangle in the upper–left corner of the cell assigned the formula in question.

Assume, for example, that background formula checking is enabled and that cell E4, which contains the PMT function in the Braden Mortgage workbook, is unlocked. Because rule 7 in Table 4–4 stipulates that a cell containing a formula must be locked, Excel displays a green triangle in the upper–left corner of cell E4.

When you select the cell with the green triangle, a Trace Error button appears next to the cell. If you click the Trace Error button, Excel displays the Trace Error menu (Figure 4–65). The first item in the menu identifies the error (Unprotected Formula). The remainder of the menu lists commands from which you can choose. The first command locks the cell. Invoking the Lock Cell command fixes the problem so that the formula no longer violates the rule. The Error Checking Options command instructs Excel to display the Excel Options dialog box with the Formulas area active, as shown in Figure 4–64.

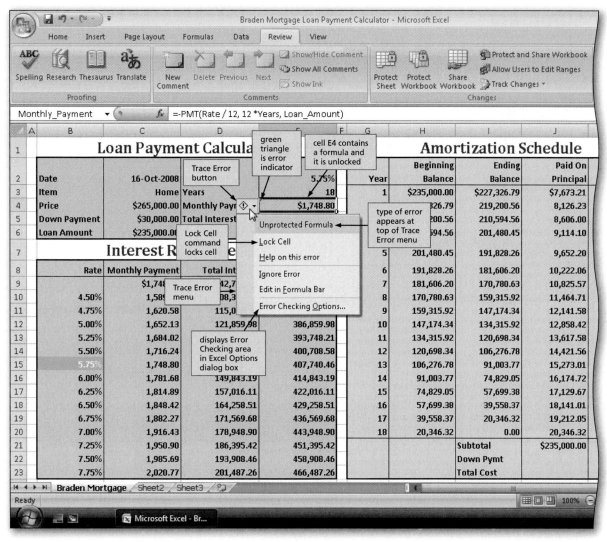

Figure 4–65

The background formula checker can become annoying when you are creating certain types of worksheets that may violate the formula rules until referenced cells contain data. It is not unusual to end up with green triangles in cells throughout your worksheet. If this is the case, then disable background formula checking by removing the check mark from the 'Enable background error checking' check box (Figure 4–64) and use the Error Checking button on the Formulas tab on the Ribbon to check your worksheet once you have finished creating it.

It is strongly recommended that you use background formula checking or the Error Checking button on the Formulas tab on the Ribbon during the testing phase to ensure the formulas in your workbook do not violate the rules listed in Table 4–4.

To Quit Excel

The following steps quit Excel.

1. Click the Close button on the right side of the title bar.

2. If Excel displays a Microsoft Office Excel dialog box, click the No button.

BTW

Certification
The Microsoft Certified Application Specialist (MCAS) program provides an opportunity for you to obtain a valuable industry credential – proof that you have the Excel 2007 skills required by employers. For more information, see Appendix G or visit the Excel 2007 Certification Web page (scsite.com/ex2007/cert).

Chapter Summary

In this chapter, you learned how to use names, rather than cell references, to enter formulas, use financial functions, such as the PMT and PV functions, analyze data by creating a data table and amortization schedule, set print options and print sections of a worksheet using names and the Set Print Area command, protect a worksheet or workbook, and hide and unhide rows, columns, sheets, and workbooks. The items listed below include all the new Excel skills you have learned in this chapter.

1. Add Custom Borders and a Background Color to a Range (EX 272)
2. Create Names Based on Row Titles (EX 276)
3. Enter the Loan Amount Formula Using Names (EX 279)
4. Enter the PMT Function (EX 280)
5. Create a Percent Series Using the Fill Handle (EX 286)
6. Define a Range as a Data Table (EX 288)
7. Add a Pointer to the Data Table (EX 292)
8. Enter the Formulas in the Amortization Schedule (EX 297)
9. Copy the Formulas to Fill the Amortization Schedule (EX 301)
10. Set Up a Worksheet to Print (EX 307)
11. Set the Print Area (EX 309)
12. Name and Print Sections of a Worksheet (EX 310)
13. Protect a Worksheet (EX 313)
14. Hide and Unhide a Sheet (EX 316)
15. Hide and Unhide a Workbook (EX 317)
16. Enable Background Formula Checking (EX 319)

If you have a SAM user profile, you may have access to hands-on instruction, practice, and assessment. Log in to your SAM account (http://sam2007.course.com) to launch any assigned training activities or exams that relate to the skills covered in this chapter.

Learn It Online

Learn It Online is a series of online student exercises that test your knowledge of chapter content and key terms.

Instructions: To complete the Learn It Online exercises, start your browser, click the Address bar, and then enter the Web address scsite.com/ex2007/learn. When the Excel 2007 Learn It Online page is displayed, click the link for the exercise you want to complete and then read the instructions.

Chapter Reinforcement TF, MC, and SA

A series of true/false, multiple choice, and short answer questions that test your knowledge of the chapter content.

Flash Cards

An interactive learning environment where you identify chapter key terms associated with displayed definitions.

Practice Test

A series of multiple choice questions that test your knowledge of chapter content and key terms.

Who Wants To Be a Computer Genius?

An interactive game that challenges your knowledge of chapter content in the style of a television quiz show.

Wheel of Terms

An interactive game that challenges your knowledge of chapter key terms in the style of the television show *Wheel of Fortune*.

Crossword Puzzle Challenge

A crossword puzzle that challenges your knowledge of key terms presented in the chapter.

Apply Your Knowledge

Reinforce the skills and apply the concepts you learned in this chapter.

Determining the Monthly Loan Payment

Instructions: Start Excel. Open the workbook Apply 4–1 Monthly Loan Payment from the Data Files for Students. See the inside back cover of this book for instructions for downloading the Data Files for Students or see your instructor for information on accessing the files required in this book.

Perform the following tasks.

1. Use the Create from Selection button in the Defined Names group on the Formulas tab to create names for cells in the range C4:C9 using the row titles in the range B4:B9.
2. Enter the formulas shown in Table 4–5.

Table 4–5 Data Table Formulas	
Cell	**Formula**
C8	=Price – Down_Payment
C9	=– PMT(Interest_Rate/12, 12 * Years, Loan_Amount)
F4	=C9
G4	=+12 * C7 * C9 + C5
H4	=G4 – C4

Continued >

Apply Your Knowledge *continued*

3. Use the Data Table button in the What–If Analysis gallery on the Data tab to define the range E4: H19 as a one–input data table. Use cell C6 (interest rate) as the column input cell. Format the data table so that it appears as shown in Figure 4–66.

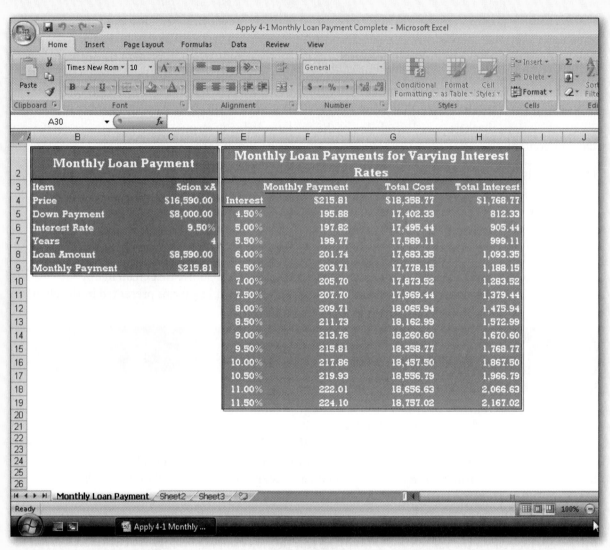

Figure 4–66

4. Use the Page Setup dialog box to select the Fit to and Black and white options. Use the Set Print Area command to select the range B2:C9 and then use the Print command on the Office Button menu to print. Use the Clear Print Area command to clear the print area. Name the following ranges: B2:C9 – Calculator; E2:H19 – Rate_Schedule; and B1:H19 – All_Sections. Print each range by selecting the name in the Name box and using the Selection option in the Print dialog box.

5. Unlock the range C3:C7. Protect the worksheet so that the user can select only unlocked cells.

6. Press CTRL+` and print the formulas version in landscape orientation. Press CTRL+` to display the values version.

7. Hide and then unhide the Monthly Loan Payment sheet. Hide and then unhide the workbook. Unprotect the worksheet and then hide columns E through H. Print the worksheet. Select columns D and I and unhide the hidden columns. Hide rows 11 through 19. Print the worksheet. Select rows 10 and 20 and unhide rows 11 through 19. Protect the worksheet.

8. Change the document properties as specified by your instructor. Change the worksheet header with your name, course number, and other information as specified by your instructor. Save the workbook using the file name, Apply 4–1 Monthly Loan Payment Complete.
9. Determine the monthly payment and print the worksheet for each data set: (a) Item = Home; Price = $310,000.00; Down Payment = $62,000.00; Interest Rate = 6.75%; Years = 20; (b) Item = Jacuzzi; Price = $19,000.00; Down Payment = $0.00; Interest Rate = 8.80%; Years = 5. You should get the following monthly payment results: (a) $1,885.70; (b) $392.57.
10. Submit the assignment as requested by your instructor.

Extend Your Knowledge

Extend the skills you learned in this chapter and experiment with new skills. You may need to use Help to complete the assignment.

Two–Input Data Table

Instructions: Start Excel. Open the workbook Extend 4–1 401(k) Planning Sheet from the Data Files for Students. See the inside back cover of this book for instructions for downloading the Data Files for Students or see your instructor for information on accessing the files required in this book. You have been asked to include a two–input data table (Figure 4–67) on the existing 401(k) Planning Sheet worksheet that shows the future value that results from varying the expected annual return (cell C8) and employee percent invested (cell C5). Complete the following tasks to create the two–input data table.

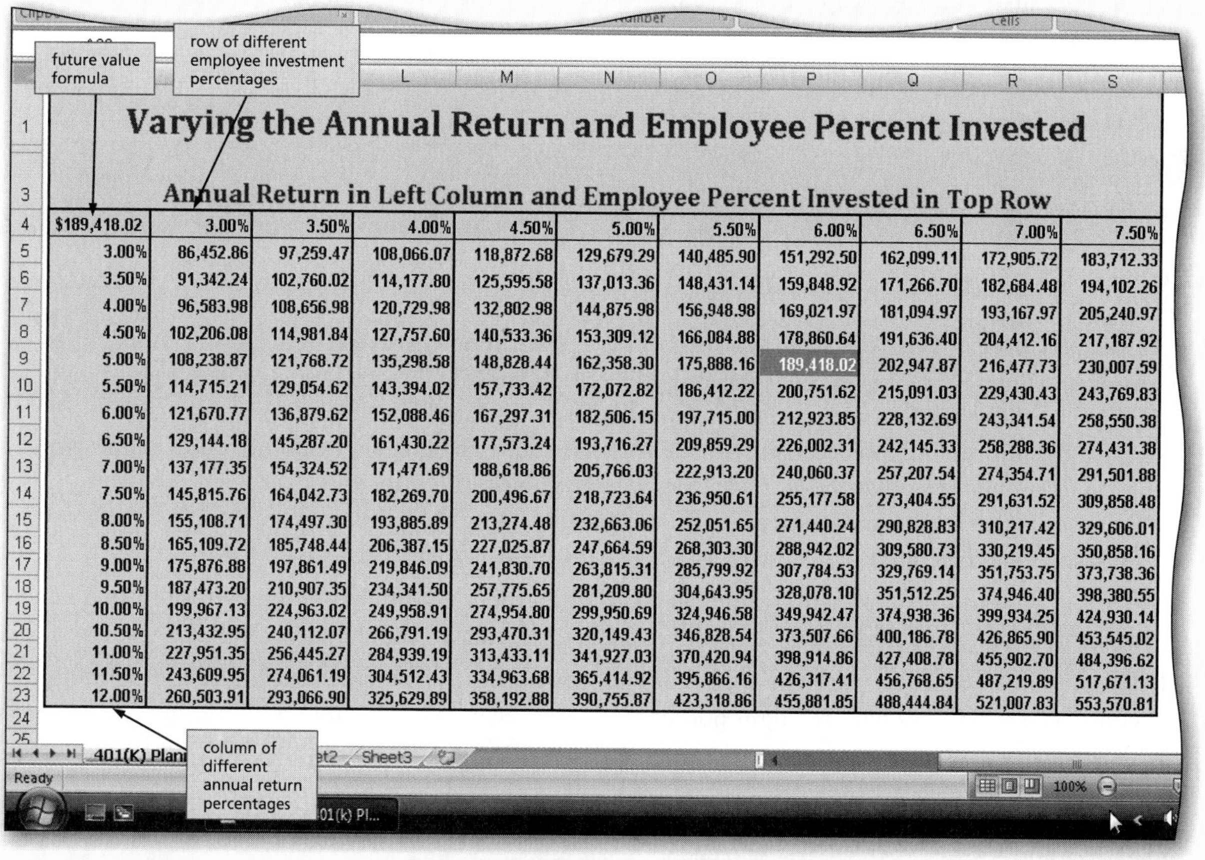

$189,418.02	3.00%	3.50%	4.00%	4.50%	5.00%	5.50%	6.00%	6.50%	7.00%	7.50%
3.00%	86,452.86	97,259.47	108,066.07	118,872.68	129,679.29	140,485.90	151,292.50	162,099.11	172,905.72	183,712.33
3.50%	91,342.24	102,760.02	114,177.80	125,595.58	137,013.36	148,431.14	159,848.92	171,266.70	182,684.48	194,102.26
4.00%	96,583.98	108,656.98	120,729.98	132,802.98	144,875.98	156,948.98	169,021.97	181,094.97	193,167.97	205,240.97
4.50%	102,206.08	114,981.84	127,757.60	140,533.36	153,309.12	166,084.88	178,860.64	191,636.40	204,412.16	217,187.92
5.00%	108,238.87	121,768.72	135,298.58	148,828.44	162,358.30	175,888.16	189,418.02	202,947.87	216,477.73	230,007.59
5.50%	114,715.21	129,054.62	143,394.02	157,733.42	172,072.82	186,412.22	200,751.62	215,091.03	229,430.43	243,769.83
6.00%	121,670.77	136,879.62	152,088.46	167,297.31	182,506.15	197,715.00	212,923.85	228,132.69	243,341.54	258,550.38
6.50%	129,144.18	145,287.20	161,430.22	177,573.24	193,716.27	209,859.29	226,002.31	242,145.33	258,288.36	274,431.38
7.00%	137,177.35	154,324.52	171,471.69	188,618.86	205,766.03	222,913.20	240,060.37	257,207.54	274,354.71	291,501.88
7.50%	145,815.76	164,042.73	182,269.70	200,496.67	218,723.64	236,950.61	255,177.58	273,404.55	291,631.52	309,858.48
8.00%	155,108.71	174,497.30	193,885.89	213,274.48	232,663.06	252,051.65	271,440.24	290,828.83	310,217.42	329,606.01
8.50%	165,109.72	185,748.44	206,387.15	227,025.87	247,664.59	268,303.30	288,942.02	309,580.73	330,219.45	350,858.16
9.00%	175,876.88	197,861.49	219,846.09	241,830.70	263,815.31	285,799.92	307,784.53	329,769.14	351,753.75	373,738.36
9.50%	187,473.20	210,907.35	234,341.50	257,775.65	281,209.80	304,643.95	328,078.10	351,512.25	374,946.40	398,380.55
10.00%	199,967.13	224,963.02	249,958.91	274,954.80	299,950.69	324,946.58	349,942.47	374,938.36	399,934.25	424,930.14
10.50%	213,432.95	240,112.07	266,791.19	293,470.31	320,149.43	346,828.54	373,507.66	400,186.78	426,865.90	453,545.02
11.00%	227,951.35	256,445.27	284,939.19	313,433.11	341,927.03	370,420.94	398,914.86	427,408.78	455,902.70	484,396.62
11.50%	243,609.95	274,061.19	304,512.43	334,963.68	365,414.92	395,866.16	426,317.41	456,768.65	487,219.89	517,671.13
12.00%	260,503.91	293,066.90	325,629.89	358,192.88	390,755.87	423,318.86	455,881.85	488,444.84	521,007.83	553,570.81

Figure 4–67

Continued >

Extend Your Knowledge *continued*

1. Enter the data table title and subtitle as shown in cells I1 and I3 in Figure 4–67. Change the width of column H to 0.50 characters. Merge and center the titles over columns I through S. Format the titles as shown using the Title cell style for both the title and subtitle, a font size of 22 for the title, and a font size of 16 for the subtitle. Change the column widths of columns I through S to 11.00 characters.

2. For a two–input data table, the formula you are analyzing must be assigned to the upper–left cell in the range of the data table. Cell C14 contains the future value formula to be analyzed. Therefore, enter =C14 in cell I4.

3. Use the fill handle to create two lists of percents (a) 3.00% through 12.00%, in increments of 0.50% in the range I5:I23; and (b) 3.00% through 7.50% in increments of 0.50% in the range J4:S4.

4. Select the range I4:S23. Click the Data tab on the Ribbon and then click the What–If Analysis button on the Ribbon. Click the Data Table command on the What–If Analysis gallery. When Excel displays the Table dialog box, enter c5 (employee percent invested) in the Row input cell box and c8 (expected annual return) in the Column input cell box. Click the OK button to populate the table.

5. Format the two–input data table as shown in Figure 4–67.

6. Use conditional formatting to change the format of the cell in the two–input data table that is equal to the future value in cell C14 to white bold font on a red background.

7. Protect the worksheet so that the user can select only unlocked cells (C3:C6 and C8:C9).

8. Change the document properties as specified by your instructor. Change the worksheet header with your name, course number, and other information requested by your instructor. Change the print orientation to landscape. Print the worksheet using the Fit to option. Print the formulas version of the worksheet.

9. Save the workbook using the file name Extend 4–1 401(k) Planning Sheet Complete.

Make It Right

Analyze a workbook and correct all errors and/or improve the design.

Functions, Custom Borders, Cell Names, What–If Analysis, and Protection

Instructions: Start Excel. Open the workbook Make It Right 4–1 Financial Calculator. See the inside back cover of this book for instructions for downloading the Data Files for Students, or see your instructor for information on accessing the files required for this book. Correct the following design and formula problems so that the worksheet appears as shown in Figure 4–68.

1. The worksheet is protected with no unprotected cells. Unprotect the worksheet so that the worksheet can be edited.

2. Correct the Monthly Payment formula in cell C7 and the Total Interest formula in cell C8. The monthly payment should equal $2,078.97 and the total interest should equal $419,214.32.

3. Change the thick box border to a dark red thick box border. Change the thick border separating columns B and C to a dark red light border.

4. Use Goal Seek to change the down payment in cell C3 so that the monthly payment is $1,850.00 as shown in Figure 4–68.

5. Name the range B1:C9, Loan_Calculator.

6. Assign the names in column E to the adjacent cells in column F. Edit the formulas in cells F5 and F6 and change the cell references to their corresponding names.

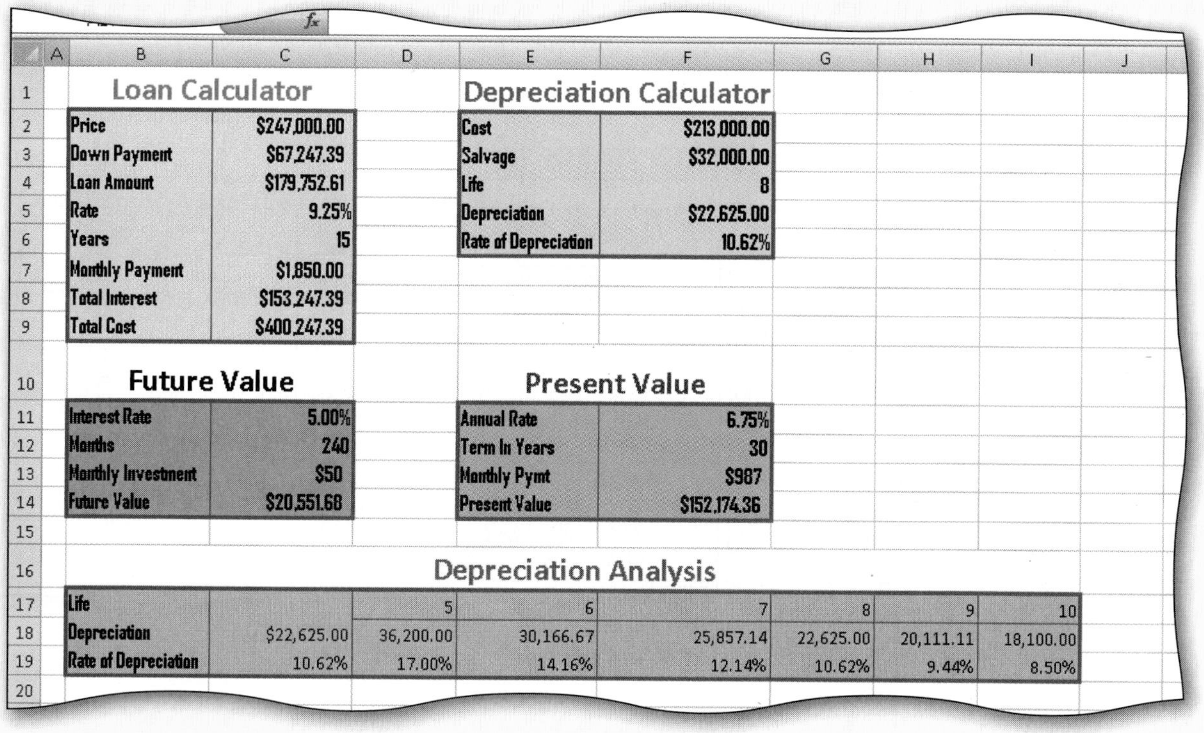

	A	B	C	D	E	F	G	H	I	J
1		Loan Calculator			Depreciation Calculator					
2		Price	$247,000.00		Cost	$213,000.00				
3		Down Payment	$67,247.39		Salvage	$32,000.00				
4		Loan Amount	$179,752.61		Life	8				
5		Rate	9.25%		Depreciation	$22,625.00				
6		Years	15		Rate of Depreciation	10.62%				
7		Monthly Payment	$1,850.00							
8		Total Interest	$153,247.39							
9		Total Cost	$400,247.39							
10		Future Value			Present Value					
11		Interest Rate	5.00%		Annual Rate	6.75%				
12		Months	240		Term In Years	30				
13		Monthly Investment	$50		Monthly Pymt	$987				
14		Future Value	$20,551.68		Present Value	$152,174.36				
15										
16					Depreciation Analysis					
17		Life		5	6	7	8	9	10	
18		Depreciation	$22,625.00	36,200.00	30,166.67	25,857.14	22,625.00	20,111.11	18,100.00	
19		Rate of Depreciation	10.62%	17.00%	14.16%	12.14%	10.62%	9.44%	8.50%	
20										

Figure 4–68

7. Correct the second and third arguments in the Future Value function in cell C14. Display the future value as a positive number.
8. Change the Present Value function in cell F14 so that the present value displays as a positive number.
9. Complete the one–input data table in the range B17:I19 that determines the depreciation and rate of depreciation for varying years of life (cell F4). Format the numbers in the data table so that they appear as shown in Figure 4–68.
10. Change the document properties as specified by your instructor. Change the worksheet header with your name, course number, and other information requested by your instructor.
11. Unlock the cells containing data (C2:C3, C5:C6, F2:F4, C11:C13, F11:F13). Protect the worksheet so that the user can select only cells with data.
12. Save the workbook using the file name, Make It Right 4–1 Financial Calculator Complete, and submit the revised workbook as requested by your instructor.

In the Lab

Create a workbook using the guidelines, concepts, and skills presented in this chapter. Labs are listed in order of increasing difficulty.

Lab 1: 401(k) Retirement Savings Model

Problem: You have been asked by the human resources department to develop a retirement planning worksheet that will allow each current and prospective employee to see the effect (dollar accumulation) of investing a percent of his or her monthly salary over a period of years (Figure 4–69 on the next page). The plan calls for the company to match an employee's investment, dollar for dollar, up to 3%. Thus, if an employee invests 6% of his or her annual salary, then the company matches the first 3%. If an employee invests only 2% of his or her annual salary, then the company matches the entire 2%. The human resources department wants a one–input data table to show the future value of the investment for different periods.

Continued >

In the Lab *continued*

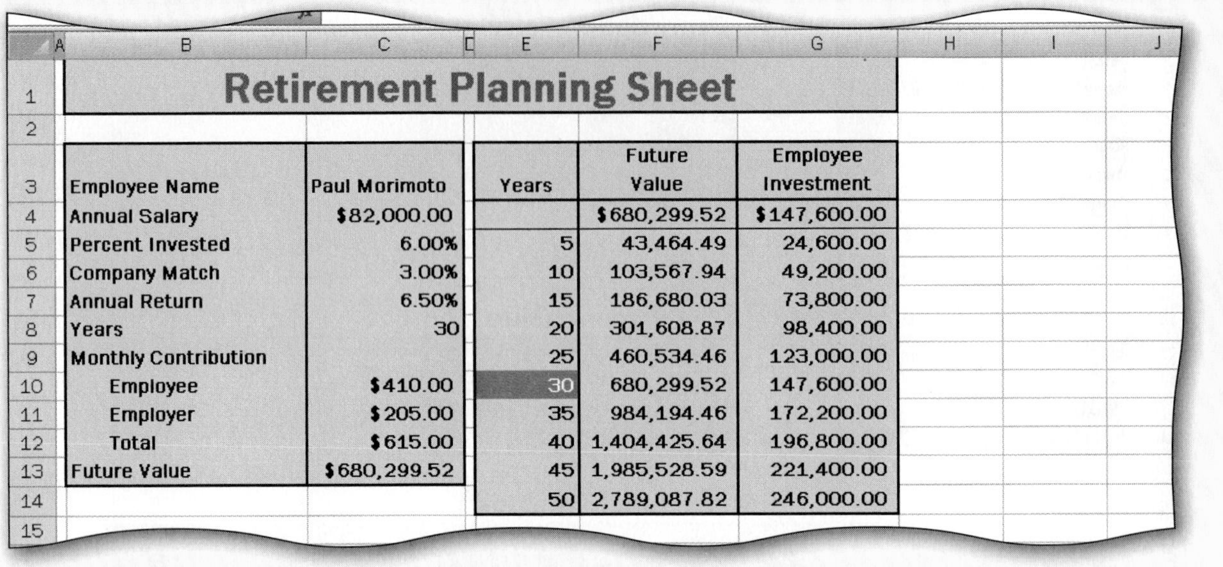

	Years	Future Value	Employee Investment
Retirement Planning Sheet			
Employee Name	Paul Morimoto		$680,299.52	$147,600.00
Annual Salary	$82,000.00	5	43,464.49	24,600.00
Percent Invested	6.00%	10	103,567.94	49,200.00
Company Match	3.00%	15	186,680.03	73,800.00
Annual Return	6.50%	20	301,608.87	98,400.00
Years	30	25	460,534.46	123,000.00
Monthly Contribution		30	680,299.52	147,600.00
Employee	$410.00	35	984,194.46	172,200.00
Employer	$205.00	40	1,404,425.64	196,800.00
Total	$615.00	45	1,985,528.59	221,400.00
Future Value	$680,299.52	50	2,789,087.82	246,000.00

Figure 4–69

Instructions: With a blank worksheet on the screen, perform the following tasks.

1. Change the font of the entire worksheet to bold and apply the Trek theme to the worksheet. Change the column widths to the following: A and D = 0.50; B = 20.00; C, F, and G = 13.00. Change the row heights to the following: 2 = 16.50; and 3 = 32.25. The height of row 1 will be adjusted automatically when a cell style is applied to the worksheet title.

2. In cell B1, enter Retirement Planning Sheet as the worksheet title. Merge and center cell B1 across columns B through G. Apply the Title cell style to cell B1, change the font size to 24 point, and change the font color to Orange, Accent 6 (column 10, row 1 in the Theme colors area on the Font Color palette). Draw a medium black border around cell B1.

3. Enter the row titles in column B, beginning in cell B3 as shown in Figure 4–69. Add the data in Table 4–6 to column C. Use the dollar and percent signs format symbols to format the numbers in the range C4:C7.

Table 4–6 401(k) Planning Sheet Employee Data	
Row Title	**Item**
Employee Name	Paul Morimoto
Annual Salary	$82,000.00
Percent Invested	6.00%
Company Match	3.00%
Annual Return	6.50%
Years	30

4. Use the Create from Selection button on the Formulas tab on the Ribbon to assign the row titles in column B (range B3:B13) to the adjacent cells in column C. Use these names to enter the following formulas in the range C10:C13. Step 4e formats the displayed results of the formulas.

    a. Employee Monthly Contribution (cell C10) = Annual_Salary * Percent_Invested / 12

    b. Employer Monthly Contribution (cell C11) = IF(Percent_Invested < Company_Match, Percent_Invested * Annual_Salary / 12, Company_Match * Annual_Salary / 12)

    c. Total Monthly Contribution (cell C12) = SUM(C10:C11)

    d. Future Value (cell C13) = –FV(Annual_Return/12, 12 * Years, Total)

    e. If necessary, use the Format Painter button on the Home tab on the Ribbon to assign the Currency style format in cell C4 to the range C10:C13.

The Future Value function (FV) in Step 4d returns to the cell the future value of the investment. The future value of an investment is its value at some point in the future based on a series of payments of equal amounts made over a number of periods earning a constant rate of return.

5. Add borders to the range B3:C13 as shown in Figure 4–69.

6. Use the concepts and techniques developed in this project to add the data table in Figure 4–69 to the range E3:G14 as follows.

   a. Enter and format the table column titles in row 3.

   b. Use the fill handle to create the series of years beginning with 5 and ending with 50 in increments of 5 in column E, beginning in cell E5.

   c. In cell F4, enter =C13 as the formula. In cell G4, enter =12 * C10 * C8 as the formula (using cell references in the formulas means Excel will copy the formats).

   d. Use the Data Table command on the What–If Analysis gallery on the Data tab on the Ribbon to define the range E4:G14 as a one–input data table. Use cell C8 as the column input cell.

   e. Format the numbers in the range F5:G14 to the Comma style format. Underline rows 3 and 4 as shown in Figure 4–69. Add borders to the range E3:G14 as shown in Figure 4–69.

7. Use the Conditional Formatting button on the Home tab on the Ribbon to add a red pointer that shows the row that equates the years in cell C8 to the Years column in the data table. Use a white font color for the pointer. Add the background color Light Yellow, Background 2 (column 3, row 1 in the Theme colors area on the Fill Color palette) as shown in Figure 4–69.

8. Change the document properties as specified by your instructor. Change the worksheet header with your name, course number, and other information as specified by your instructor.

9. Spell check and formula check the worksheet. Use Range Finder (double–click cell) to check all formulas.

10. Print the worksheet.

11. Print the formulas version of the worksheet.

12. Unlock the cells in the range C3:C8. Protect the worksheet. Allow users to select only unlocked cells.

13. Save the workbook using the file name Lab 4–1 Retirement Planning Sheet.

14. Hide and then unhide the Retirement Planning Sheet sheet. Hide and then unhide the Workbook. Unprotect the worksheet and then hide columns D through G. Print the worksheet. Select columns C and H and unhide the hidden columns. Hide rows 1 and 2. Print the worksheet. Click the Select All button and unhide rows 1 and 2.

15. Close the workbook without saving changes. Open the workbook Lab 4–1 Retirement Planning Sheet. Determine the future value for the data in Table 4–7. Print the worksheet for each data set. The following Future Value results should display in cell C13: Data Set 1 = $165,108.38; Data Set 2 = $549,735.86; and Data Set 3 = $1,241,885.59. Quit Excel without saving the workbook.

16. Submit the assignment as requested by your instructor.

Table 4–7 Future Value Data			
	Data Set 1	**Data Set 2**	**Data Set 3**
Employee Name	Paula Rios	Sam Vinci	Gupta Ghandi
Annual Salary	$101,000.00	$78,000.00	$41,000.00
Percent Invested	2.00%	4.5%	6%
Company Match	2.00%	3%	3%
Annual Return	6.50%	7.00%	8.5%
Years	20	30	40

In the Lab

Lab 2: Quarterly Income Statement and Break–Even Analysis

Problem: You are a consultant to The Bean Bag Game Company. Your area of expertise is cost–volume–profit or CVP (also called break–even analysis), which investigates the relationship among a product's expenses (cost), its volume (units sold), and the operating income (gross profit). Any money a company earns above the break–even point is called operating income, or gross profit (row 21 in the Break–Even Analysis table in Figure 4–70). You have been asked to prepare a quarterly income statement and a data table that shows revenue, expenses, and income for units sold between 40,000 and 120,000 in increments of 5,000.

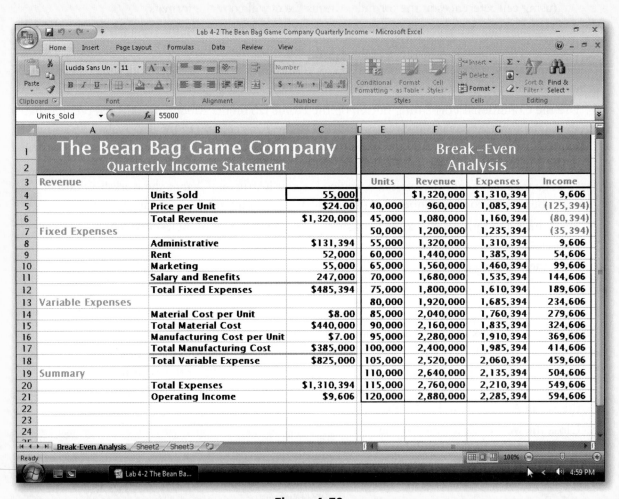

Figure 4–70

Instructions: With a blank worksheet on the screen, perform the following tasks.

1. Apply the Concourse theme to the worksheet. Change the font of the entire worksheet to bold. Change the column widths to the following: A = 21.00; B= 26.00; C = 12.78; D = 0.50; E= 7.44; and F through H = 11.22. Change the heights of rows 1 and 2 to 30.00 and 19.50 respectively. Name the sheet tab Break–Even Analysis and color the tab Orange, Accent 3 (column 7, row 1 on the Tab Color palette).

2. Enter the worksheet titles: `The Bean Bag Game Company` in cell A1, and `Quarterly Income Statement` in cell A2. Apply the Title cell style to both cells. Change the font sizes in cells A1 and A2 to 24 and 16 respectively. One at a time, merge and center cells A1 and A2 across columns A through C. Change the background color of cells A1 and A2 to Orange, Accent 3 (column 7, row 1 on the Fill Color palette). Change the font color to White, Background 1 (column 1, row 1 on the Font Color palette). Add a thick border to the range A1:A2.

3. Enter the row titles in columns A and B as shown in Figure 4–70. Change the font size of the row titles in column A to 12–point and change the font color to Orange, Accent 3. Add the data shown in Table 4–8 in column C. Use the dollar sign ($) and comma (,) format symbols to format the numbers in column C as you enter them.

Table 4–8 Annual Income Data		
Title	Cell	Item
Units Sold	C4	55,000
Price per Unit	C5	$24.00
Administrative	C8	$131,394
Rent	C9	$52,000
Marketing	C10	$55,000
Salary and Benefits	C11	$247,000
Material Cost per Unit	C14	$8.00
Manufacturing Cost per Unit	C16	$7.00

4. Use the Create from Selection button on the Formulas tab on the Ribbon to assign the row titles in column B in the range B4:B21 to the adjacent cells in column C. Use these names to enter the following formulas in column C:

a. Total Revenue (cell C6) = Units Sold * Price per Unit (or =C4 * C5)

b. Total Fixed Expenses (cell C12) = SUM(C8:C11)

c. Total Material Cost (cell C15) = Units Sold * Material Cost per Unit (or =C4 * C14)

d. Total Manufacturing Cost (cell C17) = Units Sold * Manufacturing Cost per Unit (or =C4 * C16)

e. Total Variable Expenses (cell C18) = Total Material Cost + Total Manufacturing Cost (or =C15 + C17)

f. Total Expenses (cell C20) = Total Fixed Expenses + Total Variable Expense (or =C12 + C18)

g. Operating Income (cell C21) = Total Revenue – Total Expenses (or =C6 – C20)

5. If necessary, use the Format Painter button on the Home tab on the Ribbon to assign the Currency style format in cell C8 to the unformatted dollar amounts in column C.

6. Add a thick orange bottom border to the ranges B5:C5, B11:C11, and B17:C17 as shown in Figure 4–70.

7. Use the concepts and techniques presented in this project to add the data table to the range E1:H21 as follows:

a. Add the data table titles and format them as shown in Figure 4–70.

b. Create the series in column E from 40,000 to 120,000 in increments of 5,000, beginning in cell E5.

c. Enter the formula =c6 in cell F4. Enter the formula =c20 in cell G4. Enter the formula =c21 in cell H4. If necessary, adjust the column widths.

d. Use the Data Table command in the What–If Analysis gallery on the Data tab on the Ribbon to define the range E4:H21 as a one–input data table. Use cell C4 (Units Sold) as the column input cell.

e. Use the Format Cells command on the shortcut menu to format the range F5:H21 to the Comma style format with no decimal places and negative numbers in red with parentheses. Add a medium outline border and light vertical borders to the range E1:H21.

Continued >

In the Lab *continued*

8. Change the document properties as specified by your instructor. Change the worksheet header with your name, course number, and other information as specified by your instructor.

9. Spell check and formula check the worksheet. Use Range Finder (double–click cell) to check all formulas.

10. Use the Page Setup Dialog Box Launcher on the Page Layout tab on the Ribbon to select the Fit to and 'Black and white' options.

11. Unlock the following cells: C4, C5, C14, and C16. Protect the workbook so the user can select only unlocked cells.

12. Save the workbook using the file name, Lab 4–2 The Bean Bag Game Company Quarterly Income.

13. Print the worksheet. Print the formulas version of the worksheet.

14. Determine the operating income for the data sets in Table 4–9. Print the worksheet for each data set. You should get the following Operating Income results in cell C21: Data Set 1 = $333,606; Data Set 2 = ($453,894); and Data Set 3 = $50,106.

15. Hide and then unhide the Break–Even Analysis sheet. Hide and then unhide the workbook. Unprotect the worksheet and then hide columns D through H. Print the worksheet. Select columns C and I and unhide the hidden columns. Hide rows 7 through 21. Print the worksheet. Select rows 6 and 22 and unhide rows 7 through 21. Do not save the workbook.

Table 4–9 Operating Income Data				
Title	**Cell**	**Data Set 1**	**Data Set 2**	**Data Set 3**
Units Sold	C4	84,000	42,000	119,000
Price per Unit	C5	$19.00	$15.00	$21.00
Material Cost per Unit	C14	$4.00	$4.75	$10.00
Manufacturing Cost per Unit	C16	$5.25	$9.50	$6.50

16. Submit the assignment as requested by your instructor.

In the Lab

Lab 3: Loan Analysis and Amortization Schedule

Problem: The manager of eLoans Unlimited, Inc., an Internet–based lending institution, has asked you to create the loan analysis worksheet shown in Figure 4–71. She also wants you to demonstrate the goal seeking capabilities of Excel.

Instructions:

1. Apply the Aspect theme to a new worksheet. Bold the entire worksheet and change all the columns to a width of 17.00. Change column A to a width of 0.41.

2. Enter the worksheet title in cell B1, apply the Title cell style, and change its font size to 24-point. Enter the worksheet subtitle in cell B2, apply the Title cell style, and change its font size to 16-point. One at a time, merge and center cells B1 and B2 across columns B through F.

3. Enter the row titles for the ranges B3:B5 and E3:E5 as shown in Figure 4–71. Use the Create from Selection button on the Formulas tab on the Ribbon to assign the row titles in the ranges B3:B5 and E3:E5 to the adjacent cells in ranges C3:C5 and F3:F5, respectively.

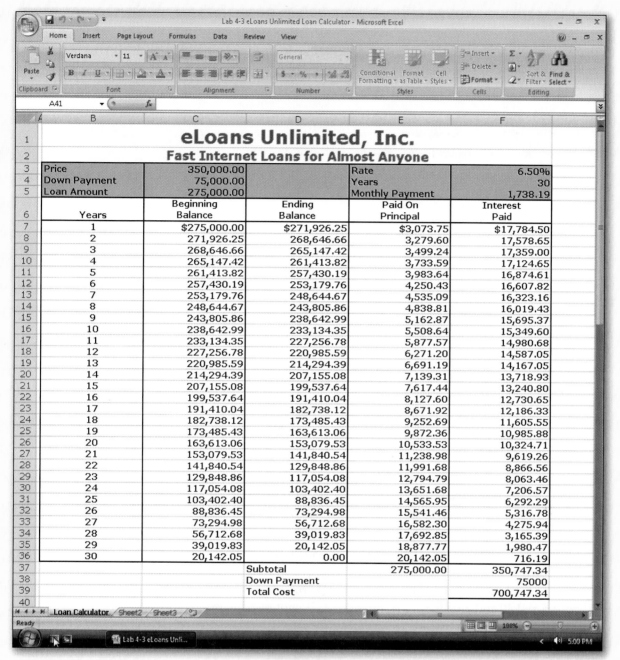

Figure 4–71

4. Enter 350000 (price) in cell C3, 75000 (down payment) in cell C4, 6.50% (interest rate) in cell F3, and 30 (years) in cell F4. Determine the loan amount by entering the formula =Price − Down_Payment in cell C5. Determine the monthly payment by entering the PMT function −PMT(Rate / 12, 12 * Years, Loan_Amount) in cell F5.

5. Create the amortization schedule in the range B6:F36 by assigning the formulas and functions to the cells indicated in Table 4–10 on the next page. Use names when appropriate. The years in column B starting at cell B7 should extend from 1 to 30 years.

6. Enter the total titles in the range D37:D39 as shown in Figure 4–71.

7. Change the sheet tab name and color as shown in Figure 4–71.

8. Change the document properties as specified by your instructor. Change the worksheet header with your name, course number, and other information requested by your instructor.

Continued >

In the Lab *continued*

9. Spell check and formula check the worksheet. Use Range Finder (double–click cell) to check all formulas listed in Table 4–10.

Table 4–10 Cell Assignments	
Cell	**Formula or Function**
C7	=C5
D7	=IF(B7 <= $F$4, PV($F$3 / 12, 12 * ($F$4 – B7), –$F$5),0)
E7	=C7 – D7
F7	=IF(C7 > 0, 12 * $F$5 – E7, 0)
C8	=D7
E37	=SUM(E7:E36)
F37	=SUM(F7:F36)
F38	=C4
F39	=E37 + F37 + F38

10. Use the Page Setup command to select the Fit to and 'Black and white' options.

11. Unlock the cells in the ranges C3:C4 and F3:F4. Protect the worksheet so that users can select any cell in the worksheet, but can change only the unlocked cells.

12. Save the workbook using the file name Lab 4–3 eLoans Unlimited Loan Calculator.

13. Print the worksheet. Print the formulas version of the worksheet.

14. Use Excel's goal seeking capabilities to determine the down payment required for the loan data in Figure 4–71 if the monthly payment is set to $1,000.00. The down payment that results for a monthly payment of $1,000.00 is $191,789.18. Print the worksheet with the new monthly payment of $1,000.00. Close the workbook without saving changes.

15. Hide and then unhide the Loan Payment Calculator sheet. Hide and then unhide the workbook. Unprotect the worksheet and then hide columns D through F. Print the worksheet. Select columns C and G and unhide the hidden columns. Hide rows 6 through 39. Print the worksheet. Select rows 5 and 40 and unhide rows 6 through 39. Do not save the workbook.

Cases and Places

Apply your creative thinking and problem solving skills to design and implement a solution.

● EASIER   ●● MORE DIFFICULT

● 1: Break–Even Analysis

You can calculate the number of units you must sell to break even (break–even point) if you know the fixed expenses, the price per unit, and the expense (cost) per unit. You have been hired by Fairview Clothing to create a data table that analyzes the break–even point for prices between $8.00 and $14.25 in increments of $0.25. The following formula determines the break–even point:

Break–Even Point = Fixed Expenses / (Price per Unit – Expense per Unit)

Assume Fixed Expenses = $800,000; Price per Unit = $8.50; and Expense per Unit = $4.10. Enter the data and formula into a worksheet and then create the data table. Use the Price per Unit as the input cell and the break–even value as the result. For a price per unit of $10.50, the data table should show a break–even point of 125,000 units. Protect the worksheet.

● 2: Salvage Value of an Asset

Jack Hollinsworth, owner of Hollinsworth Bakery, recently purchased a new commercial–sized oven for his business. Jack wants a worksheet that uses the financial function SLN to show the oven's straight–line depreciation and a formula to determine the annual rate of depreciation. Straight–line depreciation is based on an asset's initial cost, how long it can be used (called useful life), and the price at which it eventually can be sold (called salvage value). Jack has supplied the following information:

Cost = $124,857; Salvage = $30,000; Life = 8 years; and Annual Rate of Depreciation = SLN / Cost

Jack is not sure what selling price the oven will bring in 8 years. Create a data table that shows straight–line depreciation and annual rate of depreciation for salvage from $25,000 to $35,000 in $500 increments. Use Excel Help to learn more about the SLN function. Protect the worksheet.

● 3: Saving for College

Your friends' dream for their one–year–old son is that one day he will attend their alma mater, Tesla University. For the next 15 years, they plan to make monthly payment deposits to a 529 College Savings plan at a local bank. The account pays 4.5% annual interest, compounded monthly. Create a worksheet for your friends that uses a financial function to show the future value (FV) of their investment and a formula to determine the percentage of the college's tuition saved. They have supplied the following information:

Out of State Annual Tuition = $40,000; Rate (per month) = 4. 5% / 12; Nper (number of monthly payments) = 15 * 12; Pmt (payment per period) = $375; and percentage of Tuition Saved = FV / Tuition for four years

Your friends are not sure how much they will be able to save each month. Create a data table that shows the future value and percentage of tuition saved for monthly payments from $250 to $850, in $50 increments. Protect the worksheet.

Continued >

Cases and Places *continued*

•• 4 Saving for a Dream Home

Make It Personal

Find a home in your area that you would like to someday purchase. Based on the estimated current price of the home, determine how much money you need to save each month so that in seven years, you have enough to make a down payment of 10% of the current estimated value. Assume that you can save the money in an account that is getting a 5.75% return. Create a worksheet that determines how much you have to save each month so that in seven years the value of the account is 10% of the current estimated value. *Hint:* Use the FV function with a monthly savings of $400. Then use the Goal Seek command to determine the monthly savings amount. Protect the worksheet.

•• 5 Paying Off a Car Loan

Working Together

Jackie Waltrip is retiring from her teaching job, but before leaving her job, she wants to settle her account with her union's credit union. Jackie has seven years remaining on a ten–year car loan, with an interest rate of 10.25% and a monthly payment of $450.00. The credit union is willing to accept the present value (PV) of the loan as a payoff. Develop an amortization schedule that shows how much Jackie must pay at the end of each of the ten years. As a team, use Excel Help to learn more about present value. Then, design and create a worksheet that includes the beginning and ending balance, the amount paid on the principal, and the interest paid for years four through ten. Because she has paid for the three years already, determine only the ending balance (present value) for year three. Submit the worksheet as requested by your instructor and include a one–page paper on one of the following topics: (1) error checking; (2) elements you can protect in a workbook; or (3) present value.

5 Creating, Sorting, and Querying a Table

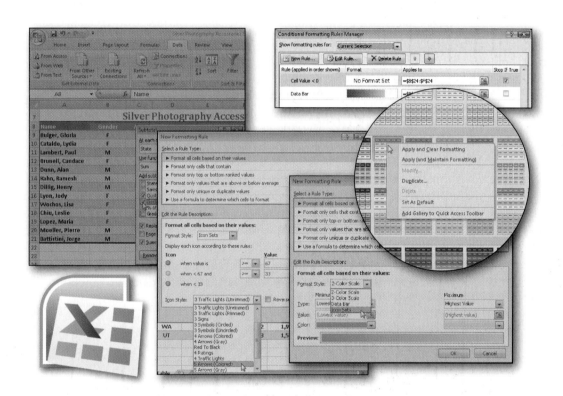

Objectives

You will have mastered the material in this chapter when you can:

- Create and manipulate a table
- Delete sheets in a workbook
- Validate data
- Add calculated columns to a table
- Use icon sets with conditional formatting
- Use the VLOOKUP function to look up a value in a table
- Print a table
- Add and delete records and change field values in a table

- Sort a table on one field or multiple fields
- Display automatic subtotals
- Use Group and Outline features to hide and unhide data
- Query a table
- Apply database functions, the SUMIF function, and the COUNTIF function
- Save a workbook in different file formats

5 | Creating, Sorting, and Querying a Table

Introduction

A **table**, also called a **database**, is an organized collection of data. For example, a list of friends, a list of students registered for a class, a club membership roster, and an instructor's grade book can be arranged as tables in a worksheet. In these cases, the data related to a person is called a **record**, and the data items that make up a record are called **fields**. For example, in a table of sales reps, each sales rep would have a separate record; each record might include several fields, such as name, age, hire date, state, and sales quota. A record in a table also can include fields (columns) that contain formulas and functions. A field, or column, that contains formulas or functions is called a **calculated column**. A calculated column displays results based on other columns in the table.

A worksheet's row-and-column structure can be used to organize and store a table. Each row of a worksheet can store a record, and each column can store a field. Additionally, a row of column headings at the top of the worksheet can store field names that identify each field. Excel's built-in data validation features help ensure data integrity of the data entered in the table.

After you enter a table onto a worksheet, you can use Excel to (1) add and delete records; (2) change the values of fields in records; (3) sort the records so Excel displays them in a different order; (4) determine subtotals for numeric fields; (5) display records that meet comparison criteria; and (6) analyze data using database functions. This chapter illustrates all six of these table capabilities.

Project — Silver Photography Accessories Sales Rep Table

The project in the chapter follows proper design guidelines and uses Excel to create the worksheet shown in Figure 5–1. Silver Photography Accessories sells equipment to photography stores throughout the western United States. The company's sales director has asked for a workbook that summarizes key information about sales reps and their performance. The data in the workbook should be easy to summarize, sort, edit, and query.

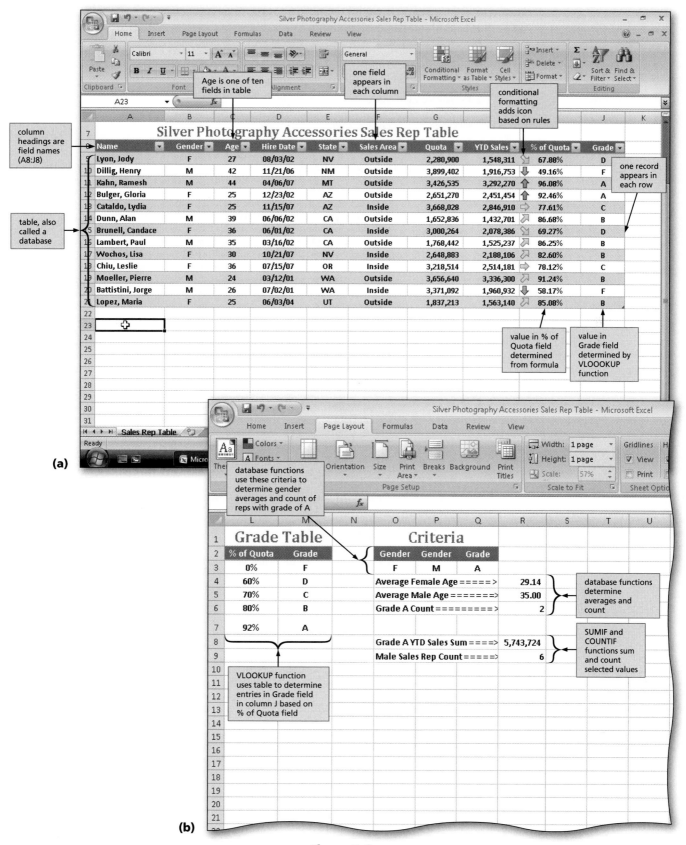

(a)

(b)

Figure 5–1

The requirements document for the Silver Photography Accessories Sales Rep table is shown in Figure 5–2. It includes the needs, source of data, calculations, special requirements, and other facts about its development.

REQUEST FOR NEW WORKBOOK

Date Submitted:	June 3, 2008
Submitted By:	Rose Veccos
Worksheet Title:	Silver Photography Accessories Sales Rep Table
Needs:	Create a sales representative table (Figure 5-3a) that can be sorted, queried, maintained, and printed to obtain meaningful information. Using the data in the table, compute statistics that include the average female age, average male age, grade A count, sum of YTD Sales for those with grade A, and the count of the male sales reps as shown in Figure 5-3b. The table field names, columns, types of data, and column widths are described in Table 5-1. Because Rose will use the table online as she travels among the offices, it is important that it be readable and that the table is visible on the screen. Therefore, some of the column widths listed in Table 5-1 are determined from the field names and not the maximum length of the data. The last two fields (located in columns I and J) use a formula and function to determine values based on data within each sales representative record.
Source of Data:	Rose will supply the sales representative data required for the table.
Calculations:	Include the following calculations: 1. % of Quota field in table = YTD Sales / Quota 2. Grade field in table = VLOOKUP function that uses the Grade table in Figure 5-3b 3. Average Female Age = AVERAGE function that uses the Criteria table in Figure 5-3b 4. Average Male Age = AVERAGE function that uses the Criteria table in Figure 5-3b 5. Grade A Count = DCOUNT function that uses the Criteria table in Figure 5-3b 6. Grade A YTD Sales Sum = SUMIF function 7. Male Sales Rep Count = COUNTIF function
Special Requirements:	1. Delete unused sheets. 2. A Criteria area will be created above the table, in rows 1 through 6, to store criteria for use in a query. An Extract area will be created below the table, beginnning in row 25, to receive records that meet a criteria. 3. Save the table as a CSV (Comma delimited) file.

Approvals

Approval Status:	X	Approved
		Rejected
Approved By:	Rose Veccos	
Date:	June 10, 2008	
Assigned To:	J. Quasney, Spreadsheet Specialist	

Figure 5–2

BTW

Excel as a Database Tool
Even though Excel is not a true database management system, such as Access or Oracle, it does give you many of the same basic capabilities. For example, in Excel you can create a list; add, change, and delete data in the list; use computational fields; sort data in the list; query the list; and create forms and reports.

The VLOOKUP function will be used to determine the grades in column J in Figure 5–1a, based on the grade table in columns L and M in Figure 5–1b. The DAVERAGE function will be used to find the average age of female and male sales reps in the table (range O4:R5 in Figure 5–1b). The DCOUNT function will be used to count the number of sales reps that received a grade of A (range O6:R6 in Figure 5–1b). These two functions require that a **criteria area** (range O1:Q3) be set up to tell Excel what items to average and count. Icon sets will be used to provide a visual means of identifying grades based on a conditional formatting rule. Finally, the SUMIF and COUNTIF functions will be used to sum selectively the sales of sales reps that received a grade of A and count the number of male sales reps in the table (range O8:R9 in Figure 5–1b).

Table 5–1 on the next page describes the field names, columns, types of data, and column widths to use when creating the table.

Overview

As you read this chapter, you will learn how to create the worksheet shown in Figure 5–1 by performing these general tasks:

- Create and format the sales rep table
- Sort the sales rep table
- Display subtotals by grouping the sales reps
- Obtain answers to questions about the sales reps using a variety of methods to query the sales rep table
- Extract records from the table based on given criteria
- Save the worksheet in different file formats

General Project Decisions

Plan
Ahead

While creating an Excel worksheet, you need to make several decisions that will determine the appearance and characteristics of the finished worksheet. As you create the worksheet required to meet the requirements shown in Figure 5–2, you should follow these general guidelines:

1. Create and format the sales rep table. The sales rep table should include the data provided in Table 5–1. The table should be formatted so that the records are easily distinguised. The data in the worksheet should start several rows from the top in order to leave room for the criteria area. Using banded rows to format the table provides greater readability. The last two columns require calculations for the % of Quota and Grade. The Grade can be obtained using Excel's VLOOKUP function. Totals also should be added to the table for the sales reps' average age, the sum of the sales reps' quotas, and the sum of the sales reps' year-to-date sales.

2. Sort the sales rep table. The user of the worksheet should be able to sort the table in a variety of manners and sort using multiple fields at the same time. Excel includes simple and advanced methods for sorting tables.

3. Display subtotals by grouping the sales reps. The user of the worksheet should be able to create subtotals of groups of sales reps after sorting the table. Excel's grouping features provide for subtotaling.

4. Obtain answers to questions (queries) about the sales reps using a variety of methods to query the sales rep table. A query can include filters, the use of which results in the table displaying only those records that meet certain criteria. Or, a query can include a calculation based on data in the table that then is displayed in the worksheet outside of the table.

5. Extract records from the table based on given criteria. A criteria area and extract area can be created on the worksheet. The criteria area can be used to enter rules regarding which records to extract, such as all female representatives with a grade of A. The extract area can be used to store the records that meet the criteria. The column headings from the table should be used as column headings in both the criteria and extract areas of the worksheet.

(continued)

Plan Ahead

(continued)

6. Save the worksheet in different file formats. A variety of circumstances may require a worksheet to be saved in a different file format. For example, the data in a worksheet may need to be used in another program that is not capable of reading the Excel file format. The CSV (comma delimited) file format is a file format that is one of the most commonly used.

In addition, using a sketch of the worksheet can help you visualize its design. The sketch of the table (Figure 5–3a) consists of the title, column headings, location of data values, and an idea of the desired formatting. The sketch does not show the criteria area above the table and the extract area below the table, which are included as requirements in the requirements document (Figure 5–2). The general layout of the grade table, criteria area, and required statistics are shown in Figure 5–3b.

When necessary, more specific details concerning the above guidelines are presented at appropriate points in the chapter. The chapter also will identify the actions you perform and decisions made regarding these guidelines during the creation of the worksheet shown in Figure 5–1 on page EX 339.

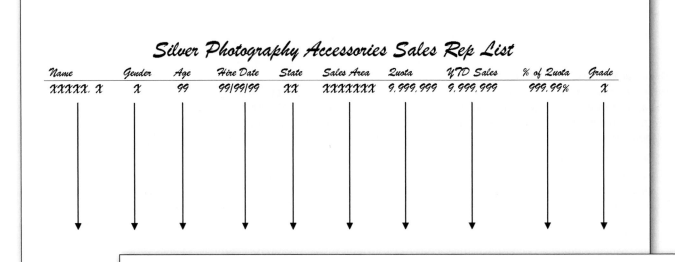

Silver Photography Accessories Sales Rep List

Name	Gender	Age	Hire Date	State	Sales Area	Quota	YTD Sales	% of Quota	Grade
XXXXX, X	X	99	99/99/99	XX	XXXXXXX	9,999,999	9,999,999	999.99%	X

(a) Table

Grade Table

% of Quota	Grade
0%	F
60%	D
70%	C
80%	B
92%	A

Criteria

Gender	Gender	Grade
F	M	A

Average Female Age ===========→ 99.99
Average Male Age ==========→ 99.99
Grade A Count =============→ 99

Grade A YTD Sales Sum=======→ 99,999,999
Male Sales Rep Count=======→ 99

(b) Grade Table, Criteria, and Statistics

Figure 5–3

With a good understanding of the requirements document, an understanding of the necessary decisions, and a sketch of the worksheet, the next step is to use Excel to create the worksheet.

Table 5–1 Column Information for Silver Photography Accessories Sales Rep Table

Column Headings (Field Names)	Column in Worksheet	Type of Data	Column Width	Description as It Pertains to a Sales Rep
Name	A	Text	16.43	Last name and first name
Gender	B	Text	11.57	Male or female
Age	C	Numeric	8.29	Age in years
Hire Date	D	Date	13.14	Date hired
State	E	Text	9.43	Sales territory
Sales Area	F	Text	14.00	Inside or outside sales
Quota	G	Numeric	13.29	Annual sales quota
YTD Sales	H	Numeric	13.29	Year-to-date sales
% of Quota	I	YTD Sales / Quota	14.57	Percent of annual quota met
Grade	J	VLOOKUP function	10.29	Grade indicates how much of quota has been met

To Start Excel

If you are using a computer to step through the project in this chapter and you want your screen to match the figures in this book, you should change your computer's resolution to 1024 × 768. For information about how to change a computer's resolution, see page APP 21 in Appendix E.

The following steps, which assume Windows is running, start Excel based on a typical installation of Microsoft Office on your computer. You may need to ask your instructor how to start Excel for your computer.

Note: If you are using Windows XP, see Appendix F for alternate steps.

1. Click the Start button on the Windows Vista taskbar to display the Start menu.
2. Click All Programs at the bottom of the left pane on the Start menu to display the All Programs list.
3. Click Microsoft Office in the All Programs list to display the Microsoft Office list.
4. Click Microsoft Office Excel 2007 to start Excel and display a blank worksheet in the Excel window.
5. If the Excel window is not maximized, click the Maximize button next to the Close button on its title bar to maximize the window.
6. If the worksheet window in Excel is not maximized, click the Maximize button next to the Close button on its title bar to maximize the worksheet window within Excel.

BTW

Starting Excel
If you plan to open an existing workbook, you can start Excel and open the workbook at the same time by double-clicking the workbook file name in Windows Explorer.

To Enter the Column Headings for a Table

Plan Ahead

> **Create and format the sales rep table.**
> One way to create a table in Excel is to follow these five steps: (1) enter the column headings (field names); (2) define a range as a table using the Format as Table command; (3) format the insert row immediately below the column headings; (4) set up data validation using the Data Validation command; and (5) enter records into the table. The following pages illustrate the process of creating the Silver Photography Accessories Sales Rep table using these five steps.

BTW

Setting Up a List
When creating a list, leave several rows empty above the list on the worksheet to set up a criteria area for querying the list. Some spreadsheet specialists also leave several columns empty to the left of the list, beginning with column A, for additional worksheet activities. A range of blank rows or columns on the side of a list is called a moat of cells.

The following steps change the column widths to those specified in Table 5–1, enter the table title, and enter and format the column headings. These steps also change the name of Sheet1 to Sales Rep Table, delete the unused sheets in the workbook, and save the workbook using the file name, Silver Photography Accessories Rep Table.

Although Excel does not require a table title to be entered, it is a good practice to include one on the worksheet to show where the table begins. With Excel, you usually enter the table several rows below the first row in the worksheet. These blank rows later will be used as a criteria area to store criteria for use in a query.

Note: The majority of tasks involved in entering and formatting the table title and column headings of a list are similar to what you have done in previous chapters. Thus, if you plan to complete this chapter on your computer and want to skip the set of steps below, open the workbook Silver Photography Accessories Sales Rep Table from the Data Files for Students.

1 Use the mouse to change the column widths as follows: A = 16.43, B = 11.57, C = 8.29, D = 13.14, E = 9.43, F = 14.00, G = 13.29, H = 13.29, I = 14.57, and J = 10.29.

2 Enter `Silver Photography Accessories Sales Rep Table` as the table title in cell A7.

3 Apply the Title cell style to cell A7. Click the Font Color button on the Home tab on the Ribbon and then click Red, Accent 2 (column 6, row 1) on the Font Color palette.

4 Select the range A7:H7. Right-click the selected range and then click Format Cells on the shortcut menu. When Excel displays the Format Cells dialog box, if necessary, click the Alignment tab, click the Horizontal box arrow in the Text alignment area, click Center Across Selection in the Horizontal list, and then click the OK button.

BTW

Merging and Centering Across a Selection
You merge and center when you want to treat the range of cells over which you center as a single cell. You center across a selection when you want the selected range of cells to be independent of one another. With most workbooks, it makes little difference whether you center using one technique or the other. Thus, most spreadsheet specialists use the merge and center technique because the procedure is available as a button on the Home tab on the Ribbon.

5 Enter the column headings in row 8 as shown in Figure 5–4. Center the column headings in the range B8:H8.

6 Apply the Heading 3 cell style to the range A8:H8.

7 Double-click the Sheet1 tab at the bottom of the screen. Type `Sales Rep Table` as the sheet name. Press the ENTER key. Right-click the tab, point to Tab Color on the shortcut menu, and then click Red, Accent 2 (column 6, row 1).

8 Click the Sheet2 tab, hold down the CTRL key, and then click the Sheet3 tab. Right-click the selected sheet tabs and then click Delete on the shortcut menu to delete the selected sheets from the workbook.

9 Update the document properties with your name and any other relevant information.

10 With a USB flash drive connected to one of the computer's USB ports, click the Save button on the Quick Access Toolbar. Save the workbook using the file name, Silver Photography Accessories Sales Rep Table on the USB flash drive. (Figure 5–4).

Q&A
When should the Center Across Selection alignment be used instead of the Merge & Center button on the Ribbon?

In Step 4, the Center Across Selection horizontal alignment was used to center the table title in row 7 horizontally across the range A7:H7. In earlier chapters, the Merge & Center button on the Home tab on the Ribbon was used to center text across a range. The major difference between the Center Across Selection horizontal alignment and the Merge & Center button is that, unlike the Merge & Center button, the Center Across Selection horizontal alignment does not merge the selected cell range into one cell.

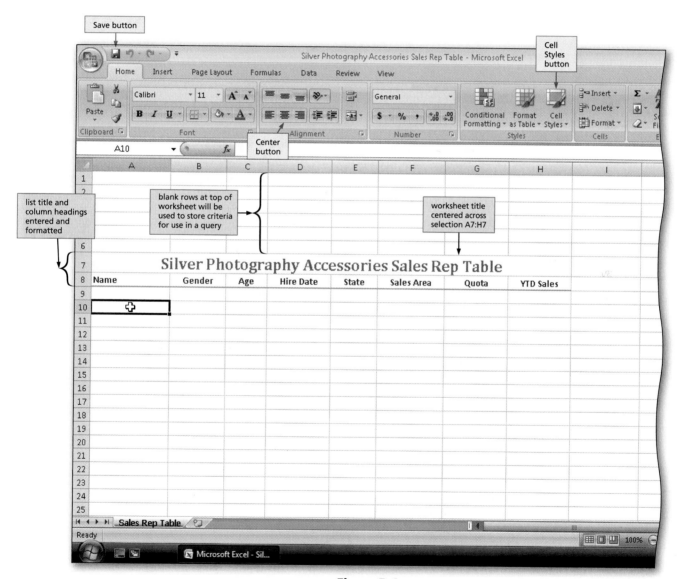

Figure 5–4

To Format a Range as a Table

The following steps define the range A8:H8 as a table by applying a table quick style to the range. Excel allows you to enter data in a range either before defining it as a table or after defining it as a table. This chapter uses the latter procedure because it offers additional tools that help ensure data integrity, such as data validation.

- Select the range A8:H8.

- Click the Format as Table button on the Home tab on the Ribbon to display the Table Style gallery (Figure 5–5).

 Experiment

- Point to a number of table quick styles in the Table Style gallery to preview them on the worksheet.

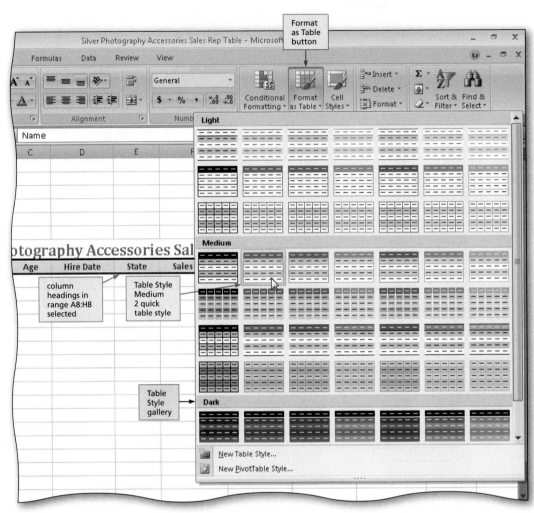

Figure 5–5

2

- Click the Table Style Medium 2 quick table style in the Table Style gallery.

- When Excel displays the Format As Table dialog box, click the 'My table has headers' check box to select it (Figure 5–6).

Q&A

Why is the range A8:H8 already selected in the Format As Table dialog box?

Because the range A8:H8 was selected before clicking the Format As Table button, Excel automatically selects this range for the 'Where is the data for your table?' box.

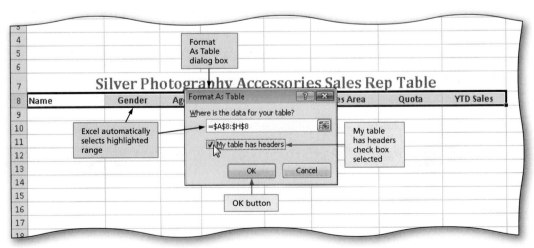

Figure 5–6

3

- Click the OK button to create a table from the selected column headings and corresponding cells in the row below it.

- Scroll down until row 7 is at the top of the worksheet window (Figure 5–7).

Q&A Why does Excel indicate that the cells in row 9 are in the table?

Excel automatically creates an empty row in the table so that you are ready to enter the first record in the table.

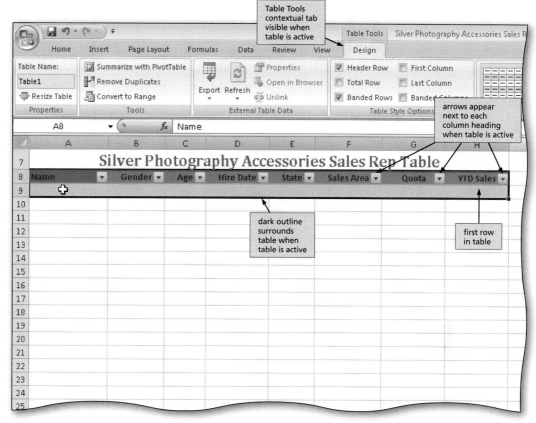

Figure 5–7

Other Ways

1. Select range, on Insert tab on Ribbon click Table, click OK button

2. Select range, press ALT+H+T, select quick style

3. Select range, press ALT+D, I, C

To Format the First Row in an Empty Table

If the table contains no data, as in Figure 5–7, then Excel sets the format of the cells in the first row to the default associated with the table quick style chosen when the table was created. That is, if you assigned any formats to the first row before it became part of a table, then those formats are lost when the table is created. For this reason, if you create an empty table and want the records to be formatted in a different manner associated with the selected quick style, you must format the first row after you create the table, as shown in the following steps.

1 Select the range B9:H9 and then click the Center button on the Home tab on the Ribbon.

2 Right-click cell D9. Click Format Cells on the shortcut menu. When Excel displays the Format Cells dialog box, click the Number tab, click Date in the Category list, click 03/14/01 in the Type list, and then click the OK button.

3 Select the range G9:H9 and then click the Comma Style button on the Ribbon. Click the Decrease Decimal button on the Ribbon twice so columns G and H will display whole numbers.

Q&A Why are no changes apparent on the worksheet?

No visible changes appear on the worksheet, because the table contains no records. As records are entered into the table, the assigned formats will apply, even as more rows are added to the table.

To Validate Data

Excel has built-in **data validation** features to ensure that the data you enter into a cell or range of cells is within limits. For example, the cells in the Gender column in Figure 5–8 should be either an F for female or an M for male. Any entry other than M or F is invalid and should not be allowed. The following steps show how to use the Data Validation button on the Data tab on the Ribbon to ensure that Excel will accept only an entry of F or M in the Gender column.

- Select cell B9, the cell in the insert row below the Gender column heading in cell B8.

- Click the Data tab on the Ribbon and then point to the Data Validation button on the Ribbon (Figure 5–8).

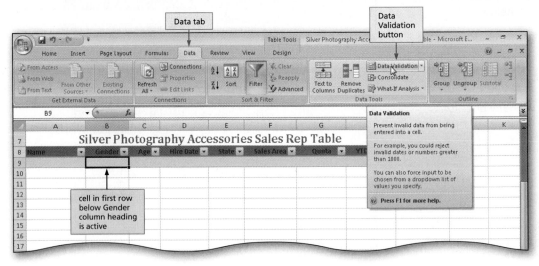

Figure 5–8

- Click the Data Validation button on the Ribbon to display the Data Validation dialog box.

- When Excel displays the Data Validation dialog box, if necessary, click the Settings tab, click the Allow box arrow, and then click List in the Allow list.

- Type F,M in the Source box.

- Click the In-cell dropdown check box to clear it (Figure 5–9).

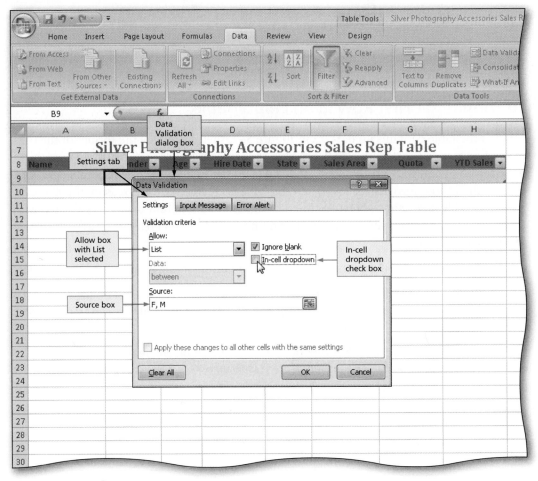

Figure 5–9

- Click the Error Alert tab.

- If necessary, click 'Show error alert after invalid data is entered' to select it.

- If necessary, click the Style box arrow and then click Stop in the Style list.

- Type Gender Invalid in the Title text box.

- Type Gender code must be an F or M. in the Error message box (Figure 5–10).

4

- Click the OK button.

Q&A

Why are no changes evident on the worksheet?

No immediate changes appear on the worksheet. If, however, you try to enter any value other than F or M in cell B9, Excel rejects the data and displays the Gender Invalid dialog box created in Step 3.

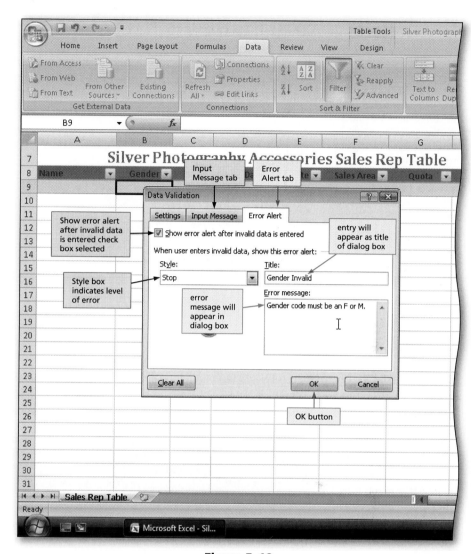

Figure 5–10

Other Ways

1. Press ALT+A, V, V

BTW

Lists

To change an active list back to a normal range of cells, right-click the range, point to Table on the shortcut menu, and then click Convert to Range on the Table submenu.

Validation
Data validation rules can be mandatory or cautionary. If the rule is mandatory (a Stop), then Excel rejects the cell entry via a dialog box (Figure 5–11) and gives you a chance to correct it. If the rule is cautionary (a Warning), Excel displays a dialog box to warn you of the invalid entry and then gives you a chance to redo the cell entry or leave it as entered.

Data Validation Errors and Criteria

The Style box in the Error Alert sheet shown in Figure 5–10 sets the level of error. Valid entries include Stop, Warning, and Information. Figure 5–11 shows the Gender Invalid dialog box that Excel displays when a user enters a value other than F or M into a cell in the Gender column in the table. The Retry button leaves the invalid value in the cell for you to change. The Cancel button removes the invalid value.

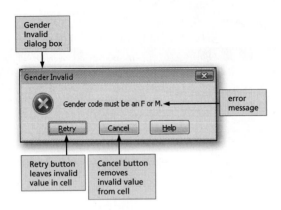

Figure 5–11

Garbage In Garbage Out (GIGO)
In information processing, the phrase "garbage in, garbage out", or GIGO (pronounced gee-go), is used to describe the output of inaccurate information that results from the input of invalid data.

Excel's built-in data validation features are powerful and easy to use. The different data validation criteria allowed by Excel and summarized in Table 5–2 can be selected in the Allow list in the Settings sheet in the Data Validation dialog box (Figure 5–9 on page EX 348).

Table 5–2 Types of Data Validation Criteria Allowed	
Allows	**Description**
Any value	Allows the user to enter anything in the cell. Any value is the default for all cells in a worksheet.
Whole number	Allows whole numbers in a specific range.
Decimal number	Allows decimal numbers in a specific range.
List	Allows the user to enter only an item from a list. Useful when working with codes, such as M for male and F for female.
Date	Allows a range of dates.
Time	Allows a range of times.
Text length	Allows a certain length of text.
Custom	Allows you to specify a formula that will validate the data entered by the user. For example, the formula <3 would require the cell entry to be less than 3.

Bypassing Validation
Excel ignores data validation when you paste data from the Office Clipboard or use the mouse to copy by dragging.

Although this chapter validates only the values entered into the Gender column, Table 5–2 shows that you can validate, in one way or another, all of the columns in the Silver Photography Accessories Sales Rep Table. For example, you can validate the data entered in the Age column by establishing limits for a whole number between 18 and 65. Or, you can validate the data entered in the Hire Date column to ensure the user enters a date between 1960 and 2008.

To Modify a Table Quick Style

Before entering records in the table, the quick style that was used to create the table should be modified to make the table more readable. A bold font style with a black font color for the table's entries makes them more readable. The following steps create a new table quick style by copying the Table Style Medium 2 quick style and then modify the new quick style to apply a bold font style and black font color to the entire table.

1

- If necessary, select cell A9 to activate the table.

- Click the Format as Table button on the Home tab on the Ribbon and then right-click the Table Style Medium 2 quick table style to display the shortcut menu (Figure 5–12).

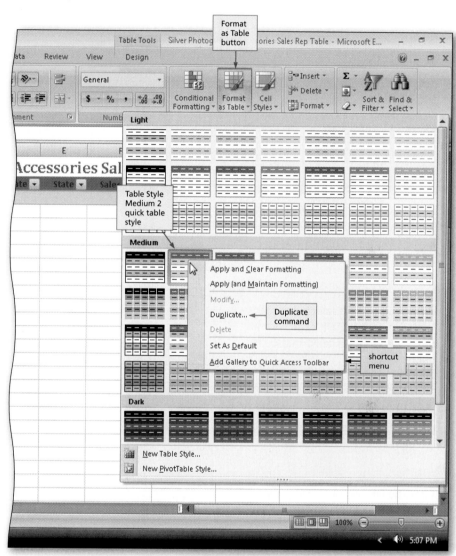

Figure 5–12

2

- Click Duplicate on the shortcut menu to display the Modify Table Quick Style dialog box.

- When Excel displays the Modify Table Quick Style dialog box, type TableStyleMedium2 – Custom in the Name text box (Figure 5–13).

Q&A What elements of a table can I customize?

The Table Element list in the Modify Table Quick Style dialog box allows you to choose almost any aspect of a table to modify. You can change the formatting for each element listed in the Table Element list by clicking the element and then clicking the Format button to display the Format Cells dialog box with which you are familiar.

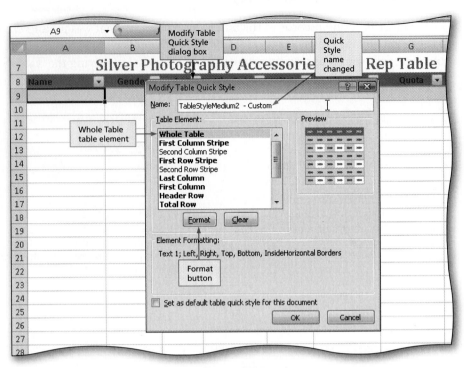

Figure 5–13

3

- With Whole Table selected in the Table Element list, click the Format button to display the Format Cells dialog box.

- Select Bold in the Font style list.

- Click the Color box arrow and then click the Black, Text 1 color (column 2, row 1) (Figure 5–14).

4

- Click the OK button to close the Format Cells dialog box.

- Click the OK button to close the Modify Table Quick Style dialog box.

- Select the range A8:H8 and then apply the White, Background 1 (column 1, row 1) font color to the range.

Q&A Why should the color of the header row be changed to white?

The white font color allows the text in the header rows to stand out against the background color of the header row.

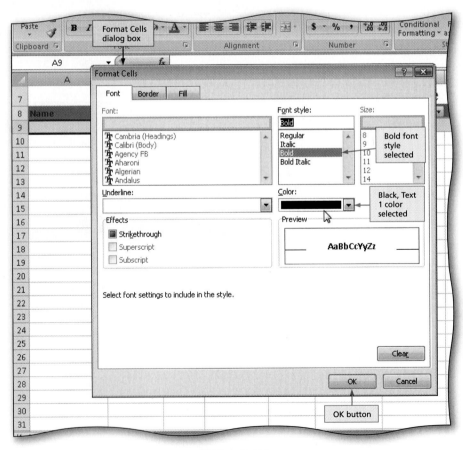

Figure 5–14

To Enter Records into a Table

The next step is to enter the sales reps' records into the table. As indicated earlier, the computational fields in columns I and J will be added after the data is in the table.

1

- If necessary, select cell A9 to activate the table.

- Type sales rep information for row 9 as shown in Figure 5–15. After typing the data for a field, press the RIGHT ARROW key to move to the next field. After you type the YTD sales, press the TAB key to start a new record.

- Type sales rep information for row 10 as shown in Figure 5–15. After typing the data for a field, press the RIGHT ARROW key to move to the next field. After you type the YTD sales, click cell A12 to select it (Figure 5–15).

Q&A Is row 10 now part of the table?

Yes. Pressing the TAB key adds the next row below the table to the table. Row 10 is now part of the sales rep table.

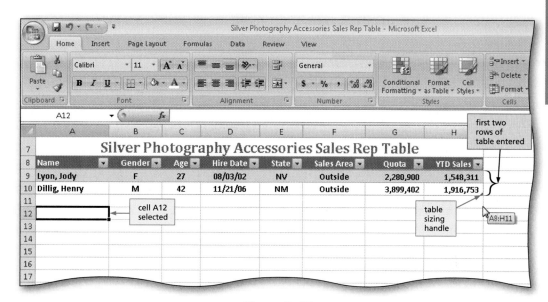

Figure 5–15

2

- Drag the table sizing handle to the top of cell H12 to add another row to the table (Figure 5–16).

Q&A Why does row 11 have a different background color than row 10?

The quick style used to create the table includes a type of formatting called row banding. **Row banding** causes adjacent rows to have different formatting so that each record in the table is distinguished from surrounding rows.

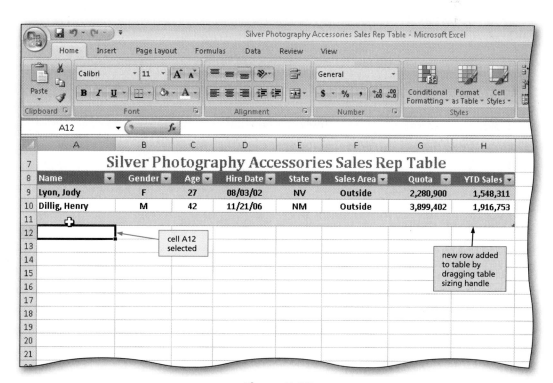

Figure 5–16

3

- Enter the sales rep record for the third sales rep as shown in Figure 5–17.

- Drag the table sizing handle to cell H21 to add 10 new rows to the table (Figure 5–17).

Q&A

Why were all of the rows not added to the table in Step 1?

Steps 1 through 3 demonstrate three different methods of adding rows to a table. The first method can be used when you are adding a number of rows to the table and do not know how many rows you are going

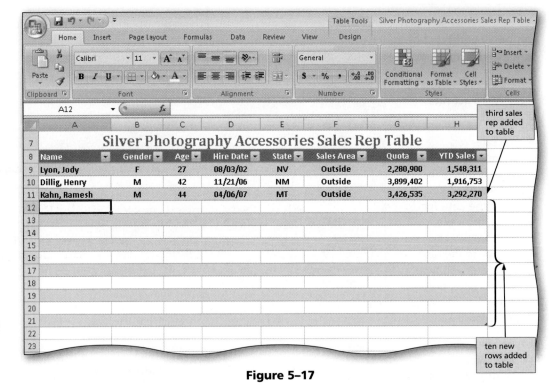

Figure 5–17

to add. The second method can be used when you need to add one additional row to a table that you previously created. The third method can be used when you know exactly how many rows you need in a table.

4

- Enter the remaining sales reps' records as shown in Figure 5–18.

- Select cell A23 (Figure 5–18).

Q&A

What happens if I enter an invalid Gender code?

If you entered an incorrect Gender code while entering the sales reps' records, then Excel should have displayed the dialog box in Figure 5–11 on page EX 350. After you click the Retry or Cancel button in the error

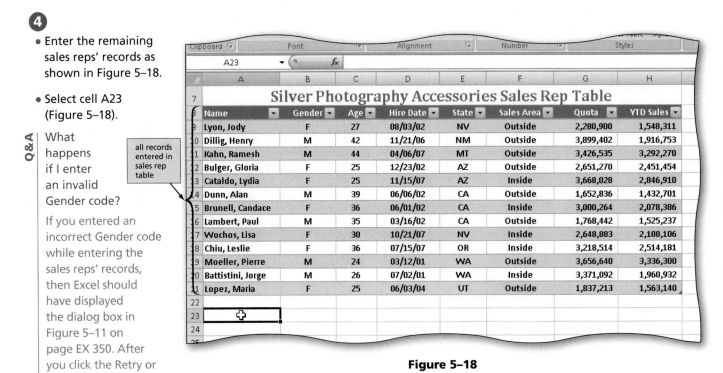

Figure 5–18

message dialog box, Excel requires you to reenter all values up to and including the value in error.

Other Ways

1. Press ALT+J, T

Adding Computational Fields to the Table

The next step is to add the computational fields % of Quota in column I and Grade in column J. The first computational field involves dividing the YTD Sales in column H by the Quota in column G. The second computational field involves a table lookup to determine a grade based upon the % of Quota in column I.

To Add New Fields to a Table

Adding new fields to a table in a worksheet illustrates another of Excel's powerful table capabilities. As shown in the following steps, if you add a new column heading in a column adjacent to the current column headings in the table, then Excel automatically adds the adjacent column to the table's range and copies the format of the table heading to the new column headings. Adding a new row to a table works in a similar manner.

The first step in adding the two new fields is to enter the two column headings, or field names, in cells I8 and J8, enter the first % of Quota formula in cell I9, and then format the two cells immediately below the new column headings. The formula for the % of Quota in cell I9 is YTD Sales / Quota or =H9 / G9. After the formula is entered in cell I9, the formula is automatically copied to the range I10:I21. When you enter a formula in the first row of a field, Excel creates a calculated column. A calculated column is a column in a table in which each row uses a common formula that references other fields in the table.

1

- Select cell I8, type % of Quota, click cell J8, type Grade.

- Select cell I9, enter =h9 / g9 as the formula, and then click the Enter button on the formula bar (Figure 5–19).

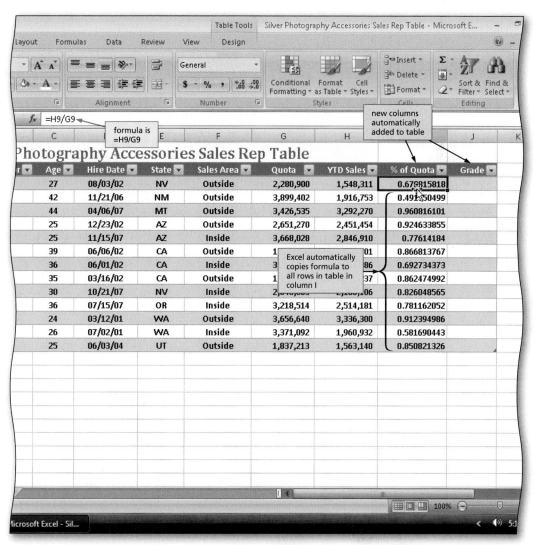

Figure 5–19

2

- Select the range I9:I21 and then click the Percent Style button on the Ribbon. Click the Increase Decimal button on the Ribbon twice.
- Click the Center button on the Ribbon to center the range I9:I21 (Figure 5–20).
- Select the range A7:J7, right-click the selected range, click Format Cells on the shortcut menu, click the Alignment tab, click the Horizontal box arrow, click Center Across Selection, and then click the OK button.

3

- Select the range J9:J21 and then click the Center button on the Home tab on the Ribbon. Select cell J9 to deselect the range J9:J21.

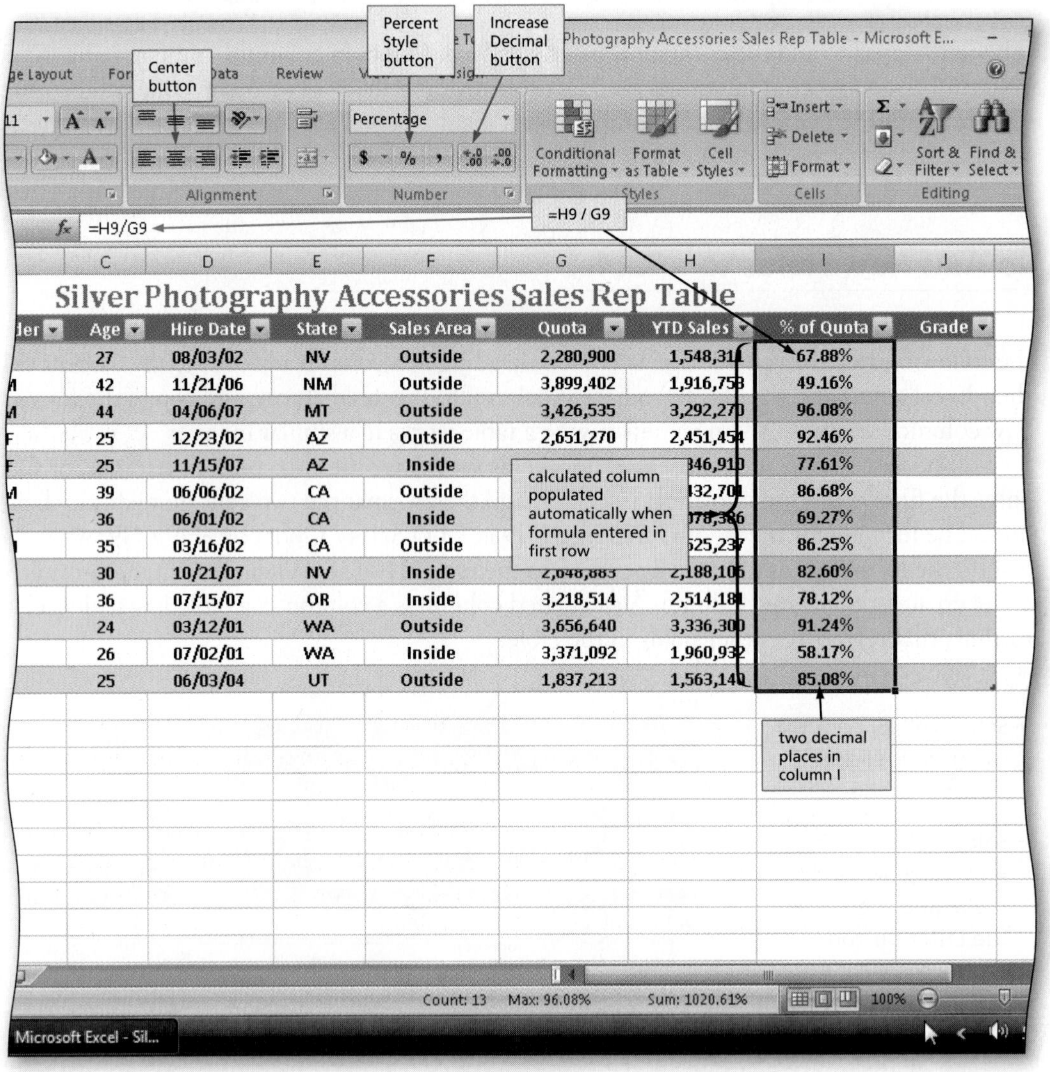

Figure 5–20

BTW

Lookup Functions
Lookup functions are powerful, useful, and interesting in the way they work. For additional information on lookup functions, enter **vlookup** in the Search box in the Excel Help window.

Adding a Lookup Table

The entries in the % of Quota column give the user an immediate evaluation of where each sales rep's YTD Sales stand in relation to their annual quota. Many people, however, dislike numbers as an evaluation tool. Most prefer simple letter grades, which, when used properly, can group the sales reps in the same way an instructor groups students by letter grades. Excel contains functions that allow you to assign letter grades based on a table.

Excel has several lookup functions that are useful for looking up values in tables, such as tax tables, discount tables, parts tables, and grade tables. The two most widely used lookup functions are the HLOOKUP and VLOOKUP functions. Both functions look up a value in a table and return a corresponding value from the table to the cell assigned the function. The **HLOOKUP function** is used when the table direction is horizontal, or across the worksheet. The **VLOOKUP function** is used when a table direction is vertical, or down the worksheet. The VLOOKUP function is by far the most often used because most tables are vertical, as is the table in this chapter.

The grading scale in this chapter (Table 5–3) is similar to one that your instructor uses to determine your letter grade. As shown in Table 5–3, any score greater than or equal to 92% equates to a letter grade of A. Scores greater than or equal to 80 and less than 92 are assigned a letter grade of B, and so on.

The VLOOKUP function requires that the table indicate only the lowest score for a letter grade. Furthermore, the table entries must be in sequence from lowest score to highest score. Thus, the entries in Table 5–3 must be resequenced for use with the VLOOKUP function so they appear as shown in Table 5–4.

The general form of the VLOOKUP function is:

=VLOOKUP(lookup_value, table_array, col_index_num)

To Create a Lookup Table

The VLOOKUP function searches the far-left column of the **table array**. The far-left column of the table_array contains what are called the **table arguments**. In this example, the table arguments are made up of percentages (see Table 5–4). The VLOOKUP function uses the % of Quota value (called the lookup_value) in the record of a sales rep to search the far-left column of the table array for a particular value and then returns the corresponding **table value** from the column indicated by the col_index_num value. In this example, the grades are in the second or far-right column.

For the VLOOKUP function to work correctly, the table arguments must be in ascending sequence, because the VLOOKUP function will return a table value based on the lookup_value being less than or equal to the table arguments. Thus, if the % of Quota value is 77.61% (fifth record in table), then the VLOOKUP function returns a grade of C, because 77.61% is greater than or equal to 70% and less than 80%.

The following steps create the grade table in the range L1:M7.

1. Select column headings L and M. Point to the boundary on the right side of the column M heading above row 1 and then drag to the right until the ScreenTip indicates, Width: 11.00 (82 pixels).

2. Select cell L1 and then enter Grade Table as the table title.

3. If necessary, scroll the worksheet to the left and click cell A7 to select it. Scroll the worksheet to the right so that cell L1 is visible. Click the Format Painter button on the Ribbon and then click cell L1. Drag through cell M1 and then click the Merge & Center button on the Home tab on the Ribbon.

4. Select the range I8:J8. While holding down the CTRL key, point to the border of the range I8:J8 and drag to the range L2:M2 to copy the column headings, % of Quota and Grade.

Table 5–3 Typical Grade Table

% of Quota	Grade
92% and higher	A
80% to 91%	B
70% to 79%	C
60% to 69%	D
0 to 59%	F

Table 5–4 Typical Grade Table Modified for VLOOKUP Function

% of Quota	Grade
0	F
60%	D
70%	C
80%	B
92%	A

BTW

The VLOOKUP Function
A score that is outside the range of the table causes the VLOOKUP function to return an error message (#N/A) to the cell. For example, any % of Quota score less than zero in column I of Figure 5–20 would result in the error message #N/A being assigned to the corresponding cell.

5 Enter the table entries in Table 5–4 in the range L3:M7. Select the range L3:M7, click the Bold button on the Ribbon, and then click the Center button on the Ribbon. Select cell J9 to deselect the range L3:M7 (Figure 5–21).

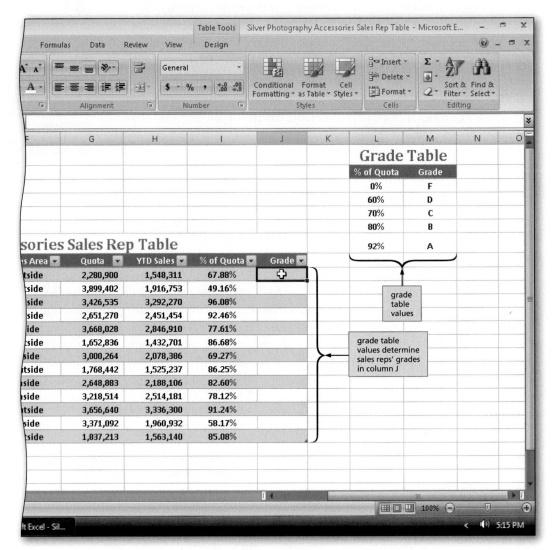

Figure 5–21

To Use the VLOOKUP Function to Determine Letter Grades

The following steps show how to use the VLOOKUP function and the grade table to determine the letter grade for each sales rep based on the sales rep's % of Quota value. In this case, cell I9 is the lookup_value; $L$3:$M$7 is the table_array; and 2 is the col_index_num in the table_array.

1

• With cell J9 selected, type =vlookup(i9, l3:m7, 2 as the cell entry (Figure 5–22).

Q&A

Why are absolute cell references used in the function?

It is most important that you use absolute cell references ($) for the table_array ($L$3:$M$7) in the VLOOKUP function or Excel will not adjust the cell references when it creates the calculated column in the next step. This will cause unexpected results in column J.

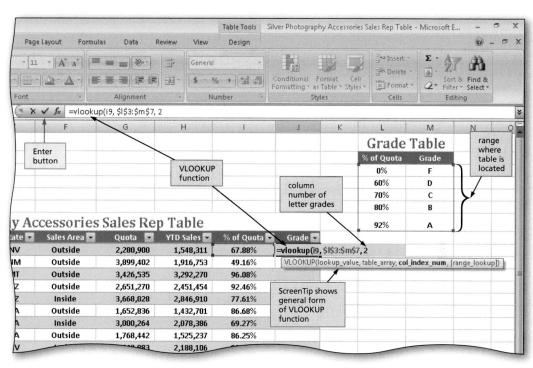

Figure 5–22

2

• Click the Enter button to create a calculated column for the Grade field (Figure 5–23).

Q&A

What happens when the Enter button is clicked?

Because the cell I9 is the first record in a table, Excel creates a calculated column in column I by copying the VLOOKUP function through row 21. As shown in Figure 5–23, any % of Quota value below 60 in column I returns a grade of F in column J. The 13th record (Lopez in row 21) receives a grade of B because its % of Quota value is 85.08%. A % of Quota value of 92% is required to move up to the next letter grade. The second record (Dillig) receives a grade of F because his % of Quota value is 49.16%, which is less than 60%.

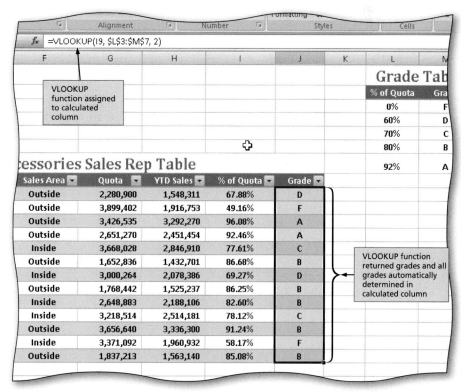

Figure 5–23

3

- Scroll the worksheet so that row 7 is the top row and then select cell A23 to show the completed sales rep table (Figure 5–24).

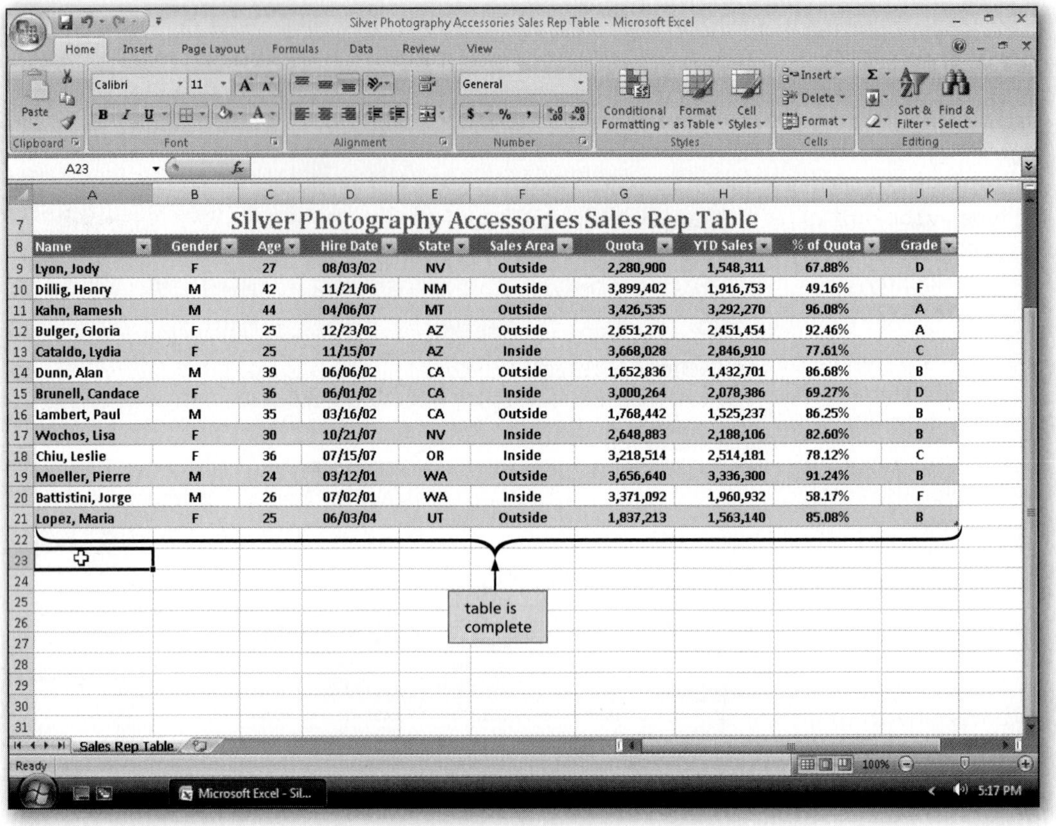

Q&A

How is the VLOOKUP function determining the grades?

From column J, you can see that the VLOOKUP function is not searching for a table argument that matches the lookup_value exactly. The VLOOKUP function begins the search at the top of the table and works downward. As soon as it finds the first table argument greater than the lookup_value, it returns the previous table value. The letter grade of F is returned for any value greater than or equal to 0 (zero) and less than 60. A score less than 0 returns an error message (#N/A) to the cell assigned the VLOOKUP function.

Figure 5–24

Other Ways

1. Click Insert Function box in formula bar, click 'Or select a category' box arrow, click Lookup & Reference, click VLOOKUP in 'Select a function' list
2. Click Formulas tab on Ribbon, click Lookup & Reference button, click VLOOKUP

BTW

Using HLOOKUP

HLOOKUP uses the same arguments as VLOOKUP, but searches rows of information instead of columns. HLOOKUP also uses the row_index_num argument instead of the col_index_num argument, as shown in Figure 5–22 on page EX 359. When using HLOOKUP, be sure to sort the values in the first row of the table_array in ascending order to find an approximate match. Otherwise, specify FALSE as the range_lookup to find an exact match.

Guidelines for Creating a Table in Excel

When you create a table in Excel, you should follow some basic guidelines, as listed in Table 5–5.

Table 5–5 Guidelines for Creating a Table in Excel
Table Size and Workbook Location
1. Do not enter more than one table per worksheet.
2. Maintain at least one blank row between a table and other worksheet entries.
3. A table can have a maximum of 16,384 fields and 1,048,576 records on a worksheet.
Column Headings (Field Names)
1. Place column headings (field names) in the first row of the table.
2. Do not use blank rows or rows with dashes to separate the column headings (field names) from the data.
3. Apply a different format to the column headings and the data. For example, bold the column headings and format the data below the column headings using a regular style. Most quick table styles follow these guidelines.
4. Column headings (field names) can be up to 32,767 characters in length. The column headings should be meaningful.
Contents of Table
1. Each column should have similar data. For example, Hire Date should be in the same column for all sales reps.
2. Format the data to improve readability, but do not vary the format of the data in a column.

Conditional Formatting

Excel provides a variety of formatting options for visually representing the value in a cell based on its value. Conditional formatting allows you to create rules that change the formatting of a cell or range of cells based on the value of a cell. Excel includes five types of conditional formats: highlight, top and bottom rules, data bars, color scales, and icon sets. You can combine different types of formats on any cell or range. For example, based on a cells value, you can format it to include both an icon and a specific background color. You also can apply multiple conditional formatting rules to a cell or range.

The Conditional Formatting Rules Manager dialog box allows you to view all of the rules for the current selection or for the entire workbook. You open the dialog box by clicking the Conditional Formatting button on the Home tab on the Ribbon and then clicking the Manage Rules command on the Conditional Formatting menu. The dialog box also allows you to view and change the order in which the rules are applied to a cell or range. You also can stop the application of subsequent rules after one rule is found to be true. For example, if the first rule specifies that a negative value in the cell results in a red background color applied to the cell, then you may not want to apply any other conditional formats to the cell. In this case, put a check mark in the Stop If True column for the rule in the Conditional Formatting Rules Manager dialog box.

The project in this chapter uses an icon set as a type of conditional format. The exercises at the end of this chapter include instructions regarding the use of other types of conditional formats.

To Add a Conditional Formatting Rule with an Icon Set

The Grade field was added to the table in order to provide a visual cue to the user of the worksheet regarding each sales rep's performance. One method to achieve a similar result is to display an icon next to the % of Quota percentage for each sales rep. Conditional formatting provides a number of icons, including icons with the appearance of traffic signals, flags, bars, and arrows. Icon sets include sets of three, four, or five icons. You use an icon set depending on how many ways you need to group your data. For example, in the case of grades for the sales reps, there are five different grades and, therefore, an icon set that includes five icons should be used. You define rules for the conditions under which each icon of the five is displayed in a cell. The following steps add a conditional format to the % of Quota field in the Sales Rep table.

- Select the range I9:I21 and then click the Conditional Formatting button on the Home tab on the Ribbon.

- Click New Rule on the Conditional Formatting menu.

- When the New Formatting Rule dialog box is displayed, click the Format Style box arrow and point to Icon Sets in the list (Figure 5–25).

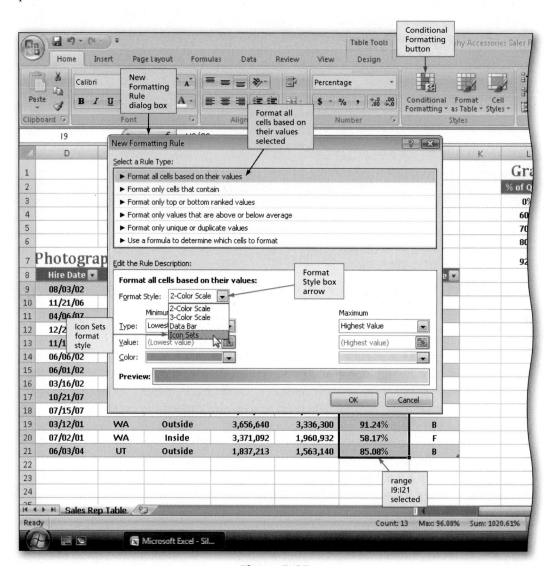

Figure 5–25

2

- Click Icon Sets in the list to display the Icon area in the Edit the Rule Description area.

- Click the Icon Style box arrow to display the Icon Style list and then scroll and point to 5 Arrows (Colored) in the list (Figure 5–26).

 Experiment

- Click a variety of icon styles in the Icon Styles list to view the options in the Edit the Rule Description area for each option.

3

- Click 5 Arrows (Colored) in the list.

- Click the top Type box arrow and then click Number in the list.

- Change the Type to Number for the remaining Type boxes.

- Type 0.92 in the first Value box, 0.8 in the second Value box, and 0.7 in the third Value box.

- Type 0.6 in the final Value box and then press the TAB key to complete the conditions (Figure 5–27).

Q&A

Why do the numbers next to each icon change as I type?

The area below the word Icon represents the current conditional formatting rule. Excel automatically updates this area as you change the conditions on the right side of the Edit the Rule Description area. Use this area as an easy-to-read status of the conditions that you are creating.

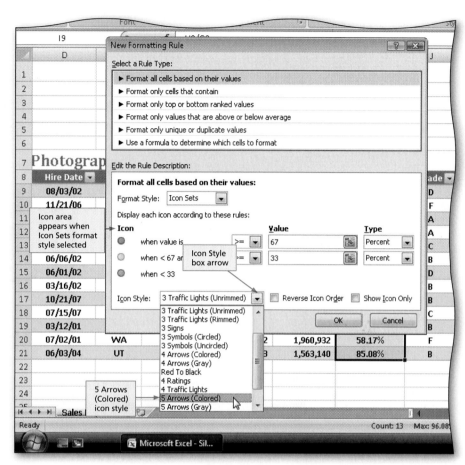

Figure 5–26

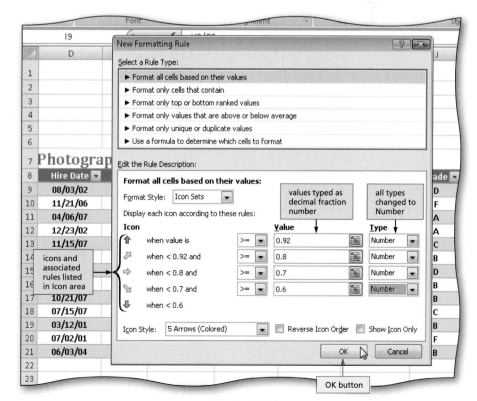

Figure 5–27

4

- Click the OK button to display icons in each row of the table in the % of Quota field.

- Select cell A23 (Figure 5–28).

Q&A

What do the icons represent?

In addition to the Grade field, the conditional formatting icons provide a visual representation of the sales reps' progress on attaining their sales quotas. The green arrow and its direction represents a grade of A, the red arrow and its direction a grade of F, and the three different yellow arrows and their directions represent the B, C, and D levels.

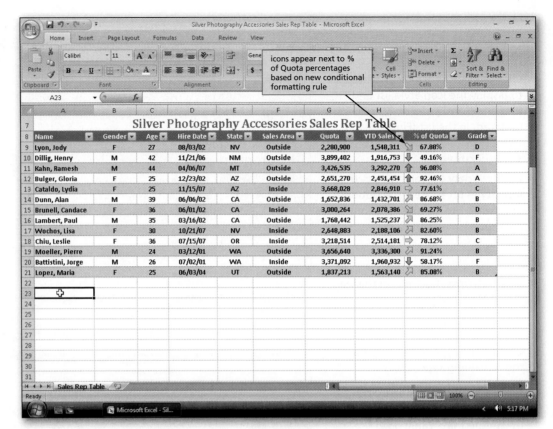

Figure 5–28

Working with Tables in Excel

When a table is active, the Design tab on the Ribbon provides powerful commands that allow you to alter the appearance and contents of a table quickly. This section explores the use of some of these commands, such as toggling total and header rows in a table.

To Use the Total Row Check Box

The Total Row check box on the Design tab allows you to insert a row at the bottom of the table called the **total row**. Within the total row, it sums the values in the far-right column of the table, if the values are numeric. If the values in the far-right column of the table are text, then Excel counts the number of records. For example, in Figure 5–30 on the next page, the 13 in cell J22 on the right side of the total row is a count of the number of sales rep records. Excel provides additional computations for the total row, as shown in the following steps.

1

- Select cell A9 to make the table active and then click the Design tab on the Ribbon (Figure 5–29).

Experiment

- Select a variety of combinations of check boxes in the Table Styles Options group on the Design tab on the Ribbon. When finished, make sure that the check boxes are set as shown in Figure 5–29.

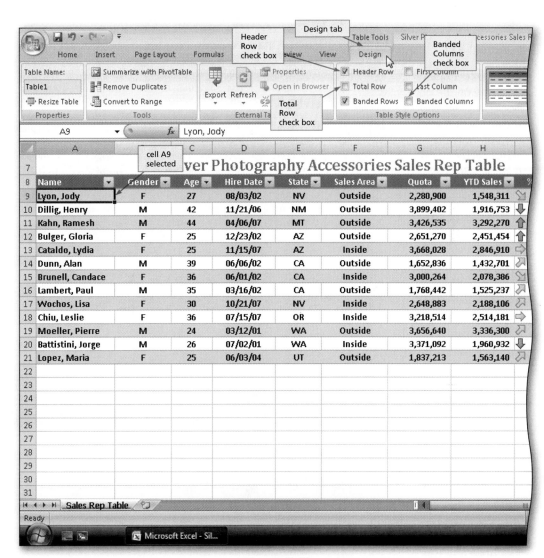

Figure 5–29

2

- Click the Total Row check box on the Ribbon to add the total row and display the record count in the far-right column of the table, column J.

- Select cell H22.

- When Excel displays an arrow on the right side of the cell, click the arrow to display a list of available statistical functions (Figure 5–30).

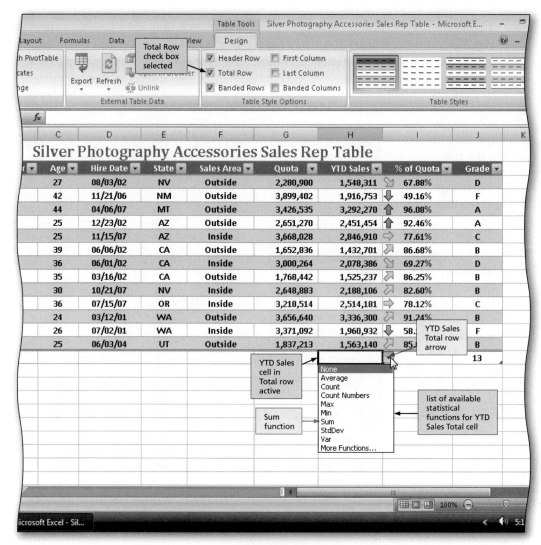

Figure 5–30

3

- Click Sum in the list.

- Select cell G22, click the arrow on the right side of the cell, and then click Sum in the list.

- Select cell C22, click the arrow on the right side of the cell, and then click Average in the list.

- Select cell A9 (Figure 5–31).

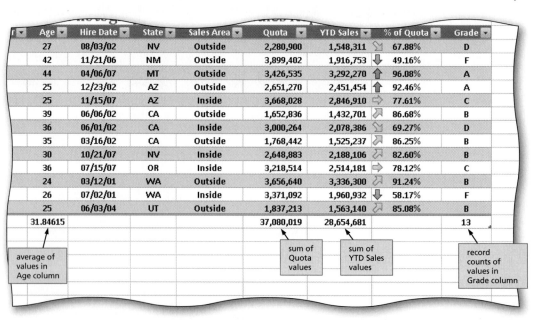

Figure 5–31

4

- Click the Total Row check box on the Ribbon to hide the total row (Figure 5–32).

Experiment

- Click the Header Row, Banded Rows, and Banded Columns check boxes on the Ribbon. When finished viewing the formatting caused by checking these check boxes, uncheck the check boxes.

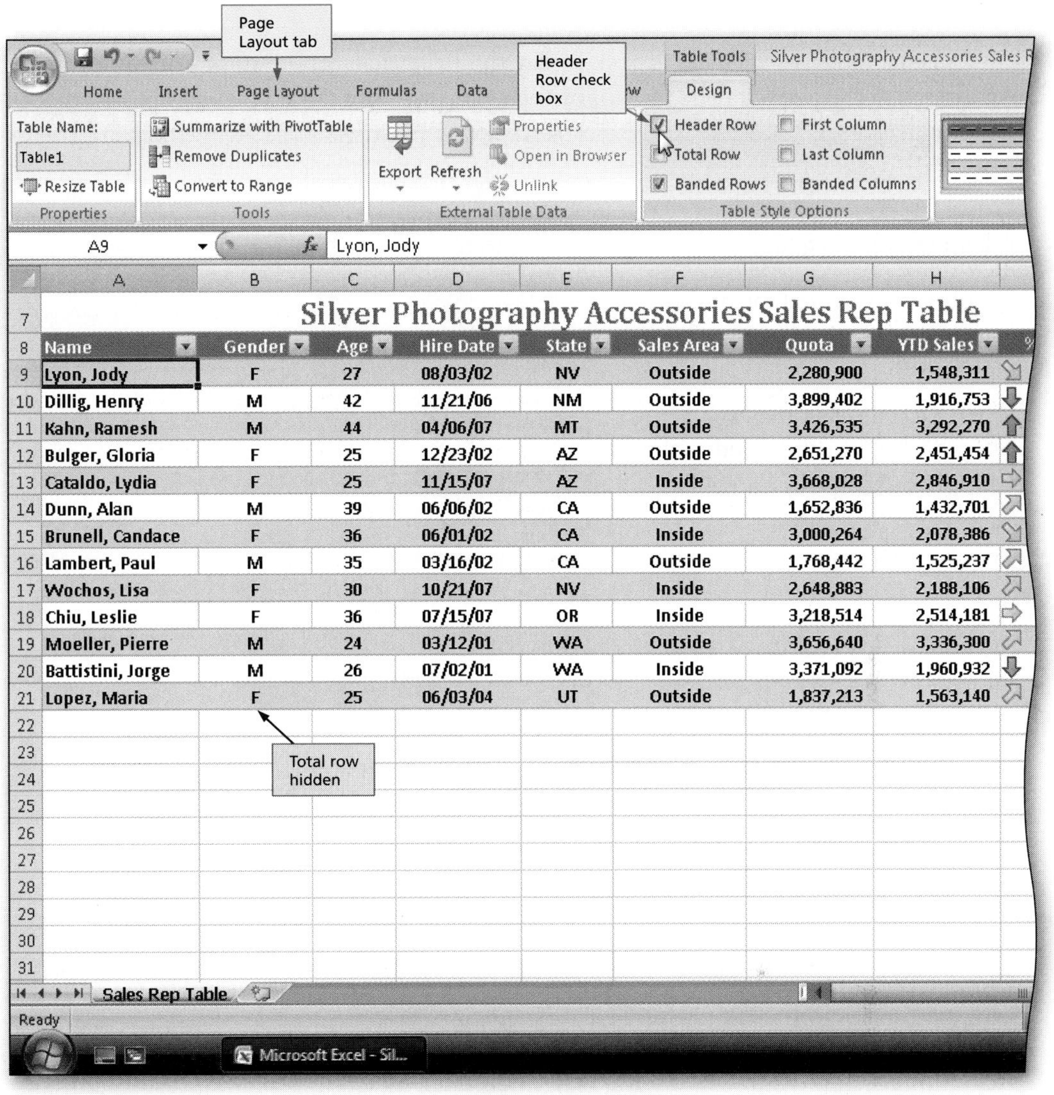
Page Layout tab
Header Row check box
Total row hidden
Silver Photography Accessories Sales Rep Table
Name | Gender | Age | Hire Date | State | Sales Area | Quota | YTD Sales
Lyon, Jody | F | 27 | 08/03/02 | NV | Outside | 2,280,900 | 1,548,311
Dillig, Henry | M | 42 | 11/21/06 | NM | Outside | 3,899,402 | 1,916,753
Kahn, Ramesh | M | 44 | 04/06/07 | MT | Outside | 3,426,535 | 3,292,270
Bulger, Gloria | F | 25 | 12/23/02 | AZ | Outside | 2,651,270 | 2,451,454
Cataldo, Lydia | F | 25 | 11/15/07 | AZ | Inside | 3,668,028 | 2,846,910
Dunn, Alan | M | 39 | 06/06/02 | CA | Outside | 1,652,836 | 1,432,701
Brunell, Candace | F | 36 | 06/01/02 | CA | Inside | 3,000,264 | 2,078,386
Lambert, Paul | M | 35 | 03/16/02 | CA | Outside | 1,768,442 | 1,525,237
Wochos, Lisa | F | 30 | 10/21/07 | NV | Inside | 2,648,883 | 2,188,106
Chiu, Leslie | F | 36 | 07/15/07 | OR | Inside | 3,218,514 | 2,514,181
Moeller, Pierre | M | 24 | 03/12/01 | WA | Outside | 3,656,640 | 3,336,300
Battistini, Jorge | M | 26 | 07/02/01 | WA | Inside | 3,371,092 | 1,960,932
Lopez, Maria | F | 25 | 06/03/04 | UT | Outside | 1,837,213 | 1,563,140

Figure 5–32

Q&A

What are banded columns?

As you have learned, banded rows include alternating colors every other row. Similarly, banded columns provide alternating colors every other column. You also can include a different color for the first and/or last column in a table. The quick style that you choose for a table must have these colors defined in the quick style. The quick style used in this chapter does not include special formatting for the first and last columns.

To Print the Table

When a table is selected and you display the Print dialog box, an option appears that allows you to print just the contents of the active table. The following steps print the table in landscape orientation using the Fit to option.

- Select cell A9 to make the table active and then click the Page Layout tab on the Ribbon.

- Click the Page Setup Dialog Box Launcher to display the Page Setup dialog box.

- When Excel displays the Page Setup dialog box, click Landscape in the Orientation area and then click Fit to in the Scaling area.

- Click the Print button to display the Print dialog box. When Excel displays the Print dialog box, click Table in the Print what area (Figure 5–33).

- Click the OK button to print the table (Figure 5–34).

- Click the Page Setup Dialog Box Launcher to display the Page Setup dialog box. Click Portrait in the Orientation area and then click Adjust to in the Scaling area.

- Click the OK button to close the Page Setup dialog box.

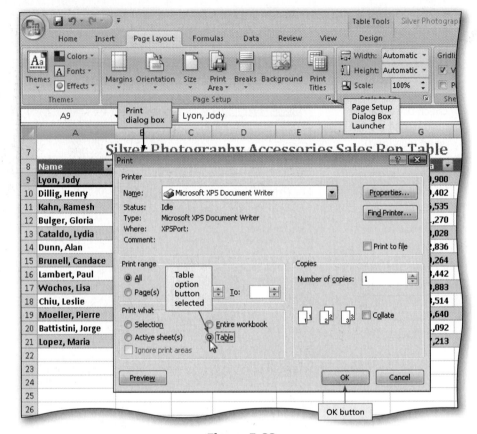

Figure 5–33

Name	Gender	Age	Hire Date	State	Sales Area	Quota	YTD Sales	% of Quota	Grade
Lyon, Jody	F	27	08/03/02	NV	Outside	2,280,900	1,548,311	67.88%	D
Dillig, Henry	M	42	11/21/06	NM	Outside	3,899,402	1,916,753	49.16%	F
Kahn, Ramesh	M	44	04/06/07	MT	Outside	3,426,535	3,292,270	96.08%	A
Bulger, Gloria	F	25	12/23/02	AZ	Outside	2,651,270	2,451,454	92.46%	A
Cataldo, Lydia	F	25	11/15/07	AZ	Inside	3,668,028	2,846,910	77.61%	C
Dunn, Alan	M	39	06/06/02	CA	Outside	1,652,836	1,432,701	86.68%	B
Brunell, Candace	F	36	06/01/02	CA	Inside	3,000,264	2,078,386	69.27%	D
Lambert, Paul	M	35	03/16/02	CA	Outside	1,768,442	1,525,237	86.25%	B
Wochos, Lisa	F	30	10/21/07	NV	Inside	2,648,883	2,188,106	82.60%	B
Chiu, Leslie	F	36	07/15/07	OR	Inside	3,218,514	2,514,181	78.12%	C
Moeller, Pierre	M	24	03/12/01	WA	Outside	3,656,640	3,336,300	91.24%	B
Battistini, Jorge	M	26	07/02/01	WA	Inside	3,371,092	1,960,932	58.17%	F
Lopez, Maria	F	25	06/03/04	UT	Outside	1,837,213	1,563,140	85.08%	B

Figure 5–34

Sorting a Table

The data in a table is easier to work with and more meaningful if the records are arranged sequentially based on one or more fields. Arranging records in a specific sequence is called **sorting**. Data is in **ascending sequence** if it is in order from lowest to highest, earliest to most recent, or alphabetically from A to Z. For example, the records in the Silver Photography Accessories Sales Rep table were entered in no particular order. Data is in **descending sequence** if it is sorted from highest to lowest, most recent to earliest, or alphabetically from Z to A. The field or fields you select to sort the records are called **sort keys**.

BTW

Sort Order
Excel uses the following order of priority: numbers from smallest to largest positive, (space), special characters, text, (blanks). For example, the sort order is: 0 1 2 3 4 5 6 7 8 9 (space) ! " # $ % & ( ) * , . / : ; ? @ [\ ] ^ _ ` { | } ~ + < = > A B C D E F G H I J K L M N O P Q R S T U V W X Y Z (blanks).

You can sort data in a table using one of the following techniques:

1. Select a cell in the field on which to sort, click the Sort & Filter button on the Home tab on the Ribbon, and then click one of the sorting options on the Sort & Filter menu.
2. With the table active, click the column heading arrow in the column on which to sort and then click one of the sorting options in the table.
3. Use the Sort button on the Data tab on the Ribbon.
4. Right-click anywhere in a table and then point to Sort on the shortcut menu to display the Sort submenu.

To Sort a Table in Ascending Sequence by Name Using the Sort & Filter Button

The following example shows how to sort the table in ascending sequence by name using the Sort & Filter button on the Home tab on the Ribbon.

1
- If necessary, click the Home tab on the Ribbon.
- Select cell A9, click the Sort & Filter button on the Ribbon, and then point to the Sort A to Z command on the Sort & Filter menu (Figure 5–35).

Q&A
What if the column I choose includes numeric or date data?

If the column you choose includes numeric data, then the Sort & Filter menu would show the Sort Smallest to Largest and Sort Largest to Smallest commands instead of the Sort A to Z and Sort Z to A commands. If the column you choose includes date data, then the Sort & Filter menu would show the Sort Oldest to Newest and Sort Newest to Oldest commands instead of the Sort A to Z and Sort Z to A commands.

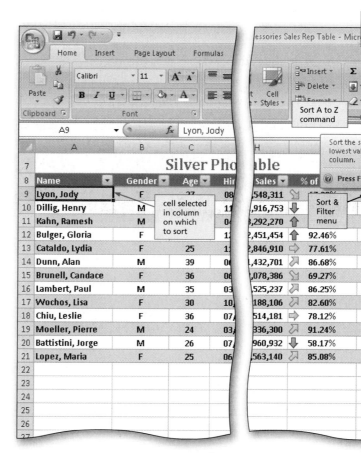

Figure 5–35

2

- Click the Sort A to Z command to sort the sales rep table in ascending sequence by name (Figure 5–36).

Experiment

- Select other fields in the table and use the same procedure to sort on the fields you choose. When you are finished, select cell A9 and repeat the first task in step 2 above.

Name	Gender	Age	Hire Date	State	Sales Area	Quota
Battistini, Jorge	M	26	07/02/01	WA	Inside	3,371,092
Brunell, Candace	F	36	06/01/02	CA	Inside	3,000,264
Bulger, Gloria	F	25	12/23/02	AZ	Outside	2,651,270
Cataldo, Lydia	F	25	11/15/07	AZ	Inside	3,668,028
Chiu, Leslie	F	36	07/15/07	OR	Inside	3,218,514
Dillig, Henry	M	42	11/21/06	NM	Outside	3,899,402
Dunn, Alan	M	39	06/06/02	CA	Outside	1,652,836
Kahn, Ramesh	M	44	04/06/07	MT	Outside	3,426,535
Lambert, Paul	M	35	03/16/02	CA	Outside	1,768,442
Lopez, Maria	F	25	06/03/04	UT	Outside	1,837,213
Lyon, Jody	F	27	08/03/02	NV	Outside	2,280,900
Moeller, Pierre	M	24	03/12/01	WA	Outside	3,656,640
Wochos, Lisa	F	30	10/21/07	NV	Inside	2,648,883

records sorted in ascending sequence by name

Figure 5–36

Other Ways

1. Select field in table, on Data tab on the Ribbon click Sort A to Z button
2. Click column heading arrow of field on which to sort, click Sort A to Z
3. Right-click column to sort, point to Sort on shortcut menu, click Sort A to Z
4. Press ALT+A, A

To Sort a Table in Descending Sequence by Name Using the Sort Z to A button on the Data Tab

The following steps show how to sort the records in descending sequence by name.

1 If necessary, select cell A9.

2 Click the Data tab on the Ribbon.

3 Click the Sort Z to A button on the Ribbon to sort the sales rep table in descending sequence by name (Figure 5–37).

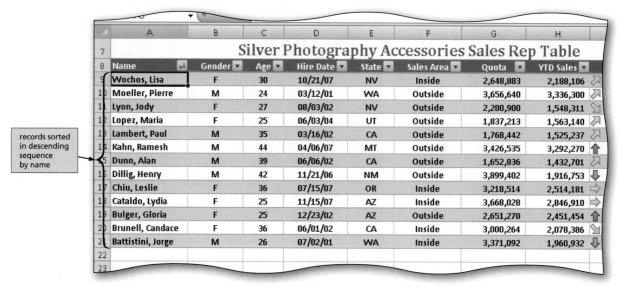

records sorted in descending sequence by name

Figure 5–37

To Sort a Table Using the Sort Command on a Column Heading AutoFilter Menu

The following step shows how to sort the table by hire date using the Sort Ascending command on a column heading list.

1

- If necessary, click the Home tab on the Ribbon.

- Click the Hire Date arrow to display the Hire Date AutoFilter menu (Figure 5–38).

- Click Sort Oldest to Newest in the Hire Date AutoFilter menu to sort the table in ascending sequence by hire date.

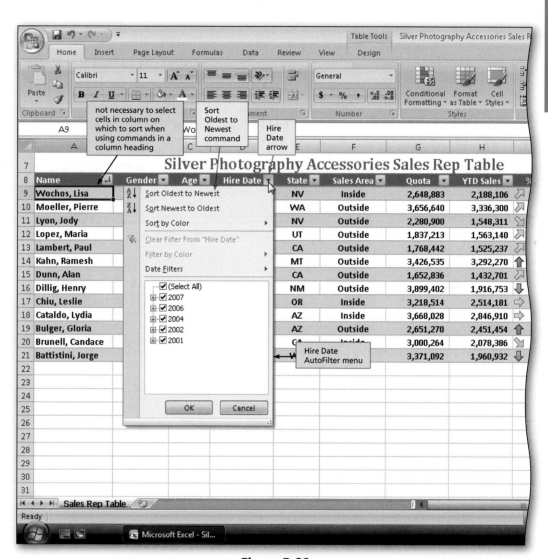

Figure 5–38

To Sort a Table on Multiple Fields Using the Custom Sort Command

Excel allows you to sort on many fields in a single sort operation. You can sort on a maximum of 256 fields in a single sort operation. For instance, the sort example that follows uses the Custom Sort command on the Sort & Filter menu to sort the Silver Photography Accessories Sales Rep table by quota (column G) within gender (column B) within sales area (column F). The Sales Area and Gender fields will be sorted in ascending sequence; the Quota field will be sorted in descending sequence.

The phrase, sort by quota within gender within sales area, means that the records in the table first are arranged in ascending sequence by sales area (Inside and Outside). Within sales area, the records are arranged in ascending sequence by gender (M or F). Within gender, the records are arranged in descending sequence by the sales rep's quota. In this case, Sales Area is the **major sort key** (Sort by field), Gender is the **intermediate sort key** (first Then by field), and Quota is the **minor sort key** (second Then by field). Sorting a table on multiple fields is illustrated below.

1

- With a cell in the table active, click the Sort & Filter button on the Home tab on the Ribbon to display the Sort & Filter menu (Figure 5–39).

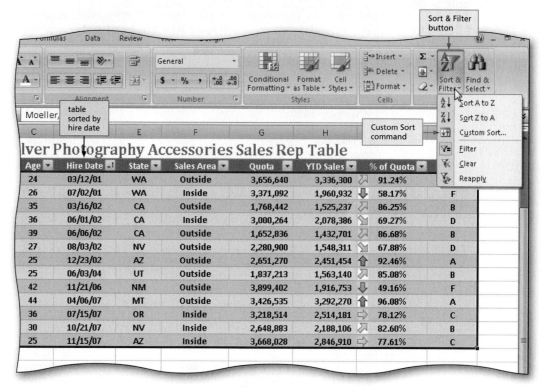

Figure 5–39

2

- Click the Custom Sort command on the Sort & Filter menu to display the Sort dialog box.

- When Excel displays the Sort dialog box, click the Sort by box arrow to display the field names in the table (Figure 5–40).

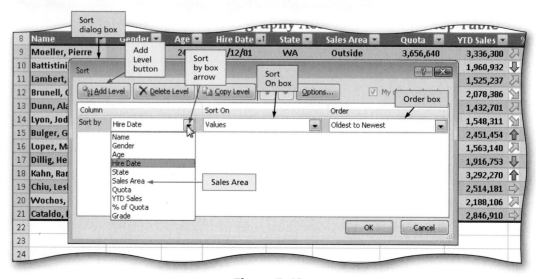

Figure 5–40

3

- Click Sales Area. If necessary, select Values in the Sort On box. If necessary, select A to Z in the Order box.

- Click the Add Level button.

- Click the Then by box arrow and then click Gender in the Then by list. If necessary, select Values in the Sort On box, and if necessary, select A to Z in the Order box.

- Click the Add Level button.

- Click the second Then by box arrow and then click Quota in the Then by list. If necessary, select Values in the Sort On box. Select Largest to Smallest in the Order box (Figure 5–41).

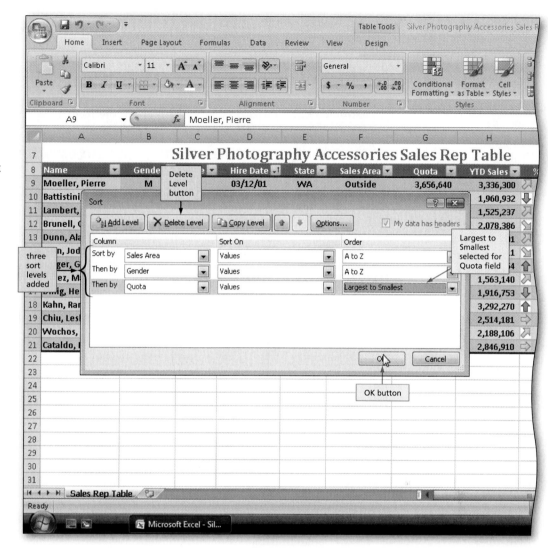

Figure 5–41

- Click the OK button to sort the table by quota within gender within sales area (Figure 5–42).

Q&A

How are the records sorted?

As shown in Figure 5–42, Excel sorts the records in ascending sequence by sales area in column F. Within each sales area, the records are in ascending sequence by gender in column B. Finally, within gender, the records are sorted in descending sequence by the quotas in column G. Remember, if you make a mistake in a sort operation, you can return the records to their original order by clicking the Undo button on the Quick Access Toolbar or by sorting the table by hire date.

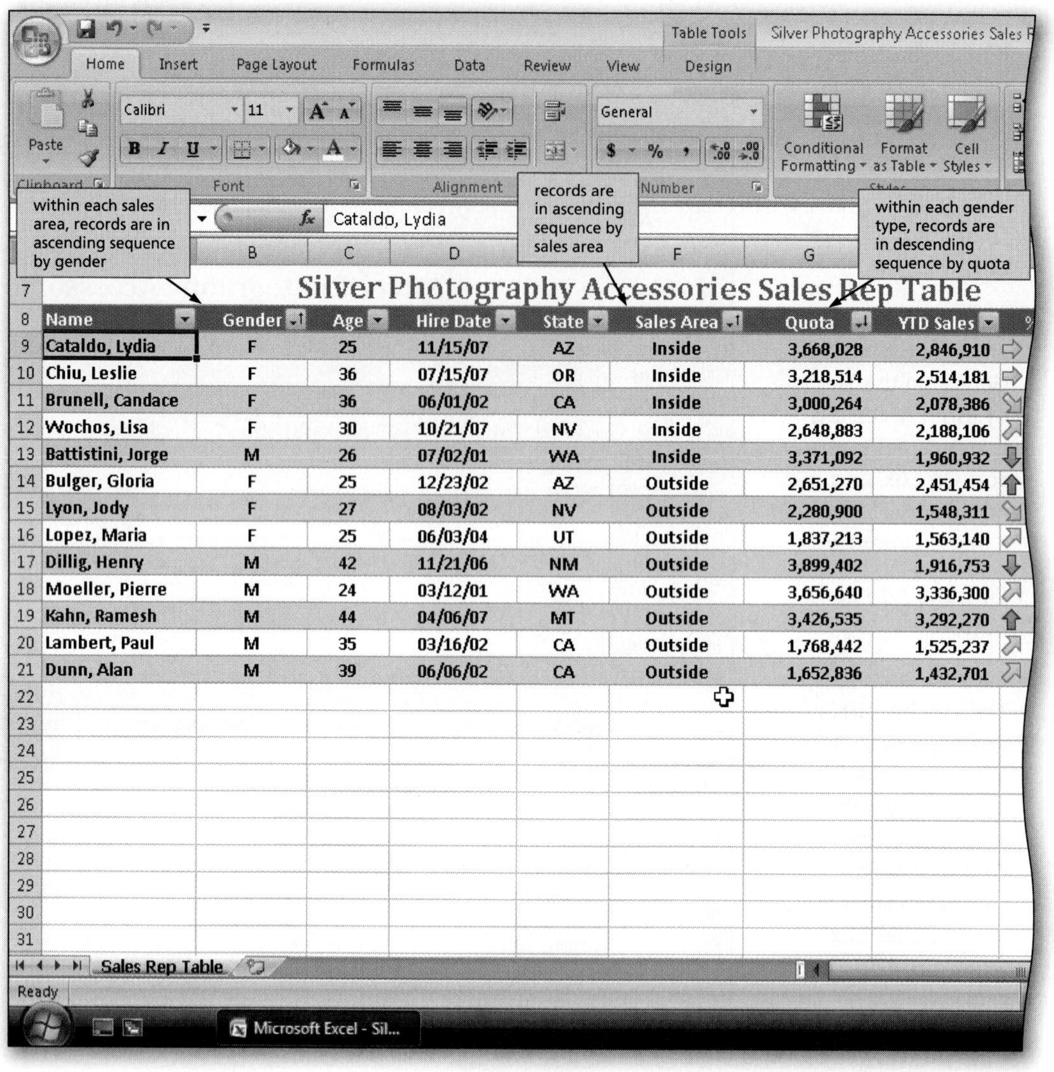

Figure 5–42

- After viewing the sorted table, click the Hire Date arrow and then click Sort Oldest to Newest in the Hire Date AutoFilter menu to sort the table into its original sequence.

Other Ways

1. Click minor field column heading arrow, click Sort Z to A button on Data tab on Ribbon, click intermediate field column heading arrow, click Sort A to Z button on Data tab on Ribbon, click major field column heading arrow, click Sort A to Z button on Data tab on Ribbon
2. Press ALT+A, S

Displaying Automatic Subtotals in a Table

Displaying **automatic subtotals** is a powerful tool for summarizing data in a table. To display automatic subtotals, Excel requires that you sort the table on the field on which the subtotals will be based, convert the table to a range, and then use the Subtotal button on the Data tab on the Ribbon. When Excel displays the Subtotal dialog box, you select the subtotal function you want to use.

The field on which you sort prior to clicking the Subtotal button is called the **control field**. When the control field changes, Excel displays a subtotal for the numeric fields selected in the Subtotal dialog box. For example, if you sort on the State field and request subtotals for the Quota and YTD Sales fields, then Excel recalculates the subtotal and grand total each time the State field changes. The most common subtotal used with the Subtotals command is the SUM function, which causes Excel to display a sum each time the control field changes.

To Display Automatic Subtotals in a Table

In addition to displaying subtotals, Excel also creates an outline for the table. The following steps show how to display subtotals for the Quota field and YTD Sales field by state.

1

- Click the State arrow in cell E8 and then click Sort A to Z in the State AutoFilter menu to sort the table in ascending order by State.

- With cell A9 active, right-click anywhere in the table and then point to the Table command on the shortcut menu to display the Table submenu (Figure 5–43).

Q&A

Why does the table need to be converted to a range?

It is most important that you convert the table to a range before attempting to click the Subtotal button. If the table is not converted to a range, then the Subtotal button on the Data tab on the Ribbon is dimmed (not available).

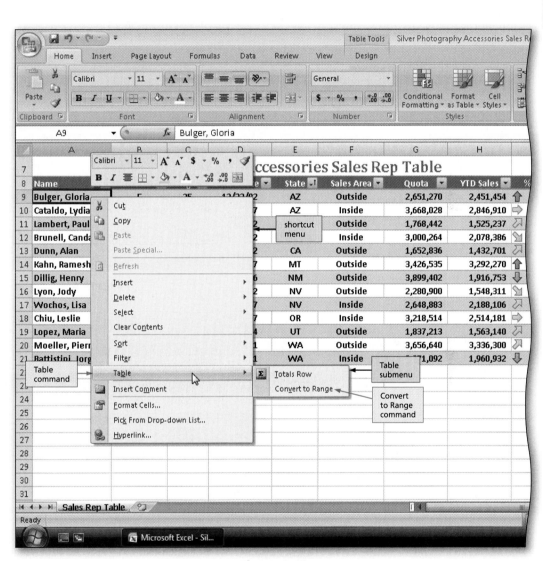

Figure 5–43

2

- Click the Convert to Range command on the Table submenu.

- When Excel displays the Microsoft Excel dialog box, click the Yes button to convert the table to a range.

- Click the Data tab on the Ribbon and then click the Subtotal button on the Ribbon to display the Subtotal dialog box.

- When Excel displays the Subtotal dialog box, click the 'At each change in' box arrow and then click State.

- If necessary, select Sum in the Use function list.

- In the 'Add subtotal to' list, click Grade to clear it and then click Quota and YTD Sales to select them (Figure 5–44).

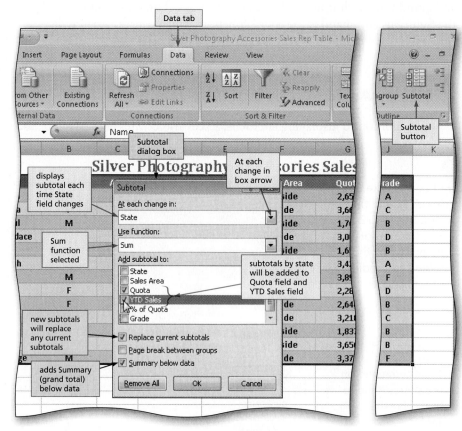

Figure 5–44

3

- Click the OK button to add subtotals to the range (Figure 5–45).

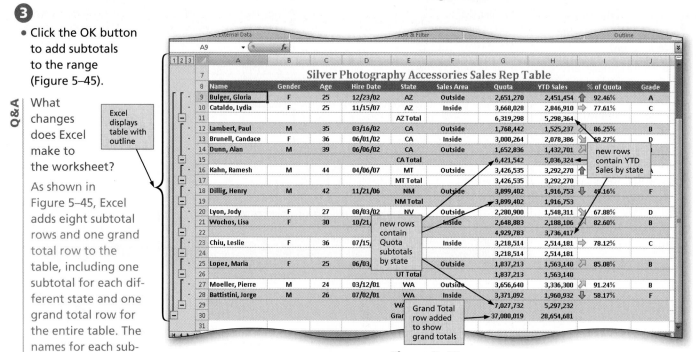

Figure 5–45

Q&A

What changes does Excel make to the worksheet?

As shown in Figure 5–45, Excel adds eight subtotal rows and one grand total row to the table, including one subtotal for each different state and one grand total row for the entire table. The names for each subtotal row are derived from the state names and appear in bold. Thus, the text, AZ Total, in cell E11 identifies the subtotal row that contains Quota and YTD Sales totals for Arizona.

Other Ways

1. Press ALT+A, B

To Zoom Out on a Subtotaled Table and Use the Outline Feature

The following steps show how to use the Zoom Out button on the status bar to reduce the magnification of the worksheet so that the table is more readable. The steps also illustrate how to use the outline features of Excel to hide and unhide data and totals.

1
- Click the Zoom Out button on the status bar once to reduce the zoom percent to 90% (Figure 5–46).

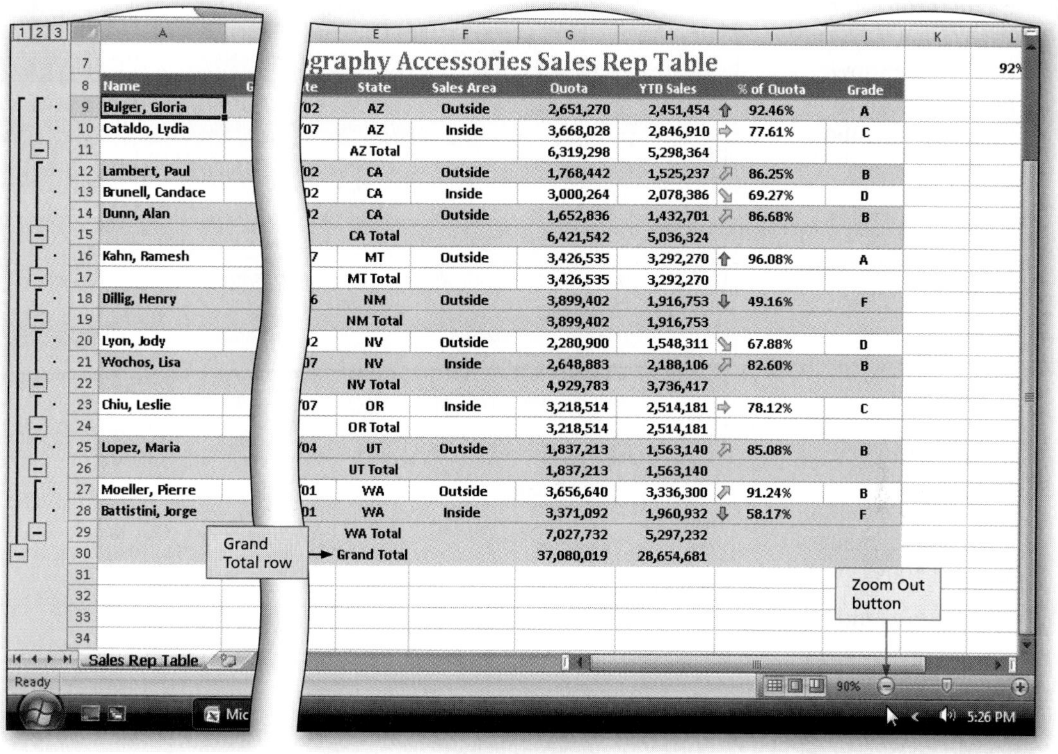

2
- Click the row level symbol 2 on the left side of the window to hide all detail rows and display only the subtotal and grand total rows (Figure 5–47).

Q&A

How can I use the outlining features?

By utilizing the **outlining features** of Excel, you quickly can hide and show detail rows. You can click the **row level symbols** to expand or collapse rows in the worksheet. Row level symbol 1, immediately below the Name box, hides all rows except the Grand Total row. Row level symbol 2 hides the detail records so the subtotal rows and Grand Total row appear as shown in Figure 5–47. Row level symbol 3 shows all rows.

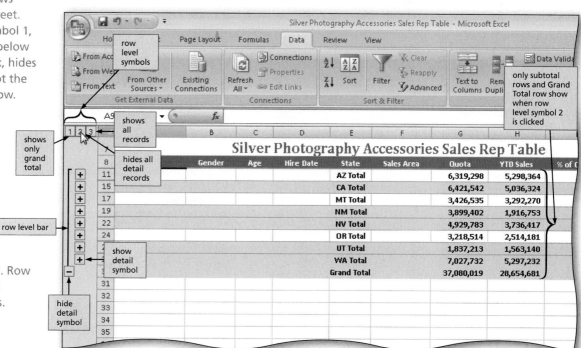

Figure 5–46

Figure 5–47

3

- Click each of the lower three show detail symbols (+) on the left side of the window to display detail records for OR, UT, and WA and change the show detail symbols to hide detail symbols (Figure 5–48).

4

- Click the row level symbol 3 on the left side of the window to show all detail rows.

- Click the Zoom In button on the status bar once to change the zoom percent back to 100%.

Q&A

Can I group and outline without subtotals?

Yes. You do not have to use the Subtotals button to outline a worksheet. You can outline a worksheet by using the Group button on the Data tab on the Ribbon. Usually, however, the Group button is useful only when you already have total lines in a worksheet.

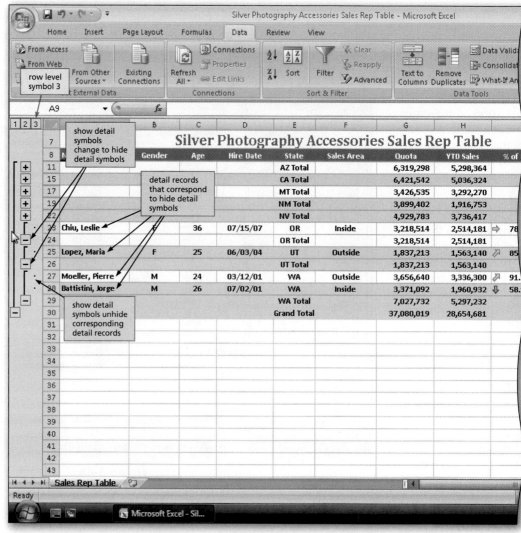

Figure 5–48

Other Ways

1. To group and outline, on Data tab on Ribbon, click Group, click Group

2. To group and outline, press ALT+A, B

3. To zoom, hold CTRL key while scrolling Intellimouse wheel towards you

4. To zoom, press ALT+W, Q, select magnification, press ENTER key

5. To zoom, click Zoom button on View tab on Ribbon, select magnification

BTW

Summarizing Data Using Named Ranges

Another way to summarize data is to use named ranges in formulas. Create a range name for one group of related data, such as WA_Total, and another range name for another group of related data, such as UT_Total. Click a blank cell and then create a formula that adds the sums of each range, using the Use in Formula button to insert range names, such as =SUM(WA_Total)+SUM(UT_Total).

To Remove Automatic Subtotals from a Table

The following steps show how to remove the subtotals and convert the range back to a table.

- Click Subtotal on the Ribbon to display the Subtotal dialog box (Figure 5–49).

- Click the Remove All button.

- Select the range A8:J21 and then click the Home tab on the Ribbon.

- Click the Format as Table button on the Ribbon and then click the Custom quick style in the Format as Table gallery.

- When Excel displays the Format As Table dialog box, click the OK button.

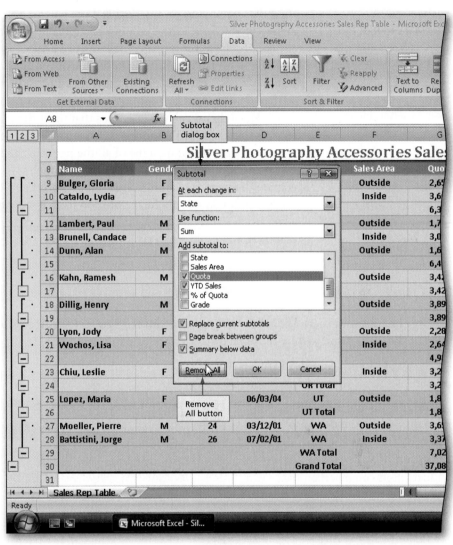

Figure 5–49

Other Ways
1. Press ALT+A, B, ALT+R

To Sort a Table Using a Column Heading List

The following steps sort the Silver Photography Accessories Sales Rep table into its previous sort order, sorted in ascending sequence by hire date.

1. Select cell A9 (or any cell in the table) to make the table active.

2. Click the Hire Date arrow and then click Sort Oldest to Newest in the Hire Date AutoFilter menu to sort the table in ascending sequence by hire date.

BTW

Sorting
Some spreadsheet specialists use the fill handle to create a series in an additional field in the list that is used only to reorder the records into their original sequence.

BTW

Sort Options
You can sort left to right across rows by clicking the Options button in the Sort dialog box (Figure 5–41 on page EX 373) and then clicking Sort left to right in the Orientation area. You also can click Case sensitive to sort lowercase letters before the same capital letters for an ascending sort.

Querying a Table Using AutoFilter

An alternative to using a data form to find records in a table that meet comparison criteria is to use the column heading arrows. The Filter button on the Data tab on the Ribbon or the Filter command on the Sort & Filter menu on the Home tab on the Ribbon places the arrows to the right of the column headings in a table. Thus, the query technique that uses the column heading arrows is called **AutoFilter**.

When you first create a table, Excel automatically enables AutoFilter; the column heading arrows thus appear to the right of the column headings. You can hide the arrows so they do not show by toggling one of the two commands listed above.

AutoFilter displays all records that meet the criteria as a subset of the table by hiding records that do not pass the test. Clicking a column heading arrow causes Excel to display, among other commands, a list of all the items in the field (column) in an AutoFilter menu. If you deselect an item from the AutoFilter menu, Excel immediately hides records that contain the item. The item you deselect from the AutoFilter menu is called the **filter criterion**. If you select a filter criterion from a second column heading while the first is still active, then Excel displays a subset of the first subset. The process of filtering activity based on one or more filter criteria is called a **query**.

To Query a Table Using AutoFilter

The following steps show how to query the Silver Photography Accessories Sales Rep table using AutoFilter, so that the table displays only those records that pass the following test:

Gender = F AND Sales Area = Inside

- Click the Gender arrow in cell B8 to display the Gender AutoFilter menu (Figure 5–50).

Q&A

What is displayed below the Text Filters command on the AutoFilter menu?

The list below the Text Filters command is a list of all of the values that occur in the selected column. The top item, (Select All), indicates that all values for this field currently are displayed in the table.

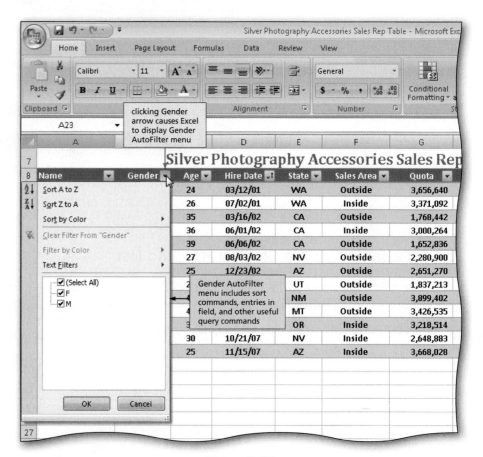

Figure 5–50

- Click M in the Gender list to remove the check mark and cause Excel to hide all records representing males, so that only records representing females appear.

- Click the OK button.

- Click the Sales Area arrow in row 8 to display the Sales Area AutoFilter menu (Figure 5–51).

Removing Duplicate Values
To maintain data integrity, you can remove a row that contains duplicate values in one column, such as Name, but not another column, such as Gender. Click in the table, click the Data tab, and then click the Remove Duplicates button in the Data Tools group. Click Unselect All, click the column in which you want Excel to look for duplicates, and then click OK to remove rows that contain duplicate data in the column you specified.

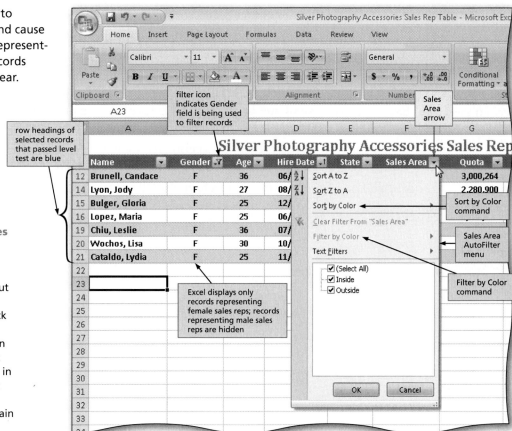

Figure 5–51

- Click Outside in the Sales Area list to remove the check mark and hide all records that represent females who are not inside sales reps (Figure 5–52).

- Click the OK button.

Why are the row headings of some rows displayed in blue?

Excel displays row headings in blue to indicate that these rows are the result of a filtering process.

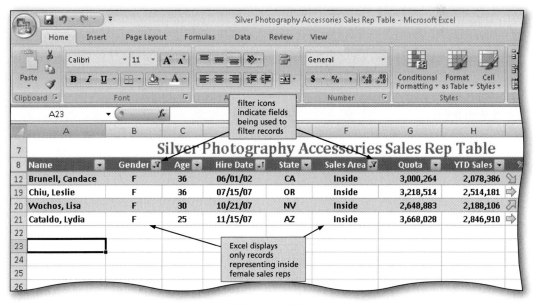

Figure 5–52

Are both filters now applied to the table?

Yes. When you select a second filter criterion, Excel adds it to the first. Hence, in the previous steps, each record must pass two tests to appear as part of the final subset of the table.

BTW

Protected Worksheets
The Sort, Subtotal, and AutoFilter commands are unavailable if the worksheet or workbook is protected, unless you selected them in the 'Allows users of this worksheet to' list in the Protect Sheet dialog box when you protect the worksheet or workbook.

BTW

Creating Formulas for Filtered Lists
Excel allows you to create formulas for filtered lists. After sorting and filtering data, click the Subtotal button on the Data tab. In the Subtotal dialog box, click the `At each change in' box arrow, select the field to sort, click the Use function box arrow, select a function (such as Sum to total the values or Count to count the values), click the check boxes of the fields you want to subtotal, and then click the OK button.

More About AutoFilter

Other important points regarding AutoFilter include the following:

1. When AutoFilter is enabled and records are hidden, Excel displays a filter icon in the table column heading arrows used to establish the filter and the row headings of the selected records in blue.

2. If the column heading arrows do not show, then you must manually enable AutoFilter by clicking the Filter command on the Sort & Filter menu on the Home tab on the Ribbon. The Filter button also is on the Data tab on the Ribbon.

3. To remove a filter criterion for a single field, select the Select All option from the column heading AutoFilter menu for that field.

4. When you create a formula in the total row of a table, the formula automatically recalculates the values even when you filter the list. For example, the results shown in the total row in Figure 5–31 on page EX 366 automatically update if you apply a filter to the table.

5. You can filter and sort a column by color or conditional formatting using the Sort by Color and Filter by Color commands on the AutoFilter menu (Figure 5–51 on the previous page).

To Show All Records in a Table

The following steps illustrate how to show all records in the table following a query.

1

- With the table active, click the Data tab on the Ribbon and then point to the Filter button on the Ribbon (Figure 5–53).

2

- Click the Filter button on the Ribbon to display all of the records in the table.

Other Ways

1. Press ALT+A, T
2. Click column heading arrow that includes a filter icon, click (Select All) in AutoFilter menu

Figure 5–53

To Enter Custom Criteria Using AutoFilter

One of the commands available in all AutoFilter menus is Custom Filter. The Custom Filter command option allows you to enter custom criteria, such as multiple options or ranges of numbers. The following steps show how to enter custom criteria to show records in the table that represent sales reps whose ages are between 30 and 40, inclusive; that is, they are greater than or equal to 30 and less than or equal to 40 ($30 \le \text{Age} \le 40$).

- Click the Filter button on the Data tab on the Ribbon to display the AutoFilter arrows in the table.

- With the table active, click the Age arrow in cell C8 to display the Age AutoFilter menu.

- When Excel displays the AutoFilter menu, point to the Number Filters command and then point to Custom Filter on the shortcut menu (Figure 5–54).

Figure 5–54

- Click Custom Filter.

- When Excel displays the Custom AutoFilter dialog box, click the top-left box arrow, click 'is greater than or equal to' in the list, and then type 30 in the top-right box.

- Click the bottom-left box arrow, click 'is less than or equal to' in the list, and then type 40 in the bottom-right box (Figure 5–55).

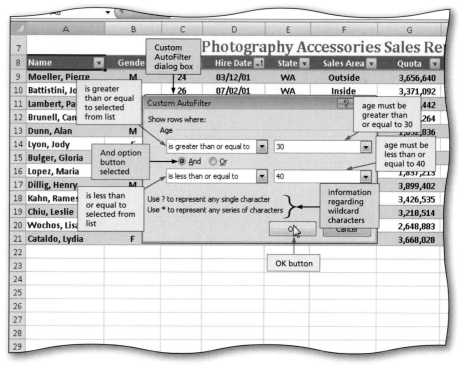

Figure 5–55

3

- Click the OK button in the Custom AutoFilter dialog box to display records in the table that represent sales reps whose ages are between 30 and 40 inclusive (Figure 5–56).

4

- After viewing the records that meet the custom criteria, click the Filter button on the Ribbon.

Experiment

- Create filters on other fields in the table, such as Gender and State. When you are finished, click the Filter button and then repeat the steps above so that the worksheet appears as it does in Figure 5–56.

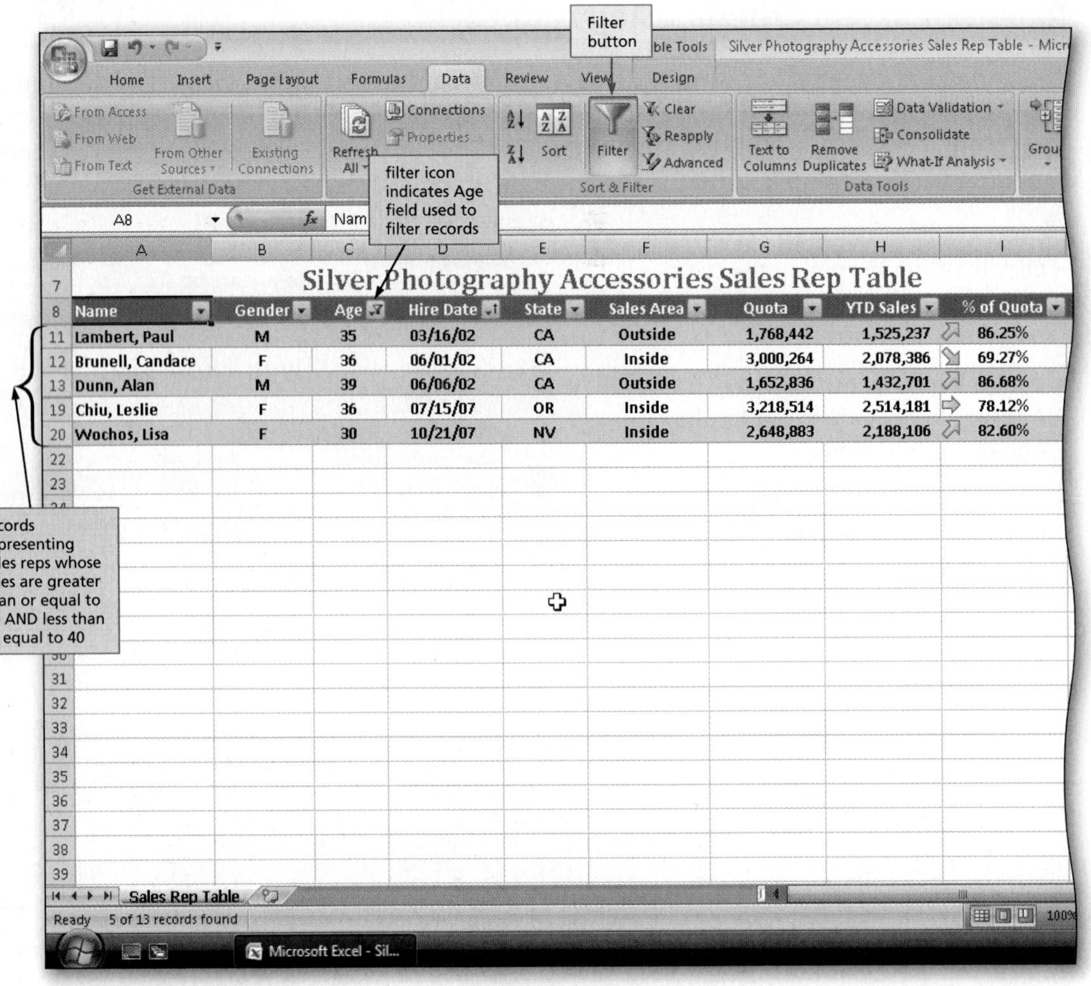

Figure 5–56

Q&A

How are the And and Or option buttons used?

You can click the And option button or the Or option button to select the AND or the OR operator. The AND operator indicates that both parts of the criteria must be true; the OR operator indicates that only one of the two must be true. Use the AND operator when the custom criteria is continuous over a range of values, such as ($30 \leq Age \leq 40$). Use the OR operator when the custom criteria is not continuous, such as Age less than or equal to 30 OR greater than or equal to 40 ($30 \leq Age \geq 40$).

Using a Criteria Range on the Worksheet

BTW

The AND and OR Operators

AND means each and every one of the comparison criteria must be true. OR means only one of the comparison criteria must be true.

You can set up a **criteria range** on the worksheet and use it to manipulate records that pass the comparison criteria. Using a criteria range on the worksheet involves two steps:

1. Create the criteria range and name it Criteria.
2. Use the Advanced button on the Data tab on the Ribbon.

To Create a Criteria Range on the Worksheet

To set up a criteria range, first copy the column headings in the table to another area of the worksheet. If possible, copy the field names to rows above the table, in case the table is expanded downward or to the right in the future. Next, enter the comparison criteria in the row immediately below the field names you just copied to the criteria range. Then use the Name box in the formula bar to name the criteria range, Criteria.

The following step shows how to create a criteria range in the range A2:J3 to find records that pass the test:

Gender = F AND Age > 25 AND Grade > C

A grade greater than or equal to C alphabetically means that only sales reps with grades of D and F pass the test.

1

- Click the Home tab on the Ribbon.

- Select the range A7:J8 and then click the Copy button on the Ribbon.

- Click cell A1 and then press the ENTER key to copy the contents on the Office Clipboard to the destination area A1:J2.

- Change the title to Criteria Area in cell A1, enter F in cell B3, enter >25 in cell C3, and then enter >C in cell J3.

- Select the range A2:J3, click the Name box in the formula bar, type Criteria as the range name, press the ENTER key, and then click cell J4 (Figure 5–57).

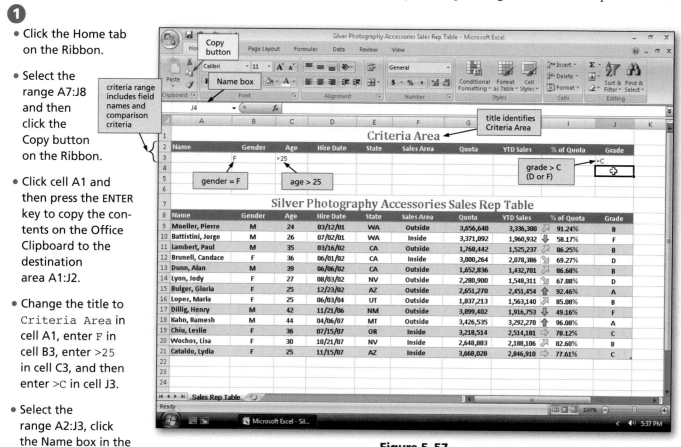

Figure 5–57

Q&A

Must the text in the column headings in the criteria range match those in the table exactly?

Yes. To ensure the column headings in the criteria range are spelled exactly the same as the column headings in the table, copy and paste the column headings in the table to the criteria range as shown in the previous set of steps.

To Query a Table Using the Advanced Filter Dialog Box

Using the Advanced Filter dialog box is similar to using the AutoFilter query technique, except that it does not filter records based on comparison criteria you select from a table. Instead, this technique uses the comparison criteria set up in a criteria range (A2:J3) on the worksheet.

The following steps show how to use the Advanced Filter dialog box to query a table and show only the records that pass the test established in the criteria range in Figure 5–57 on the previous page (Gender = F AND Age > 25 AND Grade > C).

1

- Select cell A9 to activate the table.
- Click the Data tab on the Ribbon and then click the Advanced button on the Ribbon to display the Advanced Filter dialog box (Figure 5–58).

Q&A What is displayed already in the Advanced Filter dialog box?

In the Action area, the 'Filter the list, in-place' option button is selected automatically. Excel automatically selects the table (range $A$8:$J$21) in the List range box. Excel also automatically selects the criteria range ($A$2:$J$3) in the Criteria range box, because the name Criteria was assigned to the range A2:J3 earlier.

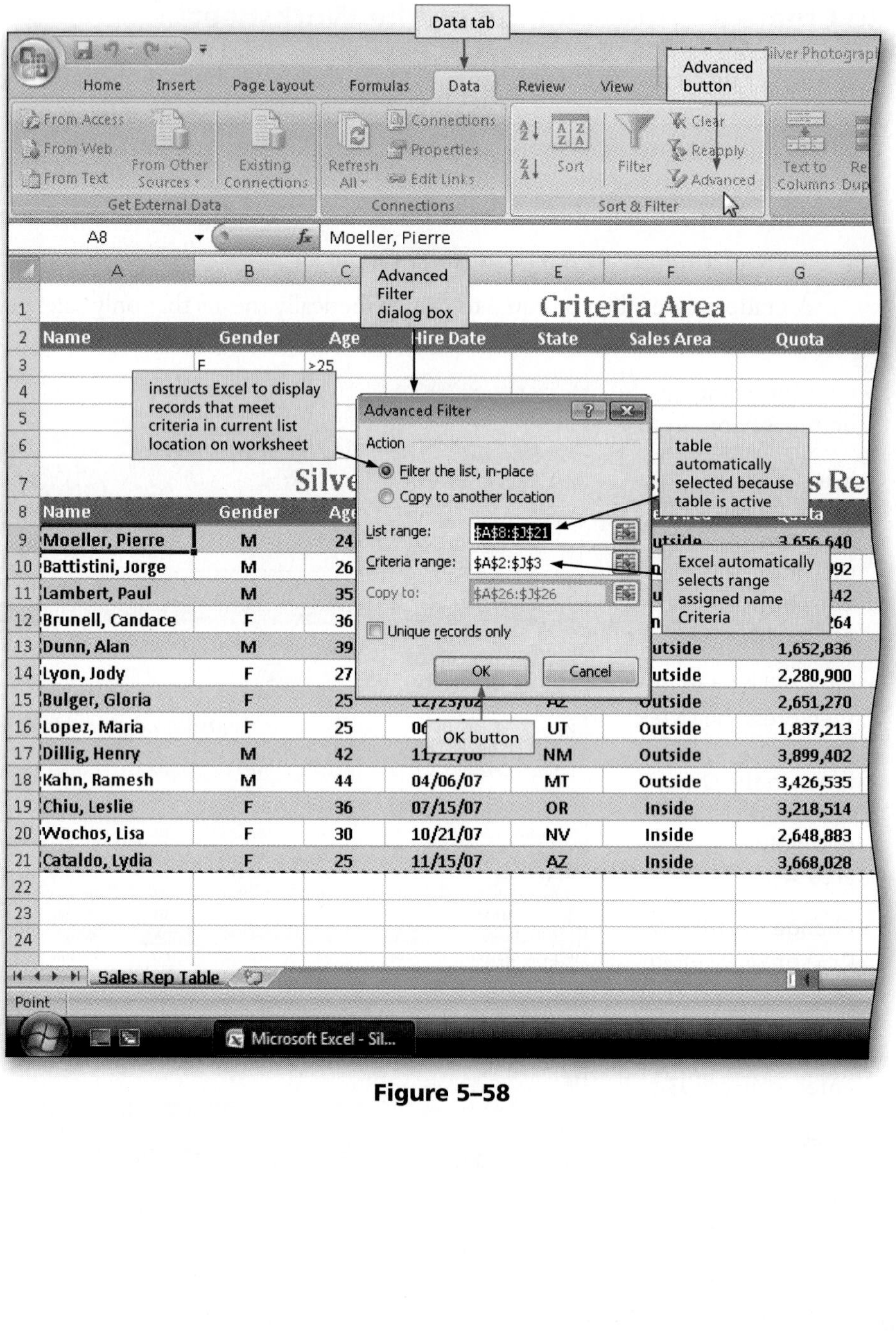

Figure 5–58

2

- Click the OK button in the Advanced Filter dialog box to hide all records that do not meet the comparison criteria (Figure 5–59).

Q&A

What is the main difference between the AutoFilter query technique and using the Advanced Filter dialog box?

Like the AutoFilter query technique, the Advanced Filter command displays a subset of the table. The primary difference between the two is that the Advanced Filter command allows you to create more complex comparison criteria, because the criteria range can be as many rows long as necessary, allowing for many sets of comparison criteria.

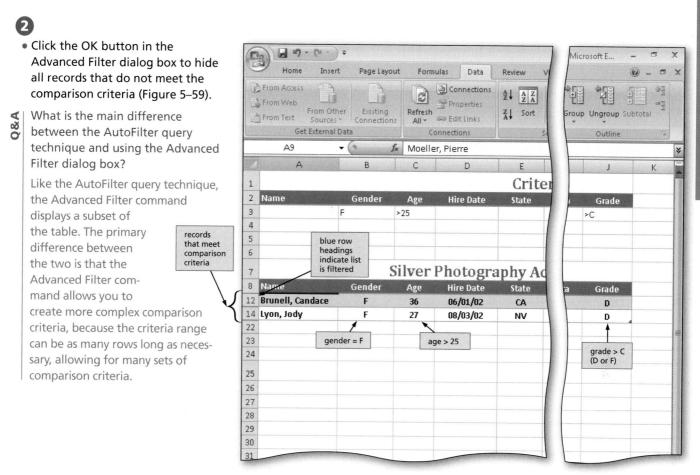

Figure 5–59

To Show All Records in a Table

The following step illustrates how to show all records in the table.

1 Click the Filter button on the Data tab on the Ribbon.

Q&A

Why was AutoFilter turned off?

When the Advanced Filter command is invoked, Excel disables the AutoFilter command, thus hiding the column heading arrows in the active table as shown in Figure 5–59.

Other Ways

1. Press ALT+A, T

Extracting Records

If you select the 'Copy to another location' option button in the Action area of the Advanced Filter dialog box (Figure 5–58), Excel copies the records that meet the comparison criteria in the criteria range to another part of the worksheet, rather than displaying them as a subset of the table. The location where the records are copied is called the **extract range**. Creating an extract range requires steps similar to those used to create a criteria range earlier in the chapter. Once the records that meet the comparison criteria in the criteria range are extracted (copied to the extract range), you can create a new table or manipulate the extracted records.

To Create an Extract Range and Extract Records

To create an extract range, copy the field names of the table and then paste them to an area on the worksheet, preferably well below the table range. Next, name the pasted range Extract by using the Name box in the formula bar. Finally, use the Advanced Filter dialog box to extract the records. The following steps show how to create an extract range below the Silver Photography Accessories Sales Rep table and then extract records that meet the following criteria, as entered earlier in the Criteria range:

Gender = F AND Age > 25 AND Grade > C

1

• Click the Home tab on the Ribbon.

• Select range A7:J8, click the Copy button on the Ribbon, select cell A25, and then press the ENTER key to copy the contents on the Office Clipboard to the destination area A25:J26.

• Select cell A25 and then type Extract Area as the title.

• Select the range A26:J26, type the name Extract in the Name box in the formula bar, and then press the ENTER key.

2

• Select cell A9 to activate the table and then click the Data tab on the Ribbon.

• Click the Advanced button on the Ribbon to display the Advanced Filter dialog box.

• When Excel displays the Advanced Filter dialog box, click 'Copy to another location' in the Action area (Figure 5–60).

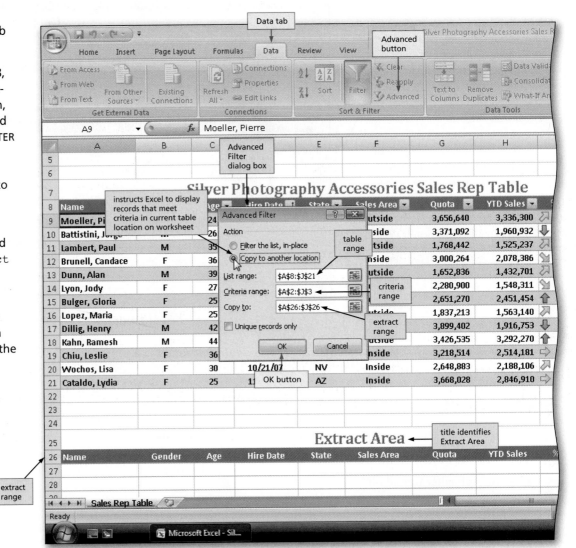

Figure 5–60

3

- Click the OK button to copy any records that meet the comparison criteria in the criteria range from the table to the extract range (Figure 5–61).

Q&A What happens to the rows in the extract range if I perform another advanced filter operation?

Each time the Advanced Filter dialog box is used and the 'Copy to another location' option button is selected, Excel clears cells below the field names in the extract range. Hence, if you change the comparison criteria in the criteria range and then use the Advanced Filter dialog box a second time, Excel clears the previously extracted records before it copies a new set of records that pass the new test.

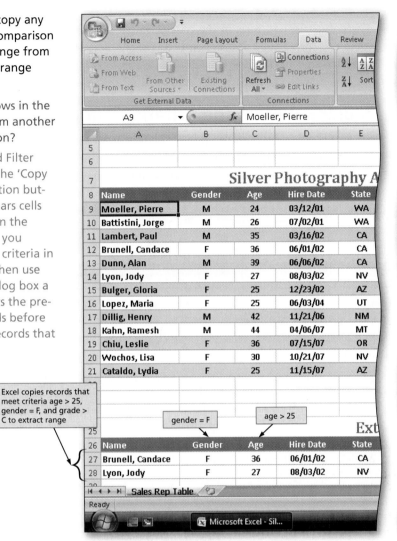

Figure 5–61

Other Ways

1. Press ALT+A, Q

To Enable AutoFilter

As indicated earlier, when the Advanced Filter dialog box is used, Excel disables AutoFilter, thus hiding the column heading arrows in an active table. The following steps show how to enable AutoFilter.

1 Click the Filter button on the Data tab on the Ribbon to display the column heading arrows in the table.

2 Click the Home tab on the Ribbon.

BTW **Setting Up the Extract Range**
When setting up the extract range, all of the column headings do not have to be copied in the list to the proposed extract range. Instead, copy only those column headings you want, in any order. You also can type the column headings rather than copy them, although this method is not recommended because it increases the likelihood of misspellings or other typographical errors.

More About the Criteria Range

The comparison criteria in the criteria range determine the records that will pass the test when the Advanced Filter dialog box is used. This section describes examples of different comparison criteria.

A Blank Row in the Criteria Range

If the criteria range contains a blank row, it means that no comparison criteria have been defined. Thus, all records in the table pass the test. For example, the blank row in the criteria range shown in Figure 5–62 means that all records will pass the test.

Figure 5–62

Using Multiple Comparison Criteria with the Same Field

If the criteria range contains two or more entries below the same field name, then records that pass either comparison criterion pass the test. For example, based on the criteria range shown in Figure 5–63, all records that represent sales reps with a State value of MT or NM will pass the test.

Figure 5–63

BTW

The Criteria Area
When you add items in multiple rows to a criteria area, you must redefine the range of the name Criteria before you use it. To redefine the name Criteria, click the Name Manager button on the Formulas tab on the Ribbon. When Excel displays the Name Manager dialog box, select Criteria in the list and then click the Delete button. Next, select the new Criteria area and name it Criteria using the Name box.

If an AND operator applies to the same field name (Age > 50 AND Age < 55), then you must duplicate the field name (Age) in the criteria range. That is, add the field name Age in cell K2 to the right of Grade and then adjust the range assigned to the name Criteria by using the Define Name command on the Formulas tab on the Ribbon.

Comparison Criteria in Different Rows and below Different Fields

When the comparison criteria below different field names are in the same row, then records pass the test only if they pass all the comparison criteria. If the comparison criteria for the field names are in different rows, then the records must pass only one of the tests. For example, in the criteria range shown in Figure 5–64, female sales reps OR outside sales reps pass the test.

Gender = F
or Sales Area
= Outside

Criteria Area

Figure 5–64

Using Database Functions

Excel has 12 **database functions** that can be used to evaluate numeric data in a table. One of the functions is called the DAVERAGE function. As the name implies, the **DAVERAGE function** is used to find the average of numbers in a table field that pass a test. This function serves as an alternative to finding an average using the Subtotal button on the Data tab on the Ribbon. The general form of the DAVERAGE function is:

=DAVERAGE(table range, "field name", criteria range)

where table range is the range of the table, field name is the name of the field in the table, and criteria range is the comparison criteria or test to pass.

Another often used table function is the DCOUNT function. The **DCOUNT function** will count the number of numeric entries in a table field that pass a test. The general form of the DCOUNT function is:

=DCOUNT(table range, "field name", criteria range)

where table range is the range of the table, field name is the name of the field in the table, and criteria range is the comparison criteria or test to pass.

To Use the DAVERAGE and DCOUNT Database Functions

The following steps use the DAVERAGE function to find the average age of female sales reps and the average age of male sales reps in the table. The DCOUNT function is used to count the number of sales reps records that have a grade of A. The first step sets up the criteria areas that are required by these two functions.

1 Select cell O1 and then enter Criteria as the criteria area title. Select cell L1, click the Format Painter button on the Ribbon, and then click cell O1. Center the title, Criteria, across the range O1:Q1.

2 Select cell O2 and then enter Gender as the field name. Select cell P2 and enter Gender as the field name. Select cell Q2 and then enter Grade as the field name. Select cell L2. Click the Format Painter button on the Ribbon. Drag through the range O2:Q2.

3 Enter F in cell O3 as the Gender code for female sales reps. Enter M in cell P3 as the Gender code for male sales reps. Enter A in cell Q3 as the Grade value. Select M3, click the Format Painter button on the Ribbon, and then drag through the range O3:Q3.

4 Enter Average Female Age = = = = = > in cell O4. Enter Average Male Age = = = = = => in cell O5. Enter Grade A Count = = = = = = = = = > in cell O6.

5 Select cell R4 and then enter =daverage(a8:j21, "Age", o2:o3) as the database function.

6 Select cell R5 and then enter =daverage(a8:j21, "Age", p2:p3) as the database function.

7 Select cell R6 and then enter =dcount(a8:j21, "Age", q2:q3) as the database function.

8 Select the range O4:R6 and then click the Bold button on the Ribbon.

9 Select the range R4:R5 and then click the Comma Style button on the Ribbon (Figure 5–65).

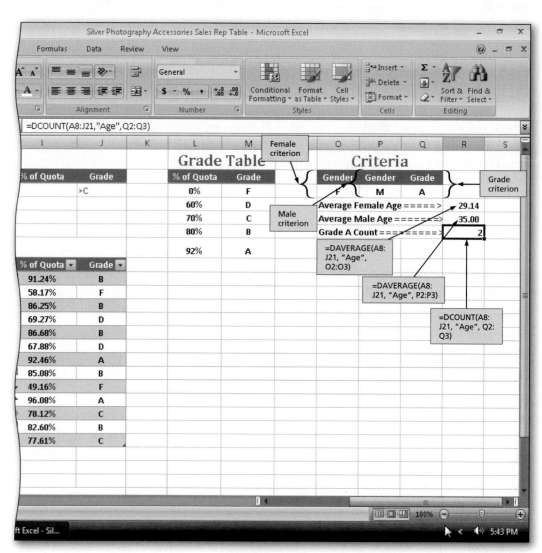

Figure 5–65

More About Using Database Functions

In Figure 5–65, the first value in the DCOUNT function, A8:J21, refers to the table range defined earlier in this chapter (range A8:J21). Instead of using the cell range, you can name the table using the Name box in the formula bar and then use the table name as the first argument in the database functions. Database is the name most often assigned to a table. If the table were named Database, then the DCOUNT function would be entered as:

=DCOUNT(Database, "Age", Q2:Q3)

Excel uses the criteria range Q2:Q3 to select the records in the range Database where the Grade is A; it then counts the numeric Age field in these records to determine the number of records that pass the criteria. Excel requires that you surround the field name Age with quotation marks unless the field has been assigned a name through the Name box in the formula bar.

The third value, Q2:Q3, is the criteria range for the grade count. In the case of the DCOUNT function, it is required that you select a numeric field to count even though the value of the numeric field itself is not used.

Other Database Functions

Other database functions that are similar to the functions described in previous chapters include the DMAX, DMIN, and DSUM functions. For a complete list of the database functions available for use with a table, click the Insert Function box in the formula bar. When Excel displays the Insert Function dialog box, select Database in the 'Or select a category' list. The 'Select a function' box displays the database functions. If you click a database function name, Excel displays a description of the function above the OK button in the Insert Function dialog box.

Using the SUMIF and COUNTIF Functions

The SUMIF and COUNTIF functions are useful when you want to sum values in a range or count values in a range only if they meet criteria. The range need not be a table. For example, assume you want to sum the YTD sales of the sales reps that have a grade of A. Or, assume you want to count the number of male sales reps. The first question can be answered by using the SUMIF function as follows:

=SUMIF(J9:J21,"A",H9:H21)

where the first argument J9:J21 is the range containing the numbers to add, the second argument "A" is the criteria, and the third argument H9:H21 is the range containing the cells with which to compare the criteria.

The second question can be answered by using the COUNTIF function as follows:

=COUNTIF(B9:B21,"M")

where the first argument B9:B21 is the range containing the cells with which to compare the criteria.

To Use the SUMIF and COUNTIF Functions

The following steps enter identifiers and these two functions in the range O8:R9.

1. Enter `Grade A YTD Sales Sum = = = =>` in cell O8.
2. Enter `Male Sales Rep Count = = = = =>` in cell O9.
3. Select cell R8 and then enter `=SUMIF(j9:j21,"A",h9:h21)` as the function.
4. Select cell R9 and then enter `=COUNTIF(b9:b21,"M")` as the function.
5. Select the range O8:R9 and then click the Bold button on the Ribbon.
6. Select cell R8, click the Comma Style button on the Ribbon, and then click the Decrease Decimal button on the Ribbon twice.

7 Double-click the right border of column heading R to change the width of column R to best fit (Figure 5–66).

Q&A Are there any differences when using these functions on a range?

Yes. The COUNTIF, SUMIF, and database functions will work on any range. The difference between using these functions on a range and table is that if the function references a table, then Excel automatically adjusts the first argument as a table grows or shrinks. The same cannot be said if the function's first argument is a range reference that is not defined as a table.

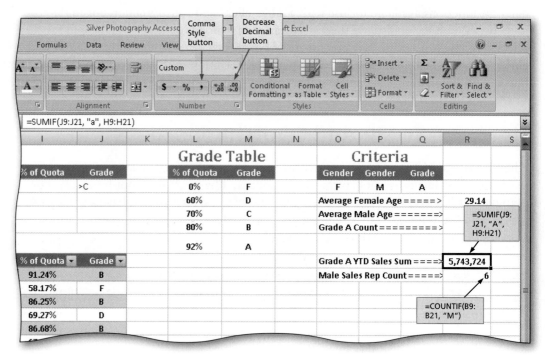

Figure 5–66

BTW

Printing
To print individual sections of the worksheet, click the Name box in the formula bar, click the name of the section (Criteria or Extract) you want to print, and then click Print on the Office Button menu. When Excel displays the Print dialog box, click Selection in the Print what area and then click the Print button.

To Print the Worksheet and Save the Workbook

The following steps print the worksheet on one page and save the workbook.

1 Select any cell outside the table.

2 Click the Page Layout tab on the Ribbon and then click the Page Setup Dialog Box Launcher to display the Page Setup dialog box.

3 Click Landscape in the Orientation area. Click Fit to in the Scaling area.

4 Click the Print button. When the Print dialog box appears, click the OK button to print the worksheet (Figure 5–67).

5 Click the Save button on the Quick Access Toolbar to save the workbook using the file name, Silver Photography Accessories Sales Rep Table.

6 Click the Page Setup Dialog Box Launcher to display the Page Setup dialog box. Click Portrait in the Orientation area and then click Adjust to in the Scaling area.

7 Click the OK button to close the Page Setup dialog box.

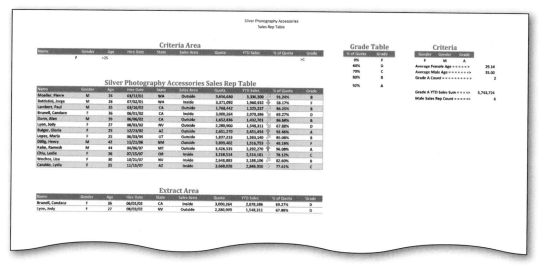

Figure 5–67

Saving a Workbook in Different File Formats

BTW

Certification
The Microsoft Certified Application Specialist (MCAS) program provides an opportunity for you to obtain a valuable industry credential – proof that you have the Excel 2007 skills required by employers. For more information, see Appendix G or visit the Excel 2007 Certification Web page (scsite.com/ex2007/cert).

Excel workbooks usually are saved in a file format called **Microsoft Excel Workbook**. A file saved in the Microsoft Excel Workbook file format has a file extension of **xlsx**. A **file extension**, which usually is three or four characters in length, is used by Windows Vista to classify files by application. By default, you do not see the file extensions when you use the Save As or Open dialog boxes, but the file extensions are appended to the file name and separated by a period. Excel allows you to save a workbook in more than 30 different file formats, so that the data can be transferred to other applications easily. Table 5–6 summarizes the more popular file formats available in Excel via the 'Save as type' box in the Save As dialog box.

Table 5–6 Popular File Formats Available with the Save As Command in Excel	
File Formats	**Extension**
Microsoft Excel Workbook	xlsx
Microsoft Excel 97 – Excel 2003 Workbook	xls
XML Spreadsheet 2003	xml
XML Data	xml
Single File Web Page	mht
Web Page	htm
Template	xltx
Text (Tab delimited)	txt
Unicode Text	txt
CSV (Comma delimited)	csv
Formatted Text (Space delimited)	prn

Plan Ahead	**Save the worksheet in a different file format.** Often, the best way to share data in a worksheet with other applications is to save the file as a text file. The CSV file format is most the most common type of text file. When saving data to a text file, Excel will place one row from the worksheet on one line of text. In this case, each sales rep record will be represented on one line of text in the CSV file. The Grade column is not included in the range to save because it is computed using the grade table, which will not be part of the new file.

To Save a Workbook in CSV File Format

The following steps show how to save the table (range A8:I21) in the Silver Photography Accessories Sales Rep Table workbook in a CSV (Comma delimited) file format so that the file can be read by most applications. In this example, the table is copied to a new workbook, saved using the CSV file format, and then displayed and printed in Notepad.

- Click the Home tab on the Ribbon.

- Select the table in the range A8:I21.

- Click the Copy button on the Ribbon.

- Click the Office Button and then click New on the Office Button menu.

- When the New Workbook dialog box is displayed, click the Create button.

- With cell A1 selected in the new workbook, click the Paste button on the Ribbon.

- Click the Select All button, point to the right border of the column A heading, and double-click to set all column widths to best fit.

- Select cell A16 (Figure 5–68).

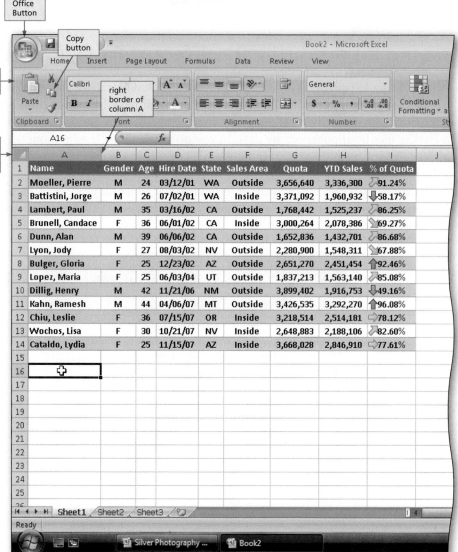

Figure 5–68

2

- With a USB flash drive connected to one of the computer's USB ports, click the Save button on the Quick Access Toolbar. Change the file name to Silver Photography Accessories Sales Rep Table CSV (Figure 5–68).

3

- Click the 'Save as type' box arrow and then scroll down and point to CSV (Comma delimited) in the 'Save as type' list as shown in Figure 5–69.

- Click CSV (Comma delimited) in the Save as type list.

- If necessary, click Computer in the Favorite Links section of the Navigation pane and then double-click UDISK 2.0 (E:) to select the USB flash drive as the new save

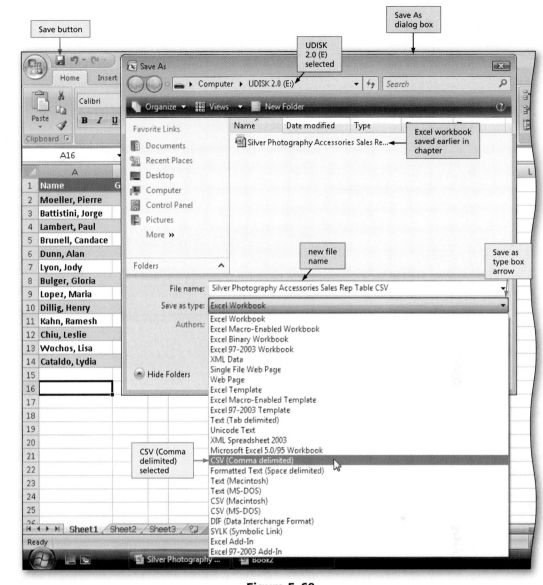

Figure 5–69

location. Click the Save button in the Save As dialog box. Click the OK button and the Yes button in the Microsoft Office Excel dialog boxes when they appear.

- Click the workbook Close button on the right side of the Excel title bar.

Can I open the CSV file in Excel?

Yes. If you open the Silver Photography Accessories Sales Rep Table CSV in Excel, it will place the fields from the CSV file in the same cells as shown in Figure 5–68, but without some of the formatting.

Other Ways

1. On Office Button menu click Save As, type file name, select file type, select drive or folder, click Save button in Save As dialog box

2. Press CTRL+S, type file name, select file type, select drive or folder, click Save button in Save As dialog box

To Use Notepad to Open and Print the CSV File

The following steps show how to use Notepad to open and print the CSV file.

1

- Click the Start button on the Windows Vista taskbar to display the Start menu and then click All Programs at the bottom of the left pane on the Start menu to display the All Programs list.

- Click Accessories in the All Programs list and then click Notepad to start Notepad.

- If the Notepad window is not maximized, click the Maximize button next to the Close button on its title bar, click File on the menu bar, and then click Open.

2

- When the Open dialog box appears, if necessary, click Computer in the Favorite Links section of the Navigation pane and then double-click UDISK 2.0 (E:) to select the USB flash drive as the new open location. Select All Files in the 'Files of type' list.

- Double-click Silver Photography Accessories Sales Rep Table CSV to display the file in Notepad (Figure 5–70).

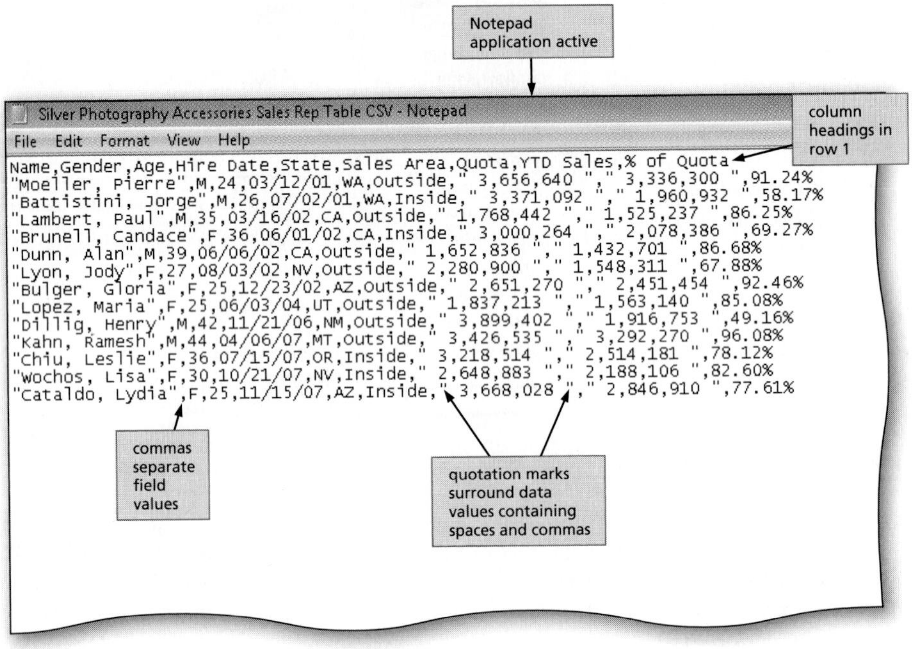

Q&A

What is shown in the CSV file?

Figure 5–70 shows the contents of the Silver Photography Accessories Sales Rep Table CSV file. The column headings are on the first line, separated by commas. Each record is on a separate line. Commas separate the fields in each record; quotation marks surround any fields with data containing spaces or commas. Data saved in this format can be read by most applications, including Excel.

Notepad
application active

column
headings in
row 1

Silver Photography Accessories Sales Rep Table CSV - Notepad

File   Edit   Format   View   Help

Name,Gender,Age,Hire Date,State,Sales Area,Quota,YTD Sales,% of Quota
"Moeller, Pierre",M,24,03/12/01,WA,Outside," 3,656,640 "," 3,336,300 ",91.24%
"Battistini, Jorge",M,26,07/02/01,WA,Inside," 3,371,092 "," 1,960,932 ",58.17%
"Lambert, Paul",M,35,03/16/02,CA,Outside," 1,768,442 "," 1,525,237 ",86.25%
"Brunell, Candace",F,36,06/01/02,CA,Inside," 3,000,264 "," 2,078,386 ",69.27%
"Dunn, Alan",M,39,06/06/02,CA,Outside," 1,652,836 "," 1,432,701 ",86.68%
"Lyon, Jody",F,27,08/03/02,NV,Outside," 2,280,900 "," 1,548,311 ",67.88%
"Bulger, Gloria",F,25,12/23/02,AZ,Outside," 2,651,270 "," 2,451,454 ",92.46%
"Lopez, Maria",F,25,06/03/04,UT,Outside," 1,837,213 "," 1,563,140 ",85.08%
"Dillig, Henry",M,42,11/21/06,NM,Outside," 3,899,402 "," 1,916,753 ",49.16%
"Kahn, Ramesh",M,44,04/06/07,MT,Outside," 3,426,535 "," 3,292,270 ",96.08%
"Chiu, Leslie",F,36,07/15/07,OR,Inside," 3,218,514 "," 2,514,181 ",78.12%
"Wochos, Lisa",F,30,10/21/07,NV,Inside," 2,648,883 "," 2,188,106 ",82.60%
"Cataldo, Lydia",F,25,11/15/07,AZ,Inside," 3,668,028 "," 2,846,910 ",77.61%

commas
separate
field
values

quotation marks
surround data
values containing
spaces and commas

Figure 5–70

3

- Click File on the menu bar and then click Print.

- When the Print dialog box appears, click the Print button to print the CSV version of the Silver Photography Accessories Sales Rep table (Figure 5–71).

- Click the Close button on the right side of the Notepad title bar to quit Notepad.

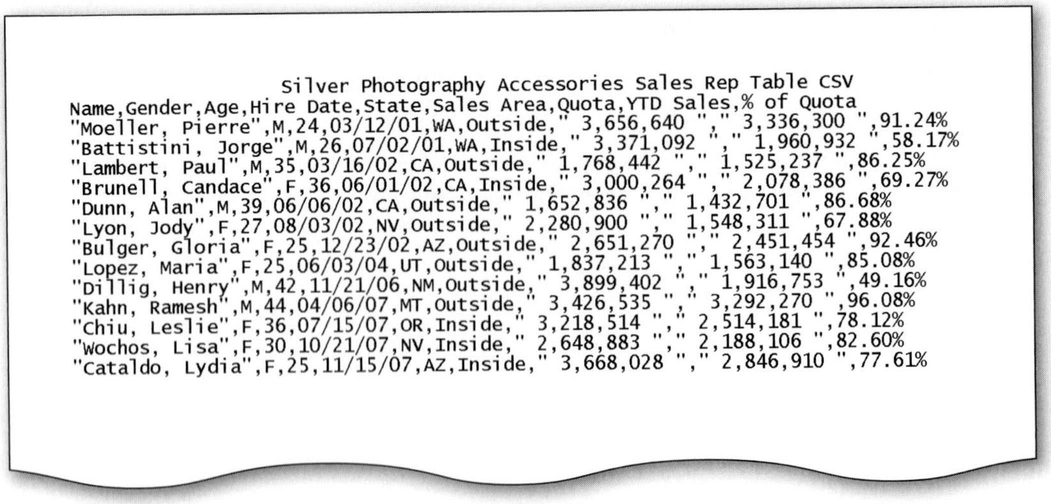

Silver Photography Accessories Sales Rep Table CSV
Name,Gender,Age,Hire Date,State,Sales Area,Quota,YTD Sales,% of Quota
"Moeller, Pierre",M,24,03/12/01,WA,Outside," 3,656,640 "," 3,336,300 ",91.24%
"Battistini, Jorge",M,26,07/02/01,WA,Inside," 3,371,092 "," 1,960,932 ",58.17%
"Lambert, Paul",M,35,03/16/02,CA,Outside," 1,768,442 "," 1,525,237 ",86.25%
"Brunell, Candace",F,36,06/01/02,CA,Inside," 3,000,264 "," 2,078,386 ",69.27%
"Dunn, Alan",M,39,06/06/02,CA,Outside," 1,652,836 "," 1,432,701 ",86.68%
"Lyon, Jody",F,27,08/03/02,NV,Outside," 2,280,900 "," 1,548,311 ",67.88%
"Bulger, Gloria",F,25,12/23/02,AZ,Outside," 2,651,270 "," 2,451,454 ",92.46%
"Lopez, Maria",F,25,06/03/04,UT,Outside," 1,837,213 "," 1,563,140 ",85.08%
"Dillig, Henry",M,42,11/21/06,NM,Outside," 3,899,402 "," 1,916,753 ",49.16%
"Kahn, Ramesh",M,44,04/06/07,MT,Outside," 3,426,535 "," 3,292,270 ",96.08%
"Chiu, Leslie",F,36,07/15/07,OR,Inside," 3,218,514 "," 2,514,181 ",78.12%
"Wochos, Lisa",F,30,10/21/07,NV,Inside," 2,648,883 "," 2,188,106 ",82.60%
"Cataldo, Lydia",F,25,11/15/07,AZ,Inside," 3,668,028 "," 2,846,910 ",77.61%

Figure 5–71

To Quit Excel

The following steps quit Excel.

1 Click the Close button on the right side of the title bar.

2 If the Microsoft Office Excel dialog box is displayed, click the No button.

Chapter Summary

In this chapter, you learned how to create, sort, and filter a table (also called a database); create subtotals; use database functions such as SUMIF and COUNTIF; and save a workbook in different file formats. The items listed below include all the new Excel skills you have learned in this chapter.

1. Format a Range as a Table (EX 346)
2. Validate Data (EX 348)
3. Modify a Table Quick Style (EX 351)
4. Enter Records in a Table (EX 353)
5. Add New Fields to a Table (EX 355)
6. Create a Lookup Table (EX 357)
7. Use the VLOOKUP Function to Determine Letter Grades (EX 359)
8. Add a Conditional Formatting Rule with an Icon Set (EX 362)
9. Use the Total Row Check Box (EX 365)
10. Print the Table (EX 368)
11. Sort a Table in Ascending Sequence by Name Using the Sort & Filter Button (EX 369)
12. Sort a Table in Descending Sequence by Name Using the Sort Z to A Button on the Data Tab (EX 370)
13. Sort a Table Using the Sort Command on a Column Heading AutoFilter Menu (EX 371)
14. Sort a Table on Multiple Fields Using the Custom Sort Command (EX 372)
15. Display Automatic Subtotals in a Table (EX 375)
16. Zoom Out on a Subtotaled Table and Use the Outline Feature (EX 377)
17. Remove Automatic Subtotals from a Table (EX 379)
18. Sort a Table Using a Column Heading List (EX 379)
19. Query a Table Using AutoFilter (EX 380)
20. Show All Records in a Table (EX 382)
21. Enter Custom Criteria Using AutoFilter (EX 383)
22. Create a Criteria Range on the Worksheet (EX 385)
23. Query a Table Using the Advanced Filter Dialog Box (EX 386)
24. Create an Extract Range and Extract Records (EX 388)
25. Use the DAVERAGE and DCOUNT Database Functions (EX 391)
26. Use the SUMIF and COUNTIF Functions (EX 393)
27. Save a Workbook in CSV File Format (EX 396)
28. Use Notepad to Open and Print the CSV File (EX 398)

If you have a SAM user profile, you may have access to hands-on instruction, practice, and assessment. Log in to your SAM account (http://sam2007.course.com) to launch any assigned training activities or exams that relate to the skills covered in this chapter.

Learn It Online

Learn It Online is a series of online student exercises that test your knowledge of chapter content and key terms.

Instructions: To complete the Learn It Online exercises, start your browser, click the Address bar, and then enter the Web address scsite.com/ex2007/learn. When the Excel 2007 Learn It Online page is displayed, click the link for the exercise you want to complete and then read the instructions.

Chapter Reinforcement TF, MC, and SA
A series of true/false, multiple choice, and short answer questions that test your knowledge of the chapter content.

Flash Cards
An interactive learning environment where you identify chapter key terms associated with displayed definitions.

Practice Test
A series of multiple choice questions that test your knowledge of chapter content and key terms.

Who Wants To Be a Computer Genius?
An interactive game that challenges your knowledge of chapter content in the style of a television quiz show.

Wheel of Terms
An interactive game that challenges your knowledge of chapter key terms in the style of the television show *Wheel of Fortune*.

Crossword Puzzle Challenge
A crossword puzzle that challenges your knowledge of key terms presented in the chapter.

Apply Your Knowledge

Reinforce the skills and apply the concepts you learned in this chapter.

Querying a List
Instructions: Assume that the figures that accompany each of the following six problems make up the criteria range for the Fritz's Luxury Kennel Guest List shown in Figure 5–72. Fill in the comparison criteria to select records from the list to solve each of these six problems. So that you understand better what is required for this assignment, the answer is given for the first problem. You can open the workbook Apply 5-1 Fritzs Luxury Kennel Guest List from the Data Files for Students and use the Filter button to verify your answers. See the inside back cover of this book for instructions for downloading the Data Files for Students or see your instructor for information on accessing the files required in this book.

Owner Name	Dog Name	Gender	Age	Breed	Cage Size
Attassi	Max	M	8	Golden Retriever	3
Koblitz	Amber	F	6	Newfoundland	3
Stanley	Goldie	F	9	Beagle	1
Athas	Muffin	M	2	Newfoundland	3
Felski	Claire	F	7	Bulldog	2
Chen	Maynard	M	5	Golden Retriever	3
Richardson	Sparky	F	4	Doberman Pinscher	3
Perez	Rocky	M	3	Bulldog	2
Dunlap	Carmy	F	1	Golden Retriever	2
Seldal	Ziggy	M	11	Beagle	1
Hong	Apollo	M	8	Doberman Pinscher	3

Figure 5–72

1. Select records that represent female dogs who are less than 5 years old.

Owner Name	Dog Name	Gender	Age	Breed	Cage Size
		F	<5		

2. Select records that have a breed of Beagle or Bulldog.

Owner Name	Dog Name	Gender	Age	Breed	Cage Size

3. Select records that represent male dogs whose owners' last names begin with the letter A and who are greater than 5 years old.

Owner Name	Dog Name	Gender	Age	Breed	Cage Size

4. Select records that represent female dogs who are at least 4 years old and need a cage size of greater than 1.

Owner Name	Dog Name	Gender	Age	Breed	Cage Size

5. Select records that represent male dogs who are Golden Retrievers or need a cage size of 3.

Owner Name	Dog Name	Gender	Age	Breed	Cage Size

6. Select records that represent dogs who are at least 4 years old and are either the Newfoundland breed or Golden Retriever breed.

Owner Name	Dog Name	Gender	Age	Breed	Cage Size

Extend Your Knowledge

Extend the skills you learned in this chapter and experiment with new skills. You may need to use Help to complete the assignment.

More Conditional Formatting

Instructions: Start Excel. Open the workbook Extend 5-1 Jensen Basketball Poles from the Data Files for Students. See the inside back cover of this book for instructions for downloading the Data Files for Students or see your instructor for information on accessing the files required in this book. You have been asked to add conditional formatting to highlight the lowest and highest total expenses, and to add conditional formatting to show data bars for net income that is greater than zero (Figure 5–73). Complete the following tasks to add and manage conditional formatting rules in the worksheet.

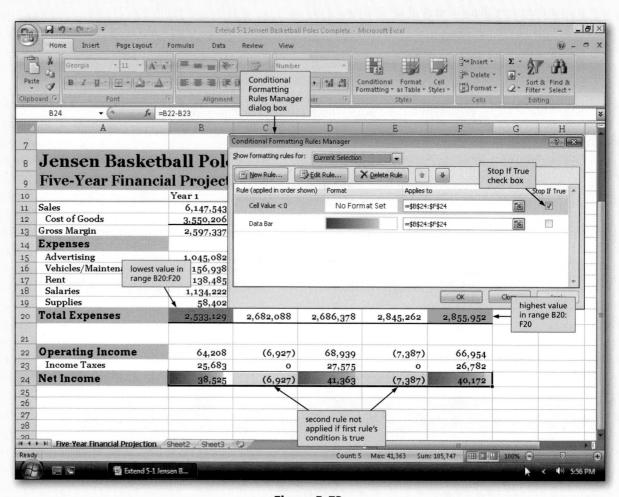

Figure 5–73

1. Save the workbook using the file name, Extend 5-1 Jensen Basketball Poles Complete. Select the range B20:F20. Click the Conditional Formatting button on the Home tab on the Ribbon and then click New Rule. When Excel displays the New Formatting Rule dialog box, select 'Format only top or bottom ranked values' in the Select a Rule Type list. In the 'Format values that rank in the' area, type 1 in the center text box. Click the Format button in the Preview area. When Excel displays the Format Cells dialog box, click the Fill tab, click the green color (column 5, row 7) in the Background Color area, and then click the OK button. Click the OK button in the New Formatting Rule dialog box.

2. With the range B20:F20 selected, add a second rule to the range following the procedure from Step 1. When creating the new rule, select Bottom in the 'Format values that rank in the' list and type 1 in the center text box. Click the Format button and then select the red color (column 2, row 7) in the Background Color area. Click the OK button in the Format Cells dialog box and then click the OK button in the New Formatting Rules dialog box.

3. With the range B20:F20 selected, click the Conditional Formatting button on the Home tab on the Ribbon and then click Manage Rules to view the rules for the range. Click the Close button in the Conditional Formatting Rules Manager dialog box.

4. Select the range B24:F24. Add a new conditional formatting rule to format all cells based on their values. Select the Data Bar format style. Select Red, Accent 1, Darker 25% (column 5, row 5) in the Bar Color palette and then close the New Formatting Rule dialog box.

5. With range B24:F24 selected, add a new conditional formatting rule. Select 'Format only cells that contain' as the rule type. Format only cells with a cell value less than zero. Do not select a format using the Format button. Make sure that the Preview area indicates that no format is set and then click the OK button to add the rule.

6. With the range B24:F24 selected, click the Conditional Formatting button on the Home tab on the Ribbon and then click Manage Rules to view the rules for the range. Click the Stop If True check box for the first rule in the dialog box to ensure that the second rule is not applied to negative values in the range (Figure 5–73). Click the OK button to close the Conditional Formatting Rules Manager dialog box.

7. Change the document properties as specified by your instructor. Change the worksheet header with your name, course number, and other information as specified by your instructor. Change the print orientation to landscape. Print the worksheet using the Fit to option. Save the workbook.

8. Select the range B15:F19. Click the Conditional Formatting button on the Home tab on the Ribbon, point to Color Scales on the Conditional Formatting menu, and then click Green – Yellow – Red Color Scale in the Color Scales gallery. Print the worksheet using the Fit to option. Do not save the workbook. Submit the assignment as requested by your instructor.

Make It Right

Analyze a workbook and correct all errors and/or improve the design.

Tables, Conditional Formatting, and Database Functions

Instructions: Start Excel. Open the workbook Make It Right 5-1 Van Dyl Kitchen Accessories Sales Rep List and then save the file using the file name, Van Dyl Kitchen Accessories Sales Rep List Complete. See the inside back cover of this book for instructions for downloading the Data Files for Students, or see your instructor for information on accessing the files required for this book. Correct the following table, conditional formatting, and database function problems so that the worksheet appears as shown in Figure 5–74.

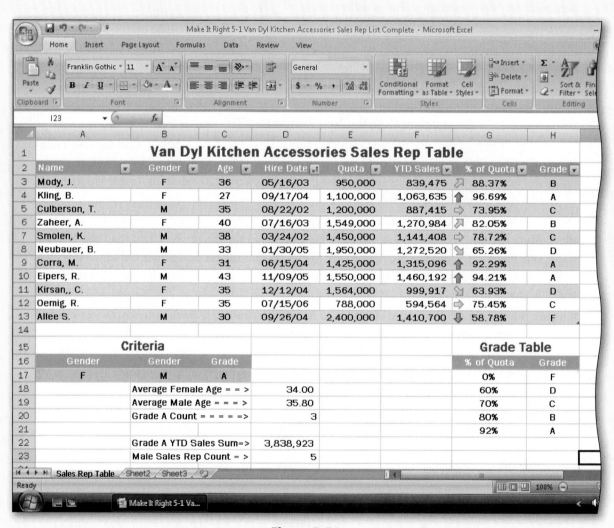

Figure 5–74

1. Use the Table Style Options group on the Design tab on the Ribbon to make certain that the table in the worksheet includes banded rows.

2. The table does not show all of the rows because the Age field is filtered. Ensure that all rows in the table are displayed.

3. The conditional formatting for the % of Quota field uses only four icons in the rule instead of five. Change the icon style of the rule to use 5 Arrows (Colored).

4. The values used by the conditional formatting rule to choose each arrow style are incorrect and should be based on the values listed in the grade table. Edit the conditional formatting rule so that the values in the grade table are reflected in the rules.

5. Correct the third argument in the DAVERAGE function used to calculate the average male age.

6. Correct the second and third arguments in the SUMIF function used to calculate the grade A YTD sales sum.

7. Change the document properties as specified by your instructor. Change the worksheet header with your name, course number, and other information requested by your instructor.

8. Save the workbook and submit the revised workbook as requested by your instructor.

In the Lab

Create a workbook using the guidelines, concepts, and skills presented in this chapter. Labs are listed in order of increasing difficulty.

Lab 1: Creating, Filtering, and Sorting a Table and Determining Subtotals

Problem: You are employed by Whitman Publishing, a company that supplies textbooks to the college market. The national sales force is divided into districts within divisions within regions. The three regions are the Southeast region (1), Midwest region (2), and Western region (3). The director of the Accounting department has asked you to create a sales rep table (Figure 5–75), run queries against the table, generate various sorted reports, and generate subtotal information.

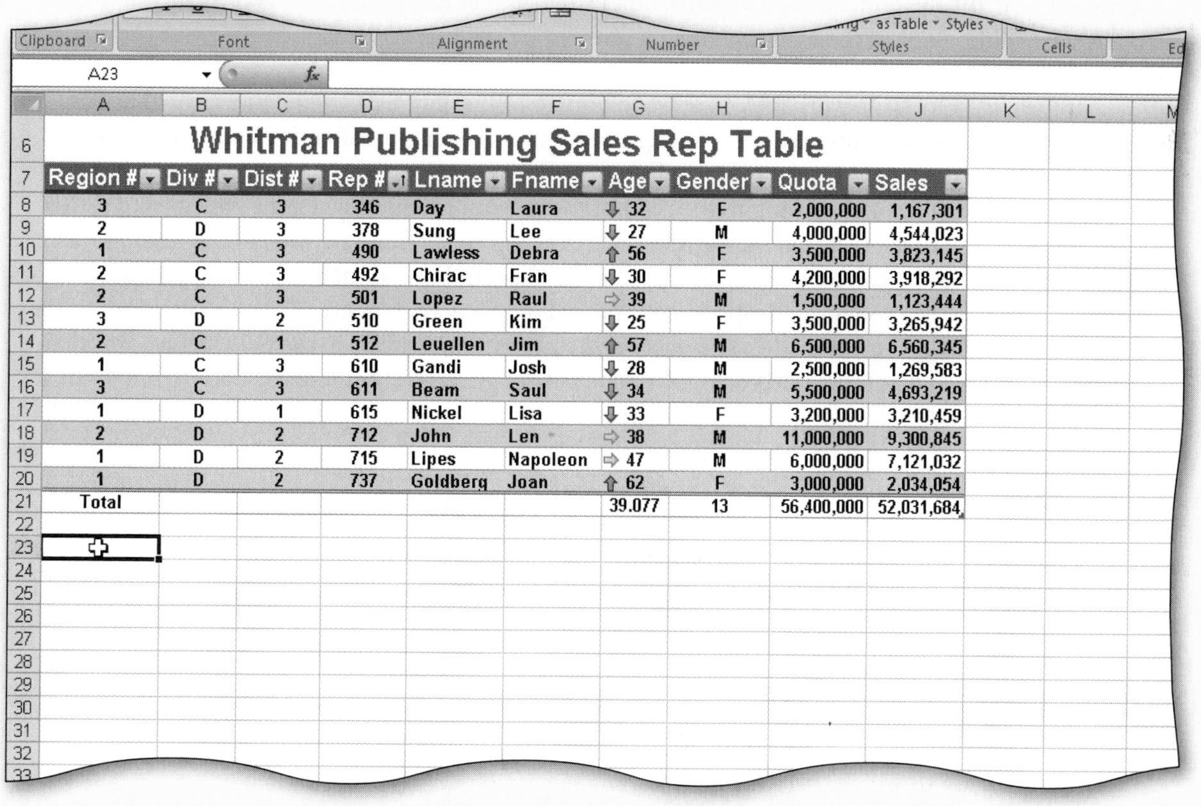

Whitman Publishing Sales Rep Table

Region #	Div #	Dist #	Rep #	Lname	Fname	Age	Gender	Quota	Sales
3	C	3	346	Day	Laura	⬇ 32	F	2,000,000	1,167,301
2	D	3	378	Sung	Lee	⬇ 27	M	4,000,000	4,544,023
1	C	3	490	Lawless	Debra	⬆ 56	F	3,500,000	3,823,145
2	C	3	492	Chirac	Fran	⬇ 30	F	4,200,000	3,918,292
2	C	3	501	Lopez	Raul	⇨ 39	M	1,500,000	1,123,444
3	D	2	510	Green	Kim	⬇ 25	F	3,500,000	3,265,942
2	C	1	512	Leuellen	Jim	⬆ 57	M	6,500,000	6,560,345
1	C	3	610	Gandi	Josh	⬇ 28	M	2,500,000	1,269,583
3	C	3	611	Beam	Saul	⬇ 34	M	5,500,000	4,693,219
1	D	1	615	Nickel	Lisa	⬇ 33	F	3,200,000	3,210,459
2	D	2	712	John	Len	⇨ 38	M	11,000,000	9,300,845
1	D	2	715	Lipes	Napoleon	⇨ 47	M	6,000,000	7,121,032
1	D	2	737	Goldberg	Joan	⬆ 62	F	3,000,000	2,034,054
Total						39.077	13	56,400,000	52,031,684

Figure 5–75

Continued >

In the Lab *continued*

Instructions Part 1: Create the table shown in Figure 5–75 on the previous page using the techniques learned in this chapter and following the instructions below.

1. Bold the entire worksheet.

2. Enter the table title in row 6 and apply the Title cell style. Enter and format the field names in row 7.

3. Use the Format as Table button on the Home tab on the Ribbon to create a table using data from the range A7:J7. Use Table Style Medium 3 to format the table. Format the first row below the field names and then enter the rows of data shown in rows 8 through 20 of Figure 5–75. Change the Sheet1 tab name to Whitman Publishing Sales Reps and delete Sheet2 and Sheet3.

4. With a cell in the table active, click the Design tab on the Ribbon and then click the Total Row check box in the Table Style Options group. Show the record count in the Gender column, the average age in the Age column, and sums in the Quota and Sales columns as shown in Figure 5–75.

5. Add the icon set 3 arrows (colored) using conditional formatting to the Age column (G8:G20): Age >=50; 35=<Age<50; Age<35 as shown in Figure 5–75. To add the conditional formatting, select the range G8:G20, click the Conditional Formatting button on the Home tab on the Ribbon, and click the New Rule command. When Excel displays the New Formatting Rule dialog box, click the Icon Style box arrow, scroll up and click 3 Arrows (Colored). Click the Value box and enter the Age limits described earlier. Change the Type boxes to Number.

6. Change the document properties as specified by your instructor. Change the worksheet header with your name, course number, and other information requested by your instructor.

7. Use the Orientation button on the Page Layout tab on the Ribbon to change the orientation to Landscape. Print the table. Save the workbook using the file name, Lab 5-1 Whitman Publishing Sales Rep Table. Submit the assignment as requested by your instructor.

Instructions Part 2: Open the workbook Lab 5-1 Whitman Publishing Sales Rep Table created in Part 1. Do not save the workbook in this part. Step through each query exercise in Table 5–7 and print (or write down for submission to your instructor) the results for each. To complete a filter exercise, use the AutoFilter technique. If the arrows are not showing to the right of the column headings when the table is active, then click the Filter button on the Data tab on the Ribbon. Select the appropriate arrow(s) to the right of the field names and option(s) on the corresponding menus. Use the Custom Filter option on the Number Filters list for field names that do not contain appropriate selections. Following each query, click the Filter button on the Data tab on the Ribbon twice to clear the query and reactivate the arrows in the field names. You should end up with the following number of records for Filters 1 through 12: 1 = 7; 2 = 6; 3 = 1; 4 = 2; 5 = 4; 6 = 1; 7 = 2; 8 = 3; 9 = 0; 10 = 4; 11 = 9; and 12 = 13. When you are finished querying the table, close the workbook without saving changes. Submit the assignment as requested by your instructor.

Table 5–7 Whitman Publishing Sales Rep Table Filter Criteria

Filter	Region	Div	Dist	Rep	Lname	Fname	Age	Gender	Quota	Sales
1								M		
2		C	3							
3	2	D	2							
4			2						>5,000,000	
5							>30	F		
6							>40 and < 50			
7							>50			>3,500,000
8	1	D								
9	1						<39	F		>4,000,000
10								M	>=5,500,000	
11				>=500						
12	All	All	All	All	All	All	All	All	All	All

Instructions Part 3: Open the workbook Lab 5-1 Whitman Publishing Sales Rep Table created in Part 1. Do not save the workbook in this part. Sort the table according to the following six sort problems. Print the table for each sort problem in landscape orientation using the Fit to option (or write down the last name in the first record for submission to your instructor). Begin problems 2 through 6 by sorting the Rep field in ascending sequence to sort the table back into its original order.

1. Sort the table in descending sequence by region.
2. Sort the table by district within division within region. All three sort keys are to be in ascending sequence.
3. Sort the table by division within region. Both sort keys are to be in descending sequence.
4. Sort the table by representative number within district within division within region. All four sort keys are to be in ascending sequence.
5. Sort the table in descending sequence by sales.
6. Sort the table by district within division within region. All three sort keys are to be in descending sequence.
7. Hide columns I and J by selecting them and pressing CTRL+0 (zero). Print the table. Select columns H and K. Press CTRL+SHIFT+RIGHT PARENTHESIS to display the hidden columns. Close the Lab 5-1 Whitman Publishing Sales Rep Table workbook without saving changes. Submit the assignment as requested by your instructor.

Instructions Part 4: Open the Lab 5-1 Whitman Publishing Sales Rep Table workbook created in Part 1 and complete the following tasks. Do not save the workbook in this part.

1. Click a cell in the table to activate the table. Click the Design tab on the Ribbon and then click the Total Row check box to remove the total row. Sort the table by district within division within region. Select ascending sequence for all three sort keys.
2. Select cell A8. Right-click anywhere in the table, point to the Table command on the shortcut menu, and then click the Convert to Range command on the Table submenu. When Excel displays the Microsoft Office Excel dialog box, click the Yes button to convert the table to a range. Click the Data tab on the Ribbon and then click the Subtotal button on the Ribbon. When Excel displays the Subtotal dialog box, click the 'At each change in' box arrow and then click Region #. If necessary, select Sum in the Use function list. In the 'Add subtotal to' list, click Quota and Sales to select them and then click the OK button. Print the table. Click row level symbol 1 and print

Continued >

In the Lab *continued*

the table. Click row level symbol 2 and print the table. Click row level symbol 3. Click the Subtotal button on the Ribbon and then click the Remove All button in the Subtotal dialog box to remove all subtotals. Close the workbook without saving changes. Submit the assignment as requested by your instructor.

Instructions Part 5:   Open the Lab 5-1 Whitman Publishing Sales Rep Table workbook created in Part 1. Copy the table (range A7:J20) to a new workbook. Save the new workbook in a CSV (Comma delimited) file format using the file name, Lab 5-1 Whitman Publishing Sales Rep Table CSV. Close the workbook. Start Notepad and open the CSV file. Print the CSV file. Close Notepad. Open the CSV file in Excel. Quit Excel. Submit the assignment as requested by your instructor.

In the Lab

Lab 2: Sorting, Finding, and Advanced Filtering

Problem: Computer Consultants, Inc. specializes in supplying computer consultants to companies in need of programmers. The company uses a table (Figure 5–76) that shows whether a consultant is knowledgeable in a programming language.

The chief financial officer, Cheryl Riiz, has asked you to sort, query, and determine some statistics from the table. Carefully label each required printout by using the part number and step. If a step results in multiple printouts, label them a, b, c, and so on.

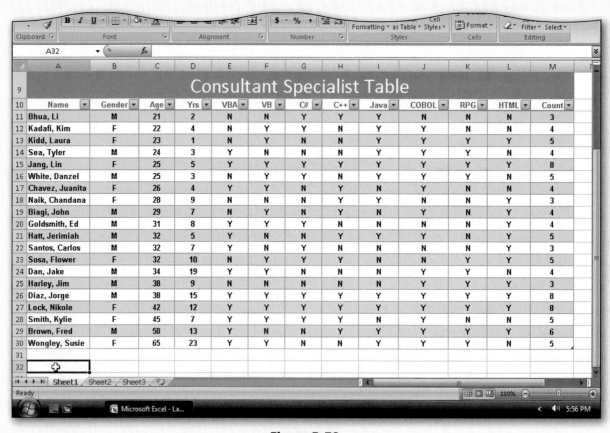

Name	Gender	Age	Yrs	VBA	VB	C#	C++	Java	COBOL	RPG	HTML	Count
Bhua, Li	M	21	2	N	N	Y	Y	Y	N	N	N	3
Kadafi, Kim	F	22	4	N	Y	Y	N	Y	Y	N	N	4
Kidd, Laura	F	23	1	N	Y	N	N	Y	Y	Y	Y	5
Sea, Tyler	M	24	3	Y	N	N	N	Y	Y	Y	N	4
Jang, Lin	F	25	5	Y	Y	Y	Y	Y	Y	Y	Y	8
White, Danzel	M	25	3	N	Y	Y	N	Y	Y	Y	N	5
Chavez, Juanita	F	26	4	Y	Y	N	Y	N	Y	N	N	4
Naik, Chandana	F	28	9	N	N	N	Y	Y	N	N	Y	3
Biagi, John	M	29	7	N	Y	N	Y	N	Y	N	Y	4
Goldsmith, Ed	M	31	8	Y	Y	Y	N	N	N	N	Y	4
Hatt, Jerimiah	M	32	5	Y	Y	N	Y	Y	Y	N	Y	5
Santos, Carlos	M	32	7	Y	N	Y	N	N	N	N	Y	3
Sosa, Flower	F	32	10	N	Y	Y	Y	N	N	Y	Y	5
Dan, Jake	M	34	19	Y	Y	N	N	N	Y	Y	N	4
Harley, Jim	M	38	9	N	N	N	N	N	Y	Y	Y	3
Diaz, Jorge	M	38	15	Y	Y	Y	Y	Y	Y	Y	Y	8
Lock, Nikole	F	42	12	Y	Y	Y	Y	Y	Y	Y	Y	8
Smith, Kylie	F	45	7	Y	Y	Y	Y	N	Y	N	N	5
Brown, Fred	M	50	13	Y	N	N	Y	Y	Y	Y	Y	6
Wongley, Susie	F	65	23	Y	Y	N	N	Y	Y	Y	N	5

Figure 5–76

Instructions Part 1: Start Excel and perform the following tasks.

1. Open the workbook Lab 5-2 Consultant Specialist Table from the Data Files for Students. See the inside back cover of this book for instructions for downloading the Data Files for Students or see your instructor for information on accessing the files required in this book. Do not save the workbook in this part.

2. Complete the following tasks:

   a. Sort the records in the table into descending sequence by name. Susie Wongley should appear first in the table. Li Bhua should appear last. Print the table. Undo the sort.

   b. Sort the records in the table by age within gender. Select ascending sequence for the age and descending sequence for gender. Li Bhua should be the first record. Print the table. Undo the sort.

   c. Sort the table by Java within C++ within C# within VB. Apply sort descending for all four fields. Sort the table first on Java, then C++, then C#, and finally VB. Those who are proficient in all four programming languages will rise to the top of the table. Jorge Diaz should be the first record. Print the table. Close the workbook without saving it. Submit the assignment as requested by your instructor.

Instructions Part 2: Open the workbook Lab 5-2 Consultant Specialist Table (Figure 5–76) from the Data Files for Students. Do not save the workbook in this part. Select a cell within the table. If the column heading arrows do not appear, then click Filter on the Data tab on the Ribbon. Use the column heading arrows to find the records that meet the criteria in items 1 through 4 below. Use the Show All command on the Filter submenu before starting items 2, 3, and 4. Print the table for each problem. You should end up with the following number of records for items 1 through 4: item 1 should have 6; item 2 should have 3; item 3 should have 3; and item 4 should have 7. Close the workbook without saving the changes. Submit the assignment as requested by your instructor.

1. Find all records that represent employees who are male and are proficient in Java.

2. Find all records that represent employees with more than 9 years of experience (Yrs) and who are certified in VB and HTML.

3. Find all records that represent female employees who are at least 30 years old and are proficient in COBOL.

4. Find all records that represent employees who have at least 5 years of experience (Yrs) and who are proficient in VBA and HTML.

Instructions Part 3: Open the workbook Lab 5-2 Consultant Specialist Table from the Data Files for Students and then save the workbook using the file name, Lab 5-2 Consultant Specialist Table Final. Perform the following tasks:.

1. Add a criteria range by copying the table title and field names (range A9:M10) to the range A1:M2 (Figure 5–77). Change cell A1 to Criteria Area and then color the title area as shown in Figure 5–77. Use the Name box in the formula bar to name the criteria range (A2:M3) Criteria.

	A	B	C	D	E	F	G	H	I	J	K	L	M	N
1						Criteria Area								
2	Name	Gender	Age	Yrs	VBA	VB	C#	C++	Java	COBOL	RPG	HTML	Count	
3		M	>30											
4														
5														
6														
7														

Figure 5–77

Continued >

In the Lab *continued*

2. Add an extract range by copying the table title and field names (range A9:M10) to the range A35:M36 (Figure 5–78). Change cell A35 to Extract Area and then color the title area as shown in Figure 5–78. Use the Name box in the formula bar to name the extract range (range A36:M36) Extract.

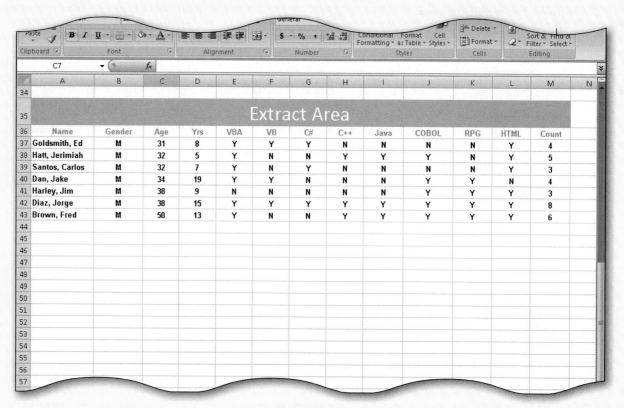

	Name	Gender	Age	Yrs	VBA	VB	C#	C++	Java	COBOL	RPG	HTML	Count
34													
35	Extract Area												
36	Name	Gender	Age	Yrs	VBA	VB	C#	C++	Java	COBOL	RPG	HTML	Count
37	Goldsmith, Ed	M	31	8	Y	Y	Y	N	N	N	N	Y	4
38	Hatt, Jerimiah	M	32	5	Y	N	N	Y	Y	Y	N	Y	5
39	Santos, Carlos	M	32	7	Y	N	Y	N	N	N	N	Y	3
40	Dan, Jake	M	34	19	Y	Y	N	N	N	Y	Y	N	4
41	Harley, Jim	M	38	9	N	N	N	N	N	Y	Y	Y	3
42	Diaz, Jorge	M	38	15	Y	Y	Y	Y	Y	Y	Y	Y	8
43	Brown, Fred	M	50	13	Y	N	N	Y	Y	Y	Y	Y	6

Figure 5–78

3. With the table active, use the Advanced button on the Data tab on the Ribbon to extract records that pass the tests listed below in a through d. Print the entire worksheet using landscape orientation and the Fit to option for each extract.

   a. Extract the records that represent employees who are male and older than 30 (Figure 5–77 on the previous page). You should extract seven records (Figure 5–78).

   b. Extract the records that represent female employees who are proficient in Java, but not in RPG. You should extract two records.

   c. Extract the records that represent male employees who are at least 35 years old and are proficient in at least four programming languages. The field Count in column M uses the COUNTIF function to count the number of Ys in a record. A count of 4 means the record represents a specialist with expertise in four areas. You should extract two records.

   d. Extract the records that represent employees who are proficient in three programming languages or fewer. You should extract 4 records.

4. Change the document properties as specified by your instructor. Change the worksheet header with your name, course number, and other information as specified by your instructor. Save the workbook using the file name, Lab 5-2 Consultant Specialist Table Final. Close the workbook. Submit the assignment as requested by your instructor.

Instructions Part 4: Open the workbook Lab 5-2 Consultant Specialist Table Final created in Part 3. If you did not complete Part 3, then open Lab 5-2 Consultant Specialist Table from the Data Files for Students. Perform the following tasks:

1. Scroll to the right to display cell G1 in the upper-left corner of the window. Enter the criteria in the range O1:Q3 as shown in Figure 5–79. Enter the row titles in cells O5:O10 as shown in Figure 5–79.

2. Use the database function DAVERAGE and the appropriate criteria in the range O2:Q3 to determine the average age of the males and females in the range. Use the table function DCOUNT and the appropriate criteria in the range O2:Q3 to determine the record count of those who are proficient in HTML. The DCOUNT function requires that you choose a numeric field in the table to count, such as Age.

3. Use the SUMIF function to determine the Java Y Sum Count in cell R9. That is, sum the Count field for all records containing a Y in the Java column. Use the COUNTIF function to determine the HTML N Count in cell R10.

4. Print the worksheet in landscape orientation using the Fit to option. Save the workbook using the file name, Lab 5-2 Consultant Specialist Table Final. Submit the assignment as requested by your instructor.

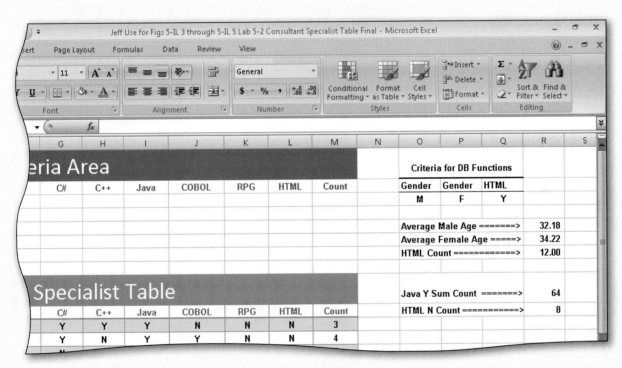

Figure 5–79

In the Lab

Lab 3: Creating a Table with a Lookup Function

Problem: You are a member of the Do-Gooders' Student Club, a club for young adults interested in helping the less fortunate. The president has asked for a volunteer to create a table of the club's members (Figure 5–80). You decide it is a great opportunity to show your Excel skills. Besides including a member's GPA in the table, the president also would like a GPA letter grade assigned to each member based on the GPA value in column G.

Instructions Part 1: Perform the following tasks to create the table shown in the range A7:H17 in Figure 5–80.

1. Bold the entire worksheet. Create the table shown in Figure 5–80 using the techniques learned in this chapter. Assign appropriate formats to row 8, the row immediately below the field names. Rename the Sheet1 tab and delete Sheet2 and Sheet3.

2. Enter the data shown in the range A8:G17.

3. Enter the Grade table in the range J6:K20. In cell H8, enter the function =vlookup(g8, j8:k20, 2) to determine the letter grade that corresponds to the GPA in cell G8. Copy the function in cell H8 to the range H9:H17.

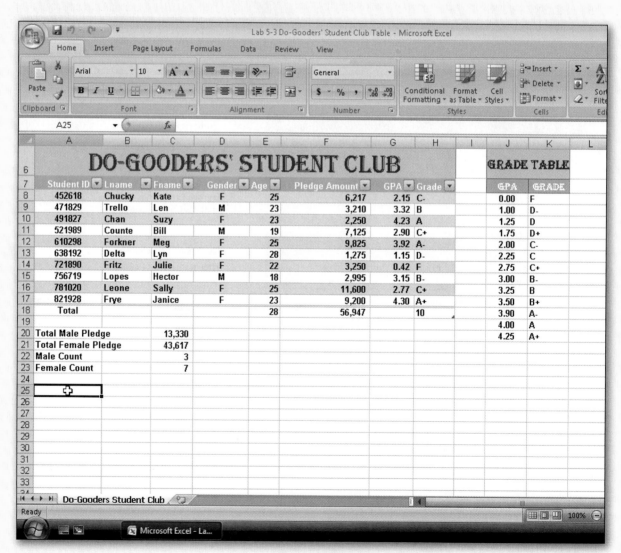

Figure 5–80

4. Select the Total Row option on the Design tab on the Ribbon to determine the maximum age, the pledge amount, and the record count in the Grade column in row 18.

5. Enter the total row headings in the range A20:A23. Use the SUMIF and COUNTIF functions to determine the totals in the range C20:C23.

6. Change the document properties as specified by your instructor. Change the worksheet header with your name, course number, and other information as specified by your instructor.

7. Save the workbook using the file name, Lab 5-3 Do-Gooders' Student Club Table. Print the worksheet in landscape orientation. At the bottom of the printout, explain why the dollar signs ($) are necessary in the VLOOKUP function in Step 3. Submit the assignment as requested by your instructor.

Instructions Part 2: Open the workbook Lab 5-3 Do-Gooders' Student Club Table. Do not save the workbook in this part. Sort the table as follows. Print the table after each sort. After completing the third sort, close the workbook without saving the changes.

1. Sort the table in ascending sequence by the Pledge Amount.

2. Sort the table by GPA within Gender. Use descending sequence for both fields.

3. Sort the table by Age within Gender. Use ascending sequence for both fields.

Instructions Part 3: Open the workbook Lab 5-3 Do-Gooders' Student Club Table and then save the file using the file name, Lab 5-3 Do Gooders' Student Club Table Final. Use the concepts and techniques presented in this chapter to set up a Criteria area above the table, set up an Extract area below the Grade table, and complete the following extractions. Extract the records that meet the following three criteria sets and print the worksheet for each:

1. Gender =F; GPA > 3.50 (Three records pass the test.)

2. Age > 23 (Four records pass the test.)

3. Gender = M; Age < 21 (Two records pass the test.)

Extract the records that meet the following criteria: 21 < Age < 25. It is necessary that you add a second field called Age to the immediate right of the Criteria range, delete the name Criteria, and then define the Criteria range to include the new field. Four records pass the final test. Select a cell outside the table and print the workbook in landscape orientation. Save the workbook with the last criteria range. Submit the assignment as requested by your instructor.

Cases and Places

Apply your creative thinking and problem solving skills to design and implement a solution.

● EASIER   ●● MORE DIFFICULT

● 1: Inventory Level Priority

Create an inventory table from the data in Table 5–8. Also include an Amount field and a Priority field. Both are calculated columns. Amount equals Inventory times Price. Create a Priority Code table in the range I1:J6 using the data shown in Table 5–9. Use the VLOOKUP function to determine the priority to assign to each record. Add the total row to the table. Print the worksheet in landscape orientation using the Fit to option. Save the workbook.

Table 5–8 Educational Percussion, Inc. Inventory List

Item number	Description	Inventory	Price
B60338	Bar Chime	619	14.25
M44910	Maraca	873	9.50
C71610	Castanet	579	17.60
S80787	Shekere	537	22.50
T36275	Tambourine	764	12.45
T74695	Triangle	208	8.30
W59366	Woodblock	268	7.95
C24890	Clave	385	13.80
C87343	Cabasa	387	14.05
W15840	Whistle	699	6.85
C49955	Cowbell	237	18.25

Table 5–9 Priority Codes

Inventory	Priority
0	1
250	2
400	3
600	4
800	5

● 2: Conditional Formatting and Sorting a Table

Open the table created in Cases and Places Exercise 1. Add conditional formatting to the Priority field using the Icon Sets format style and the 5 Ratings icon style. Complete the following three sorts, print each sorted version of the table, and then undo the sorts in preparation for the next sort: (a) sort the table in ascending sequence (smallest to largest) by inventory, (b) sort the table by amount (ascending) within priority code (descending), and (c) sort the table in descending sequence by priority code. With the table sorted by priority, toggle off the total row, convert the table to a range, and then use the Subtotal button on the Data tab on the Ribbon to determine subtotals for each priority code. Print the table with the subtotals. Save the workbook with the subtotals.

● 3: Filtering a Table and Multiple Conditional Formats

Open the table created in Cases and Places Exercise 1. Add a second conditional format to the priority code field using a Data Bar format style and a Bar color of your choice. If necessary remove the subtotals and then convert the range back to a table. Filter (query) the table using the column heading arrows. Make sure you show all records before each query. Print the table for each of the following queries: (1) priority code equal to 2, (2) inventory greater than 250 and less than 600, (3) priority code equals 1 and inventory greater than 30, and (4) price greater than 9.00. The number of records that show in the queries are: (1) 3, (2) 5, (3) 2, and (4) 8.

● ● 4: Creating a Table of Companies

Make It Personal

Gather information about companies at which you may want to work in your next job. Obtain information for at least ten companies in five different states. Include company name, state, city, miles from your current residence, and assign a rating for each company between 1 and 4, with 4 being the most preferred. Add a conditional format using the Data Bar format style, edit the formatting rule to show only bars, and change the width of the column to at least 20 characters. Complete the following sorts, print each sorted version of the table, and then undo the sorts in preparation for the next sort: (a) alphabetically (A to Z) by state, and (b) descending (smallest to largest) by miles from home. Filter the list for records with a preference greater than 2. Print the table and then show all of the records. Group the records by state, using the Average function in the Use function list in the Subtotal dialog box. Print the worksheet.

● ● 5: Creating a Table of Students

Working Together

Have your group design a table that includes a row for each student. The table should contain the following information: (1) last initial and first initial, (2) gender, (3) age, (4) college start date, (5) resident state, (6) major, (7) credit hours required for degree, (8) credit hours towards degree, (9) percent of degree completed (computational field), (10) anticipated graduation year, and (11) letter grade based on GPA (1 = D, 2 = C, 3 = B, and 4 = A). Use the concepts and techniques introduced in this chapter to design and create a table from the data collected along with a grade field that corresponds to the GPA. Add conditional formatting to the gender, age, percent of degree completed, and anticipated graduation year fields. Also, run sorts, determine subtotals, and use the database, COUNTIF, and SUMIF functions to generate statistics.

6 Creating Templates and Working with Multiple Worksheets and Workbooks

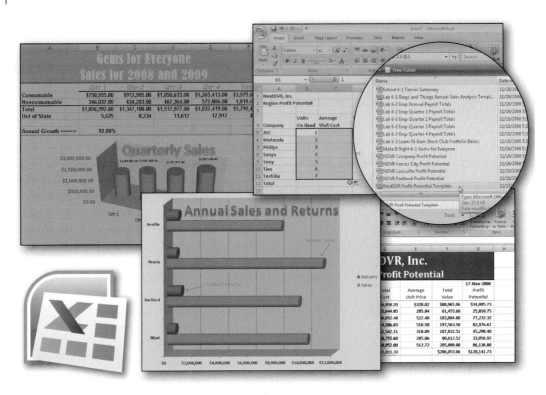

Objectives

You will have mastered the material in this chapter when you can:

- Create and use a template
- Use the ROUND function
- Utilize custom format codes
- Define, apply, and remove a style
- Add a worksheet to a workbook
- Create formulas that use 3-D cell references
- Draw a Clustered Cone chart
- Use WordArt to create a title and create and modify shapes
- Add a header or footer, change margins, and insert and move a page break
- Save a workbook as a PDF or XPS file
- Use the Find and Replace commands
- Create a workspace
- Consolidate data by linking workbooks

6 | Creating Templates and Working with Multiple Worksheets and Workbooks

Introduction

Many business applications require data from several worksheets to be summarized on one worksheet. For example, a company may keep data from various regions in different worksheets. If you enter each region's inventory data on a worksheet in a workbook, you can click the sheet tabs at the bottom of the Excel window to move from worksheet to worksheet, or region to region. On another, separate worksheet, you then can enter formulas that reference cells on the other worksheets, which allows you to summarize worksheet data. The process of summarizing data included on multiple worksheets on one worksheet is called **consolidation**.

Another important concept presented in this chapter is the use of a template. A **template** is a special workbook you can create and then use as a pattern to create new, similar workbooks or worksheets. A template usually consists of a general format (worksheet title, column and row titles, and numeric format) and formulas that are common to all the worksheets. One efficient way to create the workbook is first to create a template, save the template, and then copy the template to a workbook as many times as necessary.

Project — Profit Potential Worksheets with Cone Chart

The project in the chapter follows proper design guidelines and uses Excel to create the worksheet shown in Figure 6–1. NextDVR sells DVR (digital video recorder) equipment to cable television providers throughout the United States. The company purchases DVR equipment from a number of suppliers and then resells the equipment to customers in three regional offices. The company's chief operating officer would like to know the profit potential of the inventory currently stored at the three regional offices. She also would like to see the regional information on separate worksheets, and then consolidated into one worksheet.

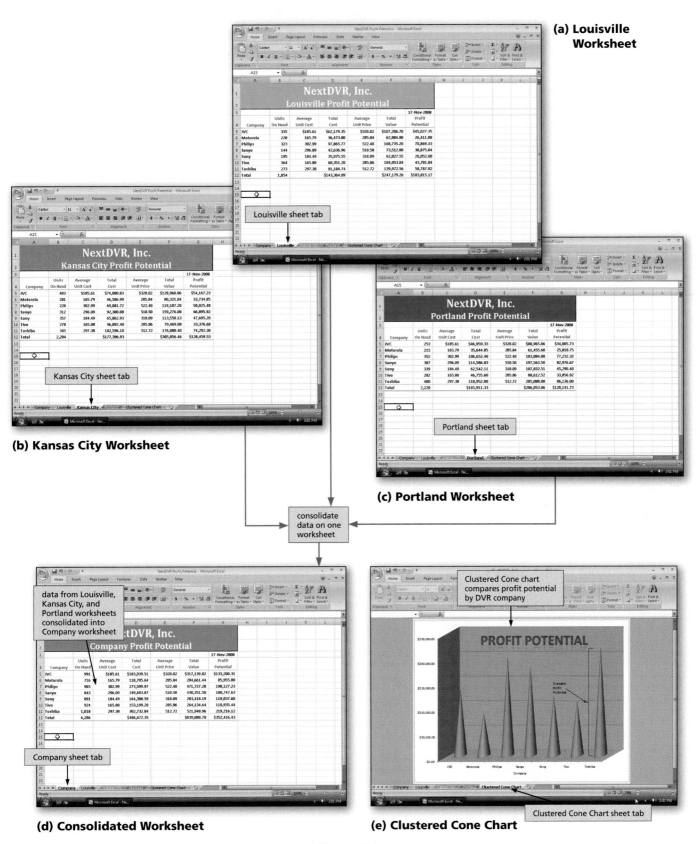

(a) Louisville Worksheet

(b) Kansas City Worksheet

(c) Portland Worksheet

(d) Consolidated Worksheet

(e) Clustered Cone Chart

Figure 6–1

The requirements document for the NextDVR Profit Potential workbook is shown in Figure 6–2. It includes the needs, source of data, summary of calculations, chart requirements, special requirements, and other facts about its development.

BTW

Workbook Survival
For workbooks to be successful and survive their expected life cycle in a business environment, they must be well documented and easy to understand. You document a workbook by adding comments to cells that contain complex formulas or to cells containing content that may not be understood easily. The documentation also should take into consideration those who will maintain the workbook after you leave. You create easy to understand workbooks by reviewing alternative designs prior to creating the workbook. The more time you spend documenting and designing a workbook, the easier it will be for users and spreadsheet maintenance specialists to understand.

REQUEST FOR NEW WORKBOOK

Date Submitted:	October 6, 2008
Submitted By:	Chip Yerkes
Worksheet Title:	NextDVR, Inc. Profit Potential
Needs:	The needs are as follows: 1. A template (Figure 6-3a) that can be used to create similar worksheets. 2. A workbook containing three worksheets for the three regions in which the company operates and one worksheet to consolidate the company data. 3. A chart (Figure 6-3b) that compares the profit potential of the different DVRs in inventory, by company or brand. The chart should be placed on a separate sheet.
Source of Data:	The data will be collected and organized by the chief financial officer, Chip Yerkes.
Calculations:	Include the following formulas in the template for each camera: 1. Total Cost = Units On Hand * Average Unit Cost 2. Average Unit Price = Average Unit Cost / (1 − .42) 3. Total Value = Units On Hand * Average Unit Price 4. Profit Potential = Total Value − Total Cost 5. Use the SUM function to determine totals. 6. After using the template to create the multiple-worksheet workbook, use the SUM function to determine the units on hand totals on the Company sheet (Figure 6-1d). **Note:** Use dummy data in the template to verify the formulas. Round the Average Unit Price to the nearest penny.
Chart Requirements:	Include a chart sheet with a Clustered Cone chart that compares the profit potential for each of the DVR brands listed on the Company sheet. Use a text box to create a callout to highlight the cone representing the DVR brand with the greatest profit potential.
Special Requirements:	Investigate a way NextDVR can consolidate data from multiple workbooks into another workbook.

Approvals

Approval Status:	X	Approved
		Rejected
Approved By:	Jason Ganden	
Date:	October 15, 2008	
Assigned To:	J. Quasney, Spreadsheet Specialist	

Figure 6–2

Overview

As you read this chapter, you will learn how to create the worksheet shown in Figure 6–1 by performing these general tasks:

- Create and format the template
- Add a worksheet to the workbook
- Reference data on other worksheets
- Create a Clustered Cone chart and add WordArt to the chart
- Print the worksheet with proper page breaks
- Create a workspace and consolidate data by linking workbooks

Plan Ahead

General Project Decisions

While creating an Excel worksheet, you need to make several decisions that will determine the appearance and characteristics of the finished worksheet. As you create the worksheet to meet the requirements shown in Figure 6–2, you should follow these general guidelines:

1. Design the template and plan the formatting. Templates help speed and simplify work because Excel users often work with the same types of problems over and over again. Using a template allows you to begin your work with a preformatted worksheet. In the case of the NextDVR Profit Potential worksheet, the template saves the work of formatting the three region worksheets and the consolidated worksheet. The formatting is done once in the template, and then that formatting automatically is carried over to the new worksheets.

2. Identify additional worksheets needed in the workbook. After the template is created using dummy data and the required formulas (Figure 6–4 on page EX 424) and then saved, it will be copied to a workbook made up of four worksheets. Actual data for the three regions will replace the dummy data on the three region worksheets. The data from the three region worksheets then will be consolidated on the company worksheet.

3. Plan the layout and location of the required chart. The chart requires additional artwork, including a callout, and would therefore be more suited for placement on a new worksheet. A Clustered Cone chart type is a proper choice for this chart because data from a few vendors is compared. The tapering of the cones allows space for additional elements, such as the callout, without any overlapping.

4. Examine the alternatives for printing a number of worksheets, including headers, margins, and page breaks. When working with multiple worksheets, using properly formatted page headers and footers is important. Excel allows you to print page numbers and the sheet name of each sheet. In addition, margins and page breaks also can be adjusted to provide professional looking printed worksheets.

5. Identify workbooks to be consolidated into a workspace and then linked to create a consolidated workbook of the initial workbooks. The special requirement for the project listed in the requirements document (Figure 6–2) asks that methods to combine workbooks together should be investigated. Each of the three regions has sent a similar workbook that represents their own profit potentials. Excel allows you to work with these workbooks in a workspace and then link the workbooks together to provide a consolidated view of the data in the workbooks.

(continued)

Plan Ahead

(continued)

In addition, using a sketch of the worksheet can help you visualize its design. The sketch of the template (Figure 6–3a) consists of titles, column and row headings, location of data values, and a general idea of the desired formatting. The sketch of the Clustered Cone chart (Figure 6–3b) consists of a chart title, which will be added using WordArt, and a callout that emphasizes the cylinder representing the greatest profit potential.

When necessary, more specific details concerning the above guidelines are presented at appropriate points in the chapter. The chapter also will identify the actions you perform and decisions made regarding these guidelines during the creation of the worksheet shown in Figure 6–1 on page EX 419.

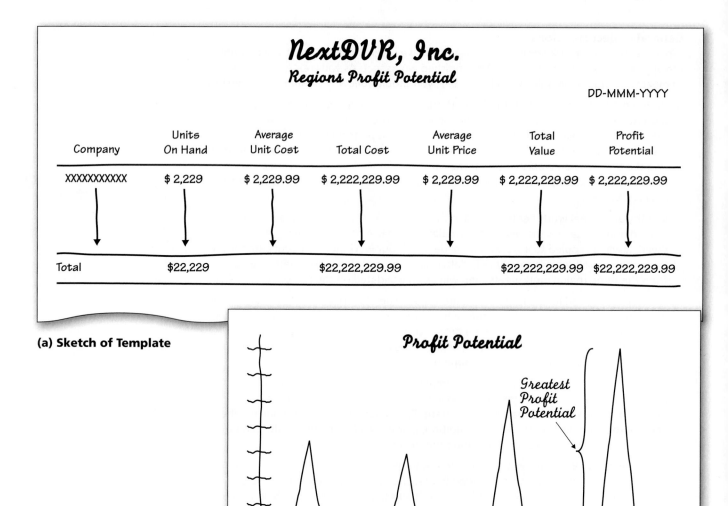

(a) Sketch of Template

(b) Sketch of Clustered Cone Chart

Figure 6–3

With a good understanding of the requirements document, an understanding of the necessary decisions, and a sketch of the template, the next step is to use Excel to create the template.

BTW

Templates
Templates are most helpful when you need to create several similar or identical workbooks. They help reduce work and ensure consistency. Templates can contain: (1) text and graphics, such as a company name and logo; (2) formats and page layouts; and (3) formulas or macros.

To Start Excel

If you are using a computer to step through the project in this chapter and you want your screen to match the figures in this book, you should change your computer's resolution to 1024 × 768. For information about how to change a computer's resolution, see page APP 21 in Appendix E.

The following steps, which assume Windows is running, start Excel based on a typical installation of Microsoft Office on your computer. You may need to ask your instructor how to start Excel for your computer.

Note: If you are using Windows XP, see Appendix F for alternate steps.

1 Click the Start button on the Windows Vista taskbar to display the Start menu.

2 Click All Programs at the bottom of the left pane on the Start menu to display the All Programs list.

3 Click Microsoft Office in the All Programs list to display the Microsoft Office list.

4 Click Microsoft Office Excel 2007 to start Excel and display a blank worksheet in the Excel window.

5 If the Excel window is not maximized, click the Maximize button next to the Close button on its title bar to maximize the window.

6 If the worksheet window in Excel is not maximized, click the Maximize button next to the Close button on its title bar to maximize the worksheet window within Excel.

Creating the Template

The first step in building the workbook is to create and save a template that contains the titles, column and row headings, formulas, and formats used on each of the sheets.

Design the template and plan the formatting.
The template will be used to create a number of other worksheets. Thus, it is important to consider the layout, cell formatting, and contents of the page.

- **Set row heights and column widths.** Row heights and column widths should be set to sizes large enough to accommodate future needs.

- **Use placeholders for data when possible.** Placeholders are used in a template to guide users of the template regarding what type of data to enter in cells. For example, the word Region should be used in the subtitle to indicate to a user of the template to place the Region name in the subtitle.

(continued)

Plan Ahead

Plan Ahead

(continued)

- **Use dummy data to verify formulas.** When a template is created, **dummy data** — that is, sample data used in place of actual data to verify the formulas in the template — should be used in place of actual data to verify the formulas in the template. Selecting simple numbers such as 1, 2, and 3 allows you to check quickly to see if the formulas are generating the proper results. In templates with more complex formulas, you may want to use numbers that test the extreme boundaries of valid data.

- **Format cells in the template.** Formatting should be applied to titles and subtitles that can be changed to provide cues to users of the worksheets. For example, by using a fill color for the title and subtitle, when each regions' worksheets are created, the fill color can be changed. All numeric cell entry placeholders – dummy data – should be properly formatted for unit numbers and currency amounts.

After the template is saved, it can be used every time a similar workbook is developed. Because templates help speed and simplify their work, many Excel users create a template for each application on which they work. Templates can be simple — possibly using a special font or worksheet title; or they can be more complex — perhaps utilizing specific formulas and format styles, such as the template for the NextDVR Profit Potential workbook.

Creating a template, as shown in Figure 6–4, follows the same basic steps used to create a workbook. The only difference between developing a workbook and a template is the file type used to save the template.

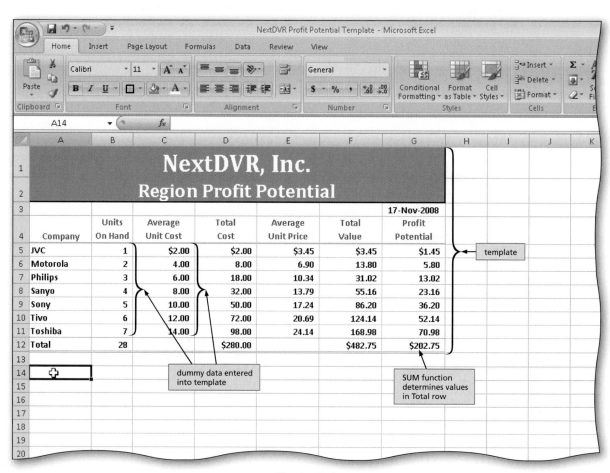

Figure 6–4

To Bold the Font and Adjust the Row Heights and Column Widths of the Template

The first step in creating the template is to change the font style to bold and adjust the height of row 4 to 30.75 points and column widths of columns A and C through G to 13.00 characters.

1 Click the Select All button immediately above row heading 1 and to the left of column heading A and then click the Bold button on the Ribbon. Select cell A1 to deselect the worksheet.

2 Drag the bottom boundary of row heading 4 down until the ScreenTip, Height 30.75 (41 pixels), appears.

3 Drag the right boundary of column heading A to the right until the ScreenTip, Width: 13.00 (96 pixels), appears.

4 Click column heading C, drag through to column heading G, and then drag the right boundary of column heading G right until the ScreenTip, Width: 13.00 (96 pixels), appears. Select cell A1 to deselect columns C through G.

To Enter the Title, Subtitle, and Row Titles in the Template

The following steps enter the titles in cells A1 and A2 and the row titles in column A.

1 Type NextDVR, Inc. in cell A1 and then press the DOWN ARROW key.

2 Type Region Profit Potential in cell A2 and then press the DOWN ARROW key twice to make cell A4 active.

3 Type Company and then press the DOWN ARROW key.

4 With cell A5 active, enter the remaining row titles in column A as shown in Figure 6–5 on the next page.

To Enter Column Titles and the System Date in the Template

The next step is to enter the column titles in row 4 and the system date in cell G3.

1 Select cell B4. Type Units and then press ALT+ENTER. Type On Hand and then press the RIGHT ARROW key.

2 Type Average and then press ALT+ENTER. Type Unit Cost and then press the RIGHT ARROW key.

3 With cell D4 active, enter the remaining column titles in row 4 as shown in Figure 6–5.

4 Select cell G3. Type =now() and then press the ENTER key. Right-click cell G3 and then click Format Cells on the shortcut menu. When Excel displays the Format Cells dialog box, click Date in the Category list and then double-click 3/14/01 13:30 in the Type list. Select cell A14 to deselect cell G3.

Q&A

Why was the date not formatted as it appears in Figure 6–4?

The format assigned to the system date in cell G3 is temporary. For now, it ensures that the system date will appear properly, rather than as a series of number signs (#). The system date will be assigned a permanent format later in this chapter.

BTW

Dummy Numbers
As you develop more sophisticated workbooks, it will become increasingly important that you create good test data to ensure your workbooks are free of errors. The more you test a workbook, the more confident you will be in the results generated. Always take the time to select test data that tests the limits of the formulas.

Figure 6–5

To Enter Dummy Data in the Template Using the Fill Handle

While creating the NextDVR template in this chapter, dummy data is used for the units on hand values in the range B5:B11 and the average unit cost values in the range C5:C11. The dummy data is entered by using the fill handle to create a series of numbers in columns B and C. The series in column B begins with 1 and increments by 1; the series in column C begins with 2 and increments by 2. Recall that you must enter the first two numbers in a series so that Excel can determine the increment amount. If the cell to the right of the start value is empty and you want to increment by 1, however, you can create a series by entering only one number as shown in the following steps.

1

- Select cell B5.

- Type 1 and then press the ENTER key.

- Select the range B5:C5.

- Drag the fill handle through cells B11 and C11. Do not release the mouse button (Figure 6–6).

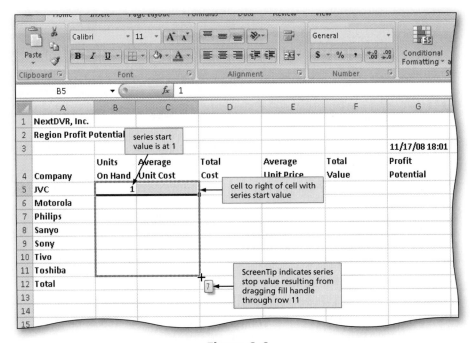

Figure 6–6

2

- Release the mouse button to create the series 1 through 7 in increments of 1 in the range B5:B11 (Figure 6–7).

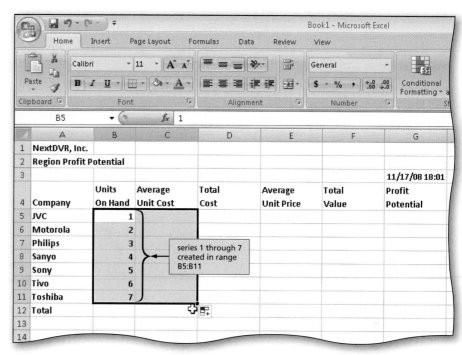

Figure 6–7

3

- Select cell C5. Type 2 and then press the DOWN ARROW key.

- Type 4 and then press the ENTER key.

- Select the range C5:C6. Drag the fill handle through cell C11 to create the series 2 through 14 in increments of 2 in the range C5:C11 (Figure 6–8).

Q&A

What other types of series can I create?

Excel allows you to create many types of series, including a **date series** (Jan, Feb, Mar, etc.), an **auto fill series** (1, 1, 1, etc.), and a **linear series** (1, 2, 3, etc. or 2, 4, 6, etc.), which was created in the previous steps. A fourth type of series is a growth series. A **growth series** multiplies values by a constant factor. You can create a growth series by entering an initial value in the first cell, selecting the range to fill, clicking the Fill button on the Home tab on the Ribbon, clicking Series, clicking Growth in the type area, and then entering a constant factor in the Step value box.

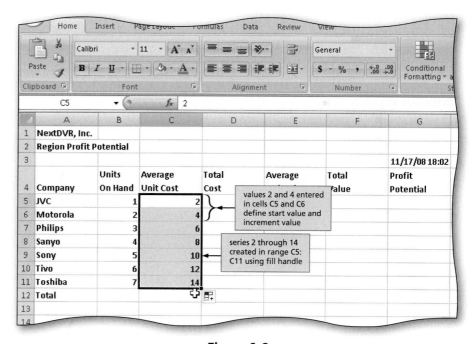

Figure 6–8

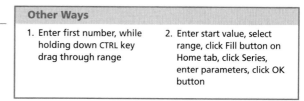

Other Ways
1. Enter first number, while holding down CTRL key drag through range	2. Enter start value, select range, click Fill button on Home tab, click Series, enter parameters, click OK button

Accuracy
The result of an arithmetic operation, such as multiplication or division, is accurate to the factor with the least number of decimal places.

The ROUND Function and Entering Formulas in the Template

The next step is to enter the four formulas for the first DVR company (JVC) in the range D5:G5. When you multiply or divide decimal numbers that result in an answer with more decimal places than the format allows, you run the risk of the column totals being off by a penny or so. For example, as shown in the worksheet sketch in Figure 6–3a on page EX 422, columns C through G use the Currency and Comma style formats with two decimal places. And yet, the formulas used to calculate values for these columns result in several additional decimal places that Excel maintains for computation purposes. For this reason, it is recommended that you use the **ROUND function** on formulas that potentially can result in more decimal places than the format displays in a given cell. The general form of the ROUND function is

=ROUND (number, number of digits)

Fractions
The forward slash (/) has multiple uses. For example, dates often are entered using the slash. In formulas, the slash represents division. What about fractions? To enter a fraction, such as ½, type .5 or 0 ½ (i.e., type zero, followed by a space, followed by the number 1, followed by a slash, followed by the number 2). If you type ½ without the preceding zero, Excel will store the value in the cell as the date January 2.

where the number argument can be a number, a cell reference that contains a number, or a formula that results in a number; and the number of digits argument can be any positive or negative number used to determine the number of places to which the number will be rounded.

The following is true about the ROUND function:

1. If the number of digits argument is greater than 0 (zero), then the number is rounded to the specified number of digits to the right of the decimal point.

2. If the number of digits argument is equal to 0 (zero), then the number is rounded to the nearest integer.

3. If the number of digits argument is less than 0 (zero), then the number is rounded to the specified number of digits to the left of the decimal point.

Table 6–1 shows the four formulas to enter in the template in the range D5:G5. The ROUND function is used to round the value resulting from the formula assigned to cell E5 to two decimal places.

Table 6–1 Formulas Used to Determine Profit Potential			
Cell	**Description**	**Formula**	**Entry**
D5	Total Cost	Units On Hand x Average Unit Cost	=B5 * C5
E5	Average Unit Price	ROUND(Average Unit Cost / (1-.42), 2)	=ROUND(C5 / (1-.42), 2)
F5	Total Value	Units On Hand x Average Unit Price	=B5 * E5
G5	Profit Potential	Total Value – Total Cost	=F5 – D5

Changing Modes
You change from Enter mode or Edit mode to Point mode by typing the EQUAL SIGN (=) followed by clicking a cell or clicking the Insert Function box on the formula bar, selecting a function, and then clicking a cell. You know you are in Point mode when the word Point appears on the left side of the status bar at the bottom of the Excel window.

The most difficult formula to understand in Table 6–1 is the one that determines the average unit price, which also is called the average selling price. To make a net profit, companies must sell their merchandise for more than the unit cost of the merchandise plus the company's operating expenses (taxes, rent, upkeep, and so forth).

To determine what selling price to set for an item, companies often first establish a desired margin and then determine a selling price. Most companies look for a margin of 30% to 75%. NextDVR, Inc., for example, tries to make a margin of 42% on each of its digital cameras. The formula for the average unit price in Table 6–1 helps the company determine the price at which to sell an item so that it ends up with a 42% margin. For example, if an item costs NextDVR $2.00 (the unit cost), then the company must sell it for $3.45 [$2.00 / (1–.42)] to make a 42% margin. Of this $3.45, $2.00 goes to pay the unit cost of the item; the other $1.45 is the gross profit potential (42% x $3.45 = $1.45).

To Enter Formulas Using Point Mode and Determine Totals in the Template

The following steps use Point mode to enter the four formulas in Table 6–1 in the range D5:G5. After the formulas are entered for JVC DVRs in row 5, the formulas will be copied for the remaining six companies. The Sum button then is used to determine the totals in row 12.

1

• Select cell D5, type = to start the formula, click cell B5, type * (asterisk), click cell C5, and then click the Enter box in the formula bar (Figure 6–9).

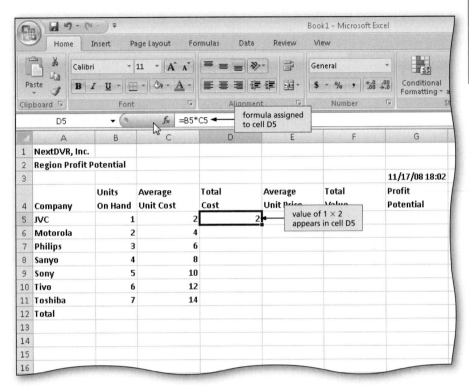

Figure 6–9

2

• Select cell E5, type =round(c5/(1-.42),2), and then click the Enter box in the formula bar to display the formula =ROUND(C5/(1-0.42), 2) in the formula bar and the value 3.45 (3.448276 rounded to two decimal places) as the average unit price in cell E5 (Figure 6–10).

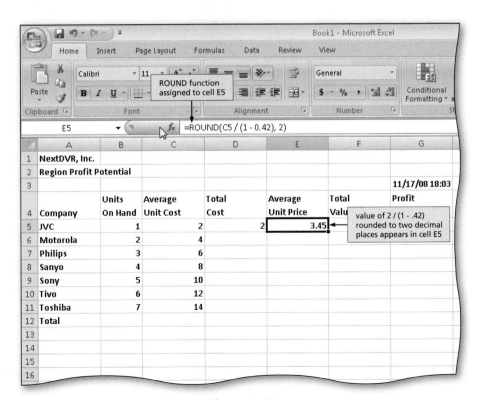

Figure 6–10

3

- Select cell F5, type = to start the formula, click cell B5, type * (asterisk), click cell E5, and then click the Enter box in the formula bar to display the formula =B5*E5 in the formula bar and the value 3.45 (1 x 3.45) as the total value in cell F5 (Figure 6–11).

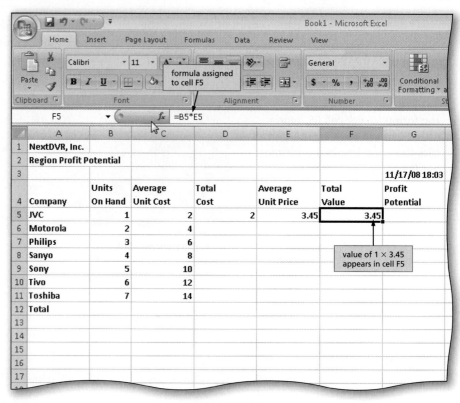

Figure 6–11

4

- Select cell G5, type = to start the formula, click cell F5, type – (minus sign), click cell D5, and then click the Enter box in the formula bar to display the formula =F5 – D5 in the formula bar and the value 1.45 (3.45 – 2) as the profit potential in cell G5 (Figure 6–12).

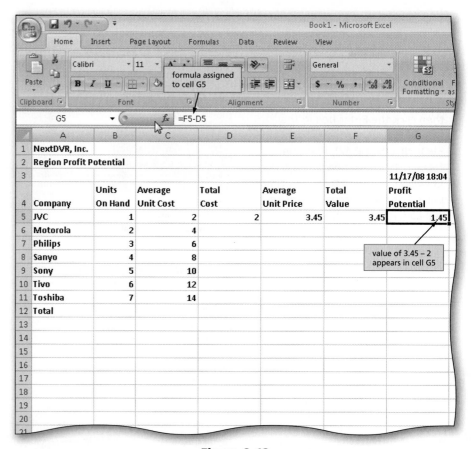

Figure 6–12

5

- Select the range
  D5:G5 and then
  point to the fill
  handle (Figure 6–13).

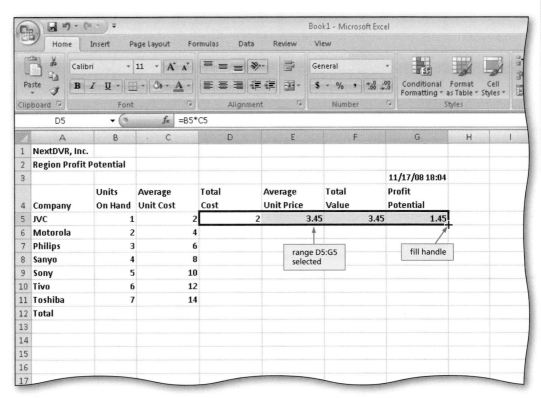

Figure 6–13

6

- Drag down through
  the range D6:G11 to
  copy the formulas in
  the range D5:G5 to
  the range D6:G11.
  Excel automatically
  adjusts the cell refer-
  ences so each formula
  references the data in
  the row to which it is
  copied (Figure 6–14).

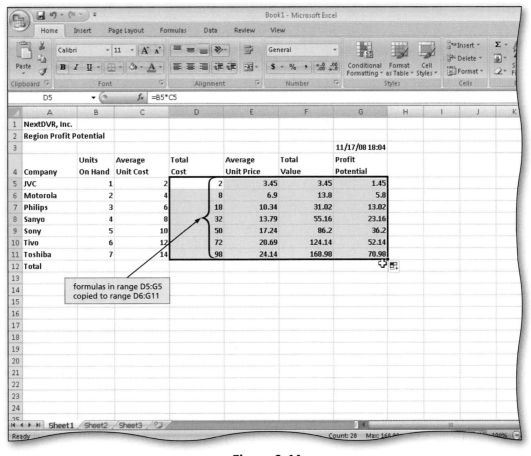

Figure 6–14

● Select cell B12, and then click the Sum button on the Ribbon twice.

● Select cell D12 and then click the Sum button twice.

● Select the range F12:G12 and then click the Sum button.

● Select cell A14 to deselect the range F12:G12 and display the values based on the dummy data entered earlier in columns B and C (Figure 6–15).

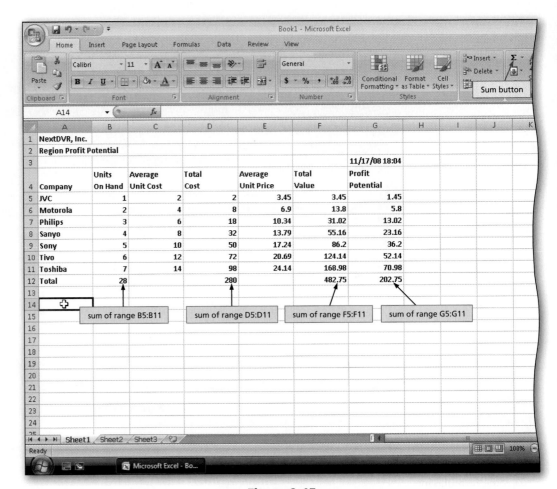

Figure 6–15

To Save the Template

Saving a template is just like saving a workbook, except that the file type Template is selected in the Save as type box in the Save As dialog box. The following steps save the template on a USB drive in drive E using the file name, NextDVR Profit Potential Template.

1

- Update the document properties with your name and any other relevant information.

- With a USB flash drive connected to one of the computer's USB ports, click the Save button on the Quick Access Toolbar to display the Save As dialog box.

- When Excel displays the Save As dialog box, type `NextDVR Profit Potential Template` in the File name box.

- Click the Save as type box arrow and then click Excel Template in the list.

- Select UDISK 2.0 (E:) as the new save location (Figure 6–16).

2

- Click the Save button in the Save As dialog box to save the template on the USB drive and display the file name, NextDVR Profit Potential Template, on the title bar (Figure 6–17 on the next page).

Q&A

Why does Excel change the folder name when the Excel Template file type is chosen?

When the Excel Template file type is chosen in the Save as type box, Excel automatically changes the contents of the Save in box to the Templates folder created when Office 2007 was installed. In a **production environment** — that is, when you are creating a template for a business, school, or personal application — the template typically would be saved in the Templates folder, not on the USB flash drive.

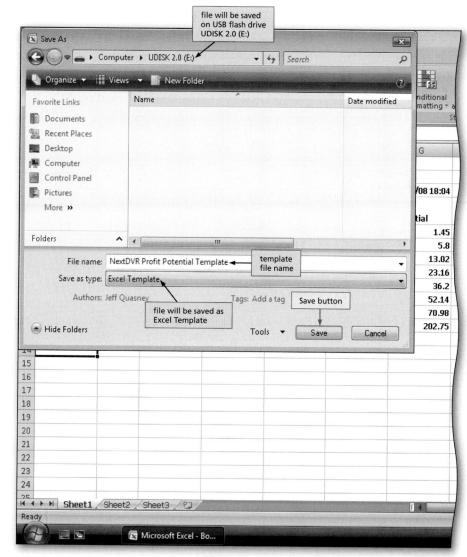

Figure 6–16

Other Ways

1. Press CTRL+S, type file name, select Excel Template in Save as type box, select drive or folder, click Save button in Save As dialog box

Formatting the Template

The next step is to format the template so it appears as shown in Figure 6–17. The following list summarizes the steps required to format the template.

1. Format the titles in cells A1 and A2.
2. Format the column titles and add borders to rows 4 and 12.
3. Assign the Currency style format with a floating dollar sign to the nonadjacent ranges C5:G5 and D12:G12.
4. Assign a Custom style format to the range C6:G11.
5. Assign a Comma style format to the range B5:B12.
6. Create a format style and assign it to the date in cell G3.

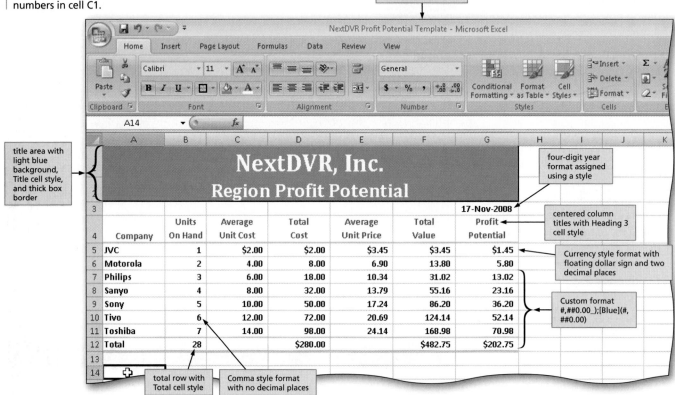

Figure 6–17

To Format the Template Title and Subtitle

The steps used to format the template title and subtitle include changing cell A1 to 28-point with the Title cell style; changing cell A2 to 22-point with the Title cell style; centering both titles across columns A through G; changing the title background color to light blue and the title font to white; and drawing a thick box border around the title area. The color scheme associated with the default Office template also will be changed to a new color scheme. One reason to change the color scheme is to add variety to the look of the worksheet that you create. The following steps format the title and subtitle.

1 Click the Page Layout tab on the Ribbon. Click the Colors button on the Ribbon and then click Apex in the Colors gallery.

2 Select the range A1:A2. Click the Home tab on the Ribbon and apply the Title cell style to the range. Select cell A1. Click the Font Size box arrow on the Ribbon and then click 28 in the Font Size list. Select the range A1:G1. Click the Merge & Center button on the Ribbon.

3 Select cell A2, click the Font Size box arrow on the Ribbon, and then click 22 in the Font Size list. Select the range A2:G2. Click the Merge & Center button on the Ribbon.

4 Select the range A1:A2, click the Fill Color button arrow on the Ribbon, and then click Light Blue (column 7, row 7) on the Fill Color palette.

5 Click the Font Color button arrow on the Ribbon and then click White, Background 1 (column 1, row 1) on the Font Color palette.

6 Click the Borders button arrow on the Ribbon and then click Thick Box Border in the Borders gallery.

7 Select cell A14 to deselect the range A1:A2.

To Format the Column Titles and Total Row

The next steps center and underline the column titles and draw a top and double bottom border on the Total row in row 12.

1 Select the range A4:G4, click the Center button on the Ribbon, and then apply the Heading 3 cell style to the range.

2 Select the range A12:G12, assign the Total cell style to the range, and then select cell A14 (Figure 6–18).

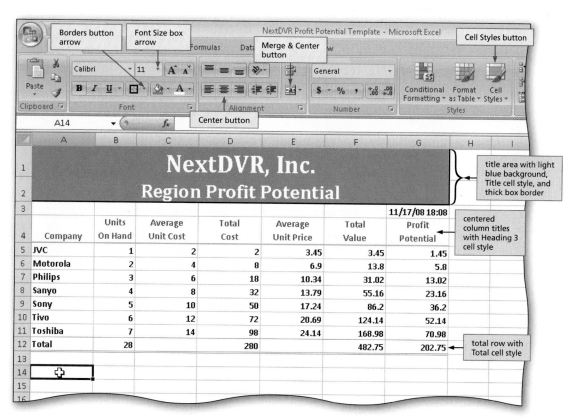

Figure 6–18

To Assign a Currency Style Using the Format Dialog Box

As shown in Figure 6–17 on page EX 434, the template for this chapter follows the **standard accounting format** for a table of numbers; that is, it contains floating dollar signs in the first row of numbers (row 5) and the totals row (row 12). Recall that while a fixed dollar sign always appears in the same position in a cell (regardless of the number of significant digits), a floating dollar sign always appears immediately to the left of the first significant digit in the cell. To assign a fixed dollar sign to rows 5 and 12, select the range and then click the Accounting Number Format button on the Home tab on the Ribbon. Assigning a floating dollar sign, by contrast, requires you to select the desired format in the Format Cells dialog box.

The following steps use the Format Cells dialog box to assign a Currency style with a floating dollar sign and two decimal places to the ranges C5:G5 and D12:G12.

- Select the range C5:G5.

- While holding down the CTRL key, select the nonadjacent range D12:G12 and then right-click the selected ranges to highlight the non-adjacent ranges and display the shortcut menu (Figure 6–19).

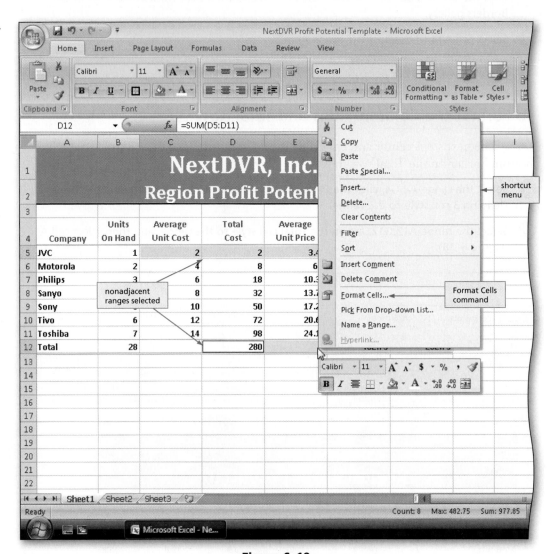

Figure 6–19

2

- Click Format Cells on the shortcut menu.

- When Excel displays the Format Cells dialog box, if necessary click the Number tab, click Currency in the Category list, and then click the red ($1,234.10) in the Negative numbers list (Figure 6–20).

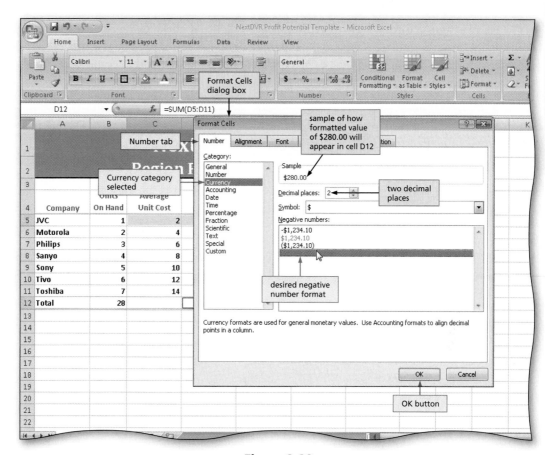

Figure 6–20

3

- Click the OK button to assign the Currency style with a floating dollar sign and two decimal places to the ranges C5:G5 and D12:G12. Select cell A14 to deselect the nonadjacent ranges (Figure 6–21).

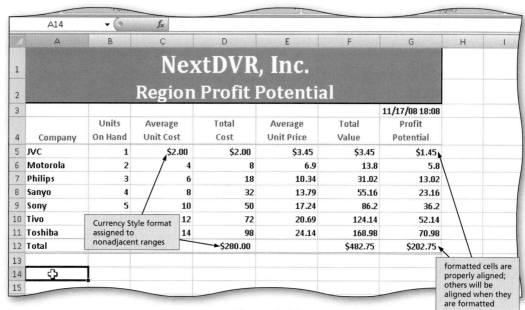

Figure 6–21

Other Ways

1. Press CTRL+1, click Number tab, select format, click OK button

To Create and Assign a Custom Format Code and a Comma Style Format

Excel assigns a format code to every format style listed in the Category list in the Number sheet in the Format Cells dialog box. As shown in Table 6–2, a **format code** is a series of format symbols that defines how a cell entry assigned a format will appear. To view the entire list of format codes that come with Excel, select Custom in the Category list (Figure 6–20 on the previous page).

Table 6–2 Format Symbols in Format Codes		
Format Symbol	**Example of Symbol**	**Description**
# (number sign)	###.##	Serves as a digit placeholder. If the value in a cell has more digits to the right of the decimal point than number signs in the format, Excel rounds the number. Extra digits to the left of the decimal point are displayed.
0 (zero)	0.00	Functions like a number sign (#), except that if the number is less than 1, Excel displays a 0 in the ones place.
. (period)	#0.00	Ensures Excel will display a decimal point in the number. The placement of period symbols determines how many digits appear to the left and right of the decimal point.
% (percent)	0.00%	Displays numbers as percentages of 100. Excel multiplies the value of the cell by 100 and displays a percent sign after the number.
, (comma)	#,##0.00	Displays a comma as a thousands separator.
( )	#0.00;(#0.00)	Displays parentheses around negative numbers.
$ or + or –	$#,##0.00; ($#,##0.00)	Displays a floating sign ($, +, or –).
* (asterisk)	$*##0.00	Displays a fixed sign ($, +, or –) to the left in the cell followed by spaces until the first significant digit.
[color]	#.##;[Red]#.##	Displays the characters in the cell in the designated color. In the example, positive numbers appear in the default color, and negative numbers appear in red.
" " (quotation marks)	$0.00 "Surplus"; $-0.00 "Shortage"	Displays text along with numbers entered in a cell.
_ (underscore)	#,##0.00_)	Skips the width of the character that follows the underscore.

Before creating custom format codes or modifying an existing custom format code, you should understand their makeup. As shown below, a format code can have up to four sections: positive numbers, negative numbers, zeros, and text. Each section is divided by a semicolon.

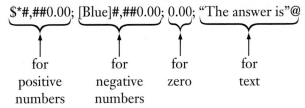

$*#,##0.00; [Blue]#,##0.00; 0.00; "The answer is"@

for	for	for	for
positive	negative	zero	text
numbers	numbers		

A format code need not have all four sections. For most applications, a format code will have only a positive section and possibly a negative section.

The next step is to create and assign a custom format code to the range C6:G11. To assign a custom format code, you select the Custom category in the Category list in the Format Cells dialog box, select a format code close to the one to be created, and then modify or customize the selected format code. The following steps create and assign a custom format code.

1

- Select the range C6:G11, right-click the selected range, and then click Format Cells on the shortcut menu.

- When Excel displays the Format Cells dialog box, if necessary, click the Number tab, and then click Custom in the Category list.

- If necessary, scroll down and then click #,##0.00_); [Red](#,##0.00) in the Type list.

- In the Type text box, change the word Red to Blue (Figure 6–22).

What is displayed in the dialog box?

The Custom format has been modified to show negative numbers in blue. In the Sample area, Excel displays a sample of the custom format assigned to the first number in the selected range.

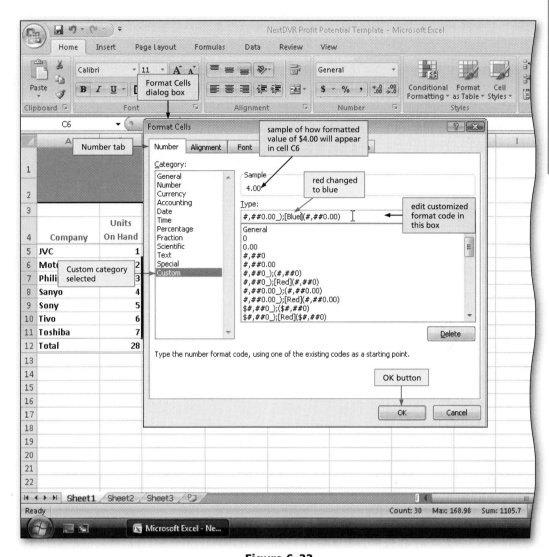

Figure 6–22

2

- Click the OK button to display the numbers in the range C6:G11 using the custom format code created in Step 1.

- Select the range B5:B12, click the Comma Style button on the Ribbon, and then click the Decrease Decimal button on the Ribbon twice to display the numbers in the range B5:B12 using the Comma style format with no decimal places (Figure 6–23).

- Select cell A14.

Q&A

Can I reuse the custom format code?

Yes. When you create a new custom format code, Excel adds it to the bottom of the Type list in the Number sheet in the Format Cells dialog box to make it available for future use.

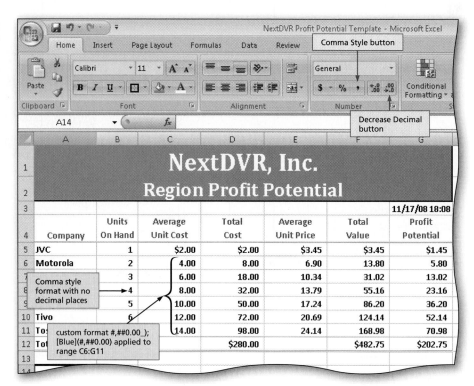

Figure 6–23

To Create a New Style

A **style** is a group of format specifications that are assigned to a style name. Most of the cell styles in the Cell Styles gallery that is displayed when you click the Cell Styles button on the Home tab include formatting only of visual characteristics, such as font, font size, font color, and fill color. Excel makes several general styles available with all workbooks and themes, as described in Table 6–3. You can apply these existing styles to a cell or cells in a worksheet, modify an existing style, or create an entirely new style.

Table 6–3 Styles Available with All Workbooks via the Cell Styles Button on the Home Tab

Style Name	Description
Normal	Number = General; Alignment = General, Bottom Aligned; Font = Arial 10; Border = No Borders; Patterns = No Shading; Protection = Locked
Comma	Number = (*#,##0.00);_(*(#,##0.00);_(*"-");_(@_)
Comma(0)	Number = (*#,##0_);_(*(#,##0);_(*"-");_(@_)
Currency	Number = ($#,##0.00_);_($*(#,##0.00);_($*"-"??_);_(@_)
Currency(0)	Number = ($#,##0_);_($*(#,##0);_($*"-");_(@_)
Percent	Number = 0%

Using the New Cell Style button in the Cell Styles gallery on the Home tab, you can create and then assign a style to a cell, a range of cells, a worksheet, or a workbook in the same way you assign a format using the buttons on the Ribbon. In fact, the Comma Style button, Currency Style button, and Percent Style button assign the Comma, Currency, and Percent styles in Table 6–3, respectively. Excel automatically assigns the Normal style in Table 6–3 to all cells when you open a new workbook.

By right-clicking styles in the Style gallery, you also can delete, modify, and duplicate styles. The Merge Styles button in the Cell Styles gallery allows you to merge styles from other workbooks. You add a new style to a workbook or merge styles when you plan to use a group of format specifications over and over.

The following steps show how to create a new style called Four-Digit Year by modifying the existing Normal style. The new style will include the following formats: Number = 14-Mar-2001 and Alignment = Horizontal Center and Bottom Aligned.

After the Four-Digit Year style is created, it will be assigned to cell G3, which contains the system date.

• Click the Cell Styles button on the Home tab on the Ribbon to display the Cell Styles gallery (Figure 6–24).

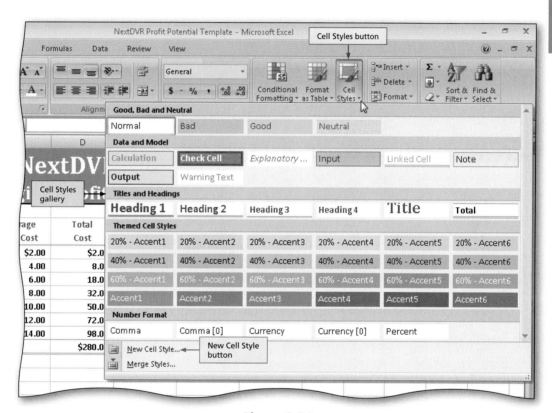

Figure 6–24

❷

• Click the New Cell Style button in the Cell Styles gallery.

• When Excel displays the Style dialog box, type Four-Digit Year as the new style name (Figure 6–25).

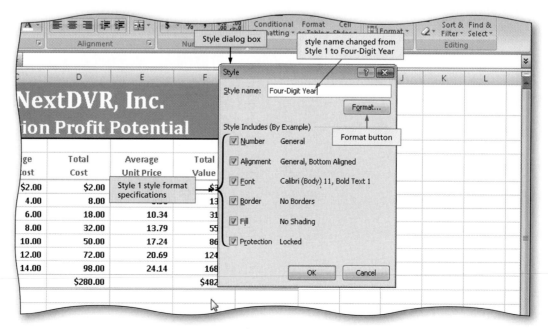

Figure 6–25

3

- Click the Format button to display the Format Cells dialog box.

- When Excel displays the Format Cells dialog box, if necessary, click the Number tab, click Date in the Category list, and then click 14-Mar-2001 in the Type list (Figure 6–26).

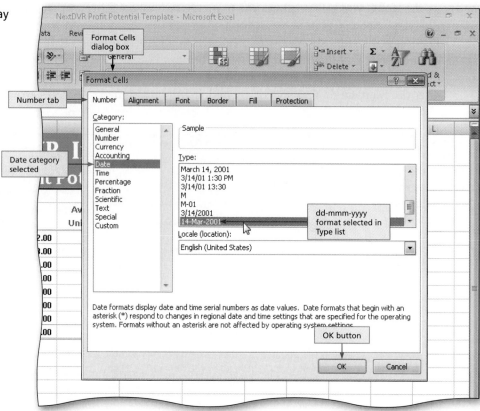

Figure 6–26

4

- Click the Alignment tab, click the Horizontal box arrow, click Center in the Horizontal list, and then click the OK button.

- When the Style dialog box becomes active, click Font, Border, Fill, and Protection to clear the check boxes (Figure 6–27).

5

- Click the OK button to add the new Four-Digit Year style to the list of styles available with the NextDVR Profit Potential Template file in the Cell Styles gallery.

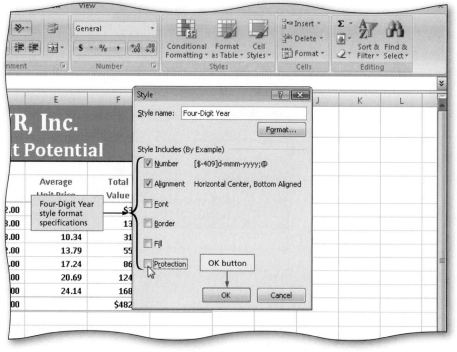

Figure 6–27

Other Ways

1. Press ALT+H, J, N

To Apply a New Style

In earlier steps, cell G3 was assigned the system date using the now() function. The next step is to assign cell G3 the Four-Digit Year style, which centers the contents of the cell and assigns it the date format dd-mmm-yyyy.

- Select cell G3 and then click the Cell Styles button on the Ribbon to display the Cell Styles gallery (Figure 6–28).

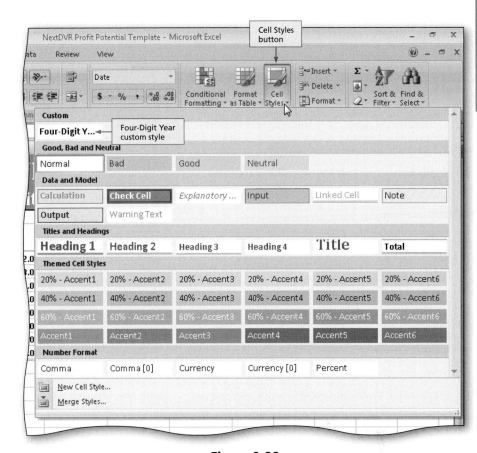

Figure 6–28

- Click the Four-Digit Year style to assign the Four-Digit Year style to cell G3 (Figure 6–29).
- Select cell A14.

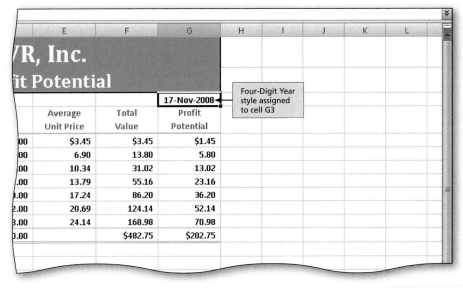

Figure 6–29

Other Ways

1. Press ALT+H, J

BTW

Creating Customized Formats
Each format symbol within the format code has special meaning. Table 6–2 on page EX 438 summarizes the more frequently used format symbols and their meanings.

More About Using Styles

Keep in mind the following additional points concerning styles:

1. A style affects the format of a cell or range of cells only if the corresponding check box is selected in the 'Style Includes area' in the Style dialog box (Figure 6–27 on page EX 442). For example, if the Font check box is not selected in the Style dialog box, then the cell assigned the style maintains the font format it had before the style was assigned.

2. If you assign two different styles to a range of cells, Excel adds the second style to the first, rather than replacing it.

3. You can merge styles from another workbook into the active workbook by using the Merge Styles button in the Cell Styles gallery. You must, however, open the workbook that contains the desired styles before you use the Merge Styles button.

4. The six check boxes in the Style dialog box are identical to the six tabs in the Format Cells dialog box (Figure 6–26 on page EX 442).

BTW

Normal Style
The Normal style is the format style that Excel initially assigns to all cells in a workbook. If you change the Normal style, Excel applies the new format specifications to all cells that are not assigned another style.

To Spell Check, Save, and Print the Template

With the formatting complete, the next step is to spell check the template, save it, and then print it.

1 Select cell A1. Click the Spelling button on the Review tab. Correct any misspelled words.

2 Click the Save button on the Quick Access Toolbar to save the workbook.

3 Print the workbook.

4 Click the Close Window button on the right side of the worksheet window to close the workbook and leave Excel open.

BTW

Opening a Workbook at Startup
You can instruct Windows to open a workbook (or template) automatically when you turn on your computer by adding the workbook (or template) to the Startup folder. Use Windows Explorer to copy the file to the Startup folder. The Startup folder is in the All Programs list.

Using Templates

Before using the template to create the NextDVR Profit Potential workbook, you should be aware of how templates are used and their importance. If you click the New command on the Office Button menu, the New Workbook dialog box is displayed (Figure 6–30). The New Workbook dialog box includes a My templates link in the Templates list, which you can click to view a list of Excel templates that you have saved on your computer in the New dialog box.

Recall that Excel automatically chose Templates as the Save in folder when the template in this chapter initially was saved (Figure 6–16 on page EX 443). Saving templates in the Templates folder, rather than in another folder, is the standard procedure in the business world. If the NextDVR Profit Potential template created in this chapter had been saved in the Templates folder, then the template would appear in the New Workbook dialog box after clicking My templates in the Templates list. The template then could have been selected to start a new workbook.

When you select a template from the New Workbook or New dialog box to create a new workbook, Excel names the new workbook using the template name with an appended digit 1 (for example, Template1). This is similar to what Excel does when you first start Excel and it assigns the name Book1 to the workbook.

Excel provides additional workbook templates, which you can access by clicking the links in the Templates list shown in Figure 6–30. Additional workbook templates also are available on the Web. To access the templates on the Web, click the links in the Microsoft Office Online section of the Templates list.

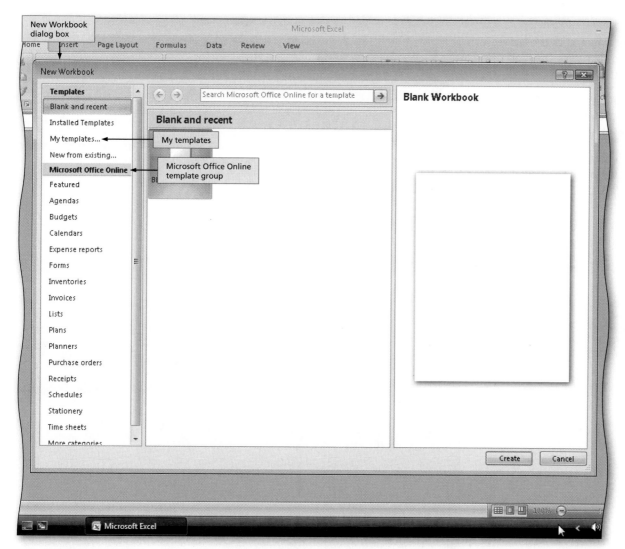

Figure 6–30

Creating a Workbook from a Template

With the template created, the next step is to use it to create the NextDVR Profit Potential workbook shown in Figure 6–1 on page EX 419.

To Open a Template and Save It as a Workbook

The following steps open the NextDVR Profit Potential template and save it as a workbook.

1
- With Excel active, click the Office Button and then click Open on the Office Button menu.

- When Excel displays the Open dialog box, select UDISK 2.0 (E:) in the Address bar.

- Click the file name NextDVR Profit Potential Template to select it (Figure 6–31).

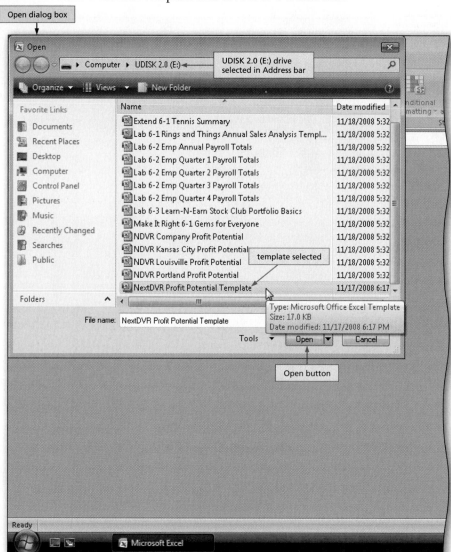

Figure 6–31

- Click the Open button in the Open dialog box.

- When Excel displays the NextDVR Profit Potential Template, click the Office Button and then click Save As on the Office Button menu.

- When the Save As dialog box appears, type `NextDVR Profit Potential` in the File name box.

- Click the Save as type box arrow and then click Excel Workbook (Figure 6–32).

- Click the Save button in the Save As dialog box to save the workbook.

Q&A

How does Excel automatically select the file type and file name?

In a production environment in which templates are saved to the Templates folder, Excel automatically selects Excel Workbook as the file type when you attempt to save a template as a workbook. Excel also appends the digit 1 to the template name as described earlier.

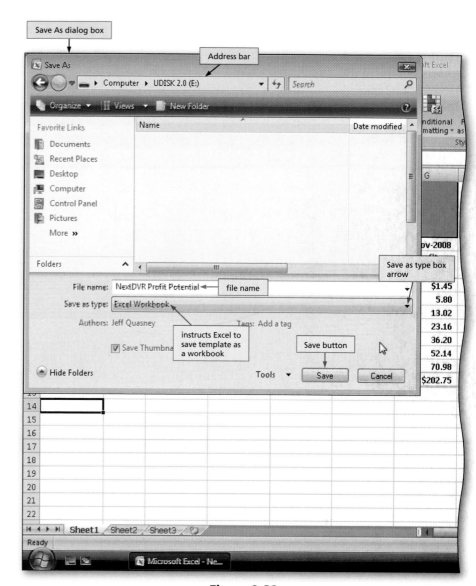

Figure 6–32

To Add a Worksheet to a Workbook

A workbook contains three worksheets by default. The number of worksheets you can have in a workbook is limited only by the amount of memory in your computer.

> **Identify additional worksheets needed in the workbook.**
> The NextDVR Profit Potential workbook requires four worksheets — one for each of the three regions and one for the company totals. Thus, a worksheet must be added to the workbook.

Plan Ahead

When you add a worksheet, Excel places the new sheet tab to the left of the active tab. To keep the worksheet with the dummy data shown in Figure 6–29 on page EX 443 on top — that is, to keep its tab (Sheet1) to the far left — spreadsheet specialists often add a new worksheet between Sheet1 and Sheet2, rather than to the left of Sheet1. The following steps select Sheet2 before adding a worksheet to the workbook.

1

• Click the Sheet2 tab at the bottom of the window and then click the Insert Cells button arrow on the Home tab on the Ribbon to display the Insert menu (Figure 6–33).

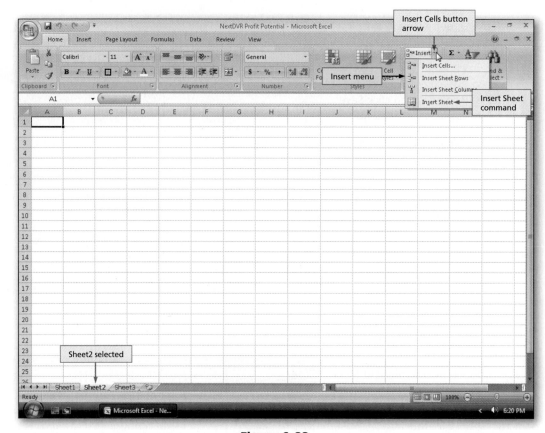

Figure 6–33

2

• Click Insert Sheet to add a fourth worksheet named Sheet 4 between Sheet 1 and Sheet 2 (Figure 6–34).

Q&A

Can I start a new workbook with more sheets?

Yes. An alternative to adding worksheets is to change the default number of worksheets before you open a new workbook. To change the default

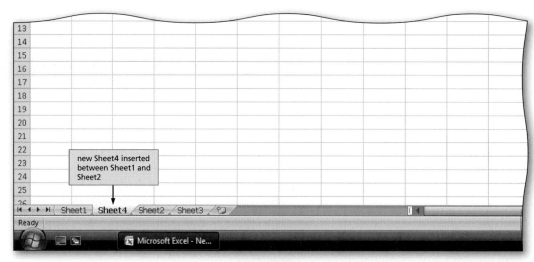

Figure 6–34

number of worksheets in a blank workbook, click the Excel Options button on the Office Button menu, and then change the number in the 'Include this many sheets' box in the 'When creating new workbooks' area of the Excel Options dialog box. Recall from Chapter 4 that you can delete a worksheet by right-clicking the sheet tab of the worksheet you want to delete and then clicking Delete on the shortcut menu.

Other Ways

1. Right-click tab, click Insert on shortcut menu
2. Press ALT+H, I, S

To Copy the Contents of a Worksheet to Other Worksheets in a Workbook

With four worksheets in the workbook, the next step is to copy the contents of Sheet1 to Sheet4, Sheet2, and Sheet3. Sheet1 eventually will be used as the Company worksheet with the consolidated data. Sheet4, Sheet2, and Sheet3 will be used for the three region worksheets.

1

- Click the Sheet1 tab.

- Click the Select All button and then click the Copy button on the Ribbon (Figure 6–35).

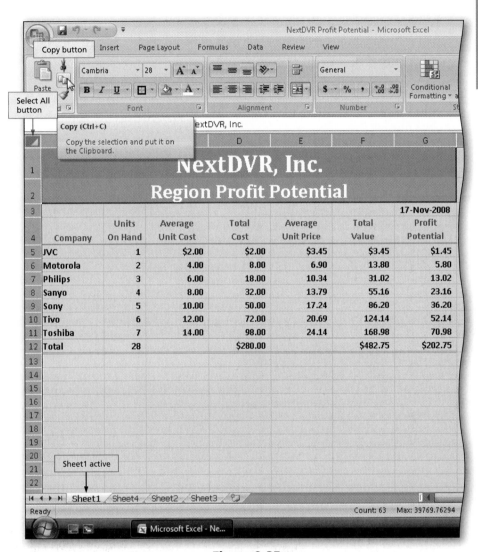

Figure 6–35

2

- Click the Sheet4 tab.

- While holding down the SHIFT key, click the Sheet3 tab so all three blank worksheets in the workbook are selected.

- Click the Paste button on the Ribbon to copy the data on the Office Clipboard to Sheet4, Sheet2, and Sheet3 (Figure 6–36).

 Why does the word Group appear on the title bar?

Because multiple worksheets are selected, the term [Group] follows the template name on the title bar.

3

- Click the Sheet1 tab and then press the ESC key to remove the marquee surrounding the selection.

- Hold down the SHIFT key and then click the Sheet3 tab. Select cell A14.

- Hold down the SHIFT key and then click the Sheet1 tab to deselect Sheet4, Sheet2, and Sheet3 (Figure 6–37).

- Click the Save button on the Quick Access Toolbar.

 Can I use the ENTER key to paste the data?

Yes. The ENTER key could have been used to complete the paste operation in Step 2, rather than the Paste button on the Ribbon. Recall that if you complete a paste operation using the ENTER key, then the marquee disappears and the Office Clipboard no longer contains the copied data following the action. Because the Paste button on the Ribbon was used, the ESC key was used in Step 3 to clear the marquee and Office Clipboard of the copied data.

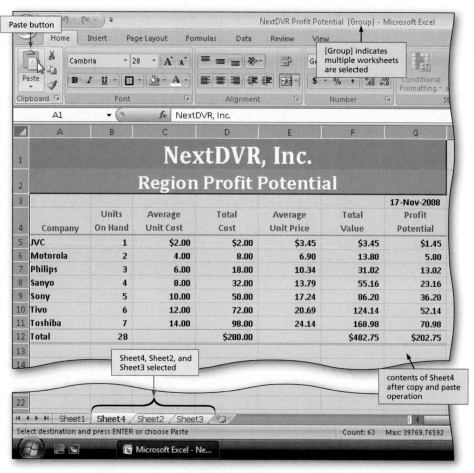

Figure 6–36

Figure 6–37

Other Ways

1. Select source area, click Copy button on Home tab, select worksheets, click Paste button on Home tab

2. Right-click source area, click Copy on shortcut menu, select worksheets, click Paste on shortcut menu

3. Select source area, press CTRL+C, select worksheets, press CTRL+V

To Drill an Entry through Worksheets

The next step is to replace the dummy numbers in the range C5:C11 with the average unit cost for each type of DVR (Table 6–4). The average unit costs for each category are identical on all four sheets. For example, the average unit cost for the JVC DVR in cell C5 is $185.61 on all four sheets. To speed data entry, Excel allows you to enter a number once and drill it through worksheets so it is entered in the same cell on all the selected worksheets. This technique is referred to as **drilling an entry**. The following steps drill the seven average unit cost entries in Table 6–4 through all four worksheets in the range C5:C11.

Table 6–4 Average Unit Cost Entries	
Company	**Average Unit Cost**
JVC	185.61
Motorola	165.79
Philips	302.99
Sanyo	296.09
Sony	184.49
Tivo	165.80
Toshiba	297.38

1

- With Sheet1 active, hold down the SHIFT key and then click the Sheet3 tab to select all four tabs at the bottom of the window.

- Select cell C5. Type 185.61 and then press the DOWN ARROW key.

- Enter the six remaining average unit costs in Table 6–4 in the range C6:C11 to display the average unit cost entries as shown in Figure 6–38.

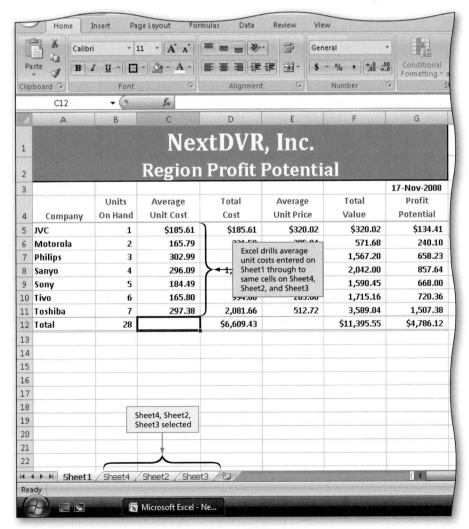

Figure 6–38

2

- Hold down the SHIFT key and then click the Sheet1 tab to deselect Sheet4, Sheet2, and Sheet3.

- One at a time, click the Sheet4 tab, the Sheet2 tab, and the Sheet3 tab to verify that all four sheets are identical (Figure 6–39).

Q&A

What is the benefit of drilling data through worksheets?

In the previous set of steps, seven new numbers were entered on one worksheet. As shown in Figure 6–39, by drilling the entries through the four other worksheets, 28 new numbers now appear, seven on each of the four worksheets. Excel's capability of drilling data through worksheets is an efficient way to enter data that is common among worksheets.

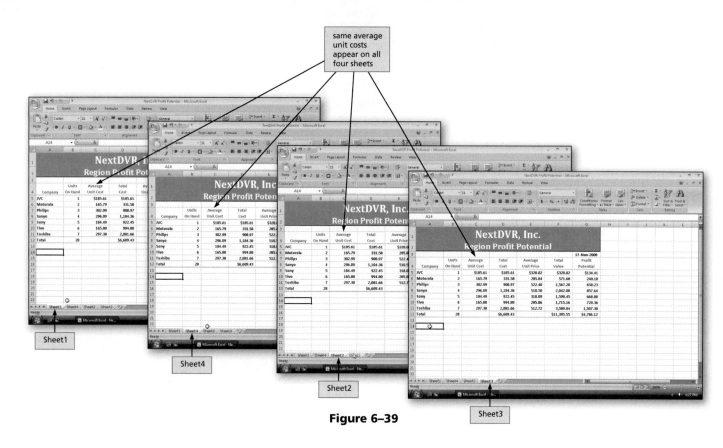

Figure 6–39

To Modify the Louisville Sheet

BTW

Drilling an Entry
Besides drilling a number down through a workbook, you can drill a format, a function, or a formula down through a workbook.

With the skeleton of the NextDVR Profit Potential workbook created, the next step is to modify the individual sheets. The following steps modify the Louisville sheet (Sheet 4) by changing the sheet name, tab color, and worksheet subtitle; changing the color of the title area; and entering the units on hand values in column B.

Table 6–5 Louisville Units On Hand	
Cell	**Units on Hand**
B5	335
B6	220
B7	323

Table 6–5 Louisville Units On Hand (continued)	
Cell	**Units on Hand**
B8	144
B9	195
B10	364
B11	273

1 Double-click the Sheet4 tab. Type `Louisville` and then press the ENTER key. Right-click the Louisville tab, point to Tab Color on the shortcut menu, and then click Light Green (column 5, row 1 in the Standard Colors area) on the Color palette.

2 Double-click cell A2, drag through the word, Region, and then type `Louisville` to change the worksheet subtitle.

3 Select the range A1:A2, click the Fill Color button arrow on the Ribbon, and then click Light Green (column 5, row 1 in the Standard Colors area) on the Fill Color palette.

4 Enter the data listed in Table 6–5 in the range B5:B11 (Figure 6–40).

5 Select cell A14 and then click the Save button on the Quick Access Toolbar.

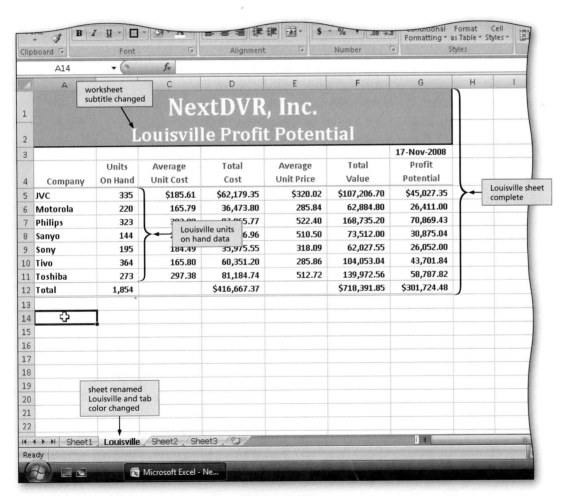

Figure 6–40

BTW

Importing Data
Costs, such as those entered into the range C5:C11, often are maintained in another workbook, a file, or a database. If the costs are maintained elsewhere, ways exist to link to a workbook or import data from a file or database into a workbook. Linking to a workbook is discussed later in this chapter. For information on importing data, see the From Other Sources button on the Data tab on the Ribbon.

To Modify the Kansas City Sheet

The following steps modify the Kansas City sheet (Sheet 2).

Table 6–6 Kansas City Units On Hand	
Cell	**Units on Hand**
B5	403
B6	281
B7	228
B8	312
B9	357
B10	278
B11	345

1 Double-click the Sheet2 tab. Type `Kansas City` and then press the ENTER key. Right-click the Kansas City tab, point to Tab Color on the shortcut menu, and then click Red (column 2, row 1 in the Standard Colors area) on the Color palette.

2 Double-click cell A2, drag through the word, Region, and then type `Kansas City` to change the worksheet subtitle.

3 Select the range A1:A2, click the Fill Color button arrow on the Ribbon, and then click Red (column 2, row 1 in the Standard Colors area) on the Fill Color palette.

4 Enter the data listed in Table 6–6 in the range B5:B11 (Figure 6–41).

5 Select cell A14 and then click the Save button on the Quick Access Toolbar.

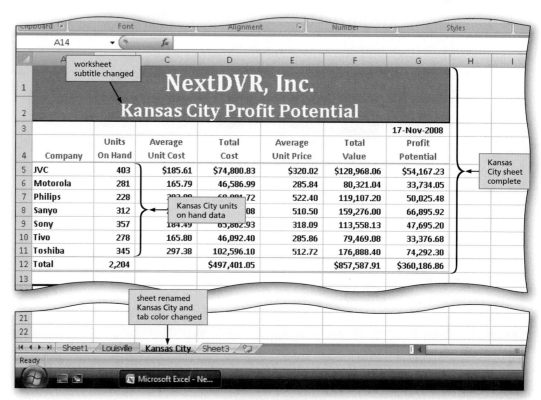

Figure 6–41

To Modify the Portland Sheet

As with the Louisville and Kansas City sheets, the sheet name, tab color, worksheet subtitle, data, and background colors must be changed on the Portland sheet. The following steps modify the Portland sheet.

Table 6–7 Portland Units On Hand	
Cell	**Units on Hand**
B5	253
B6	215
B7	352
B8	387
B9	339
B10	282
B11	400

1 Double-click the Sheet3 tab. Type `Portland` and then press the ENTER key. Right-click the Portland tab, point to Tab Color on the shortcut menu, and then click Purple (column 10, row 1 in the Standard Colors area) on the Color palette.

2 Double-click cell A2, drag through the word, Region, and then type `Portland` to change the worksheet subtitle.

3 Select the range A1:A2, click the Fill Color button arrow on the Ribbon, and then click Purple (column 10, row 1 in the Standard Colors area) on the Fill Color palette.

4 Enter the data listed in Table 6–7 in the range B5:B11 (Figure 6–42).

5 Select cell A14 and then click the Save button on the Quick Access Toolbar.

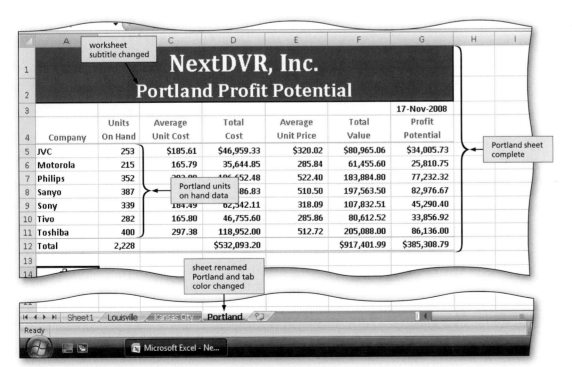

Figure 6–42

Referencing Cells in Other Sheets in a Workbook

With the three region sheets complete, the next step is to modify Sheet1, which will serve as the consolidation worksheet containing totals of the data on the Louisville, Kansas City, and Portland sheets. Because this sheet contains totals of the data, you need to understand how to reference cells in other sheets in a workbook before modifying Sheet1.

To reference cells in other sheets in a workbook, you use the sheet name, which serves as the **sheet reference**, and the cell reference. For example, you refer to cell B5 on the Louisville sheet as shown below.

=Louisville!B5

Using this method, you can sum cell B5 on the three region sheets by selecting cell B5 on the Sheet1 sheet and then entering:

= Louisville!B5 + Kansas City!B5 + Portland!B5

A much quicker way to total the three cells is to use the SUM function as follows:

=SUM(Louisville:Portland!B5)

The SUM argument (Louisville:Portland!B5) instructs Excel to sum cell B5 on each of the three sheets (Louisville, Kansas City, and Portland). The colon (:) between the first sheet name and the last sheet name instructs Excel to include these sheets and all sheets in between, just as it does with a range of cells on a sheet. A range that spans two or more sheets in a workbook such as Louisville:Portland!B5 is called a **3-D range**. The reference to this range is a **3-D reference**.

A sheet reference such as Portland! always is absolute. Thus, the sheet reference remains constant when you copy formulas.

BTW

Circular References
A circular reference is a formula that depends on its own value. The most common type is a formula that contains a reference to the same cell in which the formula resides.

Entering a Sheet Reference

You can enter a sheet reference in a cell by typing the sheet reference or by clicking the appropriate sheet tab while in Point mode. When you click the sheet tab, Excel activates the sheet and automatically adds the sheet name and an exclamation point after the insertion point in the formula bar. Next, select or drag through the cells you want to reference on the sheet.

If the range of cells to be referenced is located on several worksheets (as when selecting a 3-D range), click the first sheet tab and then select the cell or drag through the range of cells. Next, while holding down the SHIFT key, click the sheet tab of the last sheet you want to reference. Excel will include the cell(s) on the first sheet, the last sheet, and any sheets in between.

To Modify the Company Sheet

BTW

3-D References
If you are summing numbers on noncontiguous sheets, hold down the CTRL key rather than the SHIFT key when selecting the sheets.

This section modifies the Company sheet by changing the sheet name, tab color, and subtitle and then entering the SUM function in each cell in the range B5:B11. The SUM functions will determine the total units on hand at the three regions, by company. Cell B5 on the Company sheet, for instance, will contain the sum of the JVC DVR units on hand in cells Louisville!B5, Kansas City!B5, and Portland!B5. Before determining the totals, the following steps change the sheet name from Sheet1 to Company, color the tab, and change the worksheet subtitle to Company Profit Potential.

1 Double-click the Sheet1 sheet tab, type `Company` and then press the ENTER key. Right-click the Company tab, point to Tab Color on the shortcut menu, and then click Light Blue (column 7, row 1 in the Standard Colors area) on the Color palette.

2 Double-click cell A2, drag through the word, Region, and then type `Company` as the worksheet subtitle. Press the ENTER key.

To Enter and Copy 3-D References Using the Paste Button Menu

The following steps enter the 3-D references used to determine the total units on hand for each of the seven DVR companies. In these steps, the Formulas command on the Paste button menu on the Ribbon is used to complete the paste operation. When the Formulas command is used, the paste operation pastes only the formulas, leaving the formats of the destination area unchanged.

1
- Select cell B5 and then click the Sum button on the Ribbon to display the SUM function and ScreenTip (Figure 6–43).

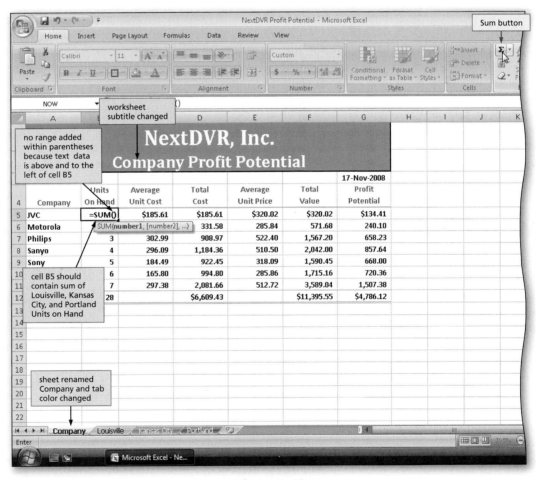

Figure 6–43

● Click the Louisville tab and then click cell B5. While holding down the SHIFT key, click the Portland tab to surround cell Louisville!B5 with a marquee (Figure 6–44).

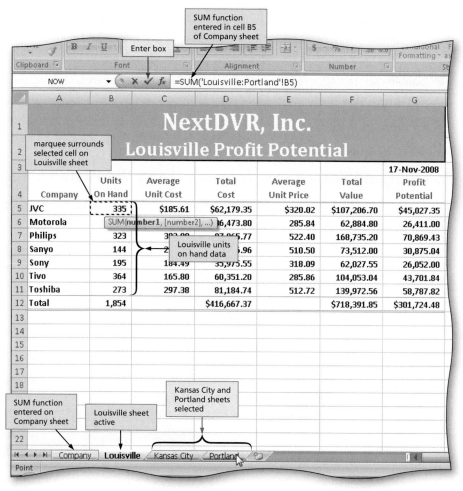

Figure 6–44

● Click the Enter box in the formula bar to enter the SUM function with the 3-D references in cell Company!B5 (Figure 6–45).

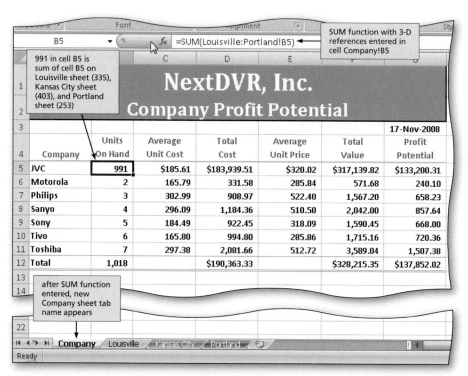

Figure 6–45

4

- With cell B5 active, click the Copy button on the Ribbon to copy the SUM function and the formats assigned to cell B5 to the Office Clipboard (Figure 6–46).

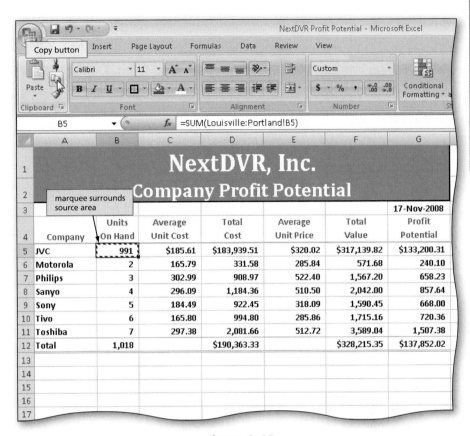

Figure 6–46

5

- Select the range B6:B11 and then click the Paste button arrow on the Ribbon to display the Paste button menu (Figure 6–47).

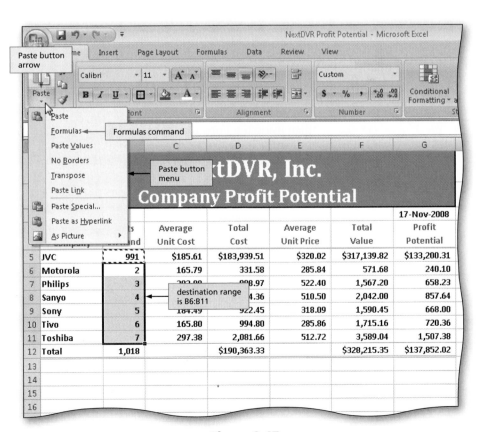

Figure 6–47

- Click Formulas on the Paste button menu to copy the SUM function in cell B5 to the range B6:B11 (Figure 6–48) and automatically adjust the cell references in the SUM function to reference the corresponding cells on the three sheets in the workbook.

- Press the ESC key to clear the marquee surrounding cell B5 and then select cell A14 to deselect the range B6:B11.

- Click the Save button on the Quick Access Toolbar to save the NextDVR Profit Potential workbook.

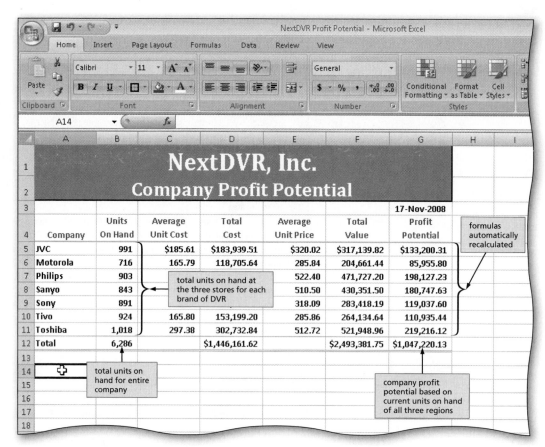

Figure 6–48

More About Pasting

If you click the Paste button on the Ribbon to complete the paste operation, rather than using the Formulas command as shown in Figure 6–47 on the previous page, then any formats assigned to cell B5 also will be copied to the range B6:B11. Completing the paste operation by using the fill handle or by pressing the ENTER key also will copy any formats from the source area to the destination area. When you use the Formulas command on the Paste button menu, Excel copies the SUM function, but not the format, assigned to cell B5. In this example, the format assigned to cell B5 is the same as the format assigned to the range B6:B11, so it does not matter if you use the Paste button or the Formulas command. In many cases, however, the formats of the source area and destination area differ; the Paste button menu, thus, is a useful option to complete the copy and paste operation. Table 6–8 summarizes the commands available on the Paste button menu, as shown in Figure 6–47.

Table 6–8 Paste Button Menu Commands

Command	Description
Paste	Pastes in the same manner as clicking the Paste button.
Formulas	Pastes the formulas from the source area, but not the formats.
Paste Values	Pastes the value of the formula from the source area, but not the formulas or formats.
No Borders	Pastes the formula and all formats from the source area, except for borders.

Table 6–8 Paste Button Menu Commands *(continued)*

Command	Description
Transpose	Pastes the formula and formats from the source area, but transposes the columns and rows. For example, if you are summing numbers in a column in the source area, then Excel will sum numbers in a row in the destination area.
Paste Link	Pastes the cell reference of the source area in the destination area.
Paste Special	Displays the Paste Special dialog box that allows you to choose what you want pasted from the source area to the destination area.
Paste as Hyperlink	Pastes the contents of the Office Clipboard as a hyperlink, which you then can edit.
As Picture	Displays the As Picture submenu, which allows you to convert the contents of the Office Clipboard to an image.

Drawing the Clustered Cone Chart

The requirements document shown in Figure 6–2 on page EX 420 requires a Clustered Cone chart. The **Clustered Cone chart** is similar to a 3-D Bar chart in that it can be used to show trends or illustrate comparisons among items.

> **Plan the layout and location of the required chart.**
> The Clustered Cone chart in Figure 6–49, for example, compares the total profit potential of the different brands of DVRs in inventory. The chart should be placed on a separate worksheet so that the company and region worksheets maintain a similar look. WordArt is used to draw the reflected chart title, Profit Potential, in an eye-catching and professional format. A text box, arrow, and brace are used to highlight the DVR brand with the greatest profit potential.

BTW

The Move Chart Button
The Move Chart button on the Design contextual tab on the Ribbon can be used to move a chart from a chart sheet to a worksheet. Click the Move Chart button on the Ribbon, select the Object in check box, and then select a destination worksheet for the chart in the Object in list in the Move Chart dialog box.

Plan Ahead

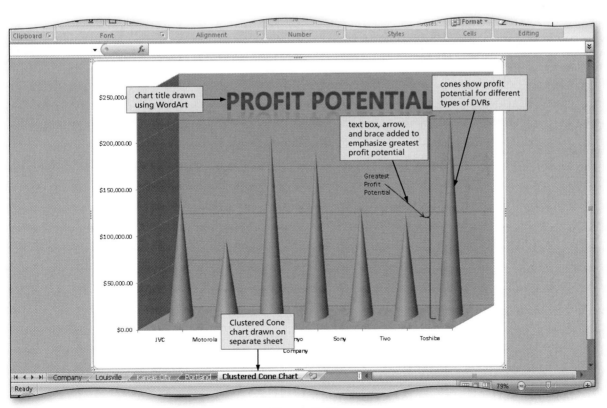

Figure 6–49

To Draw the Clustered Cone Chart

The following steps add a Clustered Cone chart to a new sheet and then change the layout of the chart to rotate it, remove the series label, and add a title to the horizontal axis.

- With the Company sheet active, select the range A5:A11.

- Hold down the CTRL key and then select the range G5:G11.

- Click the Insert tab on the Ribbon.

- Click the Column button on the Ribbon and then click Clustered Cone (column 1, row 4) in the Column gallery to insert a Clustered Cone chart (Figure 6–50).

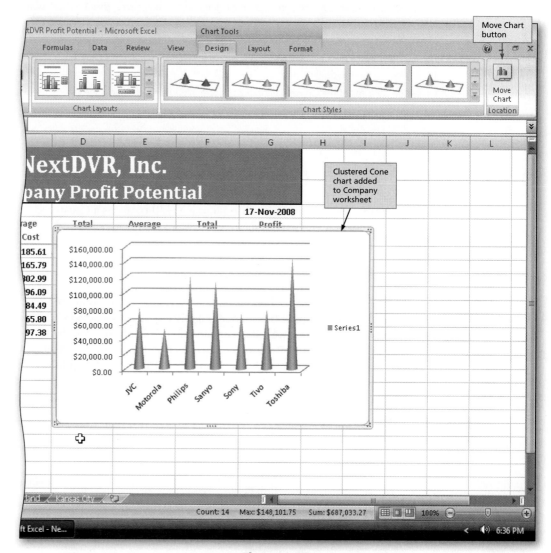

Figure 6–50

BTW

Moving Charts
To move an embedded chart to a new sheet, right-click the chart edge, click the Move Chart command, click the New sheet option button, type a sheet name, and then click the OK button. To move a chart to a chart sheet, click the chart, display the Chart Tools Design tab, and then click the Move Chart button. In the Move Chart dialog box, click the Object in option button, click the Object in box arrow, click a sheet name, and then click the OK button.

- Click the Move Chart button on the Ribbon.

- When Excel displays the Move Chart dialog box, click New sheet and then type `Clustered Cone Chart` as the sheet name.

- Click the OK button in the Move Chart dialog box to move the chart to a new sheet (Figure 6–51).

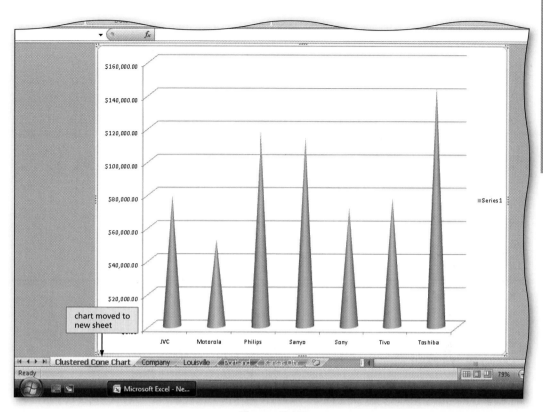

Figure 6–51

3

- Click the Layout tab on the Ribbon and then click the 3-D Rotation button on the Ribbon to display the Format Chart Area dialog box.

- Type `70` in the X text box in the Rotation area to rotate the chart 70% along the X-axis.

- Type `30` in the Y text box in the Rotation area to rotate the chart 30% along the Y-axis.

- Click the Close button in the Format Chart Area dialog box (Figure 6–52).

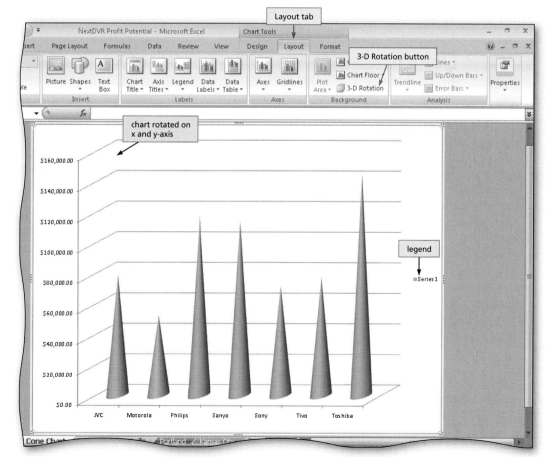

Figure 6–52

4

- Click the Legend button on the Ribbon and then click None to remove the legend from the right side of the chart (Figure 6–53).

5

- Click the Axis Titles button on the Ribbon to display the Axis Titles menu.

- Point to Primary Horizontal Axis Title on the Axis Titles menu and then click Title Below Axis in the Primary Horizontal Axis Title gallery to add a title to the horizontal axis.

- Select the horizontal axis title and type Company as the new title (Figure 6–54).

Q&A

What does the chart show?

The Clustered Cone chart compares the profit potential of the seven different brands of digital cameras. You can see from the chart that, of the DVRs in inventory, the Toshiba brand DVRs have the greatest profit potential and the Motorola brand cameras have the least profit potential.

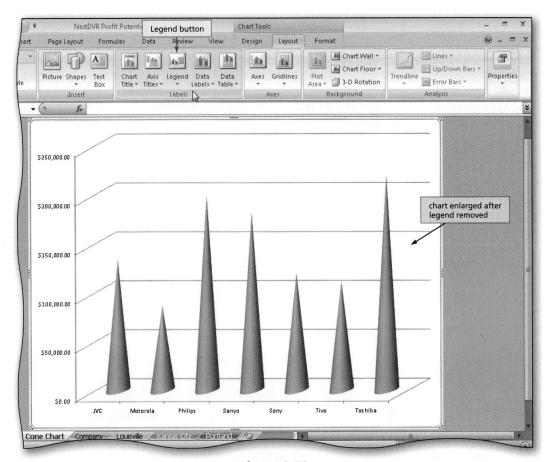

Figure 6–53

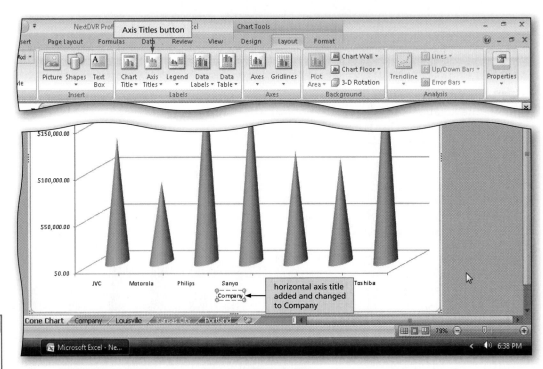

Figure 6–54

Other Ways

1. Select range, click Chart type button in Charts group on Insert tab, click Chart type in gallery
2. Select range, press F11

To Format the Clustered Cone Chart

The following steps color the sheet tab, move the sheet, change the color of the cylinders and the chart walls, and format the y-axis (values axis) and x-axis (category axis).

1 Right-click the Clustered Cone Chart sheet tab, point to Tab Color on the shortcut menu, and then click Aqua, Accent 3 (column 7, row 1) on the Color palette.

2 If necessary, drag the tab split box (Figure 6–55) to the right to ensure all five tabs show. Drag the Clustered Cone Chart sheet tab to the right of the Portland sheet tab.

3 Click the chart wall behind the cones, click the Home tab on the Ribbon, click the Fill Color button arrow on the Ribbon, and then click Lavender, Accent 5, Lighter 40% (column 9, row 4) on the Fill Color palette.

4 Click the floor of the chart below the cones, click the Fill Color button arrow on the Ribbon, and then click White, Background 1, Darker 15% (column 1, row 3) on the Fill Color palette.

5 Click one of the cylinders to select all the cones, click the Fill Color button arrow on the Ribbon, and then click Aqua, Accent 3 (column 7, row 1) on the Fill Color palette.

6 Click the x-axis and then click the Bold button on the Ribbon. Click the y-axis and then click the Bold button on the Ribbon. Click outside the chart area to display the chart as shown in Figure 6–55.

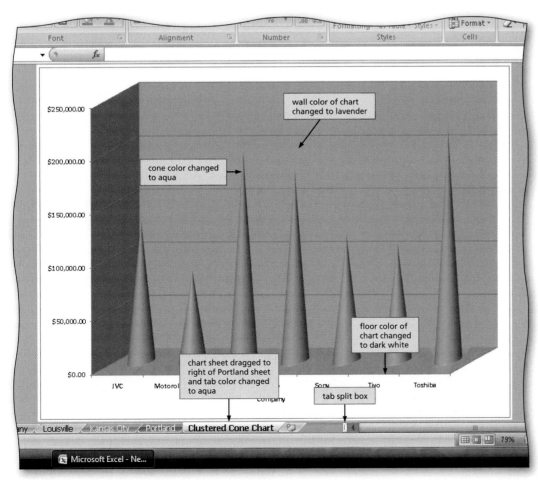

Figure 6–55

To Add a Chart Title Using the WordArt Tool

Earlier, you learned how to add a chart title by using the Chart Title button on the Layout tab on the Chart Tools contextual tab on the Ribbon. You also learned how to format it using the Home tab on the Ribbon. You also can create a chart title using the WordArt tool. The **WordArt tool** allows you to create shadowed, skewed, rotated, and stretched text on a chart sheet or worksheet and apply other special text formatting effects. The WordArt text added to a worksheet is called an **object**. The following steps show how to add a chart title using the WordArt tool.

- With the Clustered Cone Chart sheet active, click anywhere on the chart, and then click the Insert tab on the Ribbon.

- Click the WordArt button on the Ribbon to display the WordArt gallery.

- When Excel displays the WordArt gallery, point to the Gradient Fill – Accent 4, Reflection (column 5, row 4) selection in the WordArt gallery (Figure 6–56).

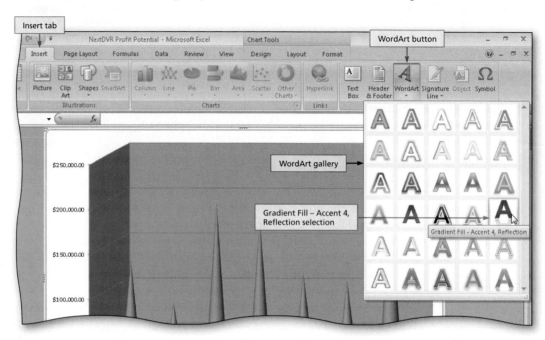

Figure 6–56

- Click the Gradient Fill – Accent 4, Reflection selection in the WordArt gallery to insert a new WordArt object.

- When Excel displays the WordArt object on the chart, type Profit Potential as the title of the Clustered Cone chart (Figure 6–57).

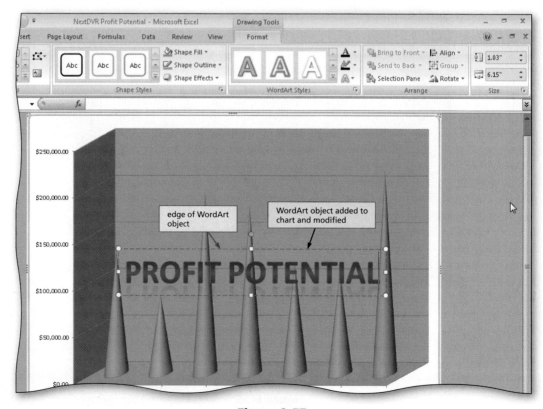

Figure 6–57

3

- Select the text in the WordArt object to display the Mini toolbar (Figure 6–58).

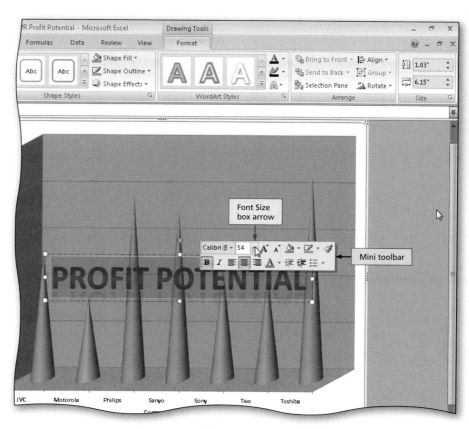

Figure 6–58

4

- Click the Font Size box arrow on the Mini toolbar and then click 44 in the Font Size list to change the font size of the WordArt object to 44 (Figure 6–59).

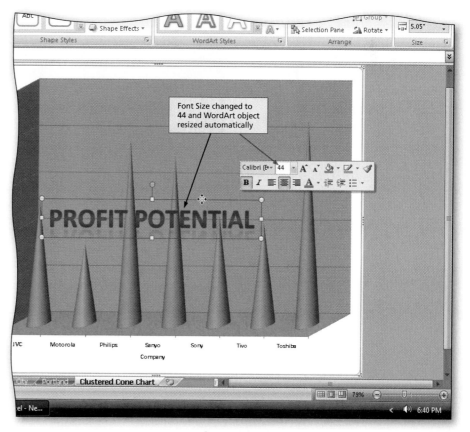

Figure 6–59

5

- Drag the top edge of the WordArt object so that the object is positioned above the cones in the chart as shown in Figure 6–60.

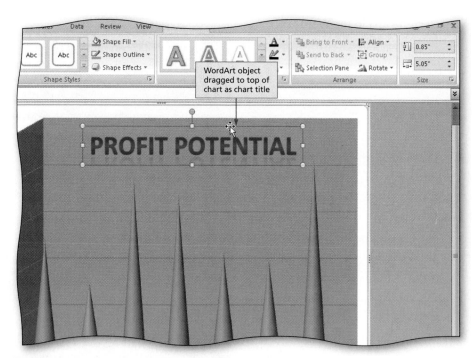

Figure 6–60

6

- Click outside the chart area to deselect the WordArt object (Figure 6–61).

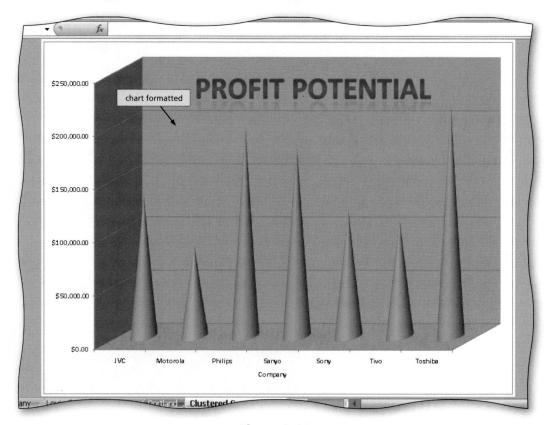

Figure 6–61

Other Ways	
1. Click WordArt button on Insert tab	2. Right-click object, click Format Shape on shortcut menu

To Add a Text Box, Arrow, and Brace to the Chart

A text box, arrow, and a brace can be used to **annotate** (call out or highlight) other objects or elements in a worksheet or chart. For example, in a worksheet, you may want to annotate a particular cell or group of cells by adding a text box, arrow, and brace. In a chart, you may want to emphasize a column or slice of a Pie chart.

A **text box** is a rectangular area of variable size in which you can add text. You use the sizing handles to resize a text box in the same manner you resize an embedded chart or a WordArt object. If the text box has the same color as the background, then the text appears as if it was written freehand, because the box itself does not show. An **arrow** allows you to connect an object, such as a text box, to an item that you want to annotate. A **brace** allows you to point out a large item or a group of items that you want to annotate.

The following steps add the text box, arrow, and brace indicated in the sketch of the chart in Figure 6–3b on page EX 422 and also shown in Figure 6–49 on page EX 461.

1

• Click the Insert tab on the Ribbon.

• Click the Shapes button on the Ribbon to display the Shapes gallery (Figure 6–62).

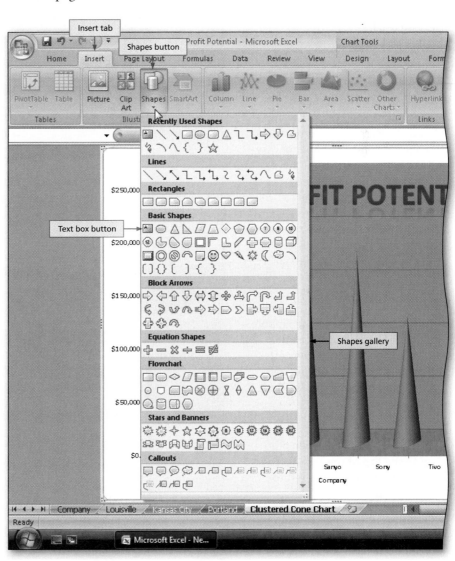

Figure 6–62

2

- Click the Text Box button (column 1, row 1 in the Basic Shapes area) in the Shapes gallery to select it.

- Point to the upper-left corner of the planned text box location, and then drag the crosshair to the lower-right corner.

- With the insertion point active in the text box, type Greatest Profit Potential as the text to display in the text box as shown in Figure 6–63.

Q&A

What if the Text Box button is not in that location in the Shapes gallery?

When Excel is first installed on a computer, it places commonly used shapes in the Recently Used Shapes area in the Shapes gallery. If users of your computer have used other shapes, they may have displaced the Text Box button in the Recently Used Shapes area. The Text Box shape also appears as the first shape in the Basic Shapes area in the Shapes gallery.

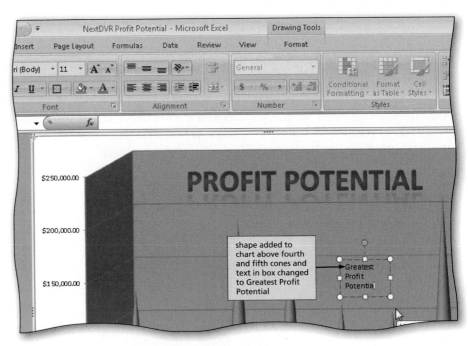

Figure 6–63

3

- Click the Insert tab on the Ribbon, click the Shapes button on the Ribbon, and then click the Left Brace button in the Shapes gallery (column 5, row 4 in the Basic Shapes area).

- Point to the bottom-left corner of the Toshiba cone and then drag up to the top of the Toshiba cone and then slightly to the left to draw the brace.

- Click the Subtle Line - Dark 1 shape style in the Shape Styles group to select it and change the color of the brace (Figure 6–64).

Q&A

Why should I add the brace before adding the arrow?

The arrow will connect the text box shape and the brace shape. Placing the start and ending points of the arrow will be easier with the targets already in place.

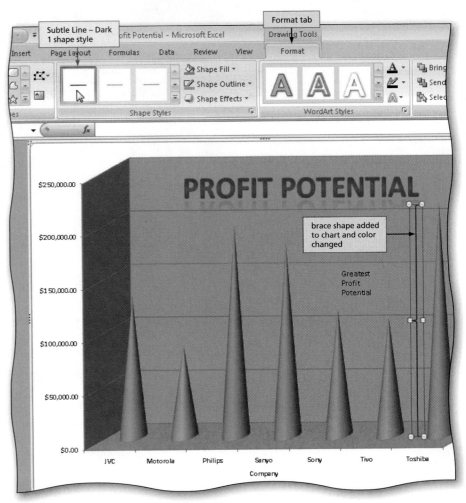

Figure 6–64

4

- Click the Insert tab on the Ribbon, click the Shapes button on the Ribbon, and then click the Arrow button in the Shapes gallery (column 2, row 1 in the Lines area).

- Point immediately to the right of the letter t in Profit in the text box, and then drag the arrow to the center of the brace to draw the arrow.

- Click the Subtle Line - Dark 1 shape style in the Shape Styles group to select it and change the color of the brace.

- Click outside the chart area to deselect the chart (Figure 6–65).

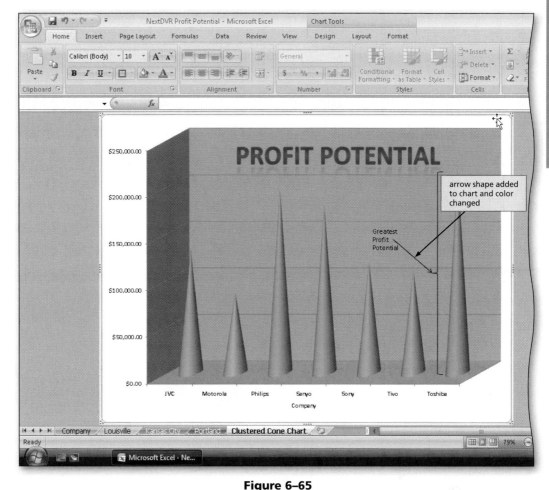

Figure 6–65

5

- Click the Company tab and then select cell A14 to deselect the chart range.

- Click the Save button on the Quick Access Toolbar to save the workbook.

Adding a Header and Footer, Changing the Margins, and Printing the Workbook

A **header** is printed at the top of every page in a printout. A **footer** is printed at the bottom of every page in a printout. By default, both the header and footer are blank. You can change either so that information, such as the workbook author, date, page number, or tab name, prints at the top or bottom of each page.

Sometimes, you will want to change the **margins** to increase or decrease the white space surrounding the printed worksheet or chart. The default margins in Excel for both portrait and landscape orientation are set to the following: Top = .75 inch; Bottom = .75 inch; Left = .7 inch; Right = .7 inch. The header and footer are set at .3 inch from the top and bottom, respectively. You also can center a printout horizontally and vertically.

Changing the header and footer and changing the margins are all part of **page setup**, which defines the appearance and format of a printed worksheet. To change page setup characteristics, select the desired sheet(s) and then click the Page Layout tab on the Ribbon. Remember to select all the sheets you want to modify before you change the headers, footers, or margins, because the page setup characteristics will change only for selected sheets. The headers and footers for chart sheets must be assigned separately from worksheets.

To Add a Header and Footer, Change Margins, and Center the Printout Horizontally

As you modify the page setup, remember that Excel does not copy page setup characteristics when one sheet is copied to another. Thus, even if you assigned page setup characteristics to the template before copying it to the NextDVR Profit Potential workbook, the page setup characteristics would not copy to the new sheet. The following steps use the Page Setup dialog box to change the headers, footers and margins and center the printout horizontally.

- With the Company sheet active, scroll to the top of the document.

- While holding down the SHIFT key, click the Portland sheet tab to select the four worksheet tabs.

- Click the Page Layout tab on the Ribbon (Figure 6–66).

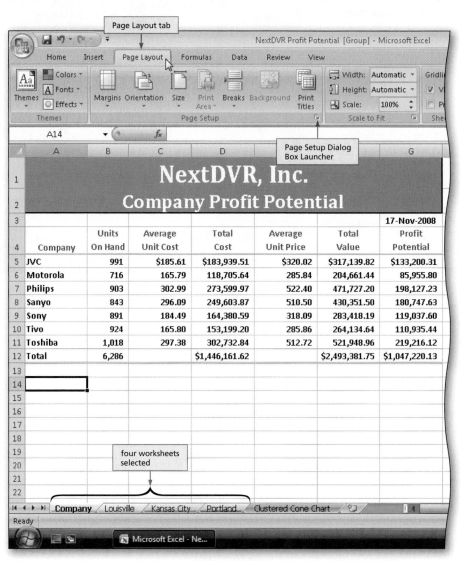

Figure 6–66

2

- Click the Page Setup Dialog Box Launcher to display the Page Setup dialog box.

- When Excel displays the Page Setup dialog box, if necessary, click the Margins tab.

- Double-click the Top box and then type 1.5 to change the top margin to 1.5 inch.

- Enter .5 in both the Left box and Right box to change the left and right margins to .5 inch.

- Click the Horizontally check box in the 'Center on page' area to select it. This will center the worksheet on the page horizontally (Figure 6–67).

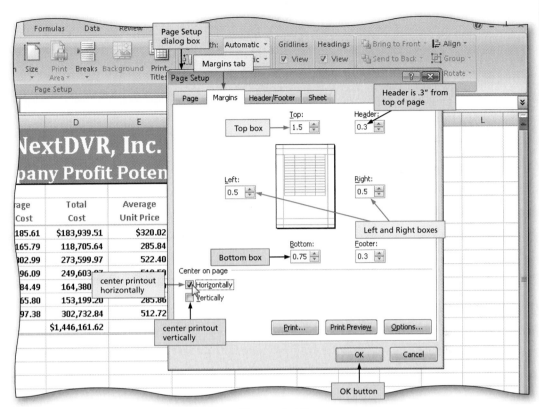

Figure 6–67

3

- Click the OK button in the Page Setup dialog box to close it.

- Click the Page Layout button on the status bar to display the worksheet in Page Layout view (Figure 6–68).

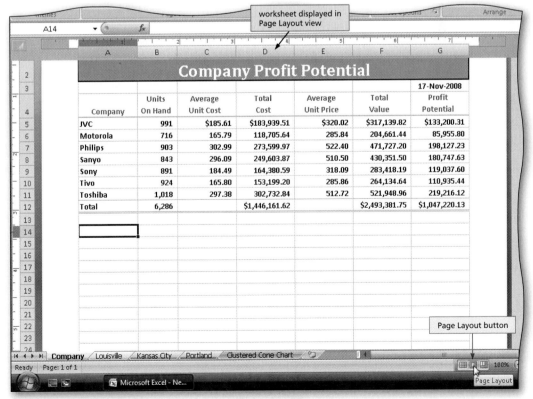

Figure 6–68

4

- If necessary, scroll the worksheet up until the Header area is displayed. Click the left Header box, type J. Quasney (or your name if you are stepping through the chapter on a computer), press the ENTER key, and then type Profit Potential to complete the entry.

- Click the center section box and then click the Sheet Name button on the Ribbon to instruct Excel to insert the sheet name that appears on the sheet tab as part of the header.

- Click the right Header box, click the Current Date button on the Ribbon, press the COMMA key, press the SPACEBAR, and then click the Current Time button on the Ribbon to insert the date and time in the Header (Figure 6–69).

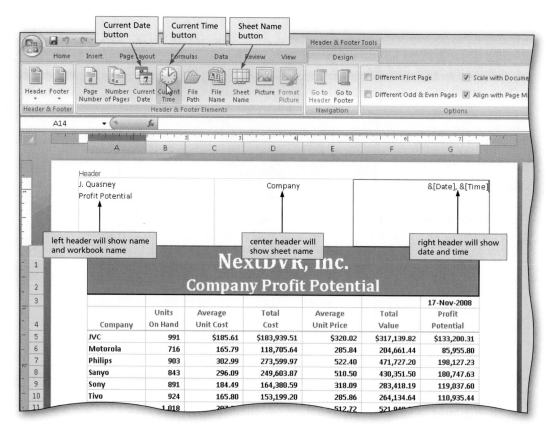

Figure 6–69

5

- Scroll the workbook down to view the Footer area.

- Click the middle section box, type Page, press the SPACEBAR, click the Page Number button on the Ribbon, press the SPACEBAR, type of, press the SPACEBAR, and then click the Number of Pages button on the Ribbon to add the footer (Figure 6–70).

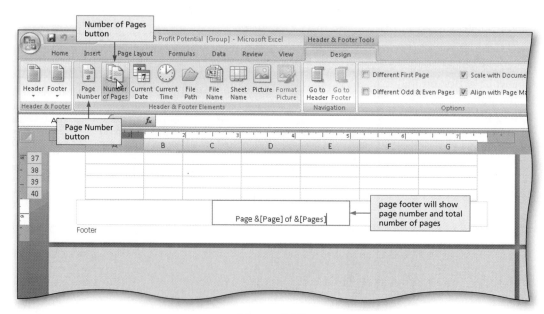

Figure 6–70

Q&A

What does Excel insert when I click a button in the Header & Footer Tools group on the Ribbon?

When you click a button in the Header & Footer Tools group on the Ribbon (Figure 6–70), Excel enters a code (similar to a format code) into the active header or footer section. A code such as &[Page] instructs Excel to insert the page number.

6

- Click anywhere on the worksheet to deselect the page footer.

- Click the Normal view button on the status bar and then select cell A14. Click the Page Layout tab on the Ribbon and then click the Page Setup Dialog Box Launcher on the Ribbon to display the Page Setup dialog box.

- Click the Print Preview button in the Page Setup dialog box to preview the Company sheet (Figure 6–71).

7

- Click the Next Page button and Previous Page button on the Print Preview tab on the Ribbon to preview the other pages.

- After previewing the printout, click the Close Print Preview button on the Ribbon.

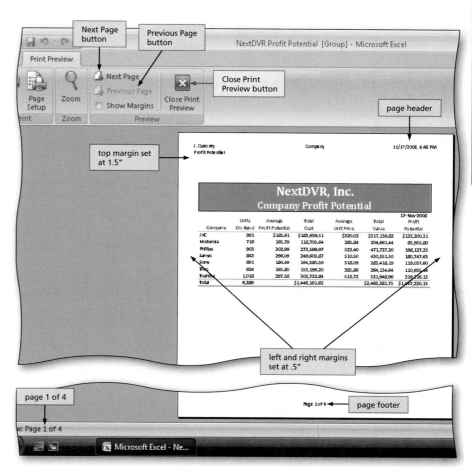

Figure 6–71

To Add a Header to the Clustered Cone Chart Sheet

The following steps add the same header applied to the four worksheets in the previous steps to the Clustered Cone Chart sheet.

1 Click the Clustered Cone Chart tab and then on the Page Layout tab, click the Page Setup Dialog Box Launcher.

2 When Excel displays the Page Setup dialog box, click the Header/Footer tab, click the Custom Header button, and in the left header box type J. Quasney (or your name if you are stepping through the chapter on a computer). Press the ENTER key and then type Profit Potential to complete the entry.

3 In the center header box, type &[Tab] to instruct Excel to print the sheet name in the Center Header section.

4 In the right header box, type &[Date], &[Time] to instruct Excel to print the date and time in the Right Header section.

5 Click the OK button in the Header dialog box and then click the OK button in the Page Setup dialog box.

6 Click the Company tab. Click the Save button on the Quick Access Toolbar to save the workbook.

To Print All Worksheets in a Workbook

The following steps print all five sheets in the workbook by selecting all the sheets before clicking the Print command on the Office Button menu.

1 Ready the printer.

2 Click the Company sheet tab. While holding down the SHIFT key, click the Clustered Cone Chart tab.

3 Click the Print command on the Office Button menu and then click the OK button in the Print dialog box to print the workbook as shown in Figure 6–72a and 6-72b.

4 Hold down the SHIFT key and then click the Company sheet tab to deselect all sheets but the Company sheet.

To Print Nonadjacent Sheets in a Workbook

In some situations, nonadjacent sheets in a workbook may need to be printed. To select nonadjacent sheets, select the first sheet and then hold down the CTRL key and click the nonadjacent sheets. The following steps show how to print the nonadjacent Company, Louisville, and Clustered Cone Chart sheets.

1 With the Company sheet active, hold down the CTRL key, click the Louisville sheet tab, and then click the Clustered Cone Chart tab.

2 Click the Print command on the Office Button menu and then click the OK button in the Print dialog box.

3 Hold down the SHIFT key and click the Company sheet tab to deselect the Louisville and Clustered Cone Chart sheets.

Selecting and Deselecting Sheets

Beginning Excel users sometimes have difficulty trying to select and deselect sheets. Table 6–9 summarizes how to select and deselect sheets.

Table 6–9 Summary of How to Select and Deselect Sheets	
Task	**How to Carry Out the Task**
Select adjacent sheets	Select the first sheet by clicking its tab and then hold down the SHIFT key and click the sheet tab at the other end of the list of adjacent sheet tabs.
Select nonadjacent sheets	Select the first sheet by clicking its tab and then hold down the CTRL key and click the sheet tabs of the remaining sheets you want to select.
Multiple sheets selected and you want to select a sheet that is selected, but not active (sheet tab name not in bold)	Click the sheet tab you want to select.
Multiple sheets selected and you want to select the active sheet (sheet tab name in bold)	Hold down the SHIFT key and then click the sheet tab of the active sheet.

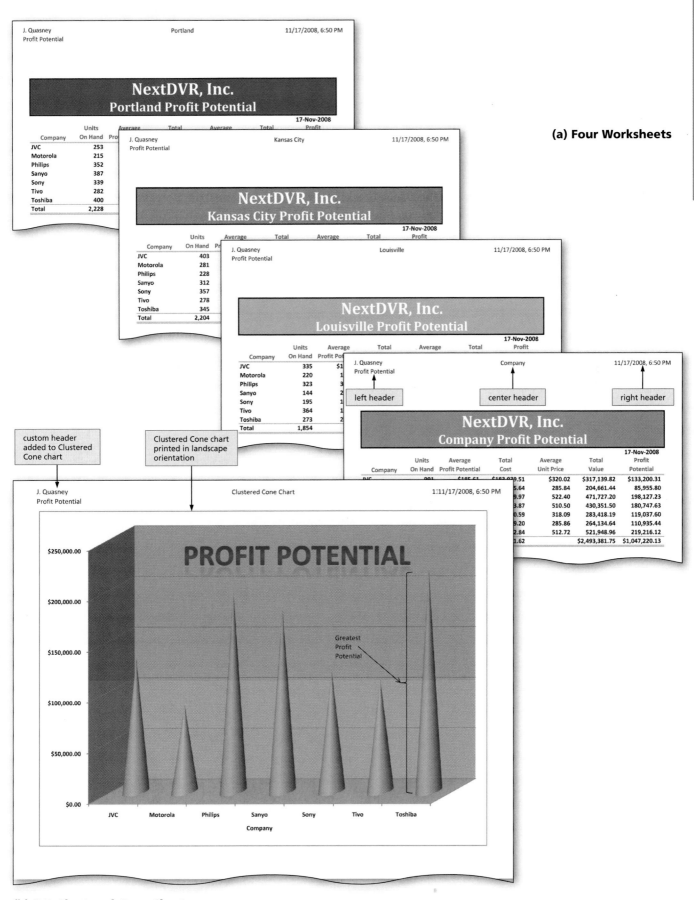

(a) Four Worksheets

custom header added to Clustered Cone chart

Clustered Cone chart printed in landscape orientation

(b) 3-D Clustered Cone Chart

Figure 6–72

To Insert and Remove a Page Break

When you print a worksheet or use the Page Setup dialog box, Excel inserts **page breaks** that show the boundaries of what will print on each page. These page breaks are based upon the margins selected in the Margins sheet in the Page Setup dialog box and the type of printer you are using. If the Page breaks option is selected, then Excel displays dotted lines on the worksheet to show the boundaries of each page. For example, the dotted line in Figure 6–73 shows the right boundary of the first page. If the dotted line does not show on your screen, then click Excel Options on the Office Button menu. When Excel displays the Excel Options dialog box, click the Advanced command to display Advanced Excel options. Scroll the window until the 'Display options for this worksheet' area appears. Click the Show page breaks check box (Figure 6–75 on page EX 480).

You can insert both horizontal and vertical page breaks in a worksheet. Manual page breaks are useful if you have a worksheet that is several pages long and you want certain parts of the worksheet to print on separate pages. For example, say you had a worksheet that comprised ten departments in sequence and each department had many rows of information. If you wanted each department to begin on a new page, then inserting page breaks would satisfy the requirement.

To insert a horizontal page break, you select a cell in column A or an entire row that you want to print on the next page and then click the Breaks button on the Page Layout tab. When the Breaks menu is displayed, click the Insert Page Break command. To insert a vertical page break, you select a cell in row 1 or an entire column that you want to print on the next page and then click the Insert Page Break command. Excel displays a dotted line to indicate the beginning of a new page. To remove a page break, you select the cell in the row immediately below or to the right of the dotted line that indicates the page break you want to remove and then click the Remove Page Break command on the Insert Breaks menu. Excel also includes a Page Break view that allows you to change page breaks by dragging them.

The following steps insert both a horizontal and vertical page break.

1

- With the Company sheet active, select cell B12 and then click the Page Layout tab on the Ribbon.

- Click the Breaks button on the Ribbon and then click Insert Page Break on the Breaks menu to insert a page break (Figure 6–73).

Q&A

What appears on the worksheet?

Excel inserts a dotted line above row 12 indicating a horizontal page break and inserts a dotted line to the left of column B indicating a vertical page break (Figure 6–73).

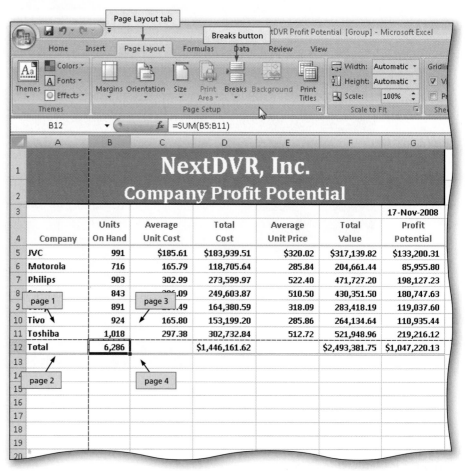

Figure 6–73

2

- With cell B12 active, click the Breaks button on the Ribbon to display the Breaks menu (Figure 6–74).

- Click Remove Page Break to remove the page breaks.

Q&A

Is there a way to move page breaks?

Yes. An alternative to using the Breaks command on the Page Layout tab on the Ribbon to insert page breaks is to click the Page Break Preview button on the status bar. When the Page Break preview appears, you can drag the blue boundaries, which represent page breaks, to new locations.

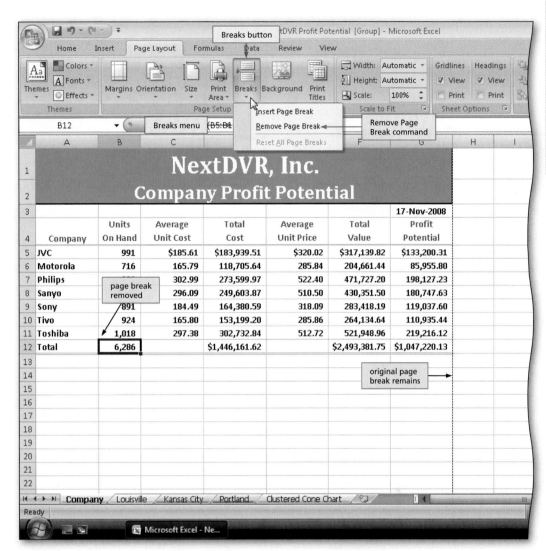

Figure 6–74

Other Ways
1. Click Page Break Preview button on View tab, click OK button, drag page breaks   2. Select cell, press ALT+P, B, I

To Hide Page Breaks

When working with a workbook, page breaks can be an unnecessary distraction, especially to users who have no interest in where pages break. The following steps show how to hide the dotted lines that represent page breaks.

1

• Click the Office Button and then click the Excel Options button on the Office Button menu.

• When Excel displays the Excel Options dialog box, click the Advanced button to display Advanced Excel options.

• Scroll the window until the 'Display options for this worksheet' area appears.

• Click the 'Show page breaks' check box to clear the check box (Figure 6–75).

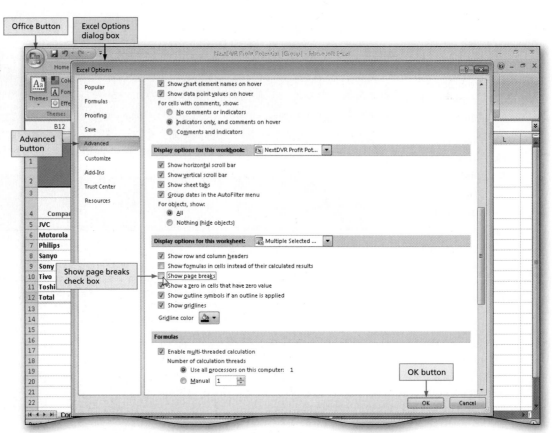

Figure 6–75

2

• Click the OK button to hide the page breaks as shown in Figure 6–76.

	Company	Units On Hand	Average Unit Cost	Total Cost	Average Unit Price	Total Value	Profit Potential
2			**Company Profit Potential**				
3							17-Nov-2008
4	Company	Units On Hand	Average Unit Cost	Total Cost	Average Unit Price	Total Value	Profit Potential
5	JVC	991	$185.61	$183,939.51	$320.02	$317,139.82	$133,200.31
6	Motorola	716	165.79	118,705.64	285.84	204,661.44	85,955.80
7	Philips	903	302.99	273,599.97	522.40		7.23
8	Sanyo	843	296.09	249,603.87	510.50		7.63
9	Sony	891	184.49	164,380.59	318.09		7.60
10	Tivo	924	165.80	153,199.20	285.86	264,134.64	110,935.44
11	Toshiba	1,018	297.38	302,732.84	512.72	521,948.96	219,216.12
12	Total	6,286		$1,446,161.62		$2,493,381.75	$1,047,220.13
13							

dotted line representing vertical page break hidden

Figure 6–76

Other Ways

1. Press ALT+P, B, R

Saving a Workbook as a PDF or XPS file

Excel provides additional options for distributing your final workbook project. Often you may want to distribute copies of a workbook to others who do not have access to Excel. The printed pages shown in Figure 6–72 on page EX 477 provide one method for distributing the workbook. Excel also allows you to distribute an electronic version of the printed pages using two different file formats: PDF and XPS. For each of these file formats, the workbook appears in an electronic format to the reader of the workbook, with one worksheet displayed as a separate page. The reader may not make changes to the documents; they, therefore, often are considered electronic printed versions of the workbook.

When you distribute a workbook as a PDF or XPS file, those who want to read the workbook must have a reader program installed. The most common PDF reader is Acrobat Reader from Adobe. Microsoft provides a reader for its newer XPS file format.

To save a workbook in the PDF and XPS file formats, you must install an add-on program from Microsoft's Web site. The add-on program is available as a free download from Microsoft, and a link to the Web site is provided in Excel Help. Once installed, the Save As submenu on the Office Button menu includes a new PDF or XPS command. When you click the command, Excel displays the Publish as PDF or XPS dialog box which allows you to choose a file name for the document, a location to save the document, and other options.

The Find and Replace Commands

A **string** can be a single character, a word, or a phrase in a cell on a worksheet. You display the Find & Select menu by clicking the Find & Select button on the Ribbon. The Find command on the Find & Select menu is used to locate a string. The Replace command on the Find & Select menu is used to locate one string and then replace it with another string. The Find and Replace commands are not available for a chart sheet.

Both the Find and Replace commands cause the Find and Replace dialog box to be displayed. The Find and Replace dialog box has two variations. One version displays minimal options, while the other version displays all of the available options. When you invoke the Find or Replace command, Excel displays the dialog box variation that was used the last time either command was invoked.

BTW

The Find Command
If you want to search only a specified range of a worksheet, then select the range before invoking the Find command. The range can consist of adjacent cells or nonadjacent cells.

To Find a String

The following steps show how to locate the string, Toshiba, in the four worksheets: Company, Louisville, Kansas City, and Portland. The Find and Replace dialog box that displays all the options will be used to customize the search to include the entire workbook and to use the match case and match entire cell contents options. **Match case** means that the search is case sensitive and the cell contents must match the word exactly the way it is typed. **Match entire cell contents** means that the string cannot be part of another word or phrase and must be unique in the cell. Unlike the Spelling command, which starts the spell checker at the active cell and works downward, the Find and Replace commands always begin at cell A1, regardless of the location of the active cell.

1
- Click the Home tab on the Ribbon.

- With the Company sheet active, click the Find & Select button on the Ribbon (Figure 6–77).

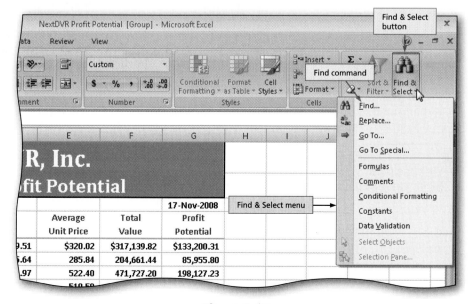

Figure 6–77

2

- Click Find.

- When Excel displays the Find and Replace dialog box, click the Options button so that it appears as shown in Figure 6–78.

- Type Toshiba in the Find what box, click the Within box arrow, select Workbook, and then click the Match case and 'Match entire cell contents' check boxes to select them (Figure 6–78).

Q&A Why does the appearance of the Options button change?

The two greater than signs pointing to the left on the Options button indicate that the more comprehensive Find and Replace dialog box is active.

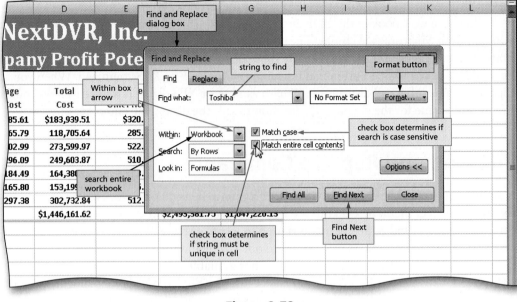

Figure 6–78

3

- Click the Find Next button to cause Excel to begin the search at cell A1 on the Company sheet and make cell A11 the active cell (Figure 6–79) because it is the first cell to match the search string.

4

- Continue clicking the Find Next button to find the string, Toshiba, on the other sheets in the workbook.

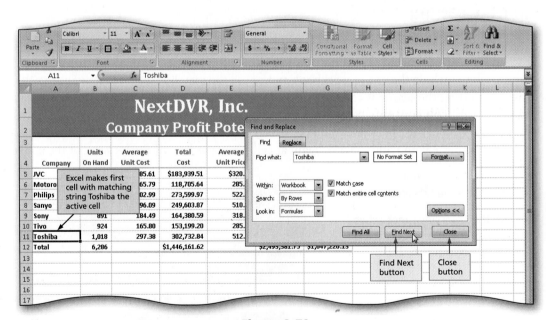

Figure 6–79

- Click the Close button in the Find and Replace dialog box to terminate the process and close the Find and Replace dialog box.

Q&A What if Excel does not find the search string?

If the Find command does not find the string for which you are searching, Excel displays a dialog box indicating it has searched the selected worksheets and cannot find the search string.

Other Ways

1. Press CTRL+F

Working with the Find and Replace Dialog Box

The Format button in the Find and Replace dialog box in Figure 6–78 allows you to fine-tune the search by adding formats, such as bold, font style, and font size, to the string. The Within box options include Sheet and Workbook. The Search box indicates whether the search will be done vertically through rows or horizontally across columns. The Look in box allows you to select Values, Formulas, or Comments. If you select Values, Excel will look for the search string only in cells that do not have formulas. If you select Formulas, Excel will look in all cells. If you select Comments, Excel will look only in comments. If you select the Match case check box, Excel will locate only cells in which the string is in the same case. For example, philips is not the same as Philips. If you select the 'Match entire cell contents' check box, Excel will locate only the cells that contain the string and no other characters. For example, Excel will find a cell entry of Philips, but not Philips DVRs.

To Replace a String with Another String

The Replace command is used to replace the found search string with a new string. You can use the Find Next and Replace buttons to find and replace a string one occurrence at a time, or you can use the Replace All button to replace the string in all locations at once. The following steps show how to use the Replace All button to replace the string, Philips, with the string, Royal Philips, formatted as red italic font.

- With the Company sheet active, click the Find & Select button on the Ribbon and then click Replace.

- When Excel displays the Find and Replace dialog box, type Philips in the Find what box and Royal Philips in the Replace with box.

- Click the Format button to the right of the Replace with box. When Excel displays the Replace Format dialog box, click the Font tab, click the Color box arrow, click Red (column 2, row 1 in the Standard colors area), click Italic in the Font style list, and then click the OK button.

- If necessary, click the Within box arrow and then click Workbook.

- If necessary, click the Match case and 'Match entire cell contents' check boxes to select them (Figure 6–80).

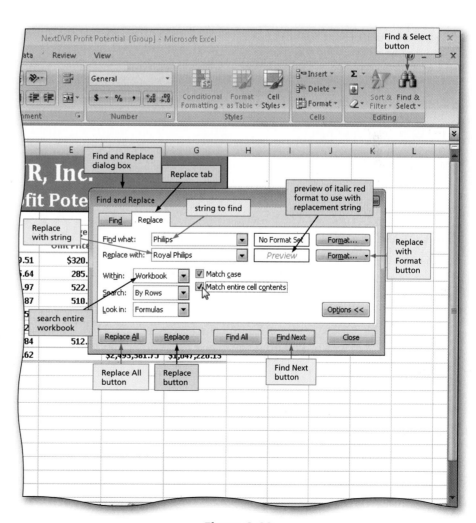

Figure 6–80

● Click the Replace All button to replace the string (Figure 6–81).

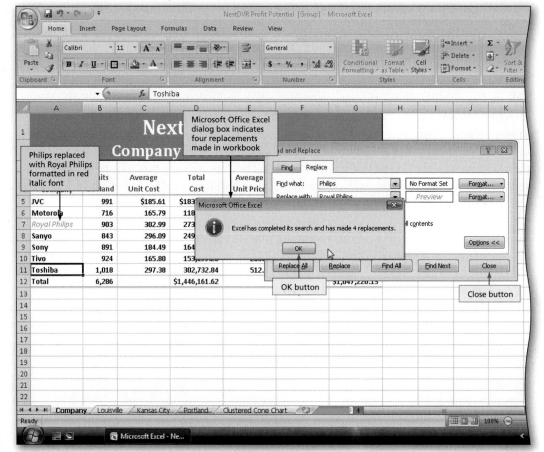

Figure 6–81

● Click the OK button in the Microsoft Office Excel dialog box.

● Click the Close button in the Find and Replace dialog box.

Q&A

What happens when Excel replaces the string?

Excel replaces the string, Philips, with the replacement string, Royal Philips (cell A7), throughout the four worksheets in the workbook. The replacement string is formatted as red italic font. Excel does not replace the string, Philips, on the Clustered Cone Chart sheet. Excel displays the Microsoft Office Excel dialog box indicating four replacements were made.

Other Ways

1. Press CTRL+H

To Quit Excel

The following steps quit Excel without saving changes to the NextDVR Profit Potential workbook.

1 Click the Close button on the right side of the Excel title bar.

2 When Excel displays the Microsoft Office Excel dialog box, click the No button.

Consolidating Data by Linking Workbooks

Earlier in this chapter, the data from three worksheets were consolidated into another worksheet in the same workbook using 3-D references. An alternative to this method is to consolidate data from worksheets in other workbooks. Consolidating data from other workbooks also is referred to as linking. A **link** is a reference to a cell or range of cells in another workbook. In this case, the 3-D reference also includes a workbook name. For example, the following 3-D reference pertains to cell B5 on the Kansas City sheet in the workbook NDVR Kansas City Profit Potential located on drive E.

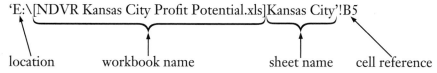

location   workbook name   sheet name   cell reference

The single quotation marks surrounding the location, workbook name, and sheet name are required if any of the three names contain spaces. If the workbook you are referring to is in the same folder as the active workbook, the location (E:\) is not necessary. The brackets surrounding the workbook name are required.

To illustrate linking cells between workbooks, the Company, Louisville, Kansas City, and Portland worksheets from the workbook created earlier in this chapter are on the Data Files for Students in separate workbooks as described in Table 6–10. In the workbook names in Table 6–10, the NDVR stands for NextDVR. The region workbooks contain the region data, but the NDVR Company workbook does not include any consolidated data. The consolidation of data from the three region workbooks into the NDVR Company Profit Potential workbook will be completed later in this section.

Table 6–10 Workbook Names	
Worksheet in NextDVR Profit Potential Workbook	**Saved on The Data Files for Students Using the Workbook Name**
Company	NDVR Company Profit Potential
Louisville	NDVR Louisville Profit Potential
Kansas City	NDVR Kansas City Profit Potential
Portland	NDVR Portland Profit Potential

The remaining sections of this chapter demonstrate how to search for the four workbooks in Table 6–10 on drive E, how to create a workspace from the four workbooks, and finally how to link the three region workbooks to consolidate the data into the NDVR Company Profit Potential workbook.

BTW

Consolidation
You also can consolidate data across different workbooks using the Consolidate button on the Data tab on the Ribbon, rather than by entering formulas. For more information on the Consolidate button, type `consolidate` in the Search box in the Excel Help dialog box, and then click the 'Consolidate data in multiple worksheets' link in the Results list.

To Search for and Open Workbooks

Excel has a powerful search tool that you can use to locate workbooks (or any file) stored on disk. You search for files using the Search text box in the Open dialog box. If you view files on the Data Files for Students, then you would see the four workbooks listed in the right column of Table 6–10. The following steps, however, show how to search for workbooks when you cannot remember exactly the name of the file or its location. In this example, the string NDVR (the first four characters in the workbook names) will be used to locate the workbooks. The located workbooks then are opened and **arranged** so that each one appears in its own window.

- Start Excel following the steps on page EX 423 and then click the Office Button.

- Click Open on the Office Button menu and then select UDISK (E:) in the Address bar (Figure 6–82).

- Type NDVR in the Search box.

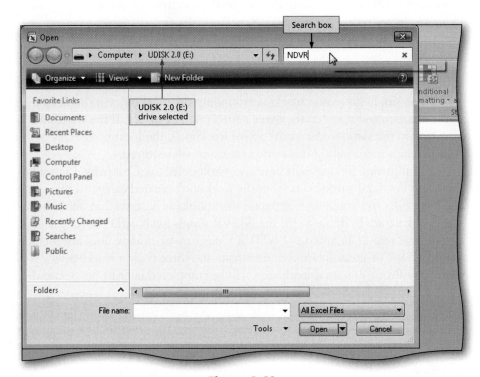

Figure 6–82

- Press the ENTER key to display a list of the four workbooks described in Table 6–10 on the previous page in the File list (Figure 6–83).

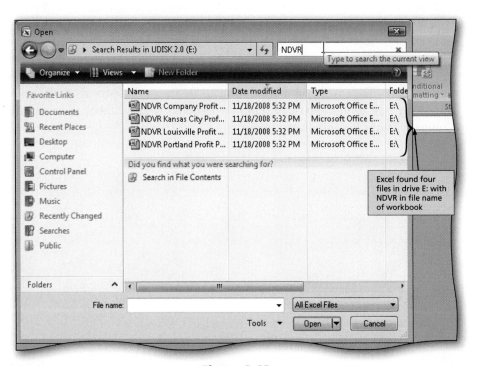

Figure 6–83

3

- In the File list, while holding down the CTRL key, click each of the three region workbook names one at a time and then click the company workbook name.

- Click the Open button to open the four workbooks.

- Click the View tab on the Ribbon and then click the Switch Windows button to display the names of the four workbooks with a check mark to the left of the active workbook (Figure 6–84).

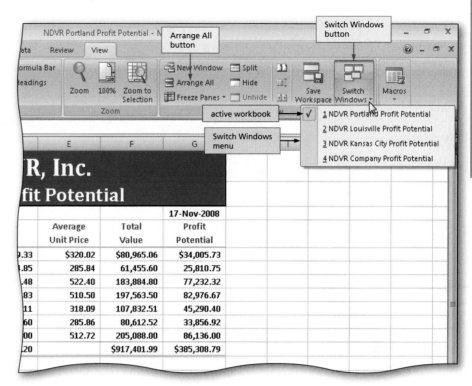

Figure 6–84

4

- Click the Arrange All button on the Ribbon.

- When Excel displays the Arrange Windows dialog box, click Vertical, and then, if necessary, click the 'Windows of active workbook' check box to clear it (Figure 6–85).

Q&A

How can I arrange workbooks in the Excel window?

As shown in Figure 6–85, multiple opened workbooks can be arranged in four ways. The option name in the Arrange Windows dialog box identifies the resulting window's configuration. You can modify any of the arranged workbooks by clicking within its window to activate it. To return to showing one workbook, double-click its title bar as described in Step 6 on the next page.

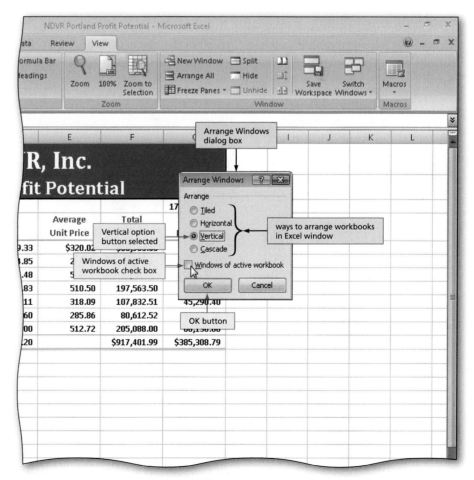

Figure 6–85

- Click the OK button in the Arrange Windows dialog box to display the four opened workbooks as shown in Figure 6–86.

- Double-click the NDVR Company Profit Potential title bar to maximize it and hide the other opened workbooks.

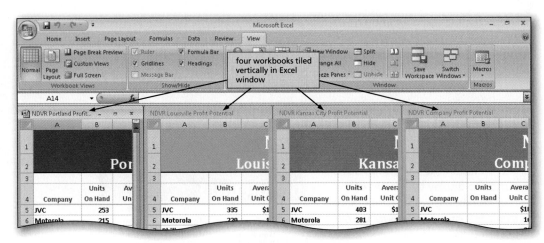

Figure 6–86

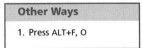

Other Ways

1. Press ALT+F, O

To Create a Workspace File

If you plan to consolidate data from other workbooks, it is recommended that you first bind the workbooks together using a workspace file. A **workspace file** saves information about all the workbooks that are open. The workspace file does not contain the actual workbooks; rather, it stores information required to open the files associated with the workspace file, including file names, which file was active at the time of the save, and other display settings. To create a workspace file, click the Save Workspace button on the View tab on the Ribbon. After you create and save a workspace file, you can open all of the associated files by opening the workspace. The following steps show how to create a workspace file from the files opened in the previous set of steps.

- With the four NDVR workbooks opened and the Company Profit Potential workbook active, if necessary, click the View tab on the Ribbon (Figure 6–87).

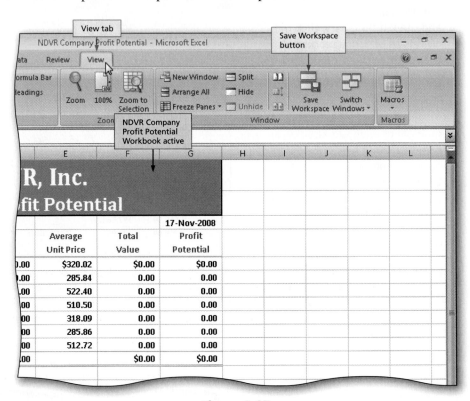

Figure 6–87

2

- Click the Save Workspace button on the Ribbon.

- When Excel displays the Save Workspace dialog box, select UDISK 2.0 (E:) in the Address bar and then type `NextDVR Workspace` in the File name box (Figure 6–88).

Q&A

Can I still open the workbooks separately or must I always open the workspace?

After the workspace is saved to disk, you can open the workbooks one at a time as you did in the past, or you can open all of the associated workbooks by opening the workspace. When you invoke the Open command, workspace file names appear in the Open dialog box, the same as any workbook file name.

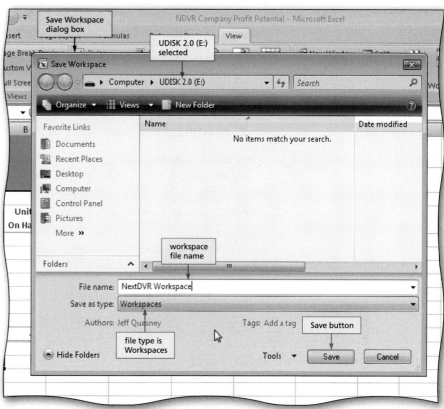

Figure 6–88

3

- Click the Save button in the Save Workspace dialog box to save the file names of the workbooks open, of the workbooks displaying, and other display settings.

- If the Microsoft Office Excel dialog box is displayed for any of the workbooks, click the No button.

- Click the Office Button and then click the Exit Excel button on the Office Button menu to quit Excel.

- If the Microsoft Office Excel dialog box is displayed for any of the workbooks, click the No button.

Other Ways
1. Press ALT+W, K

To Consolidate Data by Linking Workbooks

The following steps show how to open the workspace file NextDVR Workspace and consolidate the data from the three region workbooks into the NDVR Company Profit Potential workbook.

1 Start Excel as described on page EX 423. Click the Office Button and then click Open on the Office Button menu. When Excel displays the Open dialog box, select UDISK 2.0 (E:) in the Address bar. Double-click NextDVR Workspace to open the four workbooks saved in the workspace. Make NDVR Company Profit Potential the active worksheet. If necessary, double-click the NDVR Company Profit Potential window title bar to maximize it.

2 Select cell B5. Click the Sum button on the Home tab on the Ribbon. Click the View tab on the Ribbon and then click the Switch Windows button arrow on the Ribbon. Click NDVR Louisville Profit Potential on the Switch Windows menu. Click cell B5. Delete the dollar signs ($) in the reference to cell B5 in the formula bar. Click immediately after B5 in the formula bar and then press the COMMA key.

BTW

Workspace Files
A workspace file saves display information about open workbooks, such as window sizes, print areas, screen magnification, and display settings. Workspace files do not contain the workbooks themselves.

3 Click the Switch Windows button arrow on the Ribbon and then click NDVR Kansas City Profit Potential. Select cell B5. Delete the dollar signs ($) in the reference to cell B5 in the formula bar. Click immediately after B5 in the formula bar and then press the COMMA key.

4 Click the Switch Windows button arrow on the Ribbon and then click NDVR Portland Profit Potential. Select cell B5. Delete the dollar signs ($) in the reference to cell B5 in the formula bar. Click the Enter box.

5 With cell B5 active in the NDVR Company Profit Potential workbook, drag the cell's fill handle through cell B11. Select cell B5 (Figure 6–89).

6 Click the Save button on the Quick Access Toolbar. If Excel displays a dialog box, select Overwrite changes. Click the OK button. Click the Office Button, click Print on the Office Button menu, and then click the OK button in the Print dialog box to print the workbook.

Q&A

Why did the formulas need to be edited for each workbook?

As you link workbooks, remember that the cell reference inserted by Excel each time you click a cell in a workbook is an absolute cell reference ($B$5). You must edit the formula and change these to relative cell references because the SUM function later is copied to the range B6:B11. If the cell references are left as absolute, then the copied function always would refer to cell B5 in the three workbooks no matter where you copy the SUM function.

BTW

Excel Help
The best way to become familiar with Excel Help is to use it. Appendix C includes detailed information about Excel Help and exercises that will help you gain confidence in using it.

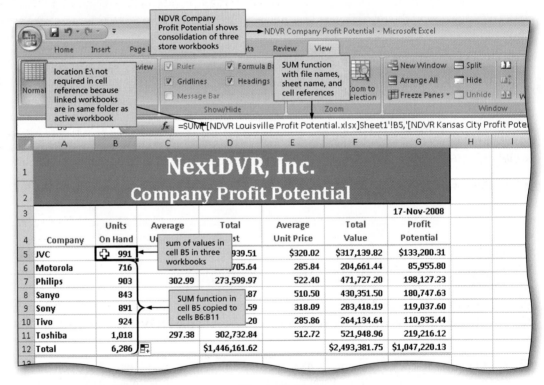

Figure 6–89

Updating Links

Later, if you open the NDVR Company Profit Potential workbook by itself, also called the **dependent workbook**, Excel will update the links automatically if the linked workbooks are open. The linked workbooks are called the **source workbooks**. If the linked workbooks are not open, then Excel displays a security warning in a pane below the Ribbon. If you click the Options button in the security warning pane, Excel displays the Microsoft

Office Security Options dialog box and asks if you would like to enable automatic update of links. If you click the 'Enable this content' option button and click the OK button in the dialog box, Excel reads the data in the source workbooks and recalculates formulas in the dependent workbook, but it does not open the source workbooks.

If the three source workbooks are open along with the dependent workbook as in the previous set of steps, Excel automatically updates the links (recalculates) in the NDVR Company Profit Potential workbook when a value changes in any one of the source workbooks.

BTW

Certification
The Microsoft Certified Application Specialist (MCAS) program provides an opportunity for you to obtain a valuable industry credential — proof that you have the Excel 2007 skills required by employers. For more information, see Appendix G or visit the Excel 2007 Certification Web page (scsite.com/ex2007/cert).

To Close All Workbooks at One Time and Quit Excel

To close all four workbooks at one time and quit Excel, complete the following steps.

1. Click the Office Button and then click the Exit Excel button on the Office Button menu.

2. If Excel displays the Microsoft Office Excel dialog box, click the No button.

Chapter Summary

In this chapter, you learned how to create and use a template, customize formats, create styles, change chart types, draw and enhance a Clustered Cone chart using WordArt, annotate using text boxes and arrows, use 3-D reference to reference cells in other sheets, add, remove, and change pages breaks, use the Find and Replace commands, and create a workspace file. The items listed below include all the new Excel skills you have learned in this chapter.

1. Save the Template (EX 433)
2. Create and Assign a Custom Format Code and a Comma Style Format (EX 438)
3. Create a New Style (EX 440)
4. Apply a New Style (EX 443)
5. Open a Template and Save It as a Workbook (EX 446)
6. Add a Worksheet to a Workbook (EX 447)
7. Copy the Contents of a Worksheet to Other Worksheets in a Workbook (EX 449)
8. Drill an Entry through Worksheets (EX 451)
9. Enter and Copy 3-D References Using the Paste Button Menu (EX 457)
10. Format the Clustered Cone Chart (EX 465)
11. Add a Chart Title Using the WordArt Tool (EX 466)
12. Add a Text Box, Arrow, and Brace to the Chart (EX 469)
13. Add a Header and Footer, Change Margins, and Center the Printout Horizontally (EX 472)
14. Add a Header to the Clustered Cone Chart Sheet (EX 475)
15. Print All Worksheets in a Workbook (EX 476)
16. Print Nonadjacent Sheets in a Workbook (EX 476)
17. Insert and Remove a Page Break (EX 478)
18. Hide Page Breaks (EX 479)
19. Find a String (EX 481)
20. Replace a String with Another String (EX 483)
21. Search for and Open Workbooks (EX 486)
22. Create a Workspace File (EX 488)
23. Consolidate Data by Linking Workbooks (EX 489)

If you have a SAM user profile, you may have access to hands-on instruction, practice, and assessment. Log in to your SAM account (http://sam2007.course.com) to launch any assigned training activities or exams that relate to the skills covered in this chapter.

Learn It Online

Learn It Online is a series of online student exercises that test your knowledge of chapter content and key terms.

Instructions: To complete the Learn It Online exercises, start your browser, click the Address bar, and then enter the Web address scsite.com/ex2007/learn. When the Excel 2007 Learn It Online page is displayed, click the link for the exercise you want to complete and then read the instructions.

Chapter Reinforcement TF, MC, and SA
A series of true/false, multiple choice, and short answer questions that test your knowledge of the chapter content.

Flash Cards
An interactive learning environment where you identify chapter key terms associated with displayed definitions.

Practice Test
A series of multiple choice questions that test your knowledge of chapter content and key terms.

Who Wants To Be a Computer Genius?
An interactive game that challenges your knowledge of chapter content in the style of a television quiz show.

Wheel of Terms
An interactive game that challenges your knowledge of chapter key terms in the style of the television show *Wheel of Fortune*.

Crossword Puzzle Challenge
A crossword puzzle that challenges your knowledge of key terms presented in the chapter.

Apply Your Knowledge

Reinforce the skills and apply the concepts you learned in this chapter.

Consolidating Data in a Workbook
Instructions: Follow the steps below to consolidate the four quarterly payroll sheets on the Annual Totals sheet in the workbook Apply 6-1 Annual Payroll Totals (Figure 6–90). At the conclusion of the instructions, the Annual Payroll Totals sheet should display as shown in the lower screen in Figure 6–90.

Perform the following tasks.

1. Start Excel. Open the workbook Apply 6-1 Annual Payroll Totals from the Data Files for Students and then save the workbook as Apply 6-1 Annual Payroll Totals Complete. See the inside back cover of this book for instructions for downloading the Data Files for Students or see your instructor for information on accessing the files required in this book. One by one, click the first four tabs and review the quarterly payroll totals. Click the Annual Totals tab.

2. Determine the annual payroll totals on the Annual Totals sheet by using the SUM function and 3-D references to sum the hours worked on the four quarterly sheets in cell B11. Do the same to determine the annual gross pay in cell C11. Copy the range B11:C11 to the range B12:C14 by using the Copy button on the Home tab on the Ribbon and the Formulas command on the Paste button menu on the Home tab on the Ribbon.

3. Change the document properties as specified by your instructor. Select all five worksheets. Add a worksheet header with your name, course number, and other information as specified by your instructor. Add the page number and total number of pages to the footer. Center all worksheets horizontally on the page and print without gridlines. Preview and print the five worksheets. Click the Annual Totals tab to select the sheet.

4. Save the workbook with the new page setup. Close the workbook.

5. Submit the assignment as requested by your instructor.

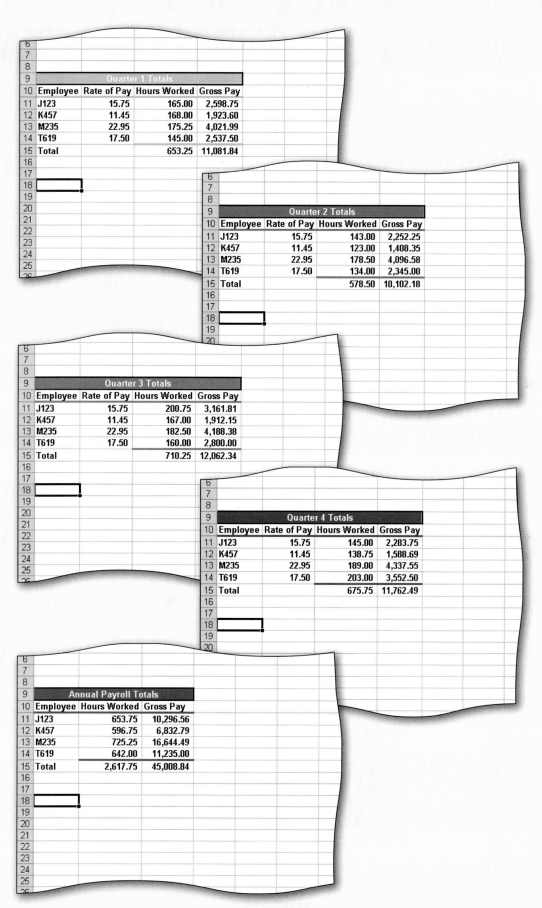

Quarter 1 Totals

Employee	Rate of Pay	Hours Worked	Gross Pay
J123	15.75	165.00	2,598.75
K457	11.45	168.00	1,923.60
M235	22.95	175.25	4,021.99
T619	17.50	145.00	2,537.50
Total		653.25	11,081.84

Quarter 2 Totals

Employee	Rate of Pay	Hours Worked	Gross Pay
J123	15.75	143.00	2,252.25
K457	11.45	123.00	1,408.35
M235	22.95	178.50	4,096.58
T619	17.50	134.00	2,345.00
Total		578.50	10,102.18

Quarter 3 Totals

Employee	Rate of Pay	Hours Worked	Gross Pay
J123	15.75	200.75	3,161.81
K457	11.45	167.00	1,912.15
M235	22.95	182.50	4,188.38
T619	17.50	160.00	2,800.00
Total		710.25	12,062.34

Quarter 4 Totals

Employee	Rate of Pay	Hours Worked	Gross Pay
J123	15.75	145.00	2,283.75
K457	11.45	138.75	1,588.69
M235	22.95	189.00	4,337.55
T619	17.50	203.00	3,552.50
Total		675.75	11,762.49

Annual Payroll Totals

Employee	Hours Worked	Gross Pay
J123	653.75	10,296.56
K457	596.75	6,832.79
M235	725.25	16,644.49
T619	642.00	11,235.00
Total	2,617.75	45,008.84

Figure 6–90

Extend Your Knowledge

Extend the skills you learned in this chapter and experiment with new skills. You may need to use Help to complete the assignment.

Making Use of the Chart Tools on the Design Tab

Instructions: Complete the following tasks.

1. Start Excel. Open the workbook Extend 6-1 Tennis Summary from the Data Files for Students and then save the workbook as Extend 6-1 Tennis Summary Complete. See the inside back cover of this book for instructions for downloading the Data Files for Students or see your instructor for information on accessing the files required in this book. Click the Chart tab. Click the chart to select it and display the Design tab on the Ribbon.

2. Click the Change Chart Type button on the Design tab on the Ribbon and then choose a Line chart to change the 3-D Bar chart to a Line chart. One at a time, repeat this step for each of the following chart types: Bar chart, Area chart, Surface chart, and Doughnut chart. Finally, choose the Column chart type 3-D Cone (column 1, row 3).

3. Click the More arrow (lower arrow) in the Chart Layouts group on the Design tab on the Ribbon to display the Chart Layouts gallery. Choose Layout 2 (column 2, row 1) in the Chart Layouts gallery. Repeat this step for the following layouts: Layout 8 and Layout 9. Finally, choose Layout 5 (column 2, row 2).

4. Click the More arrow (lower arrow) in the Chart Styles group on the Design tab on the Ribbon to display the Chart Styles gallery. One at a time, choose three different Chart Styles. Finally, choose Style 38 (column 6, row 5) as shown in Figure 6–91. Remove the axis title from the left side of the chart.

5. Change the document properties as specified by your instructor. Change the Chart sheet header with your name, course number, and other information as specified by your instructor. Change the print orientation to landscape. Print the Chart sheet using the Fit to option. Save the workbook.

6. Submit the assignment as requested by your instructor.

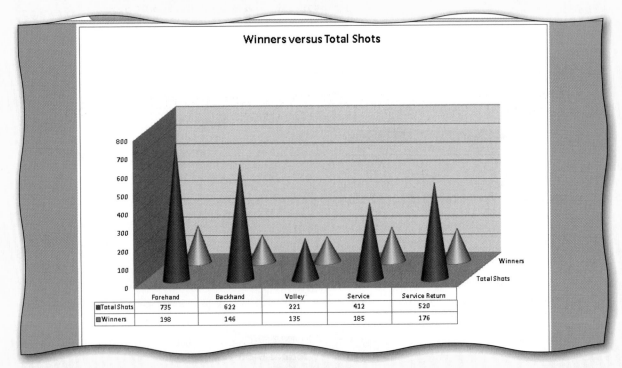

Figure 6–91

Make It Right

Analyze a workbook and correct all errors and/or improve the design.

Chart Manipulation, Using WordArt, and Correcting 3-D Cell References

Instructions: Start Excel. Open the workbook Make It Right 6-1 Gems for Everyone and then save the workbook as Make It Right 6-1 Gems for Everyone Complete. See the inside back cover of this book for instructions for downloading the Data Files for Students or see your instructor for information on accessing the files required in this book. Correct the following design and formula problems so that the Company Totals sheet appears with an embedded chart as shown in Figure 6–92.

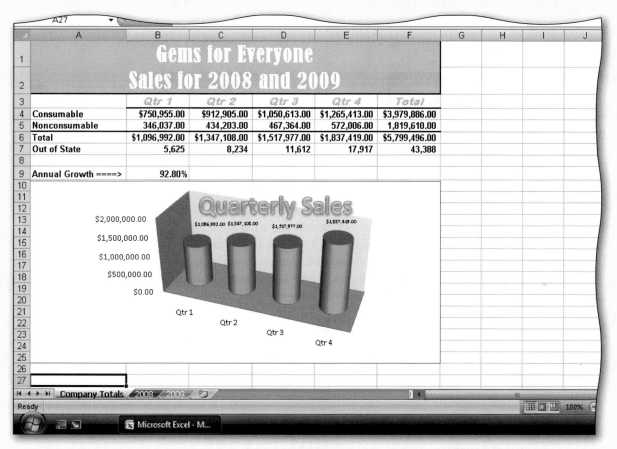

Figure 6–92

Perform the following tasks:

1. Click the Chart sheet tab to display the 3-D Pie chart and then click the chart.

2. Click the Design tab on the Ribbon and then complete the following chart tasks:

   a. Change the 3-D Pie Chart to Clustered Cylinder Chart (column 1, row 2 in the Column area).

   b. Change the chart layout to Layout 4 by clicking the More arrow (lower arrow) in the Chart Layouts group and choosing Layout 4. One at a time, select each of the total numbers at the top of the columns. Change the font size to 6 by typing 6 in the Font Size box on the Home tab on the Ribbon. Drag the total numbers above the cylinders. Delete the Series 1 label below the chart.

   c. Click the More arrow (lower arrow) in the Chart Styles group on the Design tab on the Ribbon to display the Chart Styles gallery. Choose Style 40 (column 8, row 5).

Continued >

Make It Right *continued*

    d. Use the WordArt button on the Insert tab on the Ribbon to add the chart title, Quarterly Sales. Choose the Fill – Accent 6, Warm Matte Bevel (column 2, row 6). Move the chart title above the chart. Change the font size of the chart title to 28.

    e. Click the Design tab on the Ribbon and then click the Move Chart button to move the chart to the Company Totals sheet. Drag the chart to the range A10:F25. Make any necessary adjustments so that the chart appears as shown in Figure 6–92 on the previous page.

3. Select cell B4, the supposed sum of cell B4 on the 2008 and 2009 sheets. Note that the SUM function is not referencing cell B4 on the 2008 sheet. Reenter the SUM function and select the appropriate range to sum. Do the same for cell B5. Copy the range B4:B5 to the range C4:E5.

4. Change the document properties as specified by your instructor. Change the three worksheet headers to include your name, course number, and other information requested by your instructor.

5. Save the workbook, and submit the revised workbook as requested by your instructor.

In the Lab

Create a workbook using the guidelines, concepts, and skills presented in this chapter. Labs are listed in order of increasing difficulty.

Lab 1: Using a Template to Create a Multiple-Sheet Workbook

Problem: Rings and Things is a company that specializes in hand jewelry for women. The company has four stores in Biloxi, Hartford, Peoria, and Seattle and a corporate office in Indianapolis. All of the stores sell their products via direct mail, telesales, and walk-ins. Every year, the corporate officers in Indianapolis use a template to create a year-end sales analysis workbook. The workbook contains four sheets, one for each of the three stores and one sheet to consolidate data and determine the company totals. The Consolidated sheet appears as shown in Figure 6–93.

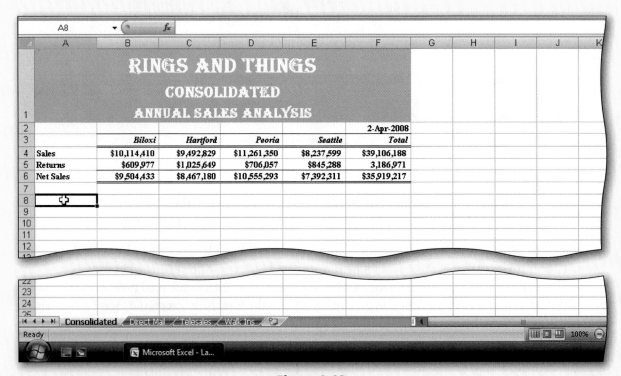

Figure 6–93

The template used to create the annual sales analysis workbook is part of the Data Files for Students. Rebecca Smart, the company's accountant, has asked you to use the template to create the year-end sales analysis workbook.

Instructions Part 1: Perform the following tasks.

1. Open the template Lab 6-1 Rings and Things Annual Sales Analysis Template from the Data Files for Students. See the inside back cover of this book for instructions for downloading the Data Files for Students or see your instructor for information on accessing the files required in this book. Save the template as a workbook using the file name, Lab 6-1 Part 1 Rings and Things Annual Sales Analysis. Make sure Excel Workbook is selected in the 'Save as type' list when you save the workbook.

2. Add a worksheet to the workbook between Sheet1 and Sheet2 and then paste the contents of Sheet1 to the three empty sheets.

3. From left to right, rename the sheet tabs Consolidated, Direct Mail, Telesales, and Walk Ins. Color the tabs as shown in Figure 6–93. On each of the three sales channel sheets, change the subtitle in cell A2 to match the tab name. Use the title, Consolidated, in cell A1 of the Consolidated worksheet. Change the title style for each title area in the range A1:F1 to match its tab color. Enter the data in Table 6–11 into the three sales channel sheets.

Table 6–11 Rings and Things Annual Sales Data by Store and Sales Channel

		Direct Mail	Telesales	Walk Ins
Biloxi	Sales	4873275	3291010	1950125
	Returns	275375	289500	45102
Hartford	Sales	5239100	2152675	2101054
	Returns	463201	500250	62198
Peoria	Sales	3925750	4235100	3100500
	Returns	225198	324519	156340
Seattle	Sales	3278109	1975200	2984290
	Returns	352679	125500	367109

4. On the Consolidated worksheet, use the SUM function, 3-D references, and copy and paste capabilities of Excel to total the corresponding cells on the three sales channel sheets. First, compute the sum in cell B4 and then compute the sum in cell B5. Copy the range B4:B5 to the range C4:E5. The Consolidated sheet should resemble Figure 6–93.

5. Change the document properties as specified by your instructor. Select all four sheets. Add a worksheet header with your name, course number, and other information requested by your instructor. Add the page number and total number of pages to the footer. Change the left and right margins to .5.

6. With the four sheets selected, preview and then print the workbook in landscape orientation and use the Black and white option.

7. Save the workbook with the new page setup characteristics. Close the workbook.

8. Submit the assignment as specified by your instructor.

Instructions Part 2: Complete the following tasks.

1. Start Excel. Open the workbook Lab 6-1 Part 1 Rings and Things Annual Sales Analysis and then save the workbook using the file name, Lab 6-1 Part 2 Rings and Things Annual Sales Analysis.

2. Create an embedded Clustered Horizontal Cylinder chart in the range A8:H25 on the Consolidated worksheet by charting the range A3:E5.

Continued >

In the Lab *continued*

3. Move the chart to a separate sheet by clicking the Move Chart button on the Design tab on the Ribbon. Name the sheet tab Chart and color the sheet tab red. Drag the Chart sheet tab to the far right.

4. Increase the font size of the labels on both axes to 12-point bold. Increase the font size of the legends on the right side of the chart to 14-point.

5. Apply the chart colors shown in Figure 6–94 to the cylinders and to the walls by right-clicking the items one at a time and selecting the appropriate commands.

6. Use the WordArt button on the Insert tab on the Ribbon to add the chart title Annual Sales and Returns. Select Fill - Accent, 2 Matte Bevel (column 3, row 6) from the WordArt gallery.

7. Add the two text boxes and arrows and change their colors to red as shown in Figure 6–94.

8. Add a header to the Chart sheet with your name, course number, and other information requested by your instructor. Add the page number and total number of pages to the footer. Preview and print all five sheets at one time. Save the workbook and then close the workbook.

9. Submit the assignment as specified by your instructor.

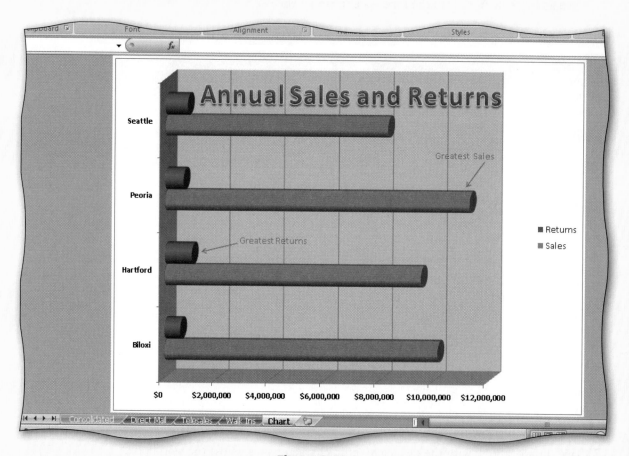

Figure 6–94

Instructions Part 3: Complete the following tasks.
1. Start Excel. Open the workbook Lab 6-1 Part 2 Rings and Things Annual Sales Analysis. Do not save the workbook in this part.

2. Select cell A1 on the Consolidated worksheet. Select all the worksheets except for the Chart sheet.

3. Use the Find & Select button on the Home tab on the Ribbon to list all occurrences of the word, Sales, in the workbook. Use the Find All button in the Find and Replace dialog box. Write down the number of occurrences and the cell locations of the word Sales.

4. Repeat Step 3, but find only cells that match exactly the word Sales. If necessary, click the Options button to display the desired check box. Use the Find & Select button to find all occurrences of the word Sales. Write down the number of occurrences and the cell locations that match exactly with the word Sales.

5. Use the Find & Select button to find all occurrences of the word, sales, in bold white font. For this find operation, clear the check mark from the Match entire cell contents check box.

6. Use the Replace command to replace the word, Sales, with the word, Revenue, on all four sheets. Print the four sheets. Close the workbook without saving changes.

7. Submit the assignment as specified by your instructor.

In the Lab

Lab 2: Consolidating Data by Linking Workbooks

Problem: The Apply Your Knowledge exercise in this chapter calls for consolidating the Hours Worked and Gross Pay from four worksheets on a fifth worksheet in the same workbook (see Figure 6–90 on page EX 493). This exercise takes the same data stored in four separate workbooks and consolidates the Hours Worked and Gross Pay by linking to a fifth workbook.

Instructions Part 1: Perform the following tasks.

1. Start Excel. Open the following five files from the Data Files for Students. See the inside back cover of this book for instructions for downloading the Data Files for Students or see your instructor for information on accessing the files required in this book. You can open them one at a time or you can open them all at one time by selecting the five files and then clicking the Open button.

   - Lab 6-2 Emp Annual Payroll Totals
   - Lab 6-2 Emp Quarter 1 Payroll Totals
   - Lab 6-2 Emp Quarter 2 Payroll Totals
   - Lab 6-2 Emp Quarter 3 Payroll Totals
   - Lab 6-2 Emp Quarter 4 Payroll Totals

2. Click the Switch Windows button on the View tab on the Ribbon and then click Lab 6-2 Emp Annual Payroll Totals.

3. Click the Save Workspace button on the View tab on the Ribbon. When the Save Workspace dialog box is displayed, save the workspace using the file name, Lab 6-2 Emp Payroll Workspace.

4. Close all the open workbooks. Open the workspace Lab 6-2 Emp Payroll Workspace. When the Lab 6-2 Emp Annual Payroll Totals window is displayed, click the Maximize button in the upper-right corner to maximize the window. Save the workbook using the file name, Lab 6-2 Part 1 Emp Annual Payroll Totals.

5. Consolidate the data in the four quarterly payroll workbooks into the range B11:C14 in the workbook Lab 6-2 Part 1 Emp Annual Payroll Totals by doing the following:

   a. Click cell B11. Click the Home tab on the Ribbon and then click Sum button.

   b. Click the Switch Windows button on the View tab on the Ribbon and then click Lab 6-2 Emp Quarter 1 Payroll Totals. When the workbook is displayed, click cell C11, click the Switch Windows button on the View tab on the Ribbon, and then click Lab 6-2 Part 1 Emp Annual

Continued >

In the Lab *continued*

Payroll Totals. Change the absolute cell reference $C$11 in the formula bar to the relative cell reference C11 by deleting the dollar signs. Click immediately after C11 in the formula bar and then press the COMMA key.

c. Click the Switch Windows button on the View tab on the Ribbon and then click Lab 6-2 Emp Quarter 2 Payroll Totals. When the workbook is displayed, click cell C11, click the Switch Windows button on the View tab on the Ribbon, and then click Lab 6-2 Part 1 Emp Annual Payroll Totals. Change the absolute cell reference $C$11 in the formula bar to the relative cell reference C11 by deleting the dollar signs. Click immediately after C11 in the formula bar and then press the COMMA key.

d. Click the Switch Windows button on the View tab on the Ribbon and then click Lab 6-2 Emp Quarter 3 Payroll Totals. When the workbook is displayed, click cell C11, click the Switch Windows button on the View tab on the Ribbon, and then click Lab 6-2 Part 1 Emp Annual Payroll Totals. Change the absolute cell reference $C$11 in the formula bar to the relative cell reference C11 by deleting the dollar signs. Click immediately after C11 in the formula bar and then press the COMMA key.

e. Click the Switch Windows button on the View tab on the Ribbon and then click Lab 6-2 Emp Quarter 4 Payroll Totals. When the workbook is displayed, click cell C11, click the Switch Windows button on the View tab on the Ribbon, and then click Lab 6-2 Part 1 Emp Annual Payroll Totals. Change the absolute cell reference $C$11 in the formula bar to the relative cell reference C11 by deleting the dollar signs. Press the ENTER key to sum the four quarter hours worked. You should end up with an annual total of 653.75 hours worked in cell B11.

f. With the workbook Lab 6-2 Part 1 Emp Annual Payroll Totals window active, select cell B11. Drag the fill handle through cell C11 to display the annual gross pay in cell C11. Select the range B11:C11. Drag the fill handle down to cell C14. When the Auto Fill Options button is displayed next to cell C14, click the Auto Fill Options button and then click the Fill Without Formatting option. The totals in row 15 should be exactly the same as the totals in row 15 in the lower figure of Figure 6–90 on page EX 493.

6. Change the document properties as specified by your instructor. Change the worksheet header with your name, course number, and other information as specified by your instructor. Preview and print the annual payroll totals. Save the workbook using the file name, Lab 6-2 Part 1 Emp Annual Payroll Totals. Close all workbooks. Submit the assignment as requested by your instructor.

Instructions Part 2: Perform the following tasks to update the hours worked for Quarter 2 and Quarter 4.

1. Start Excel. Open Lab 6-2 Emp Quarter 2 Payroll Totals from the Data Files for Students. Change the hours worked for employee K457 in row 12 from 123.00 to 223.25. Save the workbook using the file name, Lab 6-2 Emp Quarter 2 Payroll Totals. Close the workbook.

2. Open Lab 6-2 Emp Quarter 4 Payroll Totals. Change the hours worked for employee M235 in row 13 from 189.00 to 211.00. Save the workbook using the file name, Lab 6-2 Emp Quarter 4 Payroll Totals. Close the workbook.

3. Open Lab 6-2 Part 1 Emp Annual Payroll Totals workbook saved earlier in Part 1 of this exercise. Save the workbook using the file name, Lab 6-2 Part 2 Emp Annual Payroll Totals. Click the Data tab on the Ribbon. Click the Edit Links button in the Connections group on the Data tab. Select each file in the Edit Links dialog box and then click the Update Values button to instruct Excel to apply the current values in the four source workbooks to the consolidated workbook (Figure 6–95).

4. Preview and print the consolidated workbook. Save the workbook. Submit the assignment as requested by your instructor.

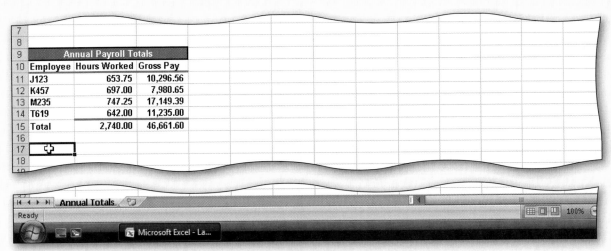

Figure 6–95

In the Lab

Lab 3: Returning Real-Time Stock Quotes to the Stock Portfolio Worksheet

Problem: You belong to the Learn-N-Earn Stock Club, which has been investing in the stock market for the past several years. As vice-president of the club, you maintain a summary of the club's stock market investments in an Excel workbook (Figure 6–96a on the next page). Each day you go through the Business section of the newspaper and manually update the current prices in column G to determine the value of the club's equities. You recently heard about the Web query capabilities of Excel and have decided to use them to update the club's stock portfolio automatically.

Instructions: Perform the following steps to have Web queries automatically update the current price in column G and the major indices in the range B12:B15 of Figure 6–96a.

1. Start Excel. Open the workbook Lab 6-3 Learn-N-Earn Stock Club Portfolio Basics from the Data Files for Students and then save the workbook using the file name, Lab 6-3 Learn-N-Earn Stock Club Portfolio. See the inside back cover of this book for instructions for downloading the Data Files for Students or see your instructor for information on accessing the files required in this book. After reviewing the worksheet, you should notice that it lacks current prices in column G and the major indices in the range B12:B15.

2. Click Sheet2 and then select cell A1. Click the Data tab on the Ribbon and then click the Existing Connections button. When Excel displays the Existing Connections dialog box, double-click MSN MoneyCentral Investor Stock Quotes. When Excel displays the Import Data dialog box, click the OK button. When Excel displays the Enter Parameter Value dialog box, click the Learn-N-Earn Portfolio sheet tab at the bottom of the screen and drag through the range B3:B10. Click the 'Use this value/reference for future refreshes' check box to select it. The Enter Parameter Value dialog box should display as shown in Figure 6–96b on the next page. Click the OK button. The Web query should return a worksheet with up-to-date stock quotes similar to the one shown in Figure 6–96c on the next page. Rename the Sheet2 tab Stock Quotes.

3. Click the Learn-N-Earn Portfolio tab. Click cell G3. Type = (equal sign). Click the Stock Quotes tab. Click cell D4. Press the ENTER key. Use the fill handle to copy cell G3 on the Learn-N-Earn Portfolio sheet to the range G4:G10. You now should have current prices for the stock portfolio that are the same as the last prices on the Stock Quotes worksheet in column D.

4. Click Sheet3 and then select cell A1. If necessary, click the Data tab on the Ribbon and then click Existing Connections. When Excel displays the Existing Connections dialog box, double-click MSN Money Central Investor Major Indices. When Excel displays the Import Data dialog box,

Continued >

In the Lab *continued*

click the OK button. Rename the Sheet3 tab Major Indices. The worksheet should be similar to the one shown in Figure 6–96d.

(a) Learn-N-Earn Portfolio Worksheet

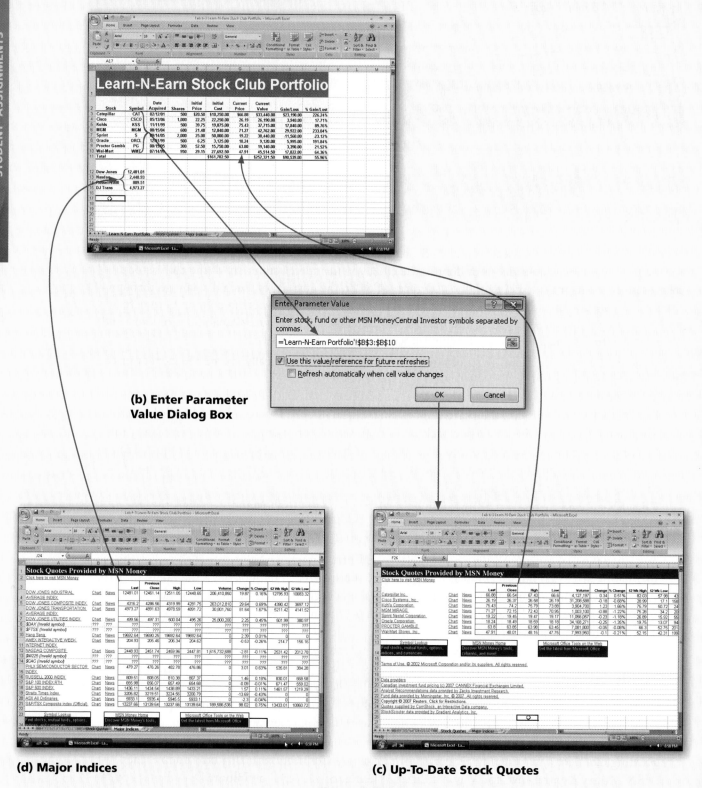

(b) Enter Parameter Value Dialog Box

(d) Major Indices

(c) Up-To-Date Stock Quotes

Figure 6–96

5. Click the Learn-N-Earn Portfolio sheet tab. Select cell B12. Type = (equal sign). Click the Major Indices sheet tab. Select cell D4 (the last Dow Jones Industrial Average Index). Press the ENTER key. Select cell B13. Type = (equal sign). Click the Major Indices tab. Select cell D12 (the last NASDAQ Composite Index). Press the ENTER key. Select cell B14. Type = (equal sign). Click the Major Indices tab. Select cell D16 (the last Russell 2000 Index). Press the ENTER key. Select cell B15. Type = (equal sign). Click the Major Indices tab. Select cell D6 (the last Dow Jones Transportation Average Index). Press the ENTER key. Select cell A16.

6. Change the document properties as specified by your instructor. Select all three worksheets and then change the header with your name, course number, and other information as specified by your instructor. Add a page number as the footer. Change the top margin to 1.5 inches. Select cell A16 and then save the workbook using the file name, Lab 6-3 Learn-N-Earn Stock Club Portfolio.

7. Print the three worksheets using the 'Black and white' option in landscape orientation. Use the Fit to option in the Page sheet in the Page Setup dialog box to print the sheets on one page.

8. Select cell A16 and then save the workbook. Submit the assignment as requested by your instructor.

Cases and Places

Apply your creative thinking and problem solving skills to design and implement a solution.

• EASIER •• MORE DIFFICULT

• 1: Public Safety Division Budget Proposal

San Pueblo's Public Safety division comprises three departments —Streets and Sanitation, Fire, and Police. The departments have submitted figures comparing this year's budget with next year's budget in four categories (Table 6–12). Develop a template that can be used to prepare each department's budget and the Public Safety division's consolidated total budget within one workbook. Include this year's budget, next year's budget, and the variance [(next year's budget – this year's budget) / this year's budget] for each expenditure. Indicate totals where appropriate. Create an embedded chart on the Public Safety division's worksheet comparing the division's expenditures this year and next.

Table 6–12 San Pueblo's Public Safety Division Expenditures						
	Streets and Sanitation		Fire		Police	
	Next Year	This Year	Next Year	This Year	Next Year	This Year
Equipment	212000	198150	62350	78345	225175	220650
Maintenance	68350	62450	22750	17000	98375	102500
Miscellaneous	48125	44520	37600	38200	47500	32800
Salaries and Benefits	116000	112400	198000	211000	150000	162750

• 2: Creating a Consolidated Balance Sheet

Jeans-For-Teens is a New York-based company that sells high-end jeans globally. After launching its Web site five years ago, the company has attracted so many clients from Europe that the owners opened a shop in Paris. The New York and Paris shops' assets last year, respectively, were: cash $825,101 and $650,450; accounts receivable $557,190 and $325,860; marketable securities $345,213 and $211,450; inventory $845,258 and $326,120; and equipment $82,250 and $56,200. The liabilities for each store were: notes payable $1,223,010 and $345,000; accounts payable $213,360 and $702,330; and income tax payable $82,100 and $125,350. The stockholders' equity was: common stock $812,300 and $235,000; and retained earnings $324,242 and $162,400.

Use the concepts and techniques presented in this project to design a template as a balance worksheet to reflect the figures above. Include totals for assets, liabilities, and stockholders' equity. Use the template to create a balance worksheet for the New York store, the Paris store, and the consolidated balance worksheet for the corporation.

•• 3: Analyzing Company Profits by Category

Elite Software sells computer software and supplies. Merchandise is divided into six categories based on profit margin: individual application packages (22%), integrated application packages (9%), entertainment software (16%), system software (25%), learning aids (18%), and supplies (10%). Last year's sales data has been collected for the State Street and Western Avenue Stores as shown in Table 6–13.

Develop a template that can be used to determine marketing strategies for next year. Include sales, profit margins, profits (sales × profit margin), total sales, total profits, and functions to determine the most and least sales, profit margins, and profits. Use the template to create a worksheet for each outlet, a consolidated worksheet for the entire company, and a chart on a separate sheet reflecting the company's profits by category.

Table 6–13 Last Year's Sales for State Street and Western Avenue Stores		
	State Street Store	**Western Avenue Store**
Individual applications	$148,812	$52,864
Integrated applications	140,135	93,182
Entertainment software	62,912	72,345
System software	22,769	25,278
Learning aids	9,562	21,397
Supplies	44,215	34,921

•• 4: Analyzing Annual College Expenses and Resources

Make It Personal

College expenses are skyrocketing and your resources are limited. To plan for the upcoming year, you have decided to organize your anticipated expenses and resources in a workbook. The data required to prepare the workbook is shown in Table 6–14.

Table 6–14 Next Year's Anticipated College Expenses and Resources			
Expenses	**Semester 1**	**Semester 2**	**Summer**
Room and Board	5750	5750	2150
Tuition	8750	8750	2200
Books	1200	1450	230
Clothes	575	350	150
Entertainment	600	500	200
Miscellaneous	400	350	175
Resources			
Savings	2500	2500	500
Parents	5000	7500	1200
Job	1000	1200	400
Financial Aid	6275	3450	2505
Scholarship	2500	2500	500

Create a template with the data for the first semester in Table 6–14 in mind. Use dummy data in the template. Sum both the expenses and resources for the semester in the template. Save the template and then use it to create a workbook with each of the three semesters on a separate worksheet. Use 3-D cell references to consolidate the data on a worksheet in the workbook. Include a 3-D pie chart that compares the annual expenses. Use the concepts and techniques described in this chapter to format the workbook and chart.

•• 5: Creating a Consolidated Budget Proposal Using Linking Techniques

Working Together

Complete the exercise outlined in Cases and Places 1 using separate workbooks for each department, rather than a single workbook. As a team, create an appropriate template. Assign each member of the team one or more of the four required workbooks to build using the template. After the workbooks have been created, use the concepts and techniques presented in this chapter to consolidate the data by creating a workspace and linking the workbooks. Test the linkage to the division workbook by changing values in the department workbooks.

Graphics Feature
SmartArt and Images

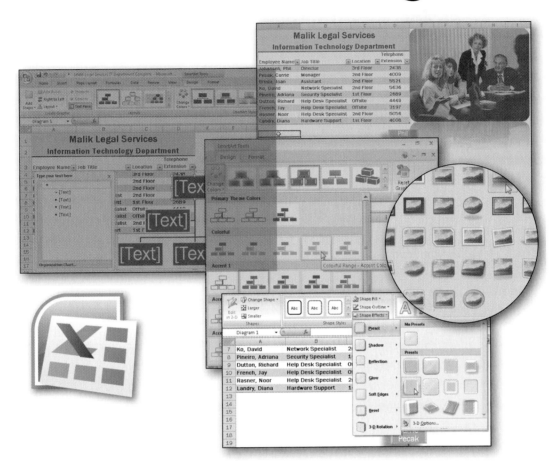

Objectives

You will have mastered the material in this Graphics feature when you can:

- Insert a SmartArt graphic on a worksheet
- Modify a SmartArt graphic
- Add effects to a SmartArt graphic
- Insert an image on a worksheet
- Modify an image on a worksheet

Graphics Feature Introduction

Like a chart, a graphic or image often conveys information or an idea better than words or numbers. You insert and modify graphics and images in order to enhance the visual appeal of an Excel workbook. Many of the skills you learn when working with graphics and images in Excel will be similar when working in Word, PowerPoint, or Outlook.

Project — Adding SmartArt and Images to a Worksheet

The director of the Malik Legal Services Information Technology department would like to enhance the department's directory to be more visually appealing to those inside and outside of the department. The directory currently exists in a table in an Excel worksheet. The director would like a photograph and department organization chart added to the directory.

Figure 1 shows the results of adding and modifying both a SmartArt graphic and an image. The SmartArt graphic is arranged as an organization chart. Other boxes and levels of the organization can be added to the graphic quickly. The SmartArt graphic also can be resized, positioned, and formatted much in the same way in which you have worked with charts in previous chapters. The image on the top right is a photograph that has been inserted into the worksheet, resized, repositioned, and formatted with a rounded corner and reflection.

Overview

As you read through this feature, you will learn how to create and modify SmartArt graphics and insert and modify images by performing the following tasks:

- Insert a SmartArt graphic on a worksheet
- Modify a SmartArt graphic
- Add effects to a SmartArt graphic
- Insert an image on a worksheet
- Modify an image on a worksheet

Plan Ahead

> **General Project Decisions**
>
> 1. **Choose the type of graphic to use for the organization chart.** The requirements for the worksheet ask for an organization chart. The SmartArt graphics provided with most Microsoft Office applications include a template for an organization chart. Using the built-in SmartArt graphics organization chart template is, therefore, a good starting point for the chart.
>
> 2. **Determine the contents and layout of the organization chart.** The organization chart reflects the hierarchy of the organization that it represents. An organization hierarchy can be inferred from the job titles shown in the table in Figure 1.
>
> 3. **Specify the formatting for the organization chart.** Because visual appeal is important, the chart should be formatted with 3-D effects, and colors should be added to make the chart more appealing.
>
> *(continued)*

(*continued*)

4. **Obtain the image to be used in the worksheet.** The image to be used is included with the Data Files for Students. Once the image is inserted on the worksheet, the image file no longer is needed because a copy of the image becomes part of the worksheet. When obtaining an image, you must use only those images for which you have permission. Several sources exist that provide royalty-free images, meaning that you do not have to pay for the image to use it.

5. **Determine placement and formatting for the image.** Placing the image to the right of the table is appropriate because the image is not likely to change size over time. The organization chart, however, may change size in the future and should be placed below the table and image. If the organization gets larger, the worksheet provides more space below the table and image for this growth. The image also can be set off from the table by using a rounded border. An artistic reflection of the image provides an additional visual enhancement to the worksheet.

When necessary, more specific details concerning the above guidelines are presented at appropriate points in the feature. The feature also will identify the actions you perform and decisions made regarding these guidelines during the addition of the organization chart and image to an existing worksheet.

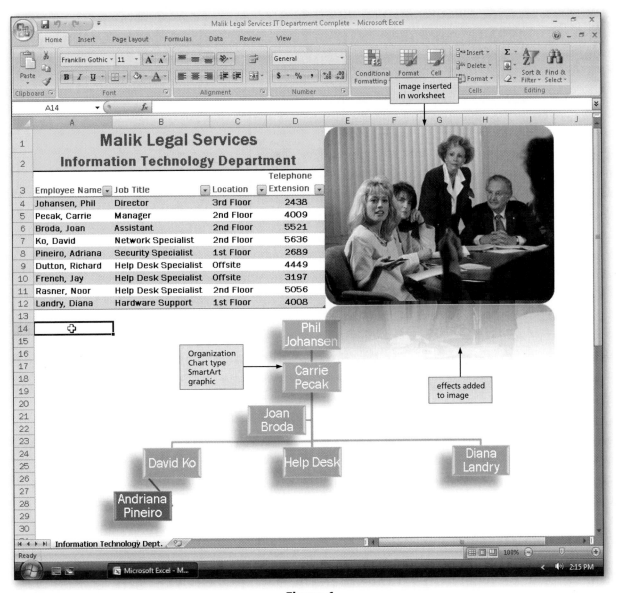

Figure 1

Working with SmartArt Graphics

A SmartArt graphic is a customizable diagram that you use to pictorially present lists, processes, and relationships. For example, the manufacturing process to produce an item can be illustrated with a SmartArt graphic. Excel includes seven types of SmartArt graphics: List, Process, Cycle, Hierarchy, Relationship, Matrix, and Pyramid. Each type of graphic includes several layouts, or templates, from which to choose. After selecting a SmartArt graphic type and layout, you customize the graphic to meet your needs and present your information and ideas in a compelling manner.

To Open a Workbook, Turn Off Gridlines, and Insert an Organization Chart

Many entities maintain an organization chart that represents the hierarchy of the employees in the organization. The following steps open a workbook that contains an employee list, and then add, move, and size a SmartArt organization chart.

- Connect a USB flash drive to one of the computer's USB ports.

- Start Excel and then open the workbook, Malik Legal Services IT Department, from the Data Files for Students.

- Save the workbook using the file name, Malik Legal Services IT Department Complete.

- Click the View tab on the Ribbon and then click the Gridlines check box to turn off gridlines on the worksheet (Figure 2).

Why should I turn off gridlines?

Although useful during the process of creating a worksheet, many spreadsheet specialists remove the gridlines to reduce the clutter on the screen. This is especially true when working with graphics and images on a worksheet.

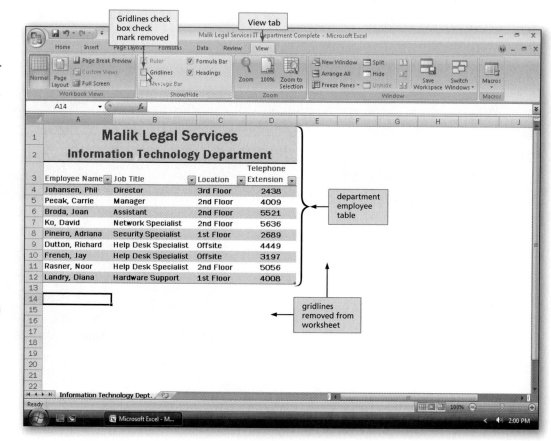

Figure 2

Excel Graphics Feature

 ❸
- Click the Insert tab on the Ribbon and then click the SmartArt button on the Ribbon to display the Choose a SmartArt Graphic dialog box.

🔍 **Experiment**
- Click a variety of SmartArt graphics types and layouts to view previews of the graphics in the preview area of the Choose a SmartArt Graphic dialog box.

❹
- Click Hierarchy in the Type list on the left side of the Choose a SmartArt Graphic dialog box. The middle portion of the dialog box (the layout list) displays a gallery of hierarchy charts, and the right side of the dialog

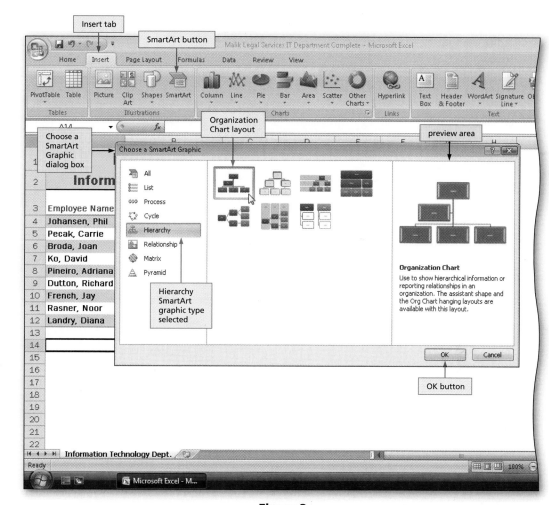

Figure 3

box (the preview area) displays a preview of the selected SmartArt graphic.

- Click Organization Chart (column 1, row 1) in the layout list to see a preview of the chart in the preview area (Figure 3).

- Click the OK button to insert an Organization Chart SmartArt graphic in the worksheet. If necessary, click the Text Pane button on the Ribbon to display the Text pane. (Figure 4).

Q&A

What is displayed on the screen?

Two panes are added to the worksheet. The left pane is the Text pane. The Text pane is displayed only when the chart is selected. The Text pane includes one line for each box in the chart and allows you to add text to the chart quickly. The right pane is the SmartArt graphic with the Hierarchy type and the Organization Chart layout. The chart is displayed over the data in the worksheet, but it will be repositioned in the following steps.

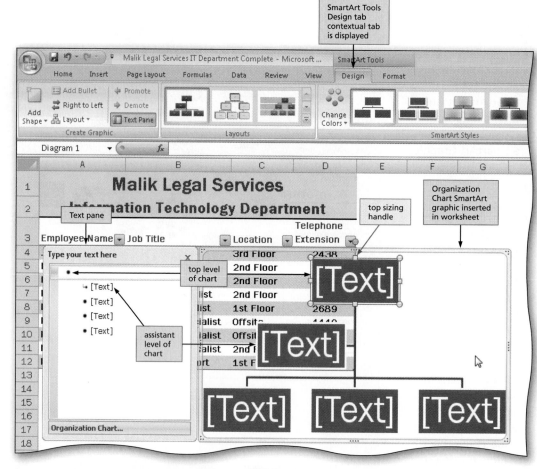

Figure 4

6

- While holding down the ALT key, click and drag the top of the chart to the bottom of row 13.

- Click the middle sizing handle on the right edge of the chart and while holding down the ALT key, drag the sizing handle until the right edge of the chart is aligned with the right edge of column H.

- Drag the Text pane to the right side of the chart (Figure 5).

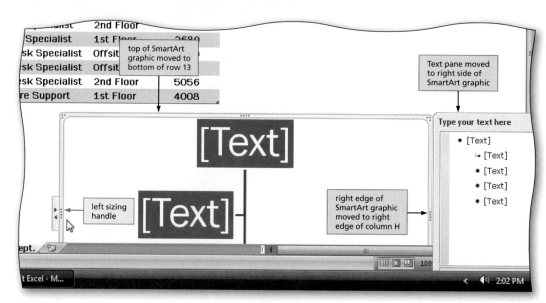

Figure 5

Q&A

Why should I drag the Text pane to the right side of the chart?

The chart will be widened further to the left. If the Text pane remains on the left side of the chart, then it will display on top of the resized chart and obscure the view of the chart.

7

- If necessary, scroll the worksheet down until row 30 is displayed.

- Click the middle sizing handle on the left edge of the chart and while holding down the ALT key, drag the sizing handle until the left edge of the chart is aligned with the right edge of column A.

- Click the middle sizing handle on the bottom edge of the chart and while holding down the ALT key, drag the sizing handle until the bottom edge of the chart is aligned with the bottom edge of row 29 (Figure 6).

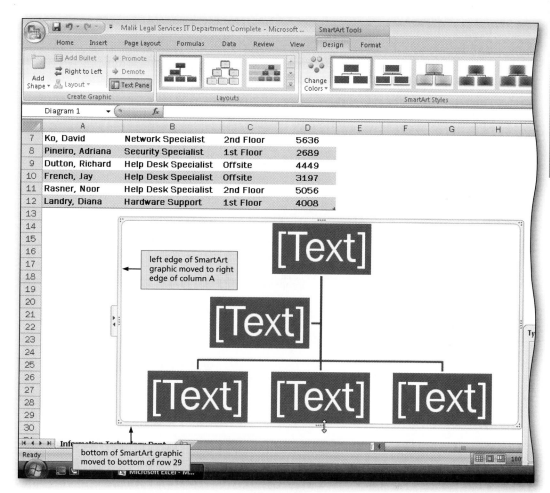

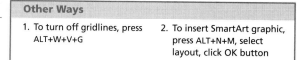

Figure 6

Other Ways	
1. To turn off gridlines, press ALT+W+V+G	2. To insert SmartArt graphic, press ALT+N+M, select layout, click OK button

To Add Shapes and Modify Text in the Organization Chart

The default organization chart layout includes five shapes: a shape for a manager at the top of the chart, a shape for the manager's assistant on the left side in the second row of the chart, and three shapes for subordinates in the third row of the chart. The Malik Legal Services Information Technology department requires two additional shapes in the organization chart: a shape at the top of the chart for the Director level of management, and a shape below the lower-left shape for the Security Specialist job title. The following steps add two new shapes to the organization chart and then modify the text in all of the shapes.

- Right-click the top shape in the organization chart to display the shortcut menu.

- Point to Add Shape on the shortcut menu to display the Add Shape submenu (Figure 7).

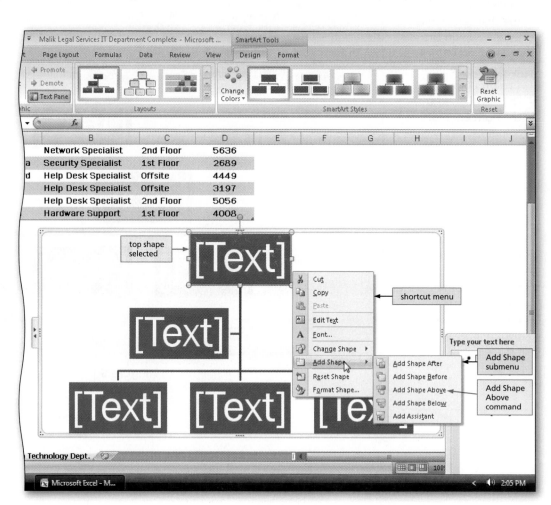

Figure 7

2

- Click Add Shape Above to add a new shape to the organization chart (Figure 8).

Why does Excel change the layout of the chart?

When a new shape is added to a SmartArt graphic, Excel rearranges the shapes in the graphic to fit in the same area. In Figure 8, the size of each shape and the font size of the text in each shape is reduced to accommodate the added shape. Excel also arranges the third level of the organization chart in a vertical alignment in order to better fit the added shape.

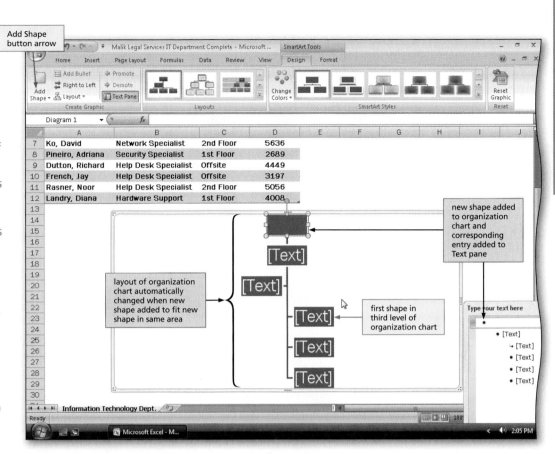

Figure 8

3

- Click the first shape in the third level of the organization chart to select it.

- Click the Add Shape button arrow on the Ribbon to display the Add Shape menu.

- Click Add Shape Below on the Add Shape menu to add a new shape below the first shape in the third level of the organization chart (Figure 9).

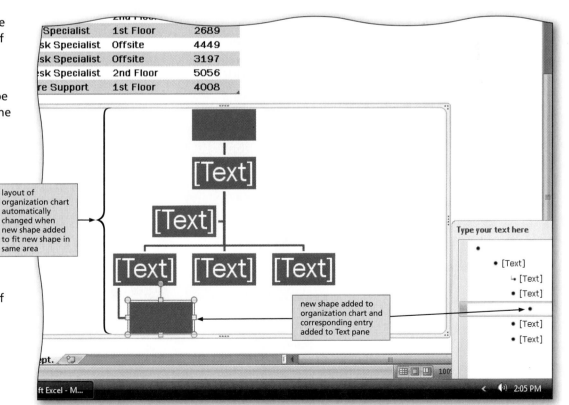

Figure 9

4

- Click the top shape in the organization chart and then type Phil Johansen to add text to the shape (Figure 10).

Q&A

Why does Excel add the same text to the Text pane?

As changes are made to text in the chart, the Text pane reflects those changes as an outline. You can type text in the shapes or type text in the Text pane, as shown in the following step.

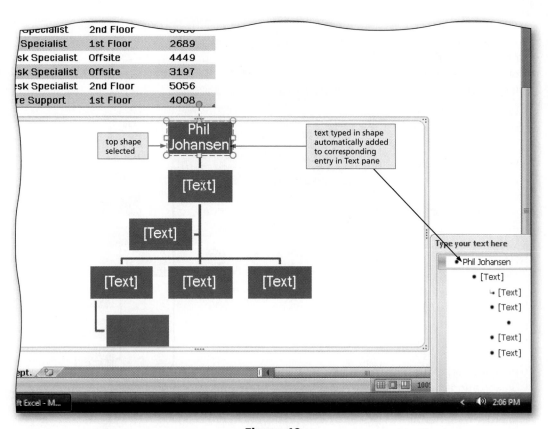

Figure 10

5

- Click the entry under Phil Johansen in the Text pane to select it.

- Type Carrie Pecak in the second line of the Text pane to change the text in the shape in the second level of the organization chart (Figure 11).

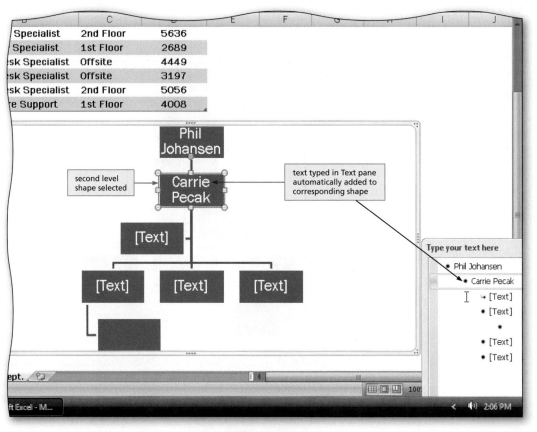

Figure 11

- Repeat Step 4 for each of the remaining shapes in the organization chart and enter text in each shape as shown in Figure 12.

- Click the Save button on the Quick Access Toolbar.

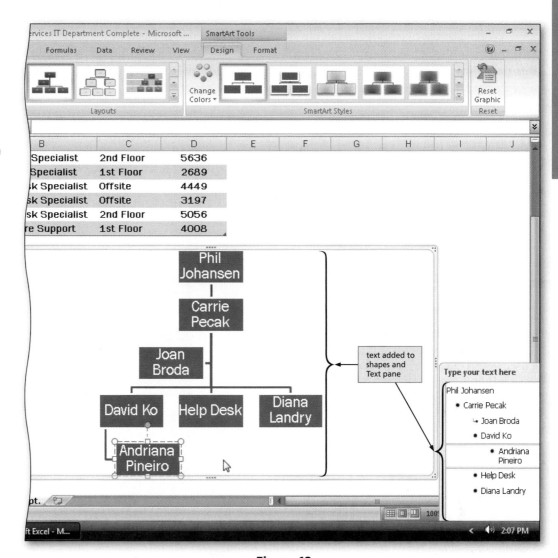

Figure 12

Other Ways

1. Click line in Text pane, press ENTER key

2. Select shape, press CTRL+C, press CTRL+V

To Change the Position of Shapes and Add Effects to the Organization Chart

With all of the necessary data in the chart, the next step is to customize the chart by changing its layout to reflect the structure of the Information Technology department. The shapes in the third and fourth rows of the organization chart should be spread out to reduce the clutter in the chart. The following steps arrange the chart to be more readable and visually appealing.

- Click the lower-right shape in the organization chart (Diana Landry) and then drag the shape to the right until the right edge of the shape is aligned with the right edge of the organization chart as shown in Figure 13.

- Click the shape containing the text, David Ko, and then drag the shape to the left until the right edge of the shape is aligned approximately with the right edge of column B as shown in Figure 13.

- Click the shape containing the text, Andriana Pineiro, and then drag the shape to the left until the lower-left corner of the shape is aligned with the lower-left corner of the organization chart as shown in Figure 13.

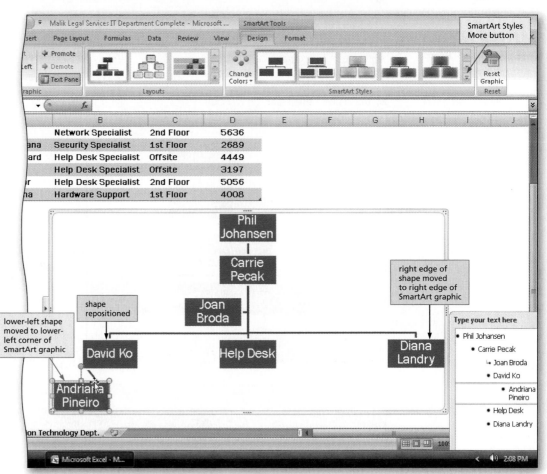

Figure 13

- Click the SmartArt Styles More button to display the SmartArt Styles gallery.

 Experiment

- Point to a variety of SmartArt styles in the SmartArt Styles gallery to preview the styles in the worksheet.

- Point to the Cartoon style in the SmartArt Styles gallery to display a preview of the style in the organization chart (Figure 14).

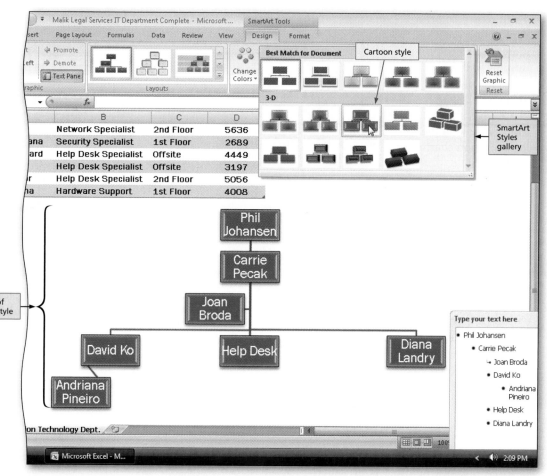

Figure 14

- Click the Cartoon style in the SmartArt Styles gallery to apply the style to the organization chart.

- Click the Change Colors button on the Ribbon to display the Change Colors gallery.

 Experiment

- Point to a variety of color schemes in the Change Colors gallery to preview the color schemes in the worksheet.

5

- Point to the Colorful Range – Accent Colors 4 to 5 color scheme in the Change Colors gallery to display a preview of the color scheme in the organization chart (Figure 15).

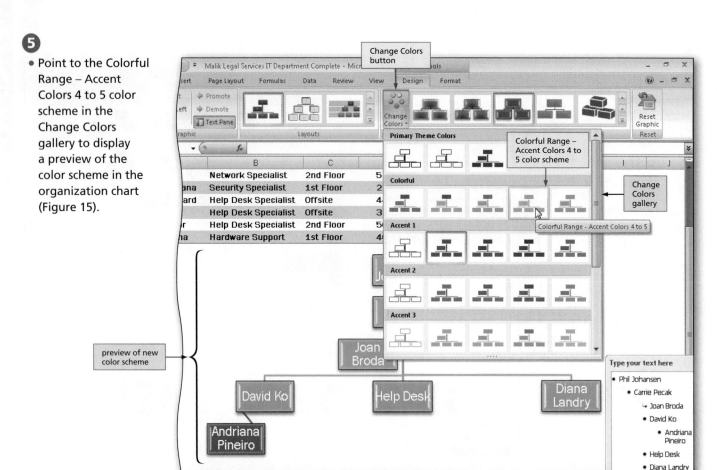

Figure 15

6

- Click the Colorful Range – Accent Colors 4 to 5 color scheme in the Change Colors gallery to apply the color scheme to the organization chart.

- Click the Format tab on the Ribbon. Click the Shape Effects button arrow to display the Shape Effects gallery.

 **Experiment**

- Point to a variety of shape effect types in the Shape Effects gallery and then point to a variety of selections in the galleries to preview the various shape effects in the worksheet.

- Point to the Preset button on the Shape Effects menu to display the Preset gallery.

- Point to the Preset 5 effect in the Preset gallery to display a preview of the effect in the organization chart (Figure 16).

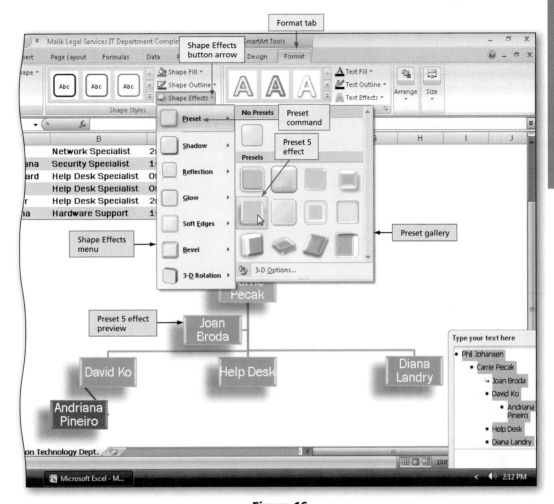

Figure 16

- If necessary, make certain that all of the names are selected in the Text pane.

- Click the Preset 5 effect in the Preset gallery to apply the effect to the organization chart.

- Select cell A14.

- Click the Save button on the Quick Access Toolbar.

Other Ways
1. To change style, select SmartArt graphic, press ALT+J+S+S, click style
2. To change color scheme, select SmartArt graphic, press ALT+J+S+C, click color scheme

Using Images on a Worksheet

Excel allows you to insert images on a worksheet and then modify the image by changing its shape and size, and adding borders and effects. You can enhance a worksheet by including an image such as a corporate logo, photograph, diagram, or map. To use an image, the image must be stored digitally in a file.

To Insert and Modify an Image in the Worksheet

The following steps insert an image of some of the Malik Legal Services Information Technology department members in the worksheet, position and resize the image, and add an effect to the image. The image, which was taken with a digital camera, is available on the Data Files for Students.

1

- Click the Insert tab on the Ribbon.

- With your USB flash drive connected to one of the computer's USB ports, click the Insert Picture from File button on the Ribbon to display the Insert Picture dialog box.

- If the Folders list is displayed below the Folders button, click the Folders button to remove the Folders list.

- If necessary, click Computer in the Favorite Links section and then scroll until UDISK 2.0 (E:) appears in the list of available drives.

- Double-click UDISK 2.0 (E:) to select the USB flash drive, drive E in this case, as the device that contains the picture. Your USB flash drive may have a different drive letter and name.

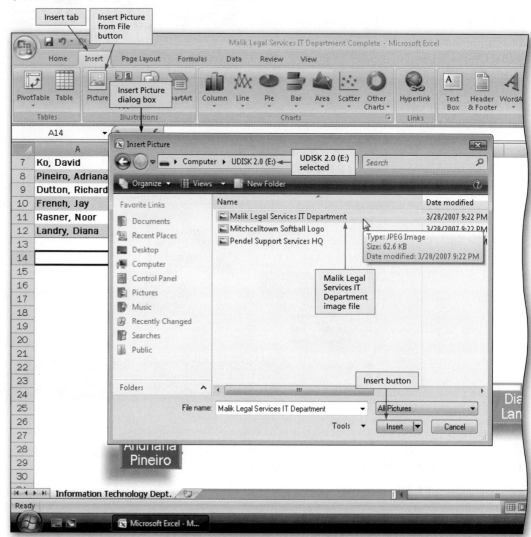

Figure 17

- Click Malik Legal Services IT Department to select the file name (Figure 17).

2

- Click the Insert button to insert the picture in the worksheet (Figure 18).

Q&A

How does Excel determine where to insert the image?

Excel inserts the image so the upper-left corner of the image is located at the upper-left corner of the selected cell, which is cell A14 in Figure 18.

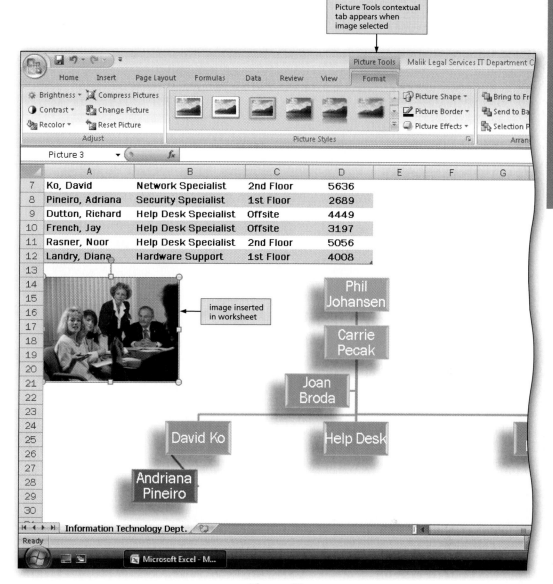

Figure 18

3

- Scroll the worksheet vertically until row 1 appears.

- Click anywhere in the image and while pressing the ALT key, drag the image so that its upper-left corner is aligned with the upper-left corner of cell E1.

- While pressing the ALT key, drag the lower-right sizing handle of the image to the lower-right corner of cell I12 (Figure 19).

Q&A

Why should I press the ALT key as I drag and resize the image?

When you press the ALT key as you drag or resize an image, Excel snaps, or aligns, the image to the borders of a cell. If you do not hold the ALT key, the corners of the image can be placed anywhere within a cell.

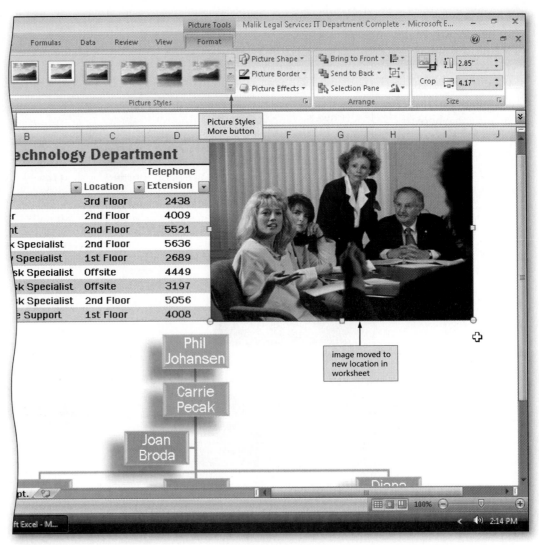

Figure 19

4

- Click the Picture Styles More button on the Ribbon to display the Picture Styles gallery.

🔍 **Experiment**

- Point to a variety of picture styles in the Picture Styles gallery and then point to a variety of styles in the galleries to preview them in the worksheet.

5

- Point to the Reflected Rounded Rectangle picture style (column 5, row 1) to see a preview of the style in the worksheet (Figure 20).

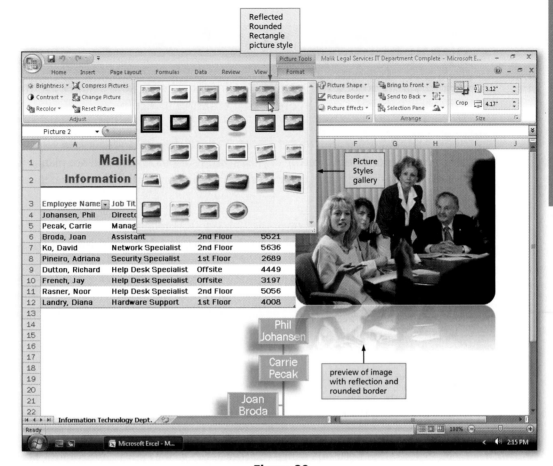

Figure 20

6

- Click the Reflected Rounded Rectangle picture style to apply the style to the image.

- Click the Save button on the Quick Access Toolbar.

Other Ways
1. Press ALT+N, P

To Quit Excel

The following steps quit Excel.

1 Click the Close button on the right side of the title bar.

2 If Excel displays a Microsoft Office Excel dialog box, click the Yes button to save the workbook.

Feature Summary

This Graphics feature introduced you to inserting and modifying SmartArt graphics and images. The items listed below include all the new Office 2007 skills you have learned in this Web feature.

1. Open a Workbook, Turn Off Gridlines, and Insert an Organization Chart (EX 510)
2. Add Shapes and Modify Text in the Organization Chart (EX 514)
3. Change the Position of Shapes and Add Effects to the Organization Chart (EX 518)
4. Insert and Modify an Image in the Worksheet (EX 522)

In the Lab

Modify a workbook using the guidelines, concepts, and skills presented in this Graphics feature. Labs are listed in order of increasing difficulty.

Lab 1: Inserting a Hierarchy Chart and Image on a Worksheet

Problem: You are the director of your town's softball league and are planning the league's playoff schedule. You want to create a worksheet that illustrates the playoff matchups for the teams in one of the divisions.

Instructions: Start Excel and open the Lab GF-1 Mitchelltown Softball League workbook from the Data Files for Students and then save it as Lab GF-1 Mitchelltown Softball League Complete. Perform the following tasks:

1. Insert a SmartArt graphic using the Hierarchy type and select the Horizontal Hierarchy layout type (column 1, row 2) in the layout area in the Choose a SmartArt Graphic dialog box.

2. Select the hierarchy chart and then click the Right to Left button on the Design tab on the Ribbon to change the layout of the hierarchy chart to read from left to right.

3. Right-click the lower shape in the middle column of the hierarchy chart, point to Add Shape on the shortcut menu, and then click Add Shape Below on the Add Shape submenu.

4. Move and resize the chart so that the upper-left corner of the chart is aligned with the upper-left corner of cell A15 and the lower-right corner of the chart is aligned with the lower-right corner of cell F30.

5. From top to bottom, change the text in the shapes in the left column of the hierarchy chart to read Angels, Sox, Mariners, and Mets. Change the text in both shapes in the middle column of the hierarchy chart to Winner Game 1. Change the text in the shape on the right side of the hierarchy chart to Division Champion.

6. Change the color scheme of the hierarchy chart to Colorful – Accent Colors (column 1, row 2) in the Change Colors gallery.

7. Change the font size of the text in the shapes to 16 using the Font Size box on the Home tab on the Ribbon.

8. Use the Shape Effects gallery to change the effects on the chart to Preset 9 in the Preset gallery.

9. Insert the Mitchelltown Softball League.jpg image file from the Data Files for Students on the worksheet.

10. Move and resize the image so that the upper-left corner of the image is aligned with the upper-left corner of cell A1 and the lower-right corner of the image is aligned with the lower-right corner of cell F6.

11. Select the image. Click the Format tab on the Ribbon and then select the Reflected Perspective Right picture style (column 5, row 4) in the Picture Styles gallery.

12. Change the document properties as specified by your instructor. Change the worksheet header with your name, course number, and other information requested by your instructor. Save the workbook. Submit the assignment as requested by your instructor.

In the Lab

Lab 2: Inserting a Balance Chart and Image on a Worksheet

Problem: Your company is considering moving to a new location. You have been asked to create a high-level overview of the pros and cons regarding the move to the location.

Instructions: Start Excel and open the Lab GF-2 Pendel Support Services workbook from the Data Files for Students and then save it as Lab GF-2 Pendel Support Services Complete. Perform the following tasks:

1. Insert a SmartArt graphic using the Relationship type and select the Balance layout type (column 1, row 1) in the layout area in the Choose a SmartArt Graphic dialog box.

2. Move and resize the chart so that the upper-left corner of the chart is aligned with the upper-left corner of cell A4 and the lower-right corner of the chart is aligned with the middle of the corner of cell H18.

3. Use the Text pane to enter text for the balance chart. Enter the values shown in Table 1, making certain that the pros column shows on the left of the chart. Be sure to delete the unused shape on the right side of the balance chart by right-clicking the shape and then clicking Cut on the shortcut menu. The upper-left shape in the chart should read Pros, and the upper-right shape in the chart should read Cons. Note that the direction of the tilt of the balance chart changes when more pros than cons are entered in the chart.

4. Change the color scheme of the hierarchy chart to Colored Fill – Accent 1 (column 2, row 3) in the Change Colors gallery.

Table 1 Pros and Cons	
Pros	**Cons**
Central Location	Expensive Lease
Convenient Parking	Congested Area
Closer to Customers	

5. Apply the Inset SmartArt style to the balance chart (column 2, row 2) on the SmartArt Styles gallery.

6. Insert the Pendel Support Services Offices.jpg image file from the Data Files for Students on the worksheet.

7. Move and resize the image so that the upper-left corner of the image is aligned with the upper-left corner of cell H4 and the lower-right corner of the image is aligned with the lower-right corner of cell M17.

8. Select the image. Click the Format tab on the Ribbon. Click the Picture Effects button on the Ribbon, point to Shadow in the Picture Effects gallery, and then select Perspective Diagonal Upper Left (column 1, row 8) in the Shadow gallery.

9. Click the Picture Effects button on the Ribbon, point to Bevel in the Picture Effects gallery, and then select Divot (column 1, row 4) in the Bevel gallery.

10. Change the document properties as specified by your instructor. Change the worksheet header with your name, course number, and other information requested by your instructor. Save the workbook. Submit the assignment as requested by your instructor.

Appendix A
Project Planning Guidelines

Using Project Planning Guidelines

The process of communicating specific information to others is a learned, rational skill. Computers and software, especially Microsoft Office 2007, can help you develop ideas and present detailed information to a particular audience.

Using Microsoft Office 2007, you can create projects such as Word documents, Excel spreadsheets, Access databases, and PowerPoint presentations. Computer hardware and productivity software such as Microsoft Office 2007 minimizes much of the laborious work of drafting and revising projects. Some communicators handwrite ideas in notebooks, others compose directly on the computer, and others have developed unique strategies that work for their own particular thinking and writing styles.

No matter what method you use to plan a project, follow specific guidelines to arrive at a final product that presents information correctly and effectively (Figure A–1). Use some aspects of these guidelines every time you undertake a project, and others as needed in specific instances. For example, in determining content for a project, you may decide that a bar chart communicates trends more effectively than a paragraph of text. If so, you would create this graphical element and insert it in an Excel spreadsheet, a Word document, or a PowerPoint slide.

Determine the Project's Purpose

Begin by clearly defining why you are undertaking this assignment. For example, you may want to track monetary donations collected for your club's fundraising drive. Alternatively, you may be urging students to vote for a particular candidate in the next election. Once you clearly understand the purpose of your task, begin to draft ideas of how best to communicate this information.

Analyze your Audience

Learn about the people who will read, analyze, or view your work. Where are they employed? What are their educational backgrounds? What are their expectations? What questions do they have?

PROJECT PLANNING GUIDELINES

1. DETERMINE THE PROJECT'S PURPOSE
Why are you undertaking the project?

2. ANALYZE YOUR AUDIENCE
Who are the people who will use your work?

3. GATHER POSSIBLE CONTENT
What information exists, and in what forms?

4. DETERMINE WHAT CONTENT TO PRESENT TO YOUR AUDIENCE
What information will best communicate the project's purpose to your audience?

Figure A–1

Design experts suggest drawing a mental picture of these people or finding photographs of people who fit this profile so that you can develop a project with the audience in mind.

By knowing your audience members, you can tailor a project to meet their interests and needs. You will not present them with information they already possess, and you will not omit the information they need to know.

Example: Your assignment is to raise the profile of your college's nursing program in the community. How much do they know about your college and the nursing curriculum? What are the admission requirements? How many of the applicants admitted complete the program? What percent pass the state Boards?

Gather Possible Content

Rarely are you in a position to develop all the material for a project. Typically, you would begin by gathering existing information that may reside in spreadsheets or databases. Web sites, pamphlets, magazine and newspaper articles, and books could provide insights of how others have approached your topic. Personal interviews often provide perspectives not available by any other means. Consider video and audio clips as potential sources for material that might complement or support the factual data you uncover.

Determine What Content to Present to your Audience

Experienced designers recommend writing three or four major ideas you want an audience member to remember after reading or viewing your project. It also is helpful to envision your project's endpoint, the key fact you wish to emphasize. All project elements should lead to this ending point.

As you make content decisions, you also need to think about other factors. Presentation of the project content is an important consideration. For example, will your brochure be printed on thick, colored paper or transparencies? Will your PowerPoint presentation be viewed in a classroom with excellent lighting and a bright projector, or will it be viewed on a notebook computer monitor? Determine relevant time factors, such as the length of time to develop the project, how long readers will spend reviewing your project, or the amount of time allocated for your speaking engagement. Your project will need to accommodate all of these constraints.

Decide whether a graph, photograph, or artistic element can express or emphasize a particular concept. The right hemisphere of the brain processes images by attaching an emotion to them, so audience members are more apt to recall these graphics long term rather than just reading text.

As you select content, be mindful of the order in which you plan to present information. Readers and audience members generally remember the first and last pieces of information they see and hear, so you should put the most important information at the top or bottom of the page.

Summary

When creating a project, it is beneficial to follow some basic guidelines from the outset. By taking some time at the beginning of the process to determine the project's purpose, analyze the audience, gather possible content, and determine what content to present to the audience, you can produce a project that is informative, relevant, and effective.

Appendix B

Introduction to Microsoft Office 2007

What Is Microsoft Office 2007?

Microsoft Office 2007 is a collection of the more popular Microsoft application software. It is available in Basic, Home and Student, Standard, Small Business, Professional, Ultimate, Professional Plus, and Enterprise editions. Each edition consists of a group of programs, collectively called a suite. Table B-1 lists the suites and their components. **Microsoft Office Professional Edition 2007** includes these six programs: Microsoft Office Word 2007, Microsoft Office Excel 2007, Microsoft Office Access 2007, Microsoft Office PowerPoint 2007, Microsoft Office Publisher 2007, and Microsoft Office Outlook 2007. The programs in the Office suite allow you to work efficiently, communicate effectively, and improve the appearance of the projects you create.

Table B–1

	Microsoft Office Basic 2007	Microsoft Office Home & Student 2007	Microsoft Office Standard 2007	Microsoft Office Small Business 2007	Microsoft Office Professional 2007	Microsoft Office Ultimate 2007	Microsoft Office Professional Plus 2007	Microsoft Office Enterprise 2007
Microsoft Office Word 2007	✓	✓	✓	✓	✓	✓	✓	✓
Microsoft Office Excel 2007	✓	✓	✓	✓	✓	✓	✓	✓
Microsoft Office Access 2007					✓	✓	✓	✓
Microsoft Office PowerPoint 2007		✓	✓	✓	✓	✓	✓	✓
Microsoft Office Publisher 2007				✓	✓	✓	✓	✓
Microsoft Office Outlook 2007	✓		✓				✓	✓
Microsoft Office OneNote 2007		✓				✓		
Microsoft Office Outlook 2007 with Business Contact Manager				✓	✓	✓		
Microsoft Office InfoPath 2007						✓	✓	✓
Integrated Enterprise Content Management						✓	✓	✓
Electronic Forms						✓	✓	✓
Advanced Information Rights Management and Policy Capabilities						✓	✓	✓
Microsoft Office Communicator 2007							✓	✓
Microsoft Office Groove 2007						✓		✓

Microsoft has bundled additional programs in some versions of Office 2007, in addition to the main group of Office programs. Table B–1 on the previous page lists the components of the various Office suites.

In addition to the Office 2007 programs noted previously, Office 2007 suites can contain other programs. Microsoft Office OneNote 2007 is a digital notebook program that allows you to gather and share various types of media, such as text, graphics, video, audio, and digital handwriting. Microsoft Office InfoPath 2007 is a program that allows you to create and use electronic forms to gather information. Microsoft Office Groove 2007 provides collaborative workspaces in real time. Additional services that are oriented toward the enterprise solution also are available.

Office 2007 and the Internet, World Wide Web, and Intranets

Office 2007 allows you to take advantage of the Internet, the World Wide Web, and intranets. The Microsoft Windows operating system includes a **browser**, which is a program that allows you to locate and view a Web page. The Windows browser is called Internet Explorer.

One method of viewing a Web page is to use the browser to enter the Web address for the Web page. Another method of viewing a Web page is clicking a hyperlink. A **hyperlink** is colored or underlined text or a graphic that, when clicked, connects to another Web page. Hyperlinks placed in Office 2007 documents allow for direct access to a Web site of interest.

An **intranet** is a private network, such as a network used within a company or organization for internal communication. Like the Internet, hyperlinks are used within an intranet to access documents, pages, and other destinations on the intranet. Unlike the Internet, the materials on the network are available only for those who are part of the private network.

Online Collaboration Using Office

Organizations that, in the past, were able to make important information available only to a select few, now can make their information accessible to a wider range of individuals who use programs such as Office 2007 and Internet Explorer. Office 2007 allows colleagues to use the Internet or an intranet as a central location to view documents, manage files, and work together.

Each of the Office 2007 programs makes publishing documents on a Web server as simple as saving a file on a hard disk. Once placed on the Web server, users can view and edit the documents and conduct Web discussions and live online meetings.

Using Microsoft Office 2007

The various Microsoft Office 2007 programs each specialize in a particular task. This section describes the general functions of the more widely used Office 2007 programs, along with how they are used to access the Internet or an intranet.

Microsoft Office Word 2007

Microsoft Office Word 2007 is a full-featured word processing program that allows you to create many types of personal and business documents, including flyers, letters, resumes, business documents, and academic reports.

Word's AutoCorrect, spelling, and grammar features help you proofread documents for errors in spelling and grammar by identifying the errors and offering suggestions for corrections as you type. The live word count feature provides you with a constantly updating word count as you enter and edit text. To assist with creating specific documents, such as a business letter or resume, Word provides templates, which provide a formatted document before you type the text of the document. Quick Styles provide a live preview of styles from the Style gallery, allowing you to preview styles in the document before actually applying them.

Word automates many often-used tasks and provides you with powerful desktop publishing tools to use as you create professional looking brochures, advertisements, and newsletters. SmartArt allows you to insert interpretive graphics based on document content.

Word makes it easier for you to share documents for collaboration. The Send feature opens an e-mail window with the active document attached. The Compare Documents feature allows you easily to identify changes when comparing different document versions.

Word 2007 and the Internet   Word makes it possible to design and publish Web pages on the Internet or an intranet, insert a hyperlink to a Web page in a word processing document, as well as access and search the content of other Web pages.

Microsoft Office Excel 2007

Microsoft Office Excel 2007 is a spreadsheet program that allows you to organize data, complete calculations, graph data, develop professional looking reports, publish organized data to the Web, and access real-time data from Web sites.

In addition to its mathematical functionality, Excel 2007 provides tools for visually comparing data. For instance, when comparing a group of values in cells, you can set cell backgrounds with bars proportional to the value of the data in the cell. You can also set cell backgrounds with full-color backgrounds, or use a color scale to facilitate interpretation of data values.

Excel 2007 provides strong formatting support for tables with the new Style Preview gallery.

Excel 2007 and the Internet   Using Excel 2007, you can create hyperlinks within a worksheet to access other Office documents on the network or on the Internet. Worksheets saved as static, or unchanging Web pages can be viewed using a browser. The person viewing static Web pages cannot change them.

In addition, you can create and run queries that retrieve information from a Web page and insert the information directly into a worksheet.

Microsoft Office Access 2007

Microsoft Office Access 2007 is a comprehensive database management system (DBMS). A **database** is a collection of data organized in a manner that allows access, retrieval, and use of that data. Access 2007 allows you to create a database; add, change, and delete data in the database; sort data in the database; retrieve data from the database; and create forms and reports using the data in the database.

Access 2007 and the Internet   Access 2007 lets you generate reports, which are summaries that show only certain data from the database, based on user requirements.

Microsoft Office PowerPoint 2007

Microsoft Office PowerPoint 2007 is a complete presentation graphics program that allows you to produce professional looking presentations. With PowerPoint 2007, you can create informal presentations using overhead transparencies, electronic presentations using a projection device attached to a personal computer, formal presentations using 35mm slides or a CD, or you can run virtual presentations on the Internet.

PowerPoint 2007 and the Internet　PowerPoint 2007 allows you to publish presentations on the Internet or other networks.

Microsoft Office Publisher 2007

Microsoft Office Publisher 2007 is a desktop publishing program (DTP) that allows you to design and produce professional quality documents (newsletters, flyers, brochures, business cards, Web sites, and so on) that combine text, graphics, and photographs. Desktop publishing software provides a variety of tools, including design templates, graphic manipulation tools, color schemes or libraries, and various page wizards and templates. For large jobs, businesses use desktop publishing software to design publications that are **camera ready**, which means the files are suitable for production by outside commercial printers. Publisher 2007 also allows you to locate commercial printers, service bureaus, and copy shops willing to accept customer files created in Publisher.

Publisher 2007 allows you to design a unique image, or logo, using one of more than 45 master design sets. This, in turn, permits you to use the same design for all your printed documents (letters, business cards, brochures, and advertisements) and Web pages. Publisher includes 70 coordinated color schemes; 30 font schemes; more than 10,000 high-quality clip art images; 1,500 photographs; 1,000 Web-art graphics; 340 animated graphics; and hundreds of unique Design Gallery elements (quotations, sidebars, and so on). If you wish, you also can download additional images from the Microsoft Office Online Web page on the Microsoft Web site.

Publisher 2007 and the Internet　Publisher 2007 allows you easily to create a multipage Web site with custom color schemes, photographic images, animated images, and sounds.

Microsoft Office Outlook 2007

Microsoft Office Outlook 2007 is a powerful communications and scheduling program that helps you communicate with others, keep track of your contacts, and organize your schedule. Outlook 2007 allows you to view a To-Do bar containing tasks and appointments from your Outlook calendar. Outlook 2007 allows you to send and receive electronic mail (e-mail) and permits you to engage in real-time communication with family, friends, or coworkers using instant messaging. Outlook 2007 also provides you with the means to organize your contacts, and you can track e-mail messages, meetings, and notes with a particular contact. Outlook's Calendar, Contacts, Tasks, and Notes components aid in this organization. Contact information is available from the Outlook Calendar, Mail, Contacts, and Task components by accessing the Find a Contact feature. **Personal information management (PIM)** programs such as Outlook provide a way for individuals and workgroups to organize, find, view, and share information easily.

Microsoft Office 2007 Help

At any time while you are using one of the Office programs, you can interact with **Microsoft Office 2007 Help** for that program and display information about any topic associated with the program. Several categories of help are available. In all programs, you can access Help by pressing the F1 key on the keyboard. In Publisher 2007 and Outlook 2007, the Help window can be opened by clicking the Help menu and then selecting Microsoft Office Publisher or Outlook Help command, or by entering search text in the 'Type a question for help' text box in the upper-right corner of the program window. In the other Office programs, clicking the Microsoft Office Help button near the upper-right corner of the program window opens the program Help window.

The Help window in all programs provides several methods for accessing help about a particular topic, and has tools for navigating around Help. Appendix C contains detailed instructions for using Help.

Collaboration and SharePoint

While not part of the Microsoft Office 2007 suites, SharePoint is a Microsoft tool that allows Office 2007 users to share data using collaborative tools that are integrated into the main Office programs. SharePoint consists of Windows SharePoint Services, Office SharePoint Server 2007, and, optionally, Office SharePoint Designer 2007.

Windows SharePoint Services provides the platform for collaboration programs and services. Office SharePoint Server 2007 is built on top of Windows SharePoint Services. The result of these two products is the ability to create SharePoint sites. A SharePoint site is a Web site that provides users with a virtual place for collaborating and communicating with their colleagues while working together on projects, documents, ideas, and information. Each member of a group with access to the SharePoint site has the ability to contribute to the material stored there. The basic building blocks of SharePoint sites are lists and libraries. Lists contain collections of information, such as calendar items, discussion points, contacts, and links. Lists can be edited to add or delete information. Libraries are similar to lists, but include both files and information about files. Types of libraries include document, picture, and forms libraries.

The most basic type of SharePoint site is called a Workspace, which is used primarily for collaboration. Different types of Workspaces can be created using SharePoint to suit different needs. SharePoint provides templates, or outlines of these Workspaces, that can be filled in to create the Workspace. Each of the different types of Workspace templates contain a different collection of lists and libraries, reflecting the purpose of the Workspace. You can create a Document Workspace to facilitate collaboration on documents. A Document Workspace contains a document library for documents and supporting files, a Links list that allows you to maintain relevant resource links for the document, a Tasks list for listing and assigning To-Do items to team members, and other links as needed. Meeting Workspaces allow users to plan and organize a meeting, with components such as Attendees, Agenda, and a Document Library. Social Meeting Workspaces provide a place to plan social events, with lists and libraries such as Attendees, Directions, Image/Logo, Things To Bring, Discussions, and Picture Library. A Decision Meeting Workspace is a Meeting Workspace with a focus on review and decision-making, with lists and libraries such as Objectives, Attendees, Agenda, Document Library, Tasks, and Decisions.

Users also can create a SharePoint site called a WebParts page, which is built from modules called WebParts. WebParts are modular units of information that contain a title bar and content that reflects the type of WebPart. For instance, an image WebPart would contain a title bar and an image. WebParts allow you quickly to create and modify a SharePoint site, and allow for the creation of a unique site that can allow users to access and make changes to information stored on the site.

Large SharePoint sites that include multiple pages can be created using templates as well. Groups needing more refined and targeted sharing options than those available with SharePoint Server 2007 and Windows SharePoint Services can add SharePoint Designer 2007 to create a site that meets their specific needs.

Depending on which components have been selected for inclusion on the site, users can view a team calendar, view links, read announcements, and view and edit group documents and projects. SharePoint sites can be set up so that documents are checked in and out, much like a library, to prevent multiple users from making changes simultaneously. Once a SharePoint site is set up, Office programs are used to perform maintenance of the site. For example, changes in the team calendar are updated using Outlook 2007, and changes that users make in Outlook 2007 are reflected on the SharePoint site. Office 2007 programs include a Publish feature that allows users easily to save file updates to a SharePoint site. Team members can be notified about changes made to material on the site either by e-mail or by a news feed, meaning that users do not have to go to the site to check to see if anything has been updated since they last viewed or worked on it. The search feature in SharePoint allows users quickly to find information on a large site.

Appendix C
Microsoft Office Excel 2007 Help

Using Microsoft Office Excel 2007 Help

This appendix shows how to use Microsoft Office Excel Help. At any time while you are using one of the Microsoft Office 2007 programs, you can use Office Help to display information about all topics associated with the program. This appendix uses Microsoft Office Excel 2007 to illustrate the use of Office Help. Help in other Office 2007 programs responds in a similar fashion.

In Office 2007, Help is presented in a window that has Web browser-style navigation buttons. Each Office 2007 program has its own Help home page, which is the starting Help page that is displayed in the Help window. If your computer is connected to the Internet, the contents of the Help page reflect both the local help files installed on the computer and material from Microsoft's Web site. As shown in Figure C–1, two methods for accessing Excel's Help are available:

1. Microsoft Office Excel Help button near the upper-right corner of the Excel window
2. Function key F1 on the keyboard

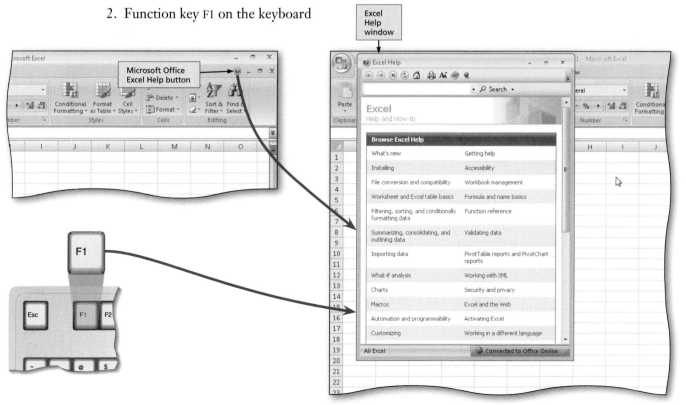

Figure C–1

To Open the Excel Help Window

The following steps open the Excel Help window and maximize the window.

1

● Start Microsoft Excel, if necessary. Click the Microsoft Office Excel Help button near the upper-right corner of the Excel window to open the Excel Help window (Figure C–2).

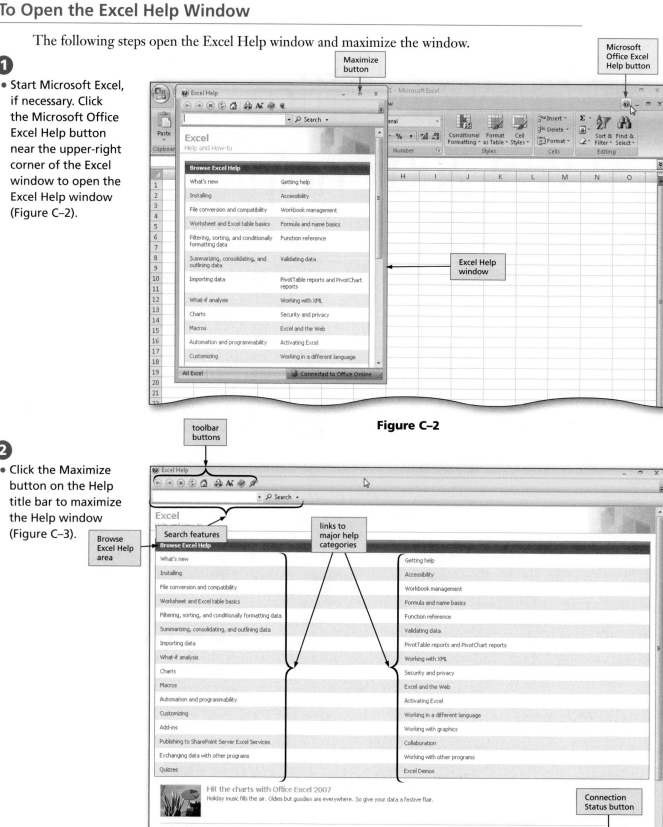

Figure C–2

2

● Click the Maximize button on the Help title bar to maximize the Help window (Figure C–3).

Figure C–3

The Excel Help Window

The Excel Help window provides several methods for accessing help about a particular topic, and also has tools for navigating around Help. Methods for accessing Help include searching the help content installed with Excel, or searching the online Office content maintained by Microsoft.

Figure C–3 shows the main Excel Help window. To navigate Help, the Excel Help window includes search features that allow you to search on a word or phrase about which you want help; the Connection Status button, which allows you to control where Excel Help searches for content; toolbar buttons; and links to major Help categories.

Search Features

You can perform Help searches on words or phrases to find information about any Excel feature using the 'Type words to search for' text box and the Search button (Figure C–4a). Click the 'Type words to search for' text box and then click the Search button or press the ENTER key to initiate a search of Excel Help.

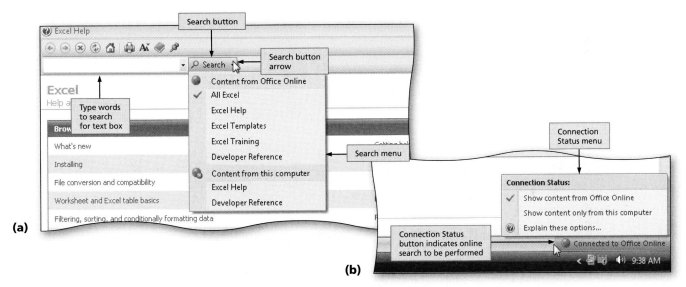

Figure C–4

Excel Help offers the user the option of searching the online Help Web pages maintained by Microsoft or the offline Help files placed on your computer when you install Excel. You can specify whether Excel Help should search online or offline from two places: the Connection Status button on the status bar of the Excel Help window, or the Search button arrow on the toolbar. The Connection Status button indicates whether Help currently is set up to work with online or offline information sources. Clicking the Connection Status button provides a menu with commands for selecting online or offline searches (Figure C–4b). The Connection Status menu allows the user to select whether help searches will return content only from the computer (offline), or content from the computer and from Office Online (online).

Clicking the Search button arrow also provides a menu with commands for an online or offline search (Figure C–4a). These commands determine the source of information that Help searches for during the current Help session only. For example, assume that your preferred search is an offline search because you often do not have Internet access. You would set Connection Status to 'Show content only from this computer'. When you have Internet access, you can select an online search from the Search menu to search Office Online for information for your current search session only. Your search will use the Office Online resources until you quit Help. The next time you start Help, the Connection Status once again will be offline. In addition to setting the source of information that Help searches for during the current Help session, you can use the Search menu to further target the current search to one of four subcategories of online Help: Excel Help, Excel Templates, Excel Training, and Developer Reference. The local search further can target one subcategory, Developer Reference.

In addition to searching for a word or string of text, you can use the links provided on the Browse Excel Help area (Figure C–3) on page APP 10 to search for help on a topic. These links direct you to major help categories. From each major category, subcategories are available to further refine your search.

Finally, you can use the Table of Contents for Excel Help to search for a topic the same way you would in a hard copy book. The Table of Contents is accessed via a toolbar button.

Toolbar Buttons

You can use toolbar buttons to navigate through the results of your search. The toolbar buttons are located on the toolbar near the top of the Help Window (Figure C–5). The toolbar buttons contain navigation buttons as well as buttons that perform other useful and common tasks in Excel Help, such as printing.

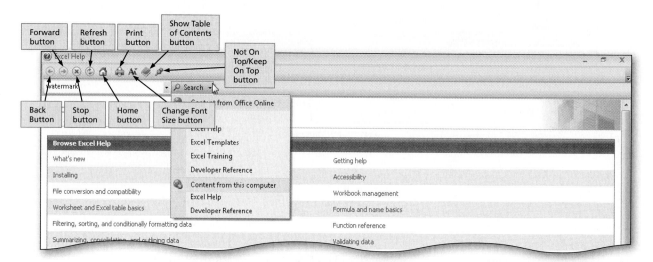

Figure C–5

The Excel Help navigation buttons are the Back, Forward, Stop, Refresh, and Home buttons. These five buttons behave like the navigation buttons in a Web browser window. You can use the Back button to go back one window, the Forward button to go forward one window, the Stop button to stop loading the current page, and the Home button to redisplay the Help home page in the Help window. Use the Refresh button to reload the information requested into the Help window from its original source. When getting Help information online, this button provides the most current information from the Microsoft Help Web site.

The buttons located to the right of the navigation buttons — Print, Change Font Size, Show Table of Contents, and Not on Top — provide you with access to useful and common commands. The Print button prints the contents of the open Help window. The Change Font Size button customizes the Help window by increasing or decreasing the size of its text. The Show Table of Contents button opens a pane on the left side of the Help window that shows the Table of Contents for Excel Help. You can use the Table of Contents for Excel Help to navigate through the contents of Excel Help much as you would use the Table of Contents in a book to search for a topic. The Not On Top button is an example of a toggle button, which is a button that can be switched back and forth between two states. It determines how the Excel Help window behaves relative to other windows. When clicked, the Not On Top button changes to Keep On Top. In this state, it does not allow other windows from Excel or other programs to cover the Excel Help window when those windows are the active windows. When in the Not On Top state, the button allows other windows to be opened or moved on top of the Excel Help window.

You can customize the size and placement of the Help window. Resize the window using the Maximize and Restore buttons, or by dragging the window to a desired size. Relocate the Help window by dragging the title bar to a new location on the screen.

Searching Excel Help

Once the Excel Help window is open, several methods exist for navigating Excel Help. You can search for help by using any of the three following methods from the Help window:

1. Enter search text in the 'Type words to search for' text box
2. Click the links in the Help window
3. Use the Table of Contents

To Obtain Help Using the Type Words to Search for Text Box

Assume for the following example that you want to know more about watermarks. The following steps use the 'Type words to search for' text box to obtain useful information about watermarks by entering the phrase, conditional formatting, as search text. The steps also navigate in the Excel Help window.

1

- **Type** conditional formatting in the 'Type words to search for' text box at the top of the Excel Help window.

- Click the Search button arrow to display the Search menu.

- If it is not selected already, click All Excel on the Search menu to select the command. If All Excel is already selected, click the Search button arrow again to close the Search menu.

Q&A

Why select All Excel on the Search menu?

Selecting All Excel on the Search menu ensures that Excel Help will search all possible sources for information on your search term. It will produce the most complete search results.

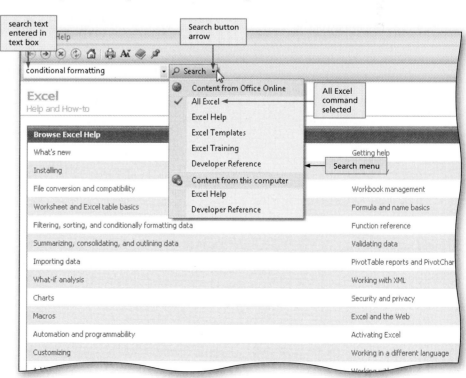

Figure C–6

● Click the Search button to display the search results (Figure C–7).

Q&A Why do my results differ?

If you do not have an Internet connection, your results will reflect only the content of the Help files on your computer. When searching for help online, results also can change as material is added, deleted, and updated on the online Help Web pages maintained by Microsoft.

Q&A Why were my search results not very helpful?

When initiating a search, keep in mind to check the spelling of the search text; and to keep your search very specific, with fewer than seven words, to return the most accurate results.

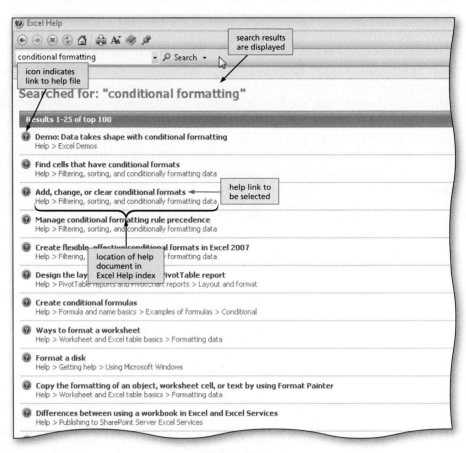

Figure C–7

● Click the 'Add, change, or clear conditional formats' link to open the Help document associated with the link in the Help window (Figure C–8).

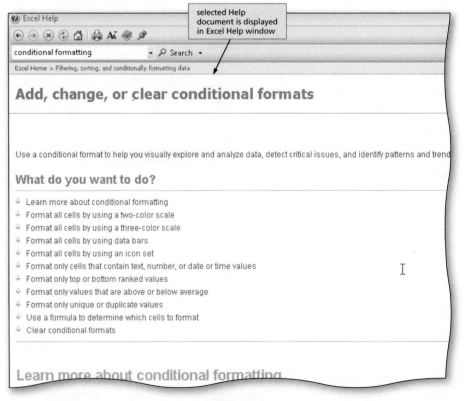

Figure C–8

4
- Click the Home button on the taskbar to clear the search results and redisplay the Excel Help home page (Figure C–9).

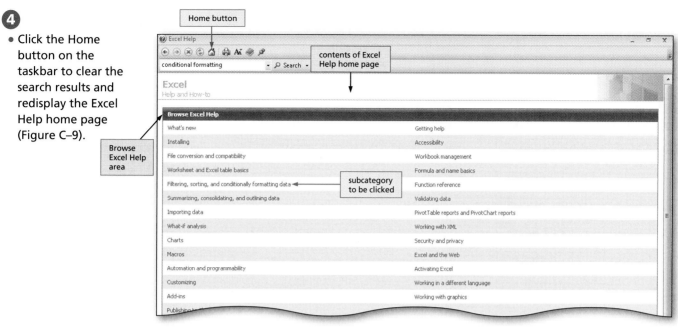

Figure C–9

To Obtain Help Using the Help Links

If your topic of interest is listed in the Browse Excel Help area, you can click the link to begin browsing Excel Help categories instead of entering search text. You browse Excel Help just like you would browse a Web site. If you know in which category to find your Help information, you may wish to use these links. The following steps find the Add, change, or clear conditional formats Help information using the category link from the Excel Help home page.

1
- Click the 'Filtering, sorting, and conditionally formatting data' link to open the Filtering, sorting, and conditionally formatting data page.

- Click the 'Add, change, or clear conditional formats' link to open the Help document associated with the link (Figure C–10).

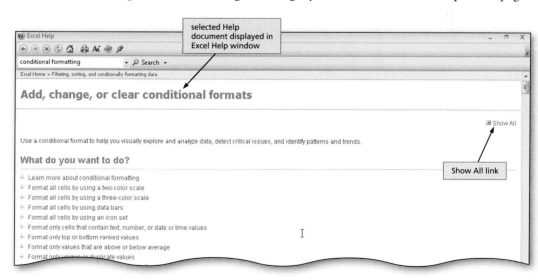

Figure C–10

Q&A What does the Show All link do?

In many Help documents, additional information about terms and features is available by clicking a link in the document to display additional information in the Help document. Clicking the Show All link opens all the links in the Help document that expand to additional text.

To Obtain Help Using the Help Table of Contents

A third way to find Help in Excel is through the Help Table of Contents. You can browse through the Table of Contents to display information about a particular topic or to familiarize yourself with Excel. The following steps access the Add, change, or clear conditional formats Help information by browsing through the Table of Contents.

1

- Click the Home button on the toolbar.

- Click the Show Table of Contents button on the toolbar to open the Table of Contents pane on the left side of the Help window. If necessary, click the Maximize button on the Help title bar to maximize the window (Figure C–11).

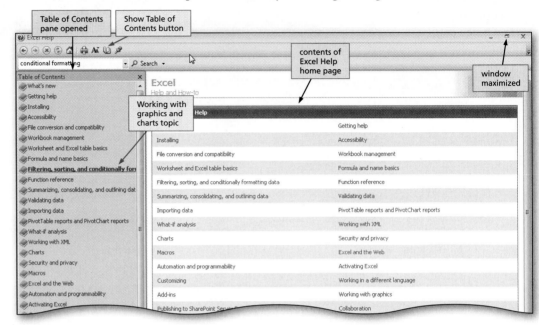

Figure C–11

2

- Click the 'Filtering, sorting, and conditionally formatting data' link in the Table of Contents pane to view a list of Help subtopics.

- Click the 'Add, change, or clear conditional formats' link in the Table of Contents pane to view the selected Help document in the right pane (Figure C–12).

 How do I remove the Table of Contents pane when I am finished with it?

The Show Table of Contents button acts as a toggle switch. When the Table of Contents pane is visible, the button changes to Hide Table of Contents. Clicking it hides the Table of Contents pane and changes the button to Show Table of Contents.

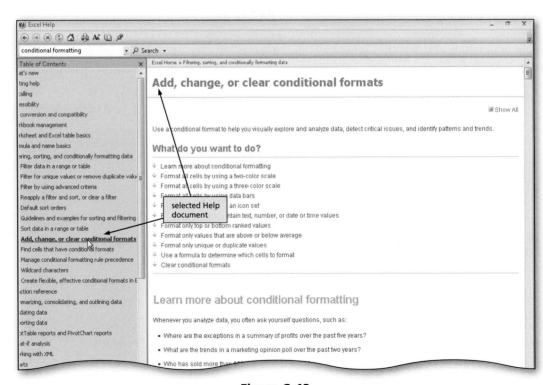

Figure C–12

Obtaining Help while Working in Excel

Often you may need help while working on a document without already having the Help window open. For example, you may be unsure about how a particular command works, or you may be presented with a dialog box that you are not sure how to use. Rather than opening the Help window and initiating a search, Excel Help provides you with the ability to search directly for help.

Figure C–13 shows one option for obtaining help while working in Excel. If you want to learn more about a command, point to the command button and wait for the Enhanced ScreenTip to appear. If the Help icon appears in the Enhanced ScreenTip, press the F1 key while pointing to the command to open the Help window associated with that command.

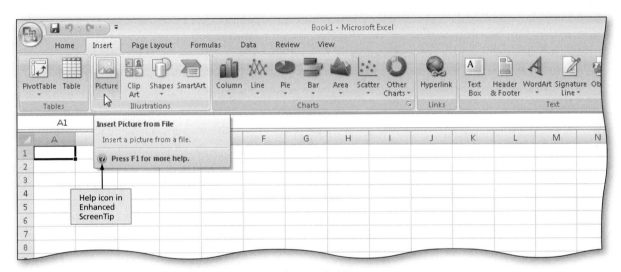

Figure C–13

Figure C–14 shows a dialog box with a Get help button in it. Pressing the F1 key while the dialog box is displayed opens a Help window. The Help window contains help about that dialog box, if available. If no help file is available for that particular dialog box, then the main Help window opens.

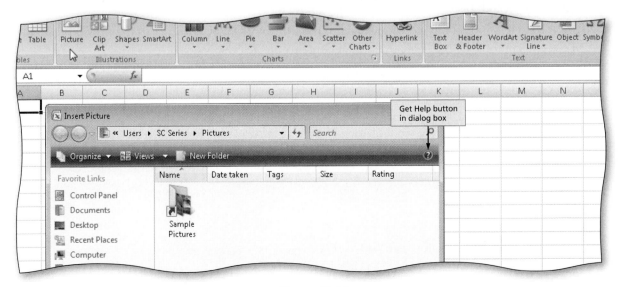

Figure C–14

Use Help

1 Obtaining Help Using Search Text

Instructions: Perform the following tasks using Excel Help.

1. Use the 'Type words to search for' text box to obtain help about landscape printing. Use the Connection Status menu to search online help if you have an Internet connection.

2. Click 'Print landscape or portrait' in the list of links in the search results. Double-click the Microsoft Office Excel Help window title bar to maximize it. Read and print the information. At the top of the printout, write down the number of links Excel Help found.

3. Use the Search menu to search for help offline. Repeat the search from Step 1. At the top of the printout, write down the number of links that Excel Help found searching offline. Submit the printouts as specified by your instructor.

4. Use the 'Type words to search for' text box to search for information online about adjusting cell width. Click the 'Change column width and row height' link in the search results. If necessary, maximize the Microsoft Office 2007 Excel Help window. Read and print the contents of the window. Close the Microsoft Office Excel Help window. Submit the printouts as specified by your instructor.

5. For each of the following words and phrases, click one link in the search results, click the Show All link, and then print the page: pie charts; formulas; print preview; Ribbon; data sorting; and accounting format. Submit the printouts as specified by your instructor.

2 Expanding on Excel Help Basics

Instructions: Use Excel Help to better understand its features and answer the questions listed below. Answer the questions on your own paper, or submit the printed Help information as specified by your instructor.

1. Use Help to find out how to customize the Help window. Change the font size to the smallest option and then print the contents of the Microsoft Office Excel Help window. Change the font size back to its original setting. Close the window.

2. Press the F1 key. Search for information about tables, restricting the search results to Excel Templates. Print the first page of the Search results. You must be working online to restrict the results to Excel templates.

3. Search for information about tables, restricting the search results to Excel Help files. Print the first page of the Search results.

4. Use Excel Help to find out what happened to the Office Assistant, a feature in the previous version of Excel. Print out the Help document that contains the answer.

Appendix D
Publishing Office 2007 Web Pages to a Web Server

With the Office 2007 programs, you use the Save As command on the Office Button menu to save a Web page to a Web server using one of two techniques: Web folders or File Transfer Protocol. A **Web folder** is an Office shortcut to a Web server. **File Transfer Protocol (FTP)** is an Internet standard that allows computers to exchange files with other computers on the Internet.

You should contact your network system administrator or technical support staff at your Internet access provider to determine if their Web server supports Web folders, FTP, or both, and to obtain necessary permissions to access the Web server. If you decide to publish Web pages using a Web folder, you must have the Office Server Extensions (OSE) installed on your computer.

Using Web Folders to Publish Office 2007 Web Pages

When publishing to a Web folder, someone first must create the Web folder before you can save to it. If you are granted permission to create a Web folder, you must obtain the Web address of the Web server, a user name, and possibly a password that allows you to access the Web server. You also must decide on a name for the Web folder. Table D–1 explains how to create a Web folder.

Office 2007 adds the name of the Web folder to the list of current Web folders. You can save to this folder, open files in the folder, rename the folder, or perform any operations you would to a folder on your hard disk. You can use your Office 2007 program or Windows Explorer to access this folder. Table D–2 explains how to save to a Web folder.

Table D–1 Creating a Web Folder
1. Click the Office Button and then click Save As or Open.
2. When the Save As dialog box (or Open dialog box) appears, click the Tools button arrow, and then click Map Network Drive... When the Map Network Drive dialog box is displayed, click the 'Connect to a Web site that you can use to store your documents and pictures' link.
3. When the Add Network Location Wizard dialog box appears, click the Next button. If necessary, click Choose a custom network location. Click the Next button. Click the View examples link, type the Internet or network address, and then click the Next button. Click 'Log on anonymously' to deselect the check box, type your user name in the User name text box, and then click the Next button. Enter the name you want to call this network place and then click the Next button. Click to deselect the 'Open this network location when I click Finish' check box, and then click the Finish button.

Table D–2 Saving to a Web Folder
1. Click the Office Button, click Save As.
2. When the Save As dialog box is displayed, type the Web page file name in the File name text box. Do not press the ENTER key.
3. Click the Save as type box arrow and then click Web Page to select the Web Page format.
4. Click Computer in the Navigation pane.
5. Double-click the Web folder name in the Network Location list.
6. If the Enter Network Password dialog box appears, type the user name and password in the respective text boxes and then click the OK button.
7. Click the Save button in the Save As dialog box.

Using FTP to Publish Office 2007 Web Pages

When publishing a Web page using FTP, you first must add the FTP location to your computer before you can save to it. An FTP location, also called an **FTP site**, is a collection of files that reside on an FTP server. In this case, the FTP server is the Web server.

To add an FTP location, you must obtain the name of the FTP site, which usually is the address (URL) of the FTP server, and a user name and a password that allows you to access the FTP server. You save and open the Web pages on the FTP server using the name of the FTP site. Table D–3 explains how to add an FTP site.

Office 2007 adds the name of the FTP site to the FTP locations list in the Save As and Open dialog boxes. You can open and save files using this list. Table D–4 explains how to save to an FTP location.

Table D–3 Adding an FTP Location

1. Click the Office Button and then click Save As or Open.

2. When the Save As dialog box (or Open dialog box) appears, click the Tools button arrow, and then click Map Network Drive... When the Map Network Drive dialog box is displayed, click the 'Connect to a Web site that you can use to store your documents and pictures' link.

3. When the Add Network Location Wizard dialog box appears, click the Next button. If necessary, click Choose a custom network location. Click the Next button. Click the View examples link, type the Internet or network address, and then click the Next button. If you have a user name for the site, click to deselect 'Log on anonymously' and type your user name in the User name text box, and then click Next. If the site allows anonymous logon, click Next. Type a name for the location, click Next, click to deselect the 'Open this network location when I click Finish' check box, and click Finish. Click the OK button.

4. Close the Save As or the Open dialog box.

Table D–4 Saving to an FTP Location

1. Click the Office Button and then click Save As.

2. When the Save As dialog box is displayed, type the Web page file name in the File name text box. Do not press the ENTER key.

3. Click the Save as type box arrow and then click Web Page to select the Web Page format.

4. Click Computer in the Navigation pane.

5. Double-click the name of the FTP site in the Network Location list.

6. When the FTP Log On dialog box appears, enter your user name and password and then click the OK button.

7. Click the Save button in the Save As dialog box.

Appendix E
Customizing Microsoft Office Excel 2007

This appendix explains how to change the screen resolution in Windows Vista to the resolution used in this book. It also describes how to customize the Excel window by changing the Ribbon, Quick Access Toolbar, and the color scheme.

Changing Screen Resolution

Screen resolution indicates the number of pixels (dots) that the computer uses to display the letters, numbers, graphics, and background you see on the screen. When you increase the screen resolution, Windows displays more information on the screen, but the information decreases in size. The reverse also is true: as you decrease the screen resolution, Windows displays less information on the screen, but the information increases in size.

The screen resolution usually is stated as the product of two numbers, such as 1024×768 (pronounced "ten twenty-four by seven sixty-eight"). A 1024×768 screen resolution results in a display of 1,024 distinct pixels on each of 768 lines, or about 786,432 pixels. The figures in this book were created using a screen resolution of 1024×768.

The screen resolutions most commonly used today are 800×600 and 1024×768, although some Office specialists set their computers at a much higher screen resolution, such as 2048×1536.

To Change the Screen Resolution

The following steps change the screen resolution from 1280×1024 to 1024×768. Your computer already may be set to 1024×768 or some other resolution.

- If necessary, minimize all programs so that the Windows Vista desktop appears.

- Right-click the Windows Vista desktop to display the Windows Vista desktop shortcut menu (Figure E–1).

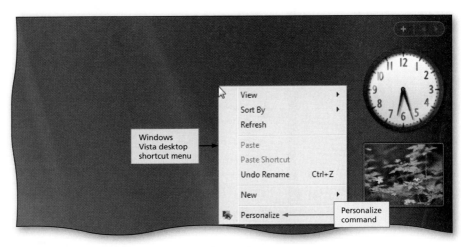

Figure E–1

- Click Personalize on the shortcut menu to open the Personalize window.

- Click Display Settings in the Personalization window to display the Display Settings dialog box (Figure E–2).

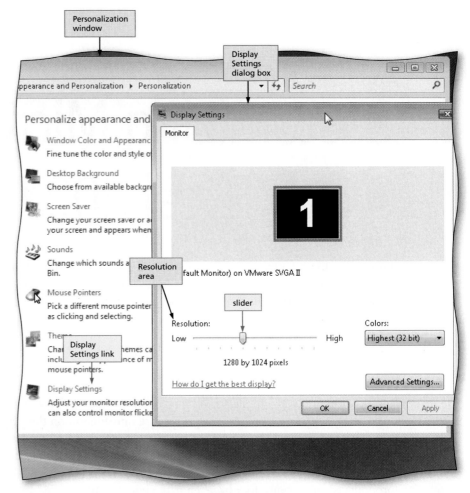

Figure E–2

- Drag the slider in the Resolution area so that the screen resolution changes to 1024 × 768 (Figure E–3).

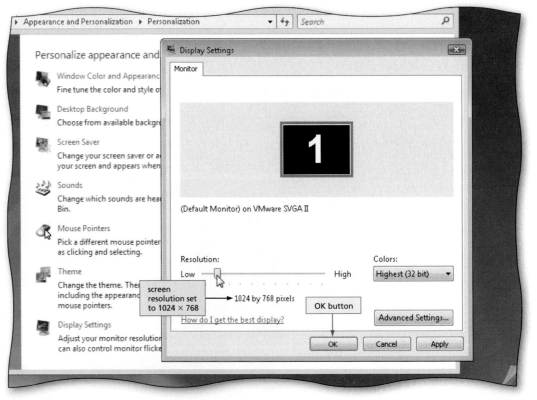

Figure E–3

4

• Click the OK button to change the screen resolution from 1280 × 1024 to 1024 × 768 (Figure E–4).

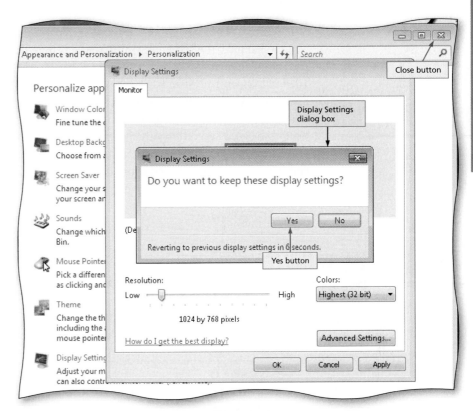

Figure E–4

5

• Click the Yes button in the Display Settings dialog box to accept the new screen resolution (Figure E–5).

 Q&A

What if I do not want to change the screen resolution after seeing it applied after I click the OK button?

You either can click the No button in the inner Display Settings dialog box, or wait for the timer to run out, at which point Windows Vista will revert to the original screen resolution.

• Click the Close button to close the Personalization Window.

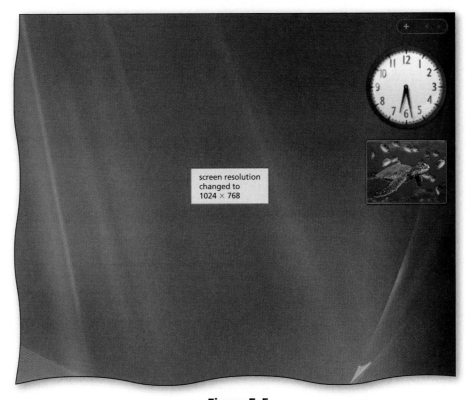

Figure E–5

Screen Resolution and the Appearance of the Ribbon in Office 2007 Programs

Changing the screen resolution affects how the Ribbon appears in Office 2007 programs. Figure E–6 shows the Word Ribbon at the screen resolutions of 800 × 600, 1024 × 768, and 1280 × 1024. All of the same commands are available regardless of screen resolution. Word, however, makes changes to the groups and the buttons within the groups to accommodate the various screen resolutions. The result is that certain commands may need to be accessed differently depending on the resolution chosen. A command that is visible on the Ribbon and available by clicking a button at one resolution may not be visible and may need to be accessed using its group button at a different resolution.

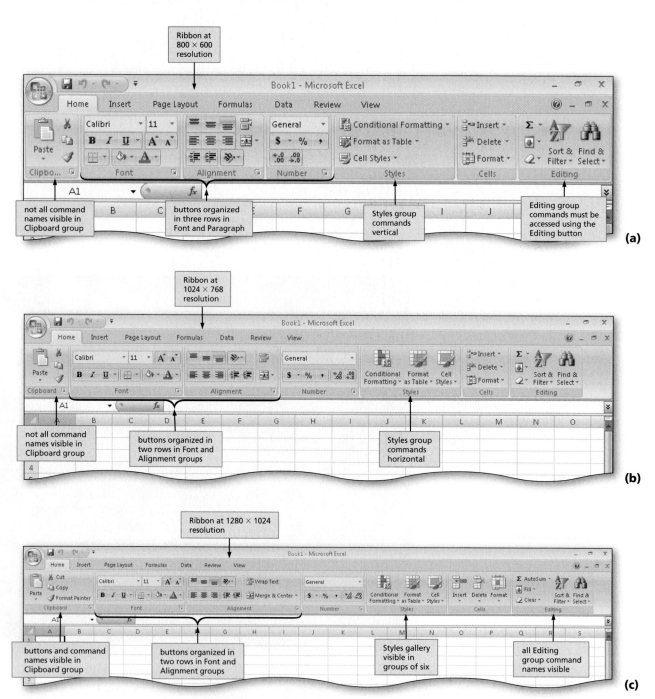

Figure E–6

Comparing the three Ribbons, notice changes in content and layout of the groups and galleries. In some cases, the content of a group is the same in each resolution, but the layout of the group differs. For example, the same buttons appear in the Font and Paragraph groups in the three resolutions, but the layouts differ. The buttons are displayed in three rows at the 800 × 600 resolution, and in two rows in the 1024 × 768 and 1280 × 1024 resolutions. In other cases, the content and layout are the same across the resolution, but the level of detail differs with the resolution. In the Clipboard group, when the resolution increases to 1280 × 1024, the names of all the buttons in the group appear in addition to the buttons themselves. At the lower resolution, only the buttons appear.

Changing resolutions also can result in fewer commands being visible in a group. Comparing the Editing groups, notice that the group at the 800 × 600 resolution consists of an Editing button, while at the higher resolutions, the group has three buttons visible. The commands that are available on the Ribbon at the higher resolutions must be accessed using the Editing button at the 800 × 600 resolution.

Changing resolutions results in different amounts of detail being available at one time in the galleries on the Ribbon. The Styles gallery in the three resolutions presented show different numbers of styles. At 800 × 600, you can scroll through the gallery three styles at a time, at 1024 × 768, you can scroll through the gallery four styles at a time, and at 1280 × 1024, you can scroll through the gallery six styles at a time.

Customizing the Excel Window

When working in Excel, you may want to make your working area as large as possible. One option is to minimize the Ribbon. You also can modify the characteristics of the Quick Access Toolbar, customizing the toolbar's commands and location to better suit your needs.

To Minimize the Ribbon in Excel

The following steps minimize the Ribbon.

1

- Start Excel.

- Maximize the Excel window, if necessary.

- Click the Customize Quick Access Toolbar button on the Quick Access Toolbar to display the Customize Quick Access Toolbar menu (Figure E–7).

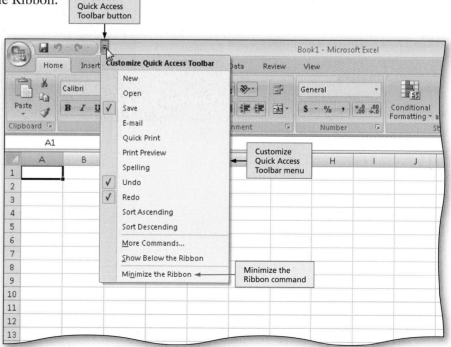

Figure E–7

2

- Click Minimize the Ribbon on the Quick Access Toolbar menu to cause the Ribbon to display just the tabs (Figure E–8).

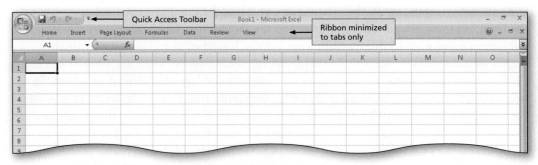

Figure E–8

Customizing and Resetting the Quick Access Toolbar

The Quick Access Toolbar, located to the right of the Office Button by default, provides easy access to some of the more frequently used commands in Excel (Figure E–7). By default, the Quick Access Toolbar contains buttons for the Save, Undo, and Redo commands. Customize the Quick Access Toolbar by changing its location in the window and by adding additional buttons to reflect which commands you would like to be able to access easily.

To Change the Location of the Quick Access Toolbar

The following steps move the Quick Access Toolbar to below the Ribbon.

1

- Double-click the Home tab to redisplay the Ribbon.

- Click the Customize Quick Access Toolbar button on the Quick Access Toolbar to display the Customize Quick Access Toolbar menu (Figure E–9).

Figure E–9

- Click Show Below the Ribbon on the Quick Access Toolbar menu to move the Quick Access Toolbar below the Ribbon (Figure E–10).

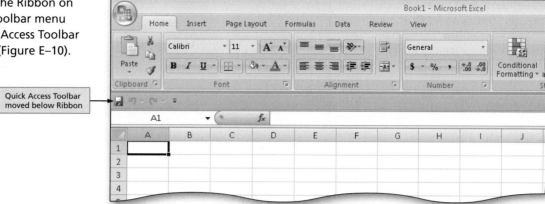

Figure E–10

To Add Commands to the Quick Access Toolbar Using the Customize Quick Access Toolbar Menu

Some of the more commonly added commands are available for selection from the Customize Quick Access Toolbar menu. The following steps add the Quick Print button to the Quick Access Toolbar.

- Click the Customize Quick Access Toolbar button to display the Customize Quick Access Toolbar menu (Figure E–11).

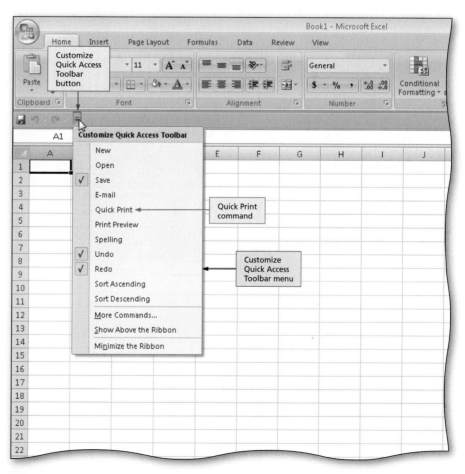

Figure E–11

- Click Quick Print on the Quick Access Toolbar menu to add the Quick Print button to the Quick Access Toolbar (Figure E–12).

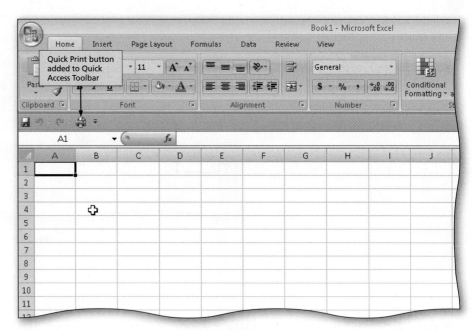

Figure E–12

To Add Commands to the Quick Access Toolbar Using the Shortcut Menu

Commands also can be added to the Quick Access Toolbar from the Ribbon. Adding an existing Ribbon command that you use often to the Quick Access Toolbar makes the command immediately available, regardless of which tab is active.

- Click the Review tab on the Ribbon to make it the active tab.

- Right-click the Spelling button on the Review tab to display a shortcut menu (Figure E–13).

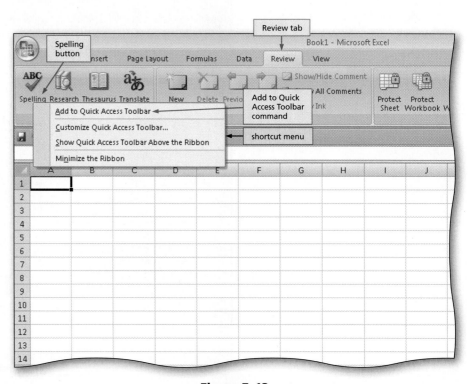

Figure E–13

2

● Click Add to Quick Access Toolbar on the shortcut menu to add the Spelling button to the Quick Access Toolbar (Figure E–14).

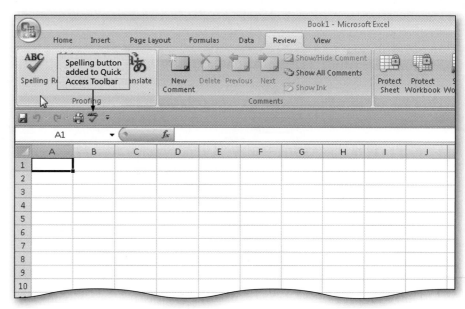

Figure E–14

To Add Commands to the Quick Access Toolbar Using Excel Options

Some commands do not appear on the Ribbon. They can be added to the Quick Access Toolbar using the Excel Options dialog box.

1

● Click the Office Button to display the Office Button menu (Figure E–15).

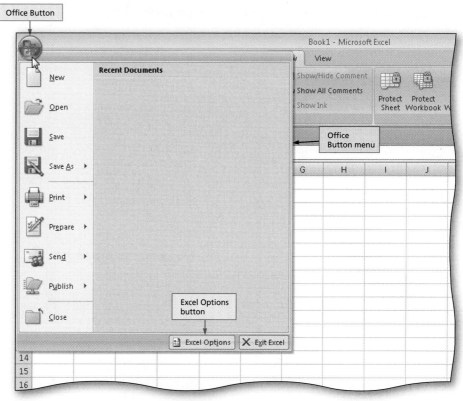

Figure E–15

2

- Click the Excel Options button on the Office Button menu to display the Excel Options dialog box (Figure E–16).

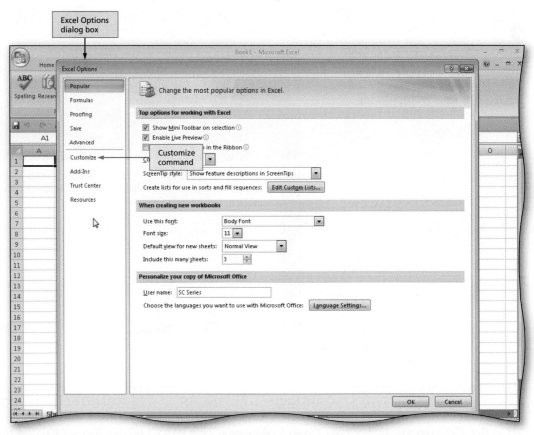

Figure E–16

3

- Click Customize in the left pane.

- Click the 'Choose commands from' box arrow to display the 'Choose commands from' list.

- Click Commands Not in the Ribbon in the 'Choose commands from' list.

- Scroll to display the Web Page Preview command.

- Click Web Page Preview to select it (Figure E–17).

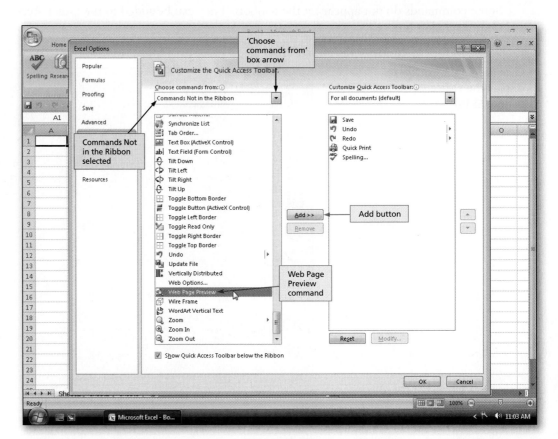

Figure E–17

4

- Click the Add button to add the Web Page Preview button to the list of buttons on the Quick Access Toolbar (Figure E–18).

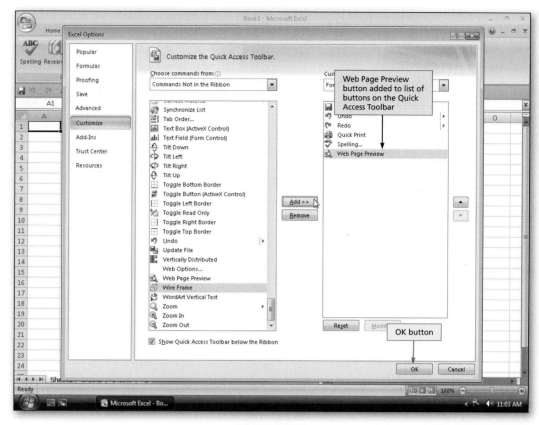

Figure E–18

5

- Click the OK button to add the Web Page Preview button to the Quick Access Toolbar (Figure E–19).

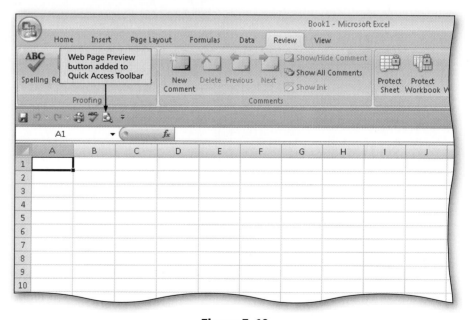

Figure E–19

Other Ways
1. Click Customize Quick Access Toolbar button, click More Commands, select commands to add, click Add button, click OK button

To Remove a Command from the Quick Access Toolbar

1

● Right-click the Web Page Preview button on the Quick Access Toolbar to display a shortcut menu (Figure E–20).

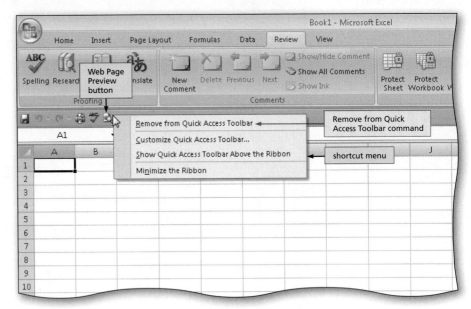

Figure E–20

2

● Click Remove from Quick Access Toolbar on the shortcut menu to remove the button from the Quick Access Toolbar (Figure E–21).

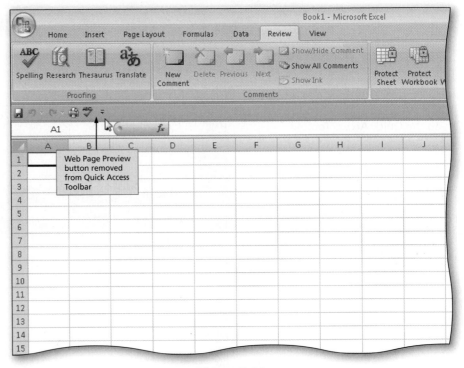

Figure E–21

Other Ways

1. Click Customize Quick Access Toolbar button, click More Commands, click the command you wish to remove in the Customize Quick Access Toolbar list, click Remove button, click OK button

2. If the command appears on the Customize Quick Access Toolbar menu, click the Customize Quick Access Toolbar button, click the command you wish to remove

To Reset the Quick Access Toolbar

1

• Click the Customize Quick Access Toolbar button on the Quick Access Toolbar.

• Click More Commands on the Quick Access Toolbar menu to display the Excel Options Dialog box.

• Click the 'Show Quick Access Toolbar below the Ribbon' check box to deselect it (Figure E–22).

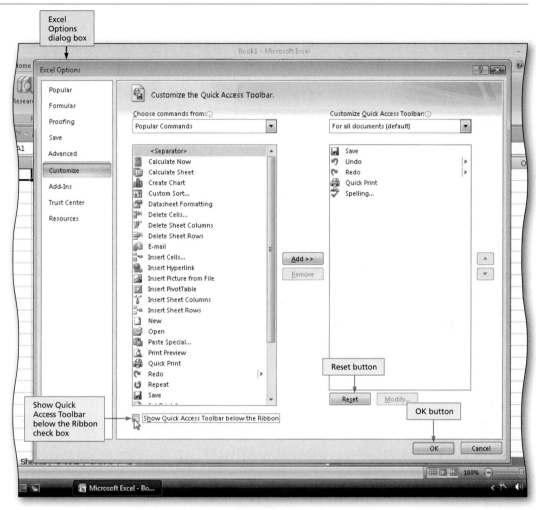

Figure E–22

• Click the Reset button, click the Yes button in the dialog box that appears, and then click the OK button in the Excel Options dialog box, to reset the Quick Access Toolbar to its original position to the right of the Office Button, with the original three buttons (Figure E–23).

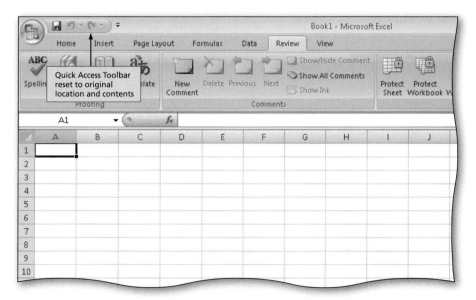

Figure E–23

Changing the Excel Color Scheme

The Microsoft Excel window can be customized by selecting a color scheme other than the default blue one. Three color schemes are available in Excel.

To Change the Excel Color Scheme

The following steps change the color scheme.

1

- Click the Office Button to display the Office Button menu.

- Click the Excel Options button on the Office Button menu to display the Excel Options dialog box.

- If necessary, click Popular in the left pane. Click the Color scheme box arrow to display a list of color schemes (Figure E–24).

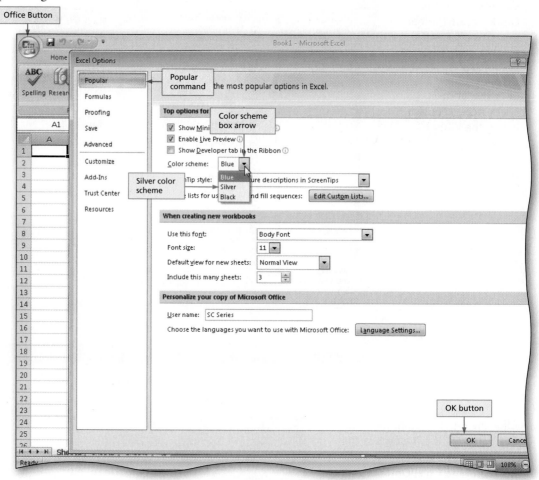

Figure E–24

2

- Click Silver in the list.

- Click the OK button to change the color scheme to silver (Figure E–25).

Q&A
How do I switch back to the default color scheme?

Follow the steps for changing the Excel color scheme, and select Blue from the list of color schemes.

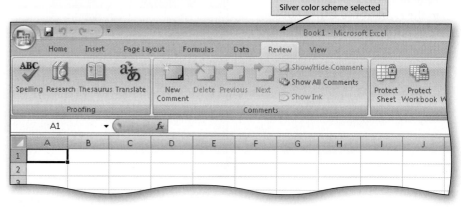

Figure E–25

Appendix F
Steps for the Windows XP User

For the XP User of this Book

For most tasks, no differences exist between using Excel under the Windows Vista operating system and using Excel under the Windows XP operating system. With some tasks, however, you will see some differences, or need to complete the tasks using different steps. This appendix shows how to Start Excel, Save a Workbook, Open a Workbook, and Insert a Picture while using Microsoft Office under Windows XP. The tasks can be accomplished in other Office programs in a similar fashion.

To Start Excel

The following steps, which assume Windows is running, start Excel based on a typical installation. You may need to ask your instructor how to start Excel for your computer.

1

- Click the Start button on the Windows taskbar to display the Start menu.

- Point to All Programs on the Start menu to display the All Programs submenu.

- Point to Microsoft Office on the All Programs submenu to display the Microsoft Office submenu (Figure F–1).

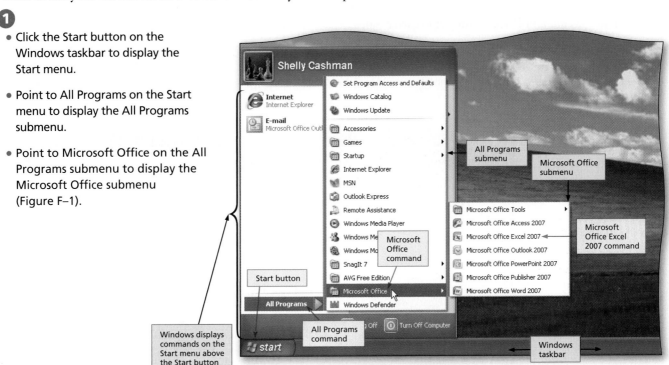

Figure F–1

2

- Click Microsoft Office Excel 2007 to start Word and display a new workbook in the Excel window (Figure F–2).

- If the Excel window is not maximized, click the Maximize button next to the Close button on its title bar to maximize the window.

3

- If the worksheet window in Excel is not maximized, click the Maximize

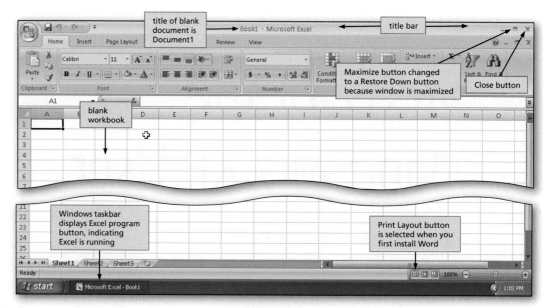

Figure F–2

button next to the Close button on its title bar to maximize the worksheet window within Excel (Figure F-2).

Other Ways	
1. Double-click Excel icon on desktop, if one is present	2. Click Microsoft Office Excel 2007 on Start menu

To Save a Workbook

After editing, you should save the document. The following steps save a document on a USB flash drive using the file name, Walk and Rock Music 1st Quarter Sales.

1

- With a USB flash drive connected to one of the computer's USB ports, click the Save button on the Quick Access Toolbar to display the Save As dialog box (Figure F–3).

Q&A

Do I have to save to a USB flash drive?

No. You can save to any device or folder. A **folder** is a specific location on a storage medium. You can save to the default folder or a different folder. You also can create your own folders, which is explained later in this book.

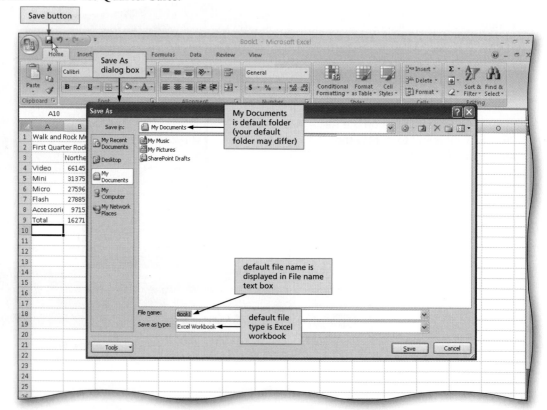

Figure F–3

2

- Type the name of your file (Walk and Rock Music 1st Quarter Sales in this example) in the File name text box to change the file name. Do not press the ENTER key after typing the file name (Figure F–4).

Q&A What characters can I use in a file name?

A file name can have a maximum of 255 characters, including spaces. The only invalid characters are the backslash (\), slash (/), colon (:), asterisk (*), question mark (?), quotation mark ("), less than symbol (<), greater than symbol (>), and vertical bar (|).

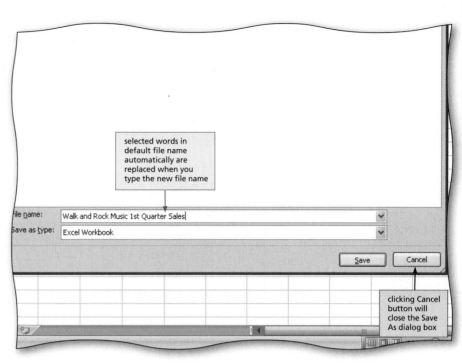

Figure F–4

3

- Click the Save in box arrow to display a list of available drives and folders (Figure F–5).

Q&A Why is my list of files, folders, and drives arranged and named differently from those shown in the figure?

Your computer's configuration determines how the list of files and folders is displayed and how drives are named. You can change the save location by clicking shortcuts on the **My Places bar**.

Q&A How do I save the file if I am not using a USB flash drive?

Use the same process, but be certain to select your device in the Save in list.

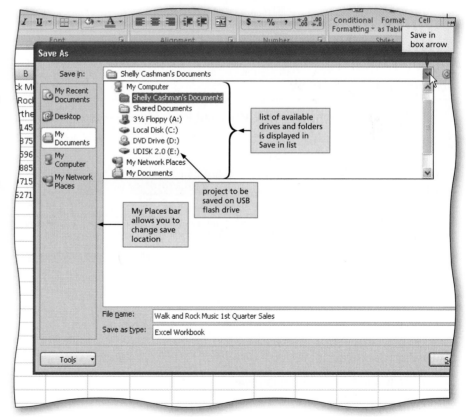

Figure F–5

4

- Click UDISK 2.0 (E:) in the Save in list to select the USB flash drive, Drive E in this case, as the new save location (Figure F–6).

- Click the Save button to save the workbook.

Q&A

What if my USB flash drive has a different name or letter?

It is very likely that your USB flash drive will have a different name and drive letter and be connected to a different port. Verify the device in your Save in list is correct.

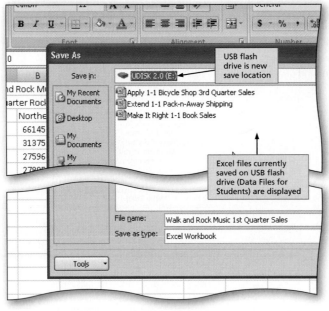
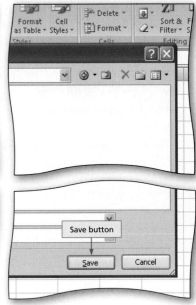

Figure F–6

Other Ways

1. Click Office Button, click Save, type file name, select drive or folder, click Save button

2. Press CTRL+S or press SHIFT+F12, type file name, select drive or folder, click Save button

To Open a Workbook

The following steps open the Walk and Rock Music 1st Quarter Sales file from the USB flash drive.

1

- With your USB flash drive connected to one of the computer's USB ports, click the Office Button to display the Office Button menu.

- Click Open on the Office Button menu to display the Open dialog box.

- If necessary, click the Look in box arrow and then click UDISK 2.0 (E:) to select the USB flash drive, Drive E in this case, in the Look in list as the new open location.

- Click Walk and Rock Music 1st Quarter Sales to select the file name (Figure F–7).

- Click the Open button to open the workbook.

Q&A

How do I open the file if I am not using a USB flash drive?

Use the same process, but be certain to select your device in the Look in list.

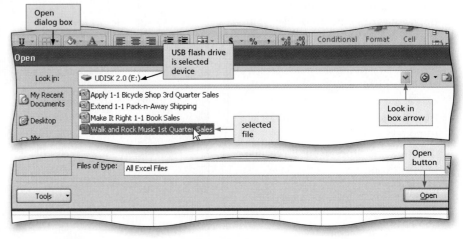

Figure F–7

Other Ways

1. Click Office Button, double-click file name in Recent Documents list

2. Press CTRL+O, select file name, press ENTER

To Insert a Picture

The following steps insert a picture, which, in this example, is located on a USB flash drive.

1 Click Insert on the Ribbon to display the Insert tab.

2 Click the Insert Picture from File button on the Insert tab to display the Insert Picture dialog box.

3 With your USB flash drive connected to one of the computer's USB ports, if necessary, click the Look in box arrow and then click UDISK 2.0 (E:) to select the USB flash drive, Drive E in this case, in the Look in list as the device that contains the picture.

4 Select the file name of the picture file.

5 Click the Insert button in the dialog box to insert the picture in the current worksheet.

Appendix G
Microsoft Business Certification Program

What Is the Microsoft Business Certification Program?

The Microsoft Business Certification Program enables candidates to show that they have something exceptional to offer – proved expertise in Microsoft Office 2007 programs. The two certification tracks allow candidates to choose how they want to exhibit their skills, either through validating skills within a specific Microsoft product or taking their knowledge to the next level and combining Microsoft programs to show that they can apply multiple skill sets to complete more complex office tasks. Recognized by businesses and schools around the world, more than 3 million certifications have been obtained in more than 100 different countries. The Microsoft Business Certification Program is the only Microsoft-approved certification program of its kind.

What Is the Microsoft Certified Application Specialist Certification?

The Microsoft Certified Application Specialist certification exams focus on validating specific skill sets within each of the Microsoft Office system programs. Candidates can choose which exam(s) they want to take according to which skills they want to validate. The available Application Specialist exams include:

- Using Windows Vista™
- Using Microsoft® Office Word 2007
- Using Microsoft® Office Excel® 2007
- Using Microsoft® Office PowerPoint® 2007
- Using Microsoft® Office Access™ 2007
- Using Microsoft® Office Outlook® 2007

> For more information and details on how Shelly Cashman Series textbooks map to Microsoft Certified Application Specialist certification, visit scsite.com/off2007/cert.

What Is the Microsoft Certified Application Professional Certification?

The Microsoft Certified Application Professional certification exams focus on a candidate's ability to use the 2007 Microsoft® Office system to accomplish industry-agnostic functions, for example Budget Analysis and Forecasting, or Content Management and Collaboration. The available Application Professional exams currently include:

- Organizational Support
- Creating and Managing Presentations
- Content Management and Collaboration
- Budget Analysis and Forecasting

Index

Quick Reference Summary

In the Microsoft Office Excel 2007 program, you can accomplish a task in a number of ways. The following table provides a quick reference to each task presented in this textbook. The first column identifies the task. The second column indicates the page number on which the task is discussed in the book. The subsequent four columns list the different ways the task in column one can be carried out.

Microsoft Office Excel 2007 Quick Reference Summary

Task	Page Number	Mouse	Ribbon	Shortcut Menu	Keyboard Shortcut
Advanced Filter	EX 386		Advanced button on Data tab		ALT+A | Q
AutoCalculate	EX 62	Select range | right-click AutoCalculate area | click calculation			
AutoFilter	EX 380		Filter button on Data tab		ALT+A | T
Bold	EX 38	Bold button on Mini toolbar	Bold button on Home tab or Font Dialog Box Launcher on Home tab | Font tab	Format Cells | Font tab | Bold in Font style list	CTRL+B
Borders	EX 111	Borders button on Mini toolbar	Borders button on Home tab or Alignment Dialog Box Launcher on Home tab | Border tab	Format Cells | Border tab	CTRL+1 | B
Cell Style, change	EX 35		Cell Styles button on Home tab		
Center	EX 113	Right-click cell | Center button on Mini toolbar	Center button on Home tab or Alignment Dialog Box Launcher on Home tab	Format Cells | Alignment tab	CTRL+1 | A
Center Across Columns	EX 40	Right-click selection | Merge & Center button on Mini toolbar	Merge & Center button on Home tab or Alignment Dialog Box Launcher on Home tab	Format Cells | Alignment tab	CTRL+1 | A
Chart, Add	EX 50, 205		Dialog Box Launcher in Charts group on Insert tab		F11

Microsoft Office Excel 2007 Quick Reference Summary (continued)

Task	Page Number	Mouse	Ribbon	Shortcut Menu	Keyboard Shortcut
Clear Cell	EX 66	Drag fill handle back	Clear button on Home tab	Clear Contents	DELETE
Clear Worksheet	EX 66		Select All button on worksheet | Clear button on Home tab		
Close All Workbooks	EX 69	Office Button | Exit Excel			ALT+F | X
Close Workbook	EX 59		Close button on Ribbon or Office Button | Close		CTRL+W
Color Background	EX 110		Fill Color button on Home tab or Font Dialog Box Launcher on Home tab	Format Cells | Fill tab	CTRL+1 | F
Color Tab	EX 216			Tab Color	
Column Width	EX 46, 122	Drag column heading boundary	Home tab | Format button | Column Width	Column Width	ALT+O | C | W
Comma Style Format	EX 44		Comma Style button on Home tab or Number Dialog Box Launcher on Home tab | Accounting	Format Cells | Number tab | Accounting	CTRL+1 | N
Conditional Formatting	EX 119, 362		Conditional Formatting button on Home tab		ALT+H | L ALT+O | D
Copy and Paste	EX 175		Copy button and Paste button on Home tab	Copy to copy; Paste to paste	CTRL+C; CTRL+V
Copy to adjacent cells	EX 27	Select source area | drag fill handle through destination cells	Select source area | click Copy button on Home tab | select destination area | click Paste button on Home tab	Right-click source area | click Copy | right-click destination area | click Paste	
Currency Style Format	EX 116		Currency Style button on Home tab or Format Cells | Number | Currency	Format Cells | Number | Currency	CTRL+1 | N
Custom Formats	EX 438		Number Dialog Box Launcher on Home tab | Custom	Format Cells | Number | Custom	ALT+H | FM
Cut	EX 64		Cut button on Home tab	Cut	CTRL+X
Data Table	EX 288	What-If Analysis button on Data tab | Data Table			ALT+A | W | T
Data Validation, Cell	EX 348	Data Validation button on Data tab			ALT+A | V | V
Date	EX 184	Insert Function button in formula bar | Date & Time | NOW	Date & Time button on Formulas tab | NOW		CTRL+SEMICOLON

Microsoft Office Excel 2007 Quick Reference Summary *(continued)*

Task	Page Number	Mouse	Ribbon	Shortcut Menu	Keyboard Shortcut
Date, Format	EX 113		Font Dialog Box Launcher on Home tab | Number tab | Date	Format Cells | Number tab | Date	
Decimal Place, Decrease	EX 115		Decrease Decimal button on Home tab or Number Dialog Box Launcher on Home tab | Number tab | Currency	Format Cells | Number tab | Currency	CTRL+1 | N
Decimal Place, Increase	EX 118		Increase Decimal button on Home tab or Number Dialog Box Launcher on Home tab | Number tab | Currency	Format Cells | Number tab | Currency	CTRL+1 | N
Delete Rows or Columns	EX 180		Home tab | Delete button arrow | Delete Sheet Rows or Home tab | Delete button arrow | Delete Sheet Columns	Delete | Entire row or Delete | Entire column	
Document Properties, Set or View	EX 55	Office Button | Prepare | Properties			ALT+F | E | P
Draft Quality	EX 309		Page Setup Dialog Box Launcher on Page Layout tab | Sheet tab		ALT+P | SP | S
E-Mail from Excel	EX 142	Office Button | Send | E-Mail			ALT+F | D | E
Embedded Chart, Delete	EX 67				Select chart, press DELETE
File Management	EX 259	Office Button | Save As | right-click file name			ALT+F | A | right-click file name
Find	EX 481		Find & Select button on Home tab | Find		CTRL+F
Fit to Print	EX 156		Page Setup Dialog Box Launcher on Page Layout tab		ALT+P | SP
Folder, New	EX 259	Office Button | Save As | Create New Folder button			ALT+F | A
Font Color	EX 39	Font Color box arrow on Mini toolbar	Font Color button arrow on Home tab or Font Dialog Box Launcher on Home tab	Format Cells | Font tab	CTRL+1 | F
Font Size, Change	EX 38	Font Size box arrow on Mini toolbar	Font Size box arrow on Home tab or Font Dialog Box Launcher on Home tab	Format Cells | Font tab	CTRL+1 | F
Font Size, Increase	EX 39	Increase Font Size button on Mini toolbar	Increase Font Size button on Home tab		

Microsoft Office Excel 2007 Quick Reference Summary *(continued)*

Task	Page Number	Mouse	Ribbon	Shortcut Menu	Keyboard Shortcut
Font Type	EX 36	Font box arrow on Mini toolbar	Font box arrow on Home tab or Font Dialog Box Launcher on Home tab	Format Cells | Font tab	CTRL+1 | F
Formula Assistance	EX 101	Insert Function button in formula bar	Insert Function button on Formulas tab		CTRL+A after you type function name
Formulas Version	EX 136				CTRL+ACCENT MARK
Freeze Worksheet Titles	EX 182		Freeze Panes button on the View tab | Freeze Panes		ALT+W | F
Full Screen	EX 9		Full Screen button on View tab		ALT+V | U
Function	EX 101	Insert Function button in formula bar	Insert Function button on Formulas tab		SHIFT+F3
Go To	EX 48	Click cell	Find & Select button on Home tab		F5
Goal Seek	EX 225		What-If Analysis button on Data tab | Goal Seek		ALT+T | G
Gridlines	EX 309, 510		Gridlines check box on View tab or Page Setup Dialog Box Launcher on Layout tab | Sheet tab		ALT+W | V | G ALT+P | V | G
Header	EX 130, 472		Page Setup Dialog Box Launcher on Page Layout tab | Header/Footer tab		ALT+P | SP | H
Help	EX 67 and Appendix C		Microsoft Office Excel Help button on Ribbon		F1
Hide Column	EX 122	Drag column heading boundary	Format button on Home tab | Hide & Unhide or Hide & Unhide button on View tab	Hide	CTRL+0 (zero) to hide CTRL+SHIFT+RIGHT PARENTHESIS to display
Hide Row	EX 126	Drag row heading boundary	Format button on Home tab | Hide & Unhide | Hide Rows	Hide	CTRL+9 to hide CTRL+SHIFT+LEFT PARENTHESIS to display
Hide Sheet	EX 316			Hide	
Hide Workbook	EX 317		Hide button on View tab		ALT+W | H
In-Cell Editing	EX 63	Double-click cell			F2
Insert Rows or Columns	EX 178		Home tab | Insert button arrow | Insert Sheet Rows or Home tab | Insert button arrow | Insert Sheet Columns	Insert	ALT+I | R or C
Insert Single Cell or Range of Cells	EX 179		Home | Insert button arrow | Insert Cells		

Microsoft Office Excel 2007 Quick Reference Summary *(continued)*

Task	Page Number	Mouse	Ribbon	Shortcut Menu	Keyboard Shortcut
Italicize	EX 203		Italic button on Home tab or Font Dialog Box Launcher on Home tab | Font tab	Format Cells | Font tab	CTRL+I
Link Update	EX 138		Existing Connections button on Data tab		ALT+A | X
Margins, Change	EX 130, 472	In Page Layout view, drag margin in ruler	Margins button on Page Layout tab or Page Setup Dialog Box Launcher | Margins tab		ALT+P | M
Merge Cells	EX 41		Merge & Center button on Home tab or Alignment Dialog Box Launcher on Home tab	Format Cells | Alignment tab	ALT+O | E | A
Move Cells	EX 177	Point to border and drag	Cut button on Home tab; Paste button on Home tab	Cut; Paste	CTRL+X; CTRL+V
Move Sheet	EX 217	Drag sheet tab to desired location		Move or Copy	
Name Cells	EX 276	Click Name box in formula bar and type name	Define Name button on Formulas tab or Create from Selection button on Formula tab or Name Manager button on Formula tab	Name a Range	ALT+M | M | D
New Workbook	EX 67	Office Button | New			CTRL+N
Open Workbook	EX 61	Office Button | Open			CTRL+O
Outline a Range	EX 273		Border button on Home tab	Format Cells | Border tab	CTRL+1 | B
Outline a Worksheet	EX 377		Group button on Data tab		ALT+A | G | G
Page Break, Insert	EX 478		Breaks button on Page Layout tab | Insert Page Break		ALT+P | B | I
Page Break, Move	EX 479	Click Page Break Preview button on status bar, drag page breaks	Page Break Preview button on View tab | drag page breaks		ALT+ W | I
Page Break, Remove	EX 478		Breaks button on Page Layout tab | Remove Page Break		ALT+P | B | R
Paste Options	EX 176		Paste button arrow on Home tab		
Percent Style Format	EX 118		Percent Style button on Home tab or Number Dialog Box Launcher on Home tab | Percentage	Format Cells | Number tab | Percentage	CTRL+1 | N or CTRL+SHIFT+%.
Picture, Insert	EX 522		Insert Picture from File button on Insert tab		ALT+N | P

Microsoft Office Excel 2007 Quick Reference Summary *(continued)*

Task	Page Number	Mouse	Ribbon	Shortcut Menu	Keyboard Shortcut
Preview Worksheet	EX 132	Office Button | Print | Print Preview			ALT+F | W | V
Print Area, Clear	EX 310		Print Area button on Page Layout tab | Clear Print Area		ALT+P | R | C
Print Area, Set	EX 309		Print Area button on Page Layout tab | Set Print Area		ALT+F | T | S
Print Row and Column Headings	EX 309		Page Setup Dialog Box Launcher on Page Layout tab | Sheet tab		ALT+P | SP | S
Print Worksheet	EX 132	Office Button | Print			CTRL+P
Protect Worksheet	EX 313		Protect Sheet button on Review tab	Protect Sheet	ALT+R | PS
Quick Style, Add	EX 440		Cell Styles button on Home tab | New Cell Style		ALT+H | J | N
Quick Style, Apply	EX 443		Cell Styles button on Home tab		ALT+H | J
Quit Excel	EX 59	Close button on title bar Office Button | Exit Excel			ALT+F4
Range Finder	EX 106	Double-click cell			
Redo	EX 65	Redo button on Quick Access Toolbar			ALT+3 or CTRL+Y
Remove Splits	EX 223	Double-click split bar	Split button on View tab		ALT+W | S
Rename Sheet tab	EX 217	Double-click sheet tab | type sheet name		Rename	
Replace	EX 483		Find & Select button on Home tab | Replace		CTRL+H
Rotate Text	EX 169		Alignment Dialog Box Launcher on Home tab	Format Cells | Alignment tab	ALT+O | E | A
Row Height	EX 125	Drag row heading boundary	Format button on Home tab | Row Height	Row Height	ALT+O | R | E
Save Workbook, Different Format	EX 395	Office Button | Save As, choose from Save as type list			ALT+F | F | O
Save Workbook, New Name	EX 57	Office Button | Save As			ALT+F | A
Save Workbook, Same Name	EX 57	Save button on Quick Access Toolbar or Office Button | Save			CTRL+S
Select All of Worksheet	EX 67	Select All button on worksheet			CTRL+A
Select Cell	EX 15	Click cell or click Name box, type cell reference, press ENTER			Use arrow keys

Microsoft Office Excel 2007 Quick Reference Summary *(continued)*

Task	Page Number	Mouse	Ribbon	Shortcut Menu	Keyboard Shortcut
Select Multiple Sheets	EX 218	CTRL+click tab or SHIFT+click tab		Select All Sheets	
Series	EX 169, 286	Drag fill handle	Fill button on Home tab	Fill Series	ALT+E | I | S ALT+H | F | I
Shortcut Menu	EX 12	Right-click object			SHIFT+F10
SmartArt	EX 510		SmartArt button on Insert tab		ALT+N | M
Spell Check	EX 127	Spelling button on Review tab			F7
Split Cell	EX 41		Merge & Center button on Home tab or Alignment Dialog Box Launcher on Home tab | click Merge cells to deselect	Format Cells | Alignment tab | click Merge cells to deselect	ALT+O | E | A
Split Window into Panes	EX 222	Drag vertical or horizontal split box	Split button on View tab		ALT+W | S
Stock Quotes	EX 138		Existing Connections button on Data tab		ALT+D | D | D ALT+A | X
Subtotals	EX 375		Subtotal button on Data tab		ALT+A | B
Subtotals, Remove	EX 379		Subtotal button on Data tab | Remove All button		ALT+A | B | ALT+R
Sum	EX 25	Function Wizard button in formula bar | SUM	Sum button on Home tab	Insert Function button on Formulas tab	ALT+=
Table, Create	EX 346		Format as Table button on Home tab or Table button on Insert tab		ALT+H | T
Table, Sort	EX 369		Sort & Filter button on Home tab or Sort A to Z button on Data tab	Sort	ALT+A | A
Table Total Row, Add	EX 365		Total Row check box on Design tab of Table Tools contextual tab		ALT+J | T | T
Table Quick Style, Modify	EX 351		Format as Table button on Home tab | right-click style | Duplicate	Duplicate	ALT+H | T
Underline	EX 203		Underline button on Home tab or Font Dialog Box Launcher on Home tab	Format Cells | Font tab	CTRL+U
Undo	EX 65	Undo button on Quick Access Toolbar			ALT+2, CTRL+Z
Unfreeze Worksheet Titles	EX 194		Freeze Panes button on View tab | Unfreeze Panes		ALT+W | F

Microsoft Office Excel 2007 Quick Reference Summary *(continued)*

Task	Page Number	Mouse	Ribbon	Shortcut Menu	Keyboard Shortcut
Unhide Column	EX 122	Drag hidden column heading boundary to right	Unhide button on View tab	Unhide	ALT+O | C | U
Unhide Row	EX 127	Drag hidden row heading boundary down	Unhide button on View tab	Unhide	ALT+O | R | U
Unhide Sheet	EX 316			Unhide	
Unhide Workbook	EX 317		Unhide button on View tab		ALT+W | H
Unlock Cells	EX 313		Font Dialog Box Launcher on Home tab | Protection tab	Format Cells | Protection tab	CTRL+1 | SHIFT+P
Unprotect Worksheet	EX 315		Unprotect Sheet button on Review tab	Unprotect Sheet	ALT+R | PS
Web Page, Save Workbook As	EX 256	Office button | Save As | Save as type: arrow | Single File Web Page or Office button | Save As | Save as type: arrow | Web Page			
WordArt	EX 466		WordArt button on Insert tab		ALT+N | W
Workbook Theme, Change	EX 109		Themes button on Page Layout tab		
Worksheet Name, Change	EX 141	Double-click sheet tab, type new name		Rename	
Workspace, Save	EX 488		Save Workspace button on View tab		ALT+W | K
Zoom	EX 220	Zoom box on status bar or Zoom In and Zoom Out buttons on status bar	Zoom button on View tab		ALT+V | Z